INNOVATIONS

The Comprehensive Toddler CURRICULUM

A complete, interactive curriculum for toddlers from 18 to 36 months

Illustrations: Joan Waites
Webs: K. Whelan Dery
Photographs: Kay Albrecht, Nancy Alexander, and CLEO Photography

Kay Albrecht / Linda G. Miller

Published by Gryphon House, Inc.
PO Box 10, Lewisville, NC 27023
800.638.0928 (toll free); 877.638.7576 (fax)

Illustrations: Joan Waites. Webs: K. Whelan Dery. Photographs: Kay Albrecht and Nancy Alexander, and CLEO Photography. Cover photograph: © 2000, Artville

Repinted March 2015

Bulk Purchase

Gryphon House books are available at special discount when purchased in bulk for special premiums and sales promotions as well as for fund-raising use. Special editions or book excerpts also can be created to specification. For details, contact the Director of Marketing at the address on this page.

Library of Congress Cataloging-in-Publication Data800.638.0928 (toll free); 877.638.7576 (fax)

Albrecht, Kay M.

Innovations : the comprehensive toddler curriculum : a complete, interactive curriculum for toddlers from 18 to 36 months / Kay Albrecht, Linda G. Miller ; illustrations, Joan Waites ; webs, K. Whelan Dery ; photographs, Kay Albrecht, Nancy Alexander, and CLE0 Photography.

p. cm.

Includes bibliographical references and index.

ISBN 978-0-87659-214-4

I. Title: Comprehensive toddler curriculm II. Miller, Linda G. III. Title.

L51140.2 A45 2000

372.19--wdc21 00-059296

Disclaimer

The publisher and the authors cannot be held responsible for injury, mishap, or damages incurred during the use of or because of the information or activities in this book. The authors recommend appropriate and reasonable supervision at all times based on the age and capability of each child.

INNOVATIONS
The Comprehensive Toddler Curriculum

Dedication

To Larry
—Kay

To Mike
—Linda

"They gave each other a smile with a future in it."
—Ring Lardner

ACKNOWLEDGMENTS

Our lives have been filled with the love of learning. We have been blessed to be a part of the lives of both children and adults together "in the moment" of education. In these moments, many people have influenced our work and helped us reach the point of publishing this book. We would like to acknowledge a few of them here.

Many children inspired us to understand and learn more about growth and development. Watching them grow, and then succeed both in school and in life proves that developmental education and experiences are great preparation for lifelong learning. Their experiences add a very rich dimension to our development as educators and to our understanding of toddlers. They have taught us that toddlerhood (like many other stages) is important, mysterious, intense, and fleeting. Education of young children is messy, and we know how parents and teachers feel when they are in the middle of it all.

The work of the teachers at HeartsHome Early Learning Center continues to inform and support our work. René Rhoads Summers, Gwen Calhoun, and Masami Mizukami, demonstrated that keeping children and teachers together over time is a formula for success—and for professional growth. We appreciate Brooke Harrington and Shien Wang, who struggled their way into brilliant ideas about discerning emergent curriculum from observation. In addition, Brenda Kerr, whose love and understanding of the developmental stage of toddlerhood is unsurpassed, and Pam Wilder, who helped flesh out the concept of primary teaching in the real world of the classroom, long before there was any written information about how to do so.

We also acknowledge the children of HeartsHome Early Learning Center, whose growth and development provides inspiration to learn and grow. We also appreciate their parents' willingness to share with readers a glimpse of children in this wonderful school setting.

Mary Jo Gibbs provided much needed support in developing the Possibilities Plans. Her creativity and experience are illuminated in the original songs, fingerplays, and other curriculum ideas she shared with us.

Once again our families made it possible to sustain the pace and intensity necessary to write – write – write. We appreciate everyone and gratefully acknowledge that we are all in this endeavor together.

Finally, this book would not have been published without the work and support of our editor, Kathy Charner. She stood by us through the process of learning about publishing while life created challenges that could have, but didn't, derail us.

Table of Contents

Introduction 13

Chapter 1—Getting Started
Developmental Tasks 18
Innovations in Observation/Assessment 18
Seeing Children as Unique 19
Insuring Developmentally Appropriate Practice 19
Using Observation and Assessment Strategies 21
Giving Feedback to Parents about Developmental Growth 22
Innovations in Child Development 22
Innovations in Interactive Experiences 22
Innovations in Teaching 23
Innovations in Parent Partnerships 24
Innovations in Environments 24
Possibilities Plans 24
Webs 25
Activities and Experiences 25
Dramatic Possibilities 25
Sensory/Art Possibilities 25
Curiosity Possibilities 26
Construction Possibilities 27
Literacy Possibilities 27
Music Possibilities 28
Movement Possibilities 29
Outdoor Possibilities 29
Project Possibilities 29
Parent Participation Possibilities 30
Concepts Learned 30
Resources 31
Picture File/Vocabulary 31
Purchased and Gathered Items 32
The Curriculum Planning Process 32
Observation—the Source of Emergent Curriculum Ideas 34

Chapter 2—Transitioning to School
Introduction 37
Innovations in Observation/Assessment 38
Observation/Assessment Instrument 38
Innovations in Child Development 40
Principles of Child Development Theory 40
Toddlers Are Not Infants! 42
Attachment and Toddlers 42
Temperament in Toddlers 43
Innovations in Interactive Experiences 45
Innovations in Teaching 47
A Family Is a Family 47
Gradual Enrollment 48
Facilitating Adjustment: What Can Teachers Do? 49
Facilitating Adjustment and Attachment 50
Participating in Groups—It's Harder than You Think! 52
Maximizing Interactions during Basic Care and Routines 53
Guidance and Discipline 54
What Is Guidance and Discipline with Toddlers? 54
Guidance 54
Distraction 54
Redirection 54
Ignoring as a Guidance Strategy 55
Teacher Competencies to Support Transitioning to School 56
Resources for Teachers 57
Innovations in Parent Partnerships 58
School- or Teacher-Initiated Activities 58
Parent Participation Possibilities 58
Parent Postcards 59
Attachment Stage 4—Stranger Anxiety: What Can Parents Do? 59
Creating a Separation and Reunion Ritual 60
Arrival and Departure Routines ARE Transitions 61
Always Say Goodbye 62
Pacifiers 63
Transitional or Security Items 64
Just How Long Will Adjustment Take? 65
Thumb and Finger Sucking 66
Facilitating Adjustment 66
Resources for Parents 67
Innovations in Environments 67
Characteristics of Toddler Environments 67
Creating a Home-Like Setting 67
Meltdown Places 67
Opportunities for Different Perspectives 68
Opportunities to Climb 69
Decreasing and Increasing Stimulation 69
Activities and Experiences vs. Centers 69
Possibilities Plan: Me and My Body 71
Web 71
Me and My Body Planning Pages 72
Dramatic Possibilities 74
Sensory/Art Possibilities 75
Curiosity Possibilities 77
Construction Possibilities 79
Literacy Possibilities 79
Music Possibilities 81
Movement Possibilities 83
Outdoor Possibilities 84
Project Possibilities 86
Parent Participation Possibilities 87
Parent Postcards 88
Every Child Is Unique! 88
You Are Your Child's Best Teacher 89
Concepts Learned in Me and My Body 90
Resources 90
Prop Boxes 90
Picture File/Vocabulary 91

Books 91
Rhymes/ Fingerplays 91
Music/Songs 92
Toys and Materials 92
Possibilities Plan: My Family 93
Web 93
My Family Planning Pages 94
Dramatic Possibilities 96
Sensory/Art Possibilities 98
Curiosity Possibilities 100
Construction Possibilities 102
Literacy Possibilities 103
Music Possibilities 105
Movement Possibilities 107
Outdoor Possibilities 108
Project Possibilities 110
Parent Participation Possibilities 111
Parent Postcards 112
We Are Now Partners 112
Creating Partnerships—Two-way Communciation 114
Concepts Learned in My Family 116
Resources 116
Prop Boxes 116
Picture File/ Vocabulary 117
Books 117
Rhymes/Fingerplays 118
Music/Songs 118
Toys and Materials 119

Chapter 3—Making Friends

Introduction 121
Innovations in Observation/Assessment 122
Observation/Assessment Instrument 122
Innovations in Child Development 124
Play 124
Piaget and Play 124
Parten and Play 125
Vygotsky and Play 125
The Importance of Friendships to Toddlers 126
Innovations in Interactive Experiences 127
Innovations in Teaching 128
Teacher as First Friend—Primary Teaching 128
Components of Primary Teaching 129
Continuity of Care and Friendship Groups 131
What to Expect Socially from Toddlers 131
Appropriate Expectations for Toddlers with Friends 132
Validating What Moms and Dads Know 132
Guidance and Discipline 133
Teaching Social Problem-solving to Toddlers 133
Patterning and Modeling with Toddlers 133
Learning Social Problem-solving Skills 134
Calling for Help 134
Trading 134
Taking Turns 134
Walking Away 135
Plan-making 135
Handling Biting in the Classroom 136
Prevention 136
Anticipation 137
Substitution 137
Supervising and Shadowing Biters 137
Teaching Toddlers Social Interaction Skills 137
Dealing with Parents about Biting 138
Teacher Competencies to Support Toddlers Making Friends 140
Resources for Teachers 140
Innovations in Parent Partnerships 142
School- or Teacher-initiated Activities 142
Parent Participation Activities 142
Parent Postcards 144
Action/Reaction Biting: Help! My Child Got Bitten, Again! 144
What Can Teachers Do to Prevent Action/Reaction Biting? 145
What Can Parents Do to Prevent Action/Reaction Biting? 147
Oh, No! Not Again: Handling Purposeful Biting 149
What Can Teachers Do to Prevent Purposeful Biting? 150
Additional Steps to Prevent Purposeful Biting 151
Teaching Social Skills to Toddlers to Reduce Biting 153
What Can Parents Do to Prevent Purposeful Biting? 154
Social Expectations for Toddlers 156
Expectations with Friends 157
Resources for Parents 157
Innovations in Environments 157
Welcoming Environments for Toddlers 157
Accessible Toys 158
Multiple Levels 159
Places to Climb and Get Away 159
Places to Be Alone 160
Spectator Areas to View Other Children and the Outdoors 160
Activities and Experiences vs. Centers 161
Possibilities Plan: My Neighborhood 163
Web 163
My Neighborhood Planning Pages 164
Dramatic Possibilities 166
Sensory/Art Possibilities 168
Curiosity Possibilities 169
Construction Possibilities 172
Literacy Possibilities 173
Music Possibilities 175
Movement Possibilities 177
Outdoor Possibilities 180
Project Possibilities 181

Parent Participation Possibilities 182
Parent Postcards 183
Do Children Learn While They Play? 183
Transmitting Values to Your Child 184
Concepts Learned in My Neighborhood 185
Resources 185
Prop Boxes 185
Picture File/Vocabulary 186
Books 187
Rhymes/Fingerplays 187
Music/Songs 187
Toys and Materials 188
Possibilities Plan: Fruits and Vegetables 191
Web 191
Fruits and Vegetables Planning Pages 192
Dramatic Possibilities 194
Sensory/Art Possibilities 195
Curiosity Possibilities 197
Construction Possibilities 198
Literacy Possibilities 199
Music Possibilities 201
Movement Possibilities 202
Outdoor Possibilities 204
Project Possibilities 205
Parent Participation Possibilities 207
Parent Postcards 208
Drive-time Activities 208
Preparing for Time Away from Your Child 209
Concepts Learned in Fruits and Vegetables 210
Resources 211
Prop Boxes 211
Picture File/Vocabulary 211
Books 212
Rhymes/Fingerplays 212
Music/Songs 212
Toys and Materials 213

Chapter 4—Exploring Roles

Introduction 215
Innovations in Observation/Assessment 217
Observation/Assessment Instrument 217
Innovations in Child Development 218
The Development of Positive Self-concept 218
Why Is Exploring Roles such an Important Task? 220
Innovations in Interactive Experiences 221
Innovations in Teaching 222
Creating Opportunities to Explore Roles 222
Creating Interactive Relationships to Enhance Exploring Roles 223
Observing to Support Exploring Roles 223
Facilitating Positive Self-Concept 224
Family-centered Practices 224
Guidance and Discipline 225
Enhancing Self Esteem through Encouragement 225
Teacher Competencies to Support Toddlers Exploring Roles 226
Resources for Teachers 227
Innovations in Parent Partnerships 227
School- or Teacher-initiated Possibilities 227
Toy Swap 227
Anecdotal Note Calendar 228
Video Diary of the Day 228
Parent Participation Activities 228
Muffins for Mom 228
Doughnuts for Dad 228
Parent Postcards 229
How Parents Support Exploring Roles 229
Facilitating Positive Self-concept for Your Child 230
Resources for Parents 230
Innovations in Environments 231
Opportunities for Side-by-side Play 231
Role of Play Cues and Play Props 231
Toy and Material Safety 233
Mirrors 233
Activities and Experiences vs. Centers 234
Possibilities Plan: Space 235
Web 235
Space Planning Pages 236
Dramatic Possibilities 238
Sensory/Art Possibilities 240
Curiosity Possibilities 243
Construction Possibilities 246
Literacy Possibilities 247
Music Possibilities 249
Movement Possibilities 250
Outdoor Possibilities 252
Project Possibilities 254
Parent Participation Possibilities 255
Parent Postcard 257
Gender Role Stereotyping 257
Concepts Learned In Space 258
Resources 258
Prop Boxes 258
Picture File/Vocabulary 259
Books 259
Rhymes/Fingerplays 259
Music/Songs 259
Toys and Materials 260
Possibilities Plan: Sky 261
Web 261
Sky Planning Pages 262
Dramatic Possibilities 264
Sensory/Art Possibilities 265
Curiosity Possibilities 267
Construction Possibilities 268
Literacy Possibilities 269
Music Possibilities 271
Movement Possibilities 273
Outdoor Possibilities 274
Project Possibilities 275
Parent Participation Possibilities 275

Parent Postcard 276
Exploring Roles at Home 276
Concepts Learned in Sky 277
Resources 277
Prop boxes 277
Picture File/Vocabulary 278
Books 278
Rhymes/Fingerplays 278
Music/Songs 278
Toys and Materials 279

Chapter 5—Communicating with Parents, Teachers, and Friends
Introduction 281
Innovations in Observation/Assessment 282
Observation/Assessment Instrument 282
Innovations in Child Development 284
Brain Growth and Development 284
Language Development 285
Expressive and Receptive Language 287
Intellectual Development 287
Piaget's Theory of Cognitive Development 289
The Development of Literacy 290
Reading in the First Three Years 291
Writing in the First Three Years 291
Getting Ready to Spell 292
Innovations in Interactive Experiences 294
Innovations in Teaching 295
What Does Brain-Based Care and Early Education Look Like in the Classroom? 295
Techniques for Stimulating Developmental Growth
Language Stimulation Techniques to Use with Toddlers 297
Building Vocabulary 298
Supporting Linguistic and Cultural Diversity 299
Stimulating Cognitive Development Using Multiple Intelligences 301
Simplifying Piaget 302
Supporting Emerging Literacy 303
Developing Reading, Writing, and Spelling Skills 303
Books for Toddlers 305
Early Identification of Developmental Challenges 306
Teacher Competencies to Support Toddlers
Communicating with Parents, Teachers, and Friends 307
Resources for Teachers 308
Innovations in Parent Partnerships 308
School- or Teacher-initiated Activities 308
Parent Participation Activities 309
Parent Postcards 310
What Is Developmentally Appropriate Care and Early Education for Toddlers?—The Role of the Teacher 310
What Is Developmentally Appropriate Care and Early Education for Toddlers?—The Role of Curriculum (Activities and Experiences) 312
Using Found and Discarded Items for Toys 313
Good Books for Toddlers 314
The Amazing Toddler Brain 315
The Windows of Learning: Brain Development and the Young Child 316
How Toddlers Learn 318
Resources for Parents 319
Innovations in Environments 319
Creating a Classroom that Values Multiple Intelligences 319
Literacy-rich Environments 320
Activities and Experiences vs. Centers 321
Possibilities Plan: Big Animals 323
Web 323
Big Animals Planning Pages 324
Dramatic Possibilities 326
Sensory/Art Possibilities 327
Curiosity Possibilities 329
Construction Possibilities 330
Literacy Possibilities 331
Music Possibilities 333
Movement Possibilities 335
Outdoor Possibilities 336
Project Possibilities 337
Parent Participation Possibilities 337
Parent Postcard 338
Teaching Your Child to Read 338
Tips for Reading to Your Child 339
Teaching Your Child to Write 341
Concepts Learned in Big Animals 342
Resources 343
Prop boxes 343
Picture File/Vocabulary 343
Books 344
Rhymes/Fingerplays 344
Music/Songs 344
Toys and Materials 345
Possibilities Plan: Little Animals 347
Web 347
Little Animals Planning Pages 348
Dramatic Possibilities 350
Sensory/Art Possibilities 351
Curiosity Possibilities 352
Construction Possibilities 353
Literacy Possibilities 354
Music Possibilities 355
Movement Possibilities 357
Outdoor Possibilities 358
Project Possibilities 359
Parent Participation Possibilities 360
Parent Postcard 361
Supporting Brain Development at Home 361
Appropriate Expectations for Learning

Academic Skills 362
Concepts Learned in Little Animals 363
Resources 364
Prop boxes 364
Picture File/Vocabulary 364
Books 364
Rhymes/Fingerplays 365
Music/Songs 365
Toys and Materials 366

Chapter 6—Problem-Solving
Introduction 367
Innovations in Observation/Assessment 368
Observation/Assessment Instrument 368
Innovations in Child Development 370
Physical Development 370
Toileting—The Ultimate Physical Challenge 371
Toilet Training—Process, Not Magic 371
Innovations in Interactive Experiences 373
Innovations in Teaching 374
Supporting Physical Development in the Classroom 374
Supporting Physical Development Outdoors 375
Supporting Learning to Toilet Independently 375
The School's Role in Supporting Toilet Training 378
Guidance and Discipline 378
Natural and Logical Consequences 378
Setting Appropriate Limits 379
Nutrition 381
What Do Toddlers Really Need to Eat? 381
24-Hour Food Guide 381
Picky Eaters 382
Health Policies 383
Illness and the Very Young Child 383
Toddler Safety 385
Get a Choke Tube and Use It! 385
Health 385
Handwashing and Diapering Procedure 385
Daily Health Conversations 386
Making Determinations about Sending Children Home 387
Safety 389
Accidents and Injuries 389
Teacher Competencies to Support Toddlers Learning to Solve Problems 390
Resources for Teachers 390
Innovations in Parent Partnerships 391
School- or Teacher-initiated Activities 391
I Can Do It! 391
Parent Participation Activities 391
Parent Postcards 392
Picky Eaters: Helping Your Toddler Eat Healthy 392
Toileting: I'm Ready, but My Child Isn't! 393
Toilet Training: Process, Not Magic 395
The School's Role 398
Natural and Logical Consequences 399
Setting Appropriate Limits 400
Resources for Parents 402
Innovations in Environment 402
Outdoor Environments for Toddlers 402
Bringing Indoor Materials Outside 404
Environmental Sanitation with Toddlers 404
Activities and Experiences vs. Centers 405
Possibilities Plan: Construction 407
Web 407
Construction Planning Pages 408
Dramatic Possibilities 410
Sensory/Art Possibilities 411
Curiosity Possibilities 412
Construction Possibilities 414
Literacy Possibilities 415
Music Possibilities 417
Movement Possibilities 419
Outdoor Possibilities 420
Project Possibilities 422
Parent Participation Possibilities 422
Parent Postcards 423
Encouraging Independence and Autonomy 423
Continuing to Support Independence and Autonomy 424
Concepts Learned in Construction 425
Resources 425
Prop Boxes 425
Picture File/Vocabulary 426
Books 426
Rhymes/Fingerplays 426
Music/Songs 426
Toys and Materials 427
Possibilities Plan: Wheels 429
Web 429
Wheels Planning Pages 430
Dramatic Possibilities 432
Sensory/Art Possibilities 433
Curiosity Possibilities 434
Construction Possibilities 436
Literacy Possibilities 437
Music Possibilities 439
Movement Possibilities 441
Outdoor Possibilities 443
Project Possibilities 445
Parent Participation Possibilities 445
Parent Postcards 446
Appropriate Expectations for Self-control 446
What If? 447
Concepts Learned in Wheels 449
Resources 449
Prop Boxes 449
Picture File/Vocabulary 450
Books 450
Rhymes/ Fingerplays 450

Music/Songs 450
Toys and Materials 451

Chapter 7: Expressing Feelings with Parents, Teachers, and Friends
Introduction 453
Innovations in Observation/Assessment 454
Observation/Assessment Instrument 454
Innovations in Child Development 456
Emotional Development 456
Innovations in Interactive Experiences 457
Innovations in Teaching 459
Facilitating Emotional Development 459
Floor Time as a Practice 460
Beyond Products: Supporting Emerging Creativity in Young Children 461
Guidance and Discipline 462
Managing Normal Aggression in Very Young Children 462
Dealing with Oppositional Behavior in Toddlers 463
Handling Temper Tantrums 466
Conferencing with Parents of Toddlers 467
Communicating with Parents of Toddlers Is Different 468
Conferences Are Parent Education 468
Re-conceptualizing Conferencing 469
Formal Conferences with Written Documentation 469
Informal Conferences with Written Documentation 470
Formal Oral Conferences 471
Informal Oral Conferences 471
Child Abuse Prevention 472
Documentation of Suspected Abuse 472
Teacher Competencies to Support Toddlers Expressing Feelings with Parents, Teachers, and Friends 473
Resources for Teachers 474
Innovations in Parent Partnerships 474
School- or Teacher-initiated Activities 474
Supporting Possibilities 474
Developmental Banners 475
Parent Participation Activities 475
Parent Day 475
Terrific Toddler Celebration 475
Parent Postcards 476
Managing Normal Aggression in Very Young Children 476
Dealing with Oppositional Behavior 478
Toddlers on the Edge 480
Handling Temper Tantrums 482
Resources for Parents 484
Innovations in Environments 484
Characteristics of Good Toddler Environments 484
Room Arrangement Guides Toddlers' Behavior 486
Activities and Experiences vs. Centers 486
Possibilities Plan: Storybook Characters 487
Web 487
Storybook Characters Planning Pages 488
Dramatic Possibilities 490
Sensory/Art Possibilities 491
Curiosity Possibilities 492
Construction Possibilities 493
Literacy Possibilities 494
Music Possibilities 497
Movement Possibilities 499
Outdoor Possibilities 500
Project Possibilities 501
Parent Participation Possibilities 502
Parent Postcards 503
Process Is the Goal 503
Concepts Learned in Storybook Characters 504
Resources 504
Prop boxes 504
Picture File/Vocabulary 505
Books 505
Rhymes/Fingerplays 505
Music/Songs 505
Toys and Materials 506
Possibilities Plan: Water 507
Web 507
Water Planning Pages 508
Dramatic Possibilities 510
Sensory/Art Possibilities 511
Curiosity Possibilities 513
Construction Possibilities 515
Literacy Possibilities 516
Music Possibilities 519
Movement Possibilities 522
Outdoor Possibilities 523
Project Possibilities 525
Parent Participation Possibilities 526
Parent Postcards 527
When Your Child's Teacher Leaves 527
When Your Child's Day Is Lengthened 528
Concepts Learned in Water 529
Resources 529
Prop boxes 529
Picture File/Vocabulary 530
Books 531
Rhymes/Fingerplays 531
Music/Songs 531
Toys and Materials 532

Appendix 535
Index 584

Introduction

As "old" educators who have been around the education block more than a few times, we have long searched for curriculum to meet the incredibly broad span of needs for teachers, parents, and the children who benefit from their efforts. Too often we have received books that have been called "curriculum," but aren't. Some "curriculum" books provide activities or ideas and expect the teacher to determine the appropriate developmental skills. Some "curriculum" books approach skill acquisition as the result of didactic teaching. Some educators equate "curriculum" with just the content that is included, as if all children need are facts to grow and learn.

All of these approaches to "curriculum" are, in our view, far too narrow. At the very least, curriculum for young children must include teacher observation, assessment, teacher training, and interactive responses; parent participation, education, and appreciation as primary educators; integration of environment, toys, materials, health and safety, and room arrangement; grounding in historical and emerging knowledge of child growth and development; and the toddler's experiences, interactions, reactions, cues, interests, and an understanding of the toddler's temperament.

The focus of curriculum, we feel, must be squarely on the child and include all of the elements mentioned thus far. ***This curriculum advocates thinking about and planning for everything that can, by the nature of the setting (school vs. home), contribute to child development and the***

teacher's relationship with the child and the family. We think this is a paradigm shift, a way to move the discussion of curriculum out of the narrow range that leads to evaluating children's potential solely by standardized testing toward a more comprehensive approach that embraces many different ways of knowing and learning. At the same time, the need for teachers to have something that is easy to use regardless of background is recognized.

Innovations: The Comprehensive Toddler Curriculum meets the needs of teachers by providing everything to implement what we feel is "real" curriculum. The following diagram illustrates what we believe is the purpose of curriculum.

Everything involved in the curriculum works together to benefit the child. Observation and assessment come first, so nothing happens to the child before the teacher learns though observing where the child is developmentally. Our view of curriculum is comprehensive—encompassing all aspects of growing and learning. It embraces the inter-relationship among teacher's planning, the child's interest and response, child development, the child's family context and culture, and the reactions and interactions of the adults and other children.

The last aspect of curriculum we embrace is the open-ended nature of the process. When activities or experiences are presented to very young children, we never know what they are going to do with the experience! This divergence is desirable, and we have included it in two ways. One is by the use of curriculum webs related to each Possibilities Plan, reinforcing once again that we cannot predict where a child's interest might take us. Thus, we need to be prepared to consider alternatives so that we can recognize them when they emerge (an idea our colleagues at Reggio Emilia also embrace). The other is the focus on the child's response as a cue to what to do next or where to go next. This is the dance between teacher and child—the gentle interplay that occurs over and over again during the day. Following children's interests is at the heart of emergent curriculum and is central to our view of curriculum with toddlers.

It is our wish that ***Innovations: The Comprehensive Toddler Curriculum*** will insure that toddlers will be supported in learning, that teachers will understand and embrace educating toddlers in a comprehensive way, and that parents and teachers will work cooperatively to make sure it all comes together.

Innovations is designed as a series. ***Innovations: The Comprehensive Toddler Curriculum*** is the second book in the series. It follows ***Innovations: The Comprehensive Infant Curriculum***. Taken together, they form a seamless, comprehensive, developmental approach to early childhood education for children from birth to three years of age.

CHAPTER 1

Getting Started

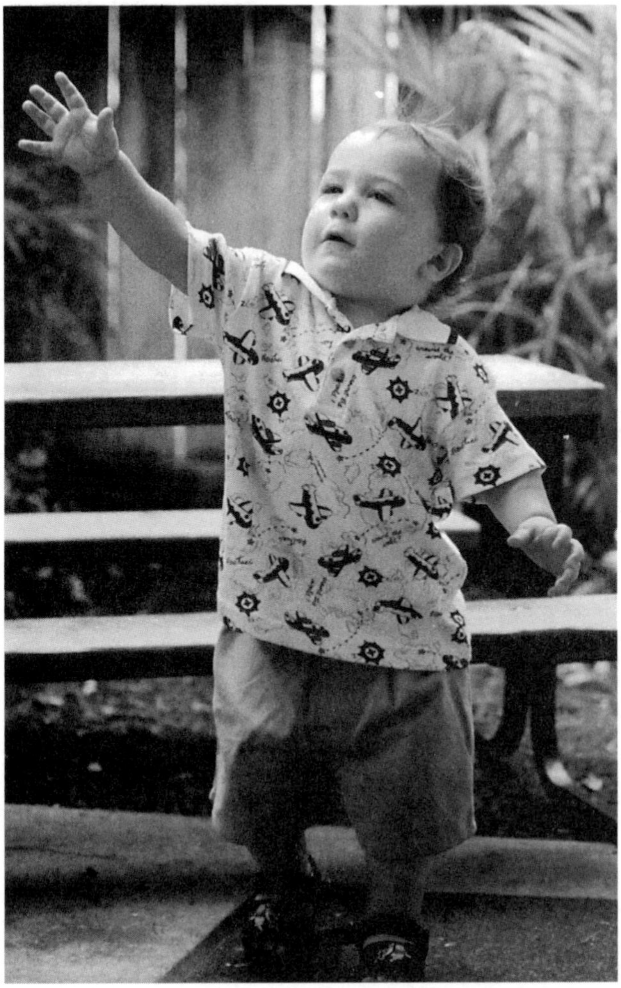

Innovations: The Comprehensive Toddler Curriculum is the second book in the ***Innovations*** series. It follows ***Innovations: The Comprehensive Infant Curriculum***. Taken together, they form a seamless, comprehensive, developmental approach to early childhood education for children from birth to three years of age. Teachers who are working with children who have just turned 18 months may benefit from looking at both books.

Innovations: The Comprehensive Toddler Curriculum is designed for teachers of children ages 18 months through 3 years. For the purposes of this curriculum, toddlerhood lasts until 3 years. In this chapter, Getting Started, you will prepare to use this book by exploring each component of the curriculum.

DEVELOPMENTAL TASKS

Chapters 2-7 each identify a major developmental challenge children experience as they learn and grow. Most curriculum models focus on the sequence of emerging development. This curriculum, however, focuses on how development is encouraged, facilitated, and stimulated. It is interactional, viewing development as the complex interplay between the child and his world.

A child's temperament, the quality of the interactions with adults (such as parents, family members, and teachers), interactions with the environment, and interactions with friends are major components of this curriculum. The intent is to identify the major interactional tasks in toddlerhood and construct a developmentally appropriate approach to dealing with each task through interactions, experiences, and activities.

The tasks are loosely sequential—that is, a teacher of toddlers could start with Chapter 2, Transitioning to School, when the child enrolls in school or at the beginning of the school year, and continue to Chapter 3, Making Friends, then to Chapter 4, Exploring Roles, and so on. Or, teachers can begin by observing children to match emerging tasks with each child's current developmental needs and then begin using the curriculum in that task.

The developmental tasks of this curriculum are Transitioning to School (Chapter 2); Making Friends (Chapter 3); Exploring Roles (Chapter 4); Communicating with Parents, Teachers, and Friends (Chapter 5); Problem-Solving (Chapter 6); and Expressing Feelings with Parents, Teachers, and Friends (Chapter 7).

INNOVATIONS IN OBSERVATION/ASSESSMENT

The National Association for the Education of Young Children (NAEYC), in its position statement on standardized testing, states that "nonstandardized assessments such as systematic observation, anecdotal records, and local and nationally developed checklists play a vital role in planning and implementing instruction and placement of children" (NAEYC, 1988). This curriculum relies on nonstandardized assessment techniques, including systematic observation, anecdotal notes, and a normative checklist, to accomplish a number of different goals. The first goal is to help the teachers and parents see the children as individuals who have unique skill repertoires. The second goal is to insure developmentally appropriate practice. The third goal is to guide curriculum development that is sensitive to children's emerging skills, but does not frustrate or overstimulate.

Seeing Children as Unique

Comparison of children begins to occur early in toddler programs. Parents, who visit the classroom upon arrival and departure, get to know the children in the group and notice the developmental changes in children. Teachers, who have watched a number of children grow and develop, sometimes compare children across time. Parents, who are watching their own child grow up in a group, often compare their child's development with the development of other children in the group. Using nonstandardized assessment techniques, particularly developmental assessments, helps parents and teachers see children as individuals. When used as an integrated part of a high-quality program, developmental assessments show progress in relation to each child's personal skill repertoire rather than comparing children to normative or group averages.

The results of systematic observation, anecdotal notes, and developmental assessments provide a common ground between parents and teachers. As they watch skills emerge, it is logical to talk about new skills and how changes give further insight into the child's individuality. Discussion of developmental maturation also serves as a marvelous parent education tool. As parents see their child grow and develop, they come to understand the sporadic nature of development as well as ways to enhance further development during time with their children. The developmental approach focuses parents' attention on the things children **can** do, instead of the things they cannot. This focus on successful activities and accomplishments enhances the child's self-esteem (Curry & Johnson, 1990).

Often there is an unexpected benefit of using assessment techniques such as these. When parents have frequent opportunities to recognize the developmental progress children are making and discuss that progress with their child's teacher, they place a higher value on what goes on during the school day. Frequent communication about emerging and developing skills also serves to alleviate parental guilt and validate the parents' decision of the choice of schools.

Insuring Developmentally Appropriate Practice

Developmentally appropriate practice guides us to modify programs to fit children rather than requiring children to fit programs. The foundation of developmentally appropriate practice is:

- Knowledge of where each individual child is on the developmental continuum in each area of development, and
- Understanding of the individuality of each child's development (Bredekamp, 1987 and Bredekamp & Copple, 1997).

Developmental assessments guide teachers to gather this information in a truly noninvasive fashion—by careful observation of children involved in daily activities.

This approach also helps to organize teacher behavior. Working with very young children requires that teachers take pleasure in the changes they see as children grow and develop. But, there are times when the sheer demands of the classroom can seem overwhelming. Developmental assessment techniques continually orient teachers' behavior toward their selected goals and allow teachers to see progress as they merge routines (such as diapering, toileting, eating, and napping) with stimulation (such as reading books, playing with stimulating toys, interacting with caregivers and friends, playing inside and outside, and so on). What children can do—the successes accomplished throughout the day—becomes the focus of teachers' interactions with children. Because teachers are carefully observing emerging skills, they can give children repeated experiences with success—doing things the child does well again and again. Success leads to enthusiasm toward new attempts and has positive impact on the child's emerging sense of self.

This approach offers another benefit. Developmental assessment tools serve as passive training tools for new or less experienced teachers to gain confidence and skill in talking to parents about how children grow and learn. Using developmental assessments helps teachers learn patterns of development, provides a common vocabulary, and builds skills in exchanging that information with parents.

Children in school have to "live" in their school settings (Greenman, 1988). Because this is the case, stimulation activities must be balanced across the important dimensions of **activity** (quiet or active), **location** (indoor or outdoor), and **initiator** (child-initiated or adult-initiated) (Bredekamp, 1987; Bredekamp & Copple, 1997; National Academy of Early Childhood Programs, 1991). Knowledge of where each child is on the developmental continuum helps teachers keep a good balance among these important dimensions. Using observation and assessment techniques helps teachers match program and stimulation needs to the developmental level of each child, preventing frustration and insuring challenge.

This kind of assessment requires that teachers observe children and use their observations to guide their interactions and the activities and experiences that they plan for children. Most of the indicators on the assessment instruments emerge from child development theory or principles of development and learning during the early years.

Skills on the continuum are categorized as 18-24 months, 24-30 months, and 30-36 months. These ages are meant to serve as guides because overlap exists throughout the continuum. In other words, a 24-month-old could still be working on some 18-24-month skills while having already perfected some 24-30-month skills. Teachers must remember this important developmental reality.

Teachers who are interested in seeing the beginning of the developmental continuum or who are serving children with special needs may need to start their observation and assessment using the assessment tools and curriculum materials from ***Innovations: The Comprehensive Infant Curriculum***, which covers birth to 18 months of age.

Using Observation and Assessment Strategies

Parent reports of children's development form the first source of anecdotal data that are collected by teachers. This information is gathered during the enrollment process and sets the stage for the regular exchange of developmental information between parents and teachers.

Teacher observations and anecdotal notes are the next source of information about the child. As teachers go about the day, they observe the child and make anecdotal notes. These notes and observations become the foundation of curriculum planning. There are many reminders to observe and take anecdotal notes throughout the curriculum, both in the interactional tasks and in the activities and experiences. And, tools for supporting observation are included (see Anecdotal Record and the Communication Sheet, pages 536 and 537, respectively, in the Appendix).

Assessment is used to identify which skills children have and what children are doing. This creates an opportunity for teachers to document, validate, and celebrate skills. Assessments are designed to help teachers observe the different areas of development and follow changes. They are not designed to compare one child to another but instead to identify each child's repertoire of skills. The results of a teacher's observations of the children in her or his group are then used to plan developmentally appropriate educational activities and experiences.

Toddlers are very easy to assess. They grow and change quickly through maturation as well as through developmental stimulation. For this reason, tools for collecting information (including checklists, note paper, and pens) need to be kept handy so that teachers can easily record data about children's emerging skills and identify the next skill to begin challenging.

Giving Feedback to Parents about Developmental Growth

There are many ways to share developmental information with parents. This curriculum provides several methods. Suggestions are included for a daily or weekly technique using written notes (see Communication Sheet in the Appendix on page 537), quarterly or semi-annual sharing that takes place in parent-teacher conferences, conversations that take place during parent participation activities (see the Observation/Assessment Instruments in the Appendix on pages 542-547), posting developmental banners, sharing documentations of children's work, and many others. Look in the Innovations in Parent Partnerships and the Possibilities Plans sections in Chapters 2-7 of the curriculum for these ideas.

All the developmental tasks are combined into a complete assessment instrument contained in the Appendix on pages 542-547. This can be used cumulatively to document individual children's movement through these developmental tasks.

INNOVATIONS IN CHILD DEVELOPMENT

Understanding child development theory, research, and best practices is the foundation of curriculum. This section explains the underlying theory or child development principles, best practices, or content knowledge leading to specific developmental tasks. It also provides a framework for specific activities that come later. Included in this section are topics such as separation anxiety, primary teaching, literacy development, temperament, and social, emotional, intellectual, and physical development theories. Teachers can discover the ***"what"*** in the developmental tasks and the activity sections, but this section on child development provides the ***"why."***

INNOVATIONS IN INTERACTIVE EXPERIENCES

Children's experiences at school have so much to do with the way they grow and develop. If they experience school as negative, frustrating, or insensitive, they will view the learning process as overwhelming and insurmountable. If, on the other hand, their experiences are supportive, nurturing, and positive, human development has an almost perfect plan for growing and learning. In fact, during the first three years, development unfolds naturally for most children.

This curriculum advocates thinking about and planning for everything that can, by the nature of the setting (school vs. home), contribute to a child's development and the teacher's relationship with the child and the family. In addition, it grounds planning in a developmental, interactive, theoretical framework. Finally, it views all children's experiences, not just formal experiences, as crucial. Children are always learning, and it is the teacher's job to support that learning in whatever form it may take.

Listed in the Innovations in Interactive Experiences are the types of experiences that teachers must be aware of, observe, plan, support, and provide. Many opportunities to capitalize on children's experiences as they happen occur during the school day. Because they are so important, these experiences should appear on curriculum plans as a validation of these crucial, often spontaneous experiences.

INNOVATIONS IN TEACHING

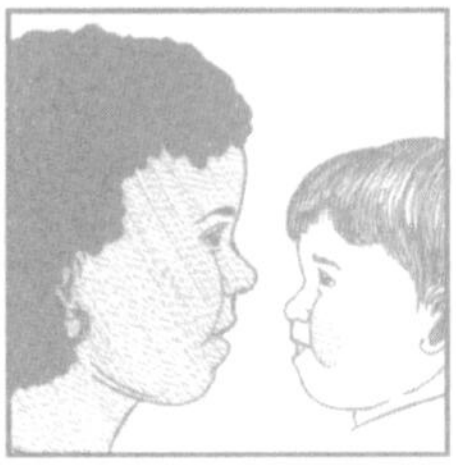

This section discusses important topics related to the developmental tasks that are important for teachers to know. How and what to do as a result of child development knowledge, theory, or best practices is often explored here. Topics covered in the Parent Postcards in the Innovations in Parent Partnerships are discussed from the teacher's point of view in this section. Expansions include the teacher's role in supporting parents as they learn more about parenting.

Teacher Competencies provides a list of behaviors teachers can use to reflect on their teaching skills. Use these skills lists to evaluate your own skill level or to have a mentor or supervisor assess your teaching competence.

Resources for Teachers contains additional suggested reading for teachers. (Complete bibliographic information for references and resources is located in the Appendix on pages 580-584.) Connection with the professional literature enhances teachers' understanding of child growth and development, theory, and best practices. Every effort was made to identify resources that lead to higher levels of understanding in these important areas. Schools are encouraged to add these resources to their professional resource libraries.

INNOVATIONS IN PARENT PARTNERSHIPS

This section gives examples of school-initiated possibilities (such as collecting materials to be made into toys for the classroom) and examples of parent participation possibilities (such as an invitation to parents to come to a parent meeting). Additionally, Innovations in Parent Partnerships includes Parent Postcards, information that may be helpful to parents as they learn more about parenting, or that schools may want parents to have about child development, best practices, or curriculum. Postcards are designed to enhance the partnership between parents and teachers by creating a shared understanding of topics and issues. Postcards can be shared with parents as they show an interest in the topic of the postcard, at appropriate times during the enrollment cycle, or as developmental issues arise with individual children. A sample chronological dissemination schedule is included in the Appendix on pages 548-550.

INNOVATIONS IN ENVIRONMENTS

Most early childhood educators think of interest or learning centers as an essential part of any classroom setting. Centers are appropriate for toddlers only when toddlers' limited social interaction skills are taken into account. For this reason, teachers must be ready to add activities to the classroom when popular activities leave room for no more additional children to participate, to help children get interested in other areas and activities that are available, and to keep toddlers in small groups that do not overwhelm their social skills. Appropriate environments can help teachers accomplish all of these goals.

POSSIBILITIES PLANS

Each of the six developmental tasks contains related curriculum plans, called Possibilities Plans. These plans give teachers a way to structure their activities and experiences with children and give parents opportunities to support teacher activities and learn songs, poems, and rhymes that toddlers are experiencing in the classroom. Plans can be used in total, or activities and experiences can be selected and pulled out to use as appropriate with children in your group. In addition, Possibilities Plans are designed to be expanded, keeping your planning and implementation of curriculum fresh and new with your own additions and expansion ideas.

Webs

Webs are used to show how this quality curriculum encourages open-ended planning. Because ***Innovations: The Comprehensive Toddler Curriculum*** is interactional, teachers adjust their plans according to how toddlers respond to the experiences. For example, the teacher's plan may focus on "my body," but children's interests may change the teacher's plan to focus on "eyes" or "things that I can do with my hands." Webbing opens up the possibilities for interactions, experiences, and activities with children. In addition, webbing allows teachers to glean topics of interest from their observations of children and create Possibilities Plans that reflect those interests.

Two pages of resources to help teachers with curriculum planning follow the web. Use these pages to plan for the individual and group needs of toddlers. Included are lists of possibilities, books, rhymes, fingerplays, music, and appropriate prop boxes. Use these as springboards to create a framework of useful support materials for your classroom.

Activities and Experiences

Each plan is accompanied by numerous activities and experiences, called possibilities, so teachers can plan quality experiences for children in the classroom. The age ranges for the activity, which are the same as those in the developmental tasks, are guidelines. Remember that these ages are just estimates—your knowledge of where your children are on the assessment continuum based on observation will help you find activities that match.

Activities are included in the following categories:

Dramatic Possibilities—Toddlers are delighted by dolls and stuffed animals. Provide a variety of simple, soft dolls representing a variety of ethnicities. Everything should be durable and washable, without eyes or parts that can come off with persistent handling. Beyond dolls, toddlers need props such as the ones they see in the real world, especially things associated with Mom or Dad (purses, hats, bracelets, toy key rings). The teacher's role includes supplying play cues, participating with children as they play, and labeling what toddlers do as they take on different roles, all helping toddlers play together. Activities contribute to vocabulary development and to children's understanding of the real world.

Sensory/Art Possibilities—Sensory, sand, and water experiences are a mainstay of any toddler program. Water is soothing; water toys stimulate play; and the splashing and slapping of water produce interesting reactions. Toddlers are ready for a sensory table in the classroom that can be used with a variety of sensory materials. The teacher's role includes very close supervision. This is an activity brought out and put away by the teacher who gauges when toddlers have had enough and are ready to get warm and dry or clean and go on to another activity.

Art activities for young children are really sensory in nature. Very young children (unlike adults) don't care about how an art activity turns out. They are experiencing the moment—enjoying the feel of the finger paint, the smell of the crayons, the texture of the paper.

Curiosity Possibilities—Young children are curious about the world in which they live. They want to find out what is in it and how everything works. They enjoy exploring new things in the environment. Manipulative toys are often favorite toys. A wide variety of manipulative toys needs to be available for *Curiosity Possibilities.* Toys need to be durable and washable, as they are mouthed and used to teethe as toddlers' teeth continue to erupt. Things to count and sort are also important. Toddlers are very interested in "more" and "less" and in "ownership" of toys and materials. So, duplicates and plenty of toys are crucial.

Repetition of movement and activity is vitally important for brain development, and manipulative toys are perfect toys to stimulate repeated actions. Repetition helps toddlers "wire" their brains and strengthens neural pathways that are developing. Lots of time with action/reaction toys that are easily gripped, manipulated, or stacked is clearly important.

Problem-solving experiences for young children involve experimenting with interesting materials, both old favorites and new ones. Easy manipulatives, puzzles, and small square blocks are also good. Plastic jars with tops to undo, simple sorting manipulatives, surprise toys such as a jack-in-the-box, and busy boxes with a variety of things to turn and push are all interesting. The role of the teacher is to interact with the children and provide plenty of invitations to play.

The last type of problem-solving experiences for toddlers involves mirrors. An important part of the toddler environment is strategically placed nonbreakable mirrors. At children's eye level, they are used to catch a view of a teacher who may be busy with other children, to discover oneself, to look at other children, and to observe the surrounding environment. Teachers at Reggio Emilia view the child's own image as one of the most interesting images children explore during the first three years (Edwards, Gandini & Forman, 1998). Mirrors facilitate the exploration and discovery of the child's physical image.

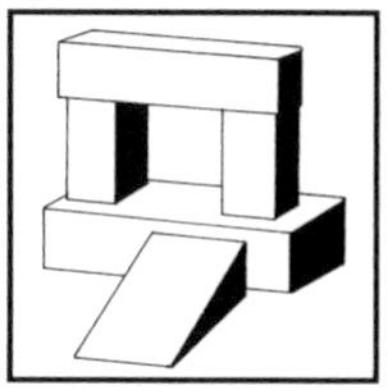

Construction Possibilities—During toddlerhood, two developments—the ability to stay occupied in a task and an increase in fine motor skills—opens up new possibilities for toddlers in construction, blocks, and block supports. Putting things together, taking things apart, building with unit and other kinds of blocks, figuring out how parts relate to the whole, discovering one-to-one correspondence, and creating and manipulating groups are all facilitated by activities and experiences in Construction Possibilities. The teacher plays an important role in introducing new materials, helping children learn to use the materials safely, and expanding learning by connecting mathematical concepts to construction and block play. Building and constructing, destroying their construction, and building them again are powerful opportunities for toddlers to experience control over their lives at school and facilitate their emerging self-control.

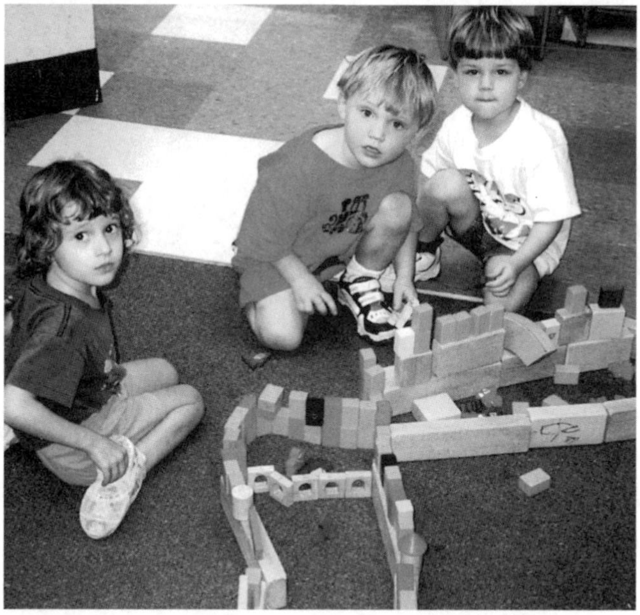

Literacy Possibilities—Reading story and picture books can be a solitary activity or a shared one for toddlers. Provide access to sturdy, inexpensive, replaceable books, including cloth books, board books, plastic books, and paper books. Display them where children can get them and put them back easily.

Give children the opportunity to experiment with and learn about books on their own, actively interacting with them. These early experiences with books as sources of interesting images and stimulation form the foundation of literacy. Be realistic about the damage that active use of books may cause. Pages may be torn and covers removed. As toddlers grow up, teachers can help children learn about the care and maintenance of books.

Teachers should read to toddlers every day. Make reading books a priority with children, one at a time or in pairs and trios. Rhymes and fingerplays are additional literacy opportunities. The rhyme and repetition in language are important for literacy development. Include many opportunities during the day to involve toddlers in this kind of interaction. Teachers can initiate these activities or follow children's lead when they get interested in them.

Music Possibilities—Music is a natural, enjoyable part of the environment for young children. Provide a variety of musical experiences (singing as well as tapes or CDs) at different times in the day. Avoid playing background music throughout the day (children cannot filter out noise as easily as adults can). This will result in escalating the noise level as the day continues. Instead, use music to accomplish specific things: transitions, calming for quiet time, and changing the pace of the day when the atmosphere becomes too energetic or not energetic enough. Music is

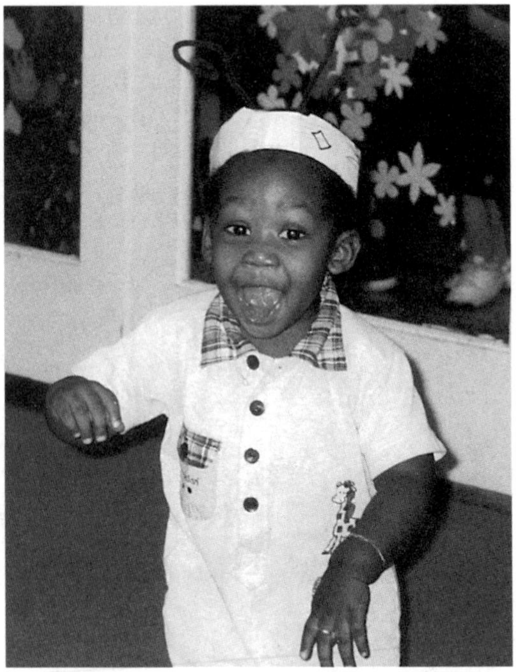

wonderful while children are involved in sensory activities and even when they are playing outside. Recent research suggests that classical music supports brain development.

Movement Possibilities—Toddlers always need a clean, padded area to stretch, wiggle, rest, and do gymnastics. A gym mat with a washable cover works well. The teacher's role is interactive. Teachers help toddlers practice skills and stay near enough to support physical exploration, while preventing serious spills and tumbles. Toddlers' balance is often unsteady as the body grows and changes. Movement experiences support re-mastery of skills after growth takes place.

Outdoor Possibilities—Outdoor time is an important part of the day for very young children. The fresh air is a nice change from the closed environment of the classroom. In addition, activities that are moved from the inside to the outside take on a new meaning. The sounds of the neighborhood, the way light changes because of clouds or shade, the feel of the breeze, running across the grass, and digging in the dirt all add to the richness of the outdoor experience. Outdoor experiences also provide a change of pace and variety for the teacher. Outdoors, the teacher's role is interactive, inviting children to learn as they explore.

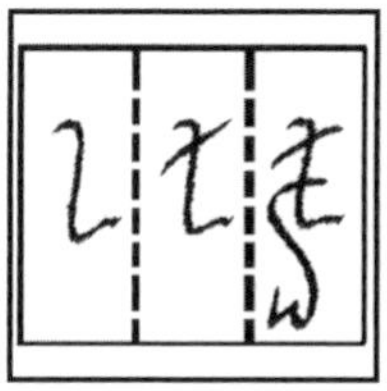

Project Possibilities—Projects are repeated activities or experiences that stretch over a period of time—instead of activities that take place in a short amount of time in one day. Projects are important because they provide continuity of experience, as well as an opportunity to practice, perfect, and enjoy experiences again and again. Unlike projects with preschoolers, which often focus on content knowledge and how children interpret this knowledge, projects with toddlers almost always focus on experiences.

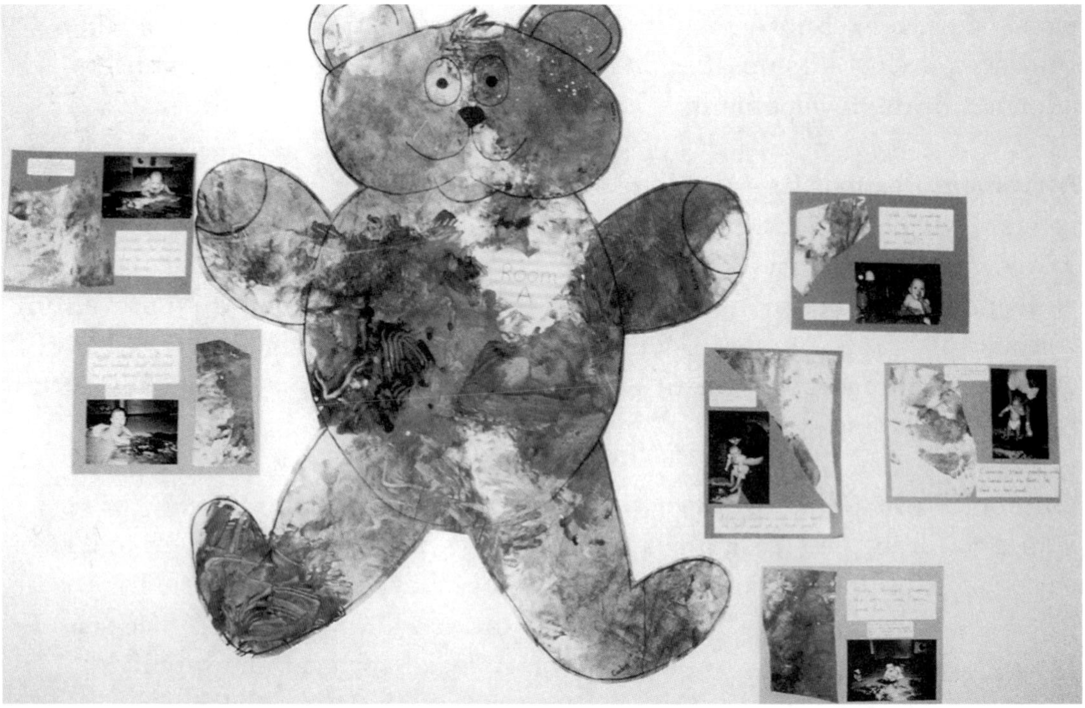

Parent Participation Possibilities—Parents are their child's first and most important teachers. For this reason, their participation in their child's school experience is crucial. Parent participation suggestions are listed here, many that are related to the Possibilities Plan. Parent Postcards are included once again in the Possibilities Plan sections. These Postcards support the plan and are natural extensions of the activities and experiences that teachers are providing for toddlers in the classroom.

Concepts Learned

What are toddlers learning from our choices of activities and experiences? Teachers often see the range and depth of children's learning in the classroom, but parents may fail to see children's playful activities as learning. The Concepts Learned list addresses this reality. The list includes content knowledge as well as process knowledge. Content knowledge includes discrete facts or concepts. Process knowledge is "how-to" knowledge learned through practice. The list includes concepts and processes that toddlers are likely learning because of the planned environment, planned interactions, and planned experiences. Concepts Learned are included in each Possibilities Plan. (Full-page versions that are suitable for copying for parents are included for all Possibilities Plans on pages 551-555 in the Appendix. Post them in the classroom for parents to read, send the list home to parents, or use them during parent conferences.)

As you expand and modify the Possibilities Plans, don't forget to add additional concepts to these lists. They will grow and expand as you follow the children's lead and add emerging curriculum interests to your plans. Keeping the Concepts Learned list up to date will support parents' understanding of the range and quality of learning and development that is taking place in your classroom.

Resources

The Resources section that accompanies each plan provides additional sources for help in planning. Because the classroom environment is an important part of a child's curriculum, suggested prop box materials, picture file/vocabulary, fingerplays, books, songs, and toys and materials important for each Possibilities Plan are included.

Picture File/Vocabulary

There is a Picture File/Vocabulary section for each plan. Toddlers are building cognitive images of the things they are experiencing. Using pictures helps give children a variety of different images. It also adds information to the images that they have already experienced. In addition, it is an inexpensive teaching tool that should be part of every toddler teacher's resources.

Collect pictures from a variety of sources, including magazines, calendars, and so on. Look for pictures that show one image clearly. Laminate them or cover with clear contact paper to extend their life, and store them in file folders or boxes by category. You might start with categories such as the Possibilities Plans topics of Me and My Body, My Family, My Neighborhood, and so on. Then, as categories become filled with pictures, separate them into smaller categories. For example, in Me and My Family, you might separate pictures into Daddies, Mommies, Sisters, Brothers, Grandparents, Extended Family, and so on. Eventually, your picture file collection will become filled with images to assist you in presenting diverse and interesting mental images to toddlers.

Don't forget photographs. Photos of the children in your group now, children in your last group, and other children you know are wonderful additions to picture files. Never throw away a photo; add it to your picture file.

There are many uses for the pictures in your file. The first is to provide interesting additions to the toddlers' near environment. Post laminated pictures at eye level for toddlers to see. Put collections of pictures in the Possibilities areas (for example, pictures of family members in the *Dramatic Possibilities* during My Family).

Second, help toddlers create connections between pictures and vocabulary by labeling the pictures. Start with one label (Daddy), and then expand your labeling (Kaylee's daddy, Jordan's daddy, Miguel's daddy). When you relate a picture to a child's experience such as this, connections between the image, the vocabulary, and the child's experience are made. These connections form the foundation on which to add additional information. The next time you talk about daddies, you can move on to what daddies do or where daddies work. Over time, toddlers will look at a picture of a daddy and connect it to ideas and images of their daddy, then to where their daddy works and what their daddy does. Next, extend toddlers' vocabulary further by adding other ways to label daddy, such as papa and padre, which will expand the image and connections even further while validating home languages.

Third, use pictures to celebrate. Images that are familiar—such as pictures of other people who look like me as well as others who don't look like me—celebrate the diversity of the human experience. Work hard to make your picture files reflect images of the children in your group as well as those that aren't. Both are important and enriching. And, remember that a child's own image is the most interesting. Celebrate the children in your classroom by enlarging great photos and including them in your picture file.

Fourth, use pictures to teach. When you want to extend a child's knowledge with mental images, use pictures. Add pictures from your file to the library shelf so children can "read" pictures as well as picture books. When a child is interested in dogs, pull out all of the pictures of dogs. When a child asks, "What's that?" as he looks at an earthworm just uncovered by digging, use pictures to help him add more information to his observation.

Purchased and Gathered Items

Purchased items are traditional equipment and supplies necessary for supporting the activities in the plan. A list of gathered items that are important for supporting each plan is also included. Although these materials are generally free or inexpensive, it does take time to collect them. Enlist the help of parents in gathering items for use in the classroom.

THE CURRICULUM PLANNING PROCESS*

Toddlerhood is a dynamic time of life. Toddlers are growing and changing quickly, but have added an interesting new dimension to enhance the teacher's curriculum planning process: Their preferences and interests are different from one another and extremely clear to the rest of the world. To make sure your curriculum planning is appropriate, follow the steps described below.

Curriculum planning always starts with observation and assessment. It is not possible to plan for children unless you know where they are developmentally and understand their interests and preferences. Observation and assessment are dynamic activities, taking place on a continual basis and, when completed, lead teachers right back to the observation and assessment process again.

Observation should focus not only on emerging development but also on emerging play themes and interests. As themes emerge (such as interest in what is under rocks or interest in baby brothers and sisters), they can be incorporated into the curriculum planning process. Expect play themes to recur in toddlers. After mommy has the baby, the toddler's interest in where babies come from and how they get here may continue to be a recurring theme. In addition, as play themes emerge, teachers have the opportunity to expand content and skill knowledge by building on previous understanding and knowledge. So, repetition isn't a negative thing—in fact, it is often a very positive one that enhances children's feelings of self-worth and accomplishment.

After you have a good picture of the preferences, interests, play themes, and ages and stages of the children in your group, most teachers turn to curriculum resources to help them flesh out an active and full plan. ***Innovations: The Comprehensive Toddler Curriculum*** encourages teachers to plan not only activities and experiences, but also environments; parent participation activities; parent education activities; interaction possibilities; what books will be available and read; which fingerplays, rhymes, and transition activities will be used; which songs will be sung or music played; and so on. This comprehensive view of planning results in rich, stimulating experiences for toddlers.

Such planning often results in more ideas than you can use. Preparing more than you need isn't a problem. In fact, it gives you the ability to modify and individualize your plans by selecting among the activities and experiences you planned for just the right one to match a child's interest or age and stage. Or, it allows you to add complexity or simplify activities based on the child's response to what you planned.

Use the materials in this curriculum as a starting place. Then, pull additional activities and experiences from the wealth of resources that contain a large number of good curriculum ideas. A list of recommended activity books follows.

The following books are good sources of activities and experiences for toddlers.

Catlin, C. (1996). ***More toddlers together: The complete planning guide for a toddler curriculum, volume II.*** Beltsville, MD: Gryphon House.

Catlin, C. (1994). ***Toddlers together: The complete planning guide for a toddler curriculum***. Beltsville, MD: Gryphon House.

Hast, F. & A. Hollyfield. (1999). ***Infant and toddler experiences.*** St. Paul, MN: Redleaf.

Herr, J. & T. Swim. (1999). ***Creative resources for infants and toddlers.*** Albany, NY: Delmar.

Miller, K. (1984). ***More things to do with toddlers and twos.*** West Palm Beach, FL: Telshare.

Miller, K. (1984). ***Things to do with toddlers and twos.*** West Palm Beach, FL: Telshare.

Miller, K. (1999). ***Simple steps.*** Beltsville, MD: Gryphon House.

Silberg, J. (1993). ***Games to play with toddlers.*** Beltsville, MD: Gryphon House.

Silberg, J. (1993). ***Games to play with two year olds.*** Beltsville, MD: Gryphon House.

Silberg, J. (1996). ***More games to play with toddlers.*** Beltsville, MD: Gryphon House.

While children are involved in the carefully planned environment and activities you have prepared, your role once again becomes that of observer. You gather valuable information about where to go next, what skills are being learned or practiced, and how learning can be shared or documented for parents. From new observations will come the knowledge of preferences, interests, play themes, and ages and stages that start the process over again.

Observation—the Source of Emergent Curriculum Ideas

Where do emergent curriculum ideas come from? They comes from observation. Developing a strategy for collecting play themes and ideas from observation of children is the challenge. Teachers may come up with many varied strategies. Here's one from Brooke Harrington and Shien Wang, primary teachers of a group of children who are now 18 months to 3 years old at HeartsHome Early Learning Center, a nationally accredited program in Houston, Texas.

Brooke and Shien do brief observations (sometimes only 5 minutes or so, sometimes as long as an hour) of children at play whenever they can garner the time. From these observations, they identify play ideas and interests of particular children. Then they synthesize the ideas they observe. Sometimes it takes only one observation to get ideas, other times it takes several observations for interests and play themes to emerge.

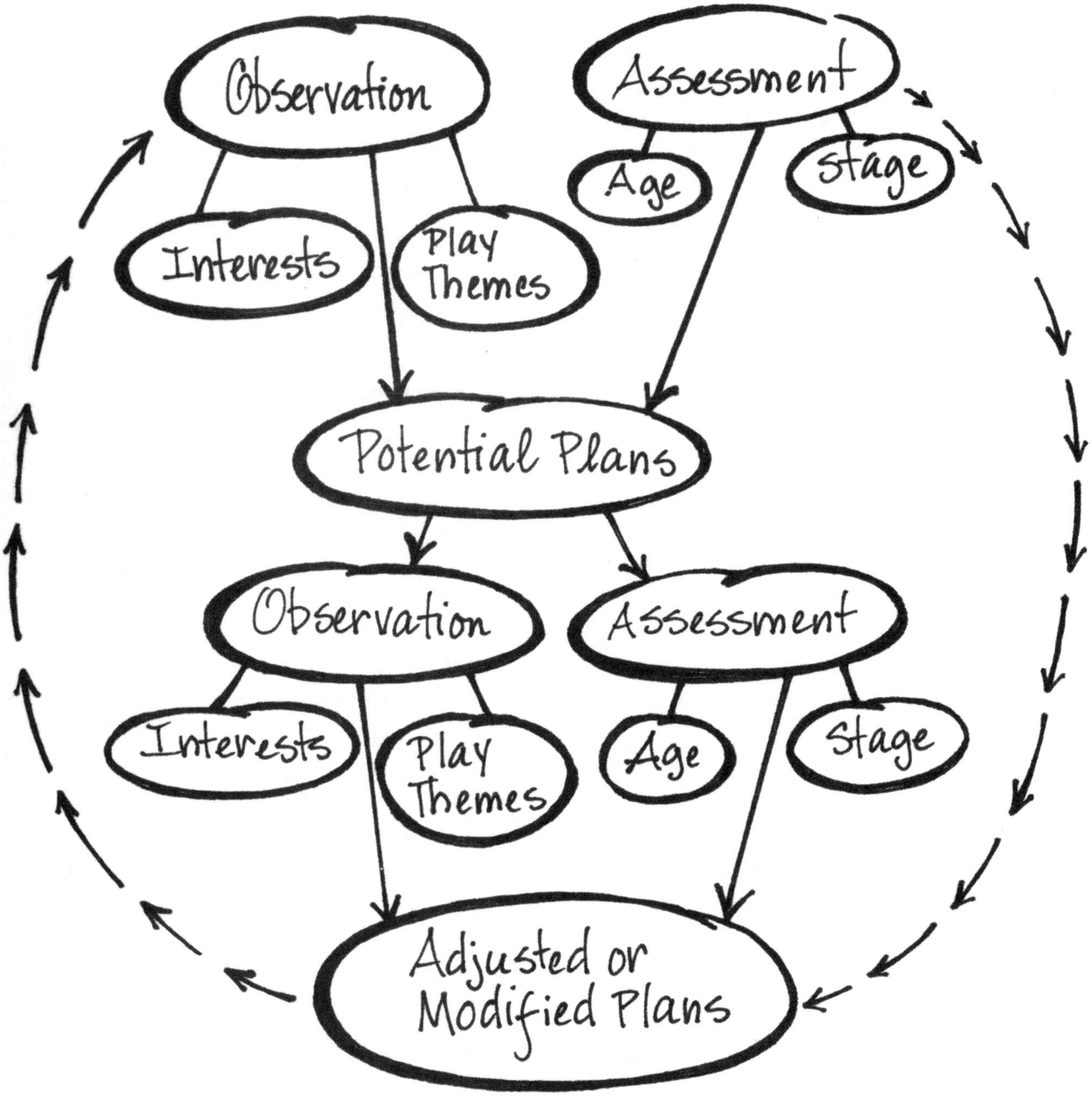

For example, here are some of the observations that these observant teachers noticed that led to experimenting with water as a curriculum plan. These observations took place over a two- to three-week time period.

- *Alli is at the sink, turning the water off and on.*
- *Emily fills cups with water at the sink and lines them up on the counter.*
- *Nathan puts a plastic cup under the faucet and watches the water overflow again and again.*

- *Lauren puts her finger on the drinking fountain spout, watching how the water squirts and splashes.*
- *Zoe imitates Lauren. Eric imitates Lauren. Emily imitates Lauren.*
- *Nathan puts his hand into a filled drinking cup, watching the water rise and overflow, then fall. He refills the cup and repeats the process again.*

These observations led these teachers to plan curriculum about experimenting with water. The resulting curriculum plan was rich with ideas that captured the children's interest in water and explored it in a variety of ways. When curriculum ideas come from children's interests, as it did here with water, children enthusiastically pursue the activities, materials, and experiences that teachers prepare for them, and teachers are able to modify them to fit individual interests—just like these children did with water.

But Brooke and Shien didn't stop here. They took their observations and their plans and clearly identified for parents what children were learning as a result of experiences. In this case, they were learning about volume, floating and sinking, how faucets work, what happens when water is displaced, and some very important skills in cleaning up the messes that water can make! This completes the cycle and makes sure that parents see the teacher's plans as good early childhood learning experiences. (The graphic on page 35 illustrates the curriculum planning process.)

Viewed this way, curriculum planning is not an event—it is an ongoing process. Use the Possibilities Plan (see pages 551-555 in the Appendix) to reflect this process as it unfolds. Post these plans where parents and visitors can see and begin to understand the complex and thorough process that leads to exciting, integrated curriculum in your classroom.

*Note: The sections on curriculum planning and observation were greatly enriched by shared experiences from toddler teachers. In particular, Brooke Harrington and Shien Wang helped develop and operationalize the ideas expanded on here. We recognize their contribution and share credit for it.

CHAPTER 2

Transitioning to School

INTRODUCTION

Toddlerhood—the period from 18 months to three years—is an exciting and challenging period for children and, often, for their parents and teachers. Marked by an emerging sense of self as separate and independent, this developmental period is given a wide variety of labels such as the terrible twos, "tantrumming" twos, tumultuous twos, the search for autonomy, or the declaration of independence.

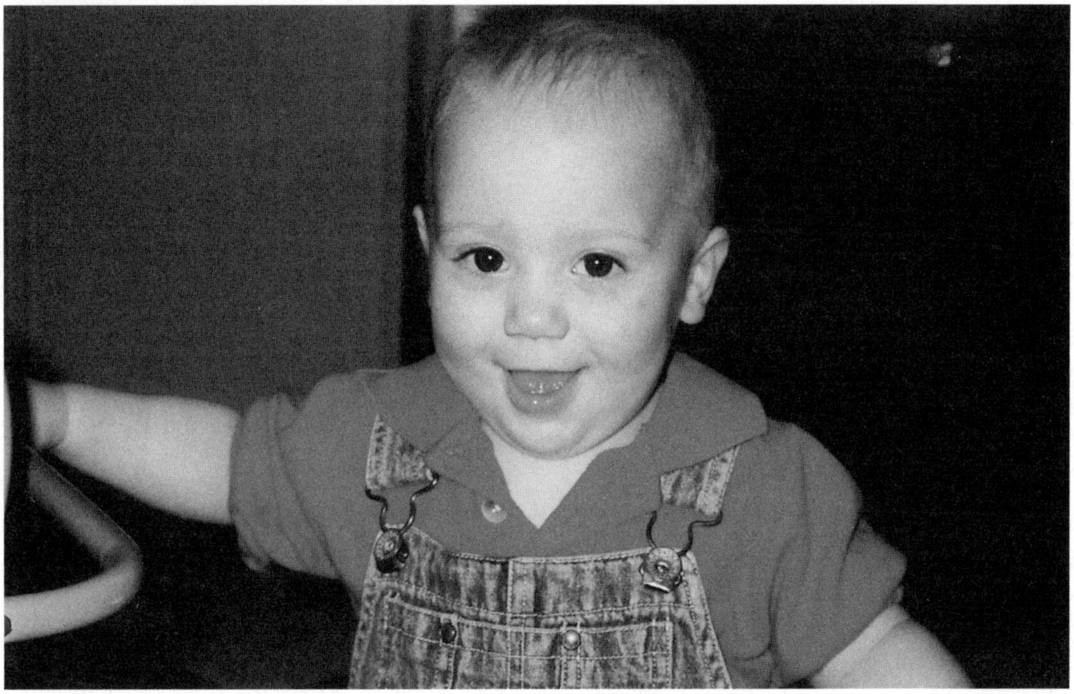

The toddler years are marked by many important transitions that continue the lifelong task of learning to separate from home and connect to the larger world. As infants become toddlers, the number of separations and connections increases, requiring children to practice and perfect the important task of transitioning among and between many different settings, experiences, and interactions.

These transitions can be small and simple, or big and challenging. Transitions from baby bed to toddler bed, from being the only child to having a sibling, from depending on others to meet most of your needs to meeting your own needs are all examples of transitions that occur during this period. As the number of transitions increases, toddlers may feel uncertain about them, often vacillating between viewing the change as exciting to feeling overwhelmed. Toddlers may reflect this uncertainty with increasing resistant and oppositional behavior.

Toddlers often enter formal early childhood education settings during this stage—expanding their interactive world dramatically. But, this expansion requires that new skills be learned. Supporting skill development and growth in transitioning is the focus of this chapter.

INNOVATIONS IN OBSERVATION/ASSESSMENT

Observation/Assessment Instrument

This assessment instrument is not just a skills checklist. Instead it is designed to guide the teacher's observation of children's development through a major interactional task of toddlerhood. The assessment's focus is on what IS happening in the child's development, not what should happen or what will happen. Use this assessment to lead to developmentally appropriate practices for toddlers.

	18-24 months	24-30 months	30-36 months
S1	a. Experienced in separating from Mom and Dad; resists initial separation in new or unusual settings, but adjusts after a few moments.	b. Experienced with separating.	c. May get into difficulty seeking and exploring interesting stimuli.
S2	a. Actively seeks new and interesting stimuli; interested in everything in the environment.	b. May get into difficulty exploring interesting stimuli.	c. Seeks novel and interesting stimuli; when presented with familiar and novel stimuli, prefers novel ones.
S3	a. Resists transitions to unfamiliar or new settings or to settings that are not familiar and preferred.	b. Transitions to familiar people in familiar settings easily.	c. Transitions to most settings without distress; when distress occurs, can be comforted or distracted.
S4	a. Separation anxiety begins to resolve.	b. Stranger anxiety emerges.	c. Stranger anxiety begins to resolve.
S5	a. Prefers predictable routines and schedule; manages changes in schedule fairly well at the time but may experience problems later.	b. Ritualistic about routines and schedule—likes to do the same thing in the same way every time; exhibits ritualistic behavior around routines; likes routines the same way every time; needs warnings of anticipated transitions and still may resist them; melts down or tantrums when schedule is changed without reminders and preparation.	c. Adapts to changes in schedule when prepared in advance; abrupt or unplanned schedule changes still present problems; adapts more readily in familiar settings except when tired, hungry or ill.
S6	a. Tries new food when presented; has strong food preferences.	b. Resists new foods on some days and not on others; reduces intake; may become picky eater or refuse to try new foods when offered. c. Has small selection of food preferences; still resists new food when presented; eats well on some days and not on others.	d. Food intake and preferences even out; will try new food after many presentations; needs encouragement to try new foods.
S7	a. Develops a sense of property rights; hoards toys and favorite objects.	b. Considers objects being played with as personal property.	c. Recognizes mine and not mine.

INNOVATIONS IN CHILD DEVELOPMENT

Principles of Child Development Theory

Which of the following diagrams do you think best represents the way children develop?

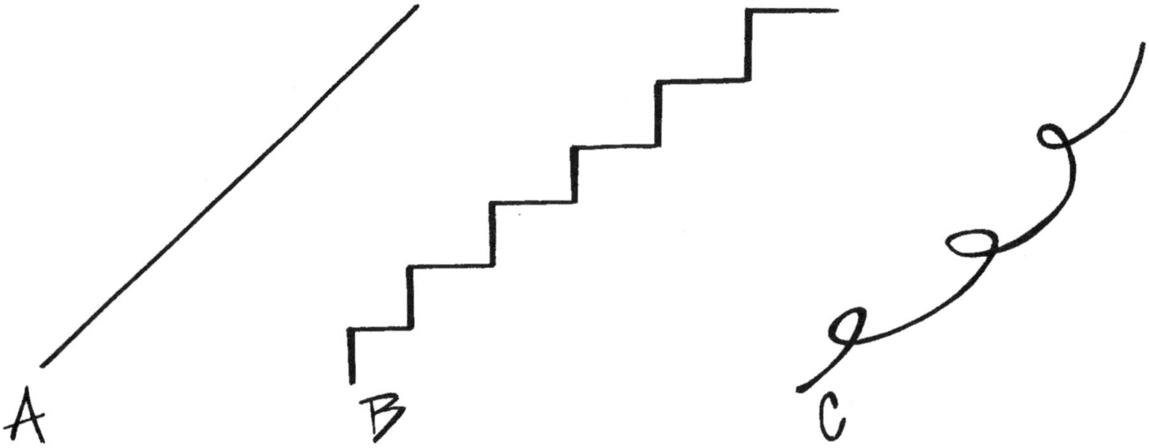

The answer is C. Development is a continuous, though uneven, cycle—a cycle of ever-increasing skills and abilities where each period of growth is preceded by a brief, sometimes turbulent regression.

Children develop in several developmental areas—physical, emotional/social, and intellectual, which includes the language and cognitive domains of development. Underlying any discussion of development is the idea of the integrated nature of child development across areas of development. Development in one sphere is closely tied to and influenced by development in another area. For example, emotional development in toddlerhood influences children's ability to access and use social skills with friends while social interest in what others are doing emerges from stability in emotional relationships. Either area can support or hinder development in both areas.

Another important developmental idea is that growth follows a universal and predictable sequence. Milestones of development can be observed and used to track children's progress along the growth continuums. The predictability of development can be seen in each area of development. For example, in the physical area, development proceeds from sitting to crawling to pulling to a stand to walking to running. Every child follows this same typical pattern of development influenced, of course, by progress in other areas of development.

Another principle of child development is that each child has an individual pattern and timing of growth. This pattern applies to areas of development as well as to development within one area. Although the sequence is predictable, each child's individual progress through the sequence is subject to variation. For example, one toddler might begin using two-word sentences at 16 or 18 months, while another might not say two-word sentences until 24-26 months.

The sporadic and uneven nature of development is a part of this principle. Developmental growth seems to come in spurts. A child might work on physical development until he or she can pull to a stand and walk and then move on to language development or cognitive skill acquisition. Or, a child might make no developmental progress at all for a few weeks, then all of a sudden make major strides, acquiring new skills in several different areas seemingly all at once. It is this characteristic of development that illustrates the uniqueness of each child.

The third principle is that development proceeds from the simple to the complex, from the general to the specific, and from externalized to internalized. Simple skills must be acquired before more complex ones can be attempted. Repeated practice of skills causes internalization (or learning) of a particular skill. For example, children always eat first with their fingers before attempting to use a spoon or fork. Controlling fingers is a simpler task than controlling an extension of the fingers, in this case, the fork. But learning to eat with a spoon or fork comes only after many experiences, first with fingers and then with many failed attempts at getting food from the plate or bowl to the mouth with utensil.

These principles must be taken into account when planning and implementing curricula for toddlers. Each one adds to the teacher's observations about the child's age, stage, and developmental growth.

Principles of Child Development

Development is a continuous, though uneven, cycle—a cycle of ever-increasing skills and abilities where each period of growth is preceded by a brief, sometimes turbulent period of regression. Development is guided by three general principles.

- Principle 1: Development is integrated across areas. Development in each area is connected to development in other areas.
- Principle 2: The sequence of development is universal and predictable, though an individual's pace through the sequence is highly variable.
- Principle 3: Development proceeds from the general to the specific, simple to the complex, and externalized to internalized.

Toddlers Are Not Infants!

For the purposes of this curriculum, toddlerhood is the period from 18-36 months. It is marked by fewer physical changes than during infancy. Toddlers are perfecting motor skills rather than acquiring lots of new ones. But, more changes are occurring in other areas of development, particularly social, emotional, and intellectual (language and cognition). This period of development has many names. It is often called the terrible twos, the declaration of independence, the search for autonomy, the "tantrumming" twos, and even the tumultuous twos. All of these names imply that the toddler years are anything but serene.

Often, curricula for children under three years of age group infancy and toddlerhood together, considering the two phases as continuing and similar. Toddler teachers know differently! Toddlerhood is a dynamic period of development. External (physical) indicators of change that were evident and ongoing in infancy decrease as internal changes in the child become the norm. The toddler years are about becoming—becoming a separate person, becoming independent enough to do things for yourself, and becoming skillful in making friends, playing roles, communicating, expressing feelings, and solving problems.

Attachment and Toddlers

During their first 18 months of life, children begin the process of attaching emotionally to significant adults in their lives. The development of attachment follows a predictable pattern, influenced by each child's temperament, individual timing, and pace of development. Most toddlers have already been through three stages of attachment. The first stage, called indiscriminant attachment, lasts from birth until about 5 or 6 months where babies will allow almost anyone who provides sensitive, responsive care to meet their needs. This stage is followed by discriminate attachment, during months 5 or 6 to 11 or 12, where babies prefer interactions with familiar adults but are still responsive to others. This normal stage 2 behavior is the reason that parents are so surprised when separation anxiety, stage 3, begins to emerge. This stage is when separations from familiar caregivers are resisted, and proximity to familiar adults is preferred. Infants become wary of strangers and resist new people, at least initially. This stage lasts from 11 or 12 months until about 17 or 18 months.

The fourth stage of attachment is called stranger anxiety. It is characterized by fear of unknown or strange adults. The cautious behavior of separation anxiety (Stage 3) is replaced with clinging, crying, screaming, and fearful responses to unfamiliar adults. Toddlers resist overtures and interactions from unknown adults and show distress when their parents and favorite alternate caregiver leaves them or moves away from them. Because of the child's individual pace through development, toddlers may be in stage 3—separation anxiety—or stage 4—stranger anxiety—during the toddler years.

These behaviors indicate that toddlers are very close to finishing the development of attachment to significant adults in their emotional world. But, they are not yet ready to let the whole world intrude on the closeness they feel with mother, father, and familiar caregivers. Strangers, therefore, pose threats. One threat is that strangers might take familiar adults away. Another threat is that strangers might take the child away from the familiar caregiver.

Temperament in Toddlers

Regardless of the imprint of biology, environment, parents, and culture, every child is born with a personality—a temperament that guides and influences her approach to the world. Genetically pre-determined, a child's temperament will manifest itself immediately in a variety of character traits (Chess & Thomas, 1987). Nine character traits have been identified to gauge a child's temperament and to help determine the most effective method of caring for each child

1. activity level, from low to high;
2. regularity of biological rhythms, including sleeping, eating, and elimination;
3. approach/withdrawal tendencies;
4. mood, positive to negative;
5. intensity of reaction, from low to high;
6. adaptability, from slow to quick;
7. sensitivity to light, touch, taste, sound, and sights;
8. distractibility; and
9. persistence.

Each of these traits varies along a continuum. Children's points on the continuum can be observed and identified. Liebermann combined the characteristics of temperament into three groups and described them as flexible, fearful, or feisty (California State Department of Education, 1990).

The traits of flexible children include regular biological rhythms, adaptability to change and new situations, low intensity, low sensitivity, and positive mood. In school, flexible children are easily recognizable, but can be overlooked because they do not demand attention. It is important to the development of flexible children that teachers devote attention to them even though such attention is not demanded.

Fearful children want to avoid new situations and are slow to warm to new people and experiences. Their cautious ways mean that teachers must go slowly with them, allowing them to observe a new activity or situation before approaching it. Teachers may also need to introduce children to new stimuli and only gradually withdraw as caution gives way to interest and enjoyment. In addition, they will need to prepare children in advance for transitions and support them through the transition process.

Feisty children are very active, intense, easily distracted, sensitive, and moody. They have irregular rhythms. Feisty children run rather than walk, push the limits, and respond impulsively to intense emotions. Well-planned transitions are very important to feisty children, who will resist being rushed. Feisty children need opportunities for active play, as well as a chance to experience quiet play when the mood strikes.

Although all children display temperamental characteristics from birth, growing through toddlerhood can magnify these traits. Evidence of this intensifying is often seen around oppositional behavior or "tantrumming"—a normal part of independence-seeking behavior. Some toddlers "tantrum" by crying, clinging, or pouting. Others become the tantrum—screaming, crying, flailing around, falling on the ground, running away, and so on. These differences are often a result of temperament. During toddlerhood, most parents and teachers are very aware of the temperamental differences in children.

Temperament interacts with and impacts development in many ways. Temperamental traits must be taken into account, along with developmental issues, when forming groups, developing curriculum, and establishing routines. Such traits must be considered in developing activities, experiences, and schedules. For example, a feisty child may need several warnings about upcoming transitions in order to prepare herself to leave what she is doing to make the transition. Or, a fearful child might need to watch a new activity from the safe haven of a familiar adult's arms before attempting the activity on her own. Flexible children, on the other hand, may look up from what they are doing and walk directly to a new activity with no preparation or support from adults.

For teachers, temperament serves as a guide—a road map that helps predict how a child might respond. This knowledge about children allows for fine tuning the interactive and stimulation relationship to enhance and support emerging development.

INNOVATIONS IN INTERACTIVE EXPERIENCES

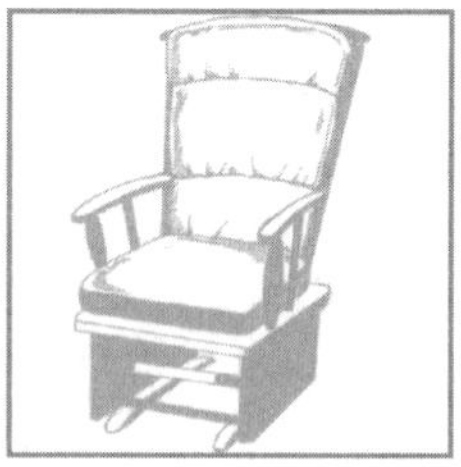

Children's experiences at school have so much to do with the way they will grow and develop. If they experience school as negative, frustrating, or insensitive, they will view the learning process as overwhelming and insurmountable. If, on the other hand, their experiences are supportive, nurturing, and positive, human development has an almost perfect plan for growing and learning. In fact, during the first three years, development unfolds naturally for most children.

Many teachers view the activities and curriculum they plan as the most important part of their job. While these tasks are important, remember that toddlers are experiencing all the time—not just when teachers are providing direct stimulation.

***Innovations: The Comprehensive Toddler Curriculum* advocates thinking about and planning for everything that can, by the nature of the setting (school vs. home), contribute to children's development and the teacher's relationship with the child and the family.** Further, it grounds planning in a developmental, interactive, theoretical framework. Finally, it views all children's experiences, not just formal experiences, as crucial. What is outside the realm of activities in the classroom (for example, a child who takes longer to prepare to transition to another place, a child who naps for a longer or shorter time than expected, a child who is suddenly fascinated with an earthworm) is all curriculum. Children are always learning, and it is the teacher's job to support that learning in whatever forms it may take.

Life's minutiae build to create experiences. Toddler teachers must be attuned to these everyday, yet important, experiences. They are truly the foundation upon which crucial skills and abilities grow. Think about the following list of experiences and make sure that the classroom reflects many of them.

- ☐ Prepare children for transitions. Until they have a great deal more experience with change, toddlers will struggle each time there is a transition. Talk to toddlers about what is going to happen to them next, and tell them what is going on. Give 5-minute, then 3-minute, then 1-minute reminders that change is about to occur.
- ☐ Leave a written record for the teacher who is arriving. This can take the form of a Communication Sheet (see page 537 in the Appendix) or a notebook with notes about what the child might need next. Written records do not rely on verbal exchanges that may get lost in the midst of the transition.
- ☐ Watch the tone of your voice and your nonverbal cues during interactions. Congruence between what you say and the way you say it, and what you do and the way you do it is communication. This is extremely important when you "tire" of toddler behaviors, such as when you leave and you know the child will get upset and cry. If you indicate that the child's feelings are not important, either intentionally or unintentionally, the message the child gets is that her feelings don't matter.
- ☐ Support children as they experience new stimuli. When new things are happening in the school environment, toddlers need support in taking in the new stimuli. Sometimes this support is preparatory, such as warning a child that the fire alarm is going to go off in a minute and make a loud noise, or reminding children that you are going to ask them to stop what they are doing and go outside.
- ☐ Provide support physically as well as visually when children experience new things. Regardless of temperament, children benefit from being close to someone that they trust while new experiences are being offered. Get down on children's eye level, hold them close, look where they look, and follow the child's lead. When physical support is no longer needed, visually support the child with eye contact and nonverbal cues such as smiling and nodding your head.

Take the time to be with the toddlers in your classroom—really be with them. Make every interaction matter, both to you and the child. When teachers invest in quality time with toddlers, all kinds of benefits result. Toddlers are easier to comfort, cues are easier to read, and children can tolerate more challenge and frustration. Remember, every experience matters!

INNOVATIONS IN TEACHING

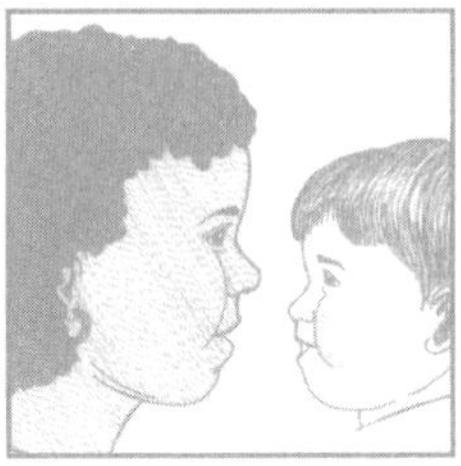

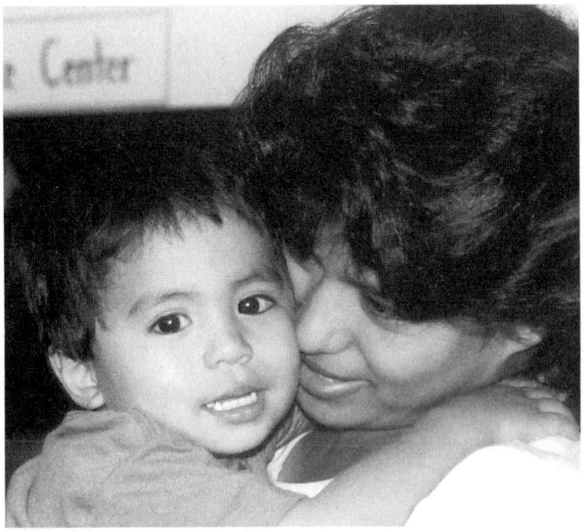

A Family Is a Family

One of a teacher's most important roles in the first three years of a child's life is viewing each child in the context of family, culture, and society (Bredekamp & Copple, 1997). For toddlers, this includes exposing the child to images and ideas about her family and culture of origin. Today, families come in all different sizes and configurations. Some families are traditional nuclear families with a mom, a dad, and children while other families might have two moms or dads, only a mom, only a dad, grandparents who are parenting, or large extended families that share child-rearing responsibilities. And families come from a wide variety of different cultures.

Teachers have a marvelous opportunity to support and validate the family and culture of every child and to begin the process of helping children understand the similarities and the differences that are a natural part of the human experience. This support and validation start with the child's family and culture—in whatever forms they may take. Photos of family members, remembrances such as clothing or gifts that are special, and warm, positive interactions between teachers and all family members are all excellent examples of ways to validate children's families.

Be careful to use images of families and cultures in your room that are representative of all of the children's experiences. Pictures and photographs should depict the types of families that are represented in your group as well as those that are not. Also, be sensitive to the issues of family structure and cultural differences when you plan events that include parents. For example, make sure you include noncustodial parents in parent conferences, even if you must conduct two conferences because the parents are unwilling to conference together. Or, make sure to invite extended family to social events if they share in the child rearing. Or, send written information to an out-of-town or traveling parent who is not able to visit the school as regularly.

A family is a family. Make sure your classroom supports and validates all the families that are represented, and broaden the view to include other family structures and cultures. Toddlers who are exposed to inclusive, multicultural environments and experiences have a better chance of growing up with a view of the world as inclusive and multicultural.

Gradual Enrollment

One of the best ways to facilitate a child's adjustment to any new early childhood experience is to encourage the parents and the child to participate with the teacher in a gradual enrollment process. Young children have little experience with change and need time to adjust to new settings. Parents need to understand how new environments work and how teachers will handle the dynamic tasks of caregiving and early education. Gradual enrollment gives children, teachers, and parents time.

Ideally, gradual enrollment would take place over a week or so with the parent and child staying 1-2 hours the first day and working up to a full day. Many parents will be able to arrange this much time for transition. Those who can't should be encouraged to do gradual enrollment for at least two days. This gives the child experience with the new environment before being left in the new setting.

If this is not possible, the parents or a familiar person should spend 20-30 minutes in the school before departing, return for lunch that day, then spend another 20-30 minutes in the school at the end of the day. Most parents can arrange this alternative.

Although gradual enrollment historically has been more than most schools require of parents, it is one of the most important components of the parent/school connection. It helps both parties understand what to expect. When parents are desperate to begin school immediately and cannot participate in the gradual enrollment process, children often have more difficulty adjusting to the school, complain more often, and drop out at a higher rate. Parents who are unsuccessful in calibrating their expectations, and who don't have the time to work cooperatively with the teacher to make sure the child's adjustment is well-planned and implemented, will have more complaints and misunderstandings.

Although there is no single correct way to do gradual enrollment, most often it looks like this.

1. The parents or a familiar person brings the child to the school.
2. The child's things are put away in an assigned cubbie.
3. The parent sits on the floor with the child or moves about the room, allowing the child to play in the environment or watch the teachers, parents, and other children.
4. The child's teacher is near during this time but is not in a hurry to interact with the child. The teacher uses this time to observe the child and the parents in action as she or he continues to care for other children and follow the day's routine.
5. As the parent and child settle in, the parent can talk with the teacher as she or he moves about the room as the day progresses. As this happens, the teacher's voice will become familiar to the child.
6. When the child needs attention, feeding, diapering or a nap, the parent proceeds with routine care. The teacher watches and observes as the parent does this.
7. Gradually, during subsequent visits or as the day progresses, the parent and the teacher reverse roles, with the parent becoming the observer and the teacher interacting directly with the child.

Don't skip gradual enrollment—it is the firm foundation upon which a mutual relationship between the parents and the teacher is built. It also gives toddlers the time they need to adjust to new places, people, and stimulation.

Facilitating Attachment: What Can Teachers Do?

Understanding stranger anxiety, an important stage of attachment, is crucial to supporting emerging independence in toddlers. Teachers can help toddlers by accepting cautious behavior and facilitating toddlers getting used to new people and settings before encouraging exploration or interaction. They can take temperament into consideration when planning new experiences or changing familiar patterns or schedules. Children who have fearful temperaments may need extra support preparing for changes and time to get used to new ideas before accepting these new ideas and participating in activities. Feisty children may need help focusing on new experiences to keep from being overwhelmed by strangers. They may also need support in handling the intense feelings and anxieties that novel experiences can create.

Although many teachers report that this is a tough stage, it signals that emotional development is right on target. Supporting children through this stage of attachment is an important part of supporting emotional growth and development.

Use the following strategies to help toddlers through stranger anxiety.

- Tell toddlers goodbye every time you leave. This continues to be an important idea well into the preschool years. When you have to leave—because it is time for your break or time to go home—tell your assigned children before you go.
- Help toddlers say goodbye, even if they resist. Use the old standbys of hugs, kisses, and a reminder to hold tight to a security item or a picture of you for comfort.
- Keep as consistent a schedule as possible. Predictability is a great comfort during this stage. It keeps toddlers from getting upset from anticipating transitions before they happen.
- When you have to leave the room and a toddler objects to your leaving, take a minute to hold her, connect with her, and assure her that you will be back. Then tell the child what you are going to do and when you will be back. When you return, go over it all again, reminding the child that you did what you said you would do. This reminder helps the next time you have to leave and can serve as a comfortable pattern for separating and reuniting.
- Prepare children for changes. Tell them what is going to happen before it happens. This helps children anticipate transitions and keeps toddlers from being upset or surprised by the change.

Facilitating Adjustment and Attachment

Researchers have expressed concerns about the development of emotional attachment of toddlers to their mothers when children begin school during toddlerhood (Belsky, 1988). As this debate continues, a quiet crisis has been occurring as the expanding demand for early education services exceeds availability (Carnegie Task Force, 1994). More and more children are spending their days at school. As a result, facilitating adjustment and attachment is a shared job facilitated by teachers.

Teachers need to differentiate the teaching role. Teachers listen to parents, suggest solutions, raise issues, point out alternatives, and provide resources to parents. These are appropriate roles for teachers. Directing child-rearing or insisting on specific expectations (like requiring the parent to take away the bottle on the first birthday) are examples of inappropriate roles for teachers. Think about the following questions to help choose appropriate boundaries.

* Who should be the first person to share the emergence of a new skill or change in growth? Parents or teachers?
* Who should decide when it is time to introduce new foods? Parents or teachers?
* Who should suggest strategies for helping toddlers learn coping skills? Parents or teachers?
* Who should be responsible for replacing disposable diapers or formula when the supply at school is depleted? Parents or teachers?

There is no absolute right answer to each of these questions. Situations will vary, and teachers need to be aware of carefully differentiating between the parenting role and the teaching role. Success in creating these boundaries will help facilitate the child's adjustment by clarifying both the teacher's and the family's unique roles.

Why does facilitating adjustment matter? For some children, these types of experiences can be life-altering. Secure attachments to significant adults (including teachers) can compensate for early deprivation and stressful experiences caused by poverty, unskilled parenting, abuse, or neglect (Schweinhart & Weikert, 1996).

What can teachers do to facilitate attachment of children to parents and then to their teachers?

- Assign a primary teacher to every child—that first friend at school who will work sensitively to match responses to cues and perfect communication, both between child and teacher and between teacher and parents.
- Resist the tendency to look at your toddlers as a group. Work hard to individualize responses to the child's cues. Congruence between toddler's nonverbal cues and quick responsiveness by the teacher will reassure the child and support the emerging relationship (Kovach & Da Ros, 1998).
- Invest in observation. Good teachers build an understanding of the toddlers in their group by being good observers. Observation informs practice and serves as the foundation for matching stimulation activities and experiences to emerging development. This match is crucial for maximizing the toddler's potential.
- Clearly differentiate the teacher's role from the parent's role. Boundaries between teachers and the families they serve are often blurred. Both seem to do the same thing during different times of the day. But the roles are not the same.

Participating in Groups—It's Harder than You Think!

One of the most frequent mistakes made during the toddler years is to assume that toddlers are ready for group participation and interaction. Although toddlers look a lot like their counterparts in preschool classrooms, they are not ready for most group activities. The reason is that toddlers are still developing their sense of selves as separate from others. The toddler's world is viewed from the perspective of **me** and **mine**!

Toddlers are egocentric—they cannot see anyone else's point of view. So, the toy I put down and walked away from is still mine, and the toy I haven't played with yet is mine also! Egocentric thought leads toddlers to conflict—conflict over toys, experiences, and people. Toddlers are also pre-verbal. They may have many receptive language skills, but they are not yet able to use expressive language to solve conflicts.

These developmental realities make the roles teachers play with toddlers crucial. The first important role is preparing the environment. Room arrangement becomes a crucial component of curriculum for toddlers. Toddlers need places to play that are not too open and yet not too intimate. Open spaces allow too many children to get into the same space—increasing the chance of conflict. Space that is too intimate makes toddlers feel territorial and possessive of the toys and materials that are available. Nooks and crannies seem to work well—places for two, or maybe three children to play together with a good selection of duplicated toys and materials.

Duplication of toys and materials serves two purposes. The first is to prevent ownership challenges and the need to hoard toys. The second is to offer enough play cues or invitations that children can play successfully near one another without having to share. A good general rule is to eliminate single toys from the environment altogether. If there is not more than one of a kind of toy, put it away until children are older. Toys do not have to be exactly alike as long as the function and use is similar. For example, a collection of three or four cars or trucks is acceptable as long as they are about the same size and type. If only one truck is a big red fire truck with a flashing light, you can count on conflict occurring, even if you have other types of cars and trucks available.

Another reason for duplication is related to the role of the teacher in toddlers' play. When children are learning to play together, teachers serve as an important source of play ideas and invitations. Joining two toddlers in the block area with the toys, rolling a car back and forth on the road, and modeling ways to play together is very important. Such invitations offer toddlers ideas about what might work and what might not, and often help get them started interacting with toys and materials.

The other crucial role of the teacher is that of facilitator—an active participant in helping children be close, share space and materials, and interact. Good toddler teachers are never far from the action—they are right in the middle of it. Proximity is the primary strategy for preventing conflict and managing normal aggression between children.

Toddlers' interactions almost always need facilitating. Facilitation can take the form of narrating what is going on, describing what might happen next, providing "provocations" or "what if" suggestions, exploring ideas that children have, and most importantly, helping toddlers take turns, ask for what they want, and wait a moment to get it.

The high energy level and distractibility of toddlers will daunt many teachers if they try to do whole-group activities. Instead, the teacher can invite children to join in activities and allow them to come and go as interest dictates. A class schedule in a toddler class is actually a schedule for the teachers—not the children. Teachers need not worry about toddlers who do not sit still long enough for a story or activity. They are just being toddlers, too involved with exploring to stay with anything for a long period of time.

Maximizing Interactions during Basic Care and Routines

Once the commitment is made to allow children to follow their own schedules, it is then easy to combine one-on-one interaction with routine activities. Time spent diapering, feeding, and putting children to sleep is also used to stimulate and encourage social, emotional, physical, language, and intellectual growth.

Reciprocity—the give and take of interactions—is virtually guaranteed during routine care. It is really difficult to serve lunch to a toddler unless the child is ready to eat, hard to change a diaper on a wiggly toddler until you get her attention. Because reciprocal interactions are so important to the development of happy, healthy children, teachers who use routines to insure a healthy dose of reciprocal exchanges are not spending too much time on routine care (Gerber, 1979). On the contrary, they make the most of the time by "ping-ponging"—getting a response and responding. Maximizing routine experiences allows children to blossom and teachers to succeed in finding time for one-on-one interchanges (Gordon, 1970).

Guidance and Discipline

What Is Guidance and Discipline with Toddlers?

Guidance refers to what teachers do before a problem is present. Discipline is what teachers do after a problem is present. Guidance techniques are preventive in nature; they guide children to maintain self-control without actual intervention by the teacher. Although self-control begins to emerge during the early childhood years, children under the age of three still depend on adults to help them maintain control, particularly in situations where there are other children present.

Toddler teachers must use children's individual schedules, daily activity schedules, classroom arrangement, and the plans they make for children's activities to help guide and direct children's behavior.

Guidance

Distraction—The younger the child is, the fewer times she should be expected to comply with verbal requests. For example, toddlers will frequently pick up food with their hands. Constant verbal reminders to "use your spoon" fail because we are expecting the child to change her behavior to suit the situation.

A better strategy is to hand the child a spoon. This encourages the child to use a spoon and increases the chance that she might do so by putting the spoon into her hand. It modifies the situation to fit the child's developmental stage.

This technique is called distraction. Distraction involves changing the child's focus from an activity that is unacceptable to one that is acceptable without directly confronting the inappropriate behavior. Use distraction when there is no danger to the child. Distraction also can be used to prevent the escalation of a minor problem into a major one. Toddlers respond very well to this guidance technique. Parents and teachers can use distraction often to modify the situation for very young children.

Redirection—Redirection is a preventive discipline strategy requiring that teachers be particularly good observers of children. Redirection involves anticipating problems and intervening before they occur. The following are examples of redirection:

- Exchanging an inappropriate toy or activity (such as eating dirt on the playground) for an appropriate one (such as handing the child a hand shovel to dig in the dirt),

- Quietly singing a song to redirect a child's focus from a separation event to what is going on in the classroom, or
- Putting something in a toddler's hand when that child is fingering another child's hair (to prevent pulling hair).

Redirection only works when alert teachers get to a situation before it erupts into a problem. Once children need more intervention, the opportunity to redirect is lost.

Ignoring as a Guidance Strategy—Ignoring inappropriate behavior is a discipline strategy that teachers often forget to use. The school day can be long, and some children exhibit behaviors that are irritating but not dangerous or really problematic. For example, toddlers often dump the contents of manipulative toy containers on the floor or tabletop. An observant teacher uses these experiences to model putting things back in the container and to encourage the toddler to help, rather than scolding the child for a normative behavior that is interesting and fun for the child.

To determine if ignoring is an appropriate strategy, ask yourself, "Is this a behavior I can live with in my classroom?" If the answer is yes, try ignoring the behavior. It goes without saying that behavior that hurts other children or destroys the environment or materials cannot be ignored.

Teacher Competencies to Support Transitioning to School

Sometimes	Usually	Always	
☐	☐	☐	Looks up, acknowledges, and greets children and parents as they arrive in the class room.
☐	☐	☐	Facilitates child's entry into the classroom and separation from parents as they leave.
☐	☐	☐	Accepts and respects each child as she is. Indicates this respect by talking about what is going to happen and waiting for indications of wants or needs before responding.
☐	☐	☐	Shows an awareness of each child's temperament and level of development.
☐	☐	☐	Responds quickly to children who need attention.
☐	☐	☐	Allows children to follow their own schedules; changes with the children as schedules fluctuate. Is an alert observer of each child in the classroom.
☐	☐	☐	Uses routines of eating, resting, and diapering as opportunities to maximize reciprocal interactions.
☐	☐	☐	Monitors children's general comfort and health (for example, warmth, dryness, noses wiped, wet clothes changed, and so on).
☐	☐	☐	Invests in quality time with infants throughout the day during routines and stimulation activities.
☐	☐	☐	Uses floor time to build relationships with children.
☐	☐	☐	Maintains a positive, pleasant attitude toward parents; thinks in terms of creating a partnership to support the child.
☐	☐	☐	Communicates regularly with parents about the child's experience at school; uses a variety of techniques to keep communication flowing freely.
☐	☐	☐	Plans, implements, and evaluates regular parent participation experiences, parent/teacher conferences, and parent education experiences.
☐	☐	☐	Supports children's developing awareness by talking about families, displaying families' photographs, and celebrating accomplishments.
☐	☐	☐	Uses books, pictures, and stories to help children identify with events that occur in the world of the family and the school.

Resources for Teachers

Belsky, J. (1988). The effects of infant day care reconsidered. ***Early Childhood Research Quarterly,*** 3, 235-272.

Blecher-Sass, H. (1997). Good-byes can build trust. ***Young Children***, 52(7), 12-15.

Bredekamp, S. & C. Copple. (1997). ***Developmentally appropriate practice in early childhood programs serving children from birth to age 8*** (exp. ed.). Washington, DC: National Association for the Education of Young Children (NAEYC).

California Department of Education. (1990). ***Flexible, fearful, or feisty: The different temperaments of infants and toddlers*** {videotape}. Sacramento, CA.

Carnegie Corporation of New York. (1994). ***Starting Points: Meeting the needs of our youngest children.*** New York: Carnegie Corporation of New York.

Chess, S. & A. Thomas. (1987). ***Know your child***. New York: Basic Books.

Gerber, M. (1979). ***Resources for infant educarers: A manual for parents and professionals***. Los Angeles, CA: Resources for Infant Educarers.

Gerber, M. & A. Johnson. (1998). ***Your self-confident baby.*** New York: Wiley.

Gordon, I. (1972). ***Baby learning through play.*** New York; St. Martin's.

Greenspan, S. & N.T. Greenspan. (1989). ***The essential partnership***. New York: Penguin.

Kovach, B.A. & D.A. Da Ros. (1998). Respectful, individual, and responsive caregiving for infants: The key to successful care in group settings. ***Young Children***, 51(1), 58-67.

Miller, K. (2000). ***Ages and stages***. West Palm Beach, FL: TelShare Publishing.

Neugebauer, B. (1992). ***Alike and different: Exploring our humanity with children***. Washington, DC: National Association for the Education of Young Children (NAEYC).

Schweinhart, L. & D.P. Weikert. (1996). ***Lasting differences: The High/Scope preschool curriculum comparison through age 23.*** Monographs of the High/Scope Educational Research Foundation, #12, Ypsilanti, MI: High/Scope Press.

Stonehouse, A. (1995). ***How does it feel?: Child care from a parent's perspective***. Redmond, WA: Exchange Press.

Teaching Tolerance Project. (1997). ***Starting small: Teaching tolerance in preschool and the early grades***. Montgomery, AL: Southern Poverty Law Center.

INNOVATIONS IN PARENT PARTNERSHIPS

School- or Teacher-initiated Activities

Pre-enrollment Visit

Plan a pre-enrollment visit for the parents and child to see the classroom and get a glimpse of what the day will be like.

Family Interview

Interview the family and let them interview the teacher. Talk about teaching philosophy and ask about parenting styles. Discuss the family's expectations for the child's school experience.

Establishing Rituals

Establish a separation and reunion routine that both the parents and the teacher will use every day. Write it down so everyone will know what the plan is.

Photo Opportunity

Photograph the parents and child together in the classroom to put in the crib or on the wall for the child to see.

Parent Participation Possibilities

Gradual Enrollment

Conduct a gradual enrollment where new families gradually increase the amount of time they spend in school—first with Mom or Dad's support and then for increasing amounts of time without Mom and Dad.

Meet-Your-Friends-at-School Book

If time allows, send home a picture book of children in the classroom to newly enrolled children. Label each child's picture with his or her name, and laminate the pages of the book. Tie the pages together with yarn or string.

Parent Postcards

Share Parent Postcards with parents as they indicate an interest, at appropriate times during the enrollment cycle, or as developmental issues arise. (See page 548 in the Appendix for a sample dissemination schedule.) Copy Postcards. Cut if necessary. Address to parent(s) and place on Communication Sheet or hand out personally.

Attachment Stage 4—Stranger Anxiety: What Can Parents Do?

The fourth stage of attachment, known as stranger anxiety, is characterized by fear of unknown or strange adults. The cautious behavior of separation anxiety, Stage 3, is replaced with clinging, crying, screaming, and fearful responses to unfamiliar adults. Toddlers resist overtures and interactions from unknown adults and show distress when their parents and favorite alternate caregiver leaves them or moves away from them. This stage emerges at 18 or 19 months and lasts until 24-26 months.

These behaviors indicate that your child is very close to finishing the development of his or her emotional attachment to you. But, your child is not yet ready to let the whole world intrude on the closeness he or she feels with you. Strangers, therefore, pose threats. The first is that they might take you away, and, secondly, they might take your child away from you. Strategies to help toddlers through this stage include the following:

- Tell your child goodbye every time you leave. This continues to be an important idea well into the preschool years. Help your child say goodbye, even if he or she resists. Use the old standbys of hugs, kisses, and a reminder to hold tight to a security item or a picture of you for comfort.
- Keep as consistent a schedule as possible. Predictability is a great comfort during this stage. It keeps toddlers from getting upset because they anticipate your return and it doesn't happen.
- When you are at home and your child objects to you leaving the room or doing tasks, take a minute to hold him or her, reconnect with your child, assure him or her that you will still be there. Then, tell him or her what you are going to do and when you will be back. Offer to take your child along, if possible.
- Prepare your child for changes. Tell him or her what is going to happen before it happens. This prepares children to anticipate transitions and keeps toddlers from being surprised by the change.

Although many parents report that this is a tough stage, it signals that your child's emotional development is right on target. Supporting your child through this last stage is an important

TO

Creating a Separation and Reunion Ritual

The way the day begins and ends for your child is so important. It sets the tone for the day and supports the task of learning to separate and reunite. What can you do to make these important times of the day work for you and your child?

Establish a predictable way to separate and reunite with your child. Having a predictable pattern helps children feel comfortable in the transition process. It also prevents children from using arrival and departure times as an opportunity to manipulate parents and teachers. Your arrival at school should look the same each day.

Come into the room, talk a minute with your child's teacher, and put your toddler's things away. Next, help your child begin to settle in by offering him or her a toy to play with or a book to read. Don't rush the separation process. It may take your child as long as 15 minutes or so to get ready for you to leave. When you are ready to leave, tell the teacher, kiss and hug your child, say goodbye and that you'll be back, and leave, blowing kisses and waving all the while.

Do the same upon your return. Instead of rushing off to gather your child's belongings to go home, cherish the reuniting process. Pick your child up, hug and kiss him or her, and then spend a few minutes getting reconnected. Don't be surprised if your child ignores you for a minute or two. He or she has just figured out that you have been somewhere else all day and may take a few minutes to get over being mad about that! Sit down and watch what your child is doing and follow his or her lead about when to try to reunite again.

TO ____________

Arrival and Departure Routines ARE Transitions

Expect arrival and departure times to be transitions. Everything in a young child's life is a transition. Some transitions are handled better than others. Most parents realize that arrival and departure times can't be abrupt and quick—transitions take time. In general, children, even very young children, resist being rushed or hurried. Parents have all been in the situation where they are running late. The harder they push, the slower and more resistant their child becomes! Knowing this is the case, plan arrival and departure routines to accept this inevitable reality.

Let your child's teacher know if your routine is going to change. Sometimes teachers can offset children's real discomfort about changes in schedule by preparing the child for the change. Even very young children know the sequence of which parent comes in first, then next, then next, and so on. If you let your teacher know, your teacher can help your child accommodate the increased time at the school without going into the "waiting" mode too soon.

Develop back-up strategies before you need them and practice these routines, too. It's going to happen—a flat tire, a car accident, a last-minute work demand that can't be postponed, more traffic than you have ever seen, the downpour that floods every street leading to the school. Plan now for these situations so that you have a backup if you cannot be predictable in your departure routine. And, don't forget to discuss the back-up plan with your child's teacher. Practice it once or twice before it is needed. Then everyone will know how to handle it if the plan is put into effect.

Predictable beginnings and ends to the day are important to you and to your child. Separations and reunions are easier for adults because we are more experienced in negotiating them. Children, particularly very young children, need lots of help from you to make them a pleasant part of their school experience.

TO

Always Say Goodbye

Leaving your child may be as hard for you as it is for him or her. It might seem that leaving without saying goodbye could save you and your toddler from suffering through another separation. In fact, the opposite is true.

During the first three years of life, children learn that the world in which they live is a predictable and responsive place to be, or that it isn't. They learn this important lesson from their caregivers. Parents and teachers who provide sensitive, responsive, and predictable care teach children to trust them.

You can help your child learn that although you may leave him or her, you will never disappear without a goodbye kiss and hug and a promise to return. At first, your child may not care too much when you leave. But as your child grows, so will his or her resistance to being separated from you. If you always say goodbye now, when it doesn't matter quite as much, when it does matter a lot, your child will remember the separation routine you have used over time and find it comforting. And, your child will learn that you mean what you say—that you will come back, just like you said you would.

TO ______________

____

____

Pacifiers

Pacifiers pose a significant challenge to toddler parents. It might seem like your growing toddler is too old for this form of soothing, and you may want to get rid of it as your child becomes more independent. Pacifiers, particularly if they are part of your toddler's calm-down routines, are hard to just take away.

As your baby matured, the sucking reflex disappeared and was replaced by your child's use of sucking the pacifier as a comfort strategy. He or she probably uses the pacifier for calming down after losing control or to relax enough to fall asleep. Both of these coping strategies are good ones, and we usually don't want to take away a coping strategy without helping children learn new ones to take the place of outdated ones.

Try the following to help your child transition from depending on a pacifier to being able to cope with newer skills.

- Start by limiting where and when your child can use the pacifier. Instead of clipping it to his or her clothing, put it in a special place—a basket or bowl—near your child's bed, or attach it to a security toy like a teddy bear or a doll.
- When your child needs to use the pacifier, send him or her to the bedroom or special place to retrieve the pacifier to use for calming down or to find the toy with the pacifier attached.
- After the child is calm, help him or her return the pacifier to the special place so it can be found when needed again. Your support in returning it to the special place will reinforce that the pacifier is still available—and in a place where your child can find it when he or she needs it.
- Help your child choose a transitional object, such as a stuffed toy, to hold on to when he or she is using the pacifier. Pairing up a transitional object with pacifier use may lead to substituting the toy for the pacifier over time.

TO

Transitional or Security Items

Parents are sometimes concerned when their toddlers use transitional or security objects. Toddlers often develop strong attachments to transitional objects such as blankets, stuffed animals, soft, silky fabric, or favorite pieces of clothing such as hats or burp cloths. For some, the item is transitory and changing as long as it is something from home. For others, the intensity of the attachment requires parents to make sure the security object is always nearby.

Like thumb or finger sucking, transitional items are a normal part of learning to separate, reunite, and transition. They can also be an excellent coping mechanism for self-quieting and soothing. In fact, children who have security items often cope better with unfamiliar situations than children who don't have transitional objects.

You might be concerned about when attachment to a security item might become a problem. Look at three issues when deciding about transitional objects:

1) the duration,
2) the intensity of the attachment, and
3) the distress caused by separation from the security item.

For example, teenagers rarely carry around transitional objects from early childhood but may, quite normally, keep them in a safe place in their rooms. Children who are traumatized if they misplace their transitional objects as they near the end of the early childhood period (which actually lasts until age 8) may be indicating the need for help to solve an underlying problem.

Take a look around school. Children of all ages and particularly very young children use a wide variety of coping mechanisms to manage separation from parents—the most important people in their lives—and transitioning to school. Your child's teacher will view this as a natural part of growing up and offer the strategies your child has learned at home as a support for encouraging adjustment and maturation.

TO

Just How Long Will Adjustment Take?

Many parents view the first few days of a child's school experience as an indication of how things will be when the child completes the adjustment process. Unfortunately, for toddlers, the initial experience is just the beginning. It is common for toddlers who are just beginning school to take up to three months to really complete adjusting. In general, though, most children are well on their way in about six weeks. What should parents expect as the adjustment process unfolds?

Children who are 18-24 months old are often very uncomfortable in new settings and resist participating. They may cling to their parents and refuse to join in activities. Give children who are in this age group plenty of time to stay close and watch while they get comfortable with the new setting. Provide nonverbal support if they do venture out (smile, nod your head, or hold a hand and go along). Expect to see lots of "tank-up behavior"—venturing out, then coming back for comfort and support, then venturing out again.

Children who are 24-30 months old may be cautious about new settings with new people, but their curiosity and interest in the environment is often enough to overcome their anxiety. Encouragement from familiar adults is usually all that is needed to bridge the gap. Or, your child may love the new setting the first time—exhibiting no resistance at all. Then, after a brief time, he or she will be ready to leave or not want to return. When this occurs, stay close during the next visit and persist in supporting participation.

Children who are 30-36 months old usually look forward to new experiences, particularly when other children are involved. It is still important to support transitions by sharing time together in the new setting and using positive nonverbal cues such as smiling and nodding your head.

TO ____________

Thumb and Finger Sucking

Most pediatricians and child development experts view thumb or finger sucking as an extension of the strong rooting and sucking reflexes with which a child is born. They consider it a normal part of early development. You may disagree. Concerns about thumb or finger sucking causing the mouth or palate to disfigure and issues about lifelong bad habits are common.

Most children give up finger or thumb sucking on their own as they learn other self-soothing and self-comforting behaviors. Don't worry too much about future problems right now. When the time is right, you and your child's teacher can work together to address this concern.

TO

Facilitating Adjustment

What can parents do to facilitate adjustment? First of all, be patient with the process. It will take a while for your child to adjust. This is normal and to be expected. Stay in close touch with your child's teacher. Good communication helps both you and your toddler succeed in adjusting. Talk about your concerns, and ask your child's teacher to tell you how she or he is helping your child adjust. Begin the transition process with shorter days. Shorter days in the new environment with new people will be easier for your toddler to handle.

Most children make the transition to school in about four to six weeks, but each child is different. Taking time during the transition process to help your toddler adjust will pay off for both of you!

TO

Resources for Parents

Bailey, Becky. (1997). ***I love you rituals***. Oviedo, FL: Loving Guidance.

Bailey, Becky. (1998). ***10 principles of positive discipline***. Oviedo, FL: Loving Guidance.

Brazelton, T. B. (1992). ***Touchpoints: The essential reference.*** Reading, MA: Addison Wesley.

Ilg, L.B. & F.L. Ames. (1976). ***Your Two Year Old***. New York: Delacorte Press.

Leach, P. (1997). ***Your baby and child: From birth to five***. New York: Knopf.

Miller, K. (2000). ***Ages and stages***. West Palm Beach, FL: TelShare.

INNOVATIONS IN ENVIRONMENTS

Characteristics of Toddler Environments

Toddler environments must meet their developmental needs. For this reason, toddler classrooms will differ significantly from those classrooms designed for infants and preschoolers. Toddlers are much more independent than infants and are beginning to explore their world in new ways.

Creating a Home-like Setting

Toddlers need a warm, home-like setting where they can feel safe and secure. Use a room arrangement that creates the nooks and crannies that they need to be able to get away from the excitement that is a natural part of the toddler experience. Soft elements help to muffle noises and create spaces where toddlers can feel cuddled.

Meltdown Places

Unlike infants, toddlers need meltdown places, places where they can be alone while they gain composure. These spaces should be carpeted and away from sharp edges of furniture. While children are losing control and then getting it back, teachers must be able to see them and support them. Sometimes, even something as simple as sitting in a box can give a toddler the feeling of being alone and of being able to regroup.

Also, unlike infants, toddlers are mobile and able to choose specific toys for play. Provide a variety of toddler toys, including manipulatives, puzzles, dolls, blocks, and books arranged on low shelves. Toddlers will choose, play with, and discard many toys as they play. Use clear containers that are labeled with a picture of the contents and the name of the objects. Putting toys in their appropriate containers can be a game at the end of play.

Opportunities for Different Perspectives

Because many toddlers must observe before they are able to join in an activity, many different perspectives must be available to them in the classroom. Multiple levels in the environment are one way to provide places for toddlers to be where they can be away from others and still observe the action. A raised platform or even foam blocks joined together can create this (perspective). Additionally, windows on walls, in doors, and between classrooms provide young children an opportunity to participate in one of their favorite activities—spectator sports. Watching other children, adults, cars, and animals can be very interesting!

Opportunities to Climb

Toddlers enjoy actively exploring their environment. They like to climb and have improved their climbing skills. Although toddlers are growing and changing physically, they are still very top-heavy. This can be a problem when climbing. Provide low climbing pieces of equipment and a cushioned fall zone.

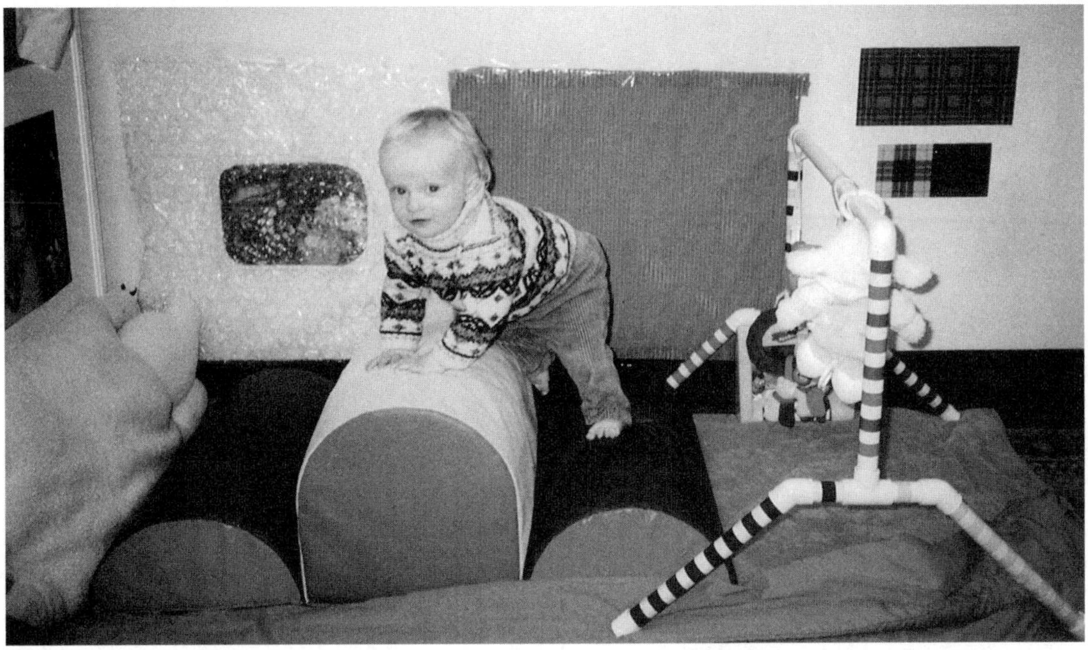

Decreasing and Increasing Stimulation

Teachers of toddlers must be able to increase and decrease the level of activity and stimulation in the classroom. Decreasing the amount of light, or increasing it, or providing incandescent as well as florescent and full-spectrum lighting are examples of ways to change stimulation levels. Adding quiet music or removing all background noise and replacing it with sounds of nature are others. Check your classroom to see which of these dimensions are under your control and can be managed as needed.

Activities and Experiences vs. Centers

Most early childhood educators think of interest or learning centers as an essential part of any classroom setting. Yet, environments for toddlers are different because toddlers are "groupie" in nature and tend to go where the action is. For this reason, teachers must bring activities and experiences to children and assist them in going to where the activities are. A wide range of activities and experiences must be available to toddlers. In each of the following Possibilities Plans, *Me and My Body* and *My Family*, activities and experiences are presented in the following areas:

- Dramatic Possibilities
- Sensory/Art Possibilities
- Curiosity Possibilities
- Construction Possibilities
- Literacy Possibilities
- Music Possibilities
- Movement Possibilities
- Outdoor Possibilities
- Project Possibilities
- Parent Participation Possibilities

When planning for a toddler classroom, consider the following when choosing furniture and equipment.

- Provide low tables and chairs where toddlers' feet touch the floor.
- Since the toddler class is where most children master independent toileting, both a diapering area with running water and a bathroom with toddler-sized toilets are needed.
- A floor that is easily mopped and sanitized is necessary, especially under eating areas, in the bathroom, and under messy sensory or art areas.
- Plan for carpeting where children play with blocks, construction toys, and manipulatives.
- Food preparation should be as far away as possible from the diapering area.
- Plan a space where toddlers can access the teacher. This may be on a rug or even in a glider or low chair.
- Finally, in addition to all the wonderful toys and equipment now available for the toddler classroom, include mirrors—large and small (cover an entire wall if possible). The mirrors will help brighten the classroom and will allow toddlers to orient themselves and others in the classroom.

Me and My Body

WEB

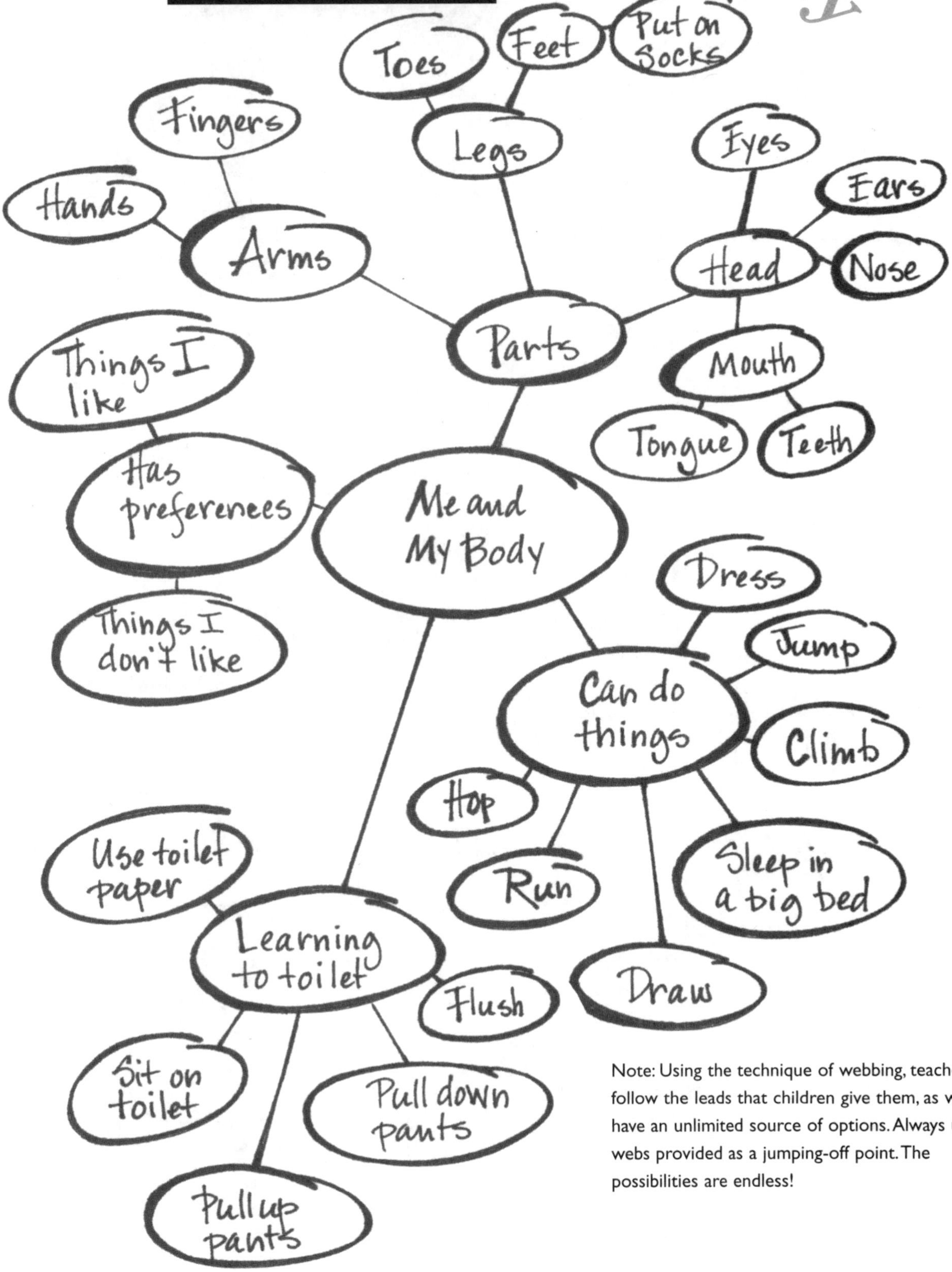

Note: Using the technique of webbing, teachers can follow the leads that children give them, as well as have an unlimited source of options. Always use the webs provided as a jumping-off point. The possibilities are endless!

PLANNING PAGES

Plan Possibilities

Dramatic

- Hidden Faces 74
- I See Me! 74
- Hands and Feet 74
- Silly Shoes 75

Sensory/Art

- Hand Mural 75
- Face Mural 76
- Smelly Paints 76
- Bubble Wrap Mittens 76

Curiosity

- Giant Texture Board 77
- Feelie Socks 78
- Fingerprints 78
- Mirror Portraits 78

Construction

- Picture Blocks 79

Literacy

- Book of Many Faces 79
- Turning Pages 80
- Glove Finger Puppets 80
- "I Can Do It!" Book 81
- Baggie Books 81

Music

- Here They Are! 81
- Clapping Hands 82
- Shake Your Shaker 82

Movement

- Thumb-in-the-Box 83
- Jumping Feet 83
- Silly Face Fun 83
- Hop a Little 84

Outdoor

- Simple Things Are Fun! ... 84
- Follow the Trail 85
- Tippy Toes 85
- Throw the Ball 86

Projects

- Body Painting 86
- Books Read List 87

Parent Participation

- Supporting Possibilities ... 87
- Boxes to Blocks 87
- Parent Postcards
  - Every Child Is Unique! .. 88
  - You Are Your Child's Best Teacher 89

Me and My Body

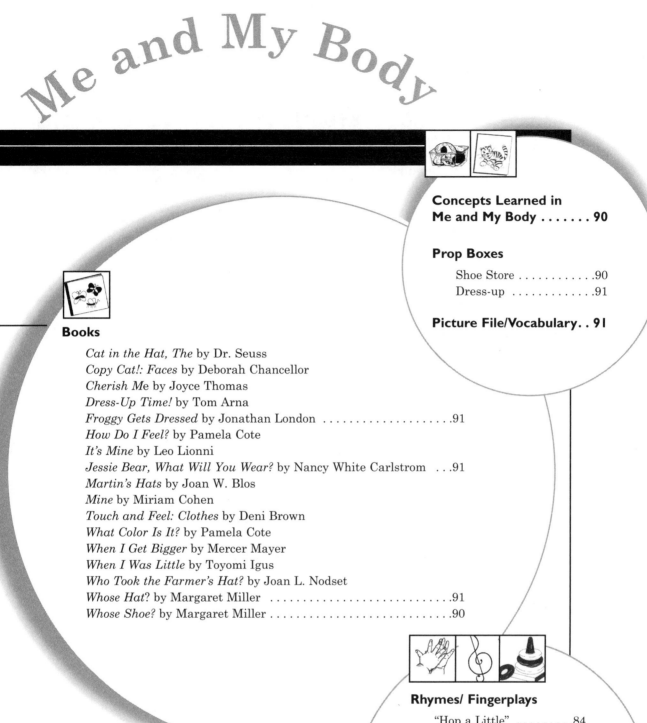

Hidden Faces

All ages

Materials
Unbreakable mirror
Curtain

Provide a mirror hanging on the wall with a curtain over it. Show children how to move the curtain aside to see themselves in the mirror. Observe their reactions.

I See Me!

18-24 months

Materials
Unbreakable mirror (locker-style)
Hook/loop (Velcro) fasteners
Hats

Teacher Talk
Use the child's name as you talk about the child's reflection in the mirror. "Who is that in the mirror, Matt? Your face is in the mirror. I see you." "You have a hat on your head."

Attach unbreakable mirrors low on the wall with hook/loop fasteners. Provide a variety of hats for toddlers to try on and look at themselves in the mirror. Show toddlers their images in the mirror.

Hands and Feet

24-30 months

Materials
Adult-size tube socks
Basket

Teacher Talk
"Marcus, you have socks on your feet. Socks keep feet warm." "I have on mittens. Mittens keep hands warm."

Place a variety of colors of adult-size tube socks and a variety of sizes of mittens in a basket for children to explore putting on and taking off. Watch for skill acquisition when toddlers perfect taking socks or mittens off, then pulling them on.

Silly Shoes

30-36 months

Materials

Old shoes big enough for children to wear over their own shoes
Spray paint
Acrylic paints and paintbrushes

Teacher Talk

Comment on how different the shoes are from children's own shoes. "You have big red shoes on your feet, Susie."

Spray paint old shoes with bright colors. When the paint is dry, use acrylic paints to make colorful designs on the shoes. Put the shoes out in Dramatic Play and observe how the children respond to them.

SENSORY/ART POSSIBILITIES

Hand Mural

All ages

Materials

Butcher paper
Paint
Sponges or paper towels

Teacher Talk

Comment on the handprints as toddlers work.

Help children press their hands onto paint-soaked sponges or paper towels and then press their painted hands onto butcher paper to make a print as an introduction to this activity. Then let children proceed without your help. Hang the completed mural on the wall at children's eye level. Repeat the process with different colors at additional times until the mural has many handprints on it. Label each child's handprint with a permanent marker and the date.

Face Mural

18-24 months

Materials
Magazine pictures
Glue sticks
Butcher paper

Teacher Talk
Talk with toddlers about the facial features on the pictures. "Madison has her finger on the eyes. Find more eyes, Josh. There they are—you found brown eyes."

Cut pictures of children's faces from magazines. Demonstrate dabbing glue on the back side of the pictures and attaching them to the paper.

Smelly Paints

24-30 months

Materials
Paint
Food flavorings
Paper
Paintbrushes

Teacher Talk
Comment on the different scents as the children paint. "What do you smell, Jodie? I smell lemon. The yellow paint smells like lemon."

Add powdered soft drink mix to the appropriate colors of paint to give the paint a scent.

Bubble Wrap Mittens

30-36 months

Materials
Plastic bubble wrap
Scissors
Duct tape
Paints
Paper

Teacher Talk
"Feel the mitten, Rico. The mitten has bubbles on it. I wonder what will happen if you paint with the mitten?"

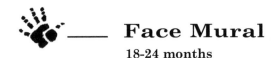

Cut bubble wrap into an eight-inch square. Fold the wrap in half and use duct tape to seal the two open sides, making a mitten with no thumb. Children slip their hands inside the mitten, then dip the mitten into paint. Demonstrate pressing the mitten onto the paper until all the paint is gone. Start with one color. Then add others to experiment with mixing colors.

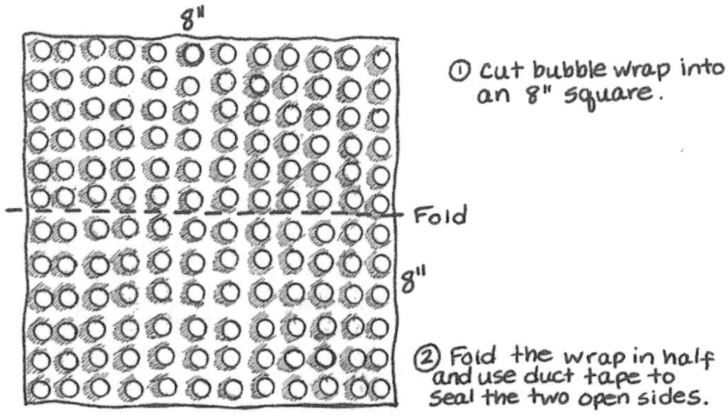

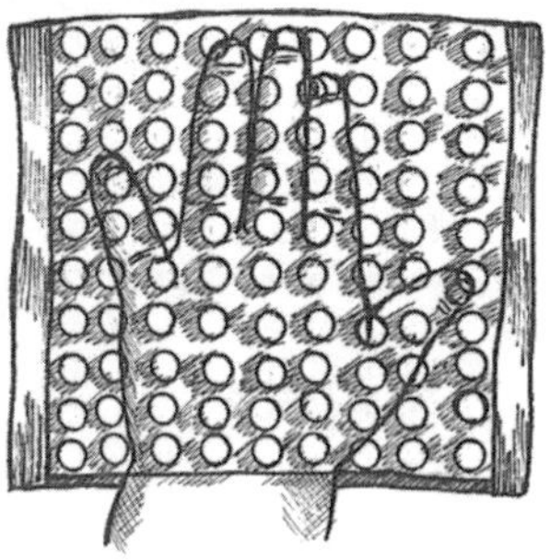

CURIOSITY POSSIBILITIES

Giant Texture Board

18-24 months

Materials

Large piece of heavy cardboard
Textured materials, such as fabric textures, wallpaper samples, cardboard egg carton, carpet pieces, cotton batting, sandpaper, piece of rubber bath tub mat, bubble wrap
Heavy-duty glue

Teacher Talk

"How does this bubble wrap feel, Julie?"

Attach a variety of textured materials to a large piece of cardboard. Mount the cardboard low on the wall, so children can explore the textures. Or, put the texture board on the floor and explore how it feels.

? Feelie Socks

24-30 months

Materials
Adult-size tube sock
Appropriate-size familiar toys

Teacher Talk
Talk about how the toy feels. "The toy is soft like Maria's blankie."

Place a familiar toy inside the sock. A child reaches inside the sock to feel the toy. Let the child then take the toy out of the sock and touch it. Use this activity as a one-on-one activity with children as they calm down for a nap, wake up from a nap, as well as any other time during the day.

? Fingerprints

24-30 months

Materials
Inkpads
Paper
Plastic magnifier

Teacher Talk
Comment on the difference in size with and without the magnifier. "Dylan's fingerprint is BIG!"

Demonstrate pressing fingers onto an inkpad, and then pressing fingers onto paper to make fingerprints. Provide magnifying glasses to investigate the prints.

? Mirror Portraits

30-36 months

Materials
Tall, unbreakable mirror
Washable nontoxic paint
Paintbrushes
Shower curtain
Wet washcloth

Teacher Talk
Cover the floor under the mirror with a shower curtain. Let one toddler paint what she sees in the mirror. After she is done, offer her a wet washcloth to clean the mirror to start over again.

CONSTRUCTION POSSIBILITIES

Picture Blocks

All ages

Materials

Photos of children
Copier
Small cardboard boxes
Newspaper
Tape
Glue
Clear contact paper

Teacher Talk

"Let's stack the blocks on the carpet. One, two, three, Darin. You stacked three of the blocks."

Make black-and-white copies of children's pictures. Gather a variety of boxes. Stuff boxes with newspaper. Tape box openings securely closed. Glue the pictures onto the cardboard boxes and cover with clear contact paper. As children grow and mature, add new pictures to new boxes until you have a set of picture blocks that are unique to the children in your classroom.

LITERACY POSSIBILITIES

Book of Many Faces

18-24 months

Materials

Magazine pictures of faces
Cardboard or poster board
Glue
Hole punch
Yarn or metal rings

Teacher Talk

"Look at this picture, Joy. What do you see? I see your teeth. Where are your teeth, Savannah?"

Glue the pictures of the different faces onto poster board pages. Punch holes in the pages and fasten them together with yarn or metal rings. Read the book to children and name the features of the faces as you look at the book together.

Turning Pages

18-24 months

Materials

Old magazines, junk-mail catalogs

Teacher Talk

"Joseph sees the doggie! There is one little doggie. What do you think is on the next page, Joseph? Turn the page and let's see. You did it! You found more doggies."

Provide toddlers with old magazines and/or junk-mail catalogs to practice turning pages. Let children experiment with page turning in this safe and inexpensive format. Observe to see who uses the whole hand to turn the pages and who begins to use the thumb and index finger to turn the pages. Point out things in the illustrations or photographs.

Glove Finger Puppets

24-30 months

Materials

White or light-colored gloves
Scissors
Permanent marker

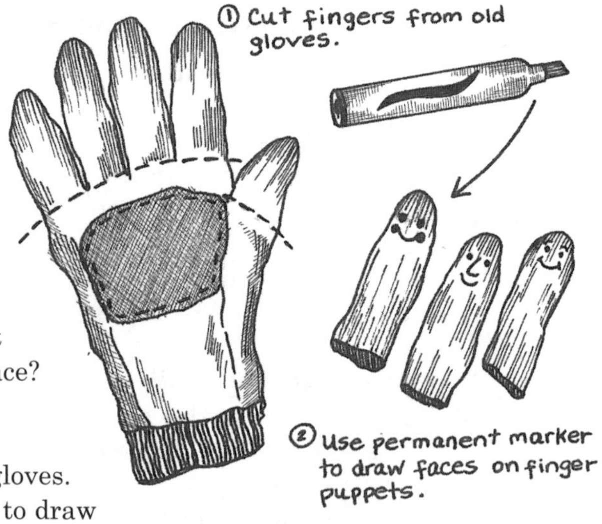

Teacher Talk

Describe the puppet's facial features and/or how to use the puppets in conjunction with fingerplays or rhymes. "My puppet has two eyes. Point to your puppet's eyes, Seth. What else is on your puppet's face? Ears! And what else?"

Cut fingers from the old gloves. Use a permanent marker to draw faces on these finger puppets. Demonstrate placing the puppets on their pointer/index fingers and how to make them move.

"I Can Do It!" Book

24-30 months

Materials

Magazine pictures
Glue
Cardboard or poster board
Hole punch
Yarn

Teacher Talk

Read the book and ask questions to help children describe what is happening in the pictures. "Caroline, I see a girl riding in the car. How about this page? What do you see?"

Collect magazine pictures of toddlers involved in typical toddler activities. Glue the pictures onto cardboard, punch holes in the pages, and fasten the pages together with yarn to make a book.

Baggie Books

30-36 months

Materials

Resealable plastic bags
Magazine pictures of people using hands and feet
Cardboard
Glue
Hole punch
Yarn

Teacher Talk

Talk about the pictures, emphasizing the use of hands and feet. "I see socks. I see feet. I see hands. What do you see?"

Cut out or collect pictures of people doing things with their hands and feet. Glue pictures onto cardboard cut to fit inside the resealable plastic bags. Punch holes in the left sides of the pages and fasten them together with yarn. Share the book with children.

MUSIC POSSIBILITIES

Here They Are!

18-24 months

Materials

None

Teacher Talk
"Where are your hands, Ethan? There they are! Your hands are ready to act out the song."

Sing the following action song with toddlers. Sing to the tune "Where Is Thumbkin?"

Here They Are!
Where are your hands? Where are your hands?
Here they are! Here they are!
Clap them together. Clap them together.
Clap, clap, clap. Clap, clap, clap.

Where are your feet? Where are your feet?
Here they are! Here they are!
Stamp them on the floor. Stamp them on the floor.
Stamp, stamp, stamp. Stamp, stamp, stamp.

Clapping Hands

24-30 months

Materials
None

Teacher Talk
"Clap your hands like me, Savannah. You did it. Now, let's clap our hands to the song."

Sing the following song with children to the tune "Skip to My Lou."

Clapping Hands
Clap, clap, clap your hands.
Clap, clap, clap your hands.
Clap, clap, clap your hands.
Clap your hands like me.

Shake Your Shaker

24-30 months

Materials
Plastic bottles or jars
Noisy materials (rice, dried beans, bells)
Glue, tape

Teacher Talk
"Follow me! Shake your shaker by your toe."

As you sing the following song, model how children are to shake the shakers. Sing the song to the tune "The Farmer in the Dell."

Shake Your Shaker
Shake your shaker high.
Shake your shaker low.
Shake it here and shake it there.
Now shake it by your toe!

MOVEMENT POSSIBILITIES

____ Thumb-in-the-Box
18-24 months

Materials
None

Teacher Talk
"Alyssa, your thumb is inside your fist. Good job! Pop your thumb out!"

Recite this fingerplay with toddlers as you talk about thumbs.

Thumb-in-the-Box
Thumb-in-the-Box, sit so still, (Make a fist by placing
the thumb inside the fingers.)
Will you come out?
Yes, I will! (Pop thumb out of fist.)

____ Jumping Feet
24-30 months

Materials
None

Teacher Talk
"Look at Michael jump! Go, Michael, jump, jump! Jump! Jump! Jump! Michael, your feet like to jump!"

Repeat the following rhyme as you show toddlers how to jump.

Jumping Feet
Jumping feet, jumping feet, jump, jump!
Up to the sky, away up high.
Jumping feet, jumping feet, jump, jump!

____ Silly Face Fun
24-30 months

Materials
None

Teacher Talk
"Ashley knows how to "beep" her nose! That's the way a mouth goes "munch." You did it!"

Use this fun action poem with children as you talk about the face.

Silly Face
These are my eye peepers, eye peepers, eye peepers.
These are my eye peepers. (Point to eyes.)
Now they're eye sleepers. (Close eyes.)
This is my nose beeper, nose beeper, nose beeper.
This is my nose beeper. (Point to nose.)
I can go beep! beep! beep! (Touch the nose.)
This is my mouth eater, mouth eater, mouth eater.
This is my mouth eater. (Point to the mouth.)
Munch! Munch! Munch! (Make chewing motions.)

Hop a Little

30-36 months

Materials
None

Teacher Talk
"Corey, hop on two feet! You did it."

Recite this poem with children. Show them how to act out the movements with you.

Hop a Little
Hop a little, jump a little,
One, two, three.
Run a little, clap a little,
Tap one knee.
Bend a little, stretch a little,
Wiggle your head.
Hop a little, jump a little

OUTDOOR POSSIBILITIES

Simple Things Are Fun!

18-24 months

Materials
Riding toys

Teacher Talk
"Run, run! Matt wants to run. I'm going to catch you, Matt." "Push with your feet, Maria. That's the way to make that car go! You did it, Maria. Feet make the car go!"

Simple games, such as chase, or simple activities, such as riding a push toy, are often just what toddlers want and need. For a game of chase, choose a grassy, sandy area of the playground. Toddlers may want to chase the teacher, or they may want the teacher to chase them. For enjoyable push-toy experiences, provide a collection of riding toys for toddlers to practice moving with their feet.

Follow the Trail
24-30 Months

Materials
Strip of paper (12" x 36")

Teacher Talk
"Josh can walk on the paper trail. That's the way, Josh, keep your feet on the trail."

Place a strip of paper approximately 12" wide and 36" long on the ground. Show toddlers how to walk on the paper.

Tippy Toes
30-36 months

Materials
None

Teacher Talk
"Look at Will standing on his tiptoes! Will can walk on his tiptoes."

Demonstrate walking on tiptoes. Tiptoe around the playground together. Use this as a transition activity to gather children to go inside.

Throw the Ball

30-36 months

Materials
Large, soft balls
Laundry basket

Teacher Talk
"Here comes the ball, Corey. Catch! Throw it back to me. That's it."
Provide several large, soft balls for children to roll to each other the playground. Or, provide a laundry basket for toddlers to throw balls into. Remember, catching is still a complex skill. When working on catching, make sure balls are large and under-inflated to avoid injury.

PROJECT POSSIBILITIES

Body Painting

All ages

Materials
Nontoxic washable paint
Paintbrushes
Tape
Permanent marker
Large pieces of paper

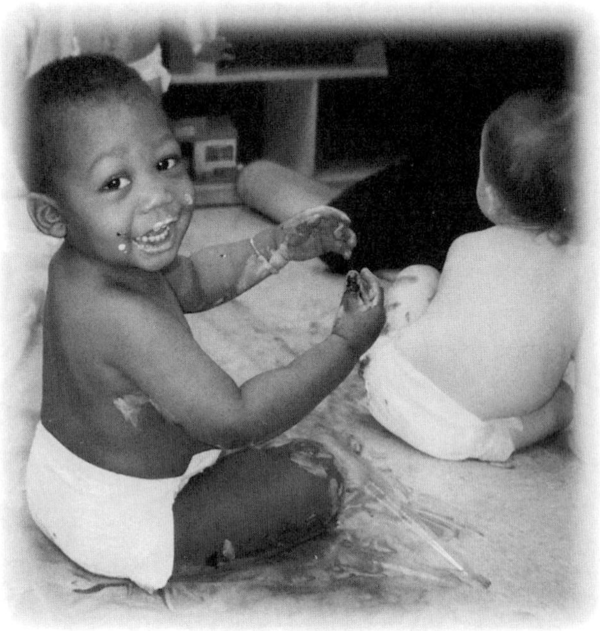

Provide times during the day when children can paint with their hands, feet, and body. Use only nontoxic, washable paint. Strip one or two toddlers to their diapers or underpants. Introduce toddlers individually to experiencing paint on their skin. Children may walk, scoot, paint, or roll on the paper. Paint will get everywhere on children and the paper. Hang the body paint pictures on the wall. The next time you want to body paint, use the same paper and a different color of paint. Date the picture each time a child adds to it. **Safety alert**: Some children will want to taste the paint. Redirect them by saying, "Paint with your fingers." Alert parents to painting activities because some paint pigment may show up in the stool of children. Post the nontoxic label to assure parents that the paint will cause no harm.

Books Read List

All ages

Materials
Pen and paper

Begin a class list of books (see page 91 for book suggestions) to read during this theme. Post the list and show parents the books children have been reading.

PARENT PARTICIPATION POSSIBILITIES

Supporting Possibilities

Send a "Wish List" to parents before the theme begins. Some items to request might be photos of their child, old magazines, clean cardboard food boxes, clear plastic bottles, and newspapers.

Boxes to Blocks Party

Invite parents to help paint and wrap cardboard boxes for the toddlers to use in their projects. Have materials ready for parents to work on the blocks. Plan several at different times, so all parents have an opportunity to attend at least one session. While parents work, talk about skills toddlers develop while playing with blocks. Serve simple refreshments. Remember to recognize parent participation by placing a "Thank You" on the Parent Board for all to see.

Parent Postcards

Parent Postcards in this section are designed to share with parents during the Possibilities Plan. The topics are natural extensions of the activities and experiences that you are planning and implementing for the toddlers in the classroom. Use the Postcards to connect parents to their children's learning.

Every Child Is Unique!

From the first experience of counting their child's fingers and toes, parents are concerned that their child is normal—like other children at the same age and stage of development. Parents worry. It's their job! The following discussion of the general principles may help you understand how children develop.

- **The first general principle is that growth follows a universal and predictable sequence. The milestones of development are observable.** The predictability of development can be seen in each area of development: physical, social, emotional, cognitive, and language. For example, in the physical domain, development proceeds from sitting to crawling, to pulling to a stand, to walking.

- **The second general principle is that development proceeds from the simple to the complex, or from the general to the specific.** Your child acquires simple skills before more complex ones can be attempted. For example, children always eat first with their fingers before attempting to use a spoon or fork. Both of these trends are influenced by children's unique pace through the developmental sequence, the unevenness of development in general, and the opportunities available for experience and practice of emerging skills.

- **The third principle is that each child has an individual pattern and timing of growth—each child is unique.** Although the sequence is predictable, each child's individual progress through the sequence is subject to variation. For example, one child may pull to a stand and walk at 7 or 8 months while another may do so at 12-13 months. Both are normal. It is normal for progress through the sequence to vary.

Enjoy your child's unique skill repertoire. Resist the temptation to compare too much, because no one else's child is just like yours!

TO

You Are Your Child's Best Teacher

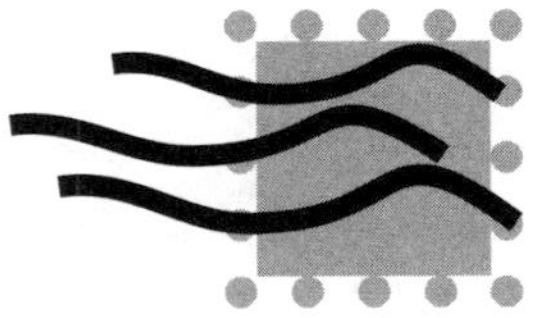

The biggest influence in a child's life is his or her parents. Teachers and extended family and friends are important, but the child's parents are his or her first and most important teachers. Parents have a profound influence on what children learn, what children feel, and how children react to the world around them.

How can parents best fill their role as teachers? The first way has to do with your involvement with your child's school. More than any other factor, parent involvement influences children's success. Parents can start early with being present in their child's school during functions and conferences. Also, very simple involvement such as collecting items for the classroom is important because it shows support for the school and the complex work teachers do.

Another way to fill the "teacher role" is to read to your child each day. This will help children become readers. Finally become partners with your child's teacher. Talk about concerns or issues before little concerns become big problems. Ask for reference material and share the ideas you find with your child's teacher. When the parent-teacher relationship works, the teacher-child relationship works, too. It is worth the effort!

TO ______________________

____

____

Concepts Learned in Me and My Body

Concepts Learned

I can recognize myself in a mirror.
I can play interactive games.
I can play near another child.
I can point to named body parts (eyes, ears, nose, mouth, chin, elbow, arm, knee, ankle, wrist, and so on).
I can name body parts.
Eyes are for seeing.
Noses are for smelling.
Mouths are for eating.
Ears are for hearing.
I can play chase.
I can climb two- or three-step stairs.
I can roll a ball.
I can turn the pages of a book.
I can ride a small riding toy without pedals.
I can jump in place.
I can hop on one foot.
I can walk with balance.
I can walk on tiptoes.
I can match pictures.
I can name pictured items.
I can use glue sticks and art materials to create a project.
I can follow one-step and two-step directions.
I can take things off.
I can put things on.

Resources

Prop Boxes

Shoe Store
- Shoe bag or shoe rack
- Shoeboxes with lids
- Shopping bags
- Variety of shoes
- *Whose Shoe?* by Margaret Miller

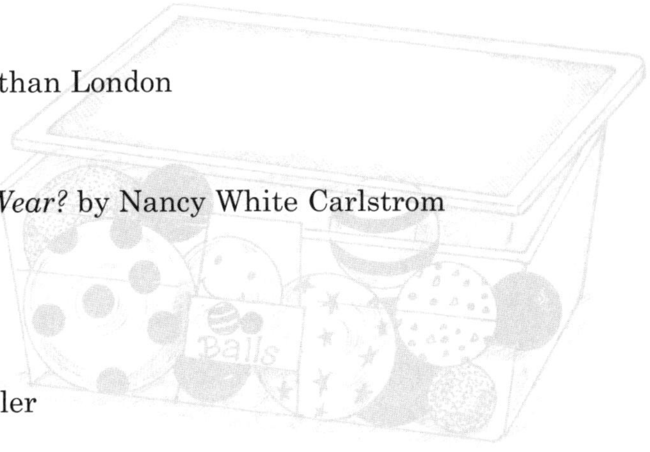

Dress-up
- Fancy dresses
- *Froggy Gets Dressed* by Jonathan London
- Gloves
- Hats
- *Jessie Bear, What Will You Wear?* by Nancy White Carlstrom
- Large boy's suit coats
- Purses
- Shoes
- Unbreakable mirrors
- *Whose Hat?* by Margaret Miller

Picture File/Vocabulary

Arms • Eyes • Face • Feet • Hair • Hands • Hats • Mittens
Mouth • Nose • Shoes • Toes

Books

- *Cat in the Hat, The* by Dr. Seuss
- *Copy Cat!: Faces* by Deborah Chancellor
- *Cherish Me* by Joyce Thomas
- *Dress-Up Time!* by Tom Arna
- *Froggy Gets Dressed* by Jonathan London (page 91)
- *How Do I Feel?* by Pamela Cote
- *It's Mine* by Leo Lionni
- *Jessie Bear, What Will You Wear?* by Nancy White Carlstrom (page 91)
- *Martin's Hats* by Joan W. Blos
- *Mine* by Miriam Cohen
- *Touch and Feel: Clothes* by Deni Brown
- *What Color Is It?* by Pamela Cote
- *When I Get Bigger* by Mercer Mayer
- *When I Was Little* by Toyomi Igus
- *Who Took the Farmer's Hat?* by Joan L. Nodset
- *Whose Hat?* by Margaret Miller (page 91)
- *Whose Shoe?* by Margaret Miller (page 90)

Rhymes/ Fingerplays

- "Hop a Little" (page 84)
- "Jumping Feet" (page 83)
- "Silly Face" (page 84)
- "Thumb-in-the Box" (page 83)

Music/Songs

"Clapping Hands" (page 82)
"Here They Are" (page 82)
"Shake Your Shaker" (page 83)

Toys and Materials

The following purchased items are important for this Possibilities Plan.

Acrylic paint and paintbrushes
Butcher paper
Clear contact paper
Crayons
Familiar toys
Glue
Glue sticks
Hats
Heavy cardboard
Hole punch
Hoop and loop fasteners (Velcro)
Inkpads
Large piece of paper
Large soft balls
Markers
Paper
Permanent markers
Plastic magnifier
Plastic spoons
Poster board
Riding toys
Scissors
Sponges/paper towels
Spray paint
Tall unbreakable mirror
Tape
Tempera paint
Yarn or metal rings

The following gathered items will help support this Possibilities Plan.

Adult shoes
Baskets (laundry and woven)
Bubble wrap
Cardboard pieces
Catalogs
Duct tape
Food flavorings
Large cardboard box
Magazines
Noisemakers (rice, dried beans, bells, metal measuring spoons, plastic rings, blocks)
Photos of children
Plastic bottles
Small curtains
Small cardboard boxes
Textured materials
Tube socks
White gloves

My Family

WEB

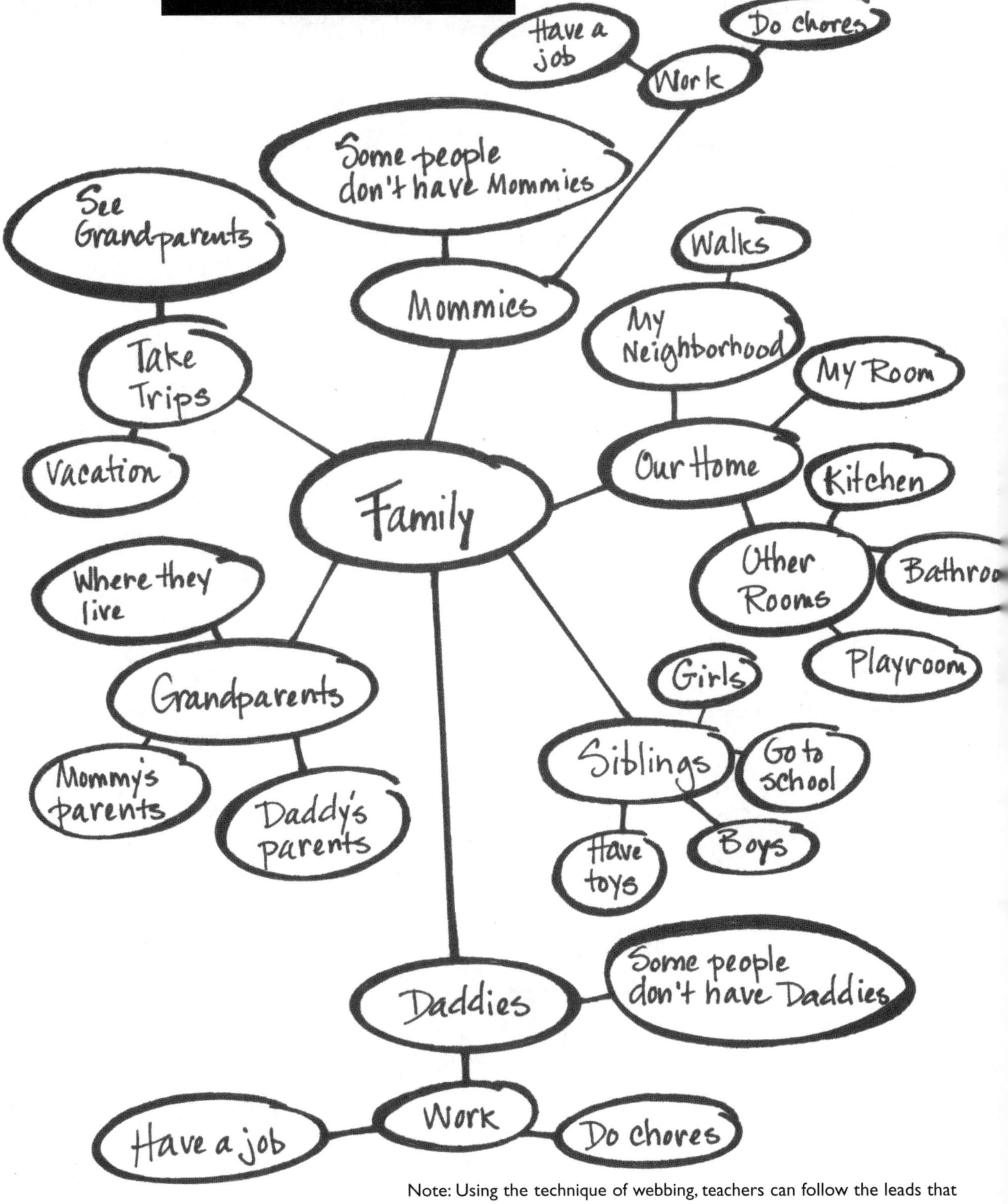

Note: Using the technique of webbing, teachers can follow the leads that children give them, as well as have an unlimited source of options. Always use the webs provided as a jumping-off point. The possibilities are endless!

PLANNING PAGES

Plan Possibilities

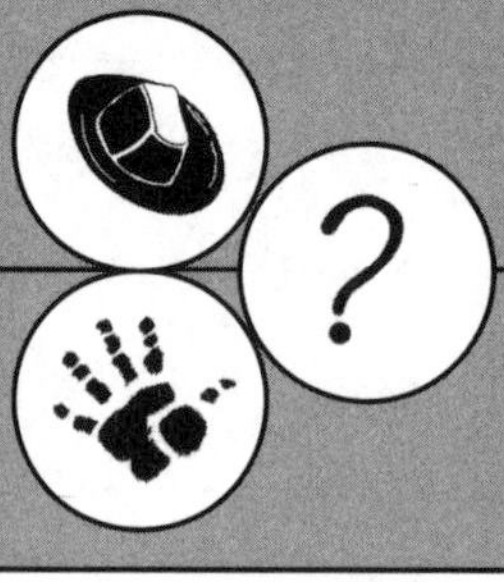

Dramatic

Sensory/Art

Curiosity

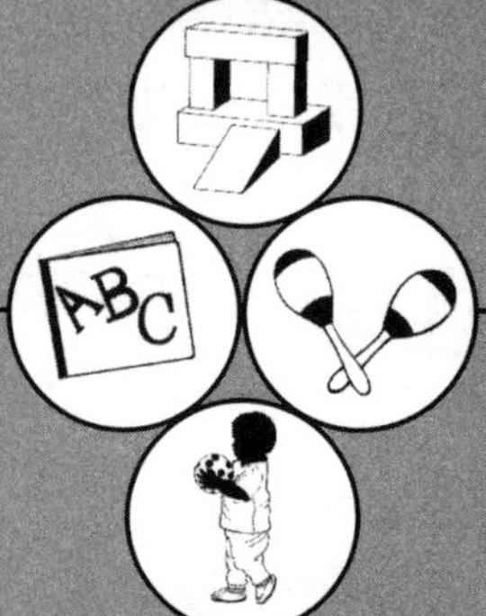

Construction

Literacy

Music

Movement

Outdoor

Project

Parent Participation

My Family

Books

Bear's Busy Family by Stella Blackstone 117
Bread and Jam for Frances by Russell Hoban
Cat in the Hat, The by Dr. Seuss 116
Gone Fishing by Earlene Long
Harry the Dirty Dog by Gene Zion 116
In My House by Susan Hood .117
Leo the Late Bloomer by Robert Kraus
My Sister and Me Outside by Lucy Dickens
Napping House, The by Audrey Woods
Runaway Bunny, The by Margaret Wise Brown
Sleeping by Jan Ormerod 117
Ten, Nine, Eight by Molly Bang
This Is the House that Jack Built by Pam Adams . . .117
Tools by Byron Barton
Touch and Feel: Home by Deni Brown 117
Wheels on the Bus, The by Maryanne Kovalski 117
Whistle for Willie by Ezra Jack Keats

DRAMATIC POSSIBILITIES

Playing Mommy or Daddy

18-24 months

Materials

Typical clothing and items that mothers or fathers of the children use each day, such as dresses, suit coats, briefcases with papers, work clothing, lunch boxes, hats, or uniforms

Teacher Talk

"Nathan has on his suit jacket. He is going to work." "You have your briefcase and are ready to go. Where are you going?"

Place a variety of clothing and work-related items that are familiar to the children in the area. Children can try on the clothing and play the roles they see their mothers and fathers do each day. Watch for children assuming different roles such as baby, pet, friend, and so on.

Doll Play

24-30 months

Materials

Dolls and equipment, such as bottles, blankets, diaper bags, stroller, bed

Teacher Talk

"Is baby going night night, Leo? Night, night, baby." "Miranda's baby is taking a bath."

Place a variety of dolls, bottles, diaper bags, and blankets for children to take care of a baby in this area. Include large furniture pieces such as a bed and stroller for children as play cues and props. Add bath time accessories, such as rubber dolls, water table, mild baby bath soap, sponges, and towels, to a water table indoors or outdoors so children can bathe the dolls. Talk about bath time with children as they play. Sing this song with children while you rock a baby doll. Sing along with your baby, too.

Rock-a-Bye, Baby

Rock-a-bye, baby, on the treetop.
When the wind blows, the cradle will rock.
When the bough breaks, the cradle will fall,
And down will come baby, cradle and all.

Sports Utility Vehicles

30-36 months

Materials
Copy paper boxes
Craft knife
Paint
Paintbrushes

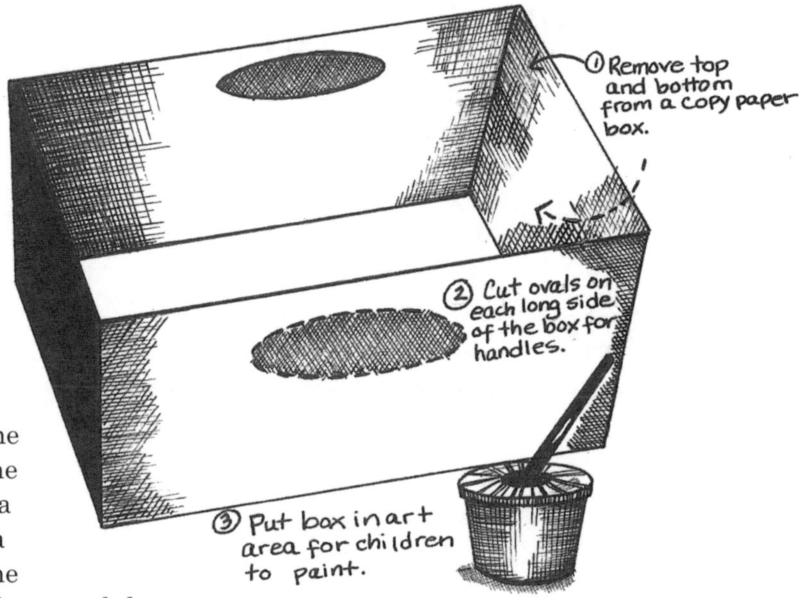

Teacher Talk
"Yes, Robbie. I see your red car."

Prepare these "sports utility vehicles" outside of the classroom. Remove the top and bottom from a copy paper box. Use a craft knife (outside the classroom) to cut ovals on each long side of the box for handles. Put the box in the art area for children to paint. Pick paint colors that match the colors of cars that children ride in to school. Demonstrate how to stand inside the box-car and pick up the car, using the handles on each side. Make sure you have several cars because this will be a popular activity.

Shopping Carts

30-36 months

Materials
Shopping carts
Food boxes
Dolls
Paper grocery bags

Teacher Talk
"Let's go shopping, Danny. Ready? Let's go!"

Provide shopping carts, real cardboard food boxes, and dolls as props for shopping.

Exploring Art

All ages

Materials

Big and little paintbrushes
Paint
Crayons
Butcherpaper
Low table
Tape
Easel

Teacher Talk

Talk about the sizes of the brushes and the designs they make on paper. "You picked the little red brush. That is the big blue brush. Look at the little yellow marks from the little yellow brush." "Tell me about what you are writing, Amy. Look at all those scribbles!"

Provide a selection of big and little paintbrushes and pots of paint. Observe as children experiment with different sizes of brushes as they paint on the easel. Or, cover a low table with butcher paper and tape it securely in place. Provide crayons for children to scribble on the paper. Observe children as they scribble. When children tire of scribbling, put the paper on the wall in the classroom. When children notice the artwork, bring it down again and work on the picture some more. Give children several opportunities to add to the paper.

Sandy Toys

18-24 months

Materials

Sand table
Plastic cups
Scoops
Funnels
Bowls
Plastic spoons

Teacher Talk

"John is stirring sand into the bowl. Are you cooking dinner?"

Place a variety of sizes and colors of plastic cups, bowls, scoops, and funnels in the sand table.

Pizza Painting

24-30 months

Materials
Masking tape
Finger paint
Pizza boards

Teacher Talk
"Look at your fingers, Aaron. You have lots of finger paint on them."

Put curls of masking tape on the bottoms of cardboard pizza boards and stick them onto the table. Provide thick finger paint for children to explore the textures of the paint on cardboard.

Dish Mop Boogie

30-36 months

① Cut 2-liter bottles in half, saving the top portion for funnels.
② Provide a sponge dish mop for each color of paint.

Materials
Sponge
Dish mop
Paint
2-liter plastic bottles
Cardboard
Music

Teacher Talk
"Let's paint fast to the fast music. Now the music is slow. Let's paint slow."

Cut 2-liter bottles in half, saving the top portion for funnels. Pour paint into the bottoms of plastic bottle containers. Provide a sponge dish mop for each color of paint. Place cardboard on a table for children to experiment with painting with the mops. Turn on music, alternating between lively music and music with a slower beat. Observe children as they paint to the rhythm of the music.

Rolling Designs

30-36 months

Materials
Cardboard tubes (paper towel or tissue cores)
Yarn
Glue

Paint
Old rectangular baking pans
Paper

Teacher Talk
Talk about the colors and textures as they explore rolling the tube on paper. "Gaylord is making a blue picture with the blue paint. Robbie is making a red picture."

Glue yarn designs onto cardboard tubes. Pour paint into baking pans. Help children dip the cardboard roll into the paint. Show them how to roll the tube on paper to make designs.

CURIOSITY POSSIBILITIES

Bathing Babies
All ages

Materials
Waterproof dolls
Shallow plastic tubs
Washcloths

Children will enjoy bathing dolls with water and washcloths. Put only a small amount of water in the shallow plastic tubs. Additional activities children will enjoy are washing plastic dishes and washing doll clothes.

Strumming the Racks
All ages

Materials
Wooden and metal racks (grill rack, oven rack, cake cooling rack, plastic-coated shelving)
Duct tape
Plastic and rubber spoons and spatulas

Teacher Talk
Describe the sounds as children play. "You are making a quiet noise with the rubber spatula, DeeDee. Here, use this plastic spoon to see what kind of noise it makes. That one makes a big noise!"

Tape the edges of the racks to the table. Provide a variety of flexible rubber and plastic spoons and spatulas for children to explore making sounds on the racks.

Find the Pictures

All ages

Materials
Photocopies of family pictures or pictures of pets
Glue
Poster board
Cardboard box
Craft knife
Sand, flour, or cornmeal

Teacher Talk
"Who's that? I see a puppy dog. I see Thomas' cat, Pebbles."

Cut off the sides of a cardboard box, leaving a two-inch lip to make shallow sides around the box. Glue family and pet pictures onto poster board and place them inside the box. Cover the pictures with clear contact paper and then with flour, sand, or cornmeal. Observe to see if children discover the pictures and see what happens next.

In and Out Box

All ages

Materials
Cardboard tubes
Marker
Scissors
Shoebox with lid
Paint
Tape

Teacher Talk
"Wesley, you are putting the tube in the box. Can you do that with this tube?"

Trace around a cardboard tube and cut holes in the shoebox lid. Tape the lid securely onto the box. Paint the cardboard tubes a variety of colors. Put the materials out in the curiosity area and see what happens. If no one puts the tubes in the box, demonstrate putting in one tube, then observe again.

Picture Box

All ages

Materials
Potato chip canister
Family photos
Glue
Clear contact paper
Small wooden blocks

Teacher Talk
When children show interest in the canisters, point to the individual pictures and ask, "Who's that?" "You found your brother's picture! Who else is on the canister?"

Glue family pictures around the outside of the potato chip canister. Cover the canister with clear contact paper. Or, place a few small wooden blocks inside the canister and put the snap-on lid in place. Observe to see if children remove the lid and play fill-and-dump games with the blocks.

CONSTRUCTION POSSIBILITIES

Family House Blocks

All ages

Materials
Small boxes
Newspaper
Tape
Pictures of children's homes or house pictures cut from magazines
Glue
Clear contact paper

Teacher Talk
Talk with children about the buildings. "Look at Mary's house. I see lots of windows."

Open boxes and stuff them with newspaper. Tape then shut. Glue pictures of the children's houses or pictures of houses cut from magazines onto the boxes. Cover the boxes with clear contact paper. Place with the blocks, so children can build with them.

Box and Bottle

18-24 months

Materials
Saltine cracker boxes
Scissors
Contact paper
2-liter plastic bottles
Noisy materials, such as rice or dried beans
Glue
Tape

Teacher Talk
"Let's put the bottle in the box. First the big part and now the little part."

Remove one end from the saltine cracker box. Cover the box with contact paper. Place noisy materials such as rice or dried beans inside the bottle. Glue and tape the cap securely in place. Place together with the blocks for children to experiment with shaking the bottle to make noise and fitting the bottle inside the cracker box.

LITERACY POSSIBILITIES

It's a Grand Book

All ages

Materials
Grandparent photos
Plastic lids
Glue
Hole punch
Metal ring

Teacher Talk
"There's Granny, Boone. Do you see Gran Gran?"

Glue pictures of each child's grandparents onto individual plastic lids. Punch a hole in each lid. Fasten the lids together with a metal ring to make each child her own grandparent book. Share the lid books with children. Point to pictures and name the pictured grandparent. Or, put one grandparent lid from each child in "Our Grandparents" class book with a lid for each child. Read the book, pointing out which grandparent goes with whom.

Family Album

18-24 months

Materials
Family photos
Poster board
Glue
Resealable plastic bags
Hole punch
Yarn or metal rings

Teacher Talk
Point to pictures and name the people in the pictures. "I see Elizabeth's mom. Now you are pointing at Dad."

Glue photos onto cardboard squares and place the pages inside a resealable plastic bag. Punch holes in the pages and fasten them together with yarn or metal rings. Make a family album for each child. Look at each child's album with the child. Give children their family albums as a reuniting experience just before or just after naptime.

Family Puppets

18-24 months

Materials
Commercial or teacher-made puppets representing a variety of family members

Teacher Talk
"Abe has the daddy puppet, and Elissa has the mommy puppet. Who wants to have the brother puppet?"

Use a variety of family-member puppets as you talk with children about families. Include culturally diverse puppets, grandparents, and siblings, as well as more stereotypical mother and father puppets. Match puppets with individual children's real family members.

Working Pictures

24-30 months

Materials
Photos of family members at work

Teacher Talk
Talk with a child about the pictures. "Let's look at your family pictures, Thomas. There is Granny. Brother is in this picture. Look, there's a picture of you."

Request that parents share photos of family members at work. Place each child's family photos in an individual album. Watch to see if children identify family members.

Peek-a-Boo Books

30-36 months

As you look at the book with the child, remove one blank strip at a time until the child can name the family member pictured behind the strips.
Glue photos to every other right hand page. Cut the blank page into three wide horizontal strips.

Materials
Notebook with side spiral
Copies of family photos
Glue
Scissors

Teacher Talk
"Who is hiding behind this paper, Sara? That's Mommy's nose. There are Mommy's eyes! That's Mommy."

Open the spiral notebook and glue photos to every other right-hand page. Cut the blank page into three wide horizontal strips. As you look at the book with a child, remove one blank strip at a time until the child can name the family member pictured behind the strips.

MUSIC POSSIBILITIES

Grandma

All ages

Materials
None

Introduce the following song to children as you talk about family members. Sing to the tune "I'm a Little Teapot."

Grandma
I have a special Grandma, I like to see.
I love her and she loves me
When I go to see her, we have fun,
From early morning 'til the day is done.

Are You Sleeping?

All ages

Materials
None

Teacher Talk
Talk about waking up in the morning. "Who wakes Gina up in the morning? Daddy wakes up Gina in the morning!"

Sing this song with children. You might substitute children's names as you sing the song, using the words brother and sister when appropriate.

Are You Sleeping?
Are you sleeping, are you sleeping,
Brother John, Brother John?
Morning bells are ringing, morning bells are ringing,
Ding, ding, dong! Ding, ding, dong!

I'm Bringing Home a Baby Bumblebee

All ages

Materials
None

Sing the song with children and help them to act out the words.

I'm Bringing Home a Baby Bumblebee
I'm bringing home a baby bumblebee, (Cup hands together)
Won't my mommy be so proud of me? (Thumbs to chest)
I'm bringing home a baby bumblebee— (Cup hands together)
Ouch! He stung me! (Clap hands loudly)

MOVEMENT POSSIBILITIES

____ This Is the Family

All ages

Materials
None

This is a fingerplay about the whole family. Help children hold up fingers, one at a time, as you recite the rhyme.

This Is the Family
This is the father short and stout. (Thumb)
This is the mother with children about. (Index finger)
This is the brother, tall you see. (Middle finger)
This is the sister with a toy on her knee. (Ring finger)
This is the baby sure to grow. (Pinky finger)
And here is the family all in a row. (All five fingers)

____ Cat Walking

24-30 months

Materials
None

Make cat sounds and move like a cat around the room. Use these types of activities (crawl like a bug, wiggle like a snake, and so on) as transitions from indoors to outdoors and back.

____ Finger Family

30-36 months

Materials
None

Recite this poem while you and a child wiggle your fingers as directed. Watch children's reactions as you introduce the rhyme.

Finger Family
Finger family up, (Wiggle fingers up)
Finger family down, (Wiggle fingers down)
Finger family dancing,
All around the town. (Wiggle fingers all around)
Dance them on your shoulders. (Wiggle fingers on shoulders)

Dance fingers on your head. (Wiggle fingers on top of head)
Dance fingers on your knees, (Wiggle fingers on knees)
And tuck them into bed. (Fold hands and put beside face)

OUTDOOR POSSIBILITIES

Pet Friends

All ages

Materials

Large cardboard box
Stuffed toy dogs
Plastic feeding dish
Empty dog food box
Large rubber bones

Teacher Talk

"The dog's bowl is empty, Holland. Let's put some food in the dog bowl, Holland."

Decorate a large cardboard box to look like a doghouse. Place a stuffed toy dog inside the doghouse. Put a plastic feeding dish, an empty dog food box, and a rubber bone nearby. Observe to see how children use the props.

Fence Rhythm Band

All ages

Materials

Large metal spoons, rubber spatulas, plastic hammers
Yarn
Chain-link fence or other metal surface

Teacher Talk

"Hit the fence like this with the spoon, Keisha. Keisha is making music on the fence."

Tie short lengths (12 inches) of yarn to each of the gathered materials and tie them securely to the fence. Show children how to strike the gadgets on the fence to make "music." Sing familiar songs that encourage children to play the "instruments."

Grandma's Cottage

18-24 months

Materials
Large cardboard box
Paint and brushes

Teacher Talk
"Who is in Grandma's cottage? It is Phillip in Grandma's cottage."

Use a craft knife (outside the classroom) to cut doors and windows in a large cardboard box. Use paint to decorate the box to look like a cottage. Children will enjoy doing this outside.

Going to Nana's

24-30 months

Materials
Tote bag
Sleep shirt or sleep toy
Riding toy

Teacher Talk
Talk with children about taking a trip to a grandparent's house. "Mary Beth has a bag on her arm. Where are you going, Mary Beth? You are going to Nana's house."

Put a sleep shirt or a sleep toy inside a tote bag. Place the bag with the riding toys.

Pet Parade

30-36 months

Materials
Stuffed toy animals, such as dogs, cats, birds
Noisemakers

Teacher Talk
"Robert, which pet would you like to carry in the parade? This doggie. Here it is."

Provide a variety of stuffed animal pets. Children can choose noisemakers such as shakers or tambourines to make noise as they walk in the parade. Some children may want to ride on a riding toy with their pet in the parade. Play some marching music and have fun being in a parade.

PROJECT POSSIBILITIES

Family House

All ages

Materials

Large cardboard box
Tape
Pictures of family members or pets (either photos or copies of photos)
Collage materials, such as felt scraps, tissue paper pieces, feathers, fabric trim, ribbons
Glue

Teacher Talk

Talk about the pets and the materials as children work on the project.

Tape the box securely closed. Provide pictures of family members and pets and a variety of collage materials for children to glue onto the cardboard box. Start by adding pictures of toddlers. Then add moms and dads, then grandparents or other relatives, then siblings, and finally pets.

Books Read List

All ages

Materials

Pen and paper

Begin a class list of books read during this theme (see suggestions on page 117). Post the list and show parents the books children have been reading. Add a copy of the list (see page 538 in the Appendix) to each child's portfolio.

Pet Lovers

Ask parents to send photos of family pets, or cut out pictures of pets from old magazines if they do not have pets at home. These pictures may be used in many different activities with children as they talk about families.

Family Visit

Family members often wonder what the day is like at school. Although you can't share everything with them, you can give them a taste of what it is like. Plan a visit for children's family members to come and play. Plan simple activities that all can enjoy while getting to know other families. Have lemonade and cookies. Encourage families to explore the class, playground, and activities their child does each day. Take pictures of this visit and display them in the classroom.

Grandparents on Tape

Ask grandparents to sing or read a story onto a blank tape. They may want to say a special greeting for their grandchild before singing or reading. Play the tape for individual children to listen to.

Parent Postcards

Parent Postcards in this section are designed to share with parents during the Possibilities Plan. The topics are natural extensions of the activities and experiences that you are planning and implementing for the toddlers in the classroom. Use the postcards to connect parents to their children's learning.

We Are Now Partners

Partnerships are special. Although no one is more important to your child than you—his or her parents—starting school means that someone else is sharing the job of providing care and early education to your toddler.

Everyone says that involvement in the school will improve the quality of the child's experience. What does involvement mean? And, how do you get involved with an already full schedule facing you every day?

Part of being involved is exchanging information with your child's teacher at the beginning or end of the day. Reading and completing the communication sheet will take care of this. Another part is looking around the room on a regular basis to see the documentation your teacher has prepared to share with you concerning your child's experiences. Look for lesson plans, photographs, developmental banners, and work samples.

There are many more ways to be involved in your child's life at school. Here is a list of ways other parents have involved themselves in school. Look through it and find out which ways might fit your schedule and available time or your particular talents and experiences. Check off the ones that you might like to try and put them in your monthly plan.

- ☐ Drop by to read a story to the children in your child's group.
- ☐ Save cereal boxes, orange juice containers, toilet paper rolls, plastic peanut butter jars, boxes with lids, margarine tubs, yogurt containers, paper towel rolls, oatmeal boxes, old magazines, and so on. Keep a paper sack at home to collect these items and bring them in to your child's teacher to convert into teacher-made toys.

TO

We Are Now Partners (continued)

- ☐ Schedule and attend conferences requested by your child's teacher. Conferences are held regularly and are an excellent time for you to get to know your child's teacher better as you discuss your child's developmental progress.
- ☐ Read the parent handbook, newsletters, and other written information shared with you by the school or your child's teacher. When the school or teacher takes the time to write something down for you, it is important for you to read it and know about it.
- ☐ Share family traditions with your child's classroom. Cultural celebrations and special family traditions make your family unique. Sharing these experiences with other children and your child's teachers adds a very special quality to your child's experience and validates his or her uniqueness.
- ☐ Share your family with us. Bring to school pictures of your child's experiences. Encourage visits to school by grandparents, relatives, and friends of your family. Come by for an extra visit when you have time. And, don't forget to share your unique expertise. Leisure activities, work-related activities, and your talents are potential resources to enrich our educational program.
- ☐ Attend special events planned by your child's teachers. Get-acquainted teas, toy swaps, book exchanges, potluck dinners, and happy hour visits are all planned to involve you and your family.

These are just a few of the ways you can be involved. Remember, we are now partners. Try these and other ways to get involved in your child's education.

TO

Creating Partnerships—Two-way Communication

As parents, you have the greatest influence in your child's life. You also have a major part in determining how satisfied and happy your child is at school. Toddlers can be sensitive to nonverbal cues. Whether you are relaxed and comfortable or anxious and uncomfortable, your toddler will know. Sometimes, school can be a source of anxiety for parents, particularly in the beginning. Almost every difficulty faced at school can be worked through using positive, two-way communication.

One way communication is encouraged is through the written communication system. All parents are asked to fill out a daily communication sheet. The purpose of this sheet is to create a written, two-way communication system between you and the school.

Teachers need to keep lots of information ready to provide what your toddler needs. Information is easily lost if parents and teachers depend just on their memories and their verbal interactions. Using a written system helps everyone keep up with information that needs to be exchanged and serves as a documentation of the progress of communicating.

Record important information about your child's time at home that might be helpful to the teacher, including how long the toddler slept, when he or she last ate, information about elimination, and any special instructions for the teacher. This information is so important. Make sure every family member who may take your child to school in the morning recognizes this. It creates a platform from which the teacher is able to anticipate and correctly interpret your child's needs.

Likewise, parents need to know information about what happened each day at school. Your child's activities (eating, sleeping, diaper changes, and so on) will be recorded. Teachers will also record developmental notes and observations.

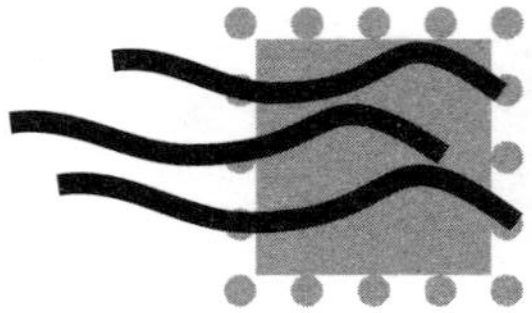

TO ______________

Creating Partnerships—Two-way Communication (continued)

Use the communication sheet to help you get a feel for how the day with your toddler went. When you enter the classroom, reunite with your child, read the communication sheet, and then ask the teacher any questions you may have.

Parents will have many other types of opportunities for communication with their child's teacher (conferences, phone calls, notes). Whenever you have a concern, talk with your child's teacher. Don't wait until your concern escalates. Your child's well-being is everyone's concern. The better the communication is between home and school and between school and home, the better the opportunity is for you and your child to feel comfortable with and enjoy his or her school experience.

TO ______________

Concepts Learned in Me and My Body

Concepts Learned

I can identify my family members (mother, father, sister, brother) in photos.
I can identify extended family members (grandparents, aunts, uncles) in photos.
I can identify pets (dog, cat, bird).
I can do housework.
I can take care of babies.
I can take care of pets.
I can make pet sounds.
I can move like pets.
I can mix two colors to make a new color.
I can use different items to make sounds.
I can name textures (soft, hard, smooth, rough).
I can put thing in and take things out of boxes.
I can fill and dump.
I can use words to describe different sizes (big, little).
I can use liquid glue and glue sticks.
I can scribble with crayons.
I can turn pages in a book.
I can read picture books.
I can act out words to songs.
I can use hands and fingers to act out fingerplays.

Resources

Prop Boxes

Pet Box
- *Cat in the Hat, The* by Dr. Seuss
- Empty food boxes
- Feeding dishes
- *Harry the Dirty Dog* by Gene Zion
- Pet brushes
- Safe pet toys
- Stuffed toy animals

Mommies and Daddies

- *Bear's Busy Family* by Stella Blackstone
- Briefcase
- Dress-up clothing
- Hard hats
- High heel shoes
- *In My House* by Susan Hood
- Lunch box
- Plastic car keys
- Purses
- *This Is the House that Jack Built* by Pam Adams
- *Touch and Feel: Home* by Deni Brown
- *Wheels on the Bus, The* by Maryanne Kovalski
- Work clothing (suit jacket, uniforms)

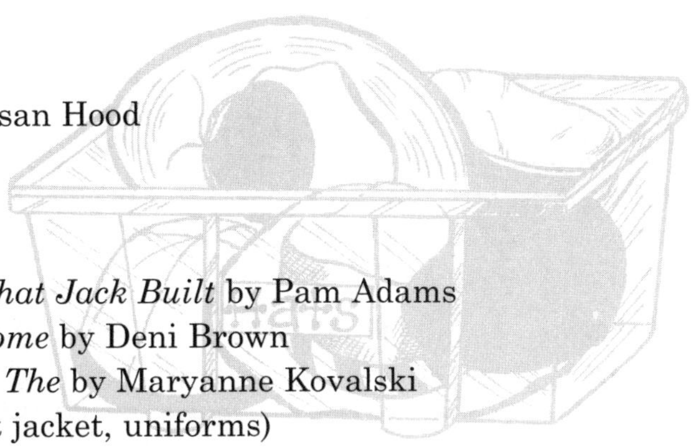

Babies

- Baby dolls
- *Bear's Busy Family* by Stella Blackstone
- Blankets
- Bottles
- Diaper bags
- Doll clothing
- Feeding dishes
- *Sleeping* by Jan Ormerod
- *Touch and Feel: Home* by Deni Brown
- *Wheels on the Bus, The* by Maryanne Kovalski

Picture File/ Vocabulary

Aunt	Big/little	Brother
Bunny	Cat	Dog
Family	Father	Grandparents
In/out	Mother	Pets
Sister	Soft/hard	Uncle

Books

Bear's Busy Family by Stella Blackstone
Bread and Jam for Frances by Russell Hoban
Cat in the Hat, The by Dr. Seuss
Gone Fishing by Earlene Long
Harry the Dirty Dog by Gene Zion
In My House by Susan Hood
Leo the Late Bloomer by Robert Kraus
My Sister and Me Outside by Lucy Dickens
Napping House, The by Audrey Woods

Runaway Bunny, The by Margaret Wise Brown
Sleeping by Jan Ormerod
Ten, Nine, Eight by Molly Bang
This Is the House that Jack Built by Pam Adams
Tools by Byron Barton
Touch and Feel: Home by Deni Brown
Wheels on the Bus, The by Maryanne Kovalski
Whistle for Willie by Ezra Jack Keats

Rhymes/ Fingerplays

"Finger Family" (page 107)
"This Is the Family" (page 107)

Music/Songs

"Are You Sleeping?" (page 106)
"Grandma" (page 106)
"I'm Bringing Home a Baby Bumblebee" (page 106)
"Rock-a-Bye, Baby" (page 96)

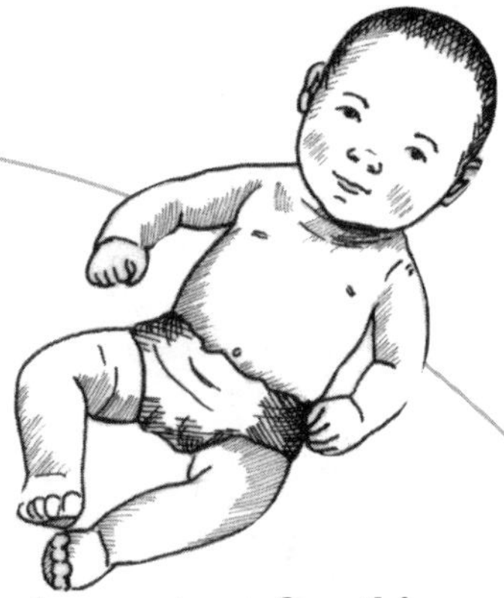

Toys and Materials

The following purchased items are important for this Possibilities Plan.

- Baby bottles
- Blankets
- Clear contact paper
- Contact paper
- Craft knife (teacher only)
- Crayons
- Doll bed
- Doll diaper bag
- Doll stroller
- Dolls (waterproof and not)
- Duct tape
- Easel
- Family puppets
- Finger paint
- Glue
- Hole punch
- Large stuffed animals
- Low table
- Markers
- Metal rings
- Music tapes
- Paint and paintbrushes (big and little)
- Paper
- Plastic bowls
- Plastic cups
- Plastic hammers
- Plastic scoops and funnels
- Plastic spoons
- Poster board
- Resealable plastic bags
- Riding toys
- Sand, flour, or cornmeal
- Sand/water table
- Scissors
- Shopping cart
- Sleep toys
- Small wooden blocks
- Spiral notebook
- Striped kitten puppet
- Stuffed toy dogs
- Tape
- Yarn

Toys and Materials (continued)

The following gathered items will help support this Possibilities Plan.

- Adult work clothes and props
- Cardboard tubes
- Chip canister
- Copy paper boxes
- Cracker box
- Dog dish
- Dog food box
- Empty food containers
- House pictures
- Large cardboard box
- Large wooden and metal spoons
- Magazines
- Newspaper
- Noisemakers
- Paper grocery bags
- Plastic tubs
- Photocopies of families and pets
- Photos of grandparents
- Photos of mom and dad at work
- Pizza boards
- Plastic bottles
- Plastic lids
- Rice and dried beans
- Rubber dog bones
- Shoeboxes
- Sleep shirts
- Small boxes
- Spatula
- Sponges and dishmops
- Toddler-safe collage materials (paper scraps, felt scraps, ribbon lengths, plastic lids, cardboard pieces)
- Tote bag
- Washcloths

CHAPTER 3

Making Friends

INTRODUCTION

A marvelous change occurs during toddlerhood. Children who spent the first 18 months of life intensely interested in themselves and their primary caregivers change. They become intensely interested in their peers—children both the same age and older become fascinating and interesting. As this interest emerges, friendships between and among children begin to emerge. Although these friendships are situational at first, eventually they become intense, joyful, and persistent.

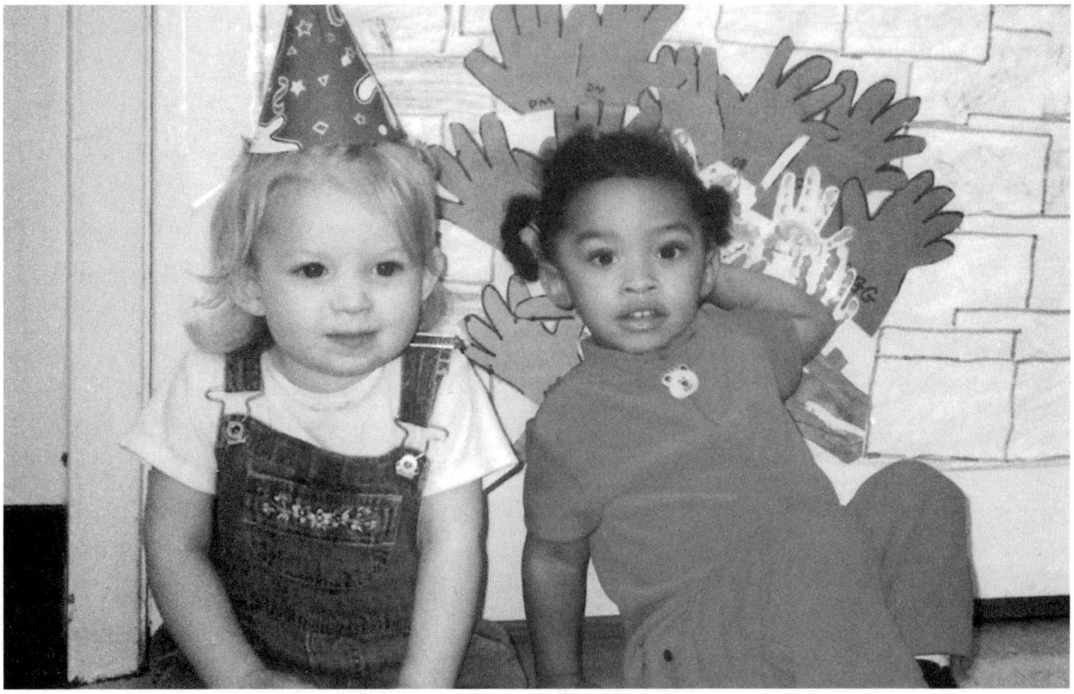

Success at making friends is so important. Some educators even believe that social skills that develop during the toddler years impact children's later success in most formal endeavors, including school and life experience. Yet, the toddler years are ones of conflict and turbulence—particularly among friends. So toddlers need supportive and capable adults to provide guidance and direction as they learn the crucial skills of making friends.

INNOVATIONS IN OBSERVATION/ASSESSMENT

Observation/Assessment Instrument

This assessment instrument is not just a skills checklist. Instead it is designed to guide the teacher's observation of children's development through a major interactional task of toddlerhood. The assessment's focus is on what IS happening in the child's development, not what should happen or what will happen. Use this assessment to lead to developmentally appropriate practices for toddlers.

	18-24 months	24-30 months	30-36 months
R1	a. Calms self with verbal support from adults and transitional objects.	b. Calms self with verbal support from adults; may look for transitional objects to help with the calm-down process after verbal support is provided. Frequency of emotional outburst begins to diminish.	c. Calms self with only verbal support. Use of transitional objects begins to decline except at bedtime and when recovering from intense emotional outbursts.
R2	a Goes to mirror to look at self; makes faces, and shows emotions like laughing, crying, and so on.	b. Calls own name when looking at photographs or in the mirror.	c. Calls names of friends in photographs.
R3	a. Develops preferences for types of play and types of toys.	b. Develops play themes that are repeated again and again (such as mommy or firefighter).	c. Begins exploration of a wider range of play themes. Themes often come from new experiences.
R4	a. Perfects gross motor skills such as running, climbing, and riding push toys. Fine motor skills with manipulatives (simple puzzles, Duplos, and so on) are emerging.	b. Likes physical challenges such as running fast, jumping high, and going up and down stairs. Plays with preferred manipulatives for increasing periods of time.	c. Competently exhibits a wide range of physical skills. Begins to be interested in practicing skills such as throwing a ball, riding a tricycle, or completing a puzzle.
R5	a. Play may be onlooker, solitary, or parallel in nature.	b. Play is predominantly parallel in nature.	c. Exhibits associative play with familiar play partners.
R6	a. Exhibits symbolic play.	b. Practices and explores a wide variety of symbolic play themes and roles.	
R7	a. Objects to strangers presence; clings, cries, and seeks support when strangers are around.	b. Objection to strangers begins to diminish; may still be wary of strangers or new situations.	c. Is able to venture into strange or new situations if prepared in advance by adults.
R8	a. Uses single words to indicate needs and wants such as "muk" for "I want milk," or "bye bye" for "Let's go bye bye."	b. Uses phrases and 2- to 3-word sentences to indicate needs and wants.	c. Uses 4- to 6-word sentences to indicate needs and wants.
R9	a. Connects emotions with behaviors; uses language to express these connections.	b. Uses emotional ideas in play. c. Elaborates on emotional ideas and understanding to play with objects.	d. Begins emotional thinking; begins to understand emotional cause-and-effect relationships.
R10	a. Takes turns with toys and materials with adult support and facilitation.	b. Takes turns with toys and materials with friend, sometimes without adult support.	
R11	a. Experiments with behavior that accomplishes a goal; may bite, pinch, poke, scratch, push, and so on while trying to make things happen.	b. Begins to anticipate what might happen when actions are taken; chooses to make things happen if outcomes are desirable (for example, trade toys with a friend who will stay and play), and resists taking action if outcomes are undesirable (for example, teacher will put markers away if child chews on the tips).	

INNOVATIONS IN CHILD DEVELOPMENT

During the first three years, the social and the emotional domains of development weave together—it is hard to know where emotional development begins or ends and social development takes over. For toddlers, it is the connected nature of these two domains that makes focusing on both important. As they move into toddlerhood, they become interested in and begin to seek out interaction with caregivers, sibling, and friends.

Attachment, as has already been discussed in Chapter 2 (see pages 42-51), plays a huge role in emerging social development. So does the environment. But more than any other developmental activity or behavior, play facilitates children's social and emotional development.

Play

The development of play overlaps all areas of development—physical, social, emotional, and intellectual, which includes cognitive and language development. In fact, we often determine where a child is on one or more developmental continua by watching him play. The developmental process guides play behavior from the simple to the complex, from concentrating on the self to interacting with others, and from the concrete to the abstract (Rogers & Sawyer, 1988).

The benefits of play for children are well documented. Through play, children are able to explore their world and learn about themselves and others. Because play is so integrated into the developmental context, it is helpful to look at the types of play behavior that have been identified and to use them to understand the social and emotional development of very young children in school.

Piaget and Play

Piaget gave us a cognitive conceptualization of play as divided into three types of play behavior—practice play, symbolic play, and play-with-rules (Piaget, 1962). Practice play, the most common type of play during the first two years of life, is composed of repetitions of the same movements and actions, both with and without objects.

Symbolic play involves the beginning of the traditional "dramatic play," where children recreate in play what they see going on in the real world. Children begin to experience symbolic play between ages 2 to 7. Play-with-rules is the last type of play behavior that emerges between ages 7 to 12.

During this type of play, children begin to impose rules to govern play or to manipulate interactions.

Toddlers are beginning to exhibit symbolic play—the ability to play out the roles and activities they see in the larger world of family, school, and community. An emerging sense of self as independent from their primary caregivers entices toddlers to explore being just like these important people, as well as to explore being very different from these important adults in their lives.

Parten and Play

As children develop socially, they experience six increasingly complex types of peer play (Parten, 1932). The first type is unoccupied play where children watch others at play. Then, onlooker play emerges where children watch others play, but seek to be near, and perhaps even respond to the play of others. Solitary independent play comes next. Children play alone with objects without interacting with others, regardless of how near. Parallel activity emerges next, with children playing along side each other with similar toys—beside each other rather than with each other. In associative play, activities occur between children although no specific roles are assigned or play goal identified. Cooperative play is the sixth form of play that finds children cooperating with others to create play situations. Group membership is defined, and group members play roles.

Six Types of Peer Play

1. Unoccupied Play
2. Onlooker Play
3. Solitary Independent Play
4. Parallel Activity
5. Associative Play
6. Cooperative Play

Toddlers may exhibit unoccupied play, solitary independent play, parallel activity, and may even participate in associative play occasionally. Understanding play behavior gives teachers cues to where children are socially and emotionally. Information about such behaviors facilitates fine-tuning the interactive relationship between teachers and toddlers.

Vygotsky and Play

Although all of these theorists believed that play links children to the larger society, Vygotsky's sociocultural theory is based on the premise that children socially construct what they know in the context of their family and cultural experiences. In Vygotsky's theory, language is viewed as the primary strategy for communication and contact with the thoughts of others (Berk, 1994). In other words, Piaget said children construct knowledge by interacting with objects and perfecting errors. Vygotsky says children construct knowledge through instructions by others, and by talking about their ideas, mistakes, and actions.

Vygotsky is best known for the idea of the zone of proximal development (ZPD), which is "the range of tasks a child cannot yet handle alone but can accomplish with the help of adults and more skilled peers" (Berk, 1994). Vygotsky believes that play creates a ZPD in the child, preparing him for the future development of abstract thought. Supportive caregivers and more competent peers can raise the level of play children use. Called scaffolding, this support is essential to social-emotional and cognitive development in the early years. Engaging in joint play with toddlers helps them develop skills that they can later use in social play with peers. Teachers can take turns with toddlers, suggest imaginative play themes, and select a level of support for play that matches the toddler's abilities. All of these supportive behaviors help toddlers practice social play with their peers.

The Importance of Friendships to Toddlers

Toddlers are fascinated by and interested in other children. This interest extends to toddlers who are familiar to them and those who are not. Spectator sports—watching what other children are doing—are highly engaging and entertaining to toddlers. In addition, toddlers may not have the social skills needed to play successfully with other children because toddlers' egocentrism focuses on their needs and wants, so interactions often result in conflict.

Most interactions between toddlers need adult support. Because they are not yet able to regulate their own emotions, toddlers have more interest in playing with other children than they have skills to do so (Stonehouse, 1988). Adult support for interactions can support emerging skills in children and help peer relationships to emerge.

Toddlers are working on developing social competence. Social competence is the ability to engage in satisfying interactions with adults and peers and, through such interactions, continue to grow socially (Katz & McClellan, 1997). Part of social competence is how children respond and are responded to by peers. Are they accepted? Rejected? Included in play? Left out of play? Is the inclusion mutual or one-sided? Some researchers view negative early peer experiences as an early indicator of potential social/emotional and academic problems (Pellegrini & Glickman, 1990).

Toddlers have many social difficulties. Major components of social development are still developing. They have limited skills in controlling impulses, delaying gratification, using expressive language, entering play, reading social cues, and regulating emotions. These difficulties can show up in different ways in different children but are most often seen in aggressive behavior. A broader discussion of managing aggression in toddlers is in chapter 7, pages 462-467.

INNOVATIONS IN INTERACTIVE EXPERIENCES

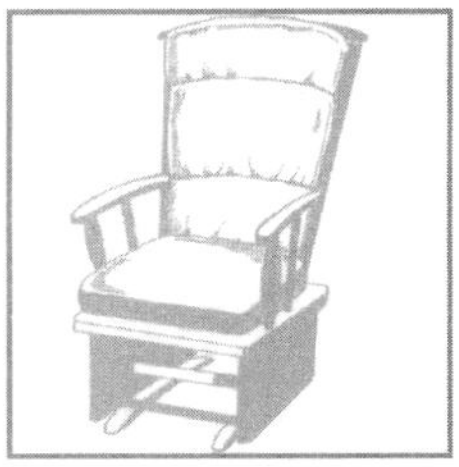

The many experiences toddlers have that stimulate social development are part of all interactions. The following list of experiences/activities for toddlers could be listed in other tasks as well. This overlap is precisely what makes it difficult to explain the important teaching that is required to stimulate social and emotional learning. Long before children begin to show others their new skills, these experiences lay the foundation for future social and emotional success.

Life's minutiae build to create experiences. Toddler teachers must be attuned to these everyday, yet important, experiences. They are truly the foundation upon which crucial skills and abilities grow.

Think about the following list of experiences and make sure that the classroom reflects many of them.

- ☐ Talk to toddlers during routines.
- ☐ Stimulate all of the senses through interaction with people, toys, and materials. Rotate toys and materials often enough to support new play themes.
- ☐ Create quiet places to play together every day with every toddler. Facilitating playtime with an important adult supports emerging social/emotional development.
- ☐ Establish a few consistent limits.
- ☐ Comment on what children are doing as they play.
- ☐ Imitate children's actions.
- ☐ Model play behaviors.
- ☐ Engage in joint pretend play with toddlers.
- ☐ Serve as a secure base for exploration of the physical and social worlds.
- ☐ Point out interesting things in the inside and outside worlds.
- ☐ Respect toddlers' intense emotions. Help children recognize and accept intense feelings of joy, anger, jealousy, sadness, fear, and so on.
- ☐ Give sympathetic attention to toddlers' intense feelings, acknowledging and labeling them for children.
- ☐ Help toddlers express their emotions by substituting appropriate behaviors for inappropriate ones.
- ☐ Encourage toddlers to control their impulses.
- ☐ Validate attempts to assert autonomy, encourage early trys and successful attempts.
- ☐ Accept the vacillation between dependence and independence as part of the toddler experience.
- ☐ Support early peer interactions by being close and scaffolding children's attempts to interact.
- ☐ Encourage children to make friends and respond appropriately to them.
- ☐ Help toddlers learn to wait—just a minute—staying near to help make it happen.

INNOVATIONS IN TEACHING

Teacher as First Friend—Primary Teaching

The child development and early childhood literature is full of references to primary teaching as a strategy for facilitating the development of children during the first three years of life (Bernhardt, 2000; Greenman & Stonehouse, 1996; Honig, 1995; Lally, 1995; Raikes, 1996; Reisenberg, 1995). Primary caregiving usually focuses on the development of an intimate, sensitive, and reciprocal relationship between a young child and his most frequent caregiver. This curriculum views primary teaching as a more comprehensive construct—one that offers schools the opportunity to develop close ties among parents, teachers, children, and school.

Powell (1998) supports this more inclusive program approach where schools work with children and parents within the family context rather than constructing a separate parent involvement component. When primary teaching is viewed this way, it creates a true partnership with families and places families at the center of the relationship, not on the periphery.

The first component is the relationship between the parents and the school. Because parents are the most significant people in a toddler's life, the relationship between the teacher and the parent is also paramount (Lally, 1995). Seeing each other as partners is an essential component of early education. The parent/teacher/school relationship needs the same timbre and trust as the teacher's relationship with the child.

Components of Primary Teaching

- Mutual relationships between parent and teacher
- Mutual teacher-child relationships
- Balance among routines, interactions, stimulation, and time alone

The second component of primary teaching is the responsive relationship between the child and teacher. This relationship is based on careful observation of each child's individuality and on "a sense of personal and emotional involvement that is mutual" (Leavitt, 1994). Many researchers, including Brazelton (1992), Erickson (1963), Gerber (1979), Shore (1997), and others have characterized the interactive relationship between caregivers and young children as crucial. Toddlers need to know that the human world in which they live is a caring one that is responsive to their bio-behavioral needs.

The concept of reciprocity and mutual trust includes much more than just stimulating interactions (Gerber & Johnson, 1998; Kovach & Da Ros, 1998; McMullen, 1999). Characteristics are:

1. interacting with, rather than reacting to, toddlers;
2. working to read and interpret verbal and nonverbal cues;
3. anticipating needs and wants;
4. responding quickly and affectionately;
5. waiting for cues from the child that he is ready for some action to take place;
6. including the child's individuality and temperament in decisions about cue interpretation;
7. including the child in the process of caregiving;
8. sensitivity to over- or under-stimulation from the environment, as well as the people (and other children) in it; and
9. individualizing the schedule or pace of the day.

When the interactive climate has these characteristics, secure relationships emerge (Gerber & Johnson, 1998; Howes & Hamilton, 1992).

Each child is unique—like no other. Primary teachers take the time to learn each child's unique ways in order to foster positive communication. Teachers gather substantive information about the child from the parents and from observations of the child with his parents at school. This information gives the teacher a start toward understanding each child's individuality so the teacher can match her or his interactive style to the young child's emotional and social needs.

The teacher-child relationship is based on mutual personal involvement between the toddler and the teacher that is reciprocal in nature. Reciprocity refers to the careful give-and-take of interactions between the child and the teacher and their mutual interdependence. Gordon (1970) calls this the "ping-ponging" of interactions—the child says a word; the adult repeats the word and smiles; the child says the word again and again; the adult smiles and expands the word into a sentence.

Experts confirm this conceptualization of the toddler and adult in an interactive and interdependent relationship (Brazelton, 1992; McMullen, 1999). It isn't just the adult's response to the toddler that makes the toddler respond or connect. The toddler is as active a participant as the adult, engaging in continued or modified interaction by his vocalizations and nonverbal responses.

The third component of primary teaching is the balance among routine, interaction, stimulation, and time alone. An unfortunate legacy of the early education movement is the mistaken idea that children need to have constant stimulation. In reality, children need balance in the interactive world. Toddlers need sensitive responses to routines; warm, caring, intimate interactions with a primary teacher; stimulation from the environment; toys, adults, and children in the environment; and, most importantly, uninterrupted time alone to integrate the experience (Gerber & Johnson, 1998; Greenman & Stonehouse, 1996; Kovach & Da Ros, 1998).

Relationships between teachers and children are not formed overnight; they develop over time. The process of becoming familiar, learning each other's interactive styles, developing a joyful interest in each other's worlds, and learning to understand each other's communication style takes time (Fein, Gariboldi & Boni, 1993). Primary teaching leads children and their teachers to form such relationships by taking time with each step of the process and by not requiring the child or the teacher to be in a relationship "all at once."

Continuity of Care and Friendship Groups

Continuity of care is an extension of primary teaching that works to keep all of the components of relationships intact. The teachers stay the same, the peers stay the same, and the context stays the same. It is worth the effort to maintain as many of these components as possible during the first three years.

Because it takes time to develop close, reciprocal relationships, teachers and children need long periods of time together. Continuity of care involves keeping all components of the child's experience continuous—the teacher, the other children in the group, and the context of the child's experience. Frequently moving children to new classrooms with new teachers disrupts the relationship-building process, forcing everyone (children, parents, and teachers) to start over.

Philosophically and experientially, primary teaching extends the length of time a teacher and a small group of children stay together in the same place. Changing any of the components of continuity should be done with great caution. Groups can stay together for at least 18 months, and may stay together for up to 3 years. The extended time together allows children to form strong ties to their primary teacher and to begin to form additional secondary relationships with other adults and children in the classroom. This much time allows parents and teachers to get to know and understand each other's needs, expectations, and talents (Edwards, Gandini & Forman, 1994).

Changes in context are also avoided. When children need changes in their environments, primary teachers make those changes in the familiar setting of the classroom, instead of requiring children to move to a new location to get these needs met.

What to Expect Socially from Toddlers

For toddlers, learning social expectations is a slow and gradual process that is tied very closely with emotional development. This isn't a good time to make a completely new group of friends, change schools, move to a new room, or find a new caregiver. Social expectations for toddlers should be grounded in their developmental context. Here are some appropriate expectations for toddlers:

- Don't expect toddlers to adjust quickly when they are left in a new situation unless there are familiar adults. So, if the primary teacher is on vacation, the substitute teacher needs to be a familiar person or someone who has spent some time in the classroom with the primary teacher before substituting.

- Children are unable to "share" until well into the third year. Teachers may help them take turns, share resources, or wait for a turn, but spontaneous sharing behavior doesn't occur consistently until after the third birthday.
- Manners are difficult for younger children. Eating with a utensil instead of your hands, staying at the table until you are finished, and not dawdling are difficult expectations until children are older. That doesn't mean you don't have rules about these issues, it just means teachers have to be the ones who enforce the rules.
- Expectations, such as touching softly, playing nicely, and keeping your hands to yourself, are also difficult for toddlers. Most children this age didn't really mean to pull a friend's hair, it just looked so interesting that it had to be touched. Stay close and help children learn these skills by modeling and supporting them.

Appropriate Expectations for Toddlers with Friends

Toddlers have a very endearing quality that can cause problems for them when they are in groups. They are very egocentric—focused on themselves. They are not able, for example, to understand that the finger in their mouths might belong to another feeling person or that the child they are stepping on might not like it. Young children can't take the point of view of another child, so they need adult support to understand if they get too close to or need to be separated from others.

A wonderful new skill is emerging in toddlers. They are beginning to develop true friendships and learn about being a friend. Having someone to play with becomes a powerful drive that helps older toddlers begin to learn more social skills. Parents and teachers alike are often pleased to see children exhibiting sympathy (feeling sad when another child is sad), empathy (understanding how a hurt child feels without being hurt themselves), and altruism (concern about the welfare of others). These new skills increase the chance that children will get along better in groups.

In a classroom where a number of toddlers are sharing the same space, remember to look at them as a group of individual, unconnected children. Stay close and help them learn the process of interacting with others as their social skills emerge and grow. Toddlers do not have the fully developed skills for social interactions, so they need the support of adults to help them function in a group setting.

Validating What Moms and Dads Know

Many parents feel insecure in their roles as their child's first and most important teachers. Some parents try to read everything possible on child rearing and development to try to overcome their feelings of uncertainty and inadequacy. Teachers can help parents by validating what parents know about their child and by supporting their parental roles.

Teachers and parents have different worldviews. Parents view the school world through their child's experience; teachers view the school world through the eyes of the group. Further, teachers often disagree with how parents are handling parenting issues because home strategies or techniques differ from those used at school. Teachers who disagree with parents may find it difficult to validate them. Strengthening relationships with parents will enable teachers to have a broad impact upon young children and their families.

Despite the fact that children may spend more waking time in the company of their teacher, parents still have a more profound effect on their children than any other factor. So, when parents want to know what they can do to help their children, embrace their interest. Encourage them to stay involved in their child's school, to read to their child each day, and to enjoy being the most influential people in their child's life.

Guidance and Discipline

Teaching Social Problem-Solving Skills to Toddlers

Patterning and Modeling with Toddlers

During the early years, toddlers take much of their social learning directly from experiences. However, we often expect them to have more sophisticated skills than they are able to acquire. What can teachers do to help children learn important social skills during this stage? Patterning and modeling are two examples of excellent teaching strategies that are very appropriate for toddler teachers to use. Patterning involves a hand-over-hand repeating of appropriate behaviors. Modeling is showing a child what you want them to do by doing it.

Patterning is appropriate to use in showing children how to touch each other softly, how to pick up toys and materials after dumping them on the floor, or how to stand back when someone wants to come in or go out the door.

Modeling is appropriate for demonstrating the appropriate use of toys and materials, demonstrating techniques such as finger painting, brush painting, stacking blocks, pushing a ball back and forth, and so on.

Use both often—they are powerful, particularly if you use language stimulation techniques (see page 297) such as self-talk or description along with the patterning and modeling.

Learning Social Problem-Solving Skills

Learning social problem-solving skills is a process—one that starts in infancy and isn't complete until adults become adept at reading social cues in different contexts. There are identifiable steps that can be taught to children during the first three years that will support emerging social relationships and facilitate emerging friendships.

Calling for Help

The tendency to call for help emerges as children develop—we usually hear about problems as soon as they begin to arise. Quick response to calls for help when toddlers get too close to each other, walk on another child's hand or foot, or get in each other's way tells children that their communication is received. When teachers validate such cries for help, children learn that the world is responsive to their needs.

Toddlers need to be reminded to call for help if the strategies they are using do not seem to be working. For example, when two toddlers want the same toy, both will grab it and begin to scream for help. Teachers must be very responsive to such situations and validate the call for help. Then, they can help children begin to understand that although grabbing didn't work, some other ideas might work.

Trading

When children's expressive language skills are not yet sophisticated enough for them to deal verbally with their peers, trading, taking turns, and walking away are good social problem-solving strategies to teach children (Albrecht & Ward, 1989). Then, toddlers need support in making plans with others to get what they want.

> The concept of sharing is difficult for toddlers to understand. However, trading something you have for something you want can be explained by sensitive adults who guide children to learn this new skill. In situations where children begin shrieking as another child grabs a favored toy, the adult hands the child who is grabbing the toy another one of equal interest to trade, saying, "Ask him to trade with you." Or, "Give her the doll in exchange for the book." Regular assistance with the concept of trading (which exchanges something for something rather than something for nothing) facilitates social skills in toddlers.

Taking Turns

After trading is learned, the concept of taking turns can be introduced. Taking turns requires children to delay gratification for a little while and participate as an onlooker until a child is ready to take a turn. Again, sensitive adults need to help children learn this skill by explaining what is happening and providing the physical support and supervision to encourage children to take turns.

Walking Away

Walking away is a technique that is used to help children begin to use words rather than actions (which are usually aggressive) to solve problems. Walking away can take two forms: I can tell you to walk away from me, or I can walk away from you if you are bothering me. Both techniques empower children to solve their own problems and to use words as problem-solving tools. However, walking away is an adult-supported activity during toddlerhood. Just telling a toddler to walk away doesn't work. He needs the teacher's gentle support to help him do so. Also, telling your friend to walk away is a supported activity. A sensitive teacher needs to be close and remind the toddler to talk to his friend who is too close and to provide the words and support the actions.

Plan-making

Finally, facilitated plan-making helps both children to get a turn. Plan-making requires adult support. Tell the children that you have an idea of how to solve the problem. Tell them that both children will get a turn. One child will get the toy for three minutes, and then you will help the toddler give the toy to the other child for three minutes. While the second child is waiting, help him choose another activity—even if that activity is sitting and waiting for three minutes with your help! Plan-making keeps teachers from feeling like referees. No one loses. One child has to delay gratification, but gets the teacher's help to do so. Plan-making has another important benefit. It keeps teachers from saying "NO." Having a plan is very different from not being able to do something.

Social Problem-Solving Skill Development—A Process over Time

Step One: Calling for Help
Step Two: Trading
Step Three: Taking Turns
Step Four: Using Words
Step Five: Walking Away
Step Six: Plan-making

Handling Biting in the Classroom

Without a doubt, biting is perceived as the most common behavior problem among children under the age of three. Dealing with biting behavior is not so difficult if the developmental reasons for biting are understood and dealt with appropriately.

Understanding why children bite is the first step in preventing biting. Noted psychologists Ilg and Ames point out that biting does not mean the child is "bad" or "cruel" (1976). Instead, it is a sign of the developmental age of the child. Children bite to explore, to get reactions, and because they lack language and social skills. They are not yet able to say, "Leave me alone," or "That's my toy." As soon as they learn to tell their peers to leave them alone, to move away from children who get too close, and to negotiate turns, the frequency of biting behavior will diminish.

***Biting in the Classroom—Three Types of Biting**

- Investigative/Exploratory Biting: For children between early infancy and about 14 or 15 months, biting is often a part of the investigation and exploration that defines babies' play. They are curious about things that get put into their mouths. They want to see what things taste and feel like. They are interested in exploring everything with their mouths.
- Action/Reaction Biting: Children between the ages of 9 and 20 months are beginning to connect actions with reactions. They are exploring interesting combinations of actions to see what reactions they might discover. Other toddlers provide a wide array of reactions to being bitten. When the toddler bites down on the finger that is gingerly exploring her face, it gets a big, loud reaction from the other child and from the adults in the room.
- Purposeful Biting: This kind of biting is a toddler's attempt to get what he wants or to change the outcome of a situation. Purposeful biting emerges at about 18 months and usually disappears as children learn language and social problem-solving skills. To adults, this stage of biting is the most difficult to handle.

Prevention

Prevention and anticipation of biting behavior are the best ways to deal with biting. The best prevention strategy is to create an environment that spreads children throughout the available space. Because toddlers tend to be "groupie" in nature (they are wherever the teacher is), it is important to arrange the classroom to limit children's ability to see everyone and everything. If children are unable to see the toys other children are playing with, they will be less likely to want to play with those specific toys and, therefore, less likely to bite to get those toys.

The best environments for toddlers are rooms full of "nooks and crannies," where children can play alone or with one or two playmates. Classrooms arranged in such a manner experience fewer biting episodes. Open, unbroken space only increases the tendency of toddlers to group together and the chances that a child will use biting behavior to meet his needs.

Anticipation

Anticipation of biting is also an important part of coping with biting behavior. Careful observation of when, where, and with whom biting occurs provides the basis for anticipating biting episodes. Once the teacher has this information, she or he will be able to limit the development of situations in which biting occurs. Separating a regular biter from his most frequent target, anticipating tired or fussy times that will likely result in conflict, and rearranging play pairs are examples of anticipation strategies for preventing biting.

Substitution

Substitution is also a strategy for helping children learn to control biting. During some ages, sore gums that need rubbing can be the cause of biting behavior. The nearest available object to soothe sore gums just might be the arms or fingers of another child. When this is the case, keep cooled teething rings or soft rubber manipulative toys available to offer to teething children.

Supervising and Shadowing Biters

The next step is a preventive one designed to teach that biting doesn't get what the child may think it does. Children who are biting frequently (for example, three or more times a day for three or more consecutive days) may need increased supervision throughout the day. Shadowing the child or limiting his freedom within the classroom by having the child hold your hand as you move around the room will reinforce the idea that biting will be controlled in your classroom.

Finally, if biting persists, the last step is to get help. Often teachers are too close to the situation to be objective. Ask another teacher to observe. Sometimes an objective eye will pinpoint something you overlooked. If all efforts fail, reach out for additional assistance. Psychologists or early childhood specialists can offer insight into chronic biting and help remedy the situation.

Teaching Toddlers Social Interaction Skills

Now is the time to teach social interaction skills to help toddlers increasingly gain control over their own behavior. Because most conflict during this stage occurs over limited resources (toys, crayons, blocks, manipulatives, the teacher's lap), the first social interaction skill a child needs is the ability to wait just a moment. This is called delaying gratification, and it a particularly difficult skill for a child to master.

Then, teach children to use their words. Start with "Mine!" As language grows, the words will get more specific ("I want the truck, please"). Then help children master the social problem-solving skills they have been practicing

When attempting to prevent action/reaction biting and to teach children social skills, remember these important points:

- Respond quickly when one toddler hurts another.
- Biting is a development phenomena that comes and goes.
- All children bite occasionally at various ages and stages.
- Comfort hurt children who are bitten quickly, hugging and cuddling them until they are calm.
- Discuss biting incidences with parents.
- Complete a written report.
- Biting disappears and is replaced by more mature skills as children grow.
- Don't let children bite without getting a negative reaction from you.
- Give older toddlers lots of attention and hugs for positive social behaviors with friends such as touching softly or taking turns.
- Talk about what children are doing and describe their actions and reactions and the actions and reactions of others as they happen.
- Model behaviors you want children to use such as talking softly, saying "please" and "thank you," and holding your hand in dangerous situations.
- Verbal children often identify the wrong child as the biter. Or, they may attribute every right and wrong in the classroom to one child. Check out the facts.
- Prevention, anticipation, and substitution take care of most biting incidences.
- Help children learn to wait for just a moment.
- Teach children to use words, walk away, trade, and take turns.
- Shadow children in new situations to prevent biting.
- Other teachers can be a resource to help in understanding biting.
- Who did the biting is not as important as the teacher's plan for handling it.
- Talk with parents about any concerns about toddlers' behaviors.
- Bites rarely cause problems from a health perspective. Concerns about infection or contracting HIV are usually unfounded.

such as walking away from a problem or asking the other child to walk away. These skills make children feel powerful and capable of solving their own problems some of the time. Next comes asking for what is wanted instead of grabbing it. "Please put that in my right hand" often works very well. The next step is trading a toy you don't want for a toy you do want. "Trade me a yellow car for the blue one," makes both children winners. Finally, help children accept no for the answer when all of these strategies don't work.

Taking turns (first me, then you) comes next, followed finally by actually sharing. Expect these skills to dramatically reduce biting specifically and aggression in general, as children master them.

Dealing with Parents about Biting

The whole subject of biting is a very emotional one for parents. When they learn that their child has been bitten, parents often feel that the teacher failed to protect their child. What many parents do not realize is that most children bite at some time in their development and that the action of biting is developmental in nature. Children bite because they have not mastered skills necessary to do things in another way. Teachers are very important to parents during this stage because they are able to offer the reassurance that many parents need. Although teachers may not want to deal with how parents are feeling about biting and other aggressive behaviors in children, it is crucial to do so in a way that keeps the lines of communication open.

Use the following approach to handling biting in your classroom. When a biting incident occurs, give your attention to the child who was bitten—not to the child who did the biting. Offer comfort and a cool washcloth or ice pack, if needed. Complete a written report (see page 539 in the Appendix), being very specific about what happened, but do not include children's names on each other's reports. Who did the biting is not as important as how you handled it and what you plan to do to prevent it in the future. Parents need to know that it is your responsibility—not theirs—to handle what happens in the classroom.

What you can do to reassure parents is to be calm and professional. Have a plan formulated and communicate that plan with parents. Emphasize that biting is a stage and that children will grow out of it as they mature and as you implement your plan.

Teacher Competencies to Support Toddlers Making Friends

Sometimes	Usually	Always	
☐	☐	☐	Spends as much or more time listening to parents than providing guidance.
☐	☐	☐	Asks questions to clarify parents' points of view or issues of concern before responding with program policies or procedures.
☐	☐	☐	Comments to parents about strengths, accomplishments, and positive attributes of the child through conversation, notes, phone calls, and so on.
☐	☐	☐	Acknowledges and compliments parents on the unique contributions they make to their child's developmental progress.
☐	☐	☐	Welcomes parents in the classroom at any time during the school day.
☐	☐	☐	Shows she or he likes children and teaching with nonverbal and verbal cues.
☐	☐	☐	Bends over, stoops down, sits, and maintains eye contact while interacting with children.
☐	☐	☐	Uses a low, calm, soothing voice.
☐	☐	☐	Avoids interruption of toddlers' activities; times requests wisely.
☐	☐	☐	Allows toddlers some flexibility in following their own routines; does not insist on scheduling compliance that conflicts with individual schedules.
☐	☐	☐	Makes mealtime and other routine interactions a time for self-help skill practice and social interaction; makes mealtime a pleasant experience.
☐	☐	☐	Actively seeks meaningful exchanges with children.
☐	☐	☐	Uses floor time to build relationships with children.
☐	☐	☐	Plays social games with toddlers.
☐	☐	☐	Takes advantage of opportunities for social play during routines.
☐	☐	☐	Structures periods of social time with other toddlers; remains available to support, facilitate, or interact while toddlers direct the activity.

Resources for Teachers

Berk, L.E. (1994). Vygotsky's theory: The importance of make-believe play. ***Young Children,*** 50(1), 30-39.

Bernhardt, J.L. (2000). A primary caregiving system for infants and toddlers: Best for everyone involved. ***Young Children,*** 55(2), 74-82,

Brazelton, T.B. (1992). ***Touchpoints: The essential reference.*** Reading MA: Addison Wesley.

Edwards, C., L. Gandini & G. Forman. (1994). The one hundred languages of children: The Reggio Emilia approach to early childhood education. Norwood, NJ: Ablex.

Erickson, E.H. (1963). ***Childhood and society.*** New York: Norton.

Fein, G.G., A. Gariboldi & R. Boni. (1993). The adjustment of infants and toddlers to group care: The first six months. ***Early Childhood Research Quarterly,*** 8, 1-14.

Gerber, M. (1979). ***Resources for infant educarers: A manual for parents and professionals.*** Los Angeles, CA: Resources for Infant Educarers.

Gerber, M. & A. Johnson. (1998). ***Your self-confident baby.*** New York: Wiley.

Gordon, I. (1970). ***Baby learning through baby play.*** New York: St. Martin's.

Greenman, J. & A. Stonehouse. (1996). Prime Times: ***A handbook for excellence in infant and toddler care.*** St. Paul, MN: Redleaf Press.

Greenspan, S., & N.T. Greenspan. (1989). ***First feelings: Milestones in the emotional development of your baby and child.*** New York: Viking Penguin.

Honig, A.S. (1995). Singing with infants and toddlers. ***Young Children,*** 50(5), 71-78.

Howes, C. & C.E. Hamilton. (1992). Children's relationships with caregivers: Mothers and child care teachers. ***Child Development,*** 64, 859-866.

Ilg, L.B. & F.L. Ames. (1976). ***Your two year old.*** New York: Delacorte Press.

Katz, E. & P. McClellan. (1997). ***Fostering social competence: The teacher's role.*** Washington, DC: National Association for the Education of Young Children (NAEYC).

Kovach, B.A. & D.A. Da Ros. (1998). Respectful, individual, and responsive caregiving for infants: The key to successful care in group settings. ***Young Children,*** (53), 61-64.

Lally, J.R. (1995). The impact of child care policies and practices on infant/toddler identity formation. ***Young Children,*** 51(1), 58-67.

Leavitt, R.L. (1994). ***Power and emotion in infant-toddler day care.*** Albany, NY: State University of New York Press.

McMullen, M.B. (1999). Achieving best practices in infant and toddler care and education. ***Young Children,*** 54(4), 69-75.

Parten, M.B. (1932). Social participation among preschool children. ***Journal of Abnormal Psychology,*** 27, 243-269.

Pelegrini, A.S. & C.D. Glickman. (1990). Measuring kindergartners' social competence, ***Young Children,*** 45(4), 40-44.

Piaget, J. (1962). ***Play, dreams, and imitation in childhood,*** C. Gattegno & F.M. Hodgson, trans. New York: Norton.

Powell, D.R. (1998). Reweaving parents into the fabric of early childhood programs. ***Young Children,*** 53(5), 60-67.

Raikes, H. (1996). Relationship duration in infant care: Time with high-ability teacher and infant-teacher attachment. ***Early Childhood Research Quarterly,*** 8, 309-325.

Reisenberg, J. (1995). Reflections on quality infant care. ***Young Children,*** 50 (6), 23-25.

Rogers, C.S. & J.K. Sawyer. (1988). ***Play in the lives of children.*** Washington, D.C.: National Association for the Education of Young Children (NAEYC).

Shore, R. (1997). ***Rethinking the brain: New insights into early development.*** New York: Families and Work.

INNOVATIONS IN PARENT PARTNERSHIPS

School- or Teacher-initiated Activities

Share Biography

Share a biography and a photo with families. In your biography, describe your philosophy of early education. Put a magnetic strip on the back of the photo and laminate it or cover it with clear contact paper, so the family can mount it on the refrigerator.

Visit Log

Keep a visit log (see Appendix page 541) in the child's file. Log each visit the parents make to the school. Use the log as an entry in the child's portfolio. Share the log with parents at parent conference time to help them see their connection (or lack of it) to school.

Parent Participation Activities

Mid-day Reunion

Plan a mid-day parent reunion, particularly for newly enrolled children. Parents may read a book or spend time interacting with their child inside or outside. Encourage parents to use the same separation and reunion routine that they use in the morning and in the afternoon when it is time to leave.

Meet-the-Parents Tea

Plan a Meet-the-Parents Tea, so parents of toddlers in your classroom can socialize and get to know each other. Parents whose children are experiencing similar stages of development can be a great resource and comfort for each other.

Disposable Camera

Ask parents to send a disposable camera to keep in their child's cubbie. Take pictures of children's everyday experiences so parents will see the rich activities their children enjoy while they are away.

Comfort from Home

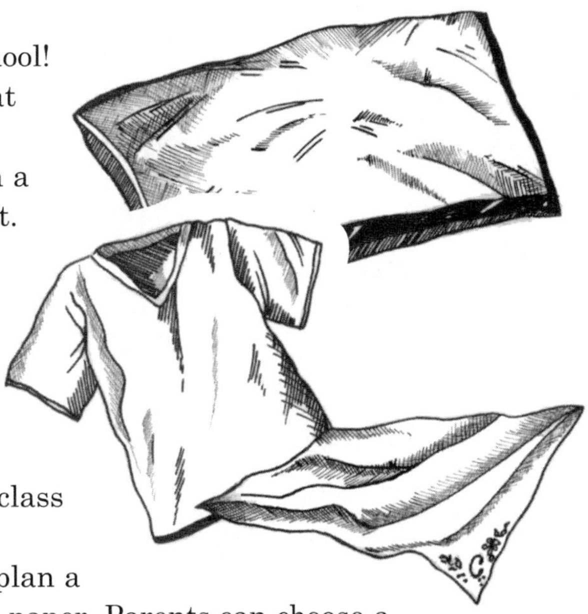

Ask parents to leave a part of themselves at school! Toddlers benefit from having a comfort item that reminds them of their parents, such as a throw pillow, a nightgown, or just a handkerchief with a little of Mom's perfume or Dad's aftershave on it. Other ideas include Mom or Dad's pillowcase (stripped right off the pillow in the morning), a T-shirt, or a soft hand towel.

Toy Swap

Plan a Toy Swap so parents of toddlers in your class can socialize, and so children can get different interesting toys to play with. If it is difficult to plan a time for the Toy Swap, wrap a box with colorful paper. Parents can choose a toy from the box and exchange it with a toy from home.

Parent Postcards

Share Parent Postcards with parents as they indicate an interest, at appropriate times during the enrollment cycle, or as developmental issues arise. (See page 548 in the Appendix for a sample dissemination schedule.) Copy Postcards. Cut if necessary. Address to parent(s) and place on Communication Sheet or hand out personally.

Action/Reaction Biting: Help! My Child Got Bitten, Again!

Again? You thought it was over when your child's friends finished teething and started playing with objects instead of putting them in their mouths. Well, not so. Investigative/exploratory biting, which usually occurs from infancy to around 14 or 15 months, is followed by biting to get a reaction (action/reaction biting).

Why does biting seem to occur among children in groups at school? The simple answer to this question, according to noted psychologists Louise Ilg and Florence Ames, is that children bite because they lack language and social skills. They view biting as a developmental phenomena—it happens at predictable times for predictable reasons tied to children's ages and stages.

This predictable stage is called action/reaction biting. When you bite down on the finger that is gingerly exploring your face, it gets a big, loud reaction from the other child and from the adults in your classroom. The ruckus that is created is interesting, different, and, yes, even fun.

Children between 9 and 20 months are beginning to connect actions with reactions. They are exploring interesting combinations of actions to see what reactions they might discover. Other children provide a wide array of interesting reactions to being bitten, whether purposefully bitten or accidentally bitten. As a result, biting may be quite an interesting activity!

TO

What Can Teachers Do to Prevent Action/Reaction Biting?

Regardless of why the child is biting, teachers have a variety of strategies for preventing it. Most of their efforts will go into close supervision, careful room arrangements that spread children out in the classroom, and, most importantly, getting to know your child's needs and temperament very well. Your child's teacher will also make sure popular toys are duplicated so that biting isn't necessary to get a toy. She or he will continue to teach your child to touch friends gently. But, even with all of these efforts, biting may still occur.

How will your teacher handle this stage of biting? Like before, the teachers' first reaction will be to comfort your child by holding and cuddling him or her. Your child's teacher will briefly isolate the biter so he or she gets the message that biting is not acceptable. At this stage, children also need to know that as interesting as the reaction to the bite was, the teacher does not approve of hurting others. The teacher will tell the biter that she or he doesn't like it. We want children to get attention from positive social behaviors, not from negative ones. The message we want to send is that the teacher will spend more time with children who have positive social behaviors than those who don't.

Your child's teacher has already started to teach your child early social problem-solving skills. The teacher started by responding quickly to calls for help from your child, validating that she or he would always be there when your child needed her or him. Your child's teacher uses narration—a kind of on-going monologue of what is going on in the child's world—to help him or her learn to pick up cues about other children's feelings and reactions. Narration helps children get information to use in their interactions with their friends.

Your child's teacher will show your child how she or he wants your child to act (called modeling). The teacher will repeat appropriate behaviors (called patterning) such as touching softly and waiting a minute for a turn. Most importantly, your child's teacher will support interactions between friends by being close to them as they play and by participating in their play.

TO

What Can Teachers Do to Prevent Action/Reaction Biting? (continued)

When your child is bitten, your teacher will always share information with you about what happened, how she or he handled it, and what she or he will do to prevent it. Your child's teacher won't be sharing with you who did the biting. Information about who it was isn't helpful because it is the teacher who must handle the situation at school. As much as you would like to help your child, you must count on the teacher to prevent biting for you during the school day.

What you can count on is accurate information about the situation and what is being done about it. Expect to receive a written report. Ask your child's teacher to tell you how she or he handles biting and what the teacher is doing specifically to prevent it in your child's classroom. Your child's teacher is a good source of information on what she or he is doing to keep biting from becoming a negative situation for you or your child. Connect with parents of older children who have passed through the action/reaction biting stage and lived to tell about it! They will help you put the experience in perspective.

TO

What Can Parents Do to Prevent Action/Reaction Biting?

The first thing you can do is respond quickly when your child is hurt by another child or a sibling. Quick responses help children build a sense of trust that their world is a safe place to be. Then, never let your child bite you without getting a negative reaction. Tell your child that you don't like it when he or she hurts you. Remind him or her that you always touch him or her softly. Then put him or her down and walk away for a minute or two to communicate that biting won't get your attention—in fact, it will make it disappear.

Work closely with your child's teacher if biting is occurring at home or in the classroom. Teachers are open to working with you to make sure biting does not become exploitive to anyone at school.

But, expect biting to come and go. It is a developmental phenomena that will be replaced by more mature skills as your younger child grows and learns. Remember these important points:

- Respond quickly when your child is hurt by another child or sibling.
- Biting is a developmental phenomena that comes and goes.
- All children bite occasionally at various ages and stages.
- Your child's teacher will comfort hurt children quickly, hugging and cuddling them until they are calm.
- Expect your teacher to talk to you about biting incidences.
- Expect to see a written report.
- Biting disappears and is replaced by more mature skills as your child's skills grow.
- Be your child's first teacher about biting—don't let him or her bite you without getting a negative reaction from you.

TO

What Can Parents Do to Prevent Action/Reaction Biting? (continued)

- Give your child lots of attention and hugs for positive social behaviors with friends and siblings such as touching softly or taking turns.
- Talk about what your child is doing and describe his or her actions and reactions and the actions and reactions of others as they happen.
- Model behaviors you want your child to use such as talking softly, saying "please" and "thank you," and holding your hand in dangerous situations.
- Parents of older children can be a resource to help you understand biting.
- Who did the biting is not as important as the teacher's plan for handling it.
- Talk to your child's teacher if you have any concerns about any of your child's behaviors.

TO ______________________

Oh, No! Not Again: Handling Purposeful Biting

By now you may be wondering if biting will become a way of life for children in your child's group at school. It may seem to you that every time you turn around children are entering another biting phase. And, now, your child will tell you all about when the bite happened, who did it, and why (although reports may bear little relationship to the facts!). Helpless feelings associated with your child's first bite may resurface, and you may be a little concerned that your child is biting, too.

Why does biting seem to occur among children in groups at school? The simple answer to this question, according to noted psychologists Louise Ilg and Florence Ames, is that children bite because they lack language and social skills. Biting is a developmental phenomena—it happens at predictable times for predictable reasons that are tied to children's ages and stages. This stage, which occurs around 18 months, is called purposeful biting. It often seems mean and malicious to adults. Further, the bites received during this stage may even leave marks.

What is going on, and what should parents do? The first step is to remember that investigative biting and action/reaction biting have come and gone. As serious as these forms of biting seemed at the time, your child passed through the stage of being bitten through investigation and biting by investigation. Then, your child also passed through the stage of being bitten for a reaction and biting for a reaction. Purposeful biting will pass as your toddler's language and social skills mature.

TO ______________________

____

____

What Can Teachers Do to Prevent Purposeful Biting?

Let's take a look at what your child's teacher will be doing to anticipate, prevent, and handle purposeful biting. Understanding why children bite is the first step in preventing biting. Biting does not mean the child is "bad" or "cruel." Children bite because they lack interaction, language, and social skills. They are not yet able to say, "Leave me alone," or "That's my toy." As soon as they learn to tell their friends to leave them alone, to move away when they get too close, and to negotiate turns, the frequency of purposeful biting diminishes.

Prevention and anticipation are two ways your child's teacher will deal with biting. She or he has created an environment that spreads children throughout the available space. Toddlers tend to be "groupie" in nature. They are wherever the teacher is. Teachers arrange the classroom to limit children's ability to see everyone and everything. If children are unable to see the toys others are playing with, they will be less likely to want to play with those specific toys and less likely to bite to get them.

Your child's teacher will also focus on anticipating biting. She or he will observe when, where, and with whom biting occurs to provide the basis for anticipating biting episodes. Your child's teacher limits the development of situations in which biting occurs by separating a regular biter from his or her most frequent target, anticipating tired or fussy times that will likely result in conflict, and rearranging play pairs.

The teacher will also use substitution to help biters learn to control biting. During some ages, sore gums that need rubbing can be the cause of biting behavior. The nearest available object to soothe sore gums just might be the arms or fingers of another child. Soft rubber manipulative toys are offered to children who are cutting teeth.

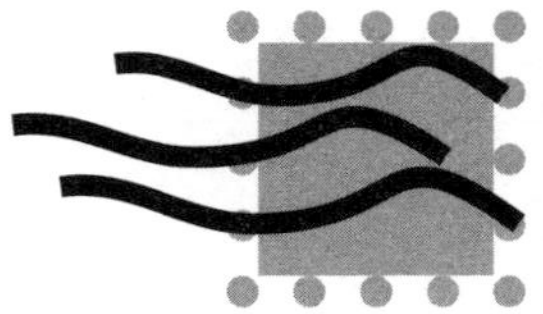

TO

Additional Steps to Prevent Purposeful Biting

Sometimes, prevention, anticipation, and substitution are not enough. When a toddler bites three or more times in one day, additional steps need to be taken. Your child's teacher will follow a three-step plan to deal with a biter once there are no more preventive measures to try. All three steps help children understand the logical consequences of biting.

The first and most important step is one your child's teacher has been using for some time—responding to the child who is bitten. If the conflict is over a toy, she or he will position herself or himself between the biter and the child who was bitten and pick up the toy. Without moving away from the biter, the teacher will comfort the toddler by holding the child near, stroking his or her back, or saying comforting things like, "I bet that hurt," or "It upsets you when Jenny bites you." This step is usually enough to help older toddlers learn that biting gets neither the toy nor attention from the teacher. In fact, the logical consequence of biting is that the other child gets attention, and the biter gets left out. Often this step is all that is needed to help a child gain control over biting.

Your teacher also has been narrating to your child. Narration is an on-going monologue of what is happening in the child's world. Teachers talk about what children are doing, how they are interacting, and how children are responding to each other's actions. Narration helps children learn to pick up cues about other children's feelings and reactions.

If the biting persists, your child's teacher will take the next step. She or he will plan a place to isolate the biter, removing him or her from the play setting and restricting the toddler's ability to play. When a child bites, the teacher will simply say to the child, "It hurts when you bite." Then the teacher will pick up the child and put him or her in the isolation place. The teacher won't be angry or disapproving, just matter-of-fact, communicating that biting just didn't work. The message the teacher is sending the biter is that you don't get to play freely in the classroom for a few minutes when you bite.

TO

Additional Steps to Prevent Purposeful Biting (continued)

Because playing is much more fun than watching others play, the biter quickly gets the message that he or she is in control of whether or not he or she can continue to play. After a minute or two, the teacher helps the biter return to play. If the child cries or is upset by the removal, the teacher will wait a minute or two for him or her to gain control. Isolation won't be very long. Toddlers have little perspective on time and will get the point after even a brief separation.

TO

Teaching Social Skills to Toddlers to Reduce Biting

Now is also the time that your child's teacher will teach social skills to help children increasingly control their own behavior. Because most conflict during this stage occurs over limited resources (toys, crayons, blocks, manipulatives, the teacher's lap), the first social skill a child needs is the ability to wait just a moment. This is called delaying gratification, and it is a particularly difficult skill for a child to master.

Then, the teacher will teach children to use their words. The teacher will start with "Mine!" As language grows, the words will get more specific ("I want the truck, please"). Then the teacher will teach children to walk away from a problem, or to ask the other child to walk away and leave them alone. This skill makes children feel powerful and capable of solving their own problems some of the time. Next comes asking for what is wanted instead of grabbing it. "Please put that in my hand," often works very well. The next step is trading a toy you don't want for a toy you do want. "Trade me a yellow car for the blue one," makes both children winners. Finally, your child's teacher will help your child accept "no" for the answer when all of these strategies don't work.

Taking turns (first me, then you) comes next, followed finally by actually sharing. As children master these skills, expect biting specifically and aggression in general to reduce.

Children who are biting frequently (for example, three or more times a day for three or more consecutive days) may need increased supervision throughout the day. Shadowing the child or limiting his or her freedom within the classroom by having the child hold the teacher's hand reinforces the idea that biting will be controlled in your child's classroom.

TO

What Can Parents Do to Prevent Purposeful Biting?

The first thing you can do is to continue responding promptly when your child is hurt by another child or a sibling. Then, never let your child bite you without getting a negative reaction. Tell your child that you don't like it when he or she hurts you. Remind your child that you always touch him or her softly. Then walk away for a minute or two to communicate that biting won't get your attention; in fact, it will make it disappear. Don't forget to reinforce and reward appropriate behaviors your child has and to show your child how you would like him or her to act. Finally, use the continuum of strategies above to help your child add these important social skills to his or her skill collection.

You should also plan to work closely with your child's teacher if biting is occurring at home and your child's classroom. Teachers are open to working with you to make sure biting does not exploit anyone at school. But, expect biting to come and go. It is a developmental phenomenon that will be replaced by more mature skills as your child grows and learns. Remember these important points:

- Respond quickly when your child is hurt by another child or a sibling.
- Biting is a developmental phenomena that comes and goes.
- All children bite occasionally at various ages and stages.
- Your child's teacher will quickly comfort hurt children who are bitten, hugging and cuddling them until they are calm.
- Expect your teacher to talk to you about biting incidences.
- Expect to see a written report.
- Biting disappears and is replaced by more mature skills as your child grows.
- Be your child's first teacher about biting. Don't let him or her bite you without getting a negative reaction from you.
- Give your older toddler lots of attention and hugs for positive social behaviors with friends and siblings such as touching softly or taking turns.

TO

What Can Parents Do to Prevent Purposeful Biting? (continued)

- Talk about what your child is doing and describe his or her actions and reactions, and the actions and reactions of others as they happen.
- Model behaviors you want your child to use such as talking softly, saying "please" and "thank you," and holding your hand in dangerous situations.
- Verbal children often identify the wrong child as the biter. Or, they may attribute every right and wrong in the classroom to one child. Check out the facts with your child's teacher.
- Prevention, anticipation, and substitution take care of most biting incidences.
- Help your child learn to wait for just a moment.
- Teach your child to use words, walk away, trade, and take turns.
- Shadow your child in new situations to prevent biting.
- Parents of older children can be a resource to help in understanding biting.
- Who did the biting is not as important as the teacher's plan for handling it.
- Talk to your child's teacher if you have any concerns about any of your toddler's behaviors.
- Bites rarely cause problems from a health perspective. Concerns about infection or contracting HIV are usually unfounded.

50

TO

Social Expectations for Toddlers

Learning social expectations is also a slow and gradual process for toddlers, which is tied very closely with emotional development. This isn't a good time to make a completely new group of friends, change schools, move to a new room, or find a new caregiver. Social expectations for all young children should be grounded in their developmental context. Here are some appropriate expectations for toddlers:

- Don't count on being able to make it through dinner when you go out to eat with children under three. You've seen it before—Dad eats while Mom walks the toddler, then they switch!
- Don't expect a younger toddler to adjust quickly when you leave him or her in a new situation unless there are familiar adults. For example, if a younger toddler hasn't seen Grandma since he or she was a baby, he or she will probably resist going with her until they have had some time to get reacquainted.
- Children are unable to "share" until well into the third year. Parents may help them take turns, share resources, or wait for a turn, but spontaneous sharing behavior doesn't occur consistently until after the third birthday.
- Manners are difficult for younger children. Eating with a utensil instead of your hands, staying at the table until you are finished, waiting for everyone to finish before getting up, and not dawdling are difficult expectations. That doesn't mean you don't have rules about these issues, it just means you will have to be the one who enforces the rules.
- Expectations such as touching softly, playing nicely, and keeping their hands to themselves are also difficult for toddlers. Most children this age didn't really mean to pull a friend's hair, it just looked so interesting that it had to be touched. Stay close and help your child learn these skills by having you model and support them.

TO

Expectations with Friends

Toddlers have a very endearing quality that can cause problems for them when they are in groups. They are very egocentric—focused on themselves. They are not able, for example, to understand that the finger in their mouths might belong to another feeling person or that the child they are crawling over might not like it. Toddlers can't take the point of view of another child, so they need adult support to understand if they get too close to or need to be separated from others.

When you get together with friends or family where babies and toddlers might get together, remember to look at them as a group of individual, unconnected children. Stay close and help them learn the process of interacting with others as their social skills emerge and grow.

TO

Resources for Parents

Add these helpful books to your parent library or post this list on your parent bulletin board.

Brazelton, T.B. (1992). ***Touchpoints: The essential reference.*** Reading, MA: Addison Wesley.

Glenn, H. & J. Nelson. (1998). ***Raising self-reliant children in a self-indulgent world.*** Rocklin, CA: Prima Publishing.

Honig, A.S. (1996). ***Talking with your baby: Family as the first school.*** Syracuse, NY: Syracuse University Press.

Lickona, T. (1994). ***Raising good children.*** New York: Bantam Doubleday Dell.

INNOVATIONS IN ENVIRONMENTS

Welcoming Environment for Toddlers

Creating different spaces within the classroom. Because the individual needs of young children vary over the period of the day or even weeks/months, different spaces are needed to meet these different needs. Create places to be alone, places to be with friends, and places to be with teacher.

Creating places to be alone is especially important in the very stimulating environments in which young children find themselves. Teachers can create these spaces without sacrificing visual supervision of all children. By breaking up large open spaces, teachers can create smaller, more intimate settings. Children will pursue activities of interest for relatively long periods of time if they are not interrupted. The smaller spaces help keep interruptions to a minimum. Low carts, duplicate toys, and activity areas can help create places to play without interruption.

Creating places to be with friends is important as children are developing a multi-sensory interest in the world around them. Spectator sports are very popular in the toddler classroom such as watching what other toddlers and adults are doing, listening to sounds and noises, sensing changes in smells in the classroom, and touching friends who are nearby. Provide enough space for toddlers to wiggle, squirm, and walk around while playing.

Creating places to be with the teacher allows the kind of intimate communication and face-to-face contact that Gerber (1998) and Greenspan (1989) term "falling in love." Such intimacy helps create a feeling of security. Diapering, toileting, and eating experiences allow the teacher and toddler to enjoy one-on-one time. Create spaces that allow toddlers to have precious time alone with their teacher. Intimacy such as this creates strong bonds between the teacher and the child and is valuable, brain-stimulating curriculum!

Accessible Toys

Very young children are constantly exploring their environment, and it is through this exploration that they learn. Carefully plan the classroom to take maximum advantage of the child's natural desire to explore and learn. The environment must be cognitively challenging, where children become involved with objects and activities that interest them (Gerber, 1998). A part of making the classroom cognitively challenging is providing a variety of appropriate toys arranged on low shelves.

Children need to be able to go to where the toys are arranged and choose toys that interest them. Always provide at least two of every toy, so toddlers are not tempted to use aggression to get the toy they desire. Toys that are piled together or in toy boxes don't offer cues as to how to use and play with the toys. Display toys separately, with just a few on each shelf. When given a choice, toddlers choose toys that are just right for their own stage of development.

Multiple Levels

Teachers in toddler environments must be able to provide variety in the perspectives that young children enjoy. One type of variety has to do with multiple levels in the classroom. Some classrooms have a raised platform that is a permanent part of the classroom, and others provide various perspectives through the use of foam structures or pits. The point is for toddlers to see the natural light from the windows, the view of other children, the sight of parents as they enter the room, and the activity of the playground or another classroom from a number of different levels. Check your classroom to see which of these dimensions are under your control.

Places to Climb and Get Away

Gross motor experiences are an important part of what toddlers need. Their bodies are changing quickly, and their physical skill repertoire is changing quickly, too. Couple this with the toddler's need to get away from the action, and the impact on room arrangement can be profound. At the very minimum, provide a place to climb, like a small climbing piece of equipment or a loft. Ride and scoot toys will provide a means for them to develop large muscles, as well as a method to get away from situations, noise, and involvement with other children in the classroom. The places to climb and the means to get away will give toddlers many different perspectives for viewing the classroom.

Places to Be Alone

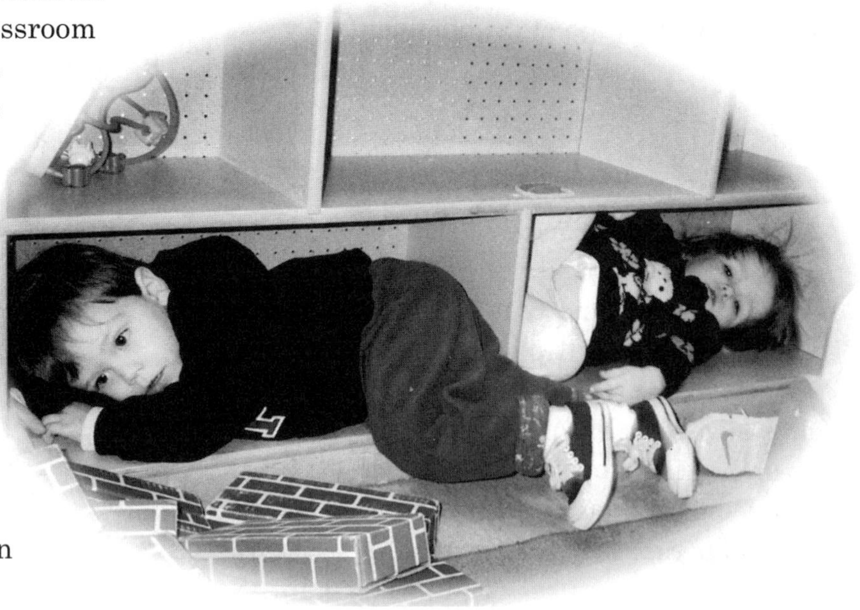

A need often neglected for toddlers in the classroom is their need to be alone. This can be problematic given the usual level of noise, activity, and involvement in the room. Places to be alone are retreats where individual children can regroup, calm themselves, and consider what to do next. Provide nooks and crannies that are too small for the entire group of toddlers to invade. Low shelves, dramatic play structures, tents, and even puppet stages can give young children the space and the break that they need. Places to be alone are not places to be unsupervised. So careful room arrangement is crucial.

Spectator Areas to View Other Children and the Outdoors

Another often-neglected need for toddlers in schools is the need to watch without being directly involved in an activity. Being a spectator is a natural role for toddlers who often watch for extended periods before they feel comfortable enough to participate or interact. Peep windows into the next classroom are a great source of enjoyment, as well as low windows that provide a view of the outside playground or even the parking lot. Provide places that are out of the flow of traffic, so toddlers can be spectators without interference from others.

Activities and Experiences vs. Centers

Most early childhood educators think of interest or learning centers as an essential part of any classroom setting. Yet, environments for toddlers are different because they are "groupie" in nature and tend to go where the action is. For this reason, teachers must bring activities and experiences to children and assist children in going to where the activities are. A wide range of activities and experiences must be available to toddlers. In each of the following Possibilities Plans, My Neighborhood and Fruits and Vegetables, activities and experiences are presented in the following areas:

- Dramatic Possibilities
- Sensory/Art Possibilities
- Curiosity Possibilities
- Construction Possibilities
- Literacy Possibilities
- Music Possibilities
- Movement Possibilities
- Outdoor Possibilities
- Project Possibilities
- Parent Participation Possibilities

My Neighborhood

WEB

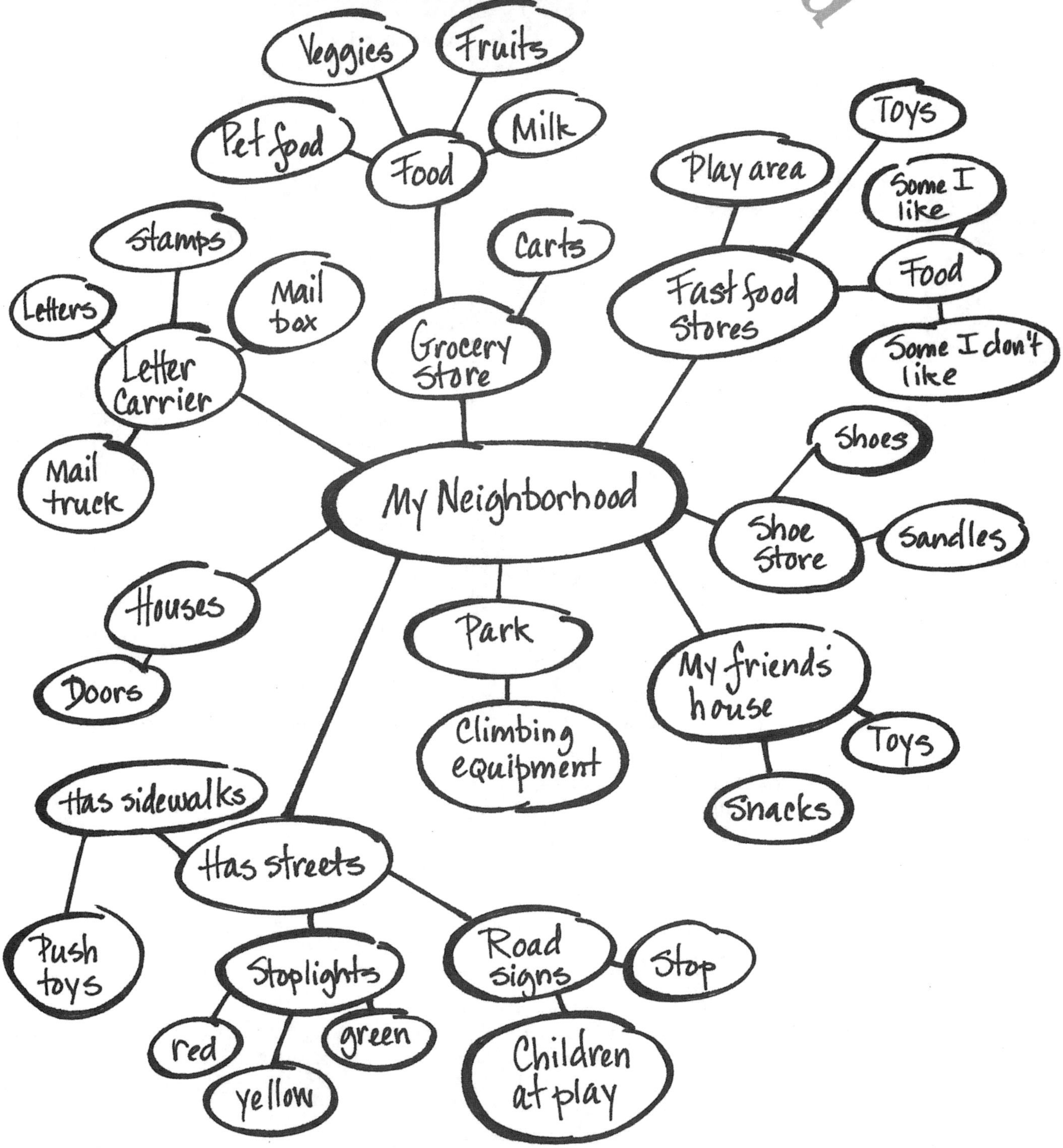

Note: Using the technique of webbing, teachers can follow the leads that children give them, as well as have an unlimited source of options. Always use the webs provided as a jumping-off point. The possibilities are endless!

Plan Possibilities

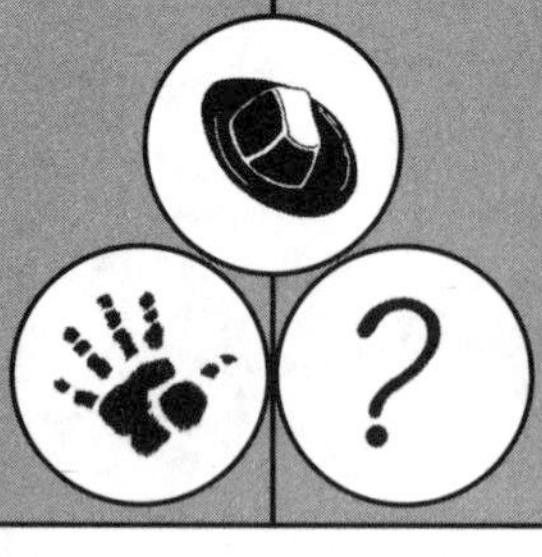

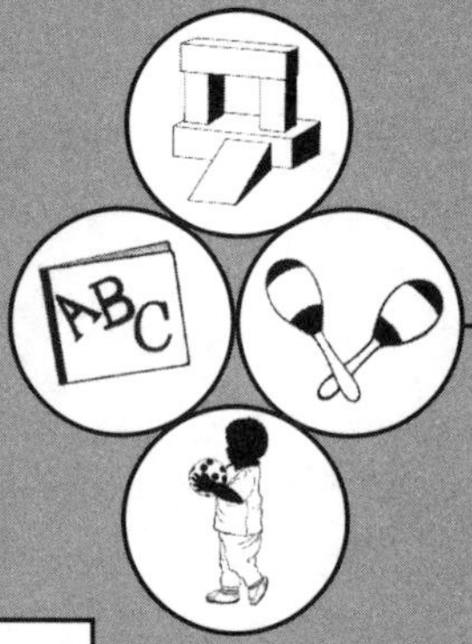

My Neighborhood

DRAMATIC POSSIBILITIES

Muffin Makers

18-24 months

Materials

Clean, empty muffin mix boxes
Paper
Tape
Metal muffin tins
Plastic bowls
Plastic spoons

Teacher Talk

"What are we having for breakfast, Joey?"

Stuff muffin mix boxes with paper and tape shut. Place muffin tins, muffin mix boxes, plastic mixing bowls, and plastic spoons in the area. Observe to see how children use the items.

Grocery Store

24-30 months

Materials

Empty food containers
Paper
Tape
Grocery advertisements
Scissors
Glue
Toy cash register, play money, wallets
Paper grocery bags or shopping cart
Clip boards and crayons

Teacher Talk

"Abby has juice in the cart."

Add various empty food containers and props to the dramatic play area. Stuff containers with paper and tape shut. Make grocery lists by cutting pictures of foods and products that are familiar to toddlers from advertisements and taping or gluing them to paper. Show children how to use the cash register and load the food items in a paper grocery bag.

Community Worker Uniforms

24-30 months

Materials

Firefighter hats, short lengths of garden hose, raincoats, rubber boots
Police officer hats, old uniform shirts
Doctor and nurse scrubs, medical kits
Fast food restaurant uniforms, fast food bags, empty fast food containers
Plastic tubs
Mirror
Camera

Teacher Talk

"You have on the firefighter's hat!"

Place various community workers' uniforms in individual plastic tubs. Observe to see who is interested in which uniforms. Join in children's play. Send children to the mirror to see themselves dressed in the uniforms. As children play, take photos of children dressed up in their favorite community workers outfits. Add the photos to the dramatic play area.

Post Office

30-36 months

Materials

Large cardboard box
Shoeboxes
Markers
Letters, stamps
Envelopes with copies of children's pictures on them

Teacher Talk

"I see Logan putting stamps on a letter."

Make a mailbox out of the large cardboard box. Make individual mailboxes out of the shoeboxes. Put the children's pictures and names on the boxes. Add the props to the Dramatic Play area and observe to see how the children use them. Help children put mail from the large mailbox into the individual mailboxes.

SENSORY/ART POSSIBILITIES

Sticky Side Out

18-24 months

Materials

One-yard length of contact paper
Tape
Toddler-safe collage materials (paper scraps, felt scraps, ribbon lengths, plastic lids, cardboard pieces)

Teacher Talk

"This paper is sticky. Try putting some of this felt on the sticky paper."

Remove the paper backing from the length of contact paper. Tape the contact paper onto a table with the sticky side facing up. Provide a variety of toddler-safe collage materials for children to place onto the sticky surface. To post where children can enjoy their work, attach contact paper to the wall or the back of a door at toddler height.

Bakery Delights

24-30 months

Materials

Playdough (salt, flour, and water)
Plastic cookie cutters
Plastic rolling pins
Cookie sheet
Spatula

Teacher Talk

"Charlie is working hard with the rolling pin."

Add playdough, rolling pins, plastic cookie cutters, cookie sheet, and spatula to the art table. Demonstrate patting and rolling to stimulate playing with the dough.

Table Painting

24-30 months

Materials

Laminated tabletop
Finger paint
Large piece of paper
Marker (teacher use)

Teacher Talk
Describe the colors and the movements the children make. "Alan and Matthew are painting with green paint on the table."

Place finger paint directly on a laminated tabletop. Let children explore the paint all over the tabletop. To save this work of cooperative art, place a large piece of paper on top of the paint and press gently to make a print of the paint design. Date the transfer and write a short description of the process to share with parents.

Filling and Pouring

30-36 months

Materials
Water table
Plastic pitchers, plastic measuring cups, plastic bottles
Black permanent marker or electrician's tape

Teacher Talk
Talk about filling and pouring as children explore the process. "Valerie is filling up the pitcher with water and pouring the water into the cup." "You stopped filling the bottle when the water reached the black line."

Place plastic pitchers, plastic measuring cups, and plastic bottles in the water table. Observe to see if children fill one container with water and pour the water into another container. Some children may be ready to pour exact amounts. Draw a line around a clear plastic cup or mark the line with electrician's tape. Observe to see if children can stop pouring when the water reaches the line.

CURIOSITY POSSIBILITIES

Wave Machine

18-24 months

Materials
Plastic jar with screw-on lid
Water
Blue food coloring
Mineral oil
Glue and tape

Teacher Talk
"There is blue water in the wave jar."

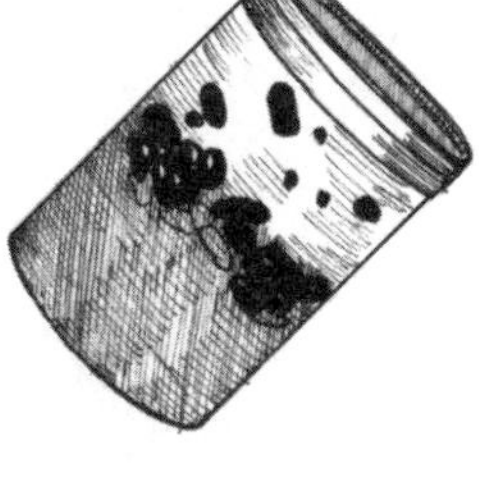

Fill a clear plastic jar two-thirds full of water. Add a few drops of blue food coloring and mix well. Finish filling the jar with clear mineral oil, getting out as many air bubbles as possible. Glue and tape the screw-on lid securely onto the jar. Demonstrate rocking the jar gently to see the changes in the water.

Noisy Roller

18-24 months

Materials

Two 2-liter clear bottles
Scissors
Large colored beads, marbles, bells, and other "noisy" materials
Clear packaging tape
Glue

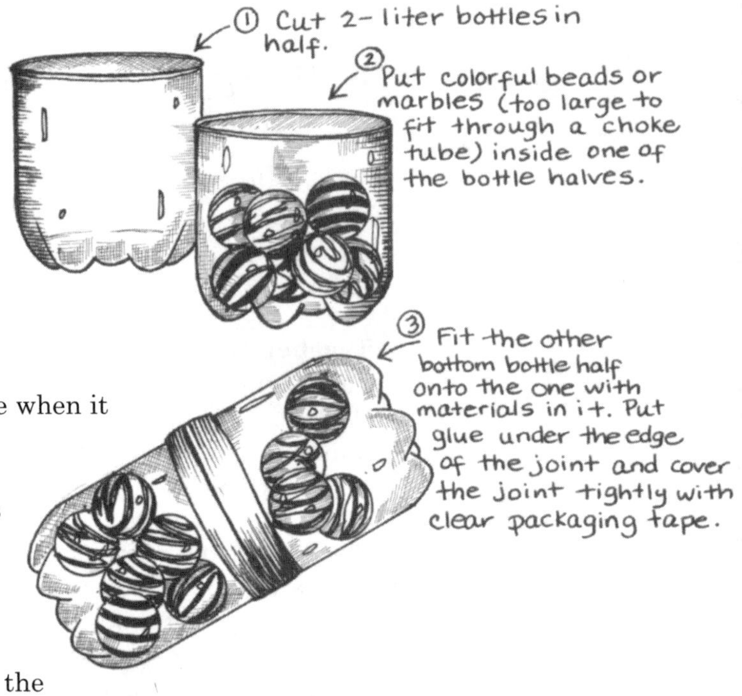

① Cut 2-liter bottles in half.
② Put colorful beads or marbles (too large to fit through a choke tube) inside one of the bottle halves.
③ Fit the other bottom bottle half onto the one with materials in it. Put glue under the edge of the joint and cover the joint tightly with clear packaging tape.

Teacher Talk

"That toy makes noise when it rolls very fast."

Cut the 2-liter bottles in half. Save the top portion for funnels in the sand/water table. Put colorful beads or marbles inside one of the bottle halves (pick materials that are too large to fit through a choke tube). Fit the other bottom bottle half onto the one with the noisy materials in it. Put glue under the edge of the joint and cover the joint tightly with clear packaging tape. Show children how to roll it across the floor or playground to make noise. Make several noisy rollers using different noisy materials.

Match the Muffin

24-30 months

Materials

Two muffin tins
Red and blue construction paper
Scissors
Tape

Teacher Talk

"You matched the red circles with the red muffin tin."

Cut 12 red circles and 12 blue circles to fit the cups of the muffin tins. Place curls of tape on the backs of 6 red and 6 blue circles and attach them inside the cups of the muffin tins. Encourage children to match the remaining red and blue circles in the appropriate muffin tins.

? Cereal Box Puzzles

24-30 Months

Materials

Colorful cereal boxes
Scissors
Markers
Resealable plastic bags

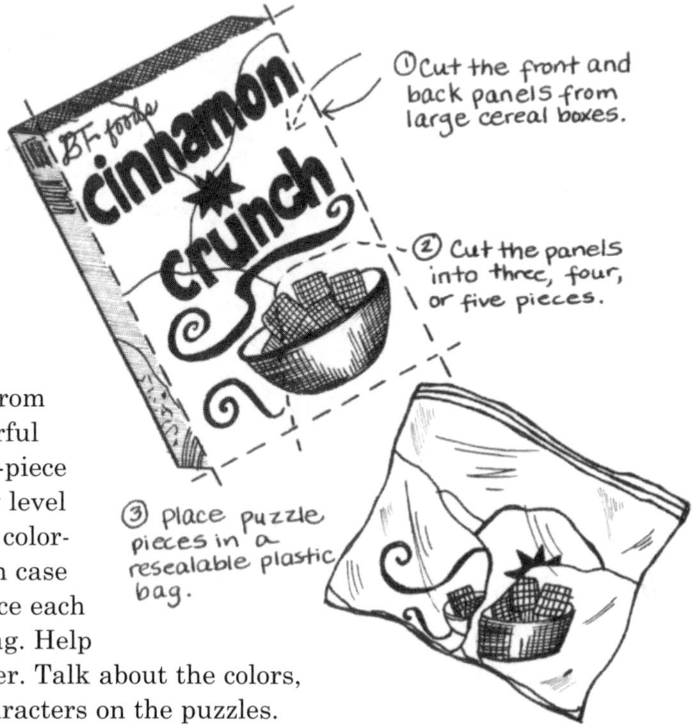

BF foods
cinnamon crunch
① Cut the front and back panels from large cereal boxes.
② Cut the panels into three, four, or five pieces.
③ Place puzzle pieces in a resealable plastic bag.

Teacher Talk

"You are putting the puzzle together, Chris."

Cut the front and back panels from large cereal boxes. Cut the colorful panels into three-, four-, or five-piece puzzles, according to the ability level of the children. Use markers to color-code the pieces of each puzzle in case puzzles get mixed together. Place each puzzle in a resealable plastic bag. Help children put the puzzles together. Talk about the colors, shapes, words, and familiar characters on the puzzles.

Note: Ask parents to bring in empty boxes of children's favorite cereal. Tell them that this is also a pre-reading activity and that familiar labels are a source of early literacy experiences for toddlers.

? Magnet Bottle

30-36 months

Materials

Clear plastic bottle with lid
Metal objects that attract to a magnet
Sand
Glue and tape
String and big bar magnet

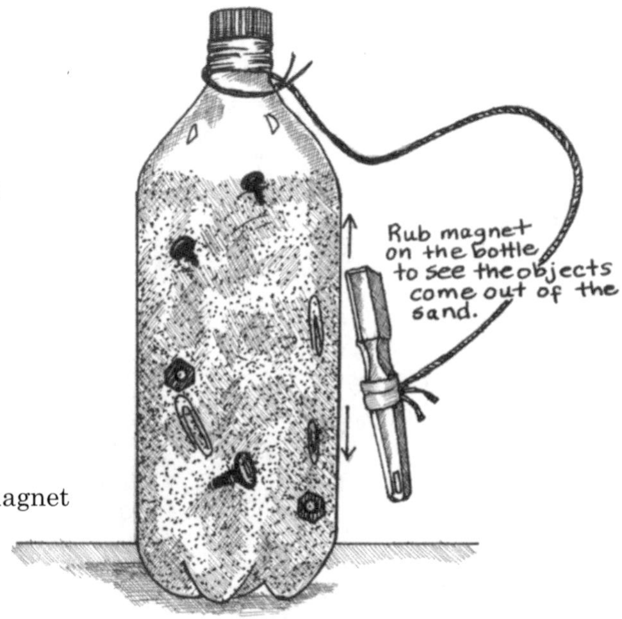

Teacher Talk

Talk about the objects in the bottle as children explore the magnetic toy.

Place metal objects that attract to a magnet inside a clear plastic bottle. Fill the bottle with sand, leaving an inch or two of air space. Glue and tape the lid securely in place. Attach a short length of string to a large bar magnet. Attach the other side of the string to the bottle. Show children how to rub the magnet on the bottle to see the objects come out of the sand. Shake the bottle and rub the bottle with the magnet again.

CONSTRUCTION POSSIBILITIES

Neighborhood Building

All ages

Materials
Shoeboxes
Newspaper
Tape
Magazines
Scissors
Glue

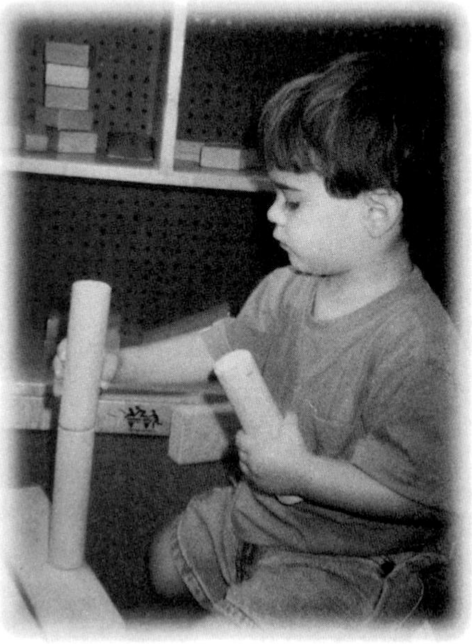

Teacher Talk
Describe what toddlers are doing as they build. "Timothy built a store. He wants you to play. Let's add some others, Angela."

Stuff shoeboxes with paper and tape shut. Glue neighborhood pictures (from magazines) onto the sides of the boxes. Add the boxes to the blocks, so toddlers can build neighborhoods.

Neighborhood Streets

All ages

Materials
White large piece of paper
Markers (without caps)
Clear contact paper

Teacher Talk
"Brandon's truck is riding on the road. John's car is parked in the parking lot."

Draw streets on the large piece of paper. Give children markers (without caps—they are a choke hazard), so they can add to the diagram. Cover with clear contact paper and use as a rug under children's block play.

Houses Book

18-24 months

② Glue different textured material on the door of each house. Punch a hole in each house and attach with a metal ring to make a book.

Materials

Poster board
Scissors
Markers (teacher use)
Textured materials (fabric, sandpaper, wallpaper samples, corrugated cardboard)
Glue
Hole punch and metal rings

Teacher Talk

Talk about hard, soft, smooth, rough, and bumpy as you and the children explore the book. "This house is blue, Sandy. How does the door feel?"

Cut house shapes from poster board. Use markers to decorate the houses. Glue a different textured material on the door of each house. Describe the different parts of each house, the colors on the houses, and the different shapes that are on each house. "Read" the book to one or two children at a time, touching the different door textures as you "read." Show children how to touch the doors to experience the different textures.

Felt Houses

18-24 months

Materials

Different colors of felt
Scissors
Flannel board

Teacher Talk

"Beth found the houses that looked alike."

Make pairs of large felt houses that are exactly the same. Help children find the matching houses and place them on the flannel board.

Neighborhood Workers

24-30 months

Materials

Pictures of familiar neighborhood workers
Poster board
Scissors
Glue
Markers (teacher use)
Resealable plastic bags
Hole punch and yarn

Collect pictures of neighborhood workers (letter carrier, police officer, firefighter, baker, grocery clerk, doctor, nurse). Cut poster board to fit inside the resealable plastic bags and glue the pictures of neighborhood workers onto the poster board pieces. Print the names of the neighborhood worker on each page. Place poster board pages inside resealable plastic bags and punch holes. Fasten the pages together with yarn. Look at the book with children. Point to the words as you say the names of each neighborhood worker. Help children name the workers.

Variation: Make a book of photographs of familiar places in the neighborhood, such as the grocery store, library, and so on.

Fast Food Bag Books

30-36 months

Materials

Bags from a variety of familiar fast food restaurants
Hole punch
Glue
Short lengths of yarn or metal rings

Teacher Talk

Talk about the fast food restaurants as part of the neighborhood. "This page says McDonald's. This one says Pizza Delivery."

Collect a variety of fast food bags. Punch holes in the bags, glue them together front to back, and fasten them together with short lengths of yarn. Read the books with children. Children will be delighted to realize they can "read" this book on their own.

Letter Writing

30-36 months

Materials

Envelopes, pencils, paper
Crayons

Stamps from junk mail
Basket

Teacher Talk
"Meredith is very busy writing this morning."

Place a variety of sizes and colors of envelopes, paper, and crayons/markers in a basket on a writing table to practice writing, folding and stuffing envelopes.

MUSIC POSSIBILITIES

The Muffin Man

All ages

Materials
Mini-muffin snacks

Teacher Talk
"Lacey is ready to sing about the muffin man."

Sing this song when you have muffins for a snack.

The Muffin Man
Oh, do you know the muffin man,
The muffin man, the muffin man?
Oh, do you know the muffin man,
Who lives in Drury Lane?

Oh, yes we know the muffin man,
The muffin man, the muffin man.
Oh, yes we know the muffin man,
Who lives on Drury Lane.

London Bridge

All ages

Materials
None

Teacher Talk
"Let's all sing 'London Bridge' while Alex and David go under the bridge."

Sing the song and help children make a bridge with their arms. Be prepared to sing it over and over again with children.

London Bridge
London Bridge is falling down, (Make a bridge with clasped hands.)
Falling down, falling down. (Children walk under the bridge.)
London Bridge is falling down.
My fair lady (gentleman)! (Catch, hug, and release the last child.)

Houses, Houses, Everywhere!

All ages

Materials
Pictures of different types of houses
Hook/loop fasteners (Velcro)
Glue
Felt board

Teacher Talk
"Look at these house pictures, Haylee."

Collect pictures of a variety of types of houses. Glue hook portion of hook and loop fasteners on the backs of the pictures. As you sing this song about houses, place pictures of houses on the felt board. Sing the song to the tune of "Twinkle, Twinkle Little Star."

Houses, Houses, Everywhere!
Houses can be made of sticks.
Houses can be made of bricks.
Houses can be short or tall.
Houses can be big or small.
Houses here and houses there;
Houses, houses, everywhere!

Pat-a-Cake

18-24 months

Materials
None

Teacher Talk
"You played Pat-a-Cake, Dana!"

Play this fun musical game with children. Help children act out the words and sing the song.

Pat-a-Cake
Pat-a-cake, pat-a-cake, baker's man. (Clap hands.)
Bake me a cake as fast as you can.
Roll it, pat it, and mark it with a "B." (Roll arms and pat hands.)
Put it in the oven for baby and me! (Hug self.)

Go In and Out the Neighborhood

30-36 months

Materials
None

Teacher Talk
"Let's hold hands, and we will play the game, Tiffany."

Hold a child's two hands as you sing and play this fun game. Sing to the tune "Go In and Out the Window."

Go In and Out the Neighborhood
Go in and out the neighborhood. (Gently pull child's body forward and backward.)
Go in and out the neighborhood.
Go in and out the neighborhood.
As you have done before. (Clap your hands together.)

MOVEMENT POSSIBILITIES

This Is Our Neighborhood

18-24 months

Materials
None

Teacher Talk
"Let's play 'This Is Our Neighborhood' and look for Shondra."

Say the rhyme several times with a child, using the child's name. After several repeats of the rhyme, use another child's name and help the child point to the named child.

This Is Our Neighborhood
This is our neighborhood where (child's name) lives.
This is our neighborhood where (child's name) lives.
Where is (child's name)? (Look all around.)
Where is (child's name)? (Look all around.)
Here he (she) is! (Hug named child.)
Here he (she) is! (Hug named child.)

____ Big Steps, Little Steps

18-24 months

Materials
None

Teacher Talk
"Kendrick, you and Carla are taking big steps and little steps together."

Say the following rhyme and act it out with children.

Big Steps, Little Steps
Big steps, big steps, big steps.
Little steps, little steps, little steps.
Big steps, little steps.
BIG STEPS!

____ The Store

24-30 months

Materials
None

Teacher Talk
"Amy! You made a store all by yourself!"

Say this fingerplay with a child while you do the actions the first few times. As the child feels comfortable, encourage the child to join you.

The Store
This is the store. (Put finger tips together for a roof.)
This is the door. (Hold hands apart.)
The windows are shiny, (Pretend to polish windows.)
And so is the floor. (Pretend to polish the floor.)
Here we buy our food, (Pretend to eat.)
This is our favorite store. (Give a "thumbs up.")

____ Shaker Up

24-30 months

Materials
Paper bags
Noisemakers (metal measuring spoons, plastic rings, blocks)
Tape

Teacher Talk
"That's the way to shake the bag, Joseph."

Place safe noisemakers inside paper bags, fold down the top of the bag, and tape it securely closed. Encourage children to shake the bags as the song directs. Sing the song to the tune of "Mary Had a Little Lamb."

Shaker Up
Shaker, shaker, up, up, up (Shake bag above your head.)
Down, down, down. (Shake bag by knees.)
Up, up, up (Shake bag above your head.)
Shaker, shaker all around. (Turn in a circle.)
All around the town. (Shake bags in a big circle.)

Here Is a House

30-36 months

Materials
None

Teacher Talk
"Jackie, let's make a house with our hands as we say the words."

Do the actions to this rhyme and encourage the children to follow your actions.

Here Is a House
Here is a house (Form a roof with hands over head.)
With an open door. (Open arms wide.)
Here are the windows, (Draw a square in the air.)
One, two, three, four. (Count with fingers.)

Here is the roof (Form a roof with hands over head.)
To keep warm and dry. (Hug yourself.)
Here is the chimney, (Raise arms higher as you say both lines.)
Way up high.

Here are the people, (Hold up both hands.)
So many, you see. (Wiggle fingers.)
And here is the place, (Form roof with hands over head.)
They like to be. (Nod "yes" and smile.)

Copy Me

30-36 months

Materials
None

Teacher Talk
"Put your hand on your head, Todd!"

Say the following rhyme with children. As children accomplish the easier directions, you may want to do two-step directions for them to copy.

Copy Me!
I put my hand on my head. (Hand on head.)
Copy me, copy me! (Child's hands on head.)
I put my hand on my knee. (Hand on knee.)
Copy me, copy me! (Child's hands on knee.)
Twiddle dee dee, twiddle dee, dee! (Hold hands and turn in a circle.)

OUTDOOR POSSIBILITIES

Neighborhood Vehicles

24-30 months

Materials
Poster board
Paint and paintbrushes
Tape or string

Teacher Talk
Talk with children about how the different vehicles work in the neighborhood. "Madison, you have mail in your mail truck. Where is the mailbox?"

Make signs by painting poster board. Make signs for a mail truck, taxi cab, pizza delivery truck, police car, and fire truck. Attach to the riding toys with tape or string.

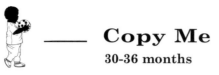

Bakery Mud Pies

24-30 months

Materials
Dirt and water
Plastic dishpans
Plastic bowls and spoons

Teacher Talk
"Look at the pie Trisha made. It looks like a big chocolate pie."

Mix dirt and water in plastic dishpans so mud is wet enough to stick together. Place plastic bowls and spoons in the dishpans. Observe to see what the children do with the mud.

Neighborhood Houses

30-36 months

Materials
Large cardboard boxes
Craft knife (teacher only)
Paint and paintbrushes
Markers (no caps)

Teacher Talk
"This house is a red house with a black roof."

Use a craft knife (outside the classroom) to make windows and doors in the cardboard boxes. Paint the houses with the children. Then, let children add decorations to the houses with markers (without caps—they are a choking hazard).

PROJECT POSSIBILITIES

Bag Buildings

All ages

Materials
Paper grocery bags
Newspapers
Tape
Construction paper doors, windows, and signs
Markers (no caps)
Glue
Play props

Teacher Talk
"I see Darren is making a grocery store."

Help children stuff newspapers inside paper grocery bags. Securely tape the stuffed bag closed. Provide children with a variety of colors, shapes, and sizes of doors and windows to glue onto the bags to make a neighborhood building. Ask children if they want to add words (like signage) to their building. When several of the bags are completed, put them out in the construction area. Add play props, such as cars, blocks, people, and road signs. Continue to add bag buildings to the construction area until there are many possibilities for play.

PARENT PARTICIPATION POSSIBILITIES

Supporting Possibilities

Send parents a list of items needed for activities. Some items parents might be able to contribute are paper grocery bags, shoeboxes, plastic bottles, large cardboard boxes, aluminum pie tins, empty food boxes, and cereal boxes. Provide a large container for parents to drop the items into when they arrive.

Neighborhood Stories

Invite parents to create a neighborhood storybook using photos of familiar neighborhood places. Plan a time to share the stories with children.

Front Door Book

Provide parents with a disposable camera, so they can take pictures of their front doors. After the pictures are developed, create a front door book. Slip photos into resealable plastic bags and join then together using metal rings or short lengths of yarn.

Picture Necklace

Take a picture of each of the children in the class while involved in some enjoyable activity. Cover with clear contact paper or laminate. Label with the child's name. Punch a hole in the upper center of the picture. String each picture onto a piece of yarn. Use the necklaces as name badges when parents attend meetings.

Parent Postcards

Parent Postcards in this section are designed to share with parents during the Possibilities Plan. The topics are natural extensions of the activities and experiences that you are planning and implementing for the toddlers in the classroom. Use the Postcards to connect parents to their children's learning.

Do Children Learn While They Play?

Play is children's work. Whether it is called symbolic play, make-believe play, fantasy play, dramatic play, or imaginative play, play is central to children's development in the first three years. Play offers children a way to explore their understanding of the world in which they live.

Will your child really learn anything from playing alone, with friends, or with you? The answer is yes! Research has documented the connection between children's play behavior during the early years and a wide range of emerging abilities, including creativity, memory, vocabulary, reasoning, and impulse control. In addition, research has documented that you serve as a guide to play, increasing your child's sophistication in play as you join in.

So, make sure you play with your toddler. Your playful interactions stimulate your child's brain and form the foundation of future life skills, including academic ones.

TO ______________________

Transmitting Values to Your Child

Parents often ask how they can be sure that they are teaching their values to their children who spend a lot of time in school. Parents have the most profound influence in their children's lives. So, chances are that children will be strongly influenced by their parents' values.

Children are much more influenced by actions than by words. Telling a child to share or to be polite is far less effective than modeling those same behaviors and clearly identifying and supporting appropriate expectations. Parents of young children can relax and enjoy their time with their children. The beginning years are not a time for lectures. They are a time for closeness, hugs, and kisses and sharing your values with your child by doing what you want them to do.

TO

Concepts Learned in My Neighborhood

Concepts Learned

I can play community workers.
I can play house.
I can experiment with a variety of textures.
I can explore filling and pouring.
I can play post office.
I can explore different sounds.
I can match colors.
I can put together simple puzzles.
I can explore the properties of magnets.
I can act out stories using a puppet.
I can enjoy looking at books.
I can turn pages in a book.
I can recognize basic colors.
I can recognize familiar symbols.
I can scribble on unlined paper.
I can name familiar places in the neighborhood.
I can play simple games with an adult.
I can develop large motor skills using my legs and arms.
I can use fine motor skills with crayons, puzzles, and paintbrushes.
I can sing simple songs.
I can follow one- and two-step directions.
I can push riding toys with my feet.

Resources

Prop Boxes

Police Officer Box
- Flashlight
- Officer hat/helmet
- Plastic badge
- Ticket book/pencil
- Toy police cars/motorcycles
- Uniform

Firefighter Box
- *Fire Fighters* by Norma Simon
- *Fire Truck* (Box Car Series)
- Firefighter helmet
- *Fireman Small to the Rescue* by Wong Herbert Lee
- Flashlight
- Raincoat
- Rubber boots
- Short lengths of garden hose
- Siren or Bell
- Toy fire trucks

Grocery Store Box
- Cash register
- Empty food containers
- *Moo Baa La La La* by Sandra Boynton
- *Old MacDonald Had a Farm* by Holly Berry
- Paper bags
- Play money
- Purse/wallet
- Shopping basket

Pizza Delivery Box
- Cardboard disk (pizza with construction paper plates)
- Money bag
- Order book/pencil
- Pizza boxes
- Pizza delivery hat
- Play money

Picture File/Vocabulary

Apartment buildings
Baker
Bakery
Doctor
Firefighter
Houses
Muffin
Neighborhood
Neighborhood buildings
Neighborhood stores
Neighborhood workers
Nurse
Police officer
Restaurant

Books

Don't Forget the Bacon by Pat Hutchins
Fire Fighters by Norma Simon (page 186)
Fire Truck (Box Car Series) (page 186)
Fireman Small to the Rescue by Wong Herbert Lee (page 186)
House Is a House for Me, A by Mary Anne Hoberman
How Can I Get There? by Pamela Cote
If You Give a Moose a Muffin by Laura Joffe Numeroff
In a People House by Theo Le Seig
Just Like Home by Elizabeth Miller
Letter to Amy by Ezra Jack Keats
Moo Baa La La La by Sandra Boynton (page 186)
Mr. Griggs Work by Cynthia Rylant
Old Henry by John W. Blos
Old MacDonald Had a Farm by Holly Berry (page 186)
Pizza Man by Marjorie Pillar
Rosie's Walk by Pat Hutchins
Shopping Basket, The by John Burningham
Street Cleaner, The by Annie Kubler
Trashy Town by Andrea Zimmerman
Where Can I Go? by Pamela Cote

Rhymes/Fingerplays

"Big Steps, Little Steps" (page 178)
"Copy Me!" (page 180)
"Here Is a House" (page 179)
"The Store" (page 178)
"This Is Our Neighborhood" (page 177)

Music/Songs

"Go In and Out the Neighborhood" (page 177)
"Houses, Houses, Everywhere!" (page 176)
"London Bridge" (page 176)
"Pat-a-Cake" (page 177)
"Shaker Up" (page 179)
"The Muffin Man" (page 175)

Toys and Materials

The following purchased items are important for this Possibilities Plan.

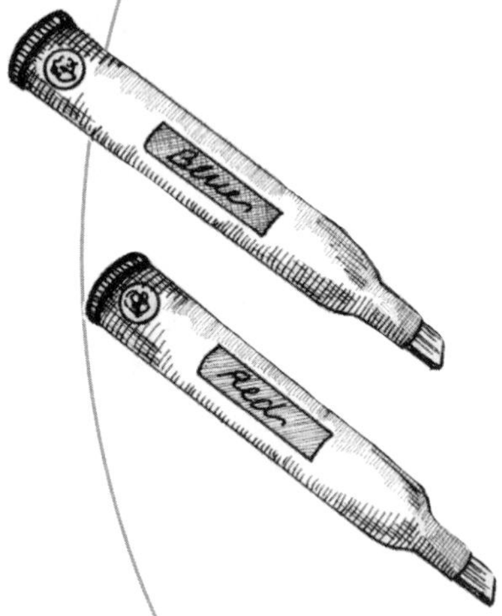

- Camera
- Clear contact paper
- Clipboards
- Contact paper—one yard
- Crayons
- Fast food uniforms
- Fingerpaint
- Firefighter hats
- FlannelboardGlue
- Gluesticks
- Hole punch
- Hoop and loop fasteners (Velcro)
- Large bar magnet
- Large piece of paper
- Markers
- Metal muffin tins
- Metal rings
- Mirror
- Paint and paintbrushes
- Paper
- Plastic bowls
- Plastic dishpans
- Plastic spoons
- Play money
- Playdough
- Police officer hats
- Posterboard
- Resealable plastic bags
- Scissors
- Shopping cart
- Tape
- Toy cash register
- Wallets
- Water table
- Yarn

The following gathered items will help support this Possibilities Plan.

Blue food coloring
Clear plastic bottle with lid
Colored construction paper
Colorful cereal boxes
Cookie sheet
Dirt and water
Electrician's tape
Empty fast food containers
Empty food containers
Envelopes with children's pictures on them
Fast food bags
Grocery advertisements
Large cardboard box
Large colored beads, bells, and other "noisy" materials
Large metal objects that attract magnet
Letters and stamps
Magazines
Mineral oil
Muffin mix boxes
Muffin tins
Newspaper
Noise makers (metal measuring spoons, plastic rings, blocks)
Paper bags
Paper grocery bags
Pictures of different types of houses
Pictures of familiar neighborhood workers
Plastic bottles
Plastic cookie cutters
Plastic dishpans
Plastic jar with screw lid
Plastic measuring cups
Plastic pitchers
Plastic rolling pins
Plastic tubs
Raincoat
Rubber boots
Sand
Shoeboxes
Short lengths of garden hose
Spatula
String
String
Toddler-safe collage materials (paper scraps, felt scraps, ribbon lengths, plastic lids, and cardboard pieces)
Two 2-liter clear bottles

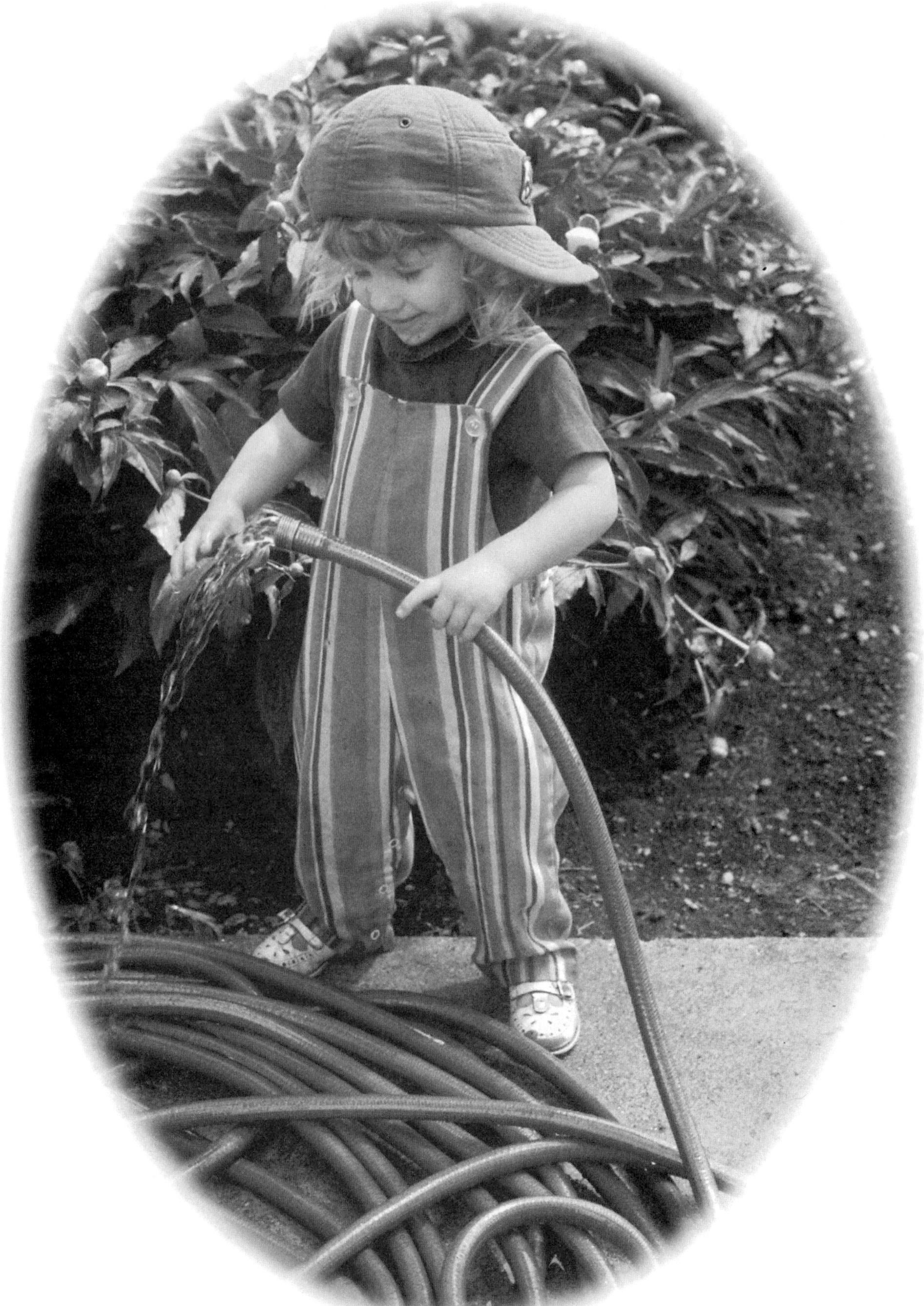

Fruits and Vegetables

WEB

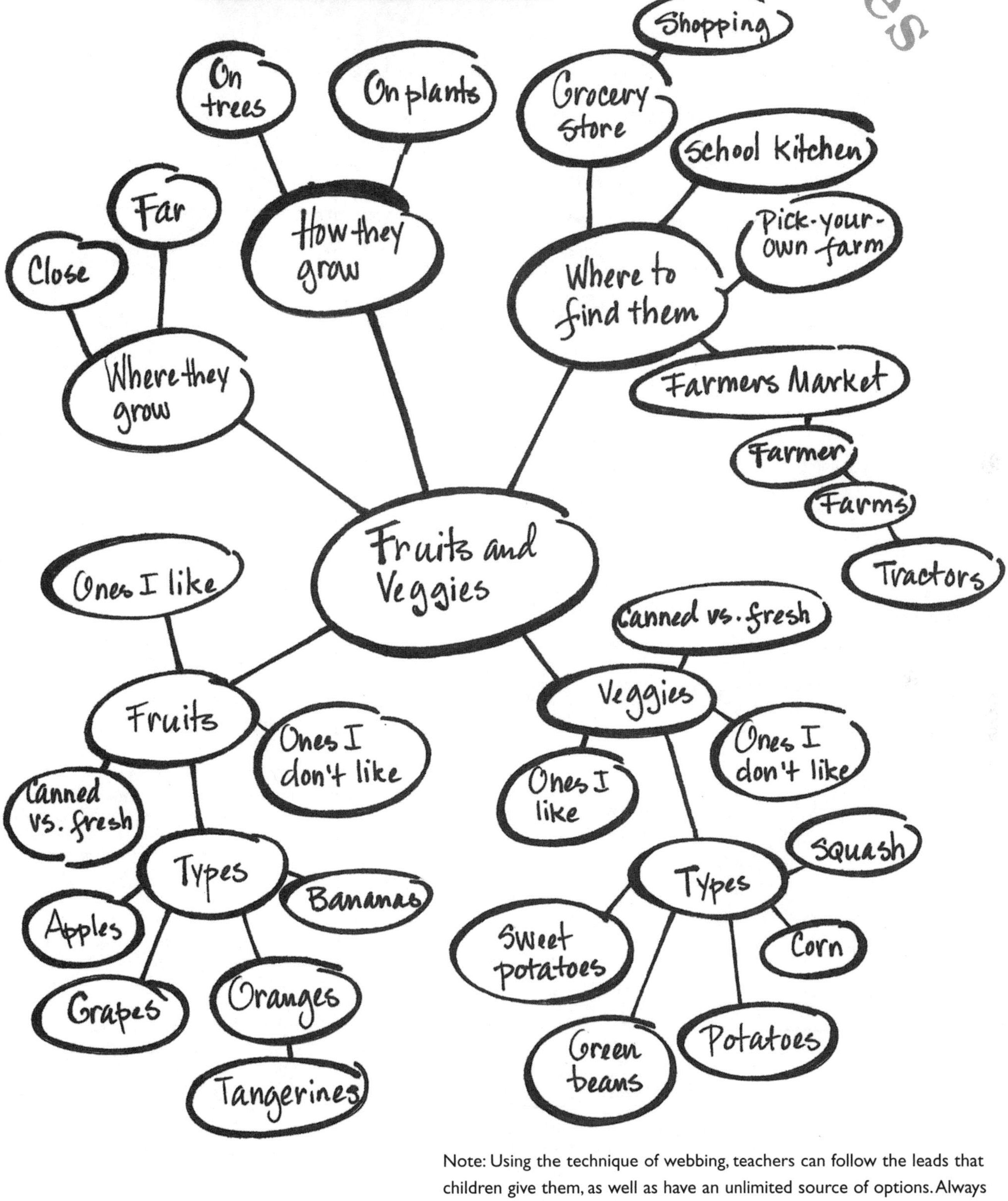

Note: Using the technique of webbing, teachers can follow the leads that children give them, as well as have an unlimited source of options. Always use the webs provided as a jumping-off point. The possibilities are endless!

PLANNING PAGES

Plan Possibilities

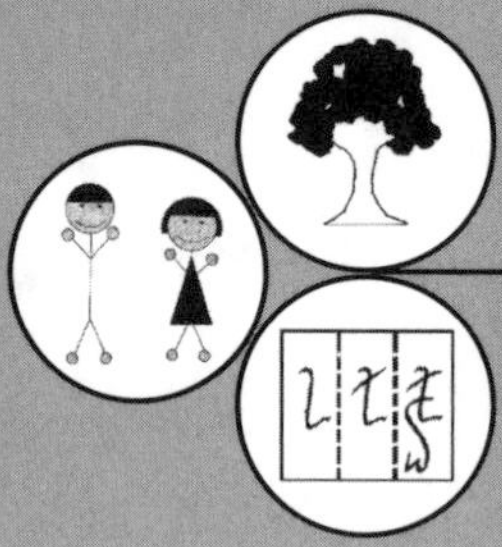

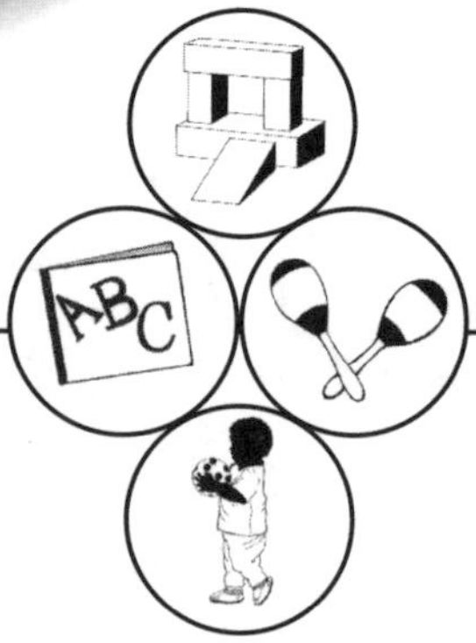

Fruits and Vegetables

Concepts Learned in Fruits and Vegetables 210

Prop Boxes

Vegetable Market 211
Cooking Box 211
Lemonade stand 211
The Very Hungry Caterpillar Box 211
The Carrot Seed Box. 211
The Little Mouse, the Red, Ripe Strawberry and the Big Hungry Bear Box 211

Picture File/Vocabulary 211

Books

Carrot Seed, The by Ruth Krauss 199
Color Fun by Deni Brown 211
Fall by Chris L. Demarest .211
Gigantic Turnip, The by Aleksei Tolstoy
I Eat Fruit! by Hannah Tofts
I Eat Vegetables! by Hannah Tofts 211
Little Mouse, the Red Ripe Strawberry & the Very Hungry Bear, The by Don & Audrey Wood 200
Patty's Pumpkin Patch by Teri Sloat
Pickin' Peas by Margaret Read MacDonald/Pat Cummins
Picnic by Emily Arnold McCully 211
Supermarket, The by Gail Gibbons 211
Tale of the Turnip, The by Brian Alderson
Ugly Vegetables by Grace Lin
Very Hungry Caterpillar, The by Eric Carle 211
What Color Is It? by Elisabeth Ivanosky 211
Yum! Yum! illustrated by Kate Gleason

Rhymes/Fingerplays

"Grow Little Seed" 203

Music/Songs

"Food Song" 202
"Oh, Do You Know Your Vegetables?" 201
"Picking Some Big Ears" 203
"Picking Up Potatoes" 204
"We Planted a Little Seed" 203

Toys and Materials 213

Food Allergies and Young Children

Experiences with food allergies or intolerance to certain foods occur often with young children. During infancy, the inability to tolerate new foods is more frequent than true allergic reactions to food but both may persist into the toddler years. In addition, allergic reactions to food can have acute onsets—they can happen all of a sudden even after the child has been exposed to the food many times before.

Symptoms of allergic reaction to food vary widely among children but can include rashes, wheezing, difficulty breathing, hives, skin welts, and itching or sometimes even vomiting and diarrhea. When these reactions occur unexpectedly, contact the child's parents immediately. Prepare to follow your school's procedure for medical emergencies even though few allergic reactions require immediate medical attention. Then, record the time, date, reaction, reactive agent, and what you did about the situation. When allergic reactions are confirmed, either by the parent or from experiences at school, make sure to update the child's file to reflect the changing situation.

When allergies are known, make sure to post a picture of the child along with the allergy where everyone who is in the classroom can see it.

DRAMATIC POSSIBILITIES

Fruit and Vegetable Market

All ages

Materials

Real vegetables (variety of potatoes, onions, turnips, squash, cabbage, jicama, kohlrabi, dry corn on the cob, and/or other seasonal vegetables)
Fruit (oranges, apples, pears, bananas)
Market baskets
Signs
Bags, cash register, play money

Teacher Talk

Describe what children are doing as they shop and fill their baskets. "Tanya is shopping at the market. Look at the potatoes and corn!"

Set up a Fruit and Vegetable Market with fresh vegetables, baskets, and bags for children to shop for foods.
Hint: Set up the market with fruits on one day and vegetables on another day.

Safety note: Use caution with children who still put things into their mouths.

What's Cooking?

18-24 months

Materials
Real pots/pans
Plastic vegetables
Dishes

Teacher Talk
Describe children's reactions as they play. "Nicole is cooking carrots in the pot."

Provide real pots and pans for children to use with toy foods as they cook.

Soup Pot

30-36 months

Materials
Large soup pot
Plastic vegetables
Big rubber or plastic spoons

Teacher Talk
Describe the vegetables as they go in the pot. "Katherine is stirring carrots in the pot."

Provide a large pot, plastic vegetables, and a rubber spoon.

SENSORY/ART POSSIBILITIES

Shucking and Printing Corn

All ages

Materials
Corn on the cob
Paper
Cardboard box lid
Paint

Teacher Talk
"Jenny is rolling the corn to make corn kernel prints."

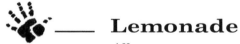

Allow the corn cob
to dry and harden.
Drop one or two
globs of paint on
paper. Roll the corn
from side to side
on the paper.

Put corn on the cob in the sensory table. Observe to see if the children take the husks off. If not, model how to husk the corn. Allow the corn on the cob to dry and harden. Place paper in the box lid. Drop one or two globs of paint on the paper. Roll the corn from side to side in the box lid, making prints with the paint. After the corn prints have dried, add more prints by adding another color of paint and repeating the process. Expand this activity by cleaning the corn on the cob in the water play table to remove the first color of paint and prepare it for another color of paint.

Pineapple Taste Test

All ages

Materials
Fresh pineapple
Knife (teacher only)

Teacher Talk
Talk about how the pineapple tastes as children enjoy the fruit. "How does the pineapple feel?"

Place a fresh pineapple in the middle of the table. Encourage children to touch it gently. Talk about how the pineapple feels. Use a knife to cut the top off the pineapple. Allow children to smell the pineapple. Cut up the pineapple into small pieces for children to taste.

Lemonade

All ages

Materials
Fresh lemons
Cutting board
Knife (teacher only)
Sugar and water
Large pitcher
Cups

Teacher Talk
"How do you think the lemon will taste, Sam?"
Wash fresh lemons and slice some for children to taste. Expect some

children to like lemon while others will not like the sour taste. After children have tasted the sour lemons, use the lemons, sugar, and water to make lemonade. Make a list of which children like lemons and which ones like lemonade.

CURIOSITY POSSIBILITIES

Bubble Scents

18-24 months

Materials

Bubble mixture
Strawberry flavoring
Plastic berry baskets

Teacher Talk

Talk about colors, sizes, and smells as children explore making bubbles. "The bubbles are tiny, Allison. How do the bubbles smell?"

Add strawberry flavoring to the bubble mixture. Use a plastic berry basket to make bubbles.

Fruity Puzzles

24-30 months

Materials

Heavy cardboard
Craft knife (teacher only)
Elastic

Teacher Talk

"Which puzzle do you want to put together. The red apple puzzle is fun, Paul."

Use a craft knife to cut fruit shapes from squares of heavy cardboard. Punch two holes in each puzzle part and use elastic to make a handle. Handles make pulling the puzzle piece easy.

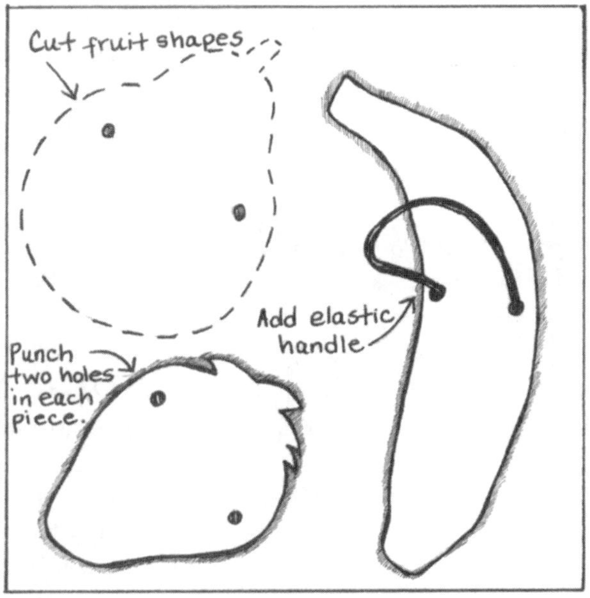

Smelling Jars

24-30 months

Materials
Plastic saltshakers with screw-on lids
Cotton balls
Fruit flavorings (lemon, orange, banana, pineapple, strawberry)

Teacher Talk
"What do you smell, Shelly? This jar does smell like a banana. Shelly likes bananas!"

Soak cotton balls in different fruit flavorings. Place the cotton balls inside the plastic saltshakers and secure the lid. Encourage children to smell the different scents. Talk about the scents. Help children name the scents.

Potato Sorting

30-36 months

Materials
Russet, red, and sweet potatoes
Three baskets

Teacher Talk
Ask children to look for the potatoes that look the same. "You chose all the red potatoes, Erik."

Place at least two of each variety of potatoes together in a basket. Place the potatoes and baskets in a play area.
Safety note: Use caution with children who still put things into their mouths.

CONSTRUCTION POSSIBILITIES

Food Box Blocks

18-24 months

Materials
Empty food boxes (cereal, crackers, cookies, macaroni/cheese, gelatin, pizza, frozen food, shoe, and/or bakery boxes)
Newspapers
Tape

Teacher Talk
"That box came with cereal in it. It will make a block when we tape the lid closed."

Collect a variety of sizes and shapes of empty food boxes. Children can help stuff the boxes with newspapers or shredded scrap paper. Tape the boxes securely closed. Put the boxes in the construction area.

Crate Building

30-36 months

Materials
Fruit and vegetable crates
Plastic fruits and vegetables

Teacher Talk
"Larry, your crate has strawberries on it. Look on the side. You are pointing to the picture of strawberries."

Collect wooden fruit and vegetable crates. Clean with soapy water, rinse, and let air dry. Sand rough edges or cover with duct tape. Add the crates to block play. Fill them with plastic fruits and vegetables and move them around the room or to the grocery store, or deliver them in push toys.

LITERACY POSSIBILITIES

The Carrot Seed

All ages

Materials
The Carrot Seed by Ruth Krauss
Fresh carrots
Plot of ground or large soil-filled container

Teacher Talk
"Look at the cover of the book. What do you think this book is about, Jada?"

Place the carrots in the pot of potting soil; then put the pot in the sensory table. Read *The Carrot Seed*. After the story, show the carrots you have planted. Pull the carrots out of the potting soil. After children have all played with the carrots and the soil, add water to the sensory table for the children to scrub and clean the carrots.

Safety note: Raw carrots can pose a choking hazard, so supervise closely.

The Little Mouse, the Red, Ripe Strawberry and the Big Hungry Bear

All ages

Materials

Little Mouse, the Red Ripe Strawberry and the Big Hungry Bear by Don and Audrey Wood
Fresh strawberries

Teacher Talk

Talk with children about how the strawberries look feel, smell, and taste. "Daniel, there is a red, ripe strawberry on the cover of this book."

Read the book with children. At the end of the story, share ripe strawberries with children.

Veggie Matching

18-24 months

Materials

Colored poster board
Scissors (teacher only)

Teacher Talk

Talk about the vegetables, colors, and shapes as you play with the children. "Yes, Darryl, you matched the two carrots. Let's see how many more matches you can make."

Cut out pairs of vegetable shapes from colored poster board. Show children how to match the pairs of vegetables.

Fruit Book

18-24 months

Materials

Pictures of fruits
Construction paper
Glue
Markers (teacher only)
Resealable plastic bags
Hole punch and yarn

Teacher Talk
Talk about names of the fruits, colors, shapes, and sizes as you share the book with children." That is a red apple, Danny. What else do you see on this page?"

Collect pictures of colorful fruits. Glue the pictures onto construction paper squares; print fruit names on the picture pages. Place the pictures inside a resealable plastic bag. Punch holes in one corner of each page. Fasten the bags together with yarn. Flip the pages to look at the book with children.

MUSIC POSSIBILITIES

Oh, Do You Know Your Vegetables?

All ages

Materials
Pictures of vegetables named in the song

Teacher Talk
"Carrie has the picture of carrots. Hold up the picture when we sing the word 'carrots.'"

Sing the following song with children. Give each child a picture of the named vegetables in the song. Point to the pictures when the vegetable's name is in the song. Sing the song to the tune "The Muffin Man."

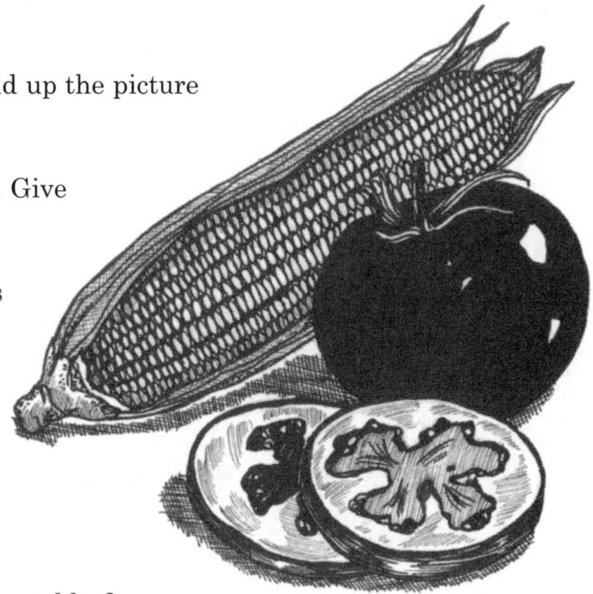

Oh, Do You Know Your Vegetables?

Oh, do you know your vegetables?
Vegetables, vegetables?
Oh, do you know your vegetables?
Veggies are so good for you!

Carrots, peas, and squash, and beans,
Broccoli, and salad greens,
Cabbage, corn, and tomatoes, too.
Veggies are so good for you!

Food Song
30-36 months

Materials
Cardboard cut into apple, cherry, strawberry, pear, pineapple, orange, carrot, and jack-o-lantern shapes

Teacher Talk
"Choose a shape to hold, Caroline."

Offer children a choice of cardboard food shapes to hold up as you sing this song. Sing the song to the tune of "I've Been Working on the Railroad."

Food Song

Red is the color for an apple to eat.
Red is the color for cherries, too.
Red is the color for strawberries.
I like red, don't you?

Yellow is the color for a great big pear.
Yellow is the color for lemonade, too.
Yellow is the color of a pineapple.
I like yellow, don't you?

Orange is the color of oranges.
Orange is the color for carrots, too.
Orange is the color of a jack-o-lantern.
I like orange, don't you?

MOVEMENT POSSIBILITIES

Grow Little Seed
All ages

Materials
Fan
Spray bottle of water

Teacher Talk
"Terrell, it rained on you while you were growing like a seed."

Recite the poem and help children act out the words.

Grow Little Seed
I'm a little seed in the deep dark soil. (Children kneel on their knees, covering their eyes.)
The warm breezes blow. (Fan the kneeling children.)
The gentle rains fall. (Lightly spray water over the children.)
The hot sun calls the seeds to rise. (Children slowly get to their feet.)
The blue sky waits for the surprise. (Children stretch their arms high over their heads.)
Happy plants grow from seeds. (Children smile.)

We Planted a Little Seed

All ages

Materials
None

Teacher Talk
"Let's sing a song about how we planted the radish seeds, Gavin."

Sing the following song with children after they have planted seeds. Show children the body movements to act out the words to the song. Sing to the tune "I'm a Little Teapot."

We Planted a Little Seed
We planted a little seed in the dark, dark ground. (Kneel and pat the floor.)
Out comes the warm sun, big and round. (Circle arms over head.)
Down comes the gentle rain, soft and slow. (Wiggle fingers for rain.)
Up comes the little seed, grow, seed, grow! (Stand with arms stretched high.)

Picking Some Big Ears

All ages

Materials
Corn on the cob in husks (real or plastic)

Teacher Talk
"Lisa knows how to pick corn!"

Sing the following song with children. Help children act out the words to the song. Sing to the tune "Skip to My Lou."

Picking Some Big Ears
Standing in the corn field out in the sun,
Picking some big ears one by one.
Cooking up the yellow corn, boy what fun!
Munching on sweet corn, yum, yum, yum!

Picking Up Potatoes

All ages

Materials
Real potatoes
Large basket

Teacher Talk
"Look at all of these potatoes on the ground! We can pick up the potatoes while we sing the song!"

Place real potatoes on the ground. Place a large basket nearby. As you sing the song, encourage children to pick up potatoes and put them in the basket as the song directs. Children may want to sing about other vegetables or fruits. Substitute the names of other fruits and vegetables in place of "potatoes." Sing the song to the tune "The Paw Paw Patch."

Picking Up Potatoes
Picking up potatoes and putting them in a basket,
Picking up potatoes and putting them in a basket,
Picking up potatoes and putting them in a basket,
Way down yonder in the potato patch!

OUTDOOR POSSIBILITIES

Veggie Path

18-24 months

Materials
Colored poster board
Scissors

Teacher Talk
"You jumped over the potatoes, Rachel."

Cut poster board into shapes of vegetables. Place the vegetable shapes on the ground close enough together for children to step or jump from one to another. Encourage children to name the vegetable as they land on them or jump over them.

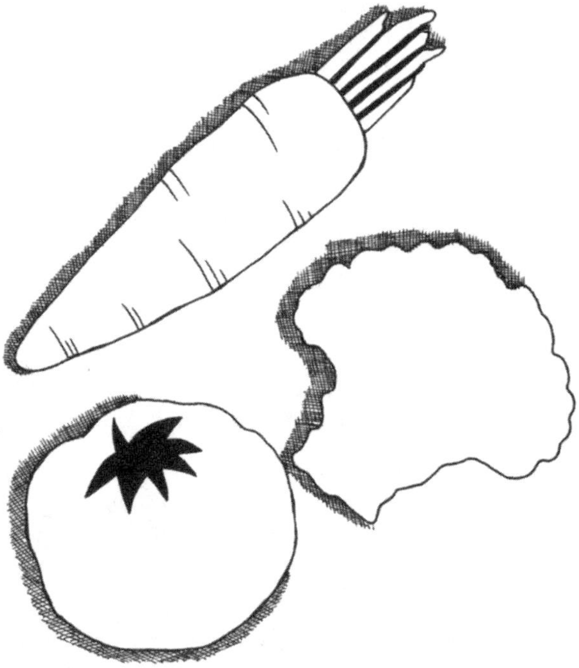

Fruit Painting

24-30 months

Materials
Cardboard fruit shapes
Easel or fence
Paint and paintbrushes

Teacher Talk
Talk about the shapes and the colors children choose to paint them. "I see Amy is painting the apple shape with red paint."

Make large cardboard fruit shapes to fasten onto an easel or the fence. Match paint colors to the colors of the fruits. Children can use paint and big brushes to paint the shapes.

Picking Berries

30-36 months

Materials
Plastic berry baskets
Plastic or poster board strawberries

Teacher Talk
"Where do you think the strawberries are, Edward?"

Place plastic or red poster board strawberries on the ground in a grassy area of the playground. Provide plastic berry baskets for children to "pick" strawberries and fill the baskets. Dump the berries out and do it all again.

PROJECT POSSIBILITIES

Books Read List

All ages

Materials
Pen and Paper

Begin a list of books to read to children during this Possibilities Plan. Post the list where parents can see it growing. Add a copy to each child's portfolio.

Fruit and Vegetable Collage

18-24 months

Materials

Butcher paper
Pictures of fruits
Glue sticks
Marker or pen (teacher only)

Teacher Talk

"The banana picture is beside the grapes, Paige. You did it all by yourself!"

Place a long piece of butcher paper on a table or on the floor. As you talk about a particular fruit or vegetable, put out pictures of that fruit or vegetable for children to glue on the butcher paper. Date each addition. Repeat the activity as you introduce each new fruit or vegetable. Take dictation of children's comments as they work. Add them to the collage.

Carrot Tops

24-30 months

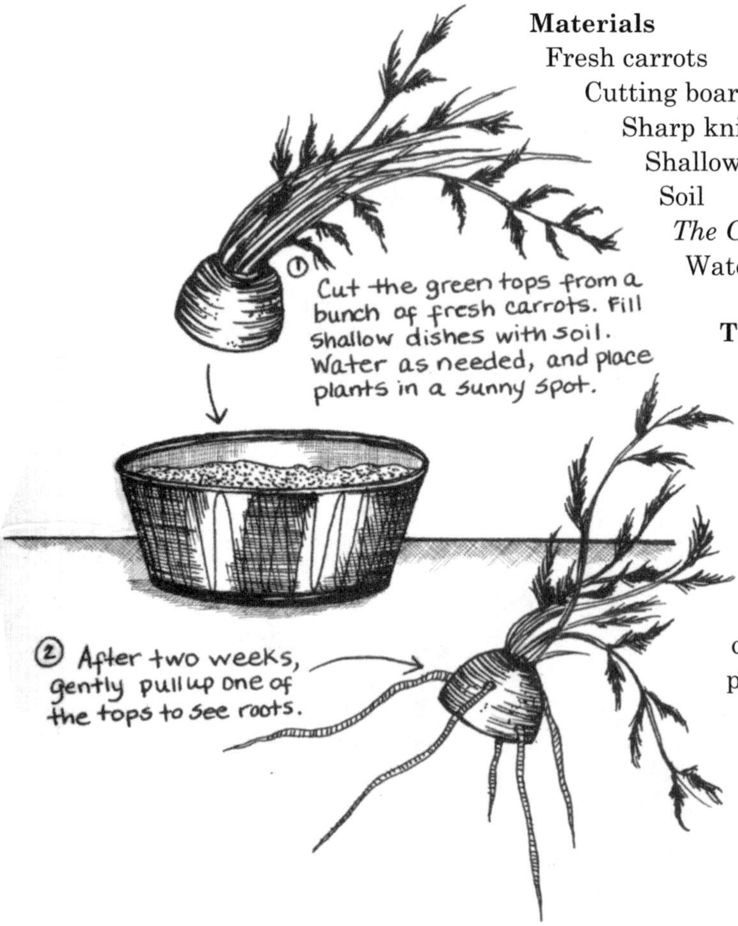

Materials

Fresh carrots
Cutting board
Sharp knife (teacher only)
Shallow dish, such as butter or margarine tubs
Soil
The Carrot Seed by Ruth Krauss
Water

Teacher Talk

"Michelle, you planted the carrot top in the soil."

Cut the green tops from a bunch of fresh carrots. Children then fill shallow dishes, such as butter tubs, with soil. Help children place the carrot tops in the soil. Read *The Carrot Seed*. Talk about the carrot and ask children what they think will happen now. Place plants in a sunny spot (preferably outside). Water as needed. After two weeks, gently pull up one of the tops to see the roots. Pull up one carrot top every two weeks to see how the roots change and grow.

PARENT PARTICIPATION POSSIBILITIES

Favorite Fruit Snack Visit

Invite parents to share a favorite fruit snack with children. Parents may want to bring the fruit to you to share with children, or they may want to share the fruit with the children at snack time.

Healthy Snacks

With a permanent marker, write a list of healthy snacks and treat ideas on the front of a canvas tote bag. Hang the bag near the classroom exit door. Encourage parents to add snacks to the bag. Then, when they anticipate being tired and hungry on the way home, they can pick a healthy snack for the road. (**Safety note**: Always eat the snack together, before getting into the car. Do not give children food to eat in the car if you cannot supervise them while they eat it.)

Parent Postcards

Parent Postcards in this section are designed to share with parents during the Possibilities Plan. The topics are natural extensions of the activities and experiences that you are planning and implementing for the toddlers in the classroom. Use the Postcards to connect parents to their children's learning.

Drive-time Activities

Often during the course of a Possibilities Plan, we will share with you a particular story, rhyme, song, or book that is being used in the classroom. This is so you will have an opportunity to support what the teacher is doing in the classroom. Additionally, your child will feel comfortable singing familiar songs, such as "Twinkle, Twinkle Little Star" or "The Wheels on the Bus." One opportune time to use these familiar elements is during Drive Time.

More and more, we are becoming a nation of drivers, where longer and longer periods of time are spent going to and from work. For parents of very young children, this can be an especially frustrating time of day. Your child wants to see more of you than the back of your head, and traffic can make the quick drive home into an arduous journey.

While you are on the road, talk with your child about your day, your child's day, what you are seeing out the window, and what you will both do when you get home. Often just the sound of your voice will be enough to calm him or her and make the time go faster. Also, try some classic songs and rhymes, and see what reaction you get. Using the same rhymes and fingerplays your teacher is using will be fun because your child has already been introduced to them. Don't let drive time be boring! Sing, talk, and rhyme away the time!

There Was a Little Turtle Who Lived in a Box

There was a little turtle who lived in a box.
He swam in the water and climbed on the rocks.
He snapped at a mosquito; he snapped at a flea.
He snapped at a minnow; and he snapped at me.
He caught the mosquito; he caught the flea.
He caught the minnow, but he didn't catch me!

TO

Preparing for Time Away from Your Child

As more and more parents are required to travel with their jobs, the issue of leaving a child for extended periods of time becomes an important one. What can parents do to make absence more bearable? Plan ahead, plan ahead, plan ahead.

Very young children have difficulty with time concepts. This is one reason why arrival and departure times at school are so important. Toddlers need to know that schedules are predictable and that parents will return. The trick with trips is being honest, but not telling young children too far in advance. Be sure that your child will be with someone familiar, in familiar surroundings, and on a familiar schedule.

The day before the trip, talk with your child. Say when the trip will be and where you will be going. Be reassuring as to who will care for your child and where your child will be. Tell why you must go (your job) and that you will telephone (as often as you can). Don't promise what you cannot deliver. Let your child know that you love him or her even when you are apart.

Details are important. Little things like having the usual clothes and shoes become more essential when a parent is away. Give your child a security item that will remind him or her of you (such as a pillowcase, a photograph, or a T-shirt). Be certain that your child has his or her usual security items, also.

Things such as emergency phone numbers, medical conditions, and where special items are located can all be written out far in advance. Then have a good trip, knowing that you have done your best to prepare.

TO

Concepts Learned in Fruits and Vegetables

Concepts Learned

I can name familiar vegetables.
I can name familiar fruits.
I can pretend to cook.
I can set the table.
Fruits have different tastes.
I can identify a star shape.
I can match smells with appropriate fruits.
I can blow bubbles.
I can put puzzles together.
Plants need water.
I can sort.
I can match.
I can name pictures in books.
I can turn pages of a book.
I can listen to a story.
I can participate in a group story activity.
Carrots grow in the ground.
Strawberries have texture, scent, and taste good!
I can name vegetables.
I can predict what happens next in a story.
I can count to five.
I can follow directions in a song.
I can move my big muscles.
I can identify colors.
I can match colors.
I can walk on a designated path.
I can jump with two feet.
I can do cross-lateral body movements.
I can play dress up.
I can place collage materials.
I can glue.
Plants have green leaves.
I can care for living plants.
Plants grow from seeds.
Plants need sun and water.
Vegetables and fruits come from plants.

Resources

Prop Boxes

Vegetable Market
- Aprons
- Bags
- Baskets
- Cash register
- *Color Fun* by Deni Brown
- *Fall* by Chris L. Demarest
- Plastic or real vegetables
- Play money
- Signs
- *What Color Is It?* by Elisabeth Ivanosky

Cooking Box
- Apron
- Chef hat
- Color Fun by Deni Brown
- Fall by Chris L. Demarest
- *Picnic* by Emily Arnold McCully
- Plastic dishes
- Plastic food
- Plastic spoons
- Pots/pans
- *Supermarket, The* by Gail Gibbons
- *What Color Is It?* by Elisabeth Ivanosky

Lemonade Stand
- Plastic cups
- Plastic lemon juice containers
- Plastic pitcher
- Sign

The Very Hungry Caterpillar Box
- Caterpillar puppet
- Food cutouts
- *Very Hungry Caterpillar, The* by Eric Carle

The Carrot Seed Box
- Carrot Seed, The by Ruth Krauss
- Container of soil
- Fresh carrots
- *I Eat Vegetables!* by Hannah Tofts

The Little Mouse, the Red, Ripe Strawberry and the Big Hungry Bear Box
- Strawberries
- *Little Mouse, the Red Ripe Strawberry & the Very Hungry Bear, The* by Don & Audrey Wood

Picture File/Vocabulary

- Baskets
- Caterpillar
- Chef
- Families cooking/shopping
- Fruits
- Gardens
- Grocery carts
- Grocery stores
- Kitchens
- Lemonade stand
- Vegetables

Books

Carrot Seed, The by Ruth Krauss (page 199)
Color Fun by Deni Brown (page 211)
Fall by Chris L. Demarest (page 211)
Gigantic Turnip, The by Aleksei Tolstoy
I Eat Fruit! by Hannah Tofts
I Eat Vegetables! by Hannah Tofts (page 211)
Little Mouse, the Red Ripe Strawberry & the Very Hungry Bear, The by Don & Audrey Wood (page 200)
Patty's Pumpkin Patch by Teri Sloat (page 211)
Pickin' Peas by Margaret Read MacDonald/Pat Cummins
Picnic by Emily Arnold McCully (page 211)
Supermarket, The by Gail Gibbons (page 211)
Tale of the Turnip, The by Brian Alderson
Ugly Vegetables by Grace Lin
Very Hungry Caterpillar, The by Eric Carle (page 211)
What Color Is It? by Elisabeth Ivanosky (page 211)
Yum! Yum! illustrated by Kate Gleason

Rhymes/Fingerplays

"Grow Little Seed" (page 203)

Music/Songs

"Food Song" (page 202)
"Oh, Do You Know Your Vegetables?" (page 201)
"Picking Some Big Ears" (page 203)
"Picking Up Potatoes" (page 204)
"We Planted a Little Seed" (page 203)

Toys and Materials

The following purchased items are important for this Possibilities Plan.

Big rubber or plastic spoons
Bubble maker
Bubble mixture
Butcher paper
Cash register
Clear contact paper
Colored poster board
Easel
Glue
Glue sticks
Hole punch
Hook and loop fasteners (Velcro)
Knife (teacher only)
Markers
Metal rings
Paint
Paintbrushes
Paper
Pen and paper
Planter with soil
Plastic dishes
Plastic fruits and vegetables
Play money
Resealable plastic bags
Scissors (teacher only)
Tape
Yarn

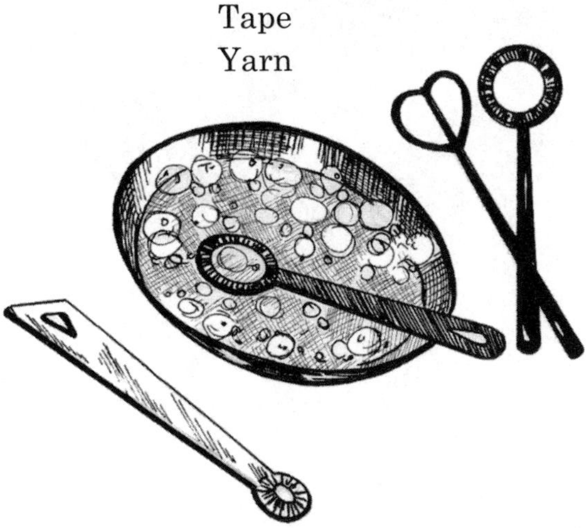

The following gathered items will help support this Possibilities Plan.

Butter or margarine tubs
Corn on the cob in husks
Cotton balls
Cutting board
Empty food boxes
Fan
Fresh carrots
Fresh lemons
Fresh pineapple
Fresh strawberries
Fruit and vegetable crates
Fruit flavorings
Heavy cardboard
Large cardboard box lid
Large plastic pitcher and cups
Large soup pot
Market baskets
Paper bags
Pictures of fruits
Pictures of vegetables
Plastic berry baskets
Plastic saltshakers with large screw-on lids
Potatoes (russet, red, and sweet)
Pots and pans
Signs
Spray water bottle
Strawberry flavoring
Sugar and water
Three baskets
Vegetables and fruits

CHAPTER 4

Exploring Roles

INTRODUCTION

Toddlerhood is characterized by changes in the way children see the world. During infancy, the focus of most interactions is on the baby. What the baby needs, wants, or is doing is the center of interactions. Infants are learning to regulate themselves and to interact with others. As children enter the second year of life, the focus on self begins to broaden to include others—other adults, other children, and other settings. During toddlerhood, children are active participants in figuring out what to do and

how they feel about their actions, as well as in interpreting what happens as a result.

As the view of self stabilizes, toddlers begin to see themselves in relation to others. From this increasing ability to evaluate "self," toddlers create a particular view of themselves. This view is commonly referred to as self-esteem or self-concept. Educators and parents know that self-concept has a great deal to do with how children continue to progress.

This view of self has lifelong implications. Children who develop views of themselves as able and competent are more likely to turn negative experiences into positive ones—to learn from their interactions and self-reflection. Creating the environment to foster feelings of self-worth and self-concept is a crucial part of the toddler teacher's role.

The way children explore their views of themselves is through play. Play provides a vehicle for exploring roles, practicing outcomes, and considering alternatives. Through play, children explore how and what to do in different play settings, increase their understanding of how others respond in a wide variety of situations, and practice a variety of roles, skills, and outcomes in the supported environment of home and school. This chapter will help teachers support these important emerging skills.

INNOVATIONS IN OBSERVATION/ASSESSMENT

Observation/Assessment Instrument

This assessment instrument is not just a skills checklist. Instead it is designed to guide the teacher's observation of children's development through major interactional tasks of toddlerhood. The assessment's focus is on what IS happening, not just what should happen or what will happen. Use this assessment to lead to developmentally appropriate practice.

Exploring Roles

	18-24 months	**24-30 months**	**30-36 months**
ER1	a. Explores roles related to self and family.	b. Explores roles related to self, friends, family, and neighborhood.	c. Explores roles related to self, friends, family, neighborhood, and the community at large.
ER2	a. Is unable to choose or modify behavior in response to physical or social cues of situations; persists in behavior that doesn't work in situations.	b. Begins to choose or modify behavior in response to physical and social cues of situations; when one behavior isn't working, may stop and try something else.	c. Chooses and modifies behavior in response to the physical and social cues of a situation; tries to choose the behaviors that will get what he or she wants; can change behaviors if they are not working.
ER3	a. Does not understand the impact of own behavior on others.	b. Begins to understand the impact of own behavior on others; shows interest and awareness of the emotional behaviors of friends and others.	c. Understands the impact of own behavior on others; anticipates how friends or others will react.
ER4	a. Uses props to play roles; becomes the occupant of the role (is superman when wearing a cape or mommy when holding a baby). Prefers familiar roles.	b. Uses props to adopt roles; abandons roles when the props are removed; changes between familiar and favorite roles in dramatic play.	c. Can play roles with or without props. Transitions between roles frequently and easily, for example, can be the mommy, then the daddy, then the monster during same play period.

INNOVATIONS IN CHILD DEVELOPMENT

The Development of Positive Self-concept

During toddlerhood, an increasing awareness of "self" leads children to view their actions, interactions, and their behavior as observers. This ability to "watch" one's own interaction and evaluate one's own "performance" is a crucial social skill that is uniquely human. It means that children can learn to anticipate the social responses and interactions of others before they occur, and choose or modify their responses to match the situation. They get ideas about how to match responses from their interactions and experiences with parents and extended family, the community, school, and peers.

This process is neither simple nor objective. Children's views of self are influenced by how they think others view them. If adults, the community, the school, and other children view them as competent, capable, and confident and are clear in communicating this view, then children are likely to view themselves as competent, capable, and confident. If adults, the community, the school, and other children view them as incompetent, incapable, or lacking in confidence, then children may view themselves similarly. So, how we see (and therefore, interact and communicate with) children directly influences their self-concepts.

The creation of self-concept begins at birth and continues to be influenced throughout life. It is an emerging process to which children contribute actively, influencing their own development. The self-concept is constantly shaped and reshaped as we interact with the important people in our lives and experience the interactive environment (Curry & Johnson, 1990).

Many theorists have contributed to our understanding of emerging self-concepts. Erickson (1963) called this period of development autonomy vs. shame and doubt. The struggles for independence were viewed as creating a feeling of autonomy ("I can do it") or a feeling of shame and doubt ("Can I do it?" "Should I do it?"). This vivid word description of the developmental challenge helps teachers see the importance of this stage. The outcome obviously contributes to how development proceeds.

Greenspan and Greenspan (1989) noted the emergence of an organized sense of self during this period. This organization leads toddlers to create and use emotional ideas, both with others and in their play (see page 456 for more on Greenspan and Greenspan's ideas). As toddlers become more aware of themselves, they organize their own emotions and coordinate their behavior with the emotions.

Curry and Johnson (1990) present self-concept as the way individuals value themselves and others. Rejecting the view that self-concept is fixed or unresponsive to change, these authors conclude that acceptance, power and control, moral virtue, and competence are the lifelong issues that impact emerging self-esteem. Each of these important issues requires consideration by teachers. Wardle (1995) expands on the issues that influence self-concept, describing themes that are present throughout life. Each theme is summarized in the following chart.

General Themes that Impact Self-Esteem or Self-Concept

Love and Acceptance	Feeling unique, special; feeling cared for and loved; feeling like a worthwhile individual.
Power and Control	Feeling in control of one's destiny; having control over some parts of one's experience.
Moral Value	A sense of belonging; feeling fairly treated; feeling like a worthy person.
Competence	Feeling like it is worth trying; feeling capable of accomplishing tasks and skills.

Notice the emphasis on "feeling." This emphasis is important because the way we "feel" about things is often different from the way things look or the way we respond. Creating feelings of acceptance, control, value, and competence is related to but different from planning activities that encourage acceptance, control, and so on. One is external to the child (plans, activities, questions, props); the other is internal (how I evaluate and feel about those activities, plans, questions, props as I experience them). It is this internal arena that is so important to the child's emerging sense of self.

Why Is Exploring Roles such an Important Task?

What, then, does exploring roles have to do with emerging self-concept? As children play, they take on different roles they see being used in the broader social setting. Toddlers observe roles such as mommy, daddy, friend, teacher, firefighter, police officer, sister, brother, puppy, fast runner, tricycle peddler, independent eater, leader, follower, helper, and many others. Then, through play, toddlers get images of themselves as they attempt to play roles such as these. Toddlers evaluate these play experiences and use their evaluations to alter their views of themselves. If toddlers positively respond to their role-playing experiences and evaluate themselves as successful in figuring out what to do and how to do it, the likely result is an enhancement of self-concept.

But children don't just have positive play experiences, particularly during the toddler years. They often have disagreements over whether others can play, what they can play with, and the possible roles they can play. It turns out that how children handle negative experiences is just as important as how they handle positive ones, and also influences self-concept. If they are able to find another way to play (such as being the puppy), joining in the play as an onlooker, finding another place to play mommy, calling to the teacher to help figure out how to play, and so on, the experience can still be self-concept enhancing. They will evaluate themselves as successful in finding a way to play. If, on the other hand, the child feels rejected and evaluates that rejection as a valid part of her view of herself, the experience can influence her self-concept negatively.

Teachers have such an important role to play in supporting children's views of themselves and the evaluation of those views. First, they are responsible for setting up the environment to facilitate taking on interesting and varied roles successfully (see the Dramatic Possibilities sections of the Possibilities Plans for lots of good ideas). Second, teachers are responsible for creating interactive relationships with children that give them many messages about love, acceptance, control, value, and competence—the themes that influence self-concept throughout life. Third, teachers have to be observant enough to help children with limited views of self or negative evaluations of self. And, lastly, teachers have to make sure that their interactions support children who are bumping up against their own or others' negative views of self.

Throughout the Innovations Series are repeated references to the importance of the interactive environment—the way adults and children interact with each other and the messages those interactions give children. It is during the toddler years that teachers begin to see the results of creating this warm, interactive environment and relationships as children approach exploring roles with confidence, competence, and capability.

INNOVATIONS IN INTERACTIVE EXPERIENCES

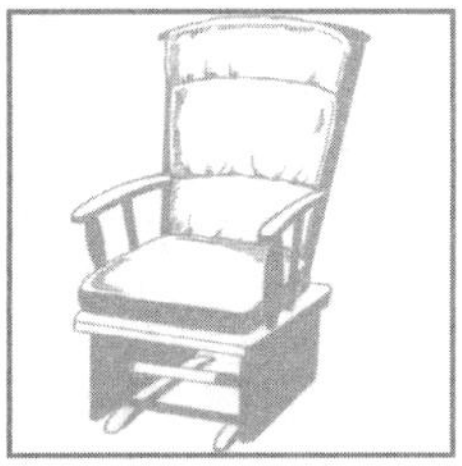

When it comes to self-concept development, children's experiences and their evaluation of themselves as participants are crucial. Teachers are always influencing a child's self-concept, sometimes positively and sometimes negatively. Children are always influencing their own self-concepts, sometimes positively and sometimes negatively. Either can become springboards for skill development. Positive experiences can lead to a feeling of competence and confidence. Negative experiences can lead to an integration of new ideas about how to succeed and motivation to do it differently next time. Or, negative experiences can stifle and damage the emerging view of self.

When teachers plan interactive experiences such as the ones that follow, children's self-concepts will have opportunities to flourish.

- ☐ Support children's feelings of belonging. Make it clear that all children belong in your classroom.
- ☐ Provide understandable and consistent limits.
- ☐ Use encouragement (instead of praise) to describe completed tasks and recognize effort.
- ☐ Validate children's uniqueness, focusing on your positive feelings about their unique qualities.
- ☐ Give children opportunities to have your undivided, personal attention regularly.
- ☐ Provide lots of opportunity for choice.
- ☐ Provide opportunities for exploration, investigation, and development of new alternatives.
- ☐ Let children know that you believe they can succeed.
- ☐ Encourage children to make and keep their own rules.
- ☐ Make sure interactions are characterized by mutual respect.
- ☐ Help children handle failure by being close and recognizing effort.
- ☐ Help children persist.
- ☐ Help children cooperate and work together to accomplish things.
- ☐ Be an ally to help identify potential solutions to solving problems.
- ☐ Accept children's solutions to their own problems.
- ☐ Prevent frustration that comes from unrealistic expectations.

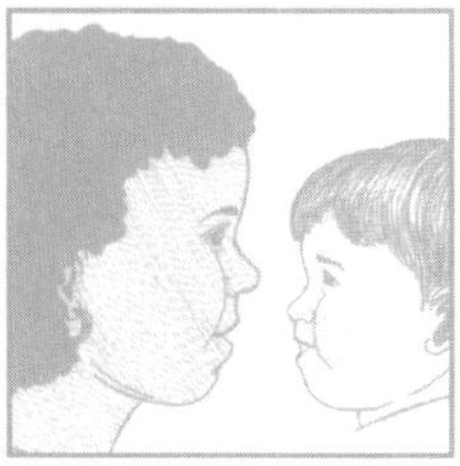

INNOVATIONS IN TEACHING

Teachers influence self-concept in many ways. It starts by creating a physical environment that leads children to experience and explore a wide variety of roles. The whole world of roles is open to toddlers. They are interested in what people do and how they do it. Toddler curiosity leads them to consider and play out many possibilities or options.

Creating Opportunities to Explore Roles

Dramatic play is the area that is most conducive to supporting the exploration of roles. For toddlers, dramatic play usually starts close to home with the roles children see their significant others filling. The roles of mommy, daddy, baby, sister, or brother are endlessly popular as toddlers explore the things these significant people do. Toddlers often move on to the roles that interest them in the wider world, frequently based on their experiences. Going grocery shopping, to the shoe store, to the doctor or hospital, and to Mommy or Daddy's work setting provide children with rich opportunities to explore roles. These interests are often followed by emerging preferences for types of materials, types of play, or types of roles. Truck driver, hairstylist, construction worker, farmer, police officer, and dance teacher all become interesting as children are exposed or introduced to these people in the course of experience.

Creating and using prop boxes gives teachers the play props children need and the ability to change the Dramatic Possibilities and create a wide variety of roles for children to explore. Every Possibilities Plan has prop box suggestions that give teachers ideas about where to start. Use these as springboards to identify additional roles that interest the children in your classroom.

Creating Interactive Relationships to Enhance Exploring Roles

Relationships form the core of curriculum in the toddler years. Teachers enhance children's self-concept by maintaining close connections to toddlers as they begin to evaluate themselves and their actions.

Teachers may want to look at their Possibilities Plans for chances to provide children with messages about love, acceptance, control, value, and competence—the themes that influence self-concept throughout life. Exposing and validating these messages is an important teaching skill. For example, when one toddler asks another if she wants to play, a sensitive teacher might point out the acceptance that the invitation to play held. "She wants you to play with her" is an example of teacher talk that labels and validates the child's acceptance.

Central to this connection is an understanding of children's uniqueness and individuality. *It is not the aim of the toddler teacher to treat every child the same.* Rather, the teacher bases interactions and teaching on her or his understanding of each child's developmental age and stage as well as on the child's uniqueness. Some children need the teacher very close to try new roles while others can pick up a prop and explore a role without much more than a smile from the teacher. Figuring out these differences is part of the observation/assessment job of the teacher. Then the teacher can modify her or his teaching to support the children who need it and smile at the ones who don't!

Observing to Support Exploring Roles

Observation emerges once again as a crucial teaching skill. In this case, teachers are observing to see when they might need to help children with self-evaluations that are challenging the child's view of self. When a child has a limited view of the roles she can play, or negatively evaluates a role-playing experience, observant teachers step in. Their goal is to help the child understand what is happening and learn from the experience.

For example, entering a playgroup is often difficult for toddlers. Some toddlers stand back and watch until others notice them and invite them in. Other toddlers jump in the middle and try to take over. One toddler might find a similar toy and begin to play beside the other players. Another toddler might begin to cry and wail that "they won't let me play." Each of these responses offers teachers an opportunity to help children learn.

The observant teacher might help the watchers to use words to ask if they can play and support them if the answer is no. The teacher might help the "jumpers" see how others feel about their intrusion into their play and explore other ways to join in. She or he might help the parallel player offer the additional toy to the players as a way to join in. The teacher might stay close to the crying child to help her see that crying isn't working but words might be worth a try. All of these examples show how dynamic the role of the teacher is in supporting children's exploration of roles and emerging self-concepts. Again, the component of teacher observation is crucial.

Facilitating Positive Self-Concept

Teachers have to make sure that their interactions support children who are bumping up against their own or others' negative views of self. Because toddlers are still learning to modify their behavior to fit the situation and to understand the impact of their behavior on the feelings of others, they need help when things don't work out. When you don't get to play, when you're not first, when someone else chooses the tricycle you wanted to ride—each of these examples creates opportunities for teachers to help children learn new social skills. In the process of social problem solving, teachers help toddlers convert an experience that could be evaluated as negative into one that recognizes a new skill is being tried out or learned. (To learn more about social problem solving, turn to page 133).

Family-centered Practices

An important part of one's self-concept comes from being a part of a family group within a culture. Cultures have different characteristics, and families within cultures vary as well. Race, ethnicity, religion, gender, primary language, family size, family composition, and cultural values are all components of culture. How the school environment responds to children's cultural differences impacts self-concept.

Teachers have a marvelous opportunity to make sure that their classrooms are culturally inclusive. They can do this by creating family-centered practices that acknowledge, respect, and support all families (McBride, 1999). These practices have particular characteristics that are under the direct control of the teacher. They begin by keeping the focus on the family rather than diverting the focus to the school. When families are validated as the primary educators of their children, teachers build bridges that will enable families to accomplish this goal.

Then, teachers develop partnerships with families to enhance school experiences and validate home experiences. Helping families stay connected to schools requires that teachers both include them in making decisions about their child's early education and respect their ideas about how to do so. Partnerships require reciprocal communication—true two-way communication aimed at acknowledging family strengths. Having a partnership also requires teachers to make sure families can be a part of the classroom by creating many ways for parents and other family members to participate and be involved.

Toddlers watch interactions. They are constantly using what they see in the interactive environment. When toddlers see teachers, parents, and other family members in partnership together, their unique cultural characteristics are validated and supported, enhancing self-concept in the process. Use the suggestions in Parent Partnerships to welcome family participation in school in many different ways. The outcome is good for children, families, and schools.

Guidance and Discipline

Enhancing Self Esteem through Encouragement

Cautions about the rampant use of praise, stickers, and other examples of external motivation are included throughout the early childhood literature, particularly the literature about self-concept development. External motivation prevents children from placing their own evaluations on their experiences. This, in turn, can interfere with the emerging sense of self. For example, toddlers often make a few marks on paper and then request another. When teachers praise children's work ("Good job!") and then ask the child to make more marks to prevent paper waste, children can be confused. If the marks were good, why are more needed? Maybe they weren't so good after all.

Some early childhood educators propose that teachers reconsider their use of praise to foster self-concept and to motivate children. Instead, they suggest that teachers use encouragement (Hitz & Driscoll, 1988). Encouragement acknowledges the effort or attributes of the work without evaluation or judgment. Encouragement has the advantage of being sincere and authentic, putting teachers in the role of honestly responding to children's experiences and efforts. These guidelines support the use of encouragement instead of praise.

- Be specific. "Your painting has lots of blue in it."
- "The paint covers all of the paper."
- "Your construction is built with lots of blocks."
- "You rode the tricycle all over the playground."
- "You chose the blue baby buggy." Encourage individually and privately. "You were able to find all the different pieces to the puzzle, Caitlin."
- "All of the star builders are in your construction!" Focus on effort, improvement, and progress rather than products or outcomes.

- "You made it all the way to the gate on the push trike."
- "You finished gluing two feathers."
- "You built with all of the Duplo blocks." Be sincere and authentic. "You worked hard on that."
- "You kept working until you finished everything." Help children see their successes. "Your tower is eight blocks tall."
- "Your baby doll is covered with a blanket and ready for bed."
- "You pulled your pants up all by yourself." Help children appreciate their own achievements. "Both feet left the ground when you hopped!"
- "You helped clean up the snack table." Avoid comparisons and competition. "You are ready to go outside."
- "You finished cleaning up."

Teacher Competencies to Support Toddlers Exploring Roles

Sometimes	Usually	Always	
☐	☐	☐	Shows support for parents as primary educators by developing partnership of respect, information exchange, and collaboration.
☐	☐	☐	Finds many different ways for family members to be involved in the school experience of the child.
☐	☐	☐	Recognizes, accepts, and celebrates cultural differences.
☐	☐	☐	Recognizes and acknowledges the unique contributions that parents make to their child's developmental progress.
☐	☐	☐	***Does not treat every child the same***—bases interactions and teaching on understanding of each child's developmental age and stage as well as on the child's uniqueness.
☐	☐	☐	Supports children's feelings of belonging—all children belong in the classroom.
☐	☐	☐	Uses encouragement (instead of praise) to describe completed tasks.
☐	☐	☐	Validates children's uniqueness, focusing on positive feelings about their unique qualities.
☐	☐	☐	Provides opportunities for exploration, investigation, and development of new alternatives.
☐	☐	☐	Assures that interactions in the classroom are characterized by mutual respect.
☐	☐	☐	Helps children handle failure by being close and recognizing effort.
☐	☐	☐	Is an ally to help identify potential solutions to solving problems.

Resources for Teachers

Curry, N.E. & C.N. Johnson. (1990). ***Beyond self-esteem: Developing a genuine sense of human value***. Washington, DC: National Association for the Education of Young Children (NAEYC).

Erickson, E.H. (1964). ***Childhood and society.*** New York: Norton.

Greenspan, S. & N.T. Greenspan. (1989). ***The essential partnership.*** New York: Penguin.

Hitz, R. & A. Driscoll. (1988). Praise or encouragement?: New insights and implications for early childhood teachers. ***Young Children,*** 43(5), 6-13.

Katz, L. & P. McClellan. (1997). ***Fostering social competence: The teacher's role.*** Washington, DC: National Association for the Education of Young Children (NAEYC).

National Association for the Education of Young Children. (1996). Responding to linguistic and cultural diversity—Recommendations for effective early childhood education. ***Young Children***, 51(2), 4-12.

Neugebauer, B. (1992). ***Alike and different: Exploring our humanity with children.*** Washington, DC: National Association for the Education of Young Children (NAEYC).

Wardle, F. (1995). How young children build images of themselves. ***Child Care Information Exchange***, 104, 44-47.

INNOVATIONS IN PARENT PARTNERSHIPS

School- or Teacher-initiated Possibilities

Toy Swap

Plan a toy swap for parents and children. Announce the swap day and invite all parents to participate. Check toys to be certain they are clean, safe, and appropriate for toddlers. Provide a choke tester for parents to test toys as they bring them into the classroom. If parents react favorably, plan additional toy swaps every three months or so. Another strategy for a toy swap is to place a box on a high shelf in the classroom and label it "toy swap." Suggest that parents check the box. If anything interests them, they can swap it with a toy from home. This becomes an ongoing activity, instead of a special event. As an extension to the toy swap activity, ask that parents provide discarded or duplicate toys they have at home for the classroom.

Anecdotal Note Calendar

Parents love to hear news about what their child experiences and accomplishes. For this activity, use calendars with plenty of space for writing. A separate calendar is needed for each child. Calendars may be bought or created with computer programs. You may even wish to draw your own and make copies. The anecdotal comments on the calendar will make a wonderful gift for parents. Some teachers like to give the special calendars to families when it is time for birthdays or when children move away. Decorate calendars using photographs you have taken of children involved in activities in the classroom and outdoors.

Video Diary of the Day

Ask parents to provide videotapes so you can create a video diary showing the events in each child's day. Tape activities, nap time, meals, and outdoor play. If the video camera you use does not have a date stamp, be certain to have the date included as part of the recording. Parents may be especially interested in shots that include them during arrival and departure time.

Parent Participation Activities

Muffins for Mom

Invite mothers to a "Muffins for Mom" informal breakfast. Make preparation easy and expect breakfast to be brief. Express your appreciation for what each mom does to support her child's learning throughout the year. A thank-you note to moms is always appreciated!

Doughnuts for Dad

Invite fathers to a "Doughnuts for Dad" informal breakfast. Make preparations easy and expect breakfast to be brief. Express your appreciation for what each dad does to support their child's learning throughout the year. A thank-you note to dads is always appreciated!

Note: With Muffins for Mom and Doughnuts for Dad, be sensitive to family configurations of the children in your class. An uncle or grandparent who is parenting the child or a same-sex parent all need to be included.

Parent Postcards

Share Parent Postcards with parents as they indicate an interest, at appropriate times during the enrollment cycle, or as developmental issues arise. (See page 548 in the Appendix for a sample dissemination schedule.) Copy Postcards. Cut if necessary. Address to parent(s) and place on Communication Sheet or hand out personally.

TO

How Parents Support Exploring Roles

A child's positive view of self emerges as a result of interactions with other children and adults. When a child has a limited view of the roles he or she can play or negatively evaluates a role-playing experience, observant parents can step in. Their goal is to help the child understand what is happening and learn from the experience.

For example, entering a play group (at home, at a family gathering, in the park, at school) is often difficult for toddlers. Some toddlers stand back and watch until others notice them and invite them in. Others jump in the middle and try to take over. Another might find a similar toy and begin to play beside the other players. Another might begin to cry and wail, "They won't let me play." Each of these responses offers parents an opportunity to help their toddler learn.

Parents might help the watcher to use words to ask if he or she can play. Of course, the parent also needs to be there to support the toddler if the answer is no. Parents might help the "jumper" see how others feel about intrusion into their play, as well as explore other ways to join in. Parents might help the parallel player offer the additional toy to the players as a way to join in. Parents might stay close to the crying child to help him or her see that crying isn't working but words might be worth a try. All of these examples show how dynamic the role of the parent can be in supporting children's exploration of roles and emerging self-concepts.

Facilitating Positive Self-concept for Your Child

Because your toddler is still learning to modify his or her behavior to fit the situation and to understand the impact of that behavior on the feelings of others, your toddler will need help when things don't work out. When you don't get to play, when you're not first, when someone else chooses the tricycle you wanted to ride—each of these examples creates opportunities for parents to help children learn new social skills. In the process of social problem solving, toddlers can learn to convert an experience that could be evaluated as negative into one that recognizes a new skill is being tried out or learned.

As your child learns to interact in new ways, you are the support. A look, a pat, a word of encouragement—all let your toddler know that you are there and that you know he or she can be successful. Validation by you is the most powerful positive message your child can receive from you. Your acceptance and love contribute to your child's emerging sense of self and clearly communicate that your child's place close to you is secure.

TO

Resources for Parents

Add these helpful books to your parent library or post this list on your parent bulletin boards.

Adams, C. & E. Fruge. (1996). ***Why children misbehave: And what to do about it***. Oakland, CA: New Harbinger.

Brazelton, T.B. (1992). ***Touchpoints: The essential reference.*** Reading, MA: Addison Wesley.

Glenn, H. & J. Nelsen, (1998). ***Raising self-reliant children in a self-indulgent world***. Rocklin, CA: Prima Publishing.

Miller, K. (2000). ***Ages and stages.*** West Palm Beach, FL: TelShare.

INNOVATIONS IN ENVIRONMENTS

Opportunities for Side-by-side Play

During the majority of the time period called toddlerhood (18-36 months), young children rarely play together. Instead they observe and copy each other. They play alongside each other in what is called parallel play, often imitating adult behaviors. Although there is little interaction, parallel play is important in providing the basis for cooperative play.

Adults are often in a hurry to get young children to share, even though they are not ready developmentally to do so. Parallel play works well for toddlers because they do not have to be involved with the same materials. Each toddler has her own toy or play prop.

When the toddler wants someone else's toy, provide a similar or duplicate item. If this is not possible or acceptable, give the toddler the words to ask for the toy after the other toddler is finished with it. "Shania, ask Timothy to give you the truck after he is finished. I will help him remember." The ability to negotiate, to wait, and to take turns are all important steps on the road to children later being able to share.

Role of Play Cues and Play Props

The play cues and props that are part of the environment invite children to play. When classrooms are full of play cues and props that lead to appropriate, exploratory play, children are able to look at an activity, area, or planned experience and figure out what to do and where to get started.

Carefully plan the classroom to take maximum advantage of toddlers' natural desire to explore and learn. Choose simple, safe toys and ordinary objects for them to explore and manipulate. Provide uninterrupted time, so toddlers can begin, explore, and elaborate without being distracted by the teacher.

Creating an environment that stimulates play is one of the teacher's most important roles. She or he is the stage manager, costume designer, orchestra conductor, and set designer. When all of these elements of the environment are planned, children can find many varied and interesting places to play, both alone and with their friends.

Both over-stimulation and under-stimulation are issues in the school setting. Over-stimulation can occur from too much noise, light, color, and activity.

Under-stimulation can occur from too little interactive experiences, physical isolation of toddlers, or too few toys and materials in the environment.

Play cues or invitations can come from many sources. The first and best source of play cues is you. When the teacher picks up a toy and plays with it, the toy becomes very interesting to toddlers. Called triangulation, this strategy for inviting play and interactions is an excellent way to initiate interactions with toddlers and to interest toddlers in new materials or props.

The second source of play cues or stimulation is color. Graphics, photographs, and pictures from the Picture File/Vocabulary lists (included for each Possibilities Plan), and colorful toys all interest toddlers. But, color also can be overwhelming. Children benefit from color in the toys they play with and colors worn by the children and adults in the environment. They need soothing, neutral colors to serve as the backdrop. Avoid adding color in bold swatches to the walls and floors of the toddler classroom. This will help insure that the stimulation comes from child-directed and -initiated activity and not from the background (Cherry, 1976).

The third source of play cues is the way toys are displayed. Make toys available where children are in the classroom, on low shelves, in clear plastic containers, in baskets, and in tubs. Provide duplicate and similar toys, so toddlers are not forced to share popular items and so toys can be removed for disinfecting after they are used. Separate toys on shelves, so children can consider each specific toy. How toys are displayed can invite children to move around the room and choose interesting things for play.

Toddlers are developing their ability to explore roles as they play. They actually become the mommy or daddy or the bear as they make use of appropriate play props provided in the Dramatic Possibilities area. Toys that are real items from the child's world (purses, wallets, pots, pans, clothes, shoes, hats) are interesting and important support for beginning role-play efforts. Continue to provide duplicate items, so children can play side by side without taking the toys away from each other.

The teacher's role is to support role-playing efforts, first by providing an appropriate environment. Observe toddlers as they begin playing roles. Limit interruptions as children explore their ideas. After the play is established, extend the experience through verbal exchanges or through adding additional items to the area. Open-ended questions such as, "Where are you taking the baby for a walk?" and "How will you build the house?" Give toddlers opportunities to add to and elaborate on the experiences they are having.

When children lose interest in the props and play cues in an area, they will let you know. They won't go there to play. This indicates that it is time to change materials, change the roles that are being explored, or supplement the area with additional props and play cues.

Toy and Material Safety

Props and play materials, both teacher-made and purchased, should be checked regularly. Check to see that the toys and materials are in good condition and that all of the parts are still sturdy, safe, and inviting. Toys that are shabby or beginning to show wear should be repaired or removed from the environment. Teacher-made toys often have a short shelf life, particularly in a busy toddler room. Don't hesitate to throw out teacher-made toys and construct new ones. These new ones will be enticing and interesting to children because they will be familiar with the toy but engaged with its newness.

Don't rely on yourself to check toy and material safety. Enlist the help of parents, who may look at the environment with a "new eye," other teachers, who may walk into or through your classroom occasionally, or even the custodian who will often be the one picking up small pieces from the floor during regular cleaning. Each will help you keep children safe from disintegrating or damaged toys and materials.

Mirrors

In the toddler environment, unbreakable mirrors are a source of interest and interaction. More than any other image, young children are drawn to the images of their own faces (Edwards, Gandini & Foreman, 1998; Shore, 1997). For toddlers, the perfect interactive experience involves discovering and exploring one's own face and the faces of others in the mirror.

Mirrors attract children's attention and allow them visually to orient themselves to others within the classroom. With large mirrors, toddlers can keep their visual connection with teachers and other children even if they are out of physical reach of them.

Place small unbreakable mirrors in boxes and containers. Imagine the delight when a toddler looks in a box and sees her own face. Small mirrors with adhesive on the backs can be placed throughout the room, so toddlers can discover and explore their own image again and again. Mirrors underneath tables, on low shelves, on the walls at various heights, on doors and windowsills, and even hidden behind curtains attached to walls will provide stimulating discoveries.

Place larger mirrors over the diaper-changing table, on walls where toddlers can see themselves eating, and in other areas of the room where children can see their entire images. If possible, cover one entire wall with a mirrored surface. This will brighten the classroom, as well as help toddlers keep an eye on their teacher.

Activities and Experiences vs. Centers

Most early childhood educators think of interest or learning centers as an essential part of any classroom setting. Yet, environments for toddlers are different because toddlers are "groupie" in nature and tend to go where the action is. For this reason, teachers must bring activities and experiences to children and assist children in going to where the activities are. A wide range of activities and experiences must be available to toddlers. In each of the following Possibilities Plans, *Space* and *Sky*, activities and experiences are presented in the following areas:

- Dramatic Possibilities
- Sensory/Art Possibilities
- Curiosity Possibilities
- Construction Possibilities
- Literacy Possibilities
- Music Possibilities
- Movement Possibilities
- Outdoor Possibilities
- Project Possibilities
- Parent Participation Possibilities

Space

WEB

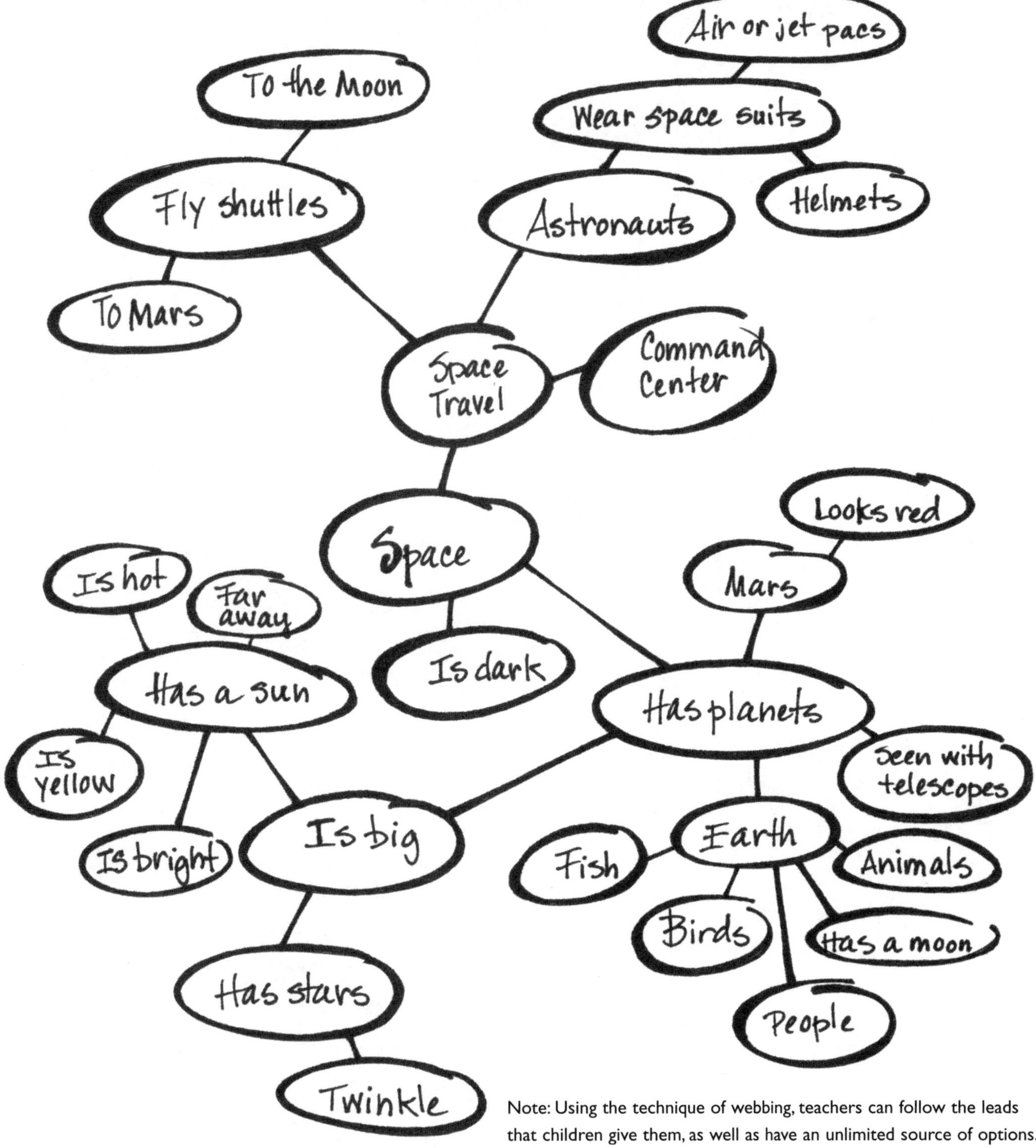

Note: Using the technique of webbing, teachers can follow the leads that children give them, as well as have an unlimited source of options. Always use the webs provided as a jumping-off point. The possibilities are endless!

PLANNING PAGES

Plan Possibilities

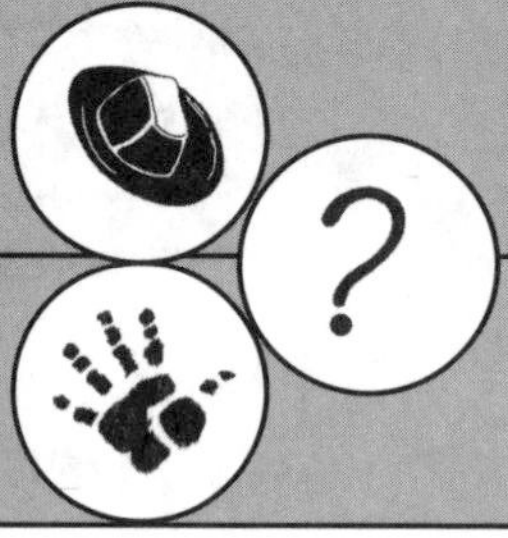

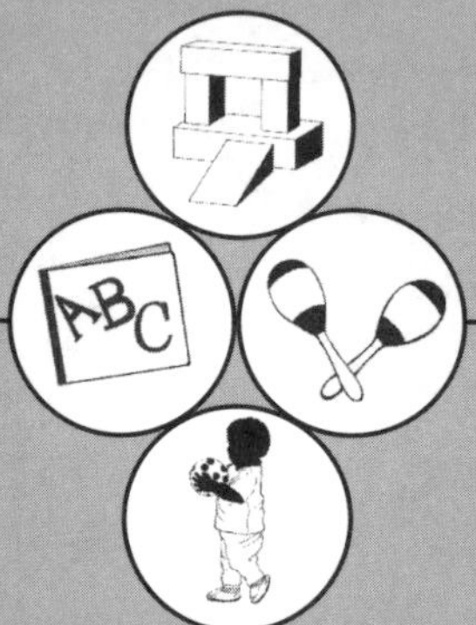

Space

Note: This Possibilities Plan was greatly enriched by shared experiences from real toddler teachers. In particular, Masami Mitzukami helped create, develop, and try out many of the ideas, activities, and experiences included here, and then shared them with us. We recognize his contribution and credit him with this Plan.

DRAMATIC POSSIBILITIES

Space Shuttle Command Center

All ages

Materials

Cardboard boxes
Paint
Paintbrushes
Toy typewriters or old keyboards with no wires
Tape recorder
Countdown tape

Teacher Talk

"Courtney is playing in the space center. Timothy looks like he wants to play with you, too."

Paint boxes to look like computers. Add a toy typewriter or an old keyboard without wires. Record yourself slowly counting backward from ten and saying, "Blast Off!" Play the tape as children play with the box computers.

Space Helmets

All ages

Materials

Fast food cardboard buckets or ice cream cartons (from ice cream parlors)
Craft knife or scissors (teacher only)
Silver duct tape
Plastic cups
Aluminum foil
One-gallon plastic milk jug, optional

Cut a rectangular hole about three inches from the bottom rim. Use duct tape to attach plastic cups around the sides and top of the bucket. Cover the helmet with aluminum foil.

Teacher Talk

Talk about the shapes and color of the helmets with children as they play. "Who is that in the space helmet?" "I hear the space ship sounds, Adam!" "You're an astronaut."

Turn the bucket upside down and cut a rectangular hole about 3" from the bottom rim. Use duct tape to attach plastic cups around the sides and on top of the bucket. Cover the helmet with aluminum foil. Tape any loose edges with silver duct tape. Children wear the helmets as they become astronauts. Or, cut the top fourth and one panel out of a one-gallon plastic milk jug. Cover the sharp edges with duct tape. Use the jug as an easy space helmet.

Space Boots

All ages

Materials

Large rubber boots
Silver nontoxic spray paint (teacher only)

Teacher Talk

Talk with children about how the space boots feel. "Trey has on space boots! They make his feet feel strange."

Spray paint rubber boots with silver nontoxic paint. Provide several pairs for children to wear in the shuttle command center.

Spaceship

All ages

Materials

Large cardboard box
Craft knife (teacher only)
Packing tape
Nontoxic silver paint
Paintbrushes
Black permanent markers (teacher only)

Create a spaceship from a very large cardboard box. Remove staples and cover any rough edges with packing tape. Children will enjoy painting the spaceship. Use black permanent markers to write "NASA" and "USA" on the completed spaceship. Cut circular windows in the sides.

Spacesuits

All ages

Materials

Large child-size coveralls
Shiny tape
Fabric paint pens

Teacher Talk

"The spacesuit has shiny tape on it."

Place strips of reflective and/or shiny tape all over the coveralls. Use fabric paint pens to write "USA Space Program" on the coveralls. Make the spacesuit with the helmet and boots available for children as they play.

Jet Packs

30-36 months

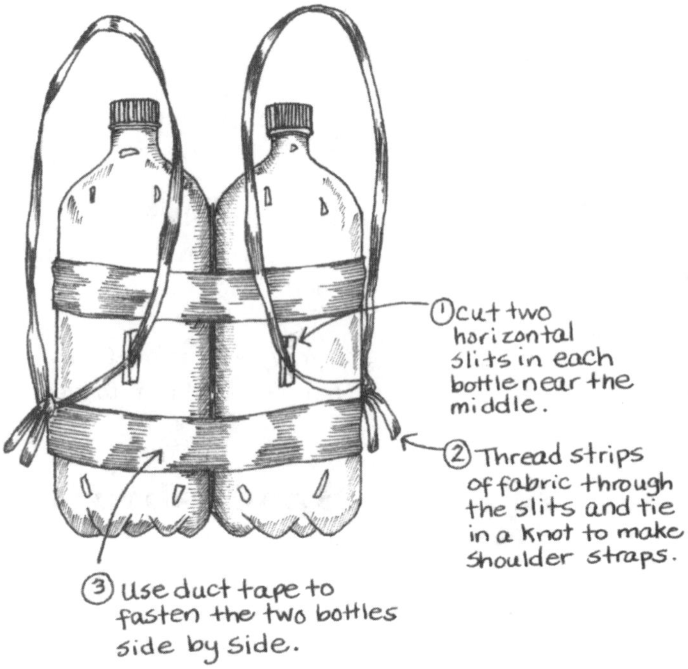

① Cut two horizontal slits in each bottle near the middle.
② Thread strips of fabric through the slits and tie in a knot to make shoulder straps.
③ Use duct tape to fasten the two bottles side by side.

Materials

Two 2-liter clear plastic bottles
Craft knife (teacher only)
Strips of fabric
Duct tape

Teacher Talk

"Scott is flying with the jet pack on his back."

Cut two horizontal slits in each bottle near the middle of the bottle. Thread strips of fabric though the slits and tie in a knot to make two loops for shoulder straps. Use duct tape to fasten the two bottles together side by side. Help children slip their arms through the fabric loops to place the jet packs onto their backs. Children wear the jet packs as they fly through space.

SENSORY/ART POSSIBILITIES

Stars

All ages

Materials

Variety of sizes of cardboard star shapes
Yellow paint
Paintbrushes

Teacher Talk

Talk about the sizes of the shapes. "That is a little star. You chose a big star and a little star."

Provide a variety of sizes of cardboard star shapes. Children choose star shapes and use yellow paint to make bright yellow stars. Observe children as they paint the stars.

Red Mars Sand

All ages

Materials
Sand and water table
Sand
Red dirt or powdered red tempera paint

Teacher Talk
Talk with children about the red planet, Mars. "This is the color of the red planet, Mars."

Mix powdered red tempera paint with fine sand to make red sand, so children can play in Mars sand.

Shiny Moons

All ages

Materials
Cardboard circles
Masking tape
Aluminum foil
Yellow finger paint

Teacher Talk
Talk about the texture of the paint and the shape of the moon as children enjoy painting. "That is a shiny moon, Tessa. How does the paint feel on your hands?"

Cover cardboard circles with aluminum foil and tape securely in place. Provide yellow finger paint for children to paint on the foil-covered circles.

Rubber Mat Prints

All ages

Materials
Rubber bathtub mat
Scissors
Paint
Paper

Teacher Talk
Talk about the prints as children continue to cover the paper with

paint. "Look at the prints on the paper. You made four blue prints, Ali."

Cut a rubber bath mat in several small pieces. Show children how to dip the piece of mat into paint and make prints on paper with the suction cup side of the piece. When the paint is dry, you may want to cut large moons or suns from the paper to decorate the room.

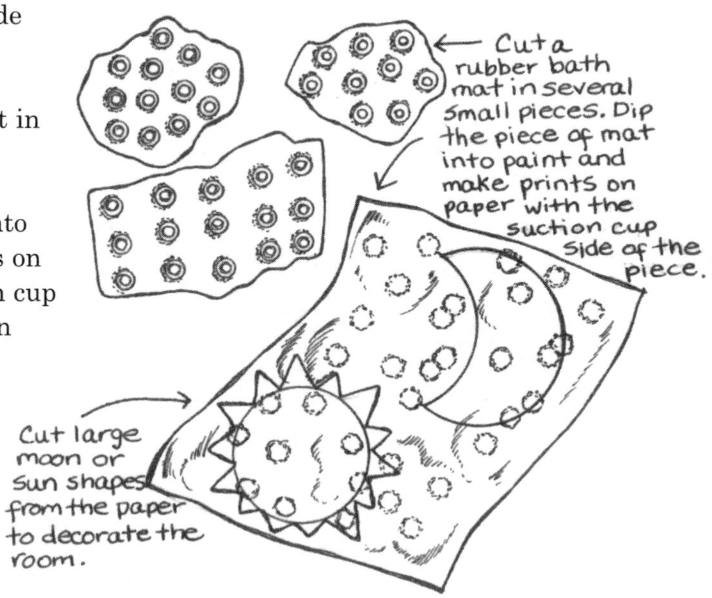

Star Dust Collage

30-36 months

Materials

Construction paper stars
Glue
Large paintbrush
Paper
Salt in a plastic shaker

Teacher Talk

Talk about colors and sizes of the stars as children work. "Claire, you have glued the star shapes on the paper. Now you are ready to make everything shiny."

Provide a variety of sizes of construction paper star shapes. Demonstrate gluing the stars onto paper. Show children how to paint glue to cover the stars. Help children shake the saltshaker over the glue. When the glue dries, the salt will glisten like stardust.

Moon Bottles

All ages

Materials

Aluminum foil
Clear plastic bottles
Water
Blue food coloring
Silver glitter
Glue
Tape

Teacher Talk

"I see the moons floating in the bottle."

Roll pieces of aluminum foil into small balls. Fill clear plastic bottles with water. Add a few drops of blue food coloring, silver glitter, and small aluminum foil balls. Secure the tops on the bottles with glue and tape. Children can shake the bottles to see the moons spin, float, and move in the bottles.

Floating Moon Rocks

All ages

Materials

Real baseball-size rocks
Silver and/or gold nontoxic spray paint (teacher only)
Aluminum foil
Water table

Teacher Talk

"Your moon rock is floating, Cherie. Which rocks will sink?"

Paint baseball-size smooth rocks with silver and/or gold spray paint. Make baseball-size aluminum foil balls. Place the balls and rocks in the water table. Watch as the children experiment and discover the difference between the two.

Cold, Cold Moon

All ages

Materials

Food coloring
Water

Plastic bowls
Freezer
Water table
Paper
Powdered tempera paint

Teacher Talk
Talk about the moon being cold and having very cold rocks. "The ice is cold. It's cold like the rocks on the moon."

Add food coloring to plastic bowls of water. Freeze the bowls of water and empty them into the water table. Children can explore the ice. When ice begins to melt, discard it before it becomes a choke hazard. Water frozen in bowls can also be used as an interesting art experience. Sprinkle large pieces of paper with powdered tempera paint and show children how to use the ice to paint with.

? Star Bottles

All ages

Materials
Clear plastic bottles
Colored hair-setting gel
Multicolored star-shaped confetti
Glitter
Glue
Tape

Teacher Talk
"There are stars in the blue bottle."
"Turn the bottle over, Quentin."

Fill clear, plastic bottles with colored hair-setting gel, leaving about 2" of air space. Pour a tablespoon of glitter into the bottle and shake the bottle to mix the glitter with the gel. Put a small package of confetti star shapes in the bottle and shake to combine with glitter and gel. Glue and tape the cap securely in place. Children move the bottle to see the stars move.

? Moon Puzzles

All ages

Materials

Large pizza boards
Yellow paint
Paintbrushes
Black permanent marker (teacher only)
Craft knife (teacher only)

Teacher Talk

"Which piece do you think goes here, Stephen? It's all done!"

Paint a large circular cardboard pizza board yellow. When the paint is dry, use a black permanent marker to draw a happy face on the moon. Use a craft knife to cut the puzzle into large pieces. Help children put the pieces together to make the happy moon puzzle.

? Moon Snacks

All ages

Materials

Raisins
Pretzels
Small marshmallows
Resealable plastic bags

Teacher Talk

"You mixed everything together to make your snack, Carlee. Squeeze the snack into your mouth, just like the astronauts do."

Children can place the items they choose in resealable plastic bags. Seal the bags. Show children how to shake the bags to mix the items to make snack. Cut off a corner of the snack bag (and discard safely). Show children how to eat the snack out of the bag like astronauts do by placing the corner of the bag to their lips. Monitor children's snacking to make sure that the resealable bags do not get into children's mouths. Discard used bags immediately after children finish eating their snacks.

CONSTRUCTION POSSIBILITIES

Space Building

All ages

Materials
Blocks
Heavy-duty foil
Tape
Paper and pen

Teacher Talk
"You are building with silver blocks, Timothy. Your building is three blocks tall."

Cover some of the blocks with foil to add interest to children's block play. Tape the foil securely to the block. Observe as they interact with each other. Record all the play partners and comments to include in children's records.

Moon or Star Building Shapes

All ages

Materials
Butcher paper
Scissors
Clear contact paper
Star builders

Teacher Talk
"The big star is yellow." "Which block do you want to use first?"

Cut very large shapes of stars or moons. Cover with clear contact paper and place on the floor in the construction area for children to build on. Also, add star builders (available from school supply stores or catalogs) to the area to add interest.

Astronaut Builders

All ages

Materials
Space boots (see page 239)
Space helmets (see page 338)

Provide space helmets and boots for children to wear as they build.

LITERACY POSSIBILITIE0S

Spaceship Book

All ages

Materials
Poster board
Pictures of things in space
Glue
Marker
Hole punch
Yarn

Teacher Talk
"The spaceship sees the moon on this page, Carmel."

Glue the pictures onto poster board pages. On the top of each page, write "Space ship, space ship, what do you see?" On the bottom of each page, write, "I see (name the picture) looking at me." Punch holes in each page and fasten them together with yarn. Read the book with children. Point to words and pictures as you read.

Hey, Diddle, Diddle

All ages

Materials
Flannel board characters
Flannel board

Teacher Talk
"Clint wants to hear the story about the cow jumping over the moon."

Use commercially made or teacher-made flannel board characters to act out the nursery rhyme. Children can name the characters and talk about what each character does in the rhyme.

Hey, Diddle, Diddle
Hey, diddle, diddle,
the cat and the fiddle
The cow jumped over the moon.
The little dog laughed to see such sport,
And the dish ran away with the spoon.

Flip Book

All ages

Materials

Space pictures
Paper plates
Glue sticks
Hole punch
Yarn or metal ring

Teacher Talk

Show the pictures to children and talk about what children see. "That's the moon."

Glue space pictures onto paper plates. Punch a hole in each plate and fasten the plates together with yarn or metal ring.

Goodnight Moon

All ages

Materials

Goodnight Moon by Margaret Wise Brown
An assortment of objects from the book, such as a toy telephone, picture of a red balloon, plastic cow, three small stuffed bears, two stuffed kittens, mittens, small dollhouse, toy mouse, comb, brush, picture of a bowl of cereal, stuffed rabbit, picture of moon and stars in a window, small clock, and socks

Teacher Talk

"Sydney, the kittens and mittens are soft. What other things are soft?"

Read the storybook aloud to children. Allow children to hold the objects. As you talk about the story, name the items children are holding. Later, place all the story props out in the Dramatic Possibilities area.

Dogs in Space

All ages

Materials

Dogs in Space by Nancy Coffelt

Read the book to children to help them get interested in the space activities.

Mister Moon

All ages

Materials
Paper plates
Markers

Teacher Talk
"Natalie is holding her paper moon."

Help children make moon puppets using paper plates and markers. Children can hold the puppets as you sing the song to the tune of "Where Is Thumbkin?".

Mister Moon
O Mister Moon, Moon,
Bright and shiny Moon,
Won't you please,
Won't you please,
Shine down on me?
Shine down on me?
Won't you please?

O Mister Moon, Moon
Bright and shiny Moon,
Won't you please,
Won't you please,
Set me fancy free?
Set me fancy free?
Won't you please?

Twinkle, Twinkle Little Star

All ages

Materials
Cardboard tubes
Craft knife (teacher only)
Star shapes
Glue

Teacher Talk
"You can sing 'Twinkle, Twinkle Little Star,' Cassie."

Cut a slit in one end of a paper towel tube with a craft knife. Slide a large star shape into the slit. Put a line of glue to hold the star in place. Children wave the star wand as they sing the song. Also, show children how to "twinkle" their fingers as you sing the song.

Twinkle, Twinkle Little Star
Twinkle, Twinkle Little Star,
How I wonder what you are.
Up above the world so high,
Like a diamond in the sky.
Twinkle, Twinkle Little Star,
How I wonder what you are.

Star Wars Space Odyssey

All ages

Materials
Tape or CD of *Star Wars* music
Tape or CD player
Scarves
Crepe paper streamers

Teacher Talk
"The scarf does look like wings, Mindy. How many ways can you move the scarf?"

Play the music from "Star Wars" and give children colorful scarves or crepe paper streamers to move to the music.

MOVEMENT POSSIBILITIES

Five Little Rockets

All ages

Materials
None

Teacher Talk
"Lonnie is holding up five fingers. Let's count to five!"

Show children how to hold up their fist with no fingers showing. Help them hold up a finger after each verse until all five fingers are showing.

Five Little Rockets
Five little rockets flying in the sky,
Come in for a landing from way up high.

The first little rocket
shining in the sun,
Is the first to land
on runway number 1.
The second little rocket
carrying its crew,
Lands very slowly on
runway number 2.

The third little rocket, such a
sight to see,
Lands quietly on runway
number 3.

The fourth little rocket can't wait
anymore.
And lands very quickly on runway
number 4.

The fifth little rocket is the last to arrive,
And finally lands on runway number 5.

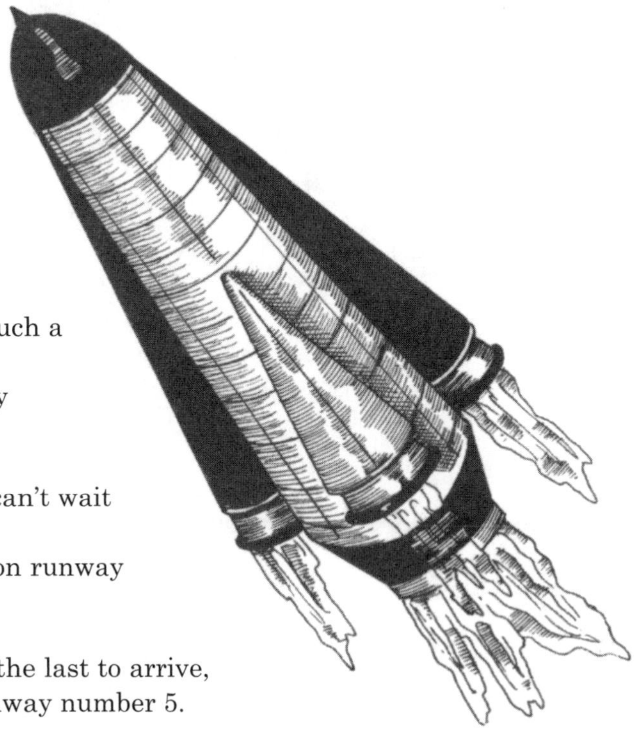

The Moon Is Out Tonight

All ages

Materials
None

Teacher Talk
"Yes, the moon is round, Alexander. You made a big round moon with your arms."

Recite the following rhyme with children. Show children how to act out the rhyme with you.

The Moon Is Out Tonight
The moon is out tonight. (Make a big circle with arms.)
The stars are shining bright. (Wiggle fingers overhead.)
My mom says it's time for bed, (Rest head on hands.)
And she's right. Goodnight!

Moon Walking

All ages

Materials
None

Show children how to walk very slowly. Use this activity to help children transition from one activity to another during the day.

OUTDOOR POSSIBILITIES

Moon Box and Moon Balls

All ages

Materials

Large cardboard box
Paint
Paintbrushes
Craft knife (teacher only)
Yarn or sock balls
Panty hose or beanbags and bucket

Teacher Talk

"Chang, your ball went inside the moon box. How many balls can you throw in the mouth, Chang?"

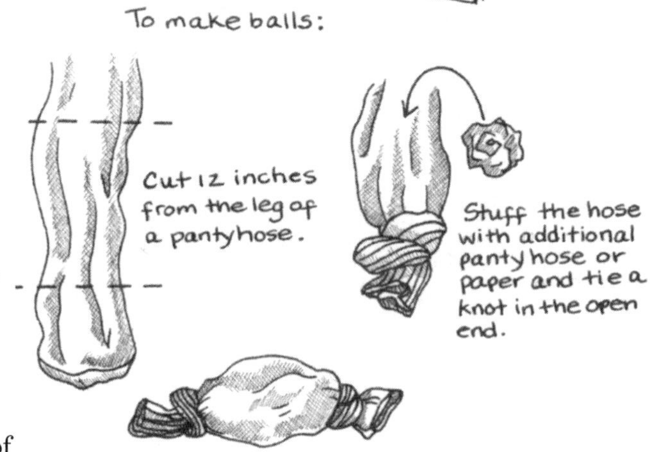

Paint a large moon face on a cardboard box. Cut out a very large mouth. Provide yarn or sock balls for children to throw into the moon's mouth. Talk about the moon and count the balls going inside the box. Cut 12" from the leg of a panty hose. Tie a knot in one end of the hose. Stuff the hose with additional panty pose or paper and tie a knot in the open end. Children can practice throwing with accuracy as they try to throw these balls into a bucket. As a variation of the activity, provide beanbags to toss.

Rocket Walk

All ages

Materials

Poster board
Markers
Scissors

Teacher Talk
"Look at Chad jump from one rocket to another one. One, two, three jumps."

Cut large rocket shapes from poster board. Use markers to add details to the shapes. Place the shapes on the ground in a path. Show children how to walk, jump, or run from one rocket shape to the next.

Moon Rocks

All ages

Materials
Very large rocks
Crayons

Provide very large rocks (too heavy for children to pick up) on the playground. Give children crayons to color the moon rocks.

Box Rocket

All ages

Materials
Copy paper boxes
Tape
Paint
Paintbrushes
Craft knife (teacher only)
Plastic lids
Spools
Poster board

Teacher Talk
"Tim is making the rocket fly. Where are you going today, Tim?"

Securely tape the boxes closed. Paint the boxes to look like rockets. Use a craft knife to cut circles from each long side of the boxes for handles. Add poster board nose cone, plastic lids for dials, and very large spools for control knobs. Observe children as they play.

Space Mural Collage

All ages

Materials

Butcher paper
Tape
Black paint
Paintbrushes
Sponges
Scissors
Low plastic trays
Construction paper
Glue sticks

Teacher Talk

Talk about the colors and shapes as children enjoy gluing shapes on paper. "The moon shape fits nicely there. Where will you put this rocket, John?"

Tape a long piece of butcher paper to a wall. Provide black pain, and paintbrushes. First give children repeated opportunities to paint the paper. Allow the paper to dry completely. Cut sponges into moon and star shapes. Next provide sponge shapes, low plastic trays, and thick tempera paint. Show children how to press the sponge into the paint and then press the sponge onto the butcher paper. Provide different colors for different days. Finally, cut construction paper into shapes of rockets, moons, stars, planets, and astronauts. Provide construction paper shapes and glue sticks for children to create a mural. Add to the mural as you discover more and more about space—stars, rockets, dogs in space, planets, astronauts, space ships, satellites, and so on. The mural can be added to throughout the Possibilities Plan.

Space Mural—Version 2

All ages

Materials

Butcher paper
Thick purple tempera paint, chilled
Thick yellow tempera paint, warmed
Thick red tempera paint with sand mixed in
Star and moon shapes
Glue sticks
Tape

Allow several days for children to bodypaint the background on the very large piece of butcher paper. On different days provide different types of paints that go with the vocabulary you are using. When you talk about Pluto, chill the purple paint in the refrigerator before you start. When you talk about the sun, make the yellow paint warm by placing it in the sun or adding warm water. On the day(s) you talk about Mars, use red paint with fine sand mixed in it. When the painting is finished, you may want to make different shapes available, so children can glue them onto the mural. The mural will be interesting over a long period of time because you will be changing the different materials. Tape the mural to the wall in between painting sessions and when it is completed.

Building a Spaceship

30-36 months

Materials

Blocks
An assortment of boxes, including cardboard tubes, shoeboxes, and oatmeal boxes
Tape, optional
Paper and pen
Camera, optional

Teacher Talk

"Jonathan, you are working hard stacking those shoeboxes. What other building materials are you going to use?"

Provide a variety of building materials for children to build their own spaceships. If possible, provide a place where "works in progress" can stay until the work is finished. Take photos of the project in its various stages of completion. Write down children's words as they work on building their space ships. Display the project, the photos, and the written words together.

PARENT PARTICIPATION POSSIBILITIES

Star Gazing

Suggest that parents look at the night sky with their children on a clear night as an at-home activity. Encourage parents to talk about the moon and the stars with their child. Encourage parents to talk, sing, and recite nursery rhymes about the moon and stars used in this Plan.

Read! Read! Read!

Encourage parents to read every day with their child. Parents may select stories about the moon, stars, or space travel to extend their child's learning. Children may choose their own favorite books for parents to read as well. Or send a space book home with children to read and return to school the next day.

Supporting Possibilities

Ask parents to save items from the gathered list, so they can be used throughout the unit. You will want to collect enough ice cream cartons (from ice cream parlors), so each child can have her own space helmet.

Parents in the Classroom

Invite parents to join in the fun on a day when children are participating in dramatic or art possibilities in space. Parents might enjoy visiting the day children have moon snacks.

Parent Postcard

The Parent Postcard in this section is designed to share with parents during the Possibilities Plan. The topic is a natural extension of the activities and experiences that you are planning and implementing for the toddlers in the classroom. Use the Postcard to connect parents to their children's learning.

Gender Role Stereotyping

From a very early age, many parents seem to be concerned about blue and pink. Whole nurseries and wardrobes are planned about the boy or girl issue. The concern doesn't stop there. Often parents are concerned about their young children's sexual orientation. When they see boys playing with purses and girls playing with trucks, they worry about the future.

Adults observe particular characteristics in young children and attribute them to the fact that a child is male or female. But, gender identification is not firmly established until children are older. In the early years they will take on the many roles they see adults around them using without awareness of the typical or stereotypical gender of those roles. Before age 5, this is normal. Later, children will begin to decide on activities and experiences based on the gender of who plays the role. For now, encourage your child to play however he or she wants to play.

Both girl and boy toddlers need a wide range of physical, intellectual, emotional, and social experiences. Of course, we want girls to grow up to be competent physically, and we certainly want boys to grow up to be loving and affectionate fathers. Thus, we must give both boys and girls chances to become the best individuals they can be. This will be accomplished through allowing many varied experiences, instead of limiting girls to playing house and boys to building with blocks.

TO ______________________

____

____

Concepts Learned in *Space*

Concepts Learned

Space is far away.
Space ships can go to space.
I can play space center activities.
Astronauts wear helmets and boots.
The moon is round.
The moon is in the sky.
I can see the moon at night.
Stars are in the night sky.
Stars twinkle.
Stars have points.
Rockets go to the moon.
Rockets go very fast.
Sand on Mars is red.
I can move my whole body to music.
I can sing simple songs.
I can recite simple rhymes.
I can use fine motor skills with my fingers.
I can be involved in imaginary play with sound effects.
I can throw.
I can jump.
I can put together simple puzzles.
I can stack more than two blocks.
I can glue.
I can use spatial awareness skills.
I can use creative materials for construction.
I can explore a variety of textures and materials.
I can use words for textures.

Resources

Prop boxes

Astronaut
- Coveralls
- Rubber boots
- Space helmet
- Toy rocket ships

Goodnight Moon

- Brush
- Comb
- *Goodnight Moon* by Margaret Wise Brown
- Mittens
- Picture of a bowl of cereal
- Picture of a red balloon
- Picture of moon and stars in a window
- Plastic cow
- Small clock
- Small dollhouse
- Socks
- Stick puppets of objects in the book
- Stuffed rabbit
- Three small stuffed bears
- Toy mouse
- Toy telephone
- Two stuffed kittens

Picture File/Vocabulary

Astronauts
Mars
Moon
Night sky
Planets
Pluto
Rocket ships
Space shuttles
Stars
Sun

Books

Dogs in Space by Nancy Coffelt (page 248)
Goodnight Moon by Margaret Wise Brown (page 248)
Grandfather Twilight by Barbara Helen Berger
Happy Birthday Moon by Frank Asch
Magic School Bus: Lost in Outer Space by Joanna Cole
Moongame by Frank Asch
Papa, Please Get the Moon for Me by Eric Carle
Sky All Around by Anna G. Hines
What Next, Baby Bear? by Jill Murphy
Why the Sun and Moon Live in the Sky by Elphinston Dayrell

Rhymes/Fingerplays

"Five Little Rockets" (page 250)
"Hey, Diddle, Diddle" (page 247)
"The Moon Is Out Tonight" (page 251)

Music/Songs

"Mister Moon" (page 249)
"Twinkle, Twinkle Little Star" (page 250)

Toys and Materials

The following purchased items are important for this Possibilities Plan.

- 2 stuffed toy kittens
- 3 small stuffed toy bears
- Aluminum foil
- Black permanent markers
- Blue food coloring
- Butcher paper
- Construction paper
- Cow and moon characters
- Craft knife (teacher only)
- Crepe paper streamers
- Fabric paint pens
- Flannel board
- Glitter
- Glue
- Hole punch
- Markers
- Metal rings
- One-gallon plastic milk jug
- Paint
- Paper
- Paper plates
- Plastic cow
- Plastic cups
- Poster board
- Pretzels
- Raisins
- Salt and shaker
- Scarves
- Scissors
- Shiny tape
- Silver and/or gold nontoxic spray paint
- Silver duct tape
- Silver paint
- Small clock
- Small dollhouse
- Small marshmallows
- Small resealable bags
- Star-shaped confetti
- Stuffed toy rabbit
- Tape
- Toy mouse
- Toy telephone
- Toy typewriters
- Water table
- Yarn
- Yarn balls
- Yellow and black paint
- Yellow fingerpaint

The following purchased items are important for this Possibilities Plan.

- Baseball-size rocks
- Cardboard
- Cardboard buckets
- Cardboard tubes
- Clear plastic bottles
- Colored hair gel
- Comb and brush
- Copy paper boxes
- Large and medium cardboard boxes
- Large pizza boards
- Large rubber boots
- Mittens
- Oatmeal boxes
- Old keyboards (no wires)
- Pantyhose
- Picture of bowl of cereal
- Picture of moon and stars in window
- Pictures of red balloon
- Pictures of things in space
- Plastic lids
- Rubber bath mat
- Several 2-liter clear plastic bottles
- Shoeboxes
- Socks
- Two fabric strips
- Used coveralls
- Very large spools

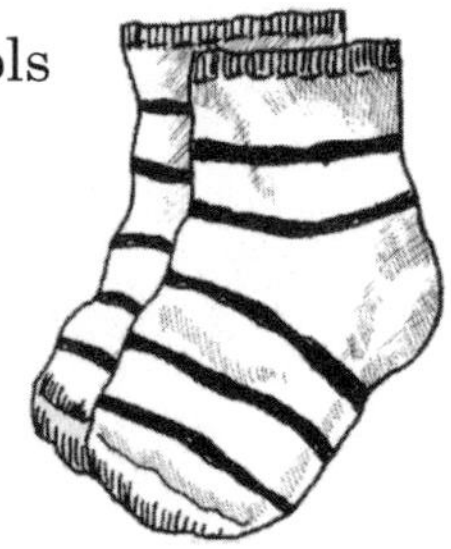

Sky

WEB

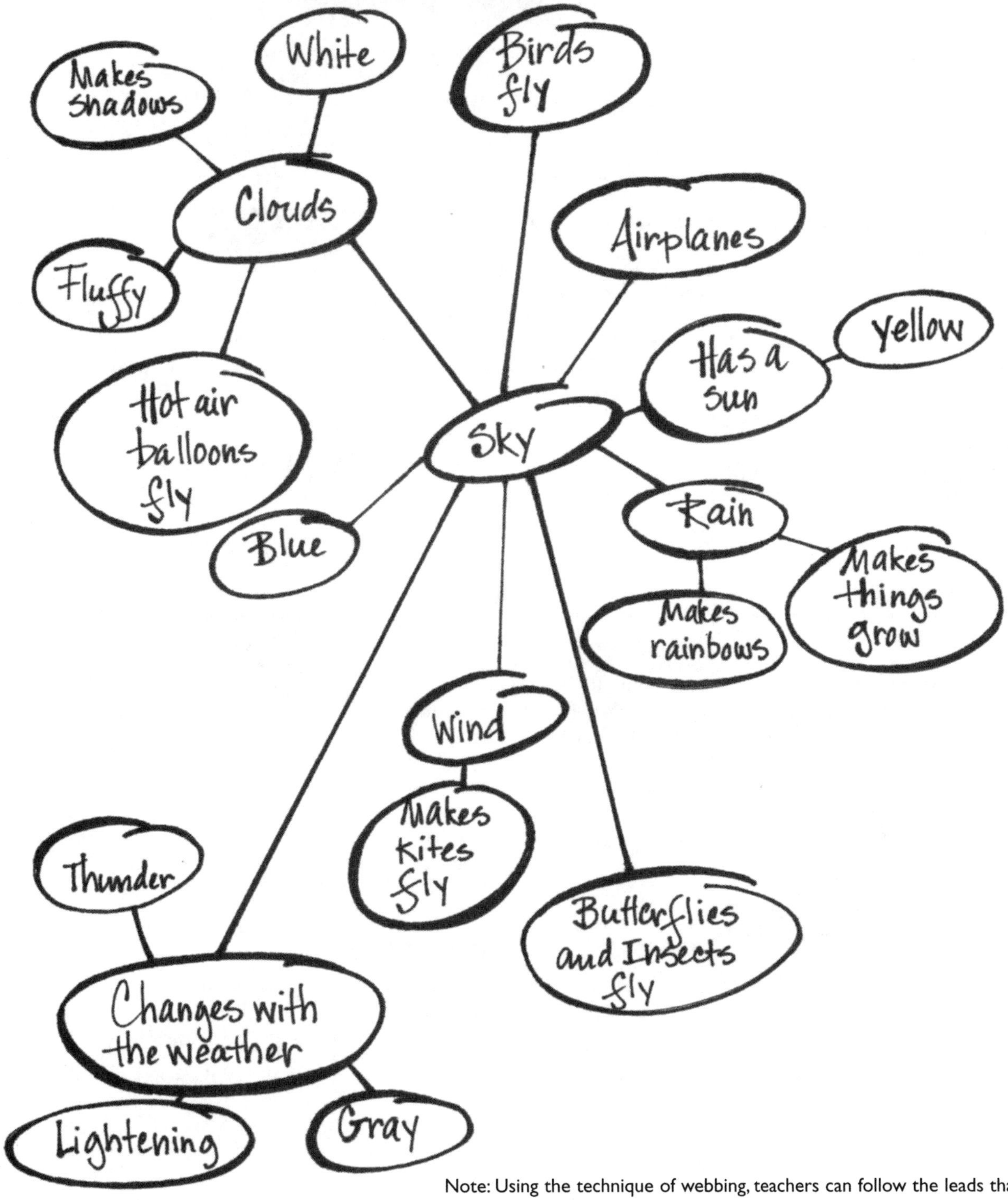

Note: Using the technique of webbing, teachers can follow the leads that children give them, as well as have an unlimited source of options. Always use the webs provided as a jumping-off point. The possibilities are endless!

PLANNING PAGES

Plan Possibilities

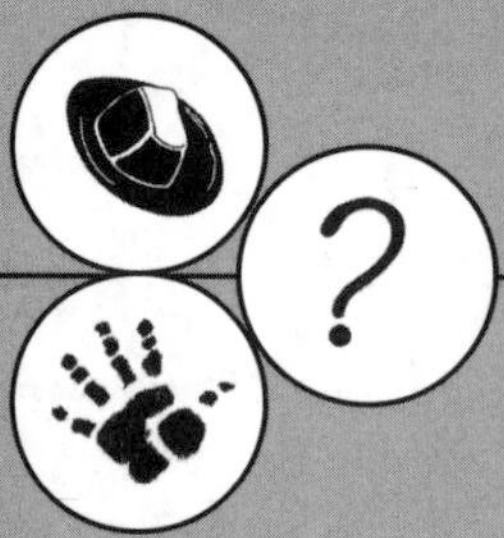

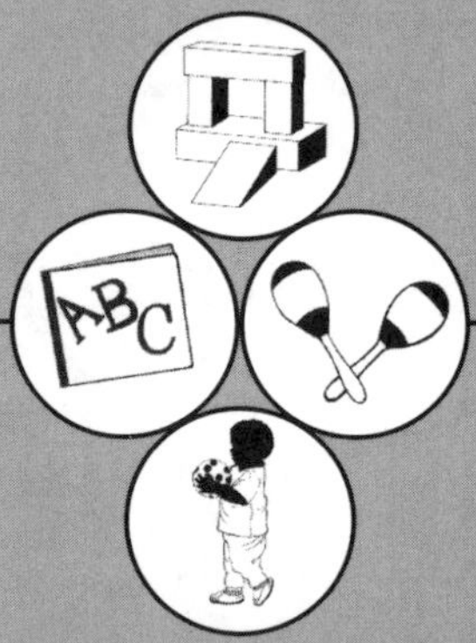

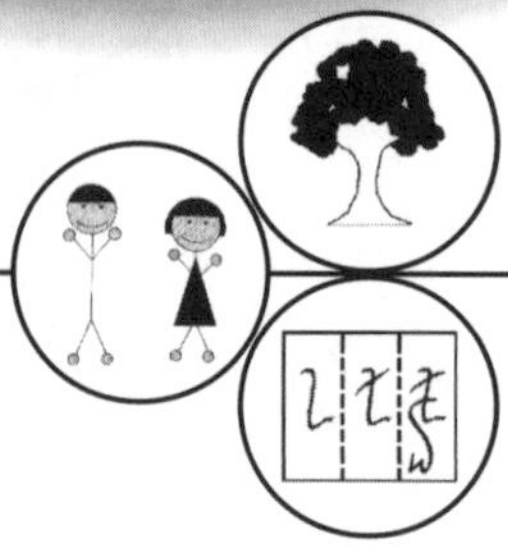

Sky

Concepts Learned in Sky 277

Prop boxes

Beach Box 277
Rainy Day 278

Picture File/Vocabulary . . 278

Books

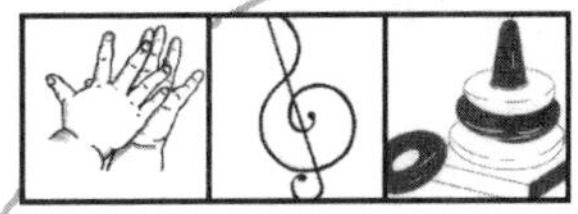

Rhymes/Fingerplays

"I Wonder Where the Clouds All Go" . .272
"The Sun" 269

Music/Songs

"Did You Ever See a Cloud?" 271
"It's Raining, It's Pouring" 271
"Rainbow Colors" 272
"Rain, Rain Go Away" 271

Toys and Materials 279

DRAMATIC POSSIBILITIES

Let's Go to the Beach!

All ages

Materials

Beach umbrella
Beach chairs
Beach towels
Beach bags
Empty suntan lotion bottles
Sun hats

Teacher Talk

Talk with children about their trip to the beach. "How are you going to the beach, Thomas?"

Provide typical beach items for children to enjoy a sunny day at the beach.

Rain Gear

All ages

Materials

Raincoats
Rain hats
Rubber boots

Teacher Talk

"You chose a big raincoat, Jeffery. The raincoat will keep you dry."

Provide a variety of raincoats, rain hats, and rubber boots for children to dress up for rainy weather.

Soft Cloud Pillows

All ages

Materials

Variety of small, soft, white pillows

Teacher Talk

"This little pillow is as soft as a cloud. What about the pillow you have, Maggie? How does it feel?"

Place a variety of small, soft, white pillows in the area for children to experience.

Sandpaper Art

All ages

Materials

Sandpaper
Chalk
Sugar water or buttermilk, optional

Teacher Talk

Talk about colors and textures as children explore. "How does the sandpaper feel, Michael?"

Provide sandpaper and colored chalk for children to experiment with drawing on the rough texture. To make chalk colors brighter, soak the chalk in a sugar water mixture or in buttermilk.

Shades of Yellow

All ages

Materials

Variety of shades of yellow paint
Assorted sizes of brushes
Paper

Teacher Talk

Talk about the colors and the sizes of the brushes as children work. "You chose the big brush, Joseph."

Provide two or three shades of yellow paint and an assortment of sizes of brushes for children to experiment painting with yellow.

Sunny Goop

All ages

Materials

Water
Cornstarch
Bowl
Yellow food coloring
Plastic pans

Teacher Talk

Talk about the texture and the changes in the mixture. "How does the goop feel in your hands, Allison?"

In a bowl, make a mixture of cornstarch, water, and a few drops of yellow food coloring. Place the mixture in plastic pans for children to explore.

Colorful Clouds

All ages

Materials
Shaving cream
Dry powdered tempera paint
Water table

Teacher Talk
Talk about the way the cream feels, looks, and smells. "Sophia, how do the clouds feel to you?"

Place shaving cream in the water table. Sprinkle two or three colors of dry powdered tempera paint on the shaving cream. Observe as children explore and investigate the shaving cream.

Cloud Art

All ages

Materials
Blue construction paper
Thick, white tempera paint
Plastic spoon

Teacher Talk
Talk about clouds and look for shapes children may recognize in the cloud designs. "Caitlin, that's the way to rub the paper with your hands. Open the paper and let's see what happened to the white paint."

Help children fold a piece of blue construction paper in half and then unfold the paper. Show children how to put spoonfuls of white paint on one side of the paper. Children can then refold the paper and rub the paper with their hands. When children open the paper they can see the white clouds in the blue sky.

Cloud Dough

All ages

Materials

Flour
Salad oil
Measuring cups
Bowl
Water
Airtight plastic container

Teacher Talk

Talk with children about how the dough feels as they squeeze it. "Squish! Squish! This dough feels squishy, Marla."

In a bowl, mix together 6 cups of flour and 1 cup salad oil. Add enough water to make the dough soft and pliable. This dough is soft and elastic and does not harden. Keep it in a sealed plastic container.

Rain Sticks

All ages

Materials

Gift wrap-size cardboard tube
Contact paper
Aluminum foil
Dry rice
Tape

Teacher Talk

"Listen, Nick. What do you hear?"

Cover one end of a cardboard tube with contact paper. Twist lengths of aluminum foil into long coils. Push the coils of foil inside the cardboard tube. Pour half a cup of dry rice into the tube. Cover the open end with contact paper. Tape all edges securely closed. Rock the tube gently to make the rice move against the foil, making sounds like rain. Help children experiment with making soft and loud rain sounds. Or, purchase a commercial rain stick and listen to the rain sounds.

Color Paddles

All ages

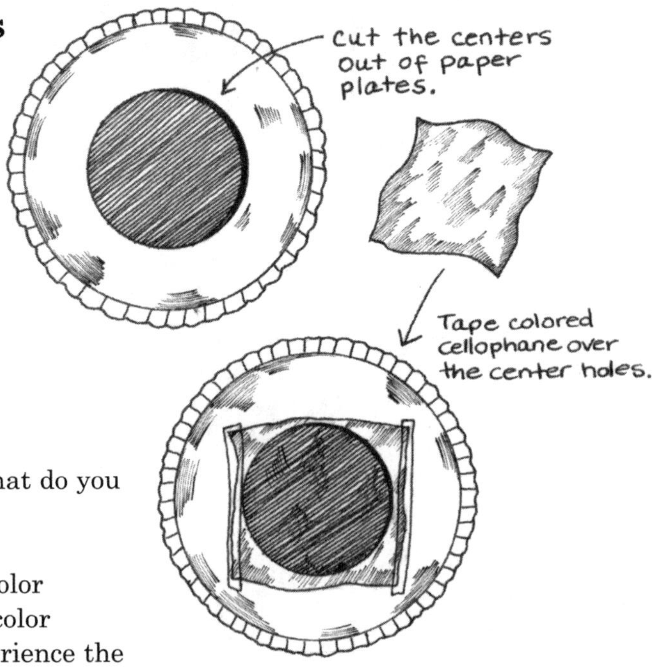
Cut the centers out of paper plates.
Tape colored cellophane over the center holes.

Materials

Purchased plastic color paddles
or
Paper plates
Scissors
Colored cellophane
Tape

Teacher Talk

Look through this, Nan. What do you see?

Provide purchased plastic color paddles or make your own color paddles for children to experience the color changes when they look through transparent colors. Cut the centers out of paper plates. Tape colored cellophane over the center holes. Children can explore their surroundings in a variety of colors using the paddles.

Prisms

30-36 months

Materials

Plastic prisms

Teacher Talk

Talk about the colors. "Look at this prism, Emilio. What colors do you see?"

Provide a prism for children to hold in the sunlight to see different colors. Show children how to hold the prism, so sunlight can shine through it to reflect colors on white paper or on the wall. Experiment to see what happens to the prism in dim light.

CONSTRUCTION POSSIBILITIES

Planes and Helicopters

All ages

Materials

Toy planes and helicopters

Teacher Talk
Use the words in the vocabulary list. "You are landing the plane on the runway, Neal."

Place toy planes and helicopters with the blocks. Attach paper with a runway and/or heliport drawn on it to the floor or tabletop. Observe children as they build.

LITERACY POSSIBILITIES

Sun Puppet
All ages

Materials
Paper plate
Yellow paint
Paintbrushes
Large craft stick
Tape

Teacher Talk
Talk about how the sun keeps the earth warm, provides light, and helps living things grow. "Listen to the poem. Now let's move the puppet the way the poem says the sun moves."

Paint a paper plate yellow and tape a large craft stick onto the back of the plate. Read the poem and show children how to move the puppet as the poem says the sun moves across the sky.

The Sun
The sun gets up from its bed,
And marches across the sky all day.
At noon it stands right overhead,
And at night it goes away.

Sun Books
All ages

Materials
Yellow paper plates
Sunny day pictures
Glue
Hole punch
Metal rings

Teacher Talk
Point to the pictures and talk about what is happening in the pictures with children. "Show me your favorite sunny pictures, Charlie."

Glue sunny day pictures onto each plate. Punch a hole in each yellow plate and fasten the plates together with a metal ring. Share the sun book with children. Encourage children to "read" the book to you.

Planting a Rainbow

All ages

Materials
Planting a Rainbow by Lois Ehlert
Felt
Scissors
Flannel board

Teacher Talk
Talk about colors. "That's the way to put the flowers on the board, Madison. You put all the pink flowers on the board."

Cut felt flowers to match the ones in the storybook, *Planting a Rainbow* by Lois Ehlert. As you read the story, take turns putting the pieces on the flannel board.

A Sunny Day Chart

30-36 months

Materials
Chart paper
Markers
Sunny day pictures

Teacher Talk
Talk about activities children like to do on a sunny day or discuss what children see in the pictures. "What can we play on a sunny day?"

Choose a sunny day for this activity, or show children pictures of people doing a variety of things on a sunny day. Write children's words on the chart paper. Title the paper and post it, so parents can enjoy their children's responses.

Rain, Rain Go Away!

All ages

Materials
None

Teacher Talk
Talk about rain and staying inside during outdoor play when it rains. "Bart, your wiggling fingers look like rain falling down."

Sing the following songs with children. When it starts to rain outside, go to the door or window and sing the rain away.

Rain, Rain Go Away
Rain, rain go away,
Come again another day.
Rain, rain go away,
Little (child's name) wants to play.

It's Raining, It's Pouring
It's raining; It's pouring,
The old man is snoring.
He snored so hard, he fell out of bed,
And bumped his head,
He couldn't get up in the morning.

Did You Ever See a Cloud?

All ages

Materials
Cloud pictures

Teacher Talk
Talk about the clouds looking like familiar animals or shapes. "Look at this picture of a cloud, Jackie. What could it be?"

Show children pictures of clouds. Sing the following song to the tune of "Did You Ever See a Lassie?" You may want to make up verses using other animals and/or shapes.

Did You Ever See a Cloud?
Did you ever see a cloud, a cloud, a cloud?
Did you ever see a cloud that looked like a sheep?
A fat one, a skinny one, a silly one, a funny one,
Did you ever see a cloud that looked like a sheep?
Did you ever see a cloud, a cloud, a cloud?

Did you ever see a cloud that looked like a car?
A big one, a little one, a fast one, a slow one.
Did you ever see a cloud that looked like a car?

I Wonder Where the Clouds All Go

All ages

Materials
None

Teacher Talk
"Yes, Abby, clouds are very quiet. Shhh, clouds move quietly."

Sing the following song with children. Encourage children to act out the song. Sing to the tune "Twinkle, Twinkle Little Star."

I Wonder Where the Clouds All Go
When I look into the sky, (Hand on brow, looking up.)
I can see the clouds go by. (Flutter fingers.)
They don't ever make a sound, (Put a finger to lips.)
Letting wind push them around. (Push with hands.)
Some go fast and some go slow. (Move hands fast, then slow.)
I wonder where the clouds all go. (Hand on brow, looking up.)

Rainbow Colors

All ages

Materials
Red, orange, yellow, green, blue, purple streamers

Teacher Talk
"See our rainbow streamers! This is fun!"

Use rainbow-colored streamers for children to wave as you sing the following song to the tune "Twinkle, Twinkle Little Star."

Rainbow Colors
When the rain falls from the sky,
Be sure to look way up high.
If the sun is shining there,
You will find a rainbow fair.
Red, orange, yellow, green, and blue,
And surely there's some purple. too.

Clouds in the Wind

All ages

Materials
Tape or CD instrumental music
Tape or CD player

Teacher Talk
"Jana is a whirling cloud. How does a cloud move slowly, Jana?"

Play music and move like clouds to the tempo of the music. Children will soon join you. Use fast tempo music, then slow tempo music as children move their bodies in rhythm to the music.

Musical Sun

30-36 months

Materials
Cardboard sun
Tape or CD of instrumental music
Tape or CD player

Children sit in a circle and pass the sun from child to child while the music plays. When the music stops, the child holding the sun can choose another place to sit in the circle. Play begins again when the music starts. Toddlers are not old enough to understand games with rules, but do respond well to repetition. Be flexible and see where the game goes.

OUTDOOR POSSIBILITIES

Rainy Painting

All ages

Materials
Plastic shower curtain squares
Dry powdered tempera paint
Plastic spray bottles
Water

Teacher Talk
Talk about what happens when the water mixes with the powdered paint. "Josh is making it rain on the plastic. What is happening to the powdered paint on the plastic?"

Place plastic on the ground or sidewalk. Sprinkle dry powdered tempera paint on the squares. Fill small plastic spray bottles with water. Show children how to spray the dry paint with water. Leave the painted plastic squares in the sun to dry.

Making Rainbows

All ages

Materials
Garden hose
Water

Teacher Talk
Name the colors. "Look, there's the rainbow, Sally. See the colors—purple, red, blue!"

On a sunny day use a garden hose to spray a fine mist of water across the sun's rays. Have the children stand with their backs to the sun and look for a rainbow in the mist.

Colored Water

All ages

Materials
Water table
Water
Food coloring
Plastic cups
Variety of sizes of plastic containers

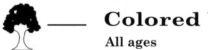

Teacher Talk
"I like blue water. Which color do you like, Debbie?"

Add a few drops of food coloring to water in the water table. Allow children to explore and investigate the water with the plastic containers.

PROJECT POSSIBILITIES

Our Weather Book

All ages

Materials
Pictures of weather from magazines
Glue
Cardboard squares

Teacher Talk
"Tell me about the weather you saw at the door, Kinsey. How did the sky look? Can you find a picture that looks like the sky looks outside?"

Go to the window or door to look at the weather. Suggest that children pick out pictures that look like what they saw to glue onto a cardboard square. Accept their choices. After the glue has dried, ask children to describe the weather. Write down their descriptions and the date. Repeat this once a week or so until you have a book of weather.

PARENT PARTICIPATION POSSIBILITIES

Rainy Day Ideas

Ask parents to share ideas for rainy day activities. Help them remember the activities they enjoyed on rainy days when they were children. Some parents may want to send special toys or treats for the children on rainy days.

Sunny Day Visit

Invite parents to visit on a sunny day, so they can play outside with their child. Encourage parents to play in the water and sand with their child. Provide simple refreshments and emphasize the pleasure of playing together.

Parent Postcard

The Parent Postcard in this section is designed to share with parents during the Possibilities Plan. The topic is a natural extension of the activities and experiences that you are planning and implementing for the toddlers in the classroom. Use the Postcard to connect parents to their children's learning.

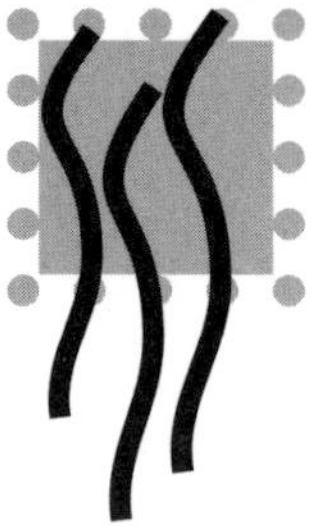

TO

Exploring Roles at Home

Home can be a wonderful place to support your child's role exploration. Whether you are sorting laundry, paying bills, or working on the computer, there are many parallel activities for your child. Provide the props needed (socks, junk mail, a notebook) and see in which direction your child takes the play.

Meal preparations can be a wonderful time to spend with your toddler. Provide pots and pans, so both of you can "cook." Talk about what you are doing and what you see your child doing. Open up the pantry and allow your child to play with the cans. They roll and stack, two skills that toddlers like to explore.

The main objective is time together. Your toddler will enjoy the attention, as well as the opportunity to do what Mommy and Daddy do!

Concepts Learned in *Sky*

Concepts Learned

The sun is in the daytime sky.
The sun is yellow.
The sun is hot.
The sun warms the earth.
The sun helps living things grow.
The sun gives light.
The sun shines at the beach.
Clouds are white.
Clouds stay in the sky.
Clouds are soft.
Rain falls from the sky.
Rain is water.
Rain waters the flowers.
Raincoats keep people dry in the rain.
Rain makes sounds.
Rainbows have many colors.
Rainbows are in the sky at special times.
Rain and sunshine make rainbows.
Some textures are soft, rough, wet, or sandy.
I understand up and down, high and low.
Words can be written on paper.
I can make large motor movements to different music rhythms.
I can strengthen my large muscles by riding toys.

Resources

Prop boxes

Beach Box
- Beach towels
- Empty suntan lotion bottles
- Plastic sunglasses
- Sand pails/shovels
- Sun hats

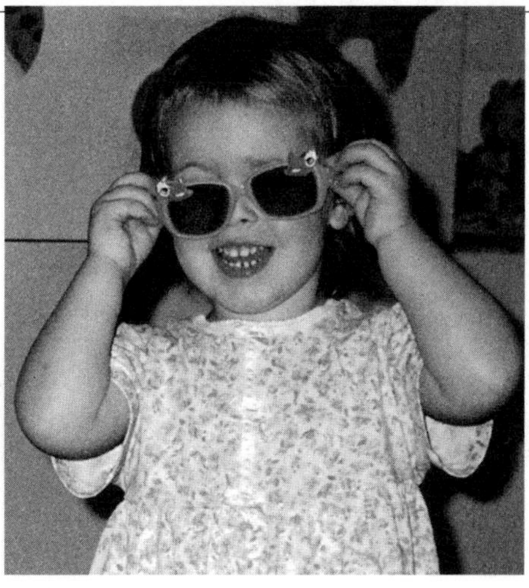

Rainy Day
- Ponchos
- Rain hats
- Raincoats
- Rubber boots

Picture File/Vocabulary

Airport
Clouds
Flowers
Helicopter
Planes
Rainbows
Rainy day pictures
Runway
Sunny day pictures
Suns

Books

Bringing the Rain to Kapiti Plain by Verna Aardema
Cloud Book by Tomie DePaola
It Looked Like Spilt Milk by Charles G. Shaw
Listen to the Rain by James Endicott, John Archambault, & Bill Martin, Jr.
Planting a Rainbow by Lois Ehlert
Rainbow of My Own, A by Don Freeman
Sun Up, Sun Down by Gail Gibbons
Way to Start a Day, The by Byrd Baylor
Why the Sun and Moon Live in the Sky by Elphinstone Dayrell

Rhymes/Fingerplays

"I Wonder Where the Clouds All Go" (page 272)
"The Sun" (page 269)

Music/Songs

"Did You Ever See a Cloud?" (page 271)
"It's Raining, It's Pouring" (page 271)
"Rainbow Colors" (page 272)
"Rain, Rain Go Away" (page 271)

Toys and Materials

The following purchased items are important for this Possibilities Plan.

Aluminum foil
Assorted brush sizes
Blue construction paper
Butcher paper
Chart paper
Color paddles or colored cellophane
Colored tissue paper
Contact paper
Cornstarch
Dry tempera paints
Felt
Flannel board
Flour
Frozen whipped topping
Ice cream scoop
Markers
Music
Nontoxic liquid starch
Nontoxic shaving cream
Paper
Paper plates (yellow, white)
Plastic cups and spoons
Plastic pans
Plastic prisms
Rainbow colors streamers
Rice (dry)
Salad oil
Sandpaper
Scissors
Tape
Thick white tempera paint
Vanilla ice cream
Variety of food coloring
Variety of shades of yellow paint
Water table

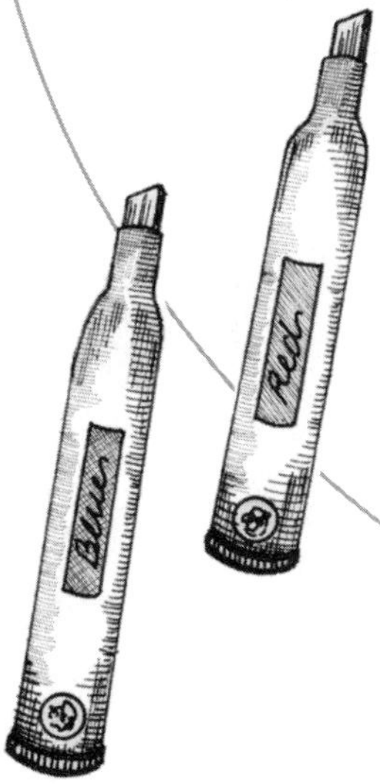

The following purchased items are important for this Possibilities Plan.

Beach bags
Beach chairs
Beach towels
Beach umbrella
Cardboard
Cloud pictures
Empty suntan lotion bottle
Garden hose
Plastic containers
Plastic shower curtain
Rain coats
Rain hats
Rubber boots
Sun hats
Sunglasses
Sunny day pictures
Variety of small, soft pillows
Water
Wrapping paper tube

CHAPTER 5

Communicating with Parents, Teachers, and Friends

INTRODUCTION

Toddlerhood marks the beginning of an exciting and challenging period in the lives of young children. Toddlers emerge from infancy with a considerable range of skills and abilities that are just beginning to be evident to unfamiliar adults. They have perfected the motor

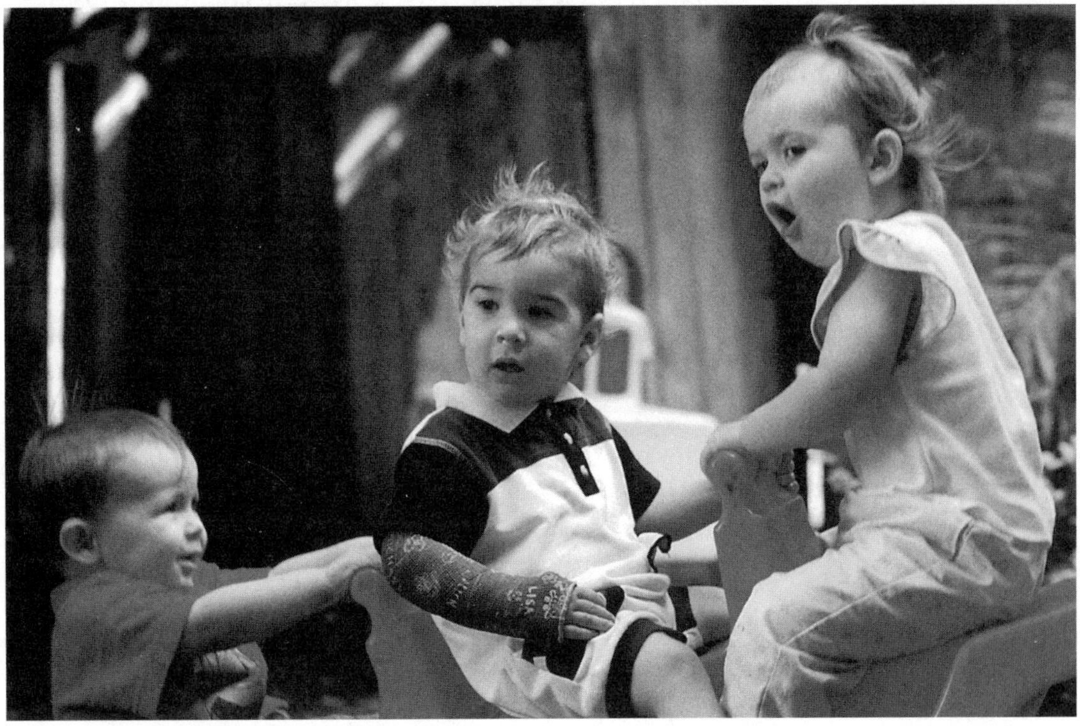

skills of getting around and eating and drinking without assistance. Toddlers have learned to understand a rather large number of words and are beginning to communicate their needs and wants with an ever-growing expressive vocabulary. And, toddlers are inquisitive about everything—wanting to interact, discover, manipulate, and explore everything in sight.

Along with this curiosity comes an emerging interest in the larger physical and social world. Exploration takes on new dimensions as the environment entices toddlers to look up as well as out, behind doors, out windows, and underneath objects, as well as at them. Viewing the room from a tabletop instead of from the floor is as interesting as viewing the underside of the table while lying on the floor.

If emotional development has proceeded normally during infancy, toddlers are also beginning to have a keen interest in others—other children and other adults. They want to interact, get to know, and play with someone rather than just with objects and toys. In fact, this interest is more developed than the associated skills needed for such interaction, and poses a major challenge for toddlers, their parents, and their teachers.

Intellectual development has also emerged. Understanding how the brain develops in the toddler years confirms that these years are learning years. Early learning is clearly seen in the curiosity of toddlers—they are interested in everything—from minute details to the "whys" of the big picture—and are trying to put together an understanding of the world in which they live.

INNOVATIONS IN OBSERVATION/ASSESSMENT

Observation/Assessment Instrument

This assessment instrument is not just a skills checklist. Instead it is designed to guide the teacher's observation of children's development through major interactional tasks of toddlerhood. The assessment's focus is on what IS happening, not just what should happen or what will happen. Use this assessment to lead to developmentally appropriate practice.

	18-24 months	24-30 months	30-36 months
CM1	a. Expressive vocabulary increases; uses about 200 words on a regular basis. Expressive language continues to be telegraphic, where single words may carry expanded meaning that is only understood by familiar caregivers.	b. Vocabulary size begins to grow rapidly; sentence length begins to increase with 3 or 4 words in some sentences.	c. Sentence length continues to grow. Four- to six-word sentences predominate expressive language. Vocabulary continues to expand; expressive vocabulary is adequate to make most needs and wants understood by others.
CM2	a. Uses a greater variety of sounds and sound combinations, simplifying the word if it is too complex (such as pane for plane, tephone for telephone); enjoys experimenting with inflection that sounds like adult speech although it is not yet understandable.	b. Rapid development of new sound combinations and new words that are understandable to adults. Begins to use language functionally—to ask for things and get needs met.	c. Is able to use language to get most needs and wants met by familiar caregivers.
CM3	a. Seeks vocal interactions with familiar people; can communicate needs and wants to familiar caregivers; begins to be wary of talking to strangers.	b. Resists interactions with strangers; hides, withdraws, or objects to encouragement to talk to strangers.	
CM4	a. 20-25% of language is intelligible to strangers. Parents and caregivers can understand more.	b. 60-65% of language is intelligible to strangers. Parents and caregivers understand most of the child's expressive language.	
CM5	a. "Reads" book from front to back; turns books right side up to look at them. b. Makes sounds that connect to pictures in books.	c. Listens to a complete story from beginning to end; asks to read familiar books over and over again.	d. Likes to look at books independently; "reads" books to self.
CM6	a. Actively experiments with the environment; follows visual displacement of objects.	b. Begins transition to symbolic thought. Uses formed mental images to solve problems. Thought processes relate to concrete experiences and objects.	c. Begins transition to pre-operational stage characterized by the beginning of symbolic thought and the use of mental images and words.

INNOVATIONS IN CHILD DEVELOPMENT

Brain Growth and Development

With the advent of new imaging technologies, neurobiologists have discovered exciting information about how the brain develops. Many of these discoveries have validated premises long held as important by early childhood teachers. New knowledge indicates that brain development is the result of a complex dance between the genetic makeup of a child, which is fixed at conception, and the child's experience, which is open to many possibilities. Scientists have always thought that this dance was a lifelong one. Brain research has now confirmed that what happens to children in the first ten years of life has a profound impact on the way the lifelong dance succeeds.

Before a child is born, neurons or brain cells develop. After birth, synapses develop between the neurons. As stimulation occurs, millions of connections are developed, creating networks for coordination and communication. This is a use-it-or-lose-it time. Neurons that aren't stimulated simply don't get connected and never have another chance to do so. So the early experiences that children have directly affect the way their brains develop and how many networks are created. Early stimulation, therefore, has lifelong impact on children, impacting the abilities children will have as adults.

After the initial connections are formed, the brain begins a lifelong process of improving the connections or highways between neurons and connecting smaller roads to larger ones. For the next 10 years or so, well-stimulated neural pathways become larger, stronger, and more coordinated, while un- or under-stimulated ones are abandoned.

Another important finding of brain research is that there are prime times for acquiring different kinds of knowledge and skills—an optimum time for stimulating and enriching children's learning (Shore, 1997). Because this is the case, negative experiences or the lack of stimulation during these prime times increase the risk of lifelong consequences for children. For very young children, two important optimum times occur before age three. The first is the foundation of emotional development, a window that opens at birth and begins to close around age two. The second is the foundation of language development that opens at birth and begins to close at about age six. As a result, continuing to support attachment between toddlers and their primary caregivers and stimulating language development are critical curricula for toddlers.

The brain research does not tell us that earlier is necessarily better. Just because the brain is developing real potential during the early years does not mean that everything can or should be stimulated during that time. In fact, the information about critical periods suggests that there are optimal times to introduce children to a wide array of stimulating information and experiences, while remembering the integrated nature of development. Optimal times take place throughout life, not just during early childhood. For example, motor development matures for children as they near the end of the early childhood period—around age 8. During this period, coordination improves, and children are intellectually ready to think about more than one thing at once—such as who is on second base and whether to run or not when a fly ball is hit. So, team sports become very popular and children are ready to benefit from these experiences. Prior to age eight, children may want to play and enjoy the experience, but their ability to do so is less coordinated.

So toddler teachers can relax about teaching academics to children and, instead, focus on the precursor skills that will lead children to be ready and able to begin their formal academic education. The first three years of life are an optimal time to keep the focus of children's educational experiences on relationship and language development.

Language Development

From 18 months to 36 months, a spectacular change takes place in children's language. They begin to make the transformation to using language in almost precisely the same way adults do—putting words together to form sentences that express ideas, and using these ideas to communicate with parents, teachers, and most importantly, their friends. This rapid growth in expressive language may seem like magic. But, like all areas of development, language follows predictable growth patterns that we can identify and follow.

Good teachers talk spontaneously to toddlers. They narrate what is going on in the classroom, talk about what children are doing, and respond to what children say to them and to others. During toddlerhood, good teachers respond even when what children say isn't completely understandable. Toddler teachers know that nonverbal communication (such as facial expressions, body language, and gestures) supports emerging expressive language and oral communication skills. Toddler teachers know that the tone and timbre of their voices mean as much to toddlers as the vocabulary or words they use.

Reciprocity—the back-and-forth of interactions between toddlers and their teachers—remains important in encouraging continued language development. No child will learn to use language in an environment that does not have a responsive adult to stimulate and respond to attempts to communicate, regardless of how well articulated or expressed.

During toddlerhood, children go from using one-word sentences (called holophrases) to speaking in grammatically correct sentences. As magical as this rapid growth seems, it follows the same developmental guidelines of all growth, from the simple to the complex and from the general to the specific.

For speech sound acquisition, the following developmental principles apply:

1. motorically simple to motorically complex; for example, (m) as in mama to (kw) as in queen
2. acoustically simple to acoustically complex; for example, (p) as in pie to (thr) as in throw
3. visible to less visible; for example, (b) as in boy to (r) as in red

The sequence of sound articulation is also predictable. During the first four years, a child will master the following groups of sounds:

(b), (p), (d), (t), (g), (k), (f), (m), (n), (ng), (w), (h), (y)

Other sounds are mastered after the fourth year.

Children's language behaviors also follow a predictable, sequential developmental pattern. The following language behaviors can be expected to emerge within one to three months of the following chronological ages:

AGE	LANGUAGE BEHAVIORS
18-24 MONTHS	• Follows simple commands without visual clues. • Enjoys books; likes being read to if book is familiar; will ask to have the same book read again and again. • Points to familiar pictures in books or magazines. • Develops a sense of "me" and "mine." • Uses a variety of common words consistently heard in the classroom or at home (usually between 10-20 words). • Refers to self by name. • Puts familiar words together to make simple sentences such as "Daddy work" or "Mommy bye-bye" and "all gone." • Talks mainly about self. • Imitates animal or object sounds. • Expresses refusal by saying "no."

AGE	LANGUAGE BEHAVIORS
24-30 MONTHS	• Likes listening to music or singing. • Sings short songs or says short fingerplays. • Imitates 3- to 4-word sentences. • Reacts to sound by telling what is heard or running to look at the source of the sound. • Continues to express refusal by saying "no." • Objects to help from others; wants to do it all by himself.
30-36 MONTHS	• Understands and uses simple verbs. • Understands pronouns, prepositions, adverbs, and adjectives such as "in," "me," "big," "go," "more," and so on. • Uses plurals. • Understands contrasts such as yes/no, come/go, run/stop, hot/cold. • Uses complete sentences frequently. • Answers simple questions from familiar people. • Uses "I" and "me."

Expressive and Receptive Language

Children have two different types of language skills. One type is children's expressive language skills, meaning those things the child can say, the size of the spoken vocabulary, and the grammar and syntax of language. Receptive language skills refer to language that is understood by children, regardless of their expressive ability. Very young children learn the meaning of language, such as "no" or "that's mine," before they are able to say those words themselves. So, stimulation of both expressive and receptive language is of critical importance. Teachers need to be skilled in using a wide variety of language-stimulation techniques that support emerging receptive and expressive language.

Intellectual Development

The intellectual development of toddlers continues to be stimulated by virtually everything children and teachers do in the classroom. In fact, during toddlerhood, intellectual and language development is stimulated naturally as children explore and interact with their environment and the people in it.

According to Jean Piaget, the most noted scholar of cognitive development in young children, children learn cognitive skills by making mistakes, by actively experimenting with the real world, and by manipulating objects as they try to understand how things work (Piaget, 1977). Throughout the early childhood years, active experimentation is the best form of intellectual stimulation. There is no need for toddler teachers to worry about teaching children numbers, colors, or any other pre-academic or academic skills. These concepts will emerge when children are older. Experiences with real things, with concrete objects, and with the environment in which toddlers live are the best ways to stimulate intellectual development.

A major change occurs to toddlers near the end of the toddler period of development. They make the transition from what Piaget called the sensori-motor stage of cognitive development to the pre-operational stage. This stage is characterized by the ability to use mental pictures and their labels to represent ideas—or the beginning of symbolic thought. During this phase, a toddler can connect the barking of a dog with its image without seeing the dog. The bark stimulates a mental picture of a dog for the child that can be recalled and applied without having physically to see the dog. This ability to recall mental images and use them is a major transition in children's cognitive abilities. It allows parents and teachers to recall experiences with children and then to build or expand on them. For many, this transition marks children's readiness for "real" learning. Good early childhood teachers know instead that real learning began at (or even before) birth, and that this is just a transition to the next stage of learning.

The chart on the next page summarizes Piaget's sensori-motor stage and pre-operational stages of cognitive development:

Piaget's Theory of Cognitive Development

Overview: Sensori-motor stage	Birth-2 years	• Adaptation (through assimilation and accommodation) to environment does not include the use of symbols or oral language. • Child develops schema (cognitive pictures).
Tertiary Circular Reactions Stage	12-18 months	• Actively experiments with environment; varies responses to obtain interesting results. • Uses trial-and-error techniques. • Object permanence advances—can follow visual sequential displacement of objects.
Imagery Stage	18 months-2 years	• Begins transition to symbolic thought. • Vocabulary grows rapidly. • Uses formed mental images to solve problems. • Thought processes relate to concrete experiences and objects.
Overview: Pre-Operational Stage	2-7 years	• Characterized by the beginning of symbolic thought and the use of mental images and words. • Has flaws in thinking: egocentrism, centration, irreversibility, transductive or illogical reasoning. • Beliefs of causal relationships: animism, artificialism, participation.
Pre-conceptual Stage	2-5 years	• Develops ability to classify objects: will group similar objects together but will not appear to have an overall plan to complete task. • Develops the ability to serialize objects: will serialize sporadically without plan or goal. • Cannot conserve quantity, substance, or volume.
Intuitive Stage	4-7 years	• Classification of objects can be done by classes and sub-classes. • Serialization develops to constructing an ordinal arrangement with some difficulty.

The Development of Literacy

Reading and writing begins to be a concern for parents and teachers almost as soon as children finish the transition from infancy to toddlerhood. As children's oral language grows to the point they can express what they know with words and ask about what they are interested in knowing, many adults think it is time to start "formal" instruction in reading and writing.

Actually, the foundations of reading and writing are formed during infancy when parents and significant adults read and responded to nonverbal cues—an important precursor skill that leads to an understanding that communication has meaning. Without meaningful relationships with others in the context of children's daily interactions, the ability to read, write, and spell cannot develop. Good teachers also know that adults have much to contribute to the development of literacy during toddlerhood.

Literacy research clearly indicates that adults can contribute to children's emerging literacy throughout the early childhood years. They start by developing positive, nurturing relationships with children, engaging them in frequent interactions. They talk to children, using language to describe and explain what is happening in the world around them. And, they expose children to books from the warm comfort of a familiar lap. They provide props, such as large and small pieces of paper, crayons, markers, tempera paint, and other artistic media for children to use to support and expand their play and facilitate the expression of ideas and thoughts. Then, they demonstrate the usefulness of representing words and ideas in a wide variety of ways, always connecting reading and writing to activities and experiences. For example, when teachers routinely record information on the Communication Sheet and toddlers see them do so over time, it isn't long before toddlers will ask to "write" notes on the sheet also. This connection between the written word and communicating with parents is a perfect example of a functional literacy experience for toddlers.

Providing print-rich environments is also supported by research (Neuman, Copple, & Bredekamp, 2000). Labeled cubbies, pictures on containers for returning manipulatives, photographs with labels on them, using pictures to check into school and out to home, real books and literature to read on your own or with an adult, materials from the environment such as logos, advertisements, cereal boxes, T-shirts, store and traffic signs, and so forth are all examples of ways to include the connection between reading and writing in toddler classrooms.

Reading in the First Three Years

By the beginning of toddlerhood, children who have been exposed to books usually love them. They like to look at them by themselves and have adults read to them. Many literacy skills are already present. For example, most toddlers position books appropriately when they pick them up—turning them upright and starting at the beginning. They are usually adept at turning pages, although the coordination to prevent crimping and tearing the pages may be intermittent. They can usually "read" the pictures, looking, pointing, identifying, and labeling concepts, ideas, and events depicted in the illustrations. And, they have developed preferences for types of books and topics that appeal to them. They ask adults to read favorite books again and again.

Many more skills will develop over the next 18 months. These skills are called "emergent literacy" skills because the process of becoming literate—able to read and write—grows and changes during the toddler years (Neuman, Copple, & Bredekamp, 2000). Literacy includes oral language, reading, and writing.

But these are not discreet areas of literacy. Children develop literacy skills in an integrated way, with skill acquisition in one area creating learning in other areas. The way children develop literacy skills is by using oral language, interpreting written language, and connecting writing to what they say and what the written word says in practical and useful ways. The process of becoming literate is an interactive one—toddlers learn as they interact and explore the functions and applications of oral language and written language.

Writing in the First Three Years

Toddlers are excellent scribblers. They enjoy making marks just about anytime and anywhere. Parents and teachers who are so anxious to see emerging intellectual skills are less excited about scribbles on the walls, floors, and tabletops! But it is precisely this intense interest in making marks that indicates so clearly that toddlers are ready for many writing experiences. And, the transition to the next stage—making marks that have circles, angles, and shapes in them—emerges after many experiences with scribbles.

Like in other areas of development, there are stages to emerging writing. First of all, children scribble, using the large muscles of the arm to make marks. Then, these marks begin to make shapes, starting usually with circles and then moving on to squiggles, angles, and other shapes. Finally, children begin to represent what they know in ways that are recognizable to adults—usually beginning with common images from the child's world, the face, the body, and the immediate world around them. Toddlers will remain in the first stage of writing well into the third year.

Getting Ready to Spell

The recognition of letters also begins to emerge during the toddler years. But the recognition is not the association of a letter name to the letter. Instead, it is an association of the patterns that letters make. For example, a toddler can usually find the pattern of his name on piece of artwork well before he can tell you the letters of his name. He is beginning to recognize the pattern that the letters of his name form—how many lines, how it begins and ends, how long or short it is, and how the middle goes up and down.

Drawing 1—The first tentative strokes; light pressure on the page; single color

Drawing 2—A month later; bold strokes; multiple colors

Drawing 3—A later drawing; circular strokes dominate

This is the foundation for spelling and later recognition that /b/ faces to the right and /d/ faces to the left. Many experiences with patterns are the very best preparation for good spelling. Puzzles, manipulatives, and blocks create many exciting patterns with lots of different shapes. These are great preparation activities for teaching the skills children will need to spell when they are older.

INNOVATIONS IN INTERACTIVE EXPERIENCES

Brain research and theories of language acquisition and intellectual development suggest that appropriate early stimulation of language and cognition results in many advantages for children later in life. For language, appropriate stimulation means giving toddlers many repeated experiences with language—hearing it used, being included in communication, having nonverbal cues interpreted correctly, receiving encouragement at communication attempts whether verbal or nonverbal, and succeeding in communicating with friends, family, and teachers.

Stimulating cognitive development almost always comes naturally as children continue the exploration of the world around them. Toddlers have two important new cognitive skills—they like to repeat actions and activities over and over as they experiment with favorite actions and reactions again and again. And, their ability to stay on task and persist in tasks is growing by leaps and bounds. The increase in task persistence is driven by emerging preferences—preferences for favorite interactions, toys, activities, and experiences.

The role of the toddler teacher is a dynamic and varied one. She or he is a planner, a facilitator, an instructor, a friend, a source of ideas for play, the director of play, and the timekeeper. The teacher helps friends stay close and work out difficulties and gives toddlers ideas of how to play together with friends. And, because toddlers are still developing expressive language skills, teachers plan experiences that support reciprocal communication and receptive and expressive language acquisition, and they work on expanding vocabulary and using language to make needs and wants known.

Make the following part of toddlers' language and cognitive experiences every day:

- ☐ Make and keep eye contact with toddlers as they play. As they make the transition from having an adult physically present to having her or him visually present, toddlers need reminders that you are still available to help if needed.
- ☐ Narrate routines as you implement them. This gives toddlers ideas about what is going to happen and serves as a reminder that the next steps are familiar and predictable.
- ☐ Converse with toddlers, labeling objects, pointing out actions, and describing actions and reactions.
- ☐ Ask simple, open-ended questions that require a real response. Avoid questions that have only one right answer or only one-word answers.
- ☐ Wait for responses to questions. Resist the tendency to answer your own questions.
- ☐ Look at objects and label them, particularly new objects in the environment.
- ☐ Sing to toddlers, dance with toddlers, and use fingerplays as routine, stimulation, and transition activities.
- ☐ Stimulate vocabulary by expanding sentences used by toddlers. Simply restate their sentences with additional words that expand the sentence complexity.
- ☐ Interpret nonverbal cues and give them word descriptions.
- ☐ Respond to toddlers' actions, particularly when they are too excited, frustrated, or angry to find the words themselves.
- ☐ Ask toddlers to show you, take you to, or point to objects of interest, particularly if you don't understand what they need or want.
- ☐ Play "what if" games.
- ☐ Support emerging concentration skills by not interrupting toddlers when they are playing (working).
- ☐ Time interruptions to avoid distracting toddlers from interesting tasks, particularly if they are favorite ones.

INNOVATIONS IN TEACHING

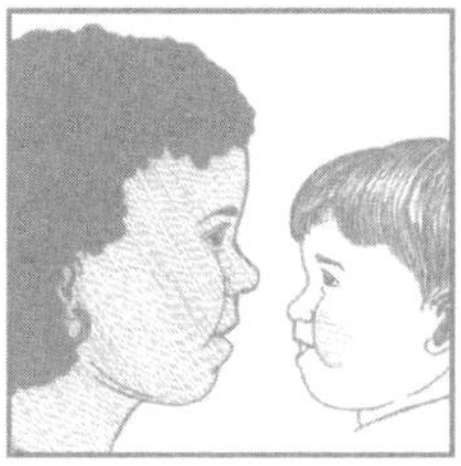

What Does Brain-Based Care and Early Education Look Like in the Classroom?

Brain-based curricula looks like developmentally appropriate curricula. It supports teachers in spending time with children to develop close connections. Children's brains work best in the context of healthy relationships. Warm, consistent, responsive care and interactions make brain growth and development emerge as nature planned. So the time teachers spend really connecting to children, increasing their understanding of nonverbal cues, observing toddlers' play, and caring for them and cuddling them is curricula for growing toddler brains.

Using warm, responsive touch to stimulate, strengthen, and reinforce neural connections is an important teaching skill in brain-based classrooms. Rough, insensitive touch, however infrequent, puts children at risk for shutting down the emotional connections that are forming between adults and children. This is particularly important when toddlers take more risks exploring the environment by climbing, reaching, and exploring every nook and cranny. When adults view risk-taking as a dangerous activity that should be stopped, the tone of their voices as well as gestures and physical constraint may convey messages that interrupt rather than encourage safe exploration of new experiences.

Toddlers are highly motivated to explore and discover their ever-widening world. A toddler's world is in the details. Toddlers see and explore minute details that interest them and are able to use a large variety of physical points of view to do so. Brain-based classrooms understand this interest and create environments that are safe to explore from different points of view. Further, exploration is viewed as important and desirable—not an activity to be curtailed or stopped. This doesn't mean that there are no rules for safety or reasonable behavior. It means that the rules and the way the teacher implements the rules are consistent with understanding exploration as a positive stimulation activity, not a negative one.

Talking to and with children is crucial to the future development of language—both the primary language of the family and the secondary language of the community or society. Starting at birth with gazing at each other, adults and children begin the communication process and tell each other that messages are being sent and received. Then, using language with children—functionally—to get needs met and understand the world around them is important. Expanding vocabularies help toddlers succeed in their interactions with peers, widening the social world in the process. Finally, the ability to initiate and interact with less support from facilitative adults launches toddlers into the world of language competency.

Stimulation that matches the child's interest and ability without overwhelming or over-stimulating is another part of brain-based curricula. This goodness of fit refers to the match between the child's individuality and the actions, interactions, and facilitation of teachers. Individualizing these interactions—making sure there is a match between the child's interest and the teacher's goals and plans—is crucial to brain development. Without this match, there is the risk of interrupting or negating the brain development under way.

Toddler teachers face the continuing challenge of helping parents see what children are learning and resisting the tendency to "push down" preschool learning into the toddler classroom. There are many supports for doing so in this curriculum. The first is the observation and assessment process. When teachers are good observers and can chart and track development, parents will see the learning that is taking place. The second is the curriculum planning process, which includes the curriculum plan, the curriculum web, and the concepts learned. All help parents see that your teaching is planned, purposeful, and designed to foster real skill acquisition and growth. The third is the Parent Postcards. Postcards make parents partners in the learning process and connect them to the breadth of knowledge teachers have about care and early education.

Teachers of toddlers (and their parents for that matter) need incredible patience during this time. Some of the most difficult and challenging behaviors children have are present during this period. Biting, toilet learning, tantrums, oppositional behavior, and the stretch for independence all create conflicts between children and the adults in their lives. In addition, giant steps forward in development are usually preceded by giant steps backward where toddlers lose skills that were easy just a few days few days before. This normal disequilibria or disintegration requires patience and understanding so it will be followed by reorganization and growth.

Techniques for Stimulating Developmental Growth

Language Stimulation Techniques to Use with Toddlers

The field of speech and language development offers several indirect language-stimulation techniques that toddler teachers will find extremely useful. These techniques, called description, parallel talk, self-talk, expansion, and expansion plus, direct the teacher's language behaviors and encourage the continuation of language development.

Description—Description is a technique in which the teacher narrates or describes what is going on in the child's world by putting word labels on things. For example, if a child looks toward the door as a parent enters the room, the adult might say, "That's Jenny's mother. She must be here to pick up Jenny." Description is also helpful in communicating mutual respect. Mutual respect advocates telling children what will happen to them before it happens and waiting for the child to indicate that he is ready (Gerber, 1979). A teacher might say, "In five minutes, it will be time to wash hands, so we can eat lunch…" as a description of what will happen to the child and when it will happen. Then, a respectful toddler teacher waits before continuing, so the child can finish what he is doing and indicate he is ready. The teacher then describes each step as it occurs, "Up go your sleeves. Now put your hands under the water. Here's the soap, so you can scrub the front, back, and in between. Now rinse your hands and dry them."

- ***Parallel Talk***—Parallel talk is a short phrase that focuses on the child's action. Parallel talk usually begins with "you." For example, "You're playing with the cars and the trucks," is parallel talk. Other examples might be, "You're putting the Duplos in the bucket," "You've got the baby doll," or "You pulled off your shoe." Focusing on the action helps the child put word labels on behavior, and more importantly, connect the word labels into a sentence describing the action.
- ***Self-Talk***—Self-talk focuses on adult behavior, labeling and describing what the adult is doing. Teachers who use self-talk usually start their utterances with "I." For example, a teacher might say to a child who is getting fussy, "I'll help you put these toys back on the shelf," or "I think it is time to take a nap." Self-talk is particularly helpful in preparing toddlers for transitions. When teachers announce and remind toddlers about transitions with self-talk, they are preparing children for the transition, a very important guidance technique. To use self-talk this way, say things such as, "I think it is almost time to put up the blocks," or, "In ten more minutes, I will get the mats down to get ready for naptime," or "In five more minutes I'll be ready for you to park the riding toys to go inside."
- ***Expansion and Expansion Plus***—Expansion and expansion plus are extremely useful techniques to use with children when their vocabularies begin to grow. These techniques take what the child says and expands on it (expansion) or adds to what the child says (expansion plus). For example, when a child says, "cracker," the teacher might say, "You want another cracker," or "Jason needs another cracker, please," to expand what the child says into a complete sentence. If the child says, "Outside," the teacher might say, "You'd like to go outside." For expansion plus, the teacher adds a little more to the sentence a child uses. An example might expand, "Go bye-bye," uttered by the child, to "It's time to get your things and go bye-bye." Expansion and expansion plus restate what the child says in complete and sometimes expanded sentence form.

Notice that these techniques require nothing of the child. The child is not asked to repeat the larger sentence, to repeat the label of an object identified by description, or to respond further to the teacher. These techniques are teaching techniques that add information to the child's language skills and foster language development. The techniques are not designed to be used as drills or exercises for very young children.

Building Vocabulary

During toddlerhood, children's expressive vocabulary increases from about 200-400 words to more than 2,000. Adults who help children learn new vocabulary fuel this growth. Teachers help children develop vocabulary when they use the following techniques:

- Provide word labels for things in the environment, increasing the sophistication of the labels as children age. For example, when you are on a walk with your toddlers, start by pointing out birds (or clouds, or trees, and so on). Then, add descriptive characteristics as you label the birds. "That's a blue bird; that one is called a mockingbird; that one's a crow."
- Use pictures to enhance and expand vocabulary. Continuing with the bird example, post pictures from your picture file of different species of birds along with their written names so that you can point out and use expanded vocabulary words. Exposing children to words, whether they use them expressively or not is a great literacy activity.

- Play word games with toddlers. Toddlers love to be silly with language—playing nonsense games with words. Encourage and expand on this interest by enjoying word games, too. Change the initial letter of a child's name (Baitlin instead of Caitlin or Mavid instead of David). Or, use sequential initial sounds such as Aitlin, Baitlin, Caitlin, Daitlin, Eitlin, Faitlin, Gaitlin, and so on, to explore initial sounds.
- Add vocabulary words to your Possibilities Plan to focus your attention on new words and to remind parents that you have identified new words for vocabulary development.

Supporting Linguistic and Cultural Diversity

English is not the primary language of a growing population of children who are in school settings (Tabors, 1998). This creates the need for increased understanding of linguistic and cultural diversity, and the strategies for supporting emerging oral language and literacy skills while accepting and validating cultural diversity.

Young children are capable of learning more than one language at a time—particularly if the adults in their lives support the process of language learning. Children learn language by having caring, responsive adults use language with them long before they begin to use language themselves. Further, there are components of language that are not specific to the language spoken. For example, nonverbal communication emerges in young children before verbal communication. Facial expressions, crying, whimpering, wiggling, running away or toward something or someone all communicate without words.

Children whose primary language is not English need support bridging the two language worlds. They need validation of their home language and time to begin the process of acquiring receptive and expressive language skills in two (or more) languages at the same time. Try some of the following suggestions to support families and children for whom English is not the primary language.

- Collaborate with parents to support the home language. Ask parents to help you learn a few words of the child's home language, particularly needs-meeting words such as "more," "mother," "daddy," the words used to express hunger, sleepiness, and fear. Specifically, learn to say "hello" and "goodbye" and how to communicate changes in routine in the child's home language.
- Use both English and the child's home language when you use these familiar words. Use the home language first and then repeat the word in English. This helps children begin to understand that the two languages they are hearing are different.
- Ask parents to help you translate fingerplays and rhymes into the home language, and to provide fingerplays and rhymes from the home language for you to use in the classroom. Encourage them to tape record lullabies, songs, and other oral language traditions in the home language for you to use at school.
- Expand your children's book collection to include some books in the home language of children in your group.
- Maintaining eye contact and physical proximity during transitions so that you can provide nonverbal cues as well as verbal ones to toddlers whose home language is not English.
- Create predictable routines—particularly those cued by oral language. For example, if you sing the clean-up song when it is time to clean up and go outside, non-English-speaking children can pick up on other cues besides the words, in this case, the tune. Think about transitions and try to support them with other cues besides language.

Stimulating Cognitive Development Using Multiple Intelligences

Gardner's theory of multiple intelligences proposes that children have several kinds of intelligence that operate at the same time in complementary ways (Gardner, 1983). But, many of the intelligences, such as logical-mathematical and spatial intelligence, seem to apply to older children, not to toddlers. Can we apply these ideas to younger children?

Gardner's Multiple Intelligence

Intelligence	Description
Linguistic	Sensitivity to the meaning and order of words
Logico-mathematical	Ability to handle chains of reasoning and recognize patterns and order
Musical	Sensitivity to pitch, melody, rhythm, and tone
Bodily-kinesthetic	Ability to use the body skillfully and handle objects adroitly
Spatial	Ability to perceive the world accurately and to recreate or transform aspects of that world
Naturalist	Ability to recognize and classify the numerous species of an environment
Interpersonal	Ability to understand people and relationships
Intrapersonal (also called emotional intelligence by Goleman)	Access to one's emotional life as a means to understand oneself and others.

Gardner's ideas are that children have lots of different types of intelligence, not just one or two. Some children have lots of musical intelligence while others have lots of logical or mathematical intelligence. Theorists and researchers who think children have multiple intelligences believe that there are many ways for children to learn and for teachers to teach.

All of the multiple intelligences begin at birth. Early indicators of different intelligences can be seen in toddlers in many ways. Some toddlers are watchers—they like to watch other toddlers try new things. Others are doers—they have to be in the middle of any experience, embracing it all. Still others listen carefully to what goes on around them before they begin to interact. These differences emerge from the individual's unique collection of intelligences and are part of what makes each of us different from one another.

One type of intelligence—intrapersonal—is a crucial type of intelligence to support during the early years. Also called emotional intelligence, this intelligence includes self-awareness, managing emotions, emotional self-control, recognizing emotions in others, and handling relationships (Goleman, 1998). Goleman believes that every interaction between infants and their parents and teachers carries emotional messages that can influence emotional intelligence. If messages are positive and responsive, infants learn that the world is a supportive and caring place. If children receive curt, insensitive responses, or worse, abusive or cruel responses, these emotional encounters will negatively mold children's views of relationships. Both of these experiences affect functioning in all realms of life, for better or worse.

The theory of multiple intelligences offers teachers of toddlers a wonderful framework for interacting with and teaching toddlers. It is very freeing for teachers to know that it is appropriate and acceptable to treat children differently—when the treatment matches the child's learning style.

Gardner's theory also proposes that interaction is cumulative—every one matters. Our actions, reactions, plans, and schedules tell children as much about how we feel about them as anything else. When all of these components support the child's emerging development, children feel valued, recognized for their individual differences and characteristics, and ready to learn and grow.

This theory validates what every toddler teacher knows—every child is unique. Such ideas help us understand individual children better and modify our programs to fit each child rather than requiring children to fit into our programs. Further, the theory of multiple intelligences helps us support parents in viewing their child's unique skills rather than comparing their child to other children—a wonderful way to guarantee that cumulative interactions of important caregivers positively affect children's potential.

Simplifying Piaget

Alice Honig, a noted early childhood specialist, simplifies Piaget's theories by synthesizing the learning tasks of childhood into 12 categories (Honig, 1982). Toddler teachers will find that they already spend an enormous amount of time exposing toddlers to these learning tasks. Each should be incorporated in planned interactions with children throughout the day.

1. Learning to make groups
2. Learning to separate parts from the big group
3. Learning to line up objects in a logical order
4. Learning time relationships
5. Learning about places and how space is organized
6. Learning what numbers mean
7. Learning to recognize change
8. Learning to use body parts together
9. Learning to reason
10. Learning to use imagination
11. Learning language and using books
12. Learning social skills

Understanding these learning tasks of the first three years allows teachers to capitalize on emerging skills by developing appropriate curriculum plans. Each of these tasks offers numerous opportunities to enhance the intellectual development of very young children.

Supporting Emerging Literacy

Developing Reading, Writing, and Spelling Skills

What teachers do in their classrooms with toddlers is so important in supporting emerging literacy. Try some of the following strategies in your classroom.

- Label your classroom with pictures and words. Both are important. Toddlers can usually read pictures easily, and connecting the picture to the word emphasizes the pattern of the word as well as its letter components. Don't go overboard. Label the important things, starting with 6-8 word/picture labels and building up to 12-15 over time.
- Label storage containers with pictures of what goes inside them. Label cubbies with pictures and names. Label coat hooks with pictures and names. And don't forget to label routinely used items such as the bleach water squirt bottle (always stored safely out of reach) or the bathroom door.

- Develop patterning skills by coding shelves with where to put things, particularly the wooden blocks in your classroom. Returning blocks to the shelves following a pattern is an excellent literacy experience as well as an appropriate mathematical experience.

- Make and use signs in your classroom. When you leave your classroom to go to the playground, put up a simple sign on the door that says so. When you close an area of the classroom, put a closed sign on it to cue children that the time to play in that area is over. When a child finds something special on the playground or on a nature walk, post a sign that tells everyone about the discovery.
- Fill your classroom with real reading materials—cookbooks, newspapers, magazines, instruction manuals for toys and materials, junk mail advertisements, and so on. These are functional reading materials, not ones just for children. They will enjoy the novelty and perfect page-turning skills in the process. And, they will see that reading materials are functional—useful for getting needed information.
- Read to children. Read to individual children, to children in small groups of three or four, and occasionally, to the whole group. Frequent book reading should be a mainstay of the toddler classroom.
- Add books and writing materials to every area of the classroom. When you consider adding or changing an area of the classroom, also consider what kinds of reading and writing materials will go along with the change. (See prop boxes for examples of how to add books, written materials, and writing materials.)
- Use narration to connect initial sounds to their word labels.
- Write down children's ideas, words, and stories. When ideas, words, and stories are written down, they take on a special meaning for children (Cooper, 1993; Paley, 1991). Toddlers can learn to dictate the words they want you to add to their work. Offer to do so often. Make your offer open-ended. "Would you like to put some words on your work?" or, "Would you like for me to put some word labels on your work?" or, "Would you like to tell me some words to write down?"
- Connect functional writing to toddlers' behavior. For example, when a child does (or doesn't) like something at snack or lunch, tell him that you will let his parents know his preference and go write it on the Communication Sheet. Later, you might ask the child if he would like to write the note to Mom or Dad to let them know about a preference or an idea the child had at school. If he says "yes," provide a piece of clean

paper and a marker or crayon for him to do so. Then, make sure you tell the parent about the importance of the written note by including additional information on the Communication Sheet. Or, if a toddler wants the toy another child is using, help him write a note to the child to remind him who to give the toy to when he is finished. Put the note near the child and tell him what it says. If the child forgets, point to the note and read it to him.

- Explore initial sounds—the beginning of names, the beginning sounds of words, and the beginning sounds of toys, objects, and materials. Notice the word exploration. Drills and direct instruction about initial sounds are still inappropriate, but songs, chants, poems, fingerplays, and action rhymes are excellent ways to explore initial sounds. For example, when you call a toddler by name, say, "Rodney, it's your turn to paint with the red paint. 'Red,' 'Rodney,' those words start with the same sound." Or, "Caitlin has carrots for lunch. Caitlin and carrots start with the sound "/k/." Or, "Thomas is reading Thomas the Tank book. The name of the book and the name of the boy are the same!" Or, use fingerplays, rhymes, and songs to reinforce the connection between sounds. "I'm Bringing Home a Baby Bumblebee" (see page 575 in the Appendix), for example, is a great song for practicing the initial sound /b/.

This exploration is teacher's work—not children's work. Teachers point out the obvious connections between sounds and letters as they use them in daily experiences. Repeated experiences with adults connecting letters and sounds facilitate phonemic awareness in toddlers that will prepare them for individual letter/sound association when they are older.

Books for Toddlers

By the age of 18 months, most toddlers are already in love with books. If parents and teachers have read to children every day, toddlers have already learned that print goes from left to right and from top to bottom, and that books are read right side up. They have learned how to turn pages and that the book goes from the front to back. And they have begun to understand that the meaning of the story is in the print as well as in the illustrations. Now they are ready for more complex stories and stories with more complex ideas.

Toddlers need books with a great deal of complexity—more pictures on the page, more details in the pictures, and more interesting story lines. They are ready to be read to in small groups as well as one on one. And, they are ready to "read" to themselves.

Try some of the following ideas for reading to toddlers:

- When you introduce a new book, don't read it. Explore it first. Name the author and the illustrator, point to pictures on the pages, and name characters. Talk about the pictures. Reading pictures is an important pre-reading skill that toddlers perfect before age three.
- Then read the book from beginning to end. Put life into your reading. Vary your voice tone. Give voices to different pictures and characters. Have fun! You may need to abbreviate the text the first few times you read a new book. Keep it simple and move quickly to keep children's interest.
- Move your finger across the page to show that reading is taking place. This helps children learn left-to-right progression—a key pre-reading skill.
- Point out familiar things first. Eyes, animals, mother, daddy, baby, car, and so on that are familiar to children's experience will keep their attention. Then, gradually add unfamiliar pictures and words as you re-read the book.
- Don't stay on one page too long. Four seconds to six seconds is about long enough for the first time with a book. For now, limit your reading to one page at a time. But over time, start to connect one page with the next, so children will see the relationship between characters or objects on subsequent pages.
- Start with books that can be used for different purposes. For example, if an alphabet book has animals (such as bears or tigers) that are associated with letters, use the book to explore the different sounds animals make, as well as reading the book to associate the letter with the animal.
- Let toddlers determine the pace. When you read to toddlers in small groups of three or four, they will tell you if your pace is on target. And, if they ask for another book when you finish the first one, your job has been well done.

Early Identification of Developmental Challenges

Teachers have many opportunities to observe children as they grow and learn. Occasionally, these observations cause teachers to have questions concerning how children are developing. When you notice that a child is outside of the age range for accomplishing a task or skill on the observation/assessment instrument, remember that differences in development are normal. For example, if a toddler is 25 months old and does not display the tasks or skills on the 18-24-month section, continue careful observations and data collection. You are probably observing the differences in the individual pace of development. If this trend continues and the toddler is still not demonstrating tasks and skills within his chronological age range, talk to the child's parents about your observations. You might want to suggest that the parents discuss what you have observed first with their pediatrician and then (if needed) with a developmental specialist such as a developmental psychologist or a specialist such as a speech pathologist, a physical therapist, or an occupational therapist.

Children who are six months or more behind their chronological age need to be evaluated further to determine if the delay you are observing is related to maturational factors or a developmental delay. Early identification of developmental delays is an important role for teachers. They are not diagnosticians, but they are excellent observers. Often intervention can completely remediate problems that are discovered early. Your careful observations can support parents in making sure that their child's needs are met.

Teacher Competencies to Support Toddlers Communicating with Parents, Teachers, and Friends

Sometimes	Usually	Always	
☐	☐	☐	States directions in positive terms.
☐	☐	☐	Communicates effectively with children and adults.
☐	☐	☐	Speaks in simple, understandable terms.
☐	☐	☐	Understands how to use voice as a teaching tool.
☐	☐	☐	Uses nonverbal techniques to communicate desired behavior.
☐	☐	☐	Uses existing materials and equipment effectively.
☐	☐	☐	Devises new materials to stimulate and challenge children.
☐	☐	☐	Rotates and adapts materials to insure children's interest.
☐	☐	☐	Encourages language by expanding sentences used by toddlers.
☐	☐	☐	Narrates routines throughout the day.
☐	☐	☐	Makes and keeps eye contact with toddlers.
☐	☐	☐	Talks with toddlers, labeling objects, pointing out actions, and describing actions and reactions.
☐	☐	☐	Waits for responses to questions.
☐	☐	☐	Asks simple, open-ended questions that require a real response.

Resources for Teachers

Bodrova, E. & D.J. Leong. (1995). ***Tools of the mind: The Vygotskyian approach to early childhood education***. New York: Prentice Hall.

Carter, Margie. (2000). Literacy Development: Back to the Real Basics, ***Child Care Information Exchange***, 14-17.

Cooper, P. (1993). ***When stories come to school: Telling, writing, and performing stories in the early childhood classroom***. New York: Teachers & Writers.

Goleman, D. (1998). ***Emotional intelligence***. New York: Bantam Doubleday Dell.

Honig, A., & H.E. Brody. (1996). ***Talking with your baby: Family as the first school***. Syracuse, NY: Syracuse University Press.

Neuman, S., C. Copple & S. Bredekamp. (2000). ***Learning to Read and Write: Developmentally Appropriate Practices for Young Children***. Washington, DC: National Association for the Education of Young Children (NAEYC).

Okagaki, L. & K.E. Diamond. (2000). Responding to cultural and linguistic differences in the beliefs and practices of families with young children. ***Young Children***, 55 (1) 74-80.

Piaget, J. (1977). ***The origins of intelligence in children***. New York: International Universities Press.

Responding to Linguistic and Cultural Diversity. (1996). Washington, DC: National Association for the Education of Young Children (NAEYC).

Rockwell, R., D. Hoge & B. Searcy. (1999). ***Linking language and literacy: Simple language and literacy throughout the curriculum***. Beltsville, MD: Gryphon House.

Schiller, P. (1999). ***Start smart: Building brain power in the early years***. Beltsville, MD: Gryphon House.

Shore, R. (1997). ***Rethinking the brain: New insights into early development.*** New York: Families and Work Institute.

Silsberg, J. (2000). ***125 Brain games for toddlers and twos***. Beltsville, MD: Gryphon House.

INNOVATIONS IN PARENT PARTNERSHIPS

School- or Teacher-initiated Activities

Picture Necklaces

Make picture necklaces for parents to use during their time at school, especially during meetings. Take a photograph and mount it on a cardboard circle. Cover with clear contact paper or laminate it. Punch a hole above the photo and string on a length of yarn. Write the parent's name above the photo and the child's name below the photo.

Parents' Voices

Toddlers love to hear their parents' voices during the day. Provide a cassette tape and recorder. Ask parents to record messages to their toddlers to be played during the day in the library or listening area.

Toy Phones

Ask parents to loan their children's toy phones, so toddlers can practice communicating. Also, ask parents to provide pictures of their child's grandparents, friends, and parents, so you can laminate them and keep them near the toy phones.

Parent Participation Activities

Tea Time to Talk

Invite parents in for tea time. Provide coffee or sodas. Use the visit as a time to talk about the importance of the Daily Communication Sheets (see page 537 in the Appendix). Make parents aware of how you use the information and how you depend on them to let you know how their child is doing.

Parent Postcards

Share Parent Postcards as parents indicate an interest, at appropriate times during the enrollment cycle, or as developmental issues arise. (See page 548 in the Appendix for a sample dissemination schedule.) Copy Postcards. Cut if necessary. Address to parent(s) and place on Communication Sheet or hand out personally.

What Is Developmentally Appropriate Care and Early Education for Toddlers?—The Role of the Teacher

Developmentally appropriate practice (DAP) is educational jargon referring to a particular approach to care and early education that has found wide acceptance in the United States. Noted early childhood specialists say DAP is the way to go. But, what is DAP for toddlers and how does it apply to your child? To answer this question, let's take a look at what developmentally appropriate care and early education for toddlers look like and how it might be different from teaching practices in programs for older children.

The role of the teacher is viewed in a special way in developmentally appropriate toddler programs. The teacher's job is to support the development of relationships between parents and their child, between the school and home, and between the teacher and the child. These mutually beneficial relationships begin with the teacher's intimate knowledge about the child, his or her family, and the child's experience at school. When teachers have these important relationships with families, they are able to modify the child's daily experiences to match the child's individual developmental needs. This congruence between what a child needs and what the program provides is the foundation of developmentally appropriate practice.

Another important role of the teacher is that of a decision-maker. Teachers make decisions constantly as they care for young children. Does the child need more challenging stimulation, less complex stimulation, a particular kind of stimulation, to be left alone to discover how something works, or be shown how it works? Each of these situations requires a different response and leads the teacher to act differently. If the toddler needs more challenging stimulation, the teacher can increase complexity by adding a more complex toy or material. If the child is frustrated, the teacher may simplify the activity to insure success. This dynamic decision-making process requires that teachers draw upon their knowledge of your child, of child development, of best care and education practices, and of the family's cultural and social expectations for the child.

TO

What Is Developmentally Appropriate Care and Early Education for Toddlers?—The Role of the Teacher (coninued)

A toddler teacher's role often looks different from the role of teachers of older children. Direct instruction—the teacher telling the child information that is important—is less prevalent. When observed over time, the role of the teacher looks much more like a dance—approaching the child who needs attention, observing children who are busy and involved with objects or activities to see how the children respond, helping children be close together in groups, intervening when children get too close, helping a child learn a discreet task (such as putting a puzzle together), and so on. The dance is sometimes fast and hectic, sometimes slow and soothing.

Teachers have another important role in toddler programs. That role is assessment of learning and development. In order to know which role to play, which activity to do, which toy to offer, which child to approach, which child to leave alone with a discovery, teachers are constantly assessing children' s learning and using that information to inform their teaching practice.

TO

What Is Developmentally Appropriate Care and Early Education for Toddlers?—The Role of Curriculum (Activities and Experiences)

The content of curriculum for toddlers is not the same as content for older children. During the first three years of life, children learn in a variety of ways. They learn by interacting with and acting on their environment—touching, tasting, smelling, feeling, manipulating, and seeing the world around them. This interaction with people and things forms the core of curriculum for very young children.

Although good early childhood settings may look similar to one another, part of curriculum is preparing the environment to have pleasing, stimulating, and interesting objects in it. What is available, what gets added or taken away, what is new, and what is familiar are all important parts of curriculum for toddlers. Adults plan experiences that will be fun to do alone, with a caring adult, or with a friend or two.

This curriculum is less didactic, or teacher-directed, than it is in the preschool classroom. Teachers of toddlers do direct instruction with children all the time, but not with a group. Direct instruction is usually at the child's initiation or request and usually with only a few other interested children. The direct instruction done by toddler teachers includes reading books; playing with children; helping children play with each other and with interesting toys; counting with children; singing; repeating fingerplays and rhymes; helping children try new motor skills or perfect emerging ones; going outside with children; preparing, serving, and eating snacks and lunch; observing children; suggesting play ideas; and supporting building with and manipulating objects. This is the curriculum for toddlers.

School for toddlers looks very different from school for preschoolers or school-agers. Toddler environments tend to be messier because toddlers love to carry things from one place to another and to hold on to what they are playing with as they observe or watch others in interesting activities. Environments for toddlers are usually more consistent than environments for older children because toddlers need and want predictable parts of their interactive and physical world. And, some activities are added and removed by the teacher as she or he modifies the classroom to fit children's changing interest. This difference is not an accident—it is desirable. It reflects what we know to be the best way to approach the care and early education of children under three years of age.

TO

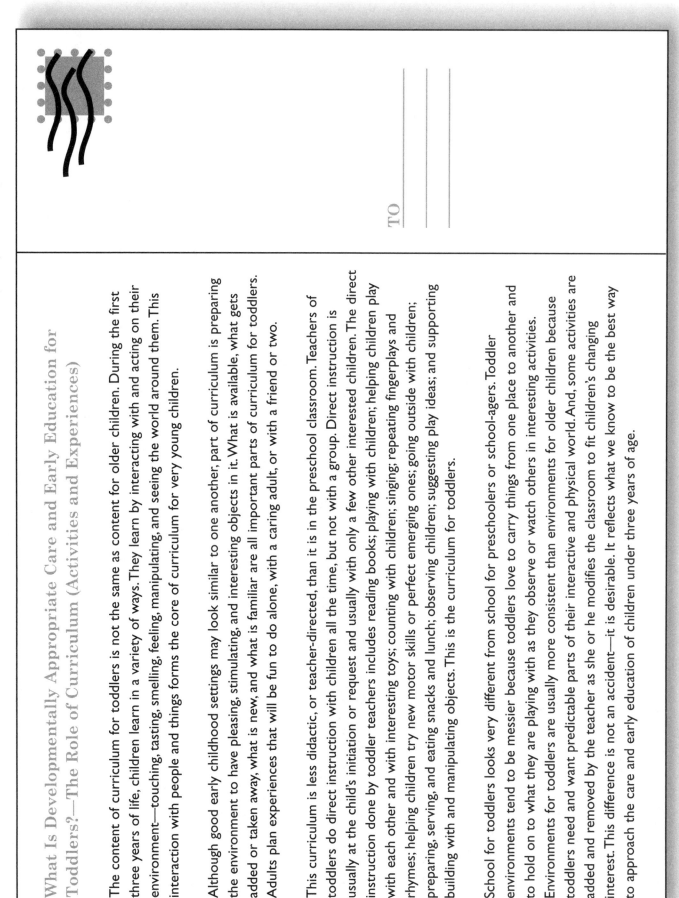

Using Found and Discarded Items for Toys

Parents want to give children what is best for them. Sometimes when we try to give a special gift, our child doesn't seem to cooperate. Instead of finding the new toy interesting, the child may find the box interesting, disappointing parents in the process!

Many items commonly found around the home are very interesting to toddlers. Pots and pans are a favorite and offer a wonderful diversion during meal preparation. Smaller ones are easier to handle and create less of a danger of pinched fingers. The shiny surfaces allow children to see their own reflections, and the noise is an added bonus.

Boxes are wonderful toys that can be used in a wide variety of ways. They can be used for stacking, carrying, nesting, filling, dumping, and matching. Large boxes make wonderful toys to climb into and out of. Very large boxes make great playhouses. Remove all staples, reinforce with tape, and eliminate all rough edges. Don't forget to add doors and windows.

Plastic bottles are another favorite. Smaller ones can be filled with glitter and water to make interesting toys. Larger bottles are great for carrying around, rolling, hitting, and knocking over. Securely glue caps onto the bottles because their small size makes them a choking hazard.

The key to using found and discarded items as toys is being open to the limitless opportunities and the imagination of a child! Think of the difference between a child having a toy phone that is always a phone and a box that can be a house, a car, a truck, a train, a step, and so on. It is the open-ended rather than closed nature of these items that makes them better than many bought toys, and a great way for your child to learn.

TO ______________

Good Books for Toddlers

Reading to young children is a great way to get them interested in books. In fact, early experiences with books help ensure that children will have successful literacy experiences later. Books are essential for the development of young children's language and literacy skills.

What kinds of books do young children need? Toddlers are still exploring things with their mouths, particularly as molars begin to emerge. Books will be explored in this same way as well. For this reason, cloth books, vinyl books, and chubby board books are all appropriate for toddlers.

Simple books are best. Books with realistic (not cartoon) illustrations are recommended. Expect children to want to read the same books over and over again. This is not a problem. Children learn from repetition (and adults get to practice patience with the repetition)!

Realize that books really are consumable. They won't last long because toddlers are still developing pre-reading skills such as page turning. Books will be mouthed, and pages will be torn. As they develop page-turning skills, books will be ruined. Still, toddlers have already learned that print goes from left to right and from top to bottom, and that books are read right side up. They are perfecting turning pages and know that the books go from the front to back. They are now ready to connect the meaning of the story to the illustrations.

When reading to your child, first read the title and the author. Then talk about what the book may be about. Read each page, pointing out things of interest in the story, as well as the illustrations. Young children have a much bigger receptive vocabulary than expressive vocabulary. They will understand far more words than they can speak. Read the book with expression. And enjoy this wonderful, close time with your child.

TO

The Amazing Toddler Brain

Everyone is talking about the brain! New imaging techniques such as PET scans are providing neurobiologists with fascinating new information about how the brain develops. This research confirms that the early years are learning years and that parents and teachers need to make them count.

Brain development is the result of a complex dance between the genetic makeup of a child, which is predetermined, and the child's experience, which is open to many possibilities. Scientists have always thought of this dance as a lifelong one. They now know that what happens to a child in the first 10 years of life has a profound impact on the way the lifelong dance proceeds.

Before a child is born, neurons or brain cells are developed. It is after birth that connections (called synapses) are developed between the neurons. From birth to about a year, millions of connections between neurons are developed—almost like making roads between towns and communities. During this stage of brain development, it is a use-it-or-lose-it time. Neurons that aren't stimulated simply don't get connected to other neurons.

After these initial connections are formed, the brain begins the process of improving the connections, or highways, between neurons and connecting smaller roads to larger ones. As this process progresses, communication and coordination among areas of the brain begin. For the next 10 or so years, well-stimulated neural pathways get bigger, stronger, and more coordinated, while under-stimulated ones are abandoned.

What makes brains strong and capable? Experience is the chief architect of the brain. Stimuli from people, places, and things provide the nutrients for healthy brain development. You have the unique responsibility of providing toddlers with most of their early experiences. What a wonderful thing to know—the way you provide early experiences to children develops their brains!

TO ______________________

Windows of Learning: Brain Development and the Young Child

While the brain has a remarkable capacity to change, the timing of experiences and stimulations that influence the change is crucial. It is during these "prime times" that the synapses (connections) and the coordination between different sections of the brain grow. After these periods, the brain's capacity to change does not disappear, but it does diminish substantially.

Prime times for learning occur throughout the early years of a child's life. Brain development occurs in "waves" with new areas of the brain responding to stimulation and experience at different times. Neurobiologists now know that windows of learning occur for emotional, visual, and motor development during the first two years. A window of learning is open between birth and age three for music and between birth and age four for thinking skills. During these windows, connections in the brain are developing at their most rapid pace and brain activity is at its greatest. Again, these areas can be stimulated throughout life, but the windows are prime times for learning.

Stimulating the emotional development of the brain comes easy for most parents. Warm, responsive, intimate relationships with primary caregivers create "construction sites" in the developing brain that buzz with activity and create synaptic connections at an amazing rate. Snuggling, holding, and loving your toddler all help develop his or her brain.

Try some of these ideas for stimulating your toddler's developing brain visually, motorically, and musically:

- Learn the fingerplays and songs that your child's teacher is using at school and teach your child your favorites from home. Shared, repeated musical and rhythmic experiences are great brain "food."
- Offer things to each of your child's hands—not only the right or the left one. This motor movement enhances connections between areas of the brain and increases coordination. It also stimulates brain connections for both sides of the brain.

TO

Windows of Learning: Brain Development and the Young Child (continued)

- March, hop, crawl, slink, creep, strut, or wiggle to get from here to there. It will be more fun and will send all kinds of stimulation messages to the developing brain.
- Read stories to your child, visually tracking the words and pointing out the pictures. Both stimulate visual acuity and increase perception skills.
- Give your child choices. Emotional health for toddlers comes from positive experiences with control and autonomy. Let them have it!

Windows of learning come and go—a part of the natural cycle of growing and developing. Don't miss the opportunity to create connections and enjoy quality interactions with your child while the windows of learning are present.

TO

How Toddlers Learn

There is a real tendency in our society to push early education down into younger years—a pressure felt by both parents and teachers. But, toddlers are not yet ready to be preschoolers. Wonderful plans for emerging development in all areas are already in place. Children are best prepared for future success by fully experiencing and growing through this stage without being hurried or pressured to perform or learn about how they will be in the next stage.

When comparisons are made, toddlers are actually much more like infants than preschoolers. Their body shapes are still disproportionate; their emotional development is experiencing a profound change as individuation creates an emerging sense of self as separate from parents and other adults; language acquisition continues to be quite rapid; and physical development is changing just as fast as body size and proportion and coordination increase.

Toddlers are learning through their senses (touching, tasting, listening, seeing, doing, manipulating). This is a period of rapid growth characterized by excitement, frustration, confusion, and wonderful feelings of accomplishment for both toddlers and their teachers. Every toddler parent knows that this is a "let me do it," not a "make me do it" time. Toddlers resist adult efforts to guide, support, and help, even though they may not be able to accomplish the tasks they are trying. It is through exploration, trial and error, and practice that toddlers perfect emerging skills.

The experiences toddlers have with books and rhymes prepare the way for learning to read. The experiences toddlers have with sorting, patterning, and grouping prepare the way for learning to add, subtract, and understand mathematics. And, the experiences toddlers have with their parents, teachers, and friends prepare them to establish and maintain relationships that will nurture future developmental growth. These are "real" learning experiences for toddlers—ones that will count now and in years to come.

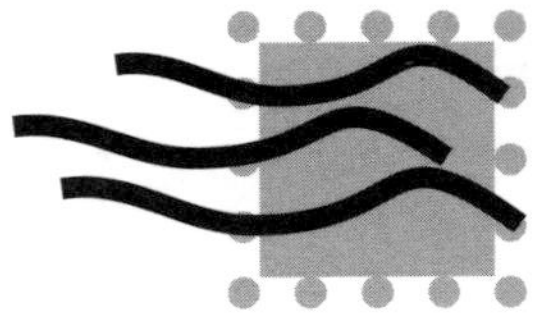

TO

Resources for Parents

Add these helpful books to your parent library or post this list on your parent bulletin board.

Herr, J. & T. Swim. (1999). ***Creative resources for infants and toddlers***. Albany, NY: Delmar.

Miller, K. (1984). ***More things to do with toddlers and twos***. West Palm Beach, FL: Telshare.

Miller, K. (1984). ***Things to do with toddlers and twos***. West Palm Beach, FL: Telshare.

Miller, K. (1999). ***Simple steps***. Beltsville, MD: Gryphon House.

Schiller, P. (1999). ***Smart start: Building brain power in the early years***. Beltsville, MD: Gryphon House.

Silberg, J. (2000). ***125 brain games for toddlers and twos***. Beltsville, MD: Gryphon House.

Silberg, J. (1993). ***Games to play with toddlers***. Beltsville, MD: Gryphon House.

Silberg, J. (1993). ***Games to play with two year olds***. Beltsville, MD: Gryphon House.

Silberg, J. (1996). ***More games to play with toddlers***. Beltsville, MD: Gryphon House.

INNOVATIONS IN ENVIRONMENTS

Creating a Classroom that Values Multiple Intelligences

What does a classroom that understands multiple intelligences look like? Toddler classrooms are characterized by individual, intimate interactions between teachers and children. Children are still allowed to follow their own schedules for eating, sleeping, and playing, and are not always required to follow a superimposed schedule. Classrooms that value multiple intelligences recognize that how long you persist in an activity or take to complete an activity is one of the variations in intelligences. Teachers make every attempt to embrace these variations rather than trying to eliminate them.

Teachers who understand multiple intelligences recognize that different children like different types of stimulation. For example, a toddler with highly complementary spatial and body kinesthetic intelligence might love exploring tight spaces such as the inside of boxes, underneath tables, and behind furniture. One who has complementary spatial and logico-mathematical intelligence might prefer to manipulate items in an open space.

These examples illustrate the individual nature and variety of multiple intelligences.

Literacy-rich Environments

A literacy-rich environment includes so much more than just books. It means creating an environment that connects children to the functional or useful aspects of the written word. Literacy-rich environments have some common characteristics.

The first is the inclusion of books of all kinds in the classroom, both in the library area as well as throughout the classroom. A literacy-rich toddler room has environmental print everywhere. Objects around the room have labels on them (printed in large, lowercase letters). Sentences are also visible (printed in large letters using both uppercase and lowercase where appropriate, as well as appropriate punctuation). Other elements of environmental print include signs, posters, books (of course), charts, big books, and art experiences where teachers have written descriptions of what actually happened in the classroom or the words that children asked to add to their work.

A literacy-rich environment has lots of places for toddlers to write (scribble) at a variety of angles (on low tables with chairs, on taller tables while standing, on easels, on fences outside, on the floor on big paper, and on a surface with little paper) with a variety of writing materials, including markers, crayons, paintbrushes, chalk, and pencils. These materials are readily available in paper bins, in notebooks, and on charts. Although all of these materials are rarely out at once in a toddler classroom, all are added as they are needed by teachers or when requested by children.

Open-ended materials are in literacy-rich environments. These materials help toddlers learn gross and fine motor control and prevent the pressure of getting something right the first time. Magic slates, clay, play dough, sand trays, flour pans, and fingerpaint, enable toddlers to practice in a "forgiving," open-ended environment.

Because toddlers are not accomplished at page turning or writing at this stage, many materials will be consumable in nature. Literacy-rich environments provide as many "free" or recycled materials as possible because toddlers are not good conservationists. They like lots of materials and may be satisfied with only one mark or dollop of paint on a page. Discarded phone books are excellent for writing practice, as well as page-turning practice. Magazines and catalogs show pictures with print, and are useful as concept books that children can hold and use. Junk mail shows how letters are sent and provides practice with opening, unfolding, holding, writing, and turning. Used copy paper and computer paper are useful as available paper in different areas of the room.

Literacy-rich environments include teachers who exhibit the teaching behaviors that support the development of young children's literacy. The most critical teaching behavior is reading to children each day. But teachers also discuss how letters, words, and sentences are formed; create group scribbling experiences; practice reading to small groups of interested children; show individual attention to children's language efforts; and narrate and describe things to toddlers throughout the day. From this rich environment, toddlers will learn that language has meaning when it is written down as well as when it is spoken. These experiences form a strong foundation for formal reading, writing, and spelling instruction to take place during the kindergarten and elementary years.

Activities and Experiences vs. Centers

Most early childhood educators think of interest or learning centers as an essential part of any classroom setting. Yet, environments for toddlers are different because they are groupie in nature and tend to go where the action is. For this reason, teachers must bring activities and experiences to children and assist children in going to where the activities are. A wide range of activities and experiences must be available to toddlers. In each of the following Possibilities Plans, *Big Animals* and *Little Animals*, activities and experiences are presented in the following areas:

- Dramatic Possibilities
- Sensory/Art Possibilities
- Curiosity Possibilities
- Construction Possibilities
- Literacy Possibilities
- Music Possibilities
- Movement Possibilities
- Outdoor Possibilities
- Project Possibilities
- Parent Participation Possibilities

Big Animals

WEB

Note: Using the technique of webbing, teachers can follow the leads that children given them, as well as have an unlimited source of options. Always use the webs provided as a jumping-off point. The possibilities are endless.

PLANNING PAGES

Plan Possibilities

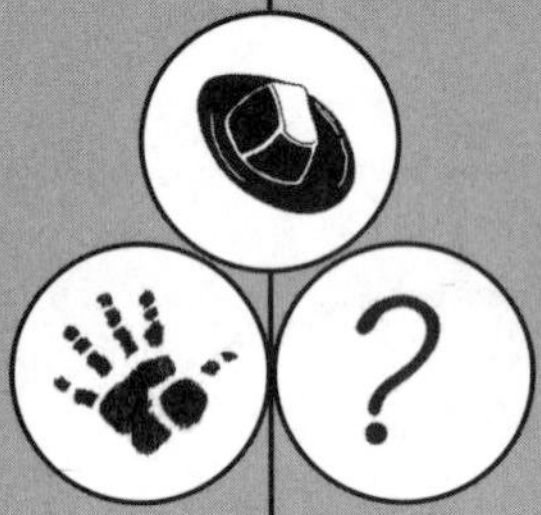

Dramatic

Big Animals 326
Cozy Cave 326
Big Feet 326

Sensory/Art

Big Animal Homes 327
Elephants and Rhinos . . . 327
Animals in the Sand 328
Sandpaper Animals 328

Curiosity

Berries for Bears 329
Big Animal Lacing 329
Animal Bottle 330
Heavy and Light 330

Construction

Plastic Animals and Fences 330
Trucks 331
Signs 331

Literacy

Elephant Rhyme. 331
Big Animals and Their Homes Chart. 332
Big Old Bear 332
Bear Puzzles 333

Music

Did You Ever See? 333
Bear Is Sleeping 334
There's an Animal 334

Movement

Walk Like the Animals . . 335
Elephant Dancing. 335
This Cow 335

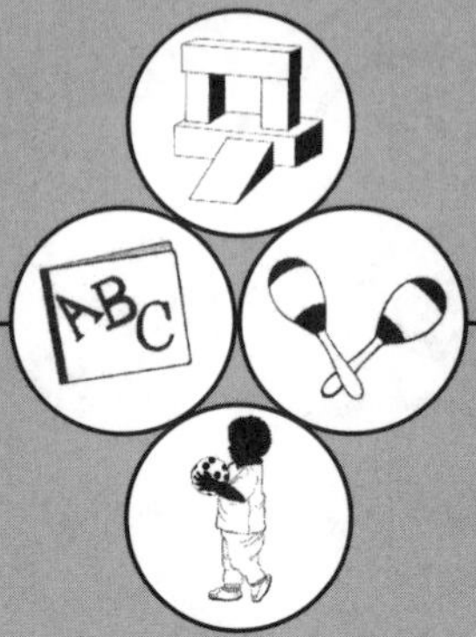

Outdoor

Bear Hunt 336
Elephant House 336
Animal Parade 336

Project

Large Elephant from Peanuts 337

Parent Participation

Story Time Props 337
Big Animal Party 338
Parent Postcards
Teaching Your Child to Read 338
Tips for Reading to Your Child 339
Teaching Your Child to Write 341

Big Animals

Books

Rhymes/ Fingerplays

Music/Songs

DRAMATIC POSSIBILITIES

Big Animals
All ages

Materials
Zoo props
Farm props

Teacher Talk
Talk about how to care for different big animals and where they live. "The horse is asleep in the barn."

Provide a variety of zoo and farm props. Observe how children use the items as they play. Include buckets and wagons for feeding animals.

Cozy Cave
All ages

Materials
Blanket
Pillows
Sheet
Toy stuffed bears

Teacher Talk
Interact with children as they play in the bear cave. "We have two children sitting in the bear cave. Where do you think bears sleep?"

Spread a blanket on the floor. Place pillows on the blanket. Drape a sheet over chairs or toy shelves to make a cave. Children enjoy crawling into a cozy place to play. Place a variety of sizes of toy stuffed bears in the area.

Big Feet
All ages

Materials
Colored poster board
Hole punch

Elastic
Gray tube socks

Teacher Talk
"I see three elephants. One, two, three."

Cut large animal-shaped feet from poster board. Punch two holes in each foot. Fasten elastic through the holes to make a loop on each foot. Slip the loops around a child's ankles with the animal foot resting on top of the child's foot. Show children how to wear the sock on an arm to make an elephant trunk. Put a variety of props in the Dramatic Possibilities area and observe what toddlers do.

SENSORY/ART POSSIBILITIES

Big Animal Homes
All ages

Materials
Large butcher paper
Variety of washable paints
Animal shapes
Sand

Teacher Talk
Talk with children about the different places animals live.

Give children opportunities to create animal environments using large pieces of butcher paper, sand, and animal shapes. Paint the jungle background with green paint; create trees using arm and hand prints. Add monkey shapes. Paint the ocean with blue paint and create an ocean collage using animal shapes. Paint the desert (savanna) using yellow paint with sand mixed in. Add zebra, elephant, and lion pictures or shapes.

Elephants and Rhinos
All ages

Materials
Gray powdered tempera paint
Thick gray tempera paint
Paintbrushes
Shaving cream

Teacher Talk
Talk about elephants and rhinos.

Provide sensory experiences to your match your discussion. Paint with thick gray paint on very large pieces of paper when you are talking about elephants. Finger paint with shaving cream sprinkled with gray powdered paint when you talk about rhinos.

Animals in the Sand

All ages

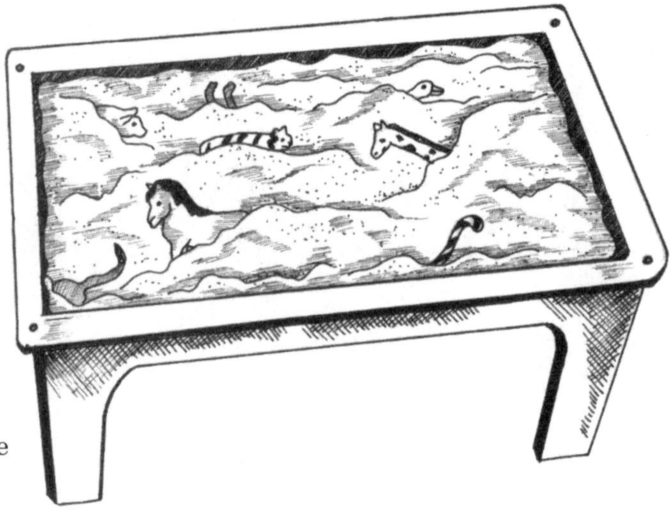

Materials

Sand box

Large plastic animals

Teacher Talk

"I hear a lion sound. Listen to Raymond roar!"

Hide large rubber or plastic animals in the sandbox. Observe children's reactions as they find the animals.

Sandpaper Animals

All ages

Materials

Sandpaper

Scissors

Colored chalk

Teacher Talk

Talk about the texture, colors, and shapes as children enjoy using chalk. "The sandpaper is rough. Look how different the camel looks."

Provide animal shapes cut from sandpaper. Model using colored chalk to color the animal shapes.

Berries for Bears

All ages

Materials

Variety of fresh berries
Small paper cups

Teacher Talk

Talk about how the berries look, taste, smell, and feel as children explore the berries. "Makela likes the strawberries best. What do you like best, Aaron?"

Provide a variety of fresh berries for children to taste

Big Animal Lacing

All ages

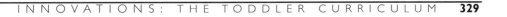

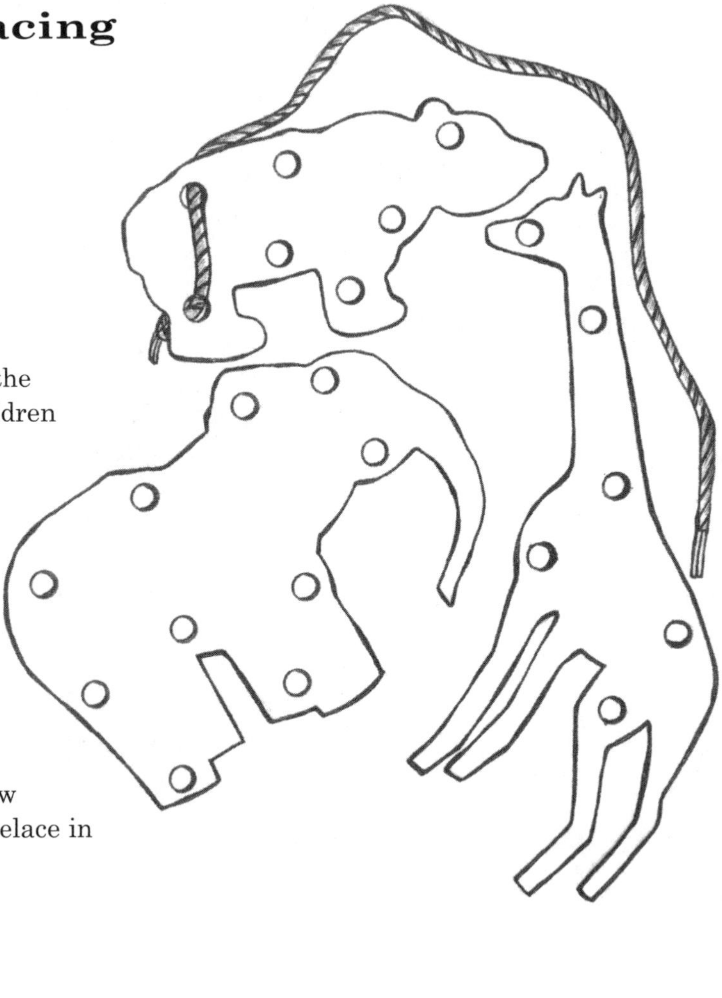

Materials

Cardboard
Craft knife (teacher only)
Hole punch
Shoelace

Teacher Talk

Talk about the shapes and the concept of in and out as children put the laces through the holes. "In goes the shoelace. Good job!"

Use a craft knife to cut bear, elephant, and giraffe shapes from cardboard. Use a hole punch to make large holes on the shapes. Attach a shoelace to each shape. Show children how to sew the shoelace in and out of the holes.

Animal Bottle

All ages

Materials

Clear plastic bottle
Sand
Small plastic animals
Glue
Tape

Teacher Talk

Name the animals and make the appropriate sounds for the animals as they are found. "What do you see, Algernon? You're right. That's a cow."

Fill a clear plastic bottle almost full of sand. Place small plastic cows, horses, bears, and/or elephants inside the bottle. Glue and tape the cap securely on the bottle. Show children how to shake or roll the bottle to see the animals.

Heavy and Light

30-36 months

Materials

Brown or white paper bags
Rice (dry)
Tape
Balance scale, optional

Teacher Talk

"Are the bags heavy? You can pick up all three, Linda!"

Fill some paper bags with a little dry rice and others with a lot of rice. Tape the openings securely closed. Explore the bags with children as they discover which ones are heavy and which ones are light. Experiment with a balance scale and the bags.

CONSTRUCTION POSSIBILITIES

Plastic Animals and Fences

All ages

Materials

Plastic animals
Plastic or teacher-made fences

Teacher Talk
Talk with the children about the animals as they play. "You put all the horses in the pen."

Add plastic animals and plastic fences to this area.

Trucks

All ages

Materials
Toy trucks of all sizes

Teacher Talk
"All the big animals are in the pen.
The little animals are in the truck."

Provide all sizes of trucks so children can move blocks and animals as they play.

Signs

All ages

Materials
Shoebox lids
Crayons
Magazines

Teacher Talk
The sign is red. The letters printed on the sign make the word animals.

Provide shoebox lids to use as signs in the construction area. Write words on the signs that children say as they play.

LITERACY POSSIBILITIES

Elephant Rhyme

All ages

Materials
Chalk
Toy elephants

Draw a spider web on the floor or sidewalk as children help. Recite the following rhyme and place toy or paper elephants on the spider web as you continue the rhyme.

One Elephant
One elephant went out to play,
Out on a spider's web one day.
He had such enormous fun,
He called for another elephant to come.

Big Animals and Their Homes Chart

All ages

Materials
Chart paper
Markers

Teacher Talk
Talk about farms, jungles, the savanna, and the ocean. "Tell me about the savanna." "Tell me about the jungle." "What do you know about the ocean?"

Make a chart named "Where Animals Live." Ask children about big animals and where they live. Write their responses on the chart. Add to the chart as children learn more and more about big animals. Remember Piaget's ideas that children learn from their mistakes. Accept answers as given from toddlers. Repeat to see if their ideas change over time.

Big Old Bear

All ages

Materials
Grocery bags
Markers
Tape

Recycle a paper grocery bag into a bear mask. Cut a large grocery bag in half. Cut a face circle in one side of the bag. Use markers to draw the shape of a bear's head with ears around the hole. Put the bags out for children to add their creative marks with markers, chalk, or paint. Watch to see if the children discover using the bags to become a bear. Repeat the following rhyme with children who wear the bear masks.

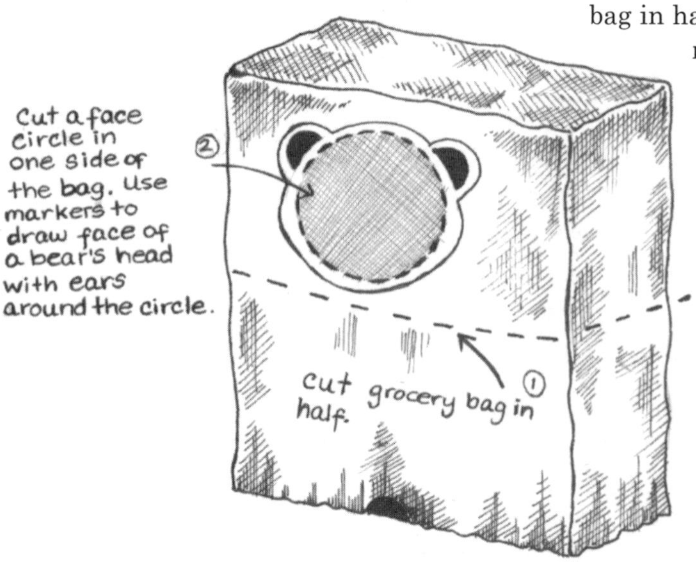

Cut a face circle in one side of the bag. Use markers to draw face of a bear's head with ears around the circle.
②
① cut grocery bag in half.

Big Old Bear
Big old bear is nice and fat.
Ready for a winter's nap.
Big old bear is fast asleep.
Safe inside her cave so deep.
Big old bear is inside her den.
When it's spring, she'll growl again!

Bear Puzzles

All ages

Materials

Poster board
Markers
Laminating or clear contact paper
Scissors

Teacher Talk

Point to the words and say the words for children. The words say, "Brown Bear."

Draw, color, and cut out large, poster board bear shapes. Write words such as "big bear," "brown bear," or "baby bear" on the bear shapes. Laminate or cover the shapes with clear contact paper. Cut the bear shapes into two or three pieces for younger children and four to six pieces for older children. Help children put the pieces together to make a bear picture.

MUSIC POSSIBILITIE

Did You Ever See?

All ages

Materials

None

Explore the movements of the song as you sing. Sing to the tune "Did You Ever See a Lassie?"

Did You Ever See?

Did you ever see an elephant, an elephant, an elephant?
Did you ever see an elephant,
Jump up and down?

Did you ever see a bear, a bear, a bear?
Did you ever see a bear,
Wiggle his nose?

(Continue with other animals.)

Bear Is Sleeping

All ages

Materials
None

Make up movements for children to do as you sing this song. Sing to the tune "Are You Sleeping?"

Bear Is Sleeping
Bear is sleeping.
Bear is sleeping.
In a cave, in a cave.
Snoring through the winter, snoring through the winter.
Snug and warm, snug and warm.

There's an Animal

All ages

Materials
Animals shapes

Children place animal shapes where the song directs. Sing to the tune "Put Your Finger in the Air."

There's an Animal
There's an animal on my head, on my head.
There's an animal on my head, on my head.
There's an animal on my head,
Oh, I wish I were in bed.
There's an animal on my head.

There's an animal on my nose, on my nose.
There's an animal on my nose, on my nose.
There's an animal on my nose,
Oh, I wish it smelled like a rose.
There's an animal on my nose.

There's an animal on my knee, on my knee.
There's an animal on my knee, on my knee.
There's an animal on my knee,
Oh, I hope it's not a bee.
There's an animal on my knee.

MOVEMENT POSSIBILITIES

____ Walk Like the Animals

All ages

Materials
None

Teacher Talk
Make the sounds the animals make as children walk.

Explore walking like a bear, elephant, or a giraffe.

____ Elephant Dancing

All ages

Materials
None

Show children how to move their arms like the elephant's trunk as you sing the following song. Sing to the tune "The Mulberry Bush."

Elephant Dancing
This is the way the elephants
dance,
The elephants dance, the
elephants dance.
This is the way the
ephants dance,
On a bright and sunny morning.

____ This Cow

All ages

Materials
None

Recite this fingerplay with children. Touch children's fingers as you say the rhyme.

This Cow
This cow eats grass.
This cow eats hay.
This cow drinks water.
This cow runs away.
This cow just moos all day.

___ Bear Hunt

All ages

Materials
Cardboard bear shapes

Teacher Talk
"You found the bear under the pillow, Jasmine. That was great!"

Hide bear shapes around the playground. Help children look for the bears. Find and hide the bears over and over with children.

___ Elephant House

All ages

Materials
Large cardboard box painted gray
Craft knife (teacher only)
Poster board
Paint
Scissors

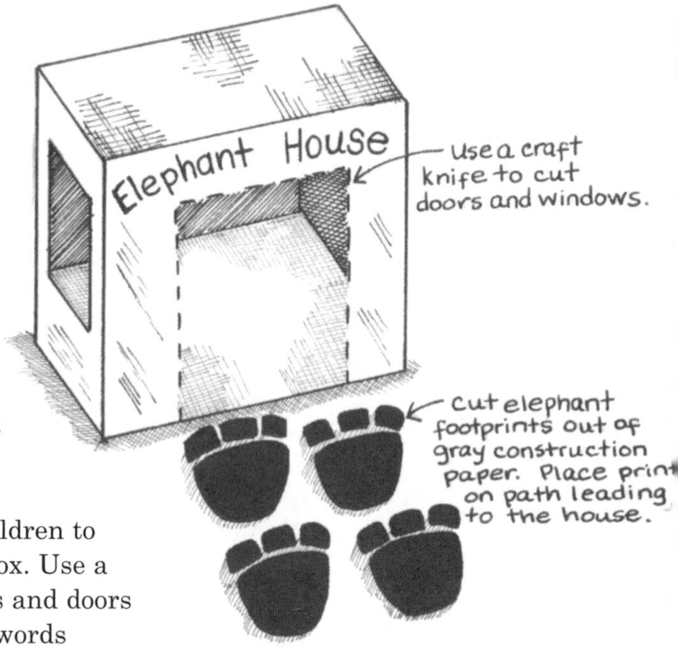
Elephant House
Use a craft knife to cut doors and windows.
Cut elephant footprints out of gray construction paper. Place prints on path leading to the house.

Teacher Talk
The sign says, "Elephant House. Look at all the elephants!"

Provide gray paint for children to paint a large cardboard box. Use a craft knife to cut windows and doors (teacher only). Write the words "Elephant House" on the box. Explore the big house where elephants live. Cut elephant footprints out of gray construction paper. Place the prints on in a path leading to the house.

___ Animal Parade

All ages

Materials
Stuffed toy animals
Music
Riding toys
Push toys

Teacher Talk

"What a big parade. Look at all the different animals!"

Put stuffed animals in shopping carts, doll strollers, or on riding toys. Play marching music and march to, from, and around the playground in a parade of animals.

PROJECT POSSIBILITIES

Large Elephant from Peanuts

All ages

Materials

Roasted peanuts
Butcher paper
Glue
Bowls

Put peanuts in the sensory table for children to manipulate. When they discover that the shells contain nuts, help them separate the shells from the peanuts. Collect the shells in a paper bag and the peanuts in a closed container. Cut a very large elephant shape from butcher paper. Provide glue for children to glue the shells onto the shape each time some peanut shells are ready. As peanuts are shelled, the elephant will get covered with peanut shells. When the elephant is completely covered with shells, it will have the rough, crinkly appearance of elephant skin.

Make peanut butter with the peanuts by processing them in a food processor or blender. (Add jelly to avoid a choke hazard.) Take photographs of peanut shelling, gluing, and making and tasting peanut butter to post by the elephant.
Note: Peanuts can be a choking hazard. Supervise closely. As with any food, check for food allergies before serving food to children.

PARENT PARTICIPATION POSSIBILITIES

Story Time Props

Ask parents to help find stuffed toy animals, puppets, and/or animal pictures to use with stories. Encourage parents to share sewing and craft-making skills to provide children with a variety of choices of props.

Big Animal Party

Invite parents to a Big Animal party. Ask parents to bring a stuffed animal to the party. Serve simple refreshments and share the peanut shell elephant. Teach parents the fingerplays you have used during this Possibilities Plan.

Parent Postcards

Parent Postcards in this section are designed to share with parents during the Possibilities Plan. The topics are natural extensions of the activities and experiences that you are planning and implementing for the toddlers in the classroom. Use the Postcards to connect parents to their children's learning.

Teaching Your Child to Read

It starts early. You want the very best for your child—the best start, the best support, the best education, and the best experiences. Sometimes it seems like parenting is a quest to figure out what to do and when to do the things that will insure that your child gets the best that you can offer.

Well, here's the good news. Teaching your child to read is a very simple process. Surprised? Puzzled? Most parents are. Reading seems like such a complex set of skills. How can we be a part of making it happen without expert assistance from educators? Only one activity predicts success in reading: being read to by parents. Research into early literacy and reading has repeatedly found that children who are read to by their parents daily are the best readers during the elementary years.

The reason for this is simple. When you read to your children, you are introducing them to the function of the written word. They are learning that letters have meaning and make words. This lesson is the first lesson in reading and writing. So get out a book and read!

TO ______________________

____

____

Tips for Reading to Your Child

- In the beginning, don't read. Point! Name objects while you point to pictures on the page. Reading pictures is an important pre-reading skill that your child will perfect first. Later, your child will realize that the meaning is in the words, and the pictures illustrate the meaning.
- Put life into your reading. Vary your voice tone. Give voices to different pictures and characters. Have fun!
- Start with easy-to-read, bright, and simple picture books. In most cases, you needn't bother with the text until your child can sit through looking at the pictures of the whole book. Then, abbreviate the text, keep it simple, and move quickly to keep your child's interest.
- Move your finger across the page to show that reading is taking place. This helps your child learn left-to-right progression—a key pre-reading skill.
- Point out familiar things first. Eyes, animals, mother, daddy, baby, car, and other things that are familiar will keep your child's attention. Then, gradually add unfamiliar pictures and words as you read the book again.
- Don't stay on one page too long. Four seconds is about long enough for very young children. Initially, limit your reading to one page at a time. But over time, start to connect one page with the next so your child will see the relationship between characters or objects on subsequent pages.
- Start with books that can be used for different purposes. For example, if a book tells a story about animals, use the book to explore the different sounds animals make as well as to tell the story.

When you don't feel like reading to your child, remember that many requests for story time are really requests for holding, cuddling, and getting reconnected emotionally. In this situation, pick a very familiar book, and let your child read to you. Your child will get the holding he or she needs, and you will marvel at how rapidly your child's pre-reading skills are growing.

TO

Tips for Reading to Your Child (continued)

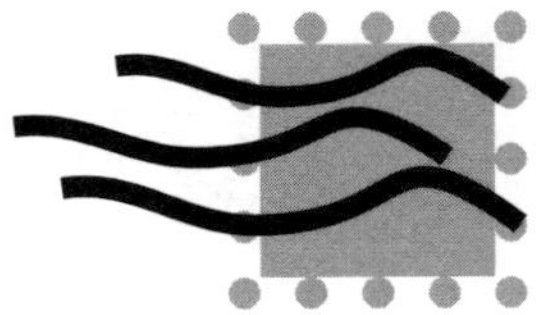

How much time is enough? This question plagues many busy parents who wonder if the time they spend with their child is enough. Start by spending 10 or 15 minutes a day reading and looking at books with your toddler. Then, as he or she grows, add 5 minutes every 6 months until you are reading to your child at least 30 minutes a day. But don't worry about the time. If you can't find 30 minutes, grab 5 minutes here and 10 minutes there to add up to a half-hour a day.

Don't forget nursery rhymes and fingerplays as reading activities. Use these childhood traditions as springboards to create your own rhyme memories with your child.

TO ______________

____

____

Teaching Your Child to Write

Writing is the other half of reading. Once children learn that symbols (letters and numbers) have meaning, they become interested in representing those symbols in writing. Like reading, learning to write is a process that begins by understanding the function of writing—why adults do it.

During toddlerhood, your child's writing skills will be limited to scribbling and making marks on paper with a variety of writing implements—crayons, markers, pencils, chalk, and so on. To encourage writing skills, let your child write when you write.

For example, when you make a grocery list, give your child a piece of scrap paper and a nontoxic marker and have him or her make a list. Or, when you sit down to pay the bills, give your child some pretend checks to write or pretend bills to pay right along with you. (Junk mail works well for this!) Whenever you use your writing skills, set your child up to use his or hers with you.

Expect your child's writing to be illegible well into the fourth year. Then, you will begin to see the letters of their names and drawings that you can recognize. Rather than focusing on whether you can read your child's writing, ask your child to tell you what it says. Remember, functional writing—applying meaning to symbols—is what is important in early writing. As long as your child thinks his or her marks have meaning, the process of learning to write is right on track!

TO ______________________

____

____

Concepts Learned in Big Animals

Concepts Learned

Some animals are big.
Bears are big animals
Bears live in caves.
Bears eat berries.
Bears sleep in winter.
Bears growl.
Elephants are gray.
Elephants have trunks.
Elephants are big animals.
Elephants eat peanuts.
Cows are big animals.
Cows live on the farm.
Cows say "moo."
Horses are big animals.
Horses live in barns.
Horses say "neigh."
Things are heavy or light.
My body goes up and down.
Sandpaper feels rough.
Big animals move in different ways.
Big and little are opposites.
Lacing uses my finger muscles.
Puzzle pieces fit together to make a picture.
Fingers can turn pages in a book.
Acting out songs exercises large muscles.
Walking, running, and jumping are ways animals move.
Moving like animals is a part of pretending to be an animal.
Painting is a way to express feelings.
Moving my body makes me feel happy.
Big brushes paint big.

Resources

Prop Boxes

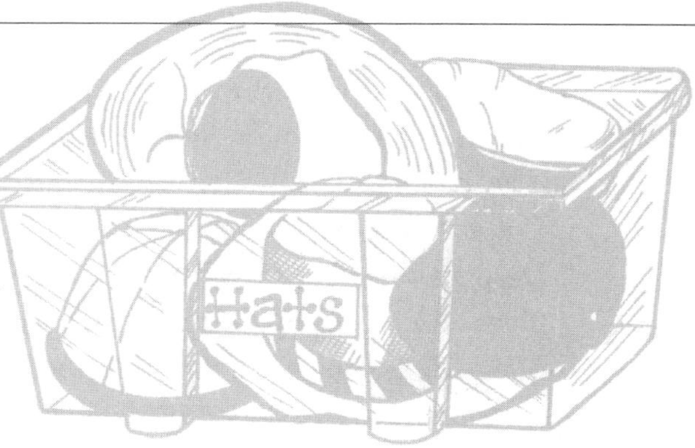

Zoo
- Animal pictures
- Feed buckets
- Zoo books and magazines
- Zoo keeper cap
- Zoo maps

Farm
- Animal pictures
- Farm books and magazines
- Feed buckets
- Gardening tools
- Jeans
- Plaid shirt
- Plastic eggs

Bear Cave
- Old sheet
- Pillows
- Stuffed bears
- *Where Do Bears Sleep?* by Barbara Shook Hazen

Elephant Box
- Gray clothing
- Gray tube socks
- *No Elephants Allowed* by Deborah Robinson
- *Trouble with Elephants, The* by Chris Riddle

Picture File/Vocabulary

Barns
Bears
Caves
Cows
Elephants
Farm
Horses
Zoos

Books

Biggest Nose, The by Kathy Caple
Blueberries for Sal by Robert McCloskey
Brown Bear, Brown Bear, What Do You See? by Bill Martin, Jr. and Eric Carle
Color Farm by Lois Ehlert
Deep in the Forest by Brinton Turkel
Farm Morning by David McPhail
Milk Makers, The by Gail Gibbons
No Elephants Allowed by Deborah Robinson (page 343)
Trouble with Elephants, The by Chris Riddle (page 343)
Where Do Bears Sleep? by Barbara Shook Hazen (page 343)

Rhymes/ Fingerplays

"Big Old Bear" (page 332)
"One Elephant" (page 332)
"This Cow" (page 335)

Music/Songs

"Bear Is Sleeping" (page 334)
"Did You Ever See?" (page 333)
"Elephant Dancing" (page 335)
"There's an Animal" (page 334)

Toys and Materials

The following purchased items are important for this Possibilities Plan:

Animal puppets (including bear and elephant)
Butcher paper
Cardboard
Chalk
Chart paper
Clear contact paper
Colored chalk
Colored poster board
Craft knife (teacher only)
Crayons
Elastic
Elephant puppet
Film and camera
Flannel board
Glue
Gray felt and white felt or yarn
Gray tempera paint
Hole punch
Jelly
Large and small plastic animals and fences
Markers
Music tapes
Push toys
Riding toys
Roasted peanuts
Sandbox
Sandpaper
Scissors
Shaving cream
Shoelaces
Sponges in animal shapes
Tape
Toy elephants
Toy stuffed animals (including bears)
Toy trucks (all sizes)
Variety of fresh fruit
Washable paint

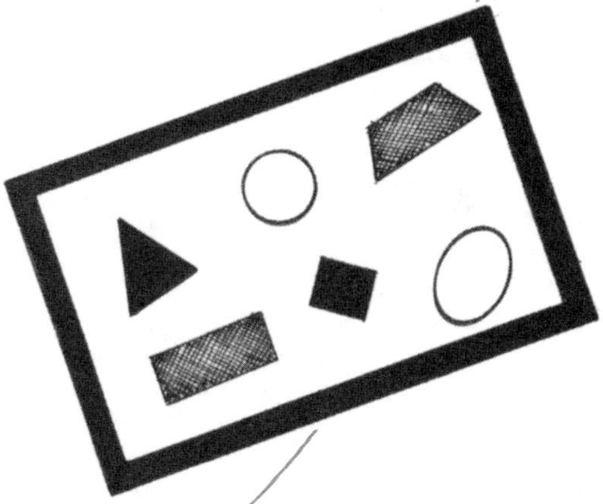

The following gathered items will help support this Possibilities Plan:

Animal pictures
Animal shapes (including bear)
Blanket
Bowls
Clear plastic bottles
Farm props
Gray tube socks
Grocery bags
Large cardboard box
Magazines
Paper bags
Peanuts
Pillows
Rice (dry)
Sand
Sheet
Shoebox lids
Small paper cups
Stuffed toy animals
Zoo props

Little Animals

WEB

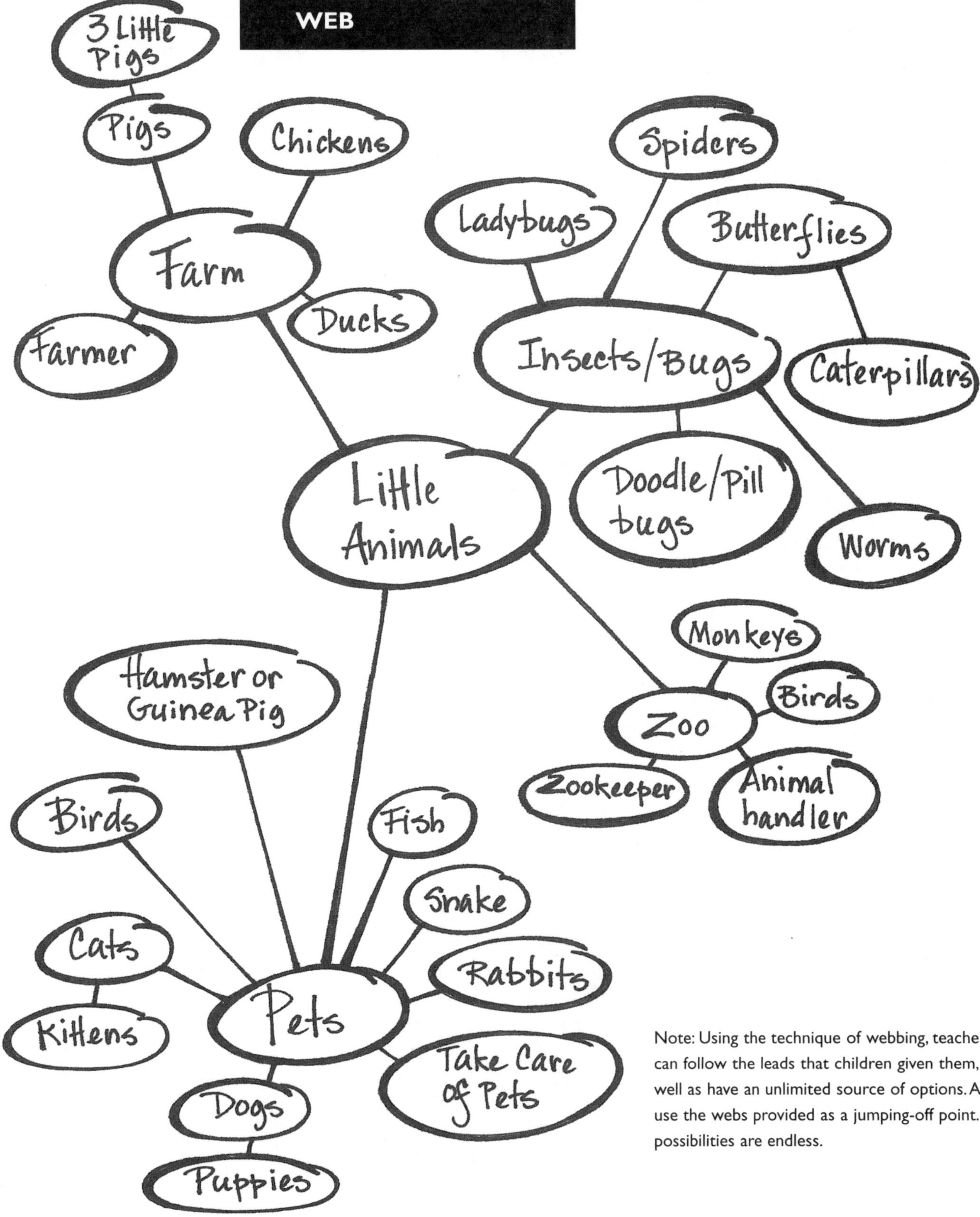

Note: Using the technique of webbing, teachers can follow the leads that children given them, as well as have an unlimited source of options. Always use the webs provided as a jumping-off point. The possibilities are endless.

PLANNING PAGES

Plan Possibilities

Little Animals

Monkey Tree

All ages

Materials

Large cardboard roll (carpet or rug)
Green butcher paper
Brown paint
Scissors
Umbrella
Tape
Small, stuffed toy monkeys
Plastic bananas, oranges, and apples
Basket

Teacher Talk

"Under the monkey tree is a nice place to sit with your doll, Lena."

Paint the cardboard roll brown. Cut leaves from the green butcher paper. Open the umbrella and place the handle inside the cardboard roll. Tape the leaves all over the open umbrella. Place toy monkeys in the tree. Children can use the tree as a place to sit or as a prop for telling stories about monkeys. Place plastic bananas, oranges, and apples in a basket.

Note: This is the type of activity that has been discouraged as too teacher-directed by some early childhood experts. The authors of this curriculum support environments that springboard children into play and interesting play extensions. Toddlers are able to read the environmental cues and then create play experiences that extend the initial cues of the environment. Although no teacher should spend an inordinate amount of time preparing teacher-made environmental props, some props add interest and fun to the learning environment and add novelty to children's day. Used in this way and for this purpose, activities such as these are appropriate.

Rabbit Hutch

All ages

Materials
Cardboard box
Craft knife
Stuffed, toy rabbits
Plastic food bowl
Plastic water bottle
Empty food boxes

Teacher Talk
"The rabbits may be hungry, Jeffrey. What can you feed them?"

Use a craft knife to cut a cardboard box to look like a rabbit cage. Place stuffed toy rabbits, plastic food, and water dishes inside the box. Children can feed and take care of the rabbits. Add other stuffed animals to the area, too.

Turtle Bowl

All ages

Materials
Plastic turtle/fish bowl
Plastic turtles
Water
Empty turtle food box

Teacher Talk
"Bhari is feeding his pet turtle."

Put a plastic turtle bowl with small toy turtles in it in the area and observe children's reactions. If permitted by regulatory agencies, arrange for real small animals to visit the classroom (gerbils, mice, lizards, cats, dogs).

SENSORY/ART POSSIBILITIES

Wash the Animals

All ages

Materials
Plastic toy animals
Sand/water table
Water
Washcloths

Teacher Talk
"Jeremy is washing all the farm animals. I see a pig, a goat, and a chicken."

Place plastic animals in the water table for children to play with and to wash. Observe children's conversations as they play to discover new words or increase the length of their sentences.

Turtle Prints

18-24 months

Materials
Sponges
Small rubber or plastic turtles
Craft knife
Paint
Paper
Tape
Aluminum pie tin

Teacher Talk
"It's a little turtle, Ross. You made a little turtle print on the paper. "

Pour paint into an aluminum pie tin. Children dip the turtles into the paint and press them onto paper to make turtle marks.

CURIOSITY POSSIBILITIES

Turtle Food

All ages

Materials
Dry cereal
Raisins
Pretzels
Large plastic bowl
Small paper cups

Teacher Talk
"Turtle food for you, Shytina?"

Pour dry cereal, raisins, and small pretzels into a large plastic bowl. Mix the ingredients well. Children scoop "turtle food" into small paper cups to enjoy a tasty and nutritious snack.

Feely Sock

24-30 months

Materials
Sock
Plastic cup
Textured items

Teacher Talk
Describe the textures for children. Explore "soft" and "rough" items. "I feel something soft in this sock, Landon."

Push a plastic cup inside the toe of a sock. Place a variety of textured items such as sandpaper, cotton balls, burlap scrap, velvet scrap, or other textures inside the cup. Show children how to reach inside and feel the items.

CONSTRUCTION POSSIBILITIES

Animals and Pens

All ages

Materials
Plastic animals
Small cardboard boxes
Twigs

Teacher Talk
"Tasha is making a fence for the sheep."

Provide plastic animals to use in the block area. Small cardboard boxes make excellent fences. Also, add twigs, small pinecones, and leaves as props.

Road Patterns and Trucks

All ages

Materials
Poster board
Makers
Commercial road carpet
Toy trucks and cars

Teacher Talk
"Amy is following the road with her blue truck."

Use a commercial road carpet or make road patterns using markers and poster board. Provide toy trucks and cars for driving on the roads.

LITERACY POSSIBILITIES

Hickory, Dickory Dock
18-24 months

Materials
Mouse puppet
Clock picture

Teacher Talk
"Yes, Scotty. That's the way to move up and down like the mouse puppet."

Explore moving the mouse puppet up and down the clock picture.

Hickory, Dickory Dock
Hickory, dickory dock.
The mouse ran up the clock.
The clock struck one,
And down he'd run.
Hickory, dickory dock.

Here's a Bunny
24-36 months

Materials
None

Teacher Talk
"Oops! That silly bunny went inside the hole, Joey."

Say the following rhyme with children, using your hand as the bunny puppet.

Here's a Bunny

Here's a bunny with ears so funny. (Point to bunny's ears.)
And here's his hole in the ground. (Point to the table.)
A sound he hears,
And perks up his ears,
And pops right into the ground. (Make bunny go under the tabletop.)

MUSIC POSSIBILITIES

Pop Goes the Bunny

18-24 months

Materials

Tape
Construction paper
Marker
Scissors

Teacher Talk

"Up pops the bunny! It's a funny bunny, Brandon!"

Tape the picture of the bunny onto a Jack-in-the-Box clown. As you sing the song, pop the bunny up on the words, "pop goes the bunny." Sing the song to the tune "Pop Goes the Weasel."

Pop Goes the Bunny

'Round and 'round the cobbler's bench,
The monkey chased the bunny.
The monkey thought it was all in fun,
'til Pop! goes the bunny.

Old Mother Turtle

24-30 months

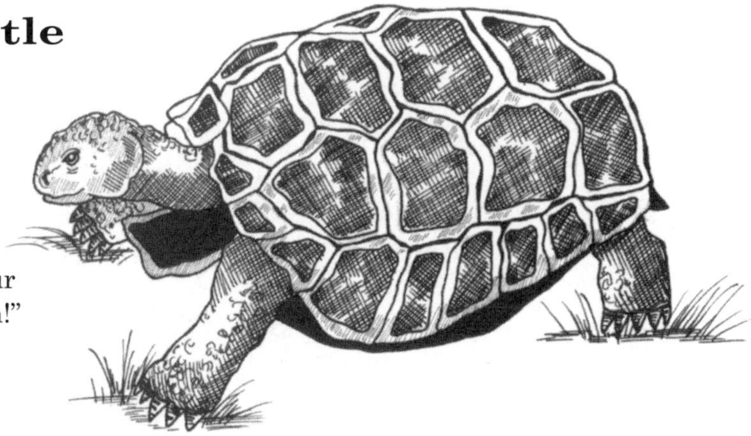

Materials

None

Teacher Talk

"Yes, that's the way to snap your fingers, Rachel. Snapping is fun!"

Sing the following song about turtles to the tune "Over in the Meadow." Encourage children to open and close their hands quickly to "snap" like turtles.

Old Mother Turtle

Over in the meadow in the sand, in the sun,
Lived an old mother turtle and her little turtle one.
"Snap!" said the mother; "I snap!" said the one,
So they snapped and they snapped in the sand, in the sun.

Monkeys Jumping on the Bed

30-36 months

Materials

None

Teacher Talk

"I see five monkeys ready for jumping, Claire."

Show children how to do the hand motions as they say the following rhyme.

Five Little Monkeys

Five little monkeys jumping on the bed. (Hold up five fingers.)
One fell off and bumped his head. (Rub head.)
Mother called the doctor. (Hold hand like talking on phone.)
And the doctor said,
"No more monkeys jumping on the bed!" (Shake finger.)

Repeat motions using the appropriate number of fingers.

Four little monkeys jumping on the bed.
One fell off and bumped his head.
Mother called the doctor.
And the doctor said,
"No more monkeys jumping on the bed!"

Three little monkeys jumping on the bed.
One fell off and bumped his head.
Mother called the doctor.
And the doctor said,
"No more monkeys jumping on the bed!"

Two little monkeys jumping on the bed.
One fell off and bumped his head.
Mother called the doctor.
And the doctor said,
"No more monkeys jumping on the bed!"

One little monkey jumping on the bed.
One fell off and bumped his head.

Mother called the doctor.
And the doctor said,
"No more monkeys jumping on the bed!"

MOVEMENT POSSIBILITIES

____ Move Like Animals

All ages

Materials
None

Teacher Talk
"You hopped like a bunny, Kaylee." "Brent is crawling like turtle."

As children transition from one area of the room to another or to go outside, invite them to move like the different animals you have been exploring. Use the rhymes in the plan to add to the fun.

____ This Is My Turtle

18-24 months

Materials
None

Teacher Talk
"Pia's turtle is sleeping inside her hand."

Recite this fingerplay with children. Demonstrate the hand movements..

This Is My Turtle
This is my turtle, (Make a fist with thumb extended.)
He lives in a shell. (Hide thumb inside fist.)
He likes his home very well.
He pokes his head out
When he wants to eat. (Extend thumb.)
He pulls it back in
When he wants to sleep. (Hide thumb inside fist.)

____ I Had a Little Turtle

24-30 months

Materials
None

Teacher Talk
"You make a great turtle, Keith! You know how to snap and catch!"

Recite the poem and act out the words with children.

I Had a Little Turtle
I had a little turtle.
I kept him in a box. (Make a box shape with hands.)
He swam in the puddles, (Make swimming motions.)
And he climbed on the rocks. (Make climbing motions.)
He snapped at a mosquito. (Open and close hands quickly.)
He snapped at a flea. (Open and close hands quickly.)
He snapped at a minnow, (Open and close hands quickly.)
And he snapped at me! (Point to self.)
He caught the mosquito. (Clap hands.)
He caught the flea. (Clap hands.)
He caught the minnow. (Clap hands.)
But he didn't catch me! (Shake head and point to self.)

OUTDOOR POSSIBILITIES

Rabbits and Carrots

All ages

Materials
Several bunches of fresh carrots with tops attached
Baskets

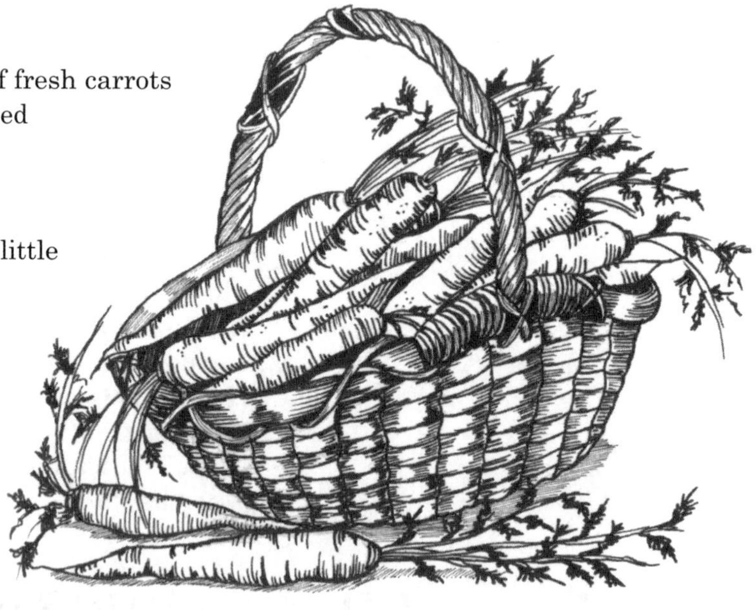

Teacher Talk
"Find the carrots, little bunnies."

Hide bunches or individual carrots on the playground for little bunnies to find. Introduce the carrot hunt on the way to the playground. Bring along baskets to put the carrots in to take back to the classroom for scrubbing in the sensory table, or scraping with spoons at the manipulatives table. Then send the carrots to the kitchen for cutting into curls for snack time.

Outside Sensory

All ages

Materials

Water table
Black, green, and blue dry tempera paint
Water
Sand
Blue food coloring
Shaving cream
Small plastic animals

Many opportunities exist for outdoor sensory experiences related to small animals. Use shaving cream with various dried tempera paints to create experiences related to water, land, and plants. Use sand for hiding and discovering animals. Create sky using shaving cream and dry blue tempera paint. Add plastic birds. Also, use the water table to create blue water for small plastic fish. All these experiences will allow children to enjoy a sensory experience related to the environment of the small animals.

Turtle Crawl

30-36 months

Materials

None

Teacher Talk

"I see Tony crawling like a turtle."

Explore crawling like a turtle.

PROJECT POSSIBILITIES

Pet Photo Albums

All ages

Materials

Photos of family pets
Pictures of pets cut from magazines
Sheet protectors
Three ring binder

Ask parents for a picture of the family pet or pets. Or, ask children to select a pet from the pictures cut from magazines. Create a pet page for each child with the picture of his or her pet, the pet's name, and a picture of the child. Put the pages into sheet protectors and place in the three ring binder. Add to the Literacy area.

PARENT PARTICIPATION POSSIBILITIES

Materials List

Ask parents to help you gather the material needed for the Little Animals theme. Post the list provided (on page 366) or make your own.

Small Animal Visitor

Invite parents to share a small pet animal such as a bunny, guinea pig, hamster, gerbil, or mouse. Parents may want to tell about the pet, show the food it eats, and the animal's toys.

Science Packet

Fill a resealable plastic bag with pictures of small animals. Encourage parents to play a matching game with their child using the animals pictures

Parent Postcards

Parent Postcards in this section are designed to share with parents during the Possibilities Plan. The topics are natural extensions of the activities and experiences that you are planning and implementing for the toddlers in the classroom. Use the Postcards to connect parents to their children's learning.

Supporting Brain Development at Home

What kinds of experiences do the best job of supporting brain development? Time, touch, talk, and training are the important sources of brain growth and development.

- **Time**—Consistent, warm, responsive caregiving is so important to children's brains during the first three years. As every toddler parent knows, responsive caregiving takes time and can't be rushed. Investing in the time it takes to make mealtime an interactive, warm experience is not a waste of time. It is a wonderful way to develop young children's brains.
- **Touch**—The very young child takes in experience through all of the senses—touch, taste, smell, sight, and sound. The brain picks up powerful messages from touch. Taking the time to hold your child, spending time being gently physical with toes, fingers, arms, and legs, touching the body to send positive messages to the developing pathways of the brain are all teaching at its best. Remember that touch is a powerful form of communication. Warm and soft touches send very different messages from rough, insensitive touches. Spend time with your child stretching, wiggling, and reaching to improve the communication between areas of the brain, which coordinate these skills. Holding hands is a powerful touching experience as toddlers walk around with your warm support.
- **Talk**—Pay attention to communication. Repetition forms connections in the brain as children are communicating all the time. The challenge is to read the verbal and nonverbal cues and interpret them accurately. Talk to your child. Describe what you are doing as you do it. "I'm going to get your pajamas now.It's almost time for your bath." Narrate what you see your child doing as he or she does it. "You see the bird! The red bird is flying to the nest!" Respond to what your child says, even if your child's articulation isn't always understandable. Tell your toddler to try again if you didn't understand and if that doesn't work, ask him or her to point, show you, or take you to what he or she is talking about.
- **Training**—The brain's connections are easily disconnected or abandoned if they are not stimulated. So very young children need lots of practice. Your toddler will like doing things again and again. In fact, this repetition is sometimes a frustrating part of parenting because children like to do both fun and interesting things again and again and irritating and inappropriate things again and again! Viewing this repetition as brain training helps parents embrace and tolerate it. Experiences that happen many times make connections, communication, and coordination among the areas of the brain stronger and more capable, actually enhancing children's potential in the process.

TO

Appropriate Expectations for Learning Academic Skills

Many child development specialists believe that the foundation for learning is built during the first three years of life. This may be a scary thought because the academic experiences we remember started at age 5 or 6. We think we have no idea how to teach our children.

Everything parents do with their children is teaching. You have actually been teaching your child for quite some time. You started by teaching your child that you love him or her. Then, you taught your baby to depend on you. Then, you helped him or her learn how to play with objects. Then, you helped your baby learn how to scoot to get something, and so forth. What you may not realize is how important these early skills are for later learning.

Each time you interact with your child, you are teaching. And each positive, playful experience a child has builds potential for academic readiness and success. Here's a list of activities that is guaranteed to lay the foundation for success in academic skills after age six. Do these now and wait until your child is ready for direct instruction in academic preparation—in about four years!

- Read to your child every day.
- Share your work with your toddler. Toddlers want to do real work all by themselves. So, let them work with you. When you sort laundry, give your toddler a pile of socks to play with. Then ask him or her to put the socks in a different pile from the towels, or count out forks for the table, plates as you take them out of the dishwasher, and stop signs as you drive along to school.
- Comment on what you are doing and why. It offers children ideas about connections that will have more meaning later.
- Use discarded cereal boxes, cartons, and cans to create fun playthings.
- Hold your child every day. Take the time to reconnect emotionally. Eye contact is very important. Emotionally stable children make good students. Supporting emotional development is one of the most important things parents can do to prepare their children for academic success.
- Avoid teaching by telling too much at this stage. The early years are years of doing and experimenting—not being taught by telling.

TO

Concepts Learned in Little Animals

Concepts Learned

Bunnies are soft animals.
Bunnies have long ears.
Bunnies eat carrots.
Bunnies hop.
Monkeys live in trees.
Monkeys are funny.
Monkeys eat fruit.
Monkeys swing from trees.
Monkeys have hands like mine.
Mice are very small animals.
Mice have long tails.
Mice scurry very fast.
Mice hide in holes.
Turtles live inside a hard shell.
Turtles crawl slowly.
Turtles are brown and green.
Some animals feel soft and fluffy.
Some animals have hard shells.
I can hop like a bunny.
I can swing my arms like a monkey.
I can crawl like a turtle.
All animals eat food.
All animals play.
Cotton balls are soft like a bunny.
I can make silly faces.
My body can move like animal bodies.
I can play follow-the-leader games.

Resources

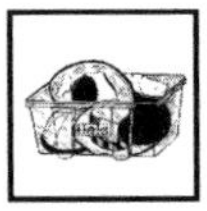

Prop Boxes

Monkey Box
- Caps
- *Caps for Sale* by Esphyr Slobodkina
- Plastic monkeys

Bunny Box
- Bunny headband
- *Peter Rabbit* by Beatrix Potter
- Plastic carrots
- Rabbit puppet

Turtle Box
- Flashlight
- *Franklin in the Dark* by Paulette Bourgeois
- Small blanket
- Turtle puppet

Picture/Vocabulary File

Faces
Fruit
Mice
Monkeys
Pets
Rabbits
Squirrels
Turtles

Books

Are You My Mother? by P. D. Eastman
Caps for Sale by Esphyr Slobodkina (page 364)
Curious George by H.A. and Margret Rey
Franklin in the Dark by Paulette Bourgeois (page 364)
Pet Show by Ezra Jack Keats
Peter Rabbit by Beatrix Potter
Play with Me by Marie Hall Ets
Squirrel Nutkin by Beatrix Potter

Rhymes/Fingerplays

"Five Little Monkeys" (page 356)
"Here's a Bunny" (page 355)
"Hickory, Dickory Dock" (page 354)
"I Had a Little Turtle" (page 358)
"This Is My Turtle" (page 357)

Music/Songs

"Old Mother Turtle" (page 356)
"Pop Goes the Bunny" (page 355)

Toys and Materials

The following purchased items are important for this Possibilities Plan:

3-ring binder
Brown paint
Construction paper (including green)
Craft knife (teacher only)
Dry tempera paint (black, green, blue)
Food coloring (including blue)
Glue
Green butcher paper
Markers (including brown)
Mouse puppet
Paint
Paper
Paper plates and cups
Plastic animals
Plastic carrots
Plastic bowl
Plastic fruit
Plastic toy animals
Plastic turtle/fish bowl
Plastic turtles
Poster board
Roads carpet
Sand/water table
Scissors
Shaving cream
Sheet protectors
Stuffed toy monkeys
Stuffed toy rabbits
Tape
Toy trucks and cars
Turtle puppet

The following gathered items will help support this Possibilities Plan:

Baskets
Blanket
Caps
Cardboard box
Carrots with tops attached
Clock picture
Dry cereal, raisins, and pretzels
Empty food boxes
Empty turtle food box
Family pet photos and magazine pictures
Flashlight
Large cardboard roll (carpet or rug roll)
Pie tin
Plastic water bottle
Sand
Sponges
Textured items
Tube sock
Umbrella
Washcloths

CHAPTER 6

Problem-solving

INTRODUCTION

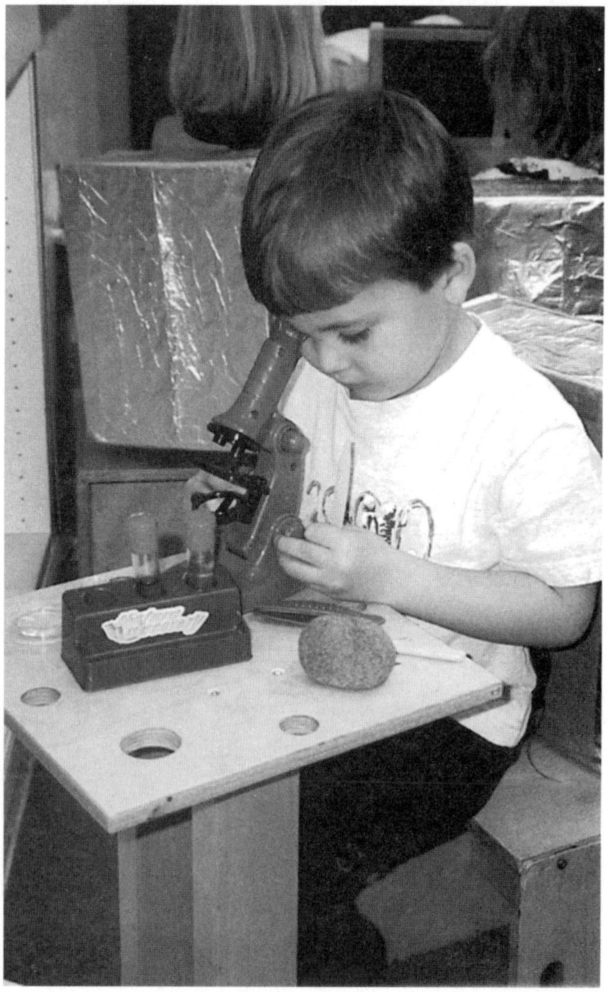

Discoveries are the purview of toddlers. During the period from 18 months to 3 years, young children make great strides in discovering how their bodies work and in connecting meaning to the world in which they live. Meaning is derived from active experimentation with people, the environment, and experiènces. Activity levels and intensity of purpose increase dramatically as children figure out that they can make things happen in their lives and take delight in sticking to tasks until they have mastered them.

Toddlers are adding new physical skills, but these skills are less dramatic than those that occurred in late infancy such as pulling to a stand, walking, and feeding oneself. New physical learning revolves around perfecting gross motor skills such as running, hopping, balancing, jumping, and coordinating the movements of the arms and legs to the movement of the torso. In the fine motor arena, attention is focused on eye-hand coordination and increasing mastery of the smaller muscles that control the fingers and hands.

The increase in fine motor skills leads to an explosion in learning about mathematical concepts. One and "more than one" are already understood, and "more" becomes interesting to explore. Manipulation of objects, toys, and materials, paired with emerging preferences for favorite manipulative experiences, join to create the ability for toddlers to stay on task in an interesting activity for quite a long time.

Understanding physical development and the way gross and fine motor skills support emerging interests in exploration of the physical world is the focus of this chapter.

INNOVATIONS IN OBSERVATION/ASSESSMENT

Observation/Assessment Instrument

This assessment instrument is not just a skills checklist. Instead it is designed to guide the teacher's observation of children's development through a major interactional task of toddlerhood. The assessment's focus is on what IS happening in the child's development, not what should happen or what will happen. Use this assessment to lead to developmentally appropriate practices for toddlers.

Problem Solving Assessment 18-36 months

	18-24 months	24-30 months	30-36 months
PS1	a. Interest in toileting is limited to watching; may show interest in flushing toilet, sitting on the toilet, or washing hands. Interest may wax and wane quickly.	b. Toilet play stage of toileting; interested in playing out toileting activities such as taking off diaper, sitting on the toilet, using toilet paper, flushing the toilet, and washing hands.	c. Toilet practice begins; likes to repeat toileting activities again and again, with or without success.
PS2	a. Activity level increases; requests and seeks out motor activities. Does not control activity level without adult support; resists adult support in modulating activity level.	b. Activity level continues to increase; continues to seek out motor activities. Begins to modulate activity levels with verbal and physical adult support.	c. Alternates between high levels of activity and periods of calm, quieter activity. Can modulate activity level with verbal reminders from adults.
PS3	a. On-task behavior begins to increase.	b. Able to sustain favorite activities for increasingly longer periods of time; extends on-task play time at favorite activities to 10 minutes. Still loses interest in other activities quickly.	c. Stays on task at favorite manipulative activities for sustained periods of time; extends on-task play time at favorite activities to 20 minutes. Still loses interest in other activities quickly.
PS4	a. Carries toys around from place to place. b. Undresses; takes off shoes, socks, and clothes. c. Turns door knob to open door.	d. Holds cup with one hand to drink. e. Shows preference for one hand.	f. Unzips zipper. g. Pulls pants up. h. Zips zipper.
PS5	a. Propels riding toys with feet. b. Runs, collapses to stop forward movement.	c. Goes up stairs without alternating feet holding on to handrail. d. Runs; begins to control starting and stopping. e. Balances on one foot.	f. Goes up stairs alternating feet holding on to handrail. g. Jumps up and down on two feet. h. Pedals tricycle.

INNOVATIONS IN CHILD DEVELOPMENT

Physical Development

During the first three years of life, a child's body changes dramatically. Seemingly helpless newborns grow into physically competent three-year-olds who are able to walk, run, climb, scribble, eat with a spoon, then with a fork, and so on. As with all development, physical development follows predictable patterns even though individual progress may be highly variable.

For physical development in general, and motor development specifically, the sequence of development is from the head to the foot and from the center to the periphery of the body. (This is called the cephalocaudal/proximodistal trend.) During infancy and toddlerhood, children develop their bodies from the top down and from the center out. For example, most children can swipe at objects by the age of 5-6 months, pick up objects between the thumb and forefinger by about 11-12 months, hold a crayon to scribble at about 18 months, eat with a fork at about 24 months, and complete simple puzzles by 26 months, illustrating the proximodistal trend. Similarly, children roll over by about 5-6 months, walk by 12-16 months, and walk up stairs at 18-20 months, illustrating the cephalocaudal trend.

Both of these trends are affected by each child's unique pace through the developmental sequence, the unevenness of development in general, and the opportunities available for experience and practice of emerging skills. In other words, children continue to have an individual pace in acquiring skills, and experience and practice can support or hinder motor development. For example, children who do not have opportunities to use stairs may seem to lag behind those who do, simply because the experience of stair climbing has not been explored, experienced, or practiced. Fortunately, physical skills such as these respond well to exposure and practice. Children who cannot climb because they have not had the experiences learn very quickly when exposed to the opportunity to practice stair climbing.

The milestones of physical development are usually broken down into two major components—gross motor and fine motor. Gross motor development refers to the large muscles of the legs, arms, and torso, whereas fine motor refers to the smaller muscles of the body including the muscles in the hands, feet, and eyes. Physical development milestones for both gross and fine motor development from 18-36 months are listed on the following page.

AGE	FINE MOTOR SKILLS	GROSS MOTOR SKILLS
18-24 MONTHS	Holds cup or glass in one hand. Unbuttons large buttons. Turns doorknobs.	Squats for long periods of time. Throws large ball. Carries large objects around. Dumps out containers of toys or materials.
24-30 MONTHS	Removes shoes, some clothing. Stacks small blocks. Fits pegs in pegboard. Pours and fills containers at sensory table. Unzips large zippers. Shows preference for one hand.	Propels riding toys with feet. Walks up stairs without alternating feet. Builds with blocks. Runs.
30-36 MONTHS	Completes puzzles. Turns pages of book, though not always one page at time. Washes hands at sink.	Walks down stairs without assistance. Balances on one foot. Jumps on two feet. Pedals tricycle.

Toileting—The Ultimate Physical Challenge

Many consider the ability to control the muscles of the bowel and bladder as an important skill that comes under voluntary control during the toddler years. In reality, most children are not completely able to control these muscles until closer to age three. However, crucial physical, emotional, social, and intellectual skills are being explored and learned to lead the way to mastery of the complex skill of bladder and bowel control.

Toilet Training—Process, Not Magic

Learning to toilet consistently is a process that begins with an interest in the toilet and what happens in bathrooms and ends with independent toileting. The developmental nature of toileting has four phases. The first phase is toilet play. Many parents and teachers view this beginning stage as readiness for toilet training when it is actually only the beginning. Toilet play is characterized by an interest in the bathroom in general and in what people, particularly parents, do in the bathroom. During this phase, children often like to get on and off the toilet (generally fully clothed!), flush repeatedly, play with toilet paper and hand washing, and watch what adults do when they are in the bathroom.

The second stage of toileting is toilet practice. Getting on and off the toilet without assistance, pulling pants down and up, taking off diapers or pull-up diapers, pretending to wipe after pretending to toilet (or after a coincidental success!), flushing the toilet, and washing hands are all part of the toilet practice stage.

The third phase is toilet training. The training part comes from cueing the children to take a reading of how their bodies are feeling and whether or not there is any bowel or bladder urgency. Some teachers mistakenly think that children are almost trained at this stage and just need to be reminded to go to the bathroom. This is not the case. During this stage, the aim of training is to help the child become increasingly conscious of what is going on internally. Asking children to check their bodies when they wake up, after breakfast, before leaving home, before getting in the bathtub, and before going to bed sets up a pattern of getting in touch with how the body feels that leads to the next stage.

The last stage is independent toileting. This is the stage that parents and teachers long for—they are not needed to remind or coax a child to toilet. Children take care of their own bodily needs without prompting or reminders. It is the culmination of a process that began with toilet play and ends with parents and teachers who are very proud of the child's accomplishments.

The Four Stages of Toilet Training

1. Toilet play
2. Toilet practice
3. Toilet training
4. Independent toileting

Take the time to understand fully the developmental nature of toileting. When teachers and parents do, children's process through learning to toileting will unfold in an environment of support, encouragement, and, in due time, success.

Toileting can be the most problematic developmental issue to understand because of the individual variations in readiness to control toileting and the integrated nature of toileting. Age is a particularly poor predictor of readiness.

Most children begin this developmental process around the age of two, but few really master toileting until age three or even later. Most children (90%) learn to toilet independently by the end of the third year. Some children master bladder control first; others master bowel control first. Some children master daytime dryness easily, only to struggle with nighttime dryness. Girls may gain control more easily than boys. Most children have accidents well into the third year.

INNOVATIONS IN INTERACTIVE EXPERIENCES

Physical development is one of the domains of development that responds so well to experience and practice. Toddlers who are confined in small spaces with limited physical challenges have few opportunities to perfect new skills. Practice is what wires the connections in the brain to bring muscles under voluntary control. In other words, toddlers need to repeat motor movements again and again. Movement sends messages to the developing brain to strengthen the connections between neurons. These connections are the roadways that send messages to the muscles about what to do. Muscles come under voluntary control as these pathways become stronger.

Provide numerous opportunities for toddlers to practice motor skills every day. They are the foundation upon which crucial skills and abilities grow. You might also want to use this list to make notes on the Communication Sheet (page 537) to document the types of experiences children have had during the day.

Be sure to plan experiences such as these for toddlers every day. In addition, don't hesitate to do them over and over again.

- ☐ Encourage flexibility.
- ☐ Provide exercise for arms and legs.
- ☐ Offer practice reaching and stretching.
- ☐ Provide toys to pull and push.
- ☐ Help toddlers practice squatting then standing then squatting.
- ☐ Add surprises to favorite experiences.
- ☐ Support toddlers' check-in behavior. (As children try new skills and practice old ones, they will periodically reconnect with adults through eye contact, touch, or proximity. They are reconnecting, so they can continue their exploration and activities after getting reassurance from the adult.)
- ☐ Provide challenges for small muscles in the hands.

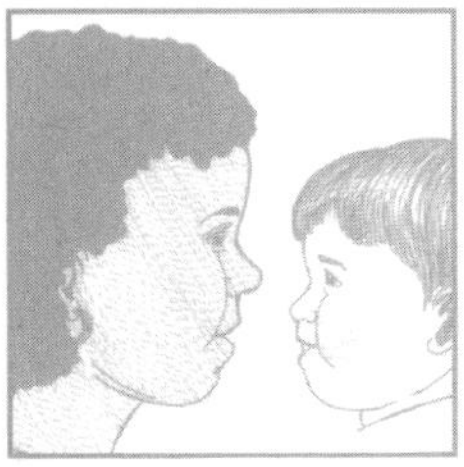

INNOVATIONS IN TEACHING

Supporting Physical Development in the Classroom

Classrooms for toddlers support physical development when they include a variety of challenging fine and gross motor activities. Fine motor activities include a wide range and variety of manipulative toys. Open-ended manipulatives, such as Duplos, Star Builders, unit blocks, shape sorters, pegged puzzles, tree blocks, and castle blocks, are popular because toddlers can be successful at early attempts in construction. Fine motor manipulatives, such as simple puzzles, inch cubes, colored blocks, and lacing cards, all exercise the small muscles of the hand while supporting increased eye-hand coordination.

Toddlers are full of energy. Using the large muscles of the arms and legs allows them to use energy in meaningful activities. Toddlers seem to be unable to resist climbing. Classrooms for toddlers can allow for climbing in appropriate ways such as into lofts and on vertical climbers that are safely placed on appropriate gym mats to prevent injuries from falls. Having appropriate places for toddlers to climb also allow teachers to redirect inappropriate or dangerous climbing, such as on tabletops, to safe climbing on a sturdy climber.

Toddlers are also pleased with new running skills. Good room arrangements divide space into functional areas that interrupt and limit running while teachers offer alternative activities such as pushing a doll stroller or a shopping cart and using ride-on push toys in Construction Possibilities and Dramatic Possibilities.

Physical development is stimulated by almost every activity and experience suggested in the Possibilities Plans. Reading books encourages fine motor skills such as visual tracking of pictures and text from top to bottom and left to right. Songs, rhymes, and fingerplays often have a physical component using fine motor movements of the fingers or gross motor movements of the body. Sensory experiences provide soothing or exciting fine motor movements while stimulating other senses. It seems that nature has an almost perfect plan for supporting physical development—the enthusiasm and energy of toddlers.

They will lead you to stay physical as they demonstrate what they can do to almost any willing audience. Play this important role whenever you have an opportunity—encouraging practice and perfection of emerging physical skills.

Supporting Physical Development Outdoors

Open the door to the outdoors and most toddlers jump up and down with glee! In fact, "out" is an operative word in toddlerhood. Toddlers intensely enjoy going and being outside. Outdoor environments interest toddlers when they offer challenge, complexity, and practice. Toddler playgrounds need sand to play in, a path for riding on push toys, climbing structures to challenge climbing and control skills, and natural environments to keep them interested.

The toddlers' micro view of the world is clearly seen when they go outside. They will notice things that most adults miss—every bug, insect, worm, leaf, or twig gets their attention. From this interest, fine motor skills of picking up, collecting, and sorting get good practice. All provide opportunities to perfect coordination and increase strength.

Sensory activities are also popular outside. Toddlers love sand, dirt, water, and creative art materials such as goop and clean mud. They enjoy adding water to things and moving natural materials around with buckets and wagons.

Discrete skills such as catching a large ball and pushing a tricycle with pedals may take more practice, and sometimes, even a little instruction to perfect. Don't hesitate to help toddlers learn skills that interest them, but don't be surprised if they abandon frustrating or difficult tasks readily. They seem to know when it is time to keep trying. When this time comes, they will persist until the coordination they need is developed. These are exciting times for toddler teachers—they are part of helping develop a new skill by supporting practice, encouraging continued effort, and celebrating success.

Supporting Learning to Toilet Independently

During the first stage of learning to toilet, called toilet play, children are just becoming keenly interested in the bathroom and what goes on in it. Expect toddlers to be curious about body parts and bodily functions—their own as well as others. Dealing matter-of-factly with this interest will help the child figure out how her body works and lead to an increased interest in wanting to control her body.

During this phase, both teachers and parents need realistic expectations. This is the beginning of toilet training. It rarely leads to successful self-control. Encourage children to "practice" toileting skills. Set up a pattern of getting on the toilet, sitting for a minute, tearing off a little bit of toilet paper, getting off the toilet, flushing, and then washing and drying hands for toddlers to repeat several times a day while they are interested in toilet play. Don't be surprised if children want to repeat this process many times. Revel in these playful activities and help children practice the skills necessary to move on to the next stage. Remember, this is play. Playing is part of getting ready for the next phase.

Often this early interest in toileting play ends as quickly as it begins. This signals that the child has answered all of her questions for the time being and is on to other discoveries—not that the process has failed. Be patient and the next stage will follow soon.

During the second stage, toilet practice, children begin to practice the range of skills they will need to toilet independently. The list of what needs to be learned is quite long. Consider this list of skills:

Body Awareness Skills	**Physical Skills**	**Language Skills**	**Cognitive Skills**	**Social-Emotional Skills**
The ability to delay gratification for a minute: "I can wait for a while, maybe 3 or 4 minutes."	Motor skills such as "I can sit still for a while, maybe 3 or 4 minutes."	"My Mommy and Daddy and I have a set of shared words for elimination--I know what to call what is happening to me."	Prediction skills such as "I may need to potty soon," or "I know what comes next when my body feels like this."	Self-confidence feelings that say, "I can be in charge of my own body!"
"I can tell when my bladder/bowel is filling up and I need to potty" and "I prefer to be clean rather than to be dirty."	Large muscle skills such as "I can pull my pants down and up without assistance from an adult."	"I can tell Mommy and Daddy what I need." "I can access and use the words I need when I need them."	Memory skills so "I won't forget to go potty while I'm busy playing."	Autonomy skills that mean "I can do it myself."
"I can stop what I am doing and go to the toilet in time."	Small muscle skills: "I can regulate the muscles that start and stop the elimination process."		"I understand that I need to think about toileting before I go outside, go down for a nap, etc."	Independence skills that mean, "I want to try to do it myself."

Body Awareness Skills	Physical Skills	Language Skills	Cognitive Skills	Social-Emotional Skills
	Motor control skills such as "I can hold my urine or bowel movement while I get to the toilet, pull my pants down, and have a seat!" and "I can wipe my bottom without adult help."			Self-esteem feelings that mean, "I don't need to make taking care of my body a power struggle."
	Bio-motor regularity skills such as "I have a prolonged periods of dryness, including waking up from sleep (nap or night time) dry."			

It is very important for teachers to continue to be excited about these small steps toward independent toileting, even if they are not accompanied with actual toileting success. Help toddlers practice the skills that interest them. Follow the child's lead as you gently assist and encourage the emerging skills of pulling pants off and on. At first, children might need a lot of assistance. But, as they practice, toddlers will need less support. Don't forget to modify your response as skill grows. Encouragement reminds toddlers that they are in charge of their bodies and keeps interest high.

The third stage of learning to toilet is toilet training. While children are in this stage, they are often surprised that the need to toilet has snuck up on them. Children wait until it is too late to get to the bathroom, pull down their pants, and get on the toilet before releasing the small muscles that control elimination. They will jump up, grab their private parts, and have an accident before they ever move toward the bathroom. It is during this stage that small muscles are strengthened enough to hold urine or stop the movement of the bowel for a minute or so while children get in the position to eliminate on the toilet.

Expect accidents to happen frequently at this stage. Validate successes and respond calmly to accidents. Approach accidents as opportunities for continued practice of the skills needed to toilet—pulling down pants, changing into clean ones, and pulling them back up. Never scold or punish children for accidents at this stage. In fact, you can foster emerging independence by helping children to clean themselves up after accidents. The more responsibility you can give children for this process, the more likely they will be interested in gaining self-control.

Independent toileting is the last stage—the one that teachers and parents are thrilled to see finally emerge. If appropriate support has been provided during the previous stages, children gradually become truly independent about toileting. Most toddler teachers will never see this stage because it may emerge as children enter the preschool years. Instead, they can be confident that progress through the first three stages during toddlerhood set the stage for success in the preschool years.

Take a developmental view of toileting. Viewed this way, toilet training never gets difficult! There are no fights, few frustrations, and no failures.

The School's Role in Supporting Toilet Training

Parents are often surprised that they are seeing different behaviors at home than the teacher is seeing at school. The school setting is very different from home, and children often change their behavior in these different settings. It is the teacher's job to explore what is happening at home and to share successes at school. Try to discover common ground between the two settings.

Cultural variations in expectations for toilet training vary widely. Explore the family's view of the process and work with them to match the child's experience at school to the experience of the home. In addition, it is the toddler teacher's job to help parents see that some toilet training strategies, such as letting the child experience repeated accidents to increase her awareness of bowel and bladder control, or frequent trips to the toilet to try and "catch" coincidental toileting, are not realistic in the school setting. Remind parents that you are responsible for a group of children and help them see that you are working on toilet training by teaching the skills listed in the table on page 376.

Guidance and Discipline

Natural and Logical Consequences

Applying natural and logical consequences is a great tool for teachers to use to help children gain self-control. A natural or logical consequence is a consequence that emerges from the situation. This important teaching skill is not one of the easiest ones to learn. And it takes time, practice, and careful response. The following example illustrates the concept of logical consequences:

Notice that there is no power struggle or disapproval in this situation. The consequences emerge from the situation and are responded to firmly but calmly. As a result, children learn to control their own behavior slowly over time as they are reminded of the consequences both by your words and your actions.

A toddler takes off toward the playground as soon as you open the door to go outside. After catching the toddler, you go back inside the building and start the transition again, saying, "I need to hold your hand before we go outside. It is dangerous to run to the playground, and I can't trust you to go with me." Then, holding the child's hand, walk to the playground. Before you exit to go to the playground the next time, remind the child that you need to hold her hand before you open the door to go outside. The logical consequence of running is a loss of the freedom of walking without holding hands. After one or two visits to the playground holding hands, tell the toddler that she is getting a chance to show you that she has learned to walk to the playground. If she succeeds, celebrate the success. If she takes off running, repeat the process until the behavior you want (controlling the impulse of running) take hold.

Setting Appropriate Limits

Teachers have two reasons to set rules and limits. The first reason is to protect children and keep them safe—reason enough for a good set of limits. The second reason teachers set limits is to help children grow toward self-control. Where do you start to establish reasonable limits and rules for your classroom? Rules should have the following elements (Marion, 1998):

- ***First, rules and limits must be humane***. There is no place for rules that are punitive in nature and/or make children feel bad about themselves. Humane rules do not humiliate, embarrass, belittle, or degrade the child. An example of an inhumane rule: "Toddlers who cry don't get to play." This kind of rule has no place in early childhood education settings.
- ***Second, limits should not be arbitrary***. Each rule should have several good reasons for existing. An example of an arbitrary rule: "I won't pick you up unless you stop crying."
- ***Third, rules should be overt (out in the open) not hidden***. Children, particularly very young children, cannot guess what the rules are. They need to be told, reminded, and reminded again. (Yes, even if it takes thousands of reminders!) If you don't want toddlers to run in the hall, you must remind them to walk before you open the door to the hallway. To determine if your rules are overt, simply watch children's behavior. If your rules are clear, most children will be learning to follow them when given supportive reminders by adults.

- ***Fourth, limits should be clearly stated and enforceable***. Rules should refer to the expected behavior and be clear enough for children to know immediately when they have broken the rule. An example of a clearly stated rule with a reference to behavior: "Leave the sand in the sandbox, or I will have to ask you to play somewhere else." Rules that end in threats such as, "I'll never let you play in the sand again," are ineffective because they are unenforceable and because very young children don't have the self-control to resist putting the sand in their mouths.
- ***Fifth, rules should be accompanied by reasons***. Research has shown that children who are given the reasons behind the rules are more likely to listen and follow the rules later without adult reminders. It is important to be brief and to the point. Children need one good reason for each rule, not three or four. Using the previously stated sand rule, an example might be: "Leave the sand in the sandbox. When you throw it, someone's eyes could be badly hurt."
- ***Sixth, remember to update your rules***. This is particularly important during the first three years when children are maturing and developing so quickly. As children mature, the limits imposed on them should be updated. As new skills emerge, limits should reflect those new skills. For example, toddler skills change quickly. As children perfect new skills, such as climbing stairs or climbing on the climbing structure, update your rules. You might say, "Hold on tight" to a child who is just learning to negotiate the stairs and then drop the rule when she becomes more skilled in climbing stairs.
- ***Seventh, rules and limits should be firmly enforced***. As children grow, they will test limits that adults set for them. If teachers use repressive controls such as coercion, testing will continue. If teachers do not set limits and do not enforce rules, children will heed no adult guidance. Firm, consistent responses to broken rules will result in children who learn to follow the rules set for them by their teachers.

The easiest way to enforce the limits you've set is to move the child to another setting when out-of-bounds behavior occurs. This technique uses logical consequences to help children remember the rules. If the child is throwing sand, take her by the hand and help her find another place to play until she can remember to leave the sand in the sandbox. If the child is climbing without holding on, take the child off of the climbing structure and ask her to find another place to play until she can remember to hold on.

Toddlers will need frequent reminders of your rules and support in complying with them. They are unable to do so just because you say so. Combine your rules with physical action (holding a child by the hand, moving a child to another place), and, later on, your toddlers will remember and comply.

Nutrition

What Do Toddlers Really Need to Eat?

Pediatric advice about what toddlers should eat varies widely. The following chart is a recommended 24-hour food guide for toddlers. Use it along with the information gathered from parents as a resource to help determine the nutritional needs of the toddlers in your classroom.

24-Hour Food Guide

	18-24 months	24-30 months	30-36 months
Milk or Formula, Yogurt, Cheese	20-24 oz. in 3-5 servings from cup	16-24 oz. in 3-5 servings from cup	16-24 oz. in 3-5 servings from cup
Water	Offer 4-6 servings of 2-4 oz. from a cup between meals; particularly in warm weather or after vigorous exercise.		
Cereals and Breads	6 or 7 servings of whole wheat or enriched bread, crackers, pasta macaroni, rice, or unsweetened cereals in ¼-½-cup serving sizes; ¼ slice of bread per serving	5-7 servings of whole wheat or enriched bread, crackers, pasta macaroni, rice, or unsweetened cereals in ¼-½-cup serving sizes; ¼ slice of bread per serving	4-6 servings of whole wheat or enriched bread, crackers, pasta macaroni, rice, or unsweetened cereals in ¼-½-cup serving sizes; ¼ slice of bread per serving
Fruits and Vegetables	4-7 servings of fresh, canned, or frozen fruits and vegetables in ⅛-¼-cup servings; or ¼ piece of fruit per serving	4-7 servings of fresh, canned, or frozen fruits and vegetables in ⅛-¼-cup servings; or ¼ piece of fruit per serving	4-7 servings of fresh, canned, or frozen fruits and vegetables in ⅛-¼-cup servings; or ¼ piece of fruit per serving
Meats and Protein	2-4 servings of lean meat, fish, poultry, eggs, dried beans, peanut butter, or tofu in 1-2 oz. servings	2-4 servings of lean meat, fish, poultry, eggs, dried beans, peanut butter, or tofu in 1-2 oz. servings	2-4 servings of lean meat, fish, poultry, eggs, dried beans, peanut butter, or tofu in 1-2 oz. servings
Fats, Oils, Sugar	Use margarine, butter, lard, mayonnaise, bacon, sausage, candy, cookies, soft drinks, and fruit punch in very limited amounts.	Use margarine, butter, lard, mayonnaise, bacon, sausage, candy, cookies, soft drinks, and fruit punch in very limited amounts.	Use margarine, butter, lard, mayonnaise, bacon, sausage, candy, cookies, soft drinks, and fruit punch in very limited amounts.

Adapted from Kendrick, Kaufman, and Messinger, 1988 and Wong, Hockenberry-Easton, Winkelstein, Wilson, & Ahmann, 1999.

Picky Eaters

A frustrating part of toddler behavior is being a picky eater. Almost all teachers and parents are concerned about how much toddlers eat (or don't eat) and whether nutritional needs are being met. There are several reasons for the pickiness of toddlers in relation to food. One reason is that the amount of food that a toddler needs drops off. The rapid growth of infancy slows down, and children need fewer calories to fuel their daily activities. Another reason is toddlers' metabolisms are changing. Infancy was characterized by eating enough to fuel activity for a few hours and then needing to eat again to keep going. Toddlers have usually stored a little body fat by the beginning of the second year of life and are able to manage without refueling as often.

Toddlers also tend to be snackers rather than eaters. They enjoy eating for a little while, then lose interest and are ready to go on to another activity. Finally, independence (and thus, oppositional behavior) is emerging—and controlling what you eat is a major act of independence—particularly if mom, dad, and teacher spend a lot of time encouraging you to eat.

Children are capable of regulating their own food intake (Clark, 1996). Nutritionists recommend letting toddlers decide what to eat—without being overruled by adults. When adults try to control children's eating by forcing, enticing, cajoling, or bribing, children begin to

What then is the best way to address eating with children? Try some of the following strategies to support picky eaters through the toddler years.

- Continue to offer toddlers new foods; it may take seeing new foods several times before it will even be tried. Taste buds are changing; a food refused yesterday may taste good today.
- Offer small portions. Be aware of serving sizes for toddlers (see the chart on page 381).
- Be a good role model. Sit with toddlers when they are eating snacks or meals; taste new foods; comment on how new foods taste.
- Don't pressure. Let toddlers control their own intake—a powerful experience with independence.
- Eat at regularly scheduled times. Toddlers need to eat more frequently than adults, perhaps 5 or 6 times a day. Three meals and two or three snacks will help children get enough nutrients across the day.
- Give children choices of nutritious foods; avoid fats and sugars that will fill up the toddler without contributing to the child's nutritional needs.
- If toddlers regularly avoid one type of food, such as vegetables or milk, introduce it in an interesting or different way. For example, if a toddler isn't drinking milk, substitute other foods high in calcium such as yogurt, cheese, or dried beans. Or, increase children's interest in the food by including a cooking or preparation activity in the classroom.
- Keep your cool. If the teacher is frantic about eating behavior, toddlers will feel like they have to continue the behavior that is problematic. If you avoid making a fuss and allow the children to control their nutritional intake, toddlers will learn to listen to the cues they are getting from their bodies about when and how much to eat—avoiding over- and under-eating.

resist eating altogether. On the other hand, if adults keep children from eating when they are hungry and ready to eat, they may overeat when they get a chance, ignoring the body's cues about fullness.

Health Policies

When to send children home and when to let them stay at school is one of the most important decisions a toddler teacher must make. And, the decision is complicated by a host of additional factors, including the family's lifestyle, the location of the parents' work, and the ability of the family to make contingency plans for sick children.

Every school needs a carefully crafted set of health policies. Clear policies are used as the foundation for determining whether or not a child can stay in school when she becomes ill or exhibits symptoms indicating the onset of illness. Policies should be developed in conjunction with consulting physicians and reviewed regularly to make sure that the latest information is used. Policies should be shared with parents in written form during the enrollment process and discussed with parents in detail by the child's teacher during gradual enrollment.

The Pennsylvania chapter of the American Academy of Pediatrics has published excellent guidelines for parents and caregivers to follow to protect both well and ill children (APHA/AAP, 1992). Though not substituting for advice from a physician, the guidelines provide an excellent starting place for writing policies that are sound and supportable. But, like so many things in toddler education, health policies are only guides to use to make good decisions about whether a child's needs can be met at school. Children's individuality and the teacher's attitude toward demanding children are variables that cannot be reduced to rules and regulations.

Helping teachers understand how to make decisions about sending children home works better than trying to make health policies cover each and every potential situation.

Illness and the Very Young Child

Every teacher has heard the accusation, "She got sick at school." The comment is usually followed by "My doctor says she shouldn't be in a school setting." Teachers are in the position of helping parents understand the infectious disease process and what steps are taken to prevent the spread of contagious diseases at school. Teachers also find that they are often the ones identifying the onset of illness.

The hardest part of understanding the spread of contagious disease is that children who do not look sick can be spreading infection by leaving their secretions around the environment. Typically, children are contagious before they show signs of illness. This makes careful observation and effective sanitation procedures in the toddler classroom even more important.

By the second year of life, patterns and characteristics of the onset of illness have emerged, and parents and teachers are usually more confident about interpreting symptoms and their accompanying behavioral cues. This knowledge can help teachers prevent the spread of infectious diseases.

Toddler teachers need to be excellent observers of children's behavior to support parents in early intervention if an illness is suspected. In general, toddlers should see a physician if they have a temperature over 101° under the arm (axillary) or have other symptoms of illness such as irritability, crying that cannot be soothed, frequent loose stools, coughing, wheezing, repeated vomiting, and so on.

Loose stools are also a normal part of toddlers' experience. New foods, too much of a favorite food, and changes in diet can cause changes in the consistency and frequency of bowel movements. Diarrhea, though, is emptying of the bowel caused by spasms in the intestinal tract that are more frequent than normal for the child. For toddlers in school settings, diarrhea is usually defined as stool that is not contained in the diaper or stool that cannot be held until the child is on the toilet. Because of the risk of contamination, children with more than one uncontained stool are usually excluded from school.

As children get older, parents and teachers become better able to differentiate behaviors and symptoms that indicate the onset of illness in children. In fact, teachers and parents often report that they are able to anticipate when a child is getting ill by observing changes in their behavior, schedule, or temperament.

Infectious diseases are diseases caused by infection with specific microorganisms such as viruses, bacteria, fungi, or parasites. Contagious diseases are infectious diseases that are spread from one person to another (Kendrick, Kaufman & Messinger, 1988). The challenge for toddler teachers is to prevent the spread of contagious diseases by careful sanitation procedures and appropriate health practices.

Preventing the onset and spread of infectious and contagious disease is partially under the control of the teacher. Careful handwashing procedures and good environmental sanitation form the first line of defense.

Toddler Safety

Get a Choke Tube and Use It!

One of the greatest risks to very young children is choking. Toddler environments are often part of schools that serve older children. Many of the toys and materials that are appropriate for preschool children pose choke threats to toddlers who still put many objects into their mouths, particularly as their molar teeth begin to emerge.

Every toddler classroom needs to have a choke tube out and available at all times. Anytime a teacher sees small items in the room, she or he should use the tube to check the items for safety. If the item fits inside of the tube, it poses a choke hazard to toddlers and must be removed immediately. If no choke tube is available, a toilet paper tube is an approximation of a choke tube and can be used until a choke tube is purchased.

The Disposable Glove Debate

Some health professionals recommend that teachers always wear disposable gloves while diapering to protect them from contamination. Because of the frequency of diapering, the intimate nature of the diapering procedure, and the possibility for one-to-one interaction to occur, gloves for routine diapering are not recommended. Careful handwashing (including the use of nailbrush) after diapering is encouraged, monitored, and expected. As long as the teacher's hands are free of cuts or sores and the child who is being diapered is healthy, gloves are not needed for routine diapering (APHA/AAP, 1992).

There are exceptions to this rule. When blood or blood containing body fluids are present, teachers should wear gloves or create barriers between themselves and blood (Rathlev, 1994). When gloves are used, they must be discarded after a single use, and careful handwashing should still occur.

Health

Handwashing and Diapering Procedure

1. Gather all of the supplies needed.
2. Wash your hands with soap, rinsing well with running water. Dry hands well with disposable toweling, and then turn off the running water with the towel covering the handle. Discard the paper towel. Remember, handwashing throughout the day is the most important method for controlling illness.
3. Cover the changing area with disposable paper. Computer paper, newspaper, or commercially prepared changing papers are all acceptable covers.
4. Pick the child up and put her on the changing table. Hold the child by the abdomen with one hand.
5. Remove the soiled diaper and place on the paper covering the diaper-changing table away from the toddler's hands and face.
6. Wash the child's bottom and genitals with warm water, using soap and

paper towels, washcloths, or wipes.

7. Pat the bottom dry with paper towels or a clean washcloth.
8. Now, dispose of the soiled diaper in a plastic bag and then in a closed container located within easy reach of the table.
9. Put on a clean diaper.
10. Examine clothes. Change any soiled or wet clothes.
11. Wash the child's hands with soap and water. Make this easy by taking time to set this up so that the child can reach the sink, soap, and toweling. By getting children into the habit of washing after diapering now, they will remember it after toileting later.
12. Return the child to a comfortable play area or assist with the transition back to the group.
13. Remove the changing table paper. Wipe the tabletop and any other surfaces that came in contact with the diaper, such as the lid of the trash can, with a weak bleach solution (¼ cup to 1 gallon of water). Also, wipe the exteriors of the entire changing station.
14. Wash your hands with soap under running water, dry hands thoroughly, and shut off the water with the paper towel.
15. Mark the child's Communication Sheet. Record the type of diaper change (urine or bowel movement) and the time.

Daily Health Conversations

An important part of every separation from parents and reunion with school should be a discussion about health. This conversation has two goals. The first is to make sure the parent who is dropping off the child at school shares information about the time spent at home. The second is to make sure the toddler is healthy enough to stay at school.

When the school day starts, teachers need the following information about time spent at home:

- What time the toddler went to sleep and how long she slept.
- What time the diaper was last changed.
- What time the child was last fed and how much was eaten.
- Changes in the child's behavior and disposition.
- Any special instructions for the child's day.

Collecting this information is important because children's health and behavior at home are often indicators of their health and behavior at school.

Use a quick health check that can be completed before parents leave for the day as an integral part of parents' drop-off procedure. The check includes a quick look at the child's general physical condition for indicators of health problems. Place a hand on the child's abdomen to determine if she is running a temperature, and look at the face, eyes, the skin on the abdomen and the inside of the arms to screen for signs of infectious or contagious disease such as rashes, bumps, or blisters.

Talk with the parent in detail about the child's behavior and disposition. Irritability, sleep interruptions, and changes in general demeanor and mood can be cues to the toddler's general health. Ask the parent if the child is on any medication.

Health checks won't prevent children from getting sick during the school day, but they will help spot ill children who are exhibiting symptoms. Health checks further assure parents that you are diligent about preventing the spread of disease.

Making Determinations about Sending Children Home

When teachers consider sending children home, a number of criteria need to be taken into consideration. Some of those are:

- ***Symptom severity.*** Severity of symptoms refers to the number and type of symptoms as well as the intensity of the symptoms. In general, the more symptoms a child has, or the more intense the symptoms, the more comfortable the teacher can be with a "go home" decision.
- ***Time of the day.*** Symptoms that begin at the end of the school day pose a different picture than symptoms that begin at the beginning of the school day. Some symptoms unrelated to disease onset are cyclical, such as having a fever after a temper tantrum or waking from a nap with an elevated temperature. Children who begin to get sick late in the day can probably stay at school until their parents pick them up. When this occurs, teachers need to make sure to tell the parents whether or not the child can return to school the next day if symptoms subside.
- ***Speed of onset of symptoms.*** Symptoms that emerge rapidly need to be recorded on the child's chart and watched for 15 to 30 minutes to determine if they go away or get worse. Don't forget to record what happens after the time lapse as well, particularly if you decide not to send the child home.
- ***Daily pattern of behavior.*** All symptoms need to be compared with the child's pattern of behavior. Two weeks of Communication Sheets (see Appendix page 537) should be kept handy. Then, teachers can look back to bring behavior changes or symptoms into focus in the broader perspective. If symptoms have a pattern (such as loose stools every afternoon after eating spinach at lunch), you can be fairly sure they are not the result of onset of illness.

- ***Consistency with health and sick child policy.*** Schools have health and sick child policies for a reason. It is to protect teachers and other children from the spread of contagious disease WHEN SOMETHING CAN BE DONE TO IMPACT THAT SPREAD.
- ***Sanitation procedures.*** Because many of the types of diseases that are contagious are contact borne, carefully follow sanitation procedures such as handwashing, toy washing, and disinfecting the diaper changing area.
- ***Review health policies.*** The first thing a teacher should do if a child exhibits symptoms is READ the school's health policies to determine any guidance for the situation she is considering. If the policy is clear and the child is exhibiting the symptoms listed, the child should be sent home. If the policy is not clear-cut, teachers may want to check out their preliminary decision with others before acting. Getting a second opinion helps teachers gain confidence in their ability to make good decisions about whether a child should be sent home or not.
- ***The family's unique situation.*** Some families have several options for the care of sick children; others do not. Think in terms of helping the family when at all possible. Sending children home must be viewed in light of what the parents are likely to be able to handle, particularly if the child's needs can be met at school. Children who are too ill to be cared for at school need to be at home. But those decisions are usually easy to make. It is more difficult to determine whether mildly ill children or those who are only exhibiting one or two symptoms should stay at school. Letting the child's teacher and the parents make that decision in conjunction with the school's health policy seems appropriate.

Parents should be informed about changes in children's health status as changes occur, even if the change does not require the child to go home. Notification of parents enables parents to begin to plan ahead should they decide the child should be at home. It allows the parents time to call their physician for advice or an appointment, and it makes the stay-at-school/send-home decision a shared one—made by the people who know the child best and who can determine if the child needs special care at home. It allows the child's teacher to consider the needs of the whole group of children. If the teacher feels she or he cannot meet the child's needs, she or he is free to say so to the parents and get their assistance in developing other strategies for getting the child's needs met.

When a child is sent home for a specific illness, or when a contagious disease is documented, parents of other children should be notified. Notification serves two purposes. One is to give parents advance warning of possible contagious diseases that their children have come in contact with as soon as they are exposed. Letting parents know in advance what to look for can limit the number of children who come to school when they are contagious because parents notice symptoms more readily when they are alerted to them. Second, working parents often need advance warning of impending absence from their jobs. Notification allows them to make some contingency plans if their child gets ill. Use the Communication Sheet (page 537) to make a note for parents to read upon reuniting with their toddler.

Safety

Accidents and Injuries

Because accidents are the most frequent cause of injury and death of children under the age of 8 years, schools take special precautions to prevent accidents. Careful accident reporting helps monitor the types of accidents that do occur and evaluate the measures taken to prevent future risks of a similar type from occurring. The teacher's role in accident reporting is to carefully fill out accident reports whenever a child or a teacher assigned to your classroom is injured. Accident reports serve as a permanent record, protecting the injured child by alerting staff to potential accidents and injuries that might need to be addressed.

Teacher Competencies to Support Toddlers Learning to Solve Problems

Sometimes	Usually	Always	
☐	☐	☐	Is aware of the activities of the entire group even when dealing with a part of it; positions self strategically, looks up often from involvement.
☐	☐	☐	Establishes and carries out reasonable limits for children and activities.
☐	☐	☐	Uses nonpunitive ways of dealing with behavior; can exert authority without requiring submission or undermining the child's sense of self.
☐	☐	☐	Redirects, distracts, or channels inappropriate behavior into acceptable outlets.
☐	☐	☐	Anticipates confrontations between children and intervenes before aggressive behavior arises.
☐	☐	☐	Anticipates problems and plans to prevent their re-occurrence.
☐	☐	☐	Does not avoid problem situations; can generate alternative ideas, and implement and evaluate solutions selected.
☐	☐	☐	Reinforces appropriate behavior by encouraging children's appropriate behavior.
☐	☐	☐	Uses praise and encouragement effectively; differentiates between the behavior and the child when using praise.
☐	☐	☐	Guides children to work out increasingly effective ways of making social contacts and solving social problems.
☐	☐	☐	Sees that children are dressed appropriately for existing temperatures throughout the day.
☐	☐	☐	Models the behavior being encouraged and taught to children.
☐	☐	☐	Assures that all children have frequent opportunities for success.
☐	☐	☐	Provides regular and varied outdoor experience.

Resources for Teachers

Adams, C. & E. Fruge. (1996). ***Why children misbehave***. Oakland, CA: New Harbinger.

Clark, S. (1996). Tips for feeding picky eaters. ***Texas Child Care***, Winter, 2-7.

Crary, E. (1993). ***Without spanking or spoiling.*** Seattle, WA: Parenting Press.

Dreikurs, R. (1964). ***Children: The challenge***. New York: Hawthorne/Dutton.

Kendrick, A.S., R. Kaufman & K.P. Messinger. (1988). ***Healthy young children: A manual for programs.*** Washington, DC: National Association for the Education of Young Children (NAEYC).

Marion, M. (1998). ***Guidance of young children.*** New York: Prentice Hall.

Mitchell, G. (1998). ***A very practical guide to discipline with young children.*** Glen Burnie, MD: Telshare.

Ratlev, M. (1994). Universal precautions in early intervention and child care. ***Infants and children***, 6(3) 54-64.

INNOVATIONS IN PARENT PARTNERSHIPS

School- or Teacher-initiated Activities

I Can Do It!

Find ways to celebrate children's developmental progress through developmental banners, notes, signs, and pictures. Invite parents to share information concerning their child's developmental progress at home. Try instituting a Parent Brag Board where parents can share information not only about the children in your classroom, but also about other children or family members.

Parent Participation Activities

We Are Family

Invite parents to be a part of school events. It is important that they bond with their child's teacher(s), the director or principal, the assistant, and teachers who will be substitutes or teachers in the next classroom. This can be accomplished through special events at the center (appreciation days for parents and staff), as well as through introductions when appropriate.

Parent Postcards

Share Parent Postcards with parents as they indicate an interest, at appropriate times during the enrollment cycle, or as developmental issues arise. (See page 548 in the Appendix for a sample dissemination schedule.) Copy Postcards. Cut if necessary. Address to parent(s) and place on Communication Sheet or hand out personally.

Picky Eaters: Helping Your Toddler Eat Healthy

Many parents report that eating behavior during the toddler years is very problematic. Either children don't eat enough or they eat too much. Both are serious problems for parents.

Nutritionists tell us that it is during toddlerhood that children learn to regulate their intake—eating when they are hungry and stopping when they are full. This is an important life lesson. They also tell us that nutritional needs during toddlerhood change—the fast-paced growth of infancy slows as toddlers work on perfecting emerging skills. This change worries many parents. What should you do to make sure your toddler develops healthy, lifelong eating behaviors? Try some of the following strategies:

- Offer new foods one at a time, and offer them several times in a row. Toddlers usually won't try a new food until they are familiar with it and have the opportunity to see it on their plate.
- Be a good role model—try new foods and comment on how they taste. Sit with your toddler when he or she is eating meals or snacks; taste new foods; comment on how new foods taste.
- Make meals a shared family time. Turn off the television and enjoy eating with your child. Sit with your toddler when he or she is eating snacks or meals; taste new foods; comment on how new foods taste.
- Don't pressure. Toddlers need to control their own intake—a powerful experience with independence. Avoid cajoling, enticing, bribing, or tricking children into eating. Let your child decide what to eat and how much. Accept your child's choices.
- Eat at regularly scheduled times; don't offer snacks in between these regularly scheduled times. Toddlers need to eat more frequently than adults, perhaps 5 or 6 times a day. Three meals and two snacks will help children get enough nutrients across the day.
- Give children choices of nutritious foods; avoid fats and sugars that will fill up your toddler without contributing to the child's nutritional needs.
- If your toddler regularly avoids one type of food, such as vegetables or milk, introduce it in an interesting or different way. For example, if he or she isn't drinking milk, substitute other foods high in calcium such as yogurt, cheese, or dried beans.
- Keep your cool. If you are frantic about eating behavior, your toddler will feel like he or she has to continue the behavior that is problematic. If you avoid making a fuss and allow the child to control his or her nutritional intake, your toddler will learn to listen to the cues from his or her body about when and how much to eat—avoiding over- and under-eating.

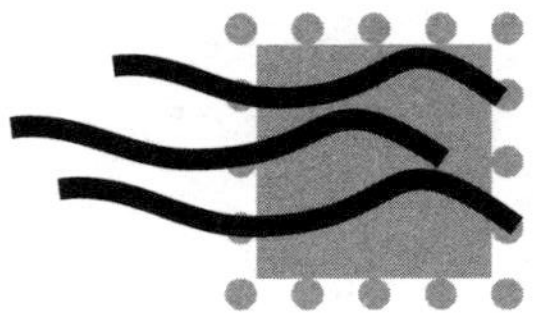

TO ______________

____

____

Toileting: I'm Ready, but My Child Isn't!

Parents look so forward to the end of the second year. They anticipate freedom from disposable diapers, changing dirty diapers, finding diaper-changing places, and washing clothes soiled by overfilled diapers. Unfortunately, for most children, independent toileting will not take place for 6 to 12 more months.

Noted pediatrician T. Berry Brazelton tells parents that 90% of children are toileting independently by the end of the third year (before the fourth birthday). He encourages parents to follow their child's lead as they begin the toilet training process rather than begin too early. When parents fail to match their child's skills and abilities and follow the developmental process of learning to toilet independently, battles and conflicts arise, particularly as your two-year-old is gaining independence skills. Controlling bodily functions is an internal process. Until your child is ready to take control of these bodily functions, no amount of coaxing, rewards, or reminders will accomplish control.

Here are some tips about how to decide if your child is ready to begin the toilet training process. Children need a variety of skills to begin the toilet training process. The first skills needed are body awareness/motor control skills. These skills include:

- Motor control skills such as, "I can sit still for a while, maybe 3 or 4 minutes."
- Skills to delay gratification such as, "I can wait for a while, maybe 3 or 4 minutes."
- Large muscle skills such as, "I can pull my pants down and up without assistance from an adult."
- Small muscle skills such as, "I can regulate the muscles that start and stop the elimination process."
- Motor control skills such as, "I can hold my urine or bowel movement while I get to the toilet, pull my pants down, and have a seat!" and "I can wipe my bottom without adult help."
- Bio-motor regularity skills such as, "I have a prolonged periods of dryness, including waking up from sleep (nap or nighttime) dry."
- Body awareness skills such as, "I can tell when my bladder/bowel is filling up and I need to potty" and "I prefer to be clean rather than dirty."

TO

Toileting: I'm Ready, but My Child Isn't! (continued)

They also need some specific language skills to be ready to toilet train. These skills include:

- My Mommy and Daddy and I have a set of shared words for elimination—I know what to call what is happening to me," and, "I can tell Mommy and Daddy what I need."

Cognitive development also gives toddlers skills that benefit the toilet training process. They include:

- Prediction skills such as, "I may need to potty soon," or "I know what comes next when my body feels like this."
- Memory skills so "I won't forget to go potty while I'm busy playing."

Finally, social/emotional development skills need to be in place to make the timing of toilet training effective. Social/emotional skills include:

- Self-confidence feelings that say, "I can be in charge of my own body!"
- Autonomy skills that mean, "I can do it myself."
- Independence skills that mean, "I want to try to do it myself!"
- Self-esteem feelings that mean "I don't need to make taking care of my body a power struggle."

TO

Toilet Training: Process, Not Magic

Learning to toilet predictably is a process that begins with an interest in the toilet and what happens in bathrooms and ends with independent toileting. The developmental nature of toileting has four phases. The first phase is toilet play. Many parents view this beginning stage as readiness for toilet training when it is actually only the first stage. Toilet play is characterized by an interest in the bathroom in general and in what people, particularly parents, do in the bathroom. During this phase, children often like to get on and off the toilet (generally fully clothed!), flush it repeatedly, play with toilet paper and handwashing, and watch what adults do when they are in the bathroom. It is often accompanied by interest in their own and others' private parts. They will want to watch and compare how they look to how others look.

During toilet play, parents need realistic expectations. This phase rarely leads to self-control directly. Encourage your child to "practice" toileting skills. Help your child learn the skills necessary to move on to the next stage—how to get on and off of the toilet and how to "wait" a minute or two between getting on and getting off. Set up a pattern of getting on the toilet, sitting for a minute, tearing off a little bit of toilet paper, getting off the toilet, flushing, and then washing and drying hands. Don't be surprised if your toddler wants to repeat this process many times. Remember, this is play for your child. Playing is part of getting ready for the next phase. Often this early interest in the bathroom and the play accompanied with it ends as quickly as they begin. This signals that your child has answered all of his or her questions for the time being and is on to other discoveries—not that the process has failed. Just be patient, and the next stage will follow soon.

Expect your child to be curious about bodily functions, his or her own as well as yours. Dealing matter-of-factly with this interest will help the child figure out how his or her body works and lead to an increased interest in wanting to control his or her body just like you do.

TO

Toilet Training: Process, Not Magic (continued)

The second stage of toileting is toilet practice. During this stage, motor skills related to toileting are practiced and perfected. Getting on and off the toilet without assistance, pulling pants down and up, taking off diapers or pull-up diapers, pretending to wipe after pretending to toilet (or after a coincidental success!), flushing the toilet, and washing hands are all part of the toilet practice stage. It is very important for parents to continue to be excited about these small steps toward independent toileting, even if they are not accompanied with actual toileting success. Help your child practice the skills that interest him or her. Follow the child's lead as you gently assist him or her. At first, your child might need a lot of assistance. But as your child practices, he or she will need less support. Don't forget to modify your response as your child's skill grows.

The third phase is toilet training. It is during this stage that children may begin to have some success and can be encouraged by caring parents to continue the process of becoming independent about toileting. During this stage, children need reminders to check their bodies to see if they are getting messages about whether they need to toilet. The training part comes from cueing the child to take a reading of how his or her body is feeling and whether or not there is any bowel or bladder urgency.

Some parents mistakenly think that their child is almost trained at this stage. This is not the case. During this stage, the training part is aimed at the child increasing his or her awareness of what is going own internally to the point that the awareness is conscious. Taking your toddler with you when you go to the bathroom, asking your child to check his or her body when waking, after breakfast, before leaving home, before getting in the bathtub, and before going to bed sets up a pattern of getting in touch with how your body feels that leads to the next stage.

Toilet Training: Process, Not Magic (continued)

Expect accidents to happen frequently at this stage. Children are just not tuned in to their bodies to adequately anticipate their needs accurately. Validate successes and respond calmly to accidents. Approach accidents as opportunities for continued practice of the skills needed to toilet—pulling down pants, changing into clean ones, and pulling them back up. Never scold or punish children for accidents at this stage. In fact, you can foster emerging independence by helping children to clean themselves up after accidents. The more responsibility you can give your child for this process, the more likely he or she will be interested in gaining self-control.

Perfecting the timing of toileting is a very difficult task for children. While children are learning to toilet independently, they are often surprised that needing to toilet has snuck up on them. Children still wait until it is too late to get to the bathroom, pull down their pants, and get on the toilet before releasing the small muscles that control elimination. They will jump up, grab their private parts, and have an accident before they even get moving toward the bathroom. It is during this stage that small muscles are strengthened enough to hold urine or stop the movement of the bowel for a minute or so while children get in the position to eliminate on the toilet.

The last stage is independent toileting. This is the stage that parents long for—they are not needed to remind or coax a child to toilet. Children take care of their own bodily needs without prompting or reminders. It is the culmination of a process that began with toilet play and ends with parents who are very proud of the child's accomplishments. Viewed this way, toilet training never gets ugly! There are no fights, no frustration, and no failures.

TO

The School's Role

Children will go through all of these stages at school as well as at home. You may find that your child's teacher will wait until you are further along in the process at home before starting the process at school. The primary reason for this is that you have one child to work with at home while teachers have a group of children to work with at school. Another reason is that children may be at very different stages in the process.

Talk to your child's teacher about what you are doing at home to see if she or he can reinforce and support your efforts at home. Don't be surprised if your child's teacher is seeing different behavior at school. The school setting is very different from home, and children often change their behavior in different settings. Try to discover where there is common ground between the two settings and start there. Also, try to avoid comparisons. It is widely thought that girls may toilet train faster that boys, but this may not be the case for your daughter or son. Some children get bladder control before bowel control, others bowel before bladder. Some children show early interest in toileting while others are oblivious to what is going on in their diapers well into the beginning of the third year. All of these variations are normal differences in the growth and development process and should never be used to evaluate a child's developmental age or stage.

TO

Natural and Logical Consequences

Natural and logical consequences are the best tools for parents to help their child gain self-control. A natural or logical consequence is a consequence that emerges from the situation. This important parent skill is not one of the easiest ones to learn. It takes time, practice, and careful response. The following examples illustrate the concept of logical consequences:

> A toddler pulls on Mommy's earring as soon as he or she gets picked up. After Mommy takes his or her hand and reminds him or her to leave the earring alone, the toddler pulls again on the earring. Mom puts the toddler down, saying, "I can't hold you if you pull on my earring. It hurts!" The logical consequence of not listening to Mommy's request is to be put down where you cannot reach her earring.

Notice that that there is no struggle for power in this situation. The consequences emerge from the situation and are responded to firmly but calmly. As a result, children learn to control their own behavior slowly over time as they come to understand the reasons they should do so and understand the consequences of not doing so.

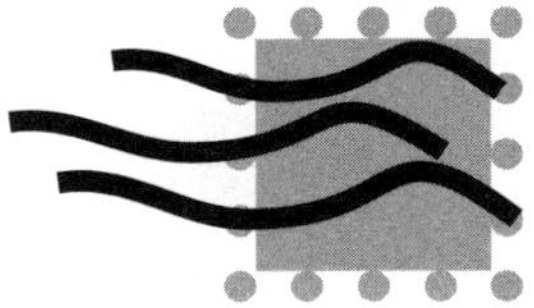

Setting Appropriate Limits

Parents have two reasons to set rules and limits. The first reason is to protect children and keep them safe—reason enough for a good set of limits. The second reason is to help children grow toward self-control. Where do you start to establish reasonable limits and rules for your home? Start by following these rules about rules.

- **First, make rules humane.** There is no place for rules that are punitive in nature and/or make children feel bad about themselves. Humane rules do not humiliate, embarrass, belittle, or degrade the child.
- **Second, limits should not be arbitrary**. Rules should convey to children that you make rules thoughtfully, not just because you can.
- **Third, rules should be out in the open, not secret**. Children, particularly very young children, cannot guess what the rules are. They need to be told, reminded, and reminded again. (Yes, even if it takes thousands of reminders!)
- **Fourth, limits should be clearly stated and enforceable**. Rules should refer to the expected behavior and be clear enough for children to know immediately when they have broken the rule. Avoid "don't" rules, such as: don't run, or don't stand on the couch. Try to state your rules from a positive perspective (walk in the house, sit on the couch).
- **Fifth, rules should be accompanied by reasons**. Research has shown that children who are given the reasons behind the rules are more likely to listen and to follow the rules without parental reminders. But, be brief and to the point. Children need one good reason for each rule, not three or four.
- **Sixth, remember to update your rules.** This is particularly important during the first three years when children are maturing and developing so quickly. Limits should reflect new skills. For example, very young children need strict climbing rules such as, "Hold on tightly with both hands when you climb." As children become proficient in climbing, the rule can simply be, "Climb safely."

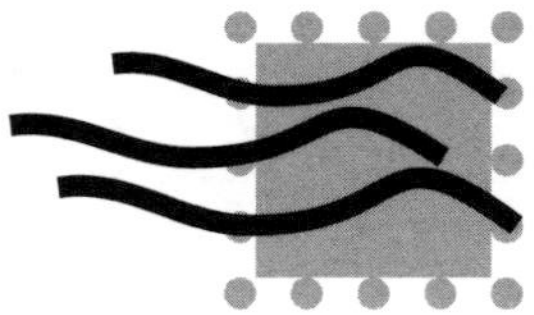

TO

Setting Appropriate Limits (continued)

- **Seventh, and most important, rules and limits should be firmly enforced.** As children grow, they will test limits that parents set for them. If parents do not set limits and do not enforce rules, children will heed no adult guidance. Firm, consistent responses to broken rules help children learn to follow the rules set for them by their parents.

Very young children get a sense of security and support from parental rules. Part of your child's rule testing is an attempt to confirm that you will set limits and keep him or her safe. Children who don't have an ordered, disciplined life struggle to find out where the limits are by testing harder and longer. Setting limits along with enforcing them is a very loving and responsive thing to do.

TO ______________________

____

____

Resources for Parents

Add these helpful books to your parent library or post this list on your parent bulletin board.

Brazelton, T. B. (1992). ***Touchpoints: The essential reference.*** Reading, MA: Addison Wesley.

Honig, A. (1989). ***Love and learn: Discipline for young children.*** Washington, DC: National Association for the Education of Young Children (NAEYC).

Miller, K. (2000). ***Ages and Stages.*** West Palm Beach, FL: TelShare.

Shelov, S. (1998). ***Caring for your baby and child.*** New York: Bantam Doubleday Dell.

INNOVATIONS IN ENVIRONMENT

Outdoor Environments for Toddlers

It is the mantra of the toddler—outside! For toddlers, one or two trips a day to the outdoors are simply not enough. They are always at the door—clamoring to go outside. This natural interest and tolerance for being outdoors is tied to the excitement of expanding skills, as well as the autonomy toddlers experience when they are outdoors acting independently as they climb, ride, or play.

Toddlers need frequent opportunities to go outside. Trips outdoors provide a change of pace, freedom from being so close to other children, and a constant source of interesting stimuli to look for, examine, and play with. Plan at least two trips to the outdoors daily.

Toddlers are climbers. As they become more interested in the world around them, toddlers become fascinated with climbing, both to try out and practice new skills, and to explore the environment from different perspectives. Both indoor and outdoor environments need a place where it is appropriate for toddlers to climb safely and appropriately.

Teachers can use the appropriate place to take children who are climbing on tables, chairs, and bookshelves, reminding them that the place to climb safely is on the climbing structure. This approach of replacing an inappropriate behavior with an appropriate one is so important because it prevents the classroom from becoming a place that restricts exploration. Although it will take many reminders, eventually toddlers will climb on appropriate equipment more often than on inappropriate equipment.

Outdoors is where toddlers can really perfect those climbing skills. Climbing structures for toddlers need to be sturdy and strong to be safe. Surround each climber with appropriate cushioning to protect toddlers from falls. Don't forget loose parts for toddlers to arrange in a variety of ways—providing experiences with controlling the environment. Toddlers like to rearrange boxes and blocks, and they like tents to create places to climb into, under, or around.

Balancing is another exciting skill to explore. Balance beams low to the ground will make sure that spills are limited to tumbles instead of falls. Investigations of how to balance on a beam compared to balancing on a climber are examples of the way toddlers create their own skill practice when the outdoor environment is conducive.

Push toys and tricycles that move through space are also popular. With paths through the playground space, these important gross motor toys also contribute to dramatic play when paired with play props and supports from the classroom.

Digging in the sand or soil is another great outdoor activity for toddlers. Not only are the materials stimulating and enjoyable, but also the ability to rearrange sand and soil makes toddlers feel capable and competent. Water, added to dry sand and soil or placed in a water table, will add interest as toddlers explore the natural world.

When toddlers are given many opportunities to play outdoors, they can practice and experience many emerging skills. The ability to impact and influence the environment, by riding a tricycle, digging in the sand, climbing on a climber, moving parts around the playground, and playing alongside and with friends, communicates powerful messages of success about the things they can do. It is for this reason that many toddlers love the outdoors—it is a "can-do" place.

But, the fast-paced activity of the outdoors can also be overstimulating and overwhelming. Don't forget to have quiet places to go to cool down or to calm down. A blanket serves nicely, and also can provide a place for toddlers to spend some time with the teacher, refueling and recharging before heading back out to explore the world again.

Bringing Indoor Materials Outside

When thinking of outdoor play, many teachers think of traditional physical education activities. These, of course, are not appropriate for toddlers. They, instead, need opportunities for sensory and physical stimulation. The very same activities that toddlers need and enjoy inside are appropriate when they go outside. Try some of these:

- Books outside provide a special time for reading on a blanket.
- Small climbers and low platforms provide opportunities to stretch and move in the fresh air.
- Dramatic play takes on a new dimension when activities take place under a shade structure or tree.
- Messy art projects that may be difficult to do in the classroom are often easier to clean up outside.

Bringing indoor materials outside helps to provide rich learning experiences for toddlers outdoors. Teachers, with careful planning and thoughtful interactions, support children as they develop socially, emotionally, physically, and intellectually when they are both in the indoor and outdoor learning environments.

Environmental Sanitation with Toddlers

Environmental sanitation involves two steps. The first is removing the warm, moist conditions under which microorganisms thrive and grow. The second is destroying or removing microorganisms that arrive at school through the respiratory tract (via secretions from the mouth, nose, lungs, or eyes); through the intestinal tract (via stool); through direct contact or touching; and through contact with blood.

Classrooms need to be well ventilated with fresh air, and children need opportunities to go outside often. As doors are opened for children to move inside and outside, fresh air is introduced into closed, centrally air-conditioned classrooms, airing out the collected airborne contaminants.

Sanitation procedures should require sanitation of surfaces that children touch, including the floors, walls, and furniture as well as the toys and materials that children put in their mouths or touch with their hands. In addition, diapering and eating areas should be as far away from each other as possible and need thorough sanitizing after each use. Bleach solution is usually the sanitizing agent of choice because it is inexpensive and easy to mix. Use ¼ cup of bleach to 1 gallon of water mixed fresh daily as a sanitizing solution.

Activities and Experiences vs. Centers

Most early childhood educators think of interest or learning centers as an essential part of any classroom setting. Yet, environments for toddlers are different because they are "groupie" in nature and tend to go where the action is. For this reason, teachers must bring activities and experiences to children and assist children in going to where the activities are. A wide range of activities and experiences must be available to toddlers. In each of the following Possibilities Plans, *Construction* and *Wheels*, activities and experiences are presented in the following areas:

- Dramatic Possibilities
- Sensory/Art Possibilities
- Curiosity Possibilities
- Construction Possibilities
- Literacy Possibilities
- Music Possibilities
- Movement Possibilities
- Outdoor Possibilities
- Project Possibilities
- Parent Participation Possibilities

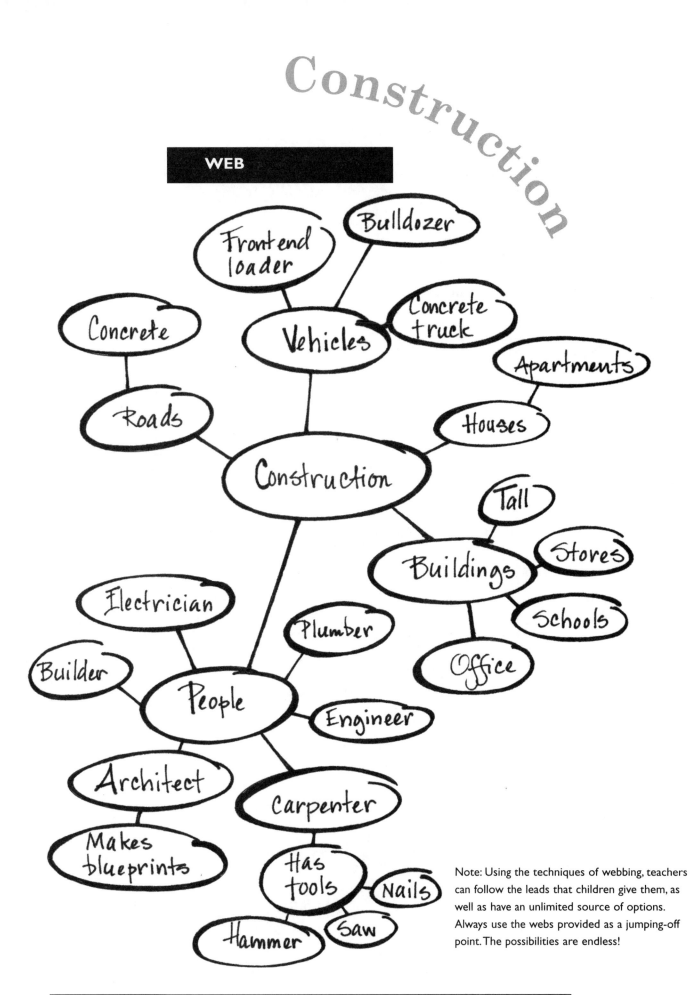

Construction

WEB

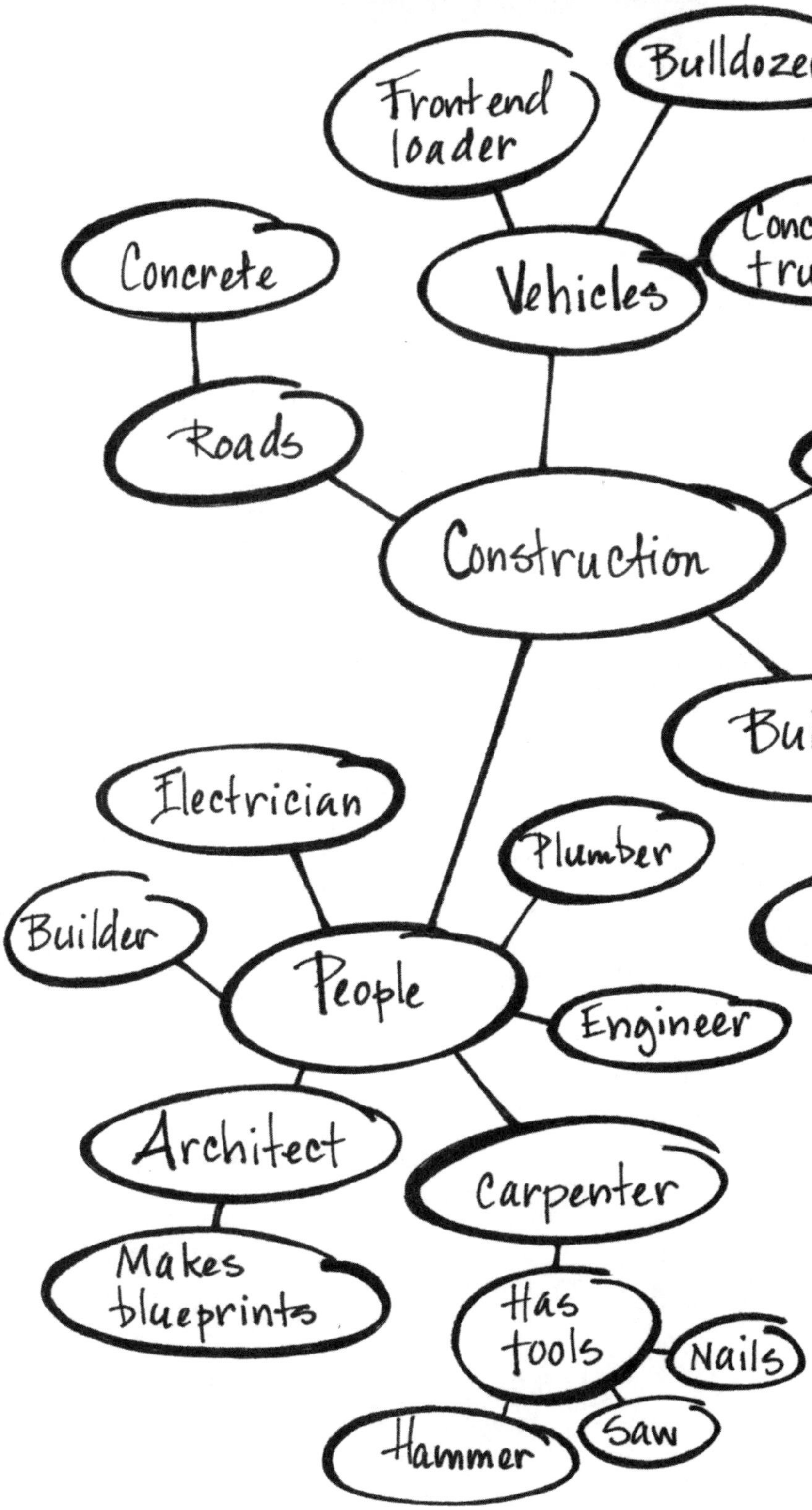

Note: Using the techniques of webbing, teachers can follow the leads that children give them, as well as have an unlimited source of options. Always use the webs provided as a jumping-off point. The possibilities are endless!

PLANNING PAGES

Plan Possibilities

Dramatic

Construction Worker 410
Plumbing Equipment 410
Pounding Bench 411

Sensory/Art

Mud Painting 411
Mounds of Dirt 411
Plunger Prints 412
Sand Painting 412

Curiosity

Construction Out the Window 412
Construction Puzzles 413
Tool Match 413
Measure It! 413

Construction

Construction Sounds 414
Building Roads 414
Construction Machines . . 415

Literacy

Class Big Book 415
Dump Truck Book 415
Tool Book 416
Apron Story 416
Construction Books 416

Music

Johnny Hammer 417
This Is the Way 417
The Dump Truck Song. . . 418

Movement

Bulldozer Moves 419
As I Was Walking 419
Drive the Truck 420

Outdoor

Wheelbarrows 420
Large Construction Toys . 421
Water Cooler 421
Construction Workers on the Job 421
Big Blocks 421

Projects

Shoebox Building 422

Parent Participation

Construction Machines/Tools 422
Songs and Fingerplays . . 422
Parent Postcards
Encouraging Independence and Autonomy 423
Continuing to Support Independence and Autonomy 424

Concepts Learned in Construction425

Prop Boxes

Construction Worker4	25
Big Machines4	26

Picture File/Vocabulary426

Books

Biggest Truck, The by David Lyon Katie and the Big Snow by Virginia Lee Burton Mike Mulligan by Virginia Lee Burton416 Mud Puddle by Robert Munsch Murmel, Murmel, Murmel by Robert Munsch Neighborhood Trucker by Louise Borden Truck by Donald Crew Truck Song by Diane Siebert Trucks by Anne Rockwell Trucks by Gail Gibbons

Construcz

Rhymes/Fingerplays

"As I Was Walking"								.419
"Drive the Truck"								.420

Music/Songs

"The Dump Truck Song"
"The Hammer Song"
"This Is the Way"

Toys and Materials427

DRAMATIC POSSIBILITIES

Construction Worker

All ages

Materials

Toy tools and toolbox
Short cloth measuring tape
Construction apron
Rulers
Lunch box
Work boots

Teacher Talk

Talk about construction workers building houses, office buildings, and bridges. "Do you need help with the tool belt, Shawn?"

Place safe, toy replicas of typical construction worker items in the area. Place a variety of plastic tools in a plastic toolbox with a lid that fastens. Children may enjoy carrying it around, filling and dumping, or "fixing" things in the area.

Plumbing Equipment

All ages

Materials

Plastic toy wrenches
Lengths of plastic pipe
Rulers
Construction apron
HVAC building plans
Plastic joint pieces
Plastic tool caddy

Teacher Talk

"You put all the wrenches and pipes in your tool caddy, Thomas."

Fill a plastic tool caddy with plastic wrenches and pieces of real plastic pipes and fittings. Observe to see how children use the items.

Pounding Bench

24-30 months

Materials

Commercially purchased pounding benches

Teacher Talk

"You are hitting the red peg with the hammer, Amalia. Yes, see the peg going in."

Place commercially purchased pounding benches in the area. Children may enjoy hitting the pegs with the hammer, putting pegs in and out, and being noisy as they play.

SENSORY/ART POSSIBILITIES

Mud Painting

All ages

Materials

Soil
Water
Cardboard
Plastic pans
Smocks

Teacher Talk

Talk about the texture as children enjoy the mud experience. "The water and the soil make mud, Laikyn."

Mix soil and water to make fingerpaint-like consistency. Show children how to use the mud to paint on cardboard.

Mounds of Dirt

All ages

Materials

Soil
Sand table

Teacher Talk

"The soil feels cool, Wade. How does the soil smell?"

Fill the sand table with soil. Observe as children explore the texture of the dirt, the smell, and how the dirt is different when it is dry and when it is damp.

Plunger Prints

24-30 months

Materials
Short-handled plungers
Shallow plastic pans
Paint
Paper

Teacher Talk
Talk about the plunger making a circle, the different colors, and the unique designs each child makes. "The red paint made a circle, Emily."

Children can use the rubber part of the plunger to dip into paint and make prints on paper.

Sand Painting

30-36 months

Materials
Glue
Sand in plastic salt shaker
Cardboard

Teacher Talk
"You can sprinkle the sand on the glue. You did it!"

Children make glue designs on cardboard. Show children how to shake sand onto the glue designs. Allow the glue to dry and then shake off excess sand.

CURIOSITY POSSIBILITIES

Construction Out the Window

All ages

Materials
Small set of curtains
Pictures showing construction scenes

Teacher Talk
Talk about what children see in the "window." "What do you see, Joseph? Yes, I see the trucks, too."

Attach curtains to a wall at the level children can reach as they stand on the floor. Underneath the curtain, attach a picture showing a construction scene. Open the curtain to show children what is in the "window." To add to the interest, change out the picture periodically.

? — Construction Puzzles

All ages

Materials
Commercially purchased or teacher-made construction puzzles

Teacher Talk
Talk about the different machines and what they do as children put the pieces together to make the pictures. "This dump truck puzzle has four big pieces, Jarrod. You put that puzzle together really fast!"

Place a variety of construction machine puzzles in the area. If purchased puzzles are not available, use pictures of construction machines glued onto cardboard. Cut the pictures into the number and sizes of pieces appropriate for the children.

? — Tool Match

24-30 months

Materials
Pairs of plastic tools

Teacher Talk
"Can you find the other hammer that looks like this one, Trevor?"

Place pairs of toy tools in a plastic box. Ask children to find the matching tools.

? — Measure It!

30-36 months

Materials
Lengths of wood

Teacher Talk
"Let's line up the pieces of wood. That piece is longest, Natasha."

Place a variety of lengths of smooth wood in a box. Show children how to line up the wood pieces. Comment on which piece is the longest.

CONSTRUCTION POSSIBILITIES

Construction Sounds

All ages

Materials
Tape recorder
Blank tape

Teacher Talk
Talk about the different sounds. "I hear a hammer, Justin. What do you hear?"

Use a blank tape to record construction sounds such as hammering, power tools, and big truck noises. Play the tape for children to hear the sounds of a construction site.

Building Roads

All ages

Materials
Blocks
Toy construction vehicles
People and animal block figures

Teacher Talk
"Andy, we can make a road together with blocks. Which blocks do you want to use first?"

Show children how to use blocks, lining them up end to end to make roads. Push small construction vehicles on the roads. Observe to see what toddlers do next.

Construction Machines

All ages

Materials

Toy dump trucks
Toy bulldozers
Toy front-end loaders

Teacher Talk

Talk about each piece of equipment and how it works as children play. "The dump truck is carrying lots of sand, Harrison."

Place small plastic dump trucks, bulldozers, and front-end loaders in the dirt. Children can explore moving the dirt with the construction machines.

LITERACY POSSIBILITIES

Class Big Book

All ages

Materials

Poster board
Large sheets of paper
Markers and pencils

Create a blank big book from poster board and large sheets of paper. Write a few words at the top of each page about trucks, construction activities, or other events children have experienced. Write children's comments, after they draw on the bottom of the page.

Dump Truck Book

All ages

Materials

Cardboard
Glue
Hole punch
Metal rings
Pictures of dump trucks

Teacher Talk

Point to pictures and talk about what is on each page. "You are right. That is a red truck, Jana."

Glue pictures of dump trucks onto cardboard. Punch holes in each page. Fasten the pages together with metal rings. Share the book with children.

Tool Book

All ages

Materials

Pictures of familiar tools
Paper plates
Glue
Hole punch
Yarn

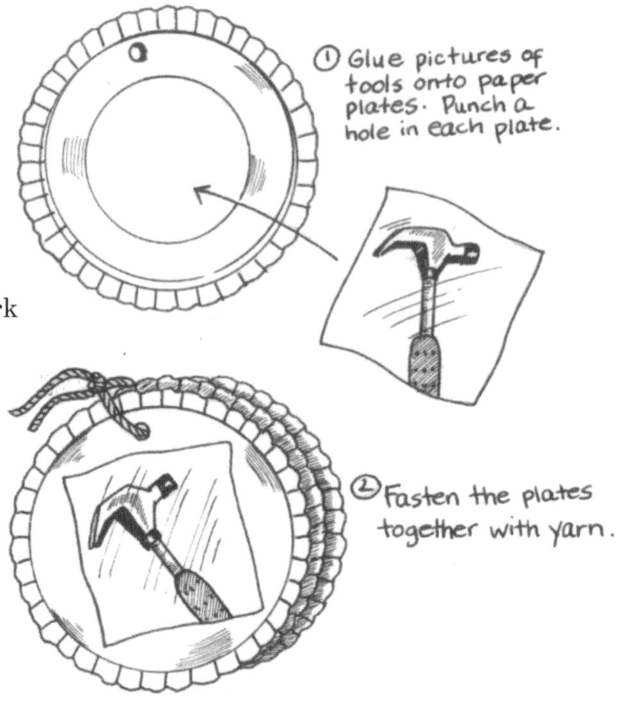

Teacher Talk

Talk about what kinds of work the tools do as you share the book. "That's a hammer, Daryl. How does a hammer sound?"

Glue pictures of tools onto paper plates. Punch a hole in each plate. Fasten the plates together with yarn. Look at the book with children.

Apron Story

All ages

Materials

Apron/smock with pockets
Small toy construction vehicles
Plastic tools

Place small toy construction vehicles in the pockets of an apron/smock. As a child pulls a vehicle out of the pocket, use it in a story, or observe to see what the child says about the vehicle.

Construction Books

All ages

Materials

Children's books about construction like *Mike Mulligan* by Virginia Lee Burton
Materials from construction prop boxes

Teacher Talk
Talk with children about what people do when they work in construction. "Yes, Abbey, construction workers make things like Mike did in the book. See the big hole that the steam shovel made?"

Read a variety of books (see page 426 for suggestions) about construction during this Possibilities Plan. Read favorites over and over again. Children will enjoy holding materials from the construction prop boxes (page 425) as you read the stories.

MUSIC POSSIBILITIES

Johnny Hammer

All ages

Materials
None

Sing the song and act out the motions with children.

The Hammer Song
Johnny hammers with one hammer, (Hammer with the right fist.)
One hammer, one hammer.
Johnny hammers with one hammer,
Then he hammers with two.

Johnny hammers with two hammers, (Hammer with right and left fists.)
Two hammers, two hammers.
Johnny hammers with two hammers,
Then he hammers with three.
Then he goes to sleep. (Place folded hands under face.)

This Is the Way

All ages

Materials
None

Teacher Talk
"Karen, I like this song, too."

Sing the song and act out the motions with children. Sing to the tune "The Mulberry Bush."

This Is the Way

This is the way we hammer the nails, (Hammer one fist on top of the other fist.)
Hammer the nails, hammer the nails.
This is the way we hammer the nails,
On a bright and sunny morning.

This is the way we saw the wood, (Make sawing motion.)
Saw the wood, saw the wood.
This is the way we saw the wood,
On a bright and sunny morning.

This is the way we tighten the bolt, (Pretend to use a wrench.)
Tighten the bolt, tighten the bolt.
This is the way we tighten the bolt,
On a bright and sunny morning.

This is the way we shovel the dirt, (Pretend to shovel dirt.)
Shovel the dirt, shovel the dirt,
This is the way we shovel the dirt,
On a bright and sunny morning.

The Dump Truck Song

All ages

Materials

None

Sing the following song and act out the words with children. Sing to the tune "The Wheels on the Bus."

The Dump Truck Song

The front-end loader fills up the truck, (Scooping motion with both hands.)
Fills up the truck, fills up the truck.
The front-end loader fills up the truck,
At the construction site.

The dump truck dumps out the dirt, (Make a dumping motion with both hands.)
Dumps out the dirt, dumps out the dirt.
The dump truck dumps out the dirt,
At the construction site.

The driver of the dump truck waves hello, (Wave hello.)
Waves hello, waves hello.

The driver of the dump truck waves hello,
At the construction site.

MOVEMENT POSSIBILITIES

Bulldozer Moves

All ages

Materials
Big construction vehicles
Roads made from butcher paper

Teacher Talk
"Yi, you are moving a big bulldozer on the roads all around the room."

Show children how to push construction vehicles around the room on the paper roads.

As I Was Walking

All ages

Materials
None

Teacher Talk
"That sounds like a dump truck, Jennifer."

Hold hands with one or more children, walk in a circle, and say the following rhyme.

As I Was Walking
As I was walking down the street, (Children move in circle.)
Down the street, down the street,
A dump truck I chanced to meet.
Hi ho, hi ho, hi ho. (Stop moving and clap hands.)

Vroom! Vroom! Vroom!
And away it went. (Children move in circle.)
Away it went, away it went.
Vroom! Vroom! Vroom!
And away it went.
Hi ho, hi ho, hi ho. (Stop moving and clap hands.)

As I was walking down the street, (Children move in circle.)
Down the street, down the street.
A cement truck I chanced to meet.
Hi ho, hi ho, hi ho. (Stop moving and clap hands.)

Grrrh! Grrrh! Grrrh!
And away it went. (Move in circle.)
Away it went, away it went.
Grrrrh! Grrrh! Grrrh!
And away it went.
Hi ho, hi ho, hi ho. (Stop moving and clap hands.)

Drive the Truck

All ages

Materials
None

Sing the following song and encourage children act out the words with you. Sing to the tune "Row, Row, Row Your Boat."

Drive the Truck
Drive, drive, drive the truck, (Pretend to steer the truck.)
Carefully down the road. (Nod head from side to side.)
Bumpity, bumpity, bumpity, bump. (Move up and down from the knees.)
Listen to my horn! (Honk!)

OUTDOOR POSSIBILITIES

Wheelbarrows

All ages

Materials
Toy wheelbarrows or wagons
Blocks
Sand
Soil

Teacher Talk
Talk about how many shovels of dirt it takes to fill the wheelbarrow and/or wagons as children work. "Your wheelbarrow is full, Jake."

Show children how to use toy wheelbarrows or wagons to move toys, blocks, sand, or soil from one place to another on the playground.

Large Construction Toys
All ages

Materials
Large toy dump trucks
Toy cement trucks
Toy bulldozers

Teacher Talk
Talk about how the wet sand feels. "The dump truck makes loud noises when it carries a heavy load, Trent. The truck is full of damp sand."

Provide large construction toys as children play in a sandbox. Dampen the sand to give children a different sand experience.

Water Cooler
All ages

Materials
Large water cooler
Paper cups

Fill a large cooler with cool water. Help children fill paper cups with water to drink while playing outside.

Construction Workers on the Job
All ages

Materials
Hard hats
Lunch boxes
Tool belts
Work boots
Work gloves

Teacher Talk
"Naomi has a hard hat on her head."

Place construction worker-related items outside for children to wear as they "work" on a construction site.

Big Blocks
All ages

Materials
Outdoor plastic blocks
Architectural blocks

Cardboard blocks
Styrofoam blocks (covered with contact paper)
Shoebox blocks
Milk carton blocks

Provide large blocks outside, so children can move around and construct using big items.

PROJECT POSSIBILITIES

Shoebox Building

All ages

Materials
Unit blocks—simple
Unit blocks—curved
Shoeboxes
Tape
People figures
Animal figures
Toy cars
Toy trucks and equipment

Begin with a small collection of simple unit blocks. After a period of time add more complex unit blocks. Over time, additional blocks or play props can be added (shoebox blocks, people figures, animal figures, and toy cars, trucks, and equipment). Take photographs of Construction Possibilities as you add enrichments and post them to the wall in the construction area. Show parents how this area has changed and grown during arrival and departure times.

PARENT PARTICIPATION POSSIBILITIES

Construction Machines/Tools

Invite parents to join you outside one the playground with tools from their tool collections. Parents may have wheelbarrows, tool belts of tools, or pole climbing equipment they can share with children. Ask parents to talk about safety rules for the tools they brought with them.

Songs and Fingerplays

This Plan contains a number of new and original fingerplays that will not be familiar to parents. Copy the words to the fingerplays and songs, post them on the bulletin board, and take the time to teach parents the songs, either at a parent meeting or informally as they arrive and depart. Pick each child's favorite song or fingerplay as a place to start.

Parent Postcards

Parent Postcards in this section are designed to share with parents during the Possibilities Plan. The topics are natural extensions of the activities and experiences that you are planning and implementing for the toddlers in the classroom. Use the postcards to connect parents to their children's learning.

Encouraging Independence and Autonomy

What are some of the ways parents can support emerging independence and autonomy? During the toddler years, toddlers are learning that they can trust the world in which they live to be a safe and responsive place. Quick responses to calls for help, sensitive matching of what you do to the toddler's cues, and warm, caring, interactions help children feel that they can trust the world around them.

Since the end of the first year, children have resisted being helped by their parents. Parents know when this happens. They pick their toddler up, and he or she immediately wants to get down. They try to put on their child's shoes on, and he or she grabs the shoes and attempts to put them on.

Encourage these early tries at independence. Tell your child "nice try," even if he or she doesn't succeed at first. Follow his or her lead on tasks where there is interest. Monitor your child's frustration level, allowing just enough to keep interest but not so much that your child gets discouraged. Expect failure and mistakes, particularly in early attempts at a new skill. Noted psychologist Jean Piaget suggests that children learn primarily by making mistakes and coming up with their own corrections. Making your own mistakes and figuring out solutions can be fun!

TO ______________________

____

____

Continuing to Support Independence and Autonomy

Avoid taking over when your child makes a mistake. Let your child know you have confidence in his or her ability. Encourage your child to keep trying or to try again. Verbal support provides important feedback that you feel your child can succeed. Talk children through what they are doing by describing their actions. "You've almost got your foot in the shoe," or "You finished all of your lunch!" These verbal cues help children see the impact of their actions as they occur and encourage a better understanding of how things work.

Expect regression as children learn and lose skills. Most emerging skills need repeated practice to be added to a child's developmental skill repertoire. Your child may accomplish a task once (such as being able to put on his or her shoes or pull off his or her clothes) and then be unable to repeat that success in many subsequent tries. Your child may also lose interest in tasks that held his or her attention for quite some time. This is a part of the natural process of learning and developing. Don't be alarmed when regression or loss of interest occurs.

Support and encourage early attempts at independence and autonomy, even though you may ultimately have to help complete the task. Early independence needs support even if the results are not quite what you expected. Success in putting on Daddy's shoes or finding one's own pajamas indicates progress toward independence. Validate these important steps as they occur with hugs, smiles, and encouragement.

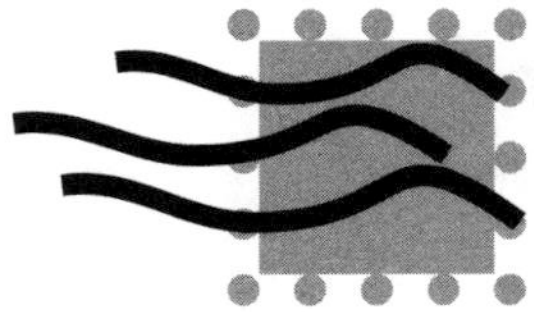

TO

Concepts Learned in Construction

Concepts Learned

Construction workers wear hard hats.
Construction workers wear tool belts.
Plumbers use pipes.
Hammers are for pounding nails.
Wrenches turn bolts.
Saws cut wood.
Measuring tapes measure the length of things.
Bulldozers make loud noises.
Bulldozers push piles of dirt.
Cement trucks carry wet cement to construction sites.
Cement trucks make grinding noises.
Dump trucks can carry heavy loads.
Dump trucks dump dirt and sand.
I can pound with a hammer.
Wet sand sticks together.
Dirt and water make mud.
I can use big boxes to make big buildings.
I can tell stories about construction machines.
I can name construction machines and familiar tools.
I can identify sounds tools make.
I can sing songs about trucks.
I can move my body in big ways.

Resources

Prop Boxes

Construction Worker

- Construction apron
- Construction magazines
- Hard hat
- House plans
- Lunch box
- Plastic hand tools
- Plastic tools
- Rulers
- Short cloth
- Measuring tape
- Small metal or plastic tool box
- Tool belt
- Tool box
- Work boots
- Writing pad and crayon

Big Machines
- Construction vehicles
- Hard hat
- Plastic construction site mat
- Roads made from paper

Picture File/Vocabulary

Bulldozers
Carpenters
Cement trucks
Construction site
Construction workers
Dump trucks
Hammers
Plumbers
Power tools
Saws
Wrenches

Books

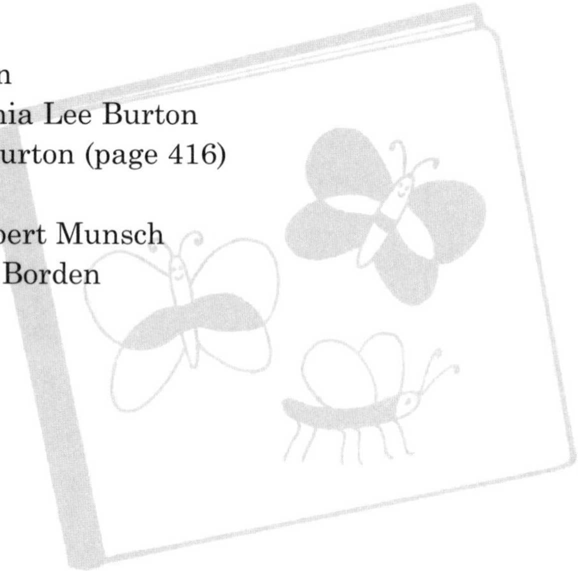

Biggest Truck, The by David Lyon
Katie and the Big Snow by Virginia Lee Burton
Mike Mulligan by Virginia Lee Burton (page 416)
Mud Puddle by Robert Munsch
Murmel, Murmel, Murmel by Robert Munsch
Neighborhood Trucker by Louise Borden
Truck by Donald Crew
Truck Song by Diane Siebert
Trucks by Anne Rockwell
Trucks by Gail Gibbons

Rhymes/Fingerplays

"As I Was Walking" (page 419)
"Drive the Truck" (page 420)

Music/Songs

"The Dump Truck Song" (page 418)
"The Hammer Song" (page 417)
"This Is the Way" (page 418)

Toys and Materials

The following purchased items are important for this Possibilities Plan:

Apron/smock with pockets
Architectural blocks
Blank tape
Blocks (variety)
Butcher paper
Cardboard
Children's wheelbarrows and wagons
Clear contact paper
Cloth measuring tape (short)
Construction puzzles
Glue
Hole punch
Lunch boxes
Outdoor plastic blocks
Paint
Paper
Paper cups
Paper plates
Pencil, markers, and crayons
People and animal block figures
Pounding bench
Rulers
Sand table
Scissors
Shallow plastic pans
Short handled plungers
Silver rings
Small and large toy construction vehicles
Smocks
Tape
Tape recorder
Toy bulldozers
Toy dump and cement trucks
Toy front-end loaders
Toy plastic tools (pairs) and tool box/caddy
Water cooler
Yarn

Toys and Materials (continued)

The following gathered items will help support this Possibilities Plan:

Big equipment sales booklets
Cardboard blocks
Construction aprons
Construction magazines
Construction pictures
Cookie sheet
Dump truck pictures
Flour
HVAC plans
Milk carton blocks
Pictures of familiar tools
Plastic pipe lengths and joints
Sand
Set of curtains
Shoebox blocks
Smooth lengths of wood
Soil
Styrofoam blocks (covered with contact paper)
Water
Work boots and gloves

Wheels

WEB

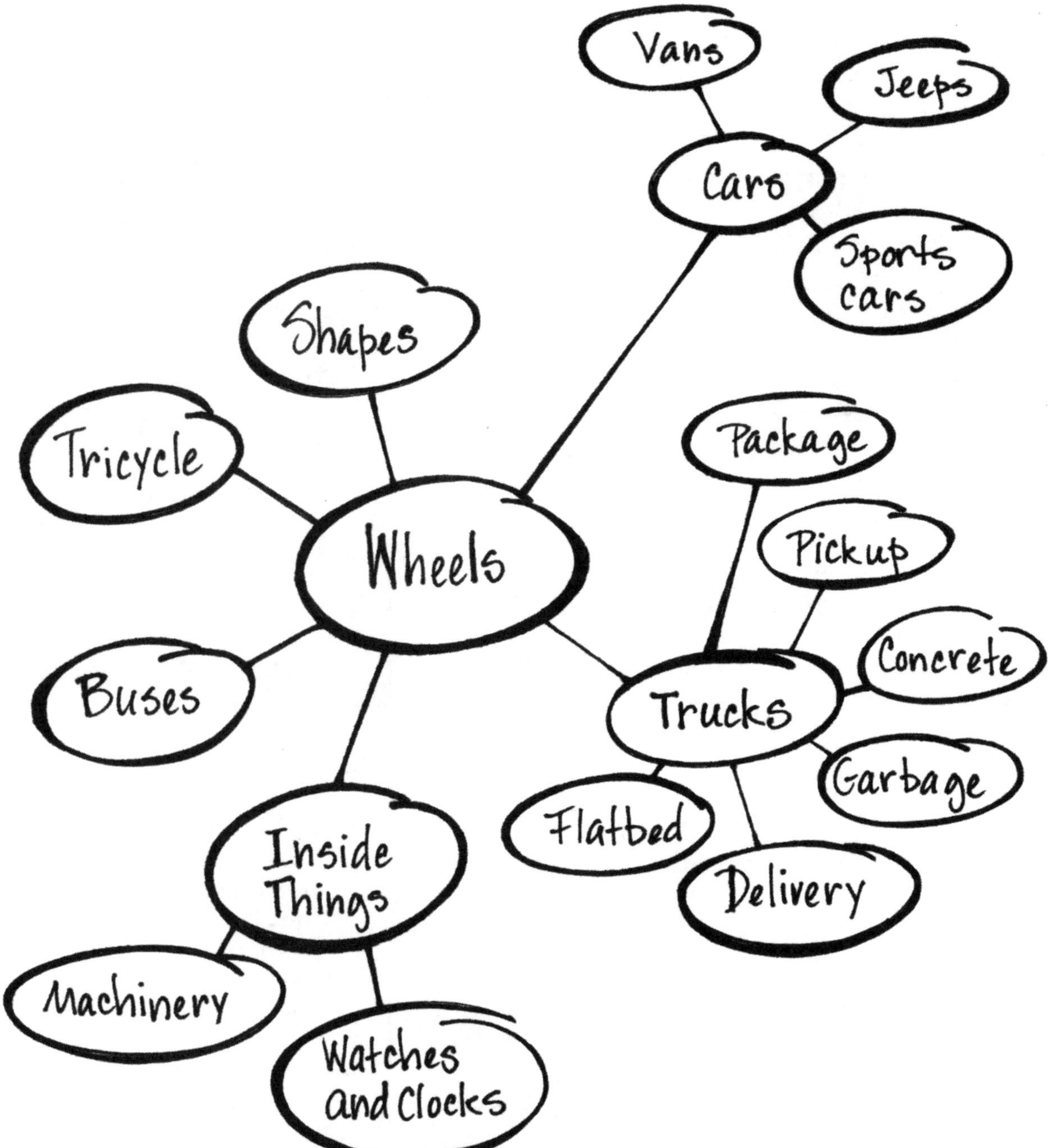

Note: Using the techniques of webbing, teachers can follow the leads that children give them, as well as have an unlimited source of options. Always use the webs provided as a jumping-off point. The possibilities are endless!

PLANNING PAGES

Plan Possibilities

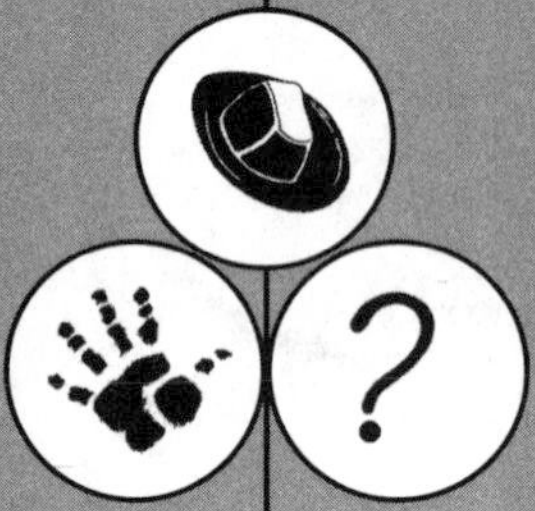

Dramatic

Sensory/Art

Wheel Prints........... 433
Big Wheels 433
Spin Art............... 434
Crayon Trails 434

Curiosity

Snack Wheel........... 434
Wheels Out the Window . 435
Paper Plate Punch and Sew 435
Attracting Wheels 435

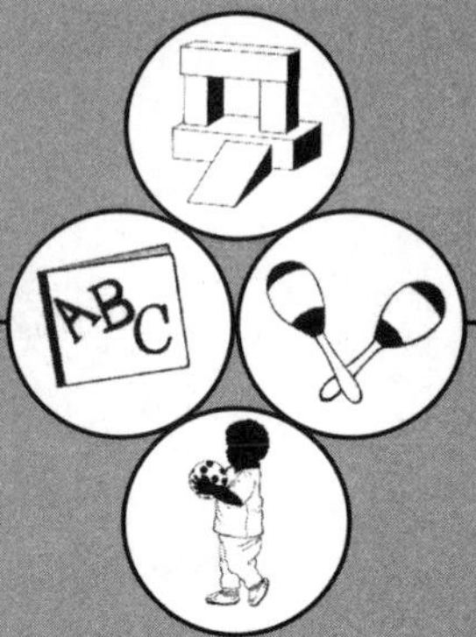

Construction

Wheeled Vehicles 436
Circle Shape 436
Shoebox Houses 437

Literacy

Wheel Book............ 437
Wheel Paper 438
Shoebox Story Kit....... 438
Chalk Writing.......... 439

Music

See the Wheels Go Round 439
Wheels................ 439
Ring Around the Rosy ... 440
Down by the Station 440
My Little Red Wagon.... 441

Movement

Heigh Ho the Derry O ... 441
Hoops................. 442
Toss It in the Wagon 442
Five Little Trucks....... 443

Outdoor

Playground Tires 443
Delivery Vehicles 443
Push/Pull Toys 444
Wheels in Sand 444
Lawn Tools 444

Projects

Parent Participation

Real Vehicles 445
Parent Postcards
Appropriate Expectations for Self-control...... 446
What If?............. 447

Wheels

DRAMATIC POSSIBILITIES

Household Wheels

All ages

Materials
Toy shopping cart
Doll stroller
Vacuum
Storage carts

Teacher Talk
"Jessica is taking the baby for a ride in the stroller."

Place a variety of real and toy wheeled household vehicles in the area for children to use as they play.

Bus

All ages

Materials
Chairs
Cardboard steering wheel
Money box (cardboard box)
Driver costume, optional

Teacher Talk
"Let's ride the bus to Main Street. Welcome aboard."

Set up chairs in rows. Place a chair in front for the driver. Place a money box beside the driver's seat. Place the cardboard steering wheel in the driver's seat. Be the bus driver and invite children to come aboard. Leave props in the area so they can revisit the activity.

Helmets

All ages

Materials
Motorcycle helmets
Bicycle helmets

Teacher Talk
"Chrissy, you need to wear a helmet when you ride your bike."

Place a variety of styles and colors of helmets in the area for children to wear as they play.

Lazy Susan

All ages

Materials

Large lazy Susan

Teacher Talk

"The lazy Susan spins around, Khasmir."

Add a large lazy Susan in the area for children to place plastic dishes on and spin around.

SENSORY/ART POSSIBILITIES

Wheel Prints

All ages

Materials

Small cars
Paint
Paper

Teacher Talk

"That's the way, Emile, roll the car on the paper."

Pour small amounts of paint in shallow pans. Children roll their cars through the paint, then run the wheels across paper to make prints. Make this a repeated experience by using different colors of paint.

Big Wheels

All ages

Materials

Plastic woven paper plate holders
Paper
Paint

Teacher Talk

"The bottom of the plate holder makes a print like a round wheel, Joel."

Children dip the bottom of the plastic plate holder into paint and press it onto paper to make big wheel prints. Offer different choices of paint, so children can choose colors.

Spin Art

All ages

Materials
Salad spinner
Paper plates
Paint

Place a paper plate inside the salad spinner. Drop teaspoons of paint onto the plate. Replace the lid and help a child turn the handle to make the plate spin around. When she has turned the handle a few times, open the salad spinner to look at the colorful design on the plate. Replace the lid and spin again to see what happens.

Crayon Trails

24-36 months

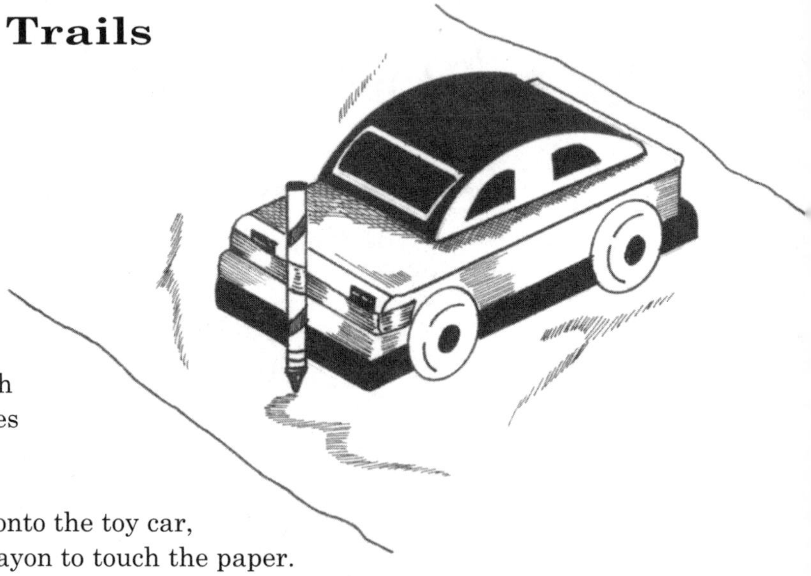

Materials
Toy cars
Crayons
Paper
Tape

Teacher Talk
"When you push the car, it makes lines, Corey."

Tape a crayon onto the toy car, allowing the crayon to touch the paper. Put different colored crayons on different cars. Show children how to push the car around the paper, making colored lines as they go.

CURIOSITY POSSIBILITIES

Snack Wheel

All ages

Materials
Lazy Susan
Round crackers
Cheese circles
Paper plates

Teacher Talk
"Here's a round paper plate for you, Maggie."

Place round crackers and cheese circles on a lazy Susan for children to enjoy round snacks.

Wheels Out the Window

All ages

Materials
Small set of curtains
Pictures of wheeled vehicles
Unbreakable mirror

Attach the curtains to the wall at child's height. Underneath, attach a picture of a vehicle with wheels. Change out the pictures periodically. Add additional interest by surprising toddlers with a mirror underneath.

Paper Plate Punch and Sew

24-36 months

Materials
Colored paper plates
Scissors
Shoestring

Teacher Talk
"You did it! Lisa can sew in and out!"

Use scissors to make quarter-size holes in colored paper plates. Tie one end of a shoestring to a hole in the plate. Show children how to lace the string in and out the plate.

Attracting Wheels

30-36 months

Materials
Metal vehicles
Large, handled magnets
Sand

Teacher Talk
"What happens when you drag the magnet across the sand, Antonio?"

Put metal vehicles in the sand. Provide large, handled magnets. Show children how to drag the magnet across the sand to make the vehicles come to the surface of the sand.

CONSTRUCTION POSSIBILITIES

Wheeled Vehicles

All ages

Materials

Blocks
Wheeled vehicles
Rug or mat with roads

Teacher Talk

"Martin, you put all of the red trucks on the road."

Provide a variety of wheeled vehicles and a rug or mat with roads in the block area for children to build with.

Circle Shape

24-36 months

Materials

Circle shape cut from butcher paper or cardboard

Teacher Talk

"You have stacked the blocks on the circle, Tomeka."

Cut a large circle shape from butcher paper or cardboard to add interest and novelty to the block area. Attach it to the floor in the block area, so children can build on it.

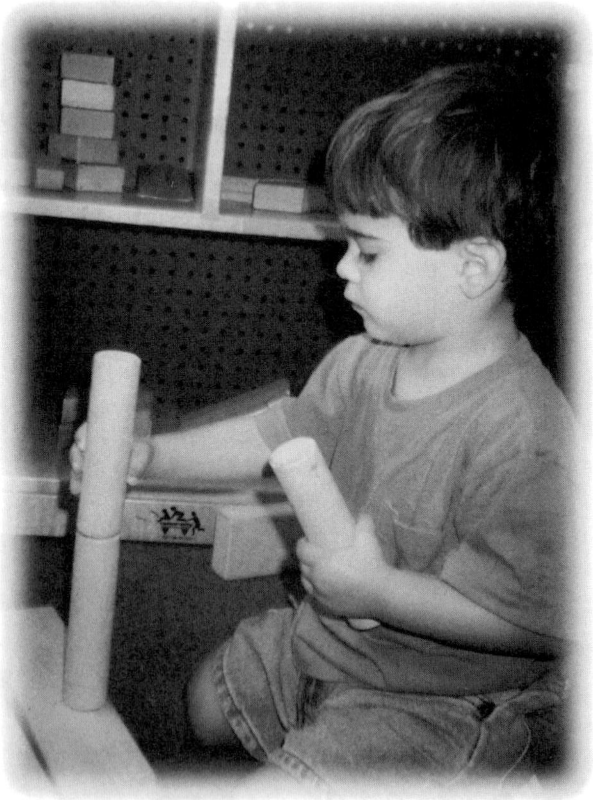

Shoebox Houses

30-36 months

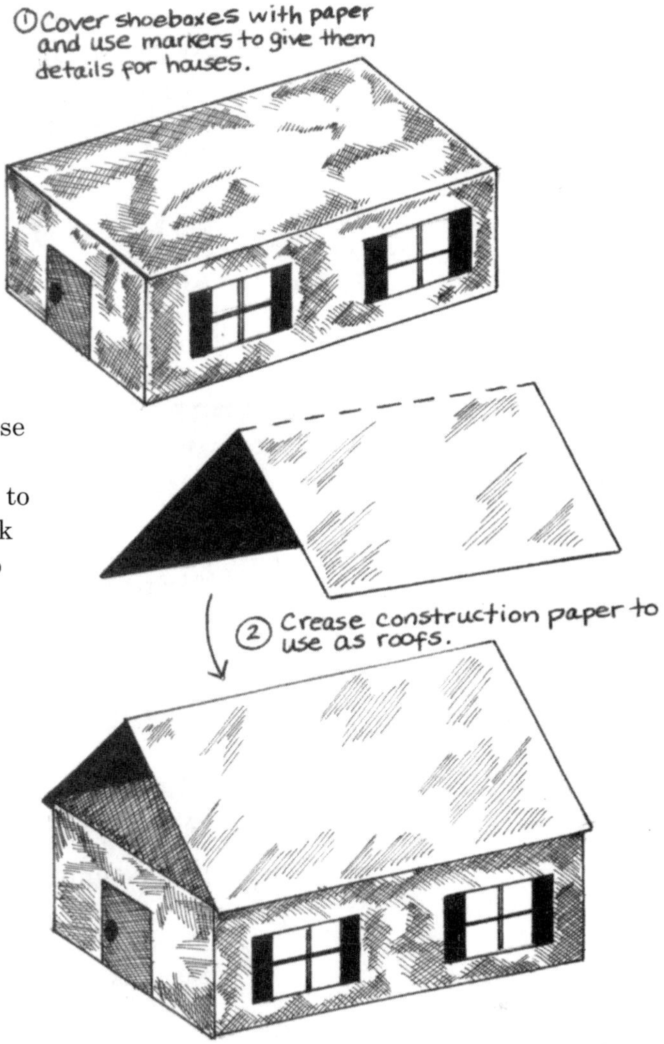

Materials

Shoeboxes
Paper grocery bags
Glue
Markers
Construction paper

Teacher Talk

"You put the roof on the house, Maxwell."

Cover shoeboxes with paper and use markers to give them details for houses. Crease construction paper to use as roofs. Add items to the block area and observe what children do with them.

LITERACY POSSIBILITIES

Wheel Book

All ages

Materials

Pictures of wheeled vehicles
Paper plates
Glue
Hole punch
Metal ring
Automobile magazines and ads

Teacher Talk
"This is a red bicycle, Amy." Talk about the vehicles, wheels, and the motion wheels make.

Glue pictures of wheeled vehicles onto paper plates. Punch a hole in each plate. Fasten the plates together with a metal ring. Share the book with children.

Wheel Paper

All ages

Materials
Paper circles
Crayons
Markers
Large pencils

Teacher Talk
"Writing on round paper is fun, Kimberly."

Place paper circles, crayons, markers, and/or pencils in the area for children, so they can write/draw on wheel shapes. If a child chooses, you may write the child's words on the circle.

Shoebox Story Kit

24-36 months

Materials
Shoebox with lid
Felt
Scissors
Glue

Teacher Talk
"Marsha has all of the felt cars lined up in a row."

Cut felt to fit the inside of the shoebox lid. Glue the felt in place. Cut felt wheeled vehicles from colored felt. Show children how the shapes will stick to the lid. Observe as children try for themselves.

① Cut felt to fit the inside of shoebox lid. glue the felt in place.
② Cut felt wheeled vehicles from colored felt. Show how shapes will stick to the lid.

Chalk Writing

30-36 months

Materials
Chalkboard
Chalk

Teacher Talk
"I would like to hear you read your story, Arlissa. Timothy wants to write with you."

Place chalkboards and chalk in the area for children to write and/or draw on.

MUSIC POSSIBILITIES

See the Wheels Go Round

All ages

Materials
Small cars

Teacher Talk
"Here's a car for you to hold while we sing about wheels, Chi Ye."

Sing the following song as children play with toy cars. Sing to the tune "My Bonnie Lies Over the Ocean."

See the Wheels Go Round
I love to play with my cars,
And push them over the ground.
Sometimes I drive them on the sidewalks,
And see the wheels go round,
Round, round, round, round.
I see the wheels go round, round, round,
Round, round, round, round.
I see the wheels go round.

Wheels

All ages

Materials
Pictures of a bus, car, bicycle, skateboard, taxi, or train

Attach pictures to the wall. Sing the following song, substituting the names of things with wheels in each verse. As you sing, point to the appropriate wheeled vehicle. Sing to the tune "The Wheels on the Bus."

Wheels
The wheels on the bus go round and round,
Round and round, round and round.
The wheels on the bus go round and round,
All over town.

Sing other verses and substitute car, bicycle, skateboard, taxi, or train.

Ring Around the Rosy

All ages

Materials
None

Teacher Talk
"Hold hands to make a big, round circle."

Hold hands with children and form a circle. Sing this song with children as you walk in a circle. Children enjoy the "all fall down" part.

Ring Around the Rosy
Ring around the rosy,
Pocket full of posies.
Ashes, ashes,
All fall down.

Down by the Station

All ages

Materials
None

Sing this song with children and show them the motions.

Down by the Station
Down by the station,
Early in the morning.
See the little puffer bellies,
All in a row.

See the engine driver,
Pull the little throttle.
Puff, puff, toot, toot!
Off we go.

My Little Red Wagon

All ages

Materials
None

Have fun as you sing this song with children. Sing to the tune "Paw-Paw Patch."

My Little Red Wagon
Bumping along in my little red wagon.
Bumping along in my little red wagon.
Bumping along in my little red wagon,
All around the town.

The wheel fell off and the wagon tipped over.
The wheel fell off and the wagon tipped over.
The wheel fell off and the wagon tipped over,
Made me bump my head.

MOVEMENT POSSIBILITIES

Heigh Ho the Derry O

All ages

Materials
None

Teacher Talk
"You make a loud horn, Jonathon."

Sing the song as you act out the words. Sing the song to the tune "The Farmer in the Dell."

Heigh Ho the Derry O
I'm riding on the bus, (Bounce up and down.)
I'm riding on the bus,
Heigh ho the derry o,
I'm riding on the bus.

I hear the horns honking, (Make a beeping motion with hands.)
I hear the horns honking,
Heigh ho the derry o,
I hear the horns honking.

I see the people walking, (Walk in place.)
I see the people walking,
Heigh ho the derry o,
I see the people walking.

I see the people jogging, (Jog in place.)
I see the people jogging,
Heigh ho the derry o,
I see the people jogging.

Hoops

All ages

Materials
Plastic hoops

Teacher Talk
"You can jump into and out of the hoop, Cassie. "

Put the plastic hoops on the ground for children to jump into and out of.

Toss It in the Wagon

All ages

Materials
Beanbags
Toy wagon

Provide beanbags for children to toss into a wagon.

Five Little Trucks

All ages

Materials
None

Show children how to hold up five fingers and put one down as each line is recited.

Five Little Trucks
Five little trucks driving down the road,
The first one said, "I'm carrying a heavy load."
The second one said, "I'm the color red."
The third one said, "I'm moving ahead."
The fourth one said, "I'm driving very slow."
The fifth one said, "Let's go and go and go!"

OUTDOOR POSSIBILITIES

Playground Tires

All ages

Materials
Car and truck tires (no radials)

Provide non-radial tires for children to climb into, out of, on, and through. Drill holes in the sidewalls of the tires, so water will not stand in them.

Delivery Vehicles

All ages

Materials
Poster board
Markers
Tape
Assorted delivery props

Teacher Talk
"You brought me a pizza!"

Use poster board and markers to make signs for various delivery vehicles such as pizza, ice cream, mail, packages, and taxi. Tape the signs onto riding toys. Provide props such as pizza boxes, ice cream boxes, mailbag, wrapped packages, and a taxi driver cap.

Push/Pull Toys

All ages

Materials
Variety of wheeled push and pull toys

Teacher Talk
"That truck is carrying lots of sand, Sara."

Provide a variety of wheeled push/pull toys for children play with outside.

Wheels in Sand

All ages

Materials
Sand table
Small, wheeled vehicles

Teacher Talk
"How did you make these tracks, Lewis?"

Place a variety of small, wheeled vehicles in the sand table, so children can make wheel tracks in the sand.

Lawn Tools

24-36 months

Materials
Toy lawn mowers
Toy wheelbarrows
Toy yard tools

Teacher Talk
"The grass looks much nicer since you mowed, Caleb."

Provide toy lawn mowers, wheelbarrows, and rakes for children to take care of the lawn.

PROJECT POSSIBILITIES

Wheel Print Mural

All ages

Materials
Butcher paper
Circular objects
Paint
Shallow trays
Pen

Completely cover a table with a large piece of butcher paper. Pour paint into shallow containers. Provide various circular objects (wheels, plastic paper plate holders, plastic bowls and saucers) for children to press into the paint and then onto the paper. Provide different colors and textures of paints on different days. Write the date and children's comments as they create the prints. Post where children and parents can enjoy.

PARENT PARTICIPATION POSSIBILITIES

Real Vehicles

Invite parents to bring a truck, motorcycle, four-wheeler, or school bus for children to explore. Children can climb on, in, and in the back of vehicles to discover more about the vehicles. Firefighter, police officer, and/or paramedic emergency vehicles can be even more fun. Supervise children closely, but allow them to sit inside, pretend to drive, and make the appropriate sounds of the emergency vehicles. Ask parents to volunteer to help you make the transition from the classroom to the vehicle safely. Activities such as these need one adult for each child.

Parent Postcards

Parent Postcards in this section are designed to share with parents during the Possibilities Plan. The topics are natural extensions of the activities and experiences that you are planning and implementing for the toddlers in the classroom. Use the Postcards to connect parents to their children's learning.

Appropriate Expectations for Self-Control

An important developmental task is learning the expectations of the family and society and matching behavior to the rules. Knowledge about these important expectations comes from exposure to expectations and support with compliance from supportive adults. Children are not born able to comply with the rules of the world; they construct this knowledge through interactions and experiences that expose them to the rules and behavioral expectations that accompany rules (for example, be quiet in church, sit down to eat, and so on). This process is called the internalization of control—becoming able to comply with expectations without reminders or support.

Toddlers are almost totally controlled externally—that is, they depend on others to keep them safe, support them in following established rules, and succeed in interactions with others. How, then, do they learn to internalize rules? The answer is simple. They learn to internalize the rules by having the rules consistently and constantly applied and followed. For example, when an older toddler picks up the television remote control, most parents take it away and tell the child that the control is for adults and not toddlers and then put it up. This rule will be explained to toddlers a thousand times over the next few months.

As the toddler gets older, he or she will pick up the remote, turn to Mom and Dad to see if they will follow the rule, and then play with it even though he or she knows the remote is off limits. This illustrates the external nature of self-control. The toddler has learned that there is a rule pertaining to the remote control but has not internalized the rule. Internalization means that the child can control his or her actions without adult support.

Toddlers still need external support to comply with rules, even when they have figured out what the rules are! In addition, they need many, many reminders to confirm that the rule really does apply every time.

TO

What If?

Do you wonder what will happen if your child is injured or hurt seriously at school? It's a natural concern. But you needn't worry. Emergency procedures are in place and practiced so that emergencies can be handled calmly, quickly, and confidently. Fire, weather, and accident drills are practiced regularly to prepare teachers to handle emergencies. These events require standard responses that are pre-planned and practiced by simulation. The most obvious indication of these plans is the evacuation notices that are posted throughout the building. Notices are signs of the planning and preparation that go into making sure your child is safe.

But what about accidents and injuries that do not require the immediate attention of medical personnel? Teachers will administer first aid, help the child calm down and get comfortable, and fill in an accident report for you to see at the end of the day. We call most of these accidents "boo-boos" because they are really a result of the normal process of growing up. A skinned knee, a pinched finger, a scratched elbow, and yes, even an unfriendly bite will all be handled calmly and comfortingly by your child's teacher.

Then we will let you know about the accident, so you don't have to figure out what happened on your own. But you might want to remember that some accidents might be so minor to your child that he or she doesn't cry or get the teacher's attention. If your teacher doesn't know what happened, she or he will tell you that she or he doesn't know and be even more diligent in trying to make sure the accident doesn't happen again without her or his knowledge.

TO

What If? (continued)

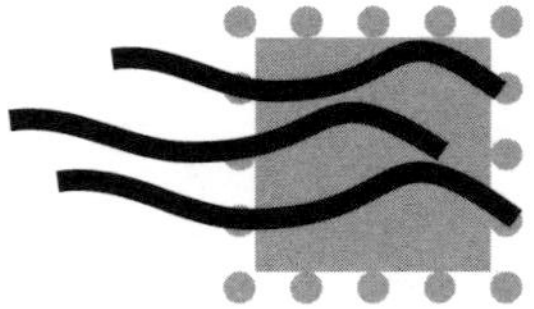

Your child's teacher will work very hard to make sure that your child is safe. But there are several things that you can do to help. Make sure we always have current telephone numbers for you and your physician. We can only contact you if we have accurate records. You might want to make a plan if voice mail answers your telephone. Who should we call to find you? Can someone be reached in person who can get in touch with you when you are not available?

Make sure that we know how to reach you if your daily schedule is different. If you are not where we usually find you, let us know in the morning during your drop-off routine. Leave an alternative number or a back-up contact for us to call instead.

Finally, make sure your alternate contacts are correct and that they expect us to call if we can't reach you. Parents within a classroom often serve as each other's alternate if other family members are not available. This is a good back-up alternate and a great way to get to know other parents in your child's classroom.

TO

Concepts Learned in Wheels

Concepts Learned

Cars have wheels.
Trucks have wheels.
Buses have wheels.
Police cars have wheels.
Fire trucks have wheels.
Some vehicles, such as cars and trucks, have four wheels.
Motorcycles and bicycles have two wheels.
Tricycles have three wheels.
Wheelbarrows have one wheel.
Trucks and buses have big wheels.
Skates and skateboards have little wheels.
Wheels roll.
Wheels are round.
Wheels help us move easier.
Push and pull toys have wheels.
Wheels are made of plastic, rubber, and metal.
Riding toys have wheels.
Wheels move around and around in a circle.

Resources

Prop Boxes

Bus Driver
- Big wallet
- Driver hat
- Money box
- Steering wheel
- Uniform
- *Wheels on the Bus, The* by Maryann Kovalski

Wheels
- Bicycle wheels
- Big wheels
- Metal wheels
- Plastic wheels
- Rubber wheels
- Skate wheels
- Small wheels
- Toy car wheels
- *Wheels Go Round* by Margaret Miller

Picture File/Vocabulary

Ambulances
Buses
Cars
Fire trucks
Four-wheelers
Motorcycles
Police cars
Skates
Taxis
Toys
Trains
Trucks
Wheels of all kinds

Books

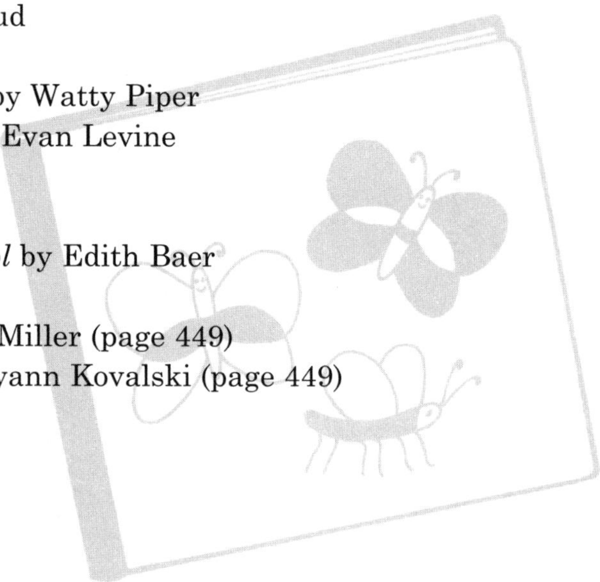

Bear's Bicycle by Emilie McCloud
Bicycle Race by Donald Crews
Little Engine That Could, The by Watty Piper
Not the Piano, Mrs. Medley! by Evan Levine
Pigs by Robert Munsch
School Bus by Donald Crews
This Is the Way We Go to School by Edith Baer
Truck by Donald Crew
Wheels Go Round by Margaret Miller (page 449)
Wheels on the Bus, The by Maryann Kovalski (page 449)

Rhymes/ Fingerplays

"Five Little Trucks" (page 440)

Music/Songs

"Down by the Station" (page 440)
"Heigh Ho the Derry O" (page 441)
"My Little Red Wagon" (page 441)
"Ring Around the Rosy" (page 440)
"See the Wheels Go Round" (page 439)
"Wheels" (page 440)

Toys and Materials

The following purchased items are important for this Possibilities Plan:

Beanbags
Butcher paper
Chairs
Chalk
Chalkboard
Colored paper plates
Construction paper
Crayons
Doll stroller
Driver costume
Drivers' caps
Felt
Glue
Hole punch
Large magnet
Large pencils
Markers
Metal rings
Metal toy vehicles
Money box
Paint
Paper
Paper plates
Plastic hoops
Poster board
Push and pull toys
Rug or mat with roads
Salad spinner
Sand table
Scissors
Shallow plastic pans
Shoestring
Small/large toy cars
Storage carts
Tape
Toy lawn mowers
Toy shopping cart
Toy vacuum
Toy wagons
Toy wheelbarrows
Toy yard tools
Unbreakable mirrors
Variety of blocks
Vehicle shape sponges

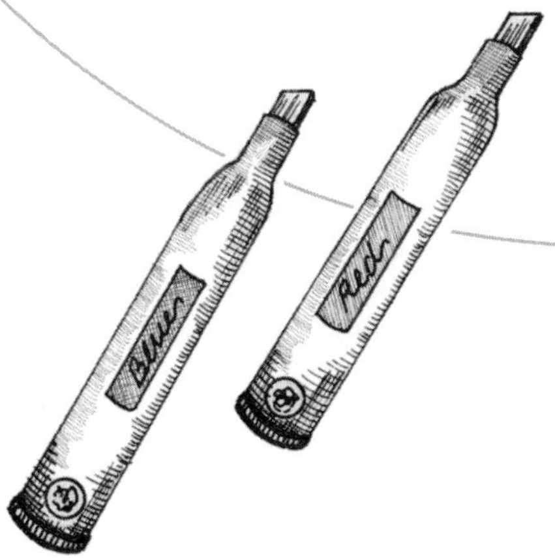

Toys and Materials (continued)

The following gathered items will help support this Possibilities Plan:

Automobile magazines and ads
Bicycle helmets
Cardboard
Delivery props
Ice cream boxes
Large lazy Susan
Money box
Motorcycle helmets
Non-radial car and truck tires
Paper grocery bags
Pictures of wheeled vehicles
Pizza box
Plastic woven paper plate holders
Sand
Set of curtains
Shoeboxes

CHAPTER 7

Expressing Feelings

INTRODUCTION

A most observable part of toddlerhood is the sincerity and intensity of expressed feelings. Although children begin expressing their feelings and emotions right after birth, it is during the period from 18-36 months that toddlers share the way they are feeling with everyone—clearly indicating whether they are happy, sad, angry,

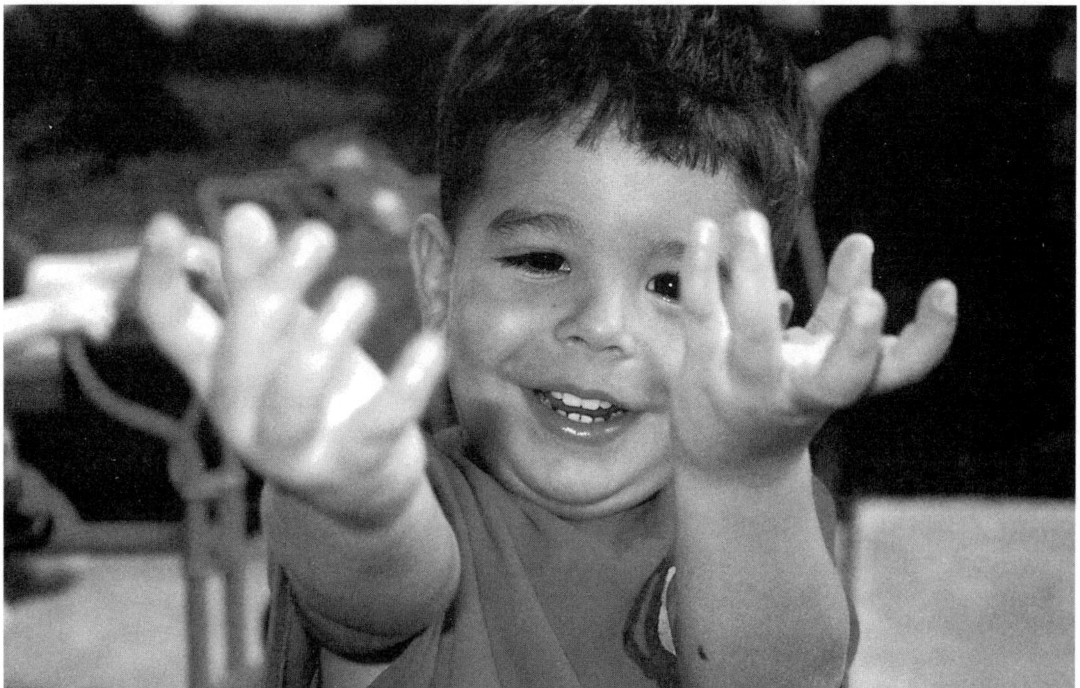

hungry, tired, mad, irritated, or just plain frustrated. Toddlers have learned to differentiate one feeling from another as well as to pair those feelings with physical expressions that convey the differences between one emotion and another. They are now ready to begin the process of managing their emotions.

Learning to express oneself and to identify and understand emotions is a crucial part of growing up. For toddlers, this process is an emerging one—one that changes over time in the context of other developmental changes taking place.

Interest in the effects of emotions on the developing brain has put emotional development in the spotlight. During the first three years, the brain grows to about two-thirds of its full size and evolves in complexity at a greater rate than it ever will again. Key learning takes place in several important developmental domains, including emotional learning. Pediatricians, educators, and other specialists emphasize the importance of supporting emotional learning right from the start. In addition, experts view emotional intelligence as important as physical, cognitive, and language intelligence. This chapter addresses curricula that supports and facilitates continued emotional development during toddlerhood.

INNOVATIONS IN OBSERVATION/ASSESSMENT

Observation/Assessment Instrument

This assessment instrument is not just a skills checklist. Instead it is designed to guide the teacher's observation of children's development through major interactional tasks of toddlerhood. The assessment's focus is on what IS happening, not just what should happen or what will happen. Use this assessment to lead to developmentally appropriate practice.

	18-24 months	24-30 months	30-36 months
E1	a. Begins to create mental images of emotional behaviors. b. Uses behavior to express emotions (i.e., stomps foot when angry, laughs when happy, etc.).	c. Distinguishes between emotions and the behaviors that go with that emotion.	d. Understands how one feeling relates to another (i.e., being disappointed about getting a toy and getting angry as a result of the disappointment).
E2	a. Emotional intensity is not regulated—minor and major events get similar reactions; falls apart easily.	b. Begins to regulate emotional intensity in some situations; falls apart less frequently.	c. Regulates emotional intensity most of the time; seldom falls apart. d. Figures out how to respond with appropriate emotions to most situations.
E3	a. Watches and remembers emotional behaviors exhibited by others; uses observations in future interactions.	b. Puts emotional mental images to work in pretend play; can make-believe or pretend to be angry, happy, sad, etc.	
E4	a. Knows rules that have been reinforced consistently but still needs reminders and physical adult support to comply.	b. Follows rules that have been reinforced consistently with verbal reminders and physical adult support.	c. Follows rules that have been reinforced consistently with just verbal reminders.
E5	a. Unable to label own feelings	b. Can label some feelings; uses the same feeling to represent many feelings (i.e., mad for angry, frustrated, irritated, unhappy, etc.).	c. Labels most of his or her own feelings; can differentiate between similar emotions and label them appropriately.
E6	a. Unable to understand how others feel.	b. Begins to understand how others feel when observing others but not when he or she is a part of the interaction.	c. Understands how others feel when the behavior exhibited is consistent with the emotion being felt (i.e., angry child is yelling, stomping foot, saying, "No!").
E7	a. Has difficulty delaying gratification.	b. Can delay gratification for a short time when supported by adults.	c. Can delay gratification for a few minutes in most situations.
E8	a. Does not separate fantasy from reality.	b. Can switch from reality to fantasy.	c. Understands "real" and "not real."
E9	a. Ambivalent about being autonomous; wants to sometimes and doesn't at other times.	b. Independent behaviors are increasing; dependent behaviors are decreasing.	c. Independent behaviors are usually present.
E10	a. Has little control over impulses.	b. Controls impulses in some situations or with support from adults.	c. Most impulses under control.
E11	a. Loses emotional control often and intensely.	b. Loss of emotional control is less frequent, less intense, and less prolonged.	c. Infrequently loses emotional control.

INNOVATIONS IN CHILD DEVELOPMENT

Emotional Development

Developmental theory tells us that children move through a predictable sequence of steps as they mature. These steps are observable and can be identified and charted. Likewise, developmental theory tells us that each and every individual has his own pace of development through the predictable sequence. This holds true for the emotional area of development. To understand the emotional development of toddlers, it is necessary to understand the stages that precede toddlerhood as well as the emotional development taking place during this period.

Innovations: The Comprehensive Toddler Curriculum views the transition from infancy to toddlerhood as taking place around 18 months. A summary of the stages before this transition follows. Stanley Greenspan and Nancy Greenspan, noted developmental psychologists, describe the stages of emotional development in infancy in the following way (Greenspan & Greenspan, 1989). In the first three months of life, infants learn to calm themselves and develop a multisensory interest in the world (touching, hearing, tasting, smelling, seeing, feeling). They are able to express personality by demonstrating individual preferences for certain kinds of sensory experiences.

The second stage of emotional development is called "a time of falling in love." This stage lasts from months two through seven. At this time, infants develop a joyful interest in the human world. This striking preference for interactions with familiar adults is an important and crucial step in emotional development.

In the third stage, from 3-10 months, babies develop intentional communication. In seeking a dialogue with the human world, infants want their caregivers to interpret and understand their nonverbal communication and to respond appropriately. As adults respond differently to infant communication cues (feed them when they are hungry and hold them when they need comforting), children learn to distinguish between their own needs and feelings.

The fourth stage, which emerges from 9 to 18 months, finds infants learning how to coordinate their behavior with their emotions. An organized sense of self begins to emerge. The infant begins to link together units of cause-and-effect into chains. He will grab the teacher's hand and take her over to the refrigerator saying "muk" instead of merely crying when he is thirsty.

Toddlerhood begins with the fifth stage, from 18 months to 3 years of age, and finds children beginning to develop the ability to create their own mental images of the world and to use behavior to express emotions. Toddlers can conjure up an image of their last interaction with a teacher or parent even when the teacher or parent is no longer present. They can watch other children and then use what they observe in future interactions.

Toddlers are also able to "make believe" or pretend. They can take the mental images that they are forming and put them to work in their play, often focusing on emotional dramas that have taken place in their lives. Toddlers at this stage are truly "thinking" in the traditional sense. This age child is beginning to internalize the rules of the family, school, and community.

During the sixth stage, between 2½ and 4 years, children expand their emotional capacities. They develop the ability to do emotional thinking—distinguishing between different emotions and the behaviors that go with those emotions, and understanding how feelings relate to one another. They can read cues from others and figure out how to respond appropriately most of the time and are beginning to have some control over their emotions, regulating the intensity of their interactions in some situations.

Notice the overlapping of ages. Emotional skills can emerge during the end of one stage or the beginning of the next. This overlap is particularly evident as toddlers acquire a skill only to lose it in subsequent similar experiences. The characteristic of growing and regressing is one of the hallmarks of all developmental experiences.

INNOVATIONS IN INTERACTIVE EXPERIENCES

Children's experiences at school have so much to do with the way they will grow and develop. If they experience school as negative, frustrating, or insensitive, they will view the learning process as overwhelming and insurmountable. If, on the other hand, their experiences are supportive, nurturing, and positive, human development has an almost perfect plan for growing and learning. In fact, during the first three years, development unfolds naturally for most children.

Many teachers view the activities they plan as the most important part of their job. Although this task is important, toddlers are experiencing all the time—not just when teachers are providing direct stimulation. ***This curriculum advocates thinking about and planning for everything that can, by the nature of the setting (school vs. home), contribute to***

children's development and the teacher's relationship with the child and the family. What is outside the realm of activities in the classroom (for example, a child who takes longer to prepare to transition to another place, a child who naps much longer or shorter than expected, a child who is suddenly fascinated with an earthworm) is all curriculum. Children are always learning, and it is the teacher's job to support that learning in whatever forms it may take.

Life's minutiae build to create experiences. Toddler teachers must be attuned to these everyday, yet important, experiences. They are truly the foundation upon which crucial skills and abilities grow.

Think about the following list of everyday experiences and make sure that the classroom reflects many of them.

- ☐ Label expressions of emotions, for example, "What a happy smile," or " That face is angry," or "You didn't want him to take that toy."
- ☐ Act authentically. Figuring out emotions requires good models. Toddlers deserve to see authentic emotional models in their classrooms.
- ☐ Support practice play that deals with emotional issues.
- ☐ Prepare toddlers before strangers enter the classroom. Stay close to them, support their interests, and protect them from getting overwhelmed.
- ☐ Keep a predictable schedule during the school day. Times may vary, but the sequence stays the same.
- ☐ Embrace stranger anxiety as a normal part of emotional development.
- ☐ Prepare children when you move around the room or leave for lunch or a break. Take toddlers who are experiencing stranger anxiety with you when you can and prepare them in advance when you can't.
- ☐ Stay nearby when toddlers are playing together. Facilitate appropriate behavior by giving toddlers the words they need to play together successfully.
- ☐ Support appropriate interactions through modeling.
- ☐ Provide multisensory experiences for toddlers.
- ☐ Spend floor time with toddlers.
- ☐ Support emerging creativity by letting children choose their activities among a selected range of appropriate ones.
- ☐ Validate novel ways of doing things. When toddlers make things happen in a new or different way, recognize and celebrate their excitement.

INNOVATIONS IN TEACHING

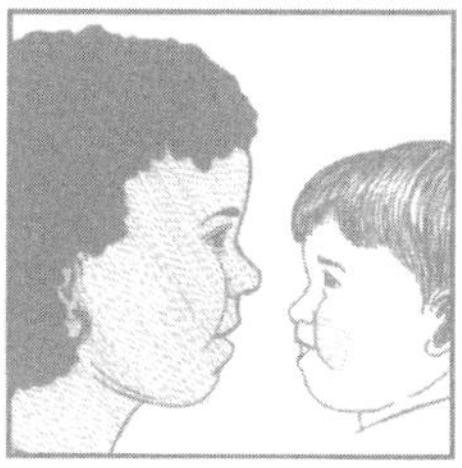

Facilitating Emotional Development

Toddlers need opportunities to test and experiment with the range of feelings they have. They are learning to understand a little bit of what another child feels (called empathy) but cannot yet really take the role of the other person in their interactions (called altruism). During this stage, toddlers begin to internalize the rules adults have had for them during infancy and need less frequent reminders about old rules. New rules, though, take a period of constant reminding before they begin to be followed. Facilitating emotional development during this stage means making rules clear and reminding children often of what they mean and what the consequence of breaking each rule is.

A dependable, familiar primary teacher is still important—particularly during times of stress or when intense negative emotions are present. Toddlers need someone to read nonverbal cues and anticipate needs just like babies do. Now, toddlers are able to think about more abstract things than when they were younger. Concentration emerges during this stage, and teachers will see children play for longer periods of time at activities that interest them or test their skill. And, play becomes more complex, often including experiences observed in the broader world of the family, school, and community.

Dramatic play is so important during this stage. Toddlers need dramatic play spaces and props that allow them to continue to express the complete range of emotions they feel—not just the positive ones. They need practice acting out anger, fear, hostility, eagerness, as well as empathy, altruism, curiosity, and so on in acceptable ways that do not cause conflict. In play, they practice the roles they see adults using in the real world. They also begin to separate what is real from what isn't and begin to understand when and how to switch from fantasy to reality.

Teachers who foster dramatic possibilities plan exciting, interesting, and changing dramatic play centers. They play along with children as they act out these experiences, facilitating and enhancing the experience. And, they spend lots of time observing children as they play, watching for emerging interests, new abilities being practiced or tried out, and for ideas about what play themes can be expanded or supported by the teacher. Teachers change the themes and props available to toddlers to refresh play ideas and offer variety. They always view play from the point of view of the emotional development of the child.

Floor Time as a Practice

This curriculum proposes that floor time be used as a practice that supports children's emotional development. Floor time looks something like this (Greenspan & Greenspan, 1989): The teacher prepares an area of the classroom with an attractive display of toys and materials, either taken from the regular toys and materials or specially planned for floor time. One or two children who are ready to play are invited to join the teacher in an area of the classroom set up for floor time. The teacher starts the practice of floor time by watching, listening, and being with the toddlers as they begin to play with the toys and with each other. She or he lets the child or children direct the time together. If a toddler smiles at the teacher, the teacher smiles back. If the children include the teacher in the play, she responds by joining in the play.

Following the child's lead is the important part of floor time. When toddlers pick up toys, the teacher expands and extends the play to enhance the child's experience. For example, if the toddler is driving miniature cars on a roadway, the teacher might describe what she sees happening and smile at the toddler to encourage him or her to continue.

Interactions such as these support interest in the child's social world and validate that the teacher is going to support being a part of the social world. These interactions also fill children with feelings of competence. Once initiated through a supportive adult, the child will be able to reconnect with the feeling without the adult's support at a later time.

Toddler teachers may find it hard to identify time when they can practice floor time with just a few children. Try some of the following ideas:

- Pick a time of day that naturally lends itself to calm play. Some ideas might be the beginning of the day as children are arriving one by one, after naptime as the first few children wake up, during the time spent in self-selected activities in the classroom, or at the end of the day as children are leaving and the group size is decreasing.

- Try to spend floor time with one or two children per day during the week. You might even want to keep track of who has had floor time each week—indicating it on your Possibilities Plan after it occurs, so you know who hasn't had special time with the teacher.
- When children are having developmental difficulties or are experiencing stress from other sources (such as a traveling parent or recovering from an illness), give them extra floor time. Stress increases children's need to feel connected to their primary caregivers. The child who is demanding the most attention may be able to cope better on his own if he gets what he needs—a feeling of being filled up with attention and connected, through play, to his teacher.
- Enlist the help of others. Invite parents, students who are studying early childhood education, and grandparents to spend some time on the floor playing with children in your group or helping in the classroom so that you are freed up to practice floor time.

Beyond Products: Supporting Emerging Creativity in Young Children

When does creativity begin? Is it always present, or do teachers help it develop? The educators at Reggio Emilia believe that creativity is not an exceptional occurrence but a characteristic way of thinking, knowing, and making choices that is innate in all children. Viewed this way, creativity is part of the childhood experience—not something that teachers need to teach children during the early childhood years.

Creativity is the production of novel thoughts, solutions, and products based on previous experience and knowledge. Creativity is the integration of learning and creative thoughts, solutions, and products—not artistic creativity, or musical creativity, or movement creativity, and so on. Viewed this way, creativity *is* an early childhood experience and can be part of every teacher's classroom.

What can teachers do to foster integration of creativity and learning? Start with choice. Creativity blossoms when children are free to choose what to do, when to do it, how to do it, whom to do it with, and where to do it! Think about the toddler classroom and the activities and experiences you plan for children. How often do you allow children to choose not only what, but also where, when, how, and with whom?

Create an environment that fosters stability and novelty? Is that possible? Aren't stability and novelty opposite ends of the same continuum? Children benefit from the stability of knowing where things are, where they will sleep, and the novelty of new, interesting, and unusual toys and experiences they encounter. Consider the following diagrams.

Teaching strategies that support emerging creativity in toddlers include listening and observing. Verbal interactions are crucial, but teachers who talk *too* much can't foster creativity. Listening, really listening, and observing children as they become fascinated by their own ideas and skills, encourage creativity. From this fascination come wonderful observations by the child, clear insight from the teacher about what the child was trying to do, and thoughtful questions to pose as children play.

Look for ideas, not answers. It is the process—the exploration—that leads to learning, not isolated facts presented to children during teacher-directed times. Instead of telling children how things work, let them find out. Instead of showing children where things are, let them search for them. Instead of anticipating the toddler's next move, wait to see if it unfolds the way that you thought it might.

Repeat experiences often. The Project Possibilities and Sensory/Art Possibilities sections of each Possibilities Plan include examples of ways to stimulate creativity with open-ended and repeated experiences. Repetition develops a crucial creative skill—persistence to task. Task persistence leads children to explore, leading to creativity.

Validate children's novel ideas and ways of doing things. Toddlers who repeat favorite activities again and again are still practicing important tasks. Don't be in a hurry to narrow children's activities into what you or parents expect. Instead, wait with patience as creativity takes its course.

Guidance and Discipline

Managing Normal Aggression in Very Young Children

Aggression is a normal part of young children's experiences. Aggression results from powerful emotions that are not yet under the child's direct control. Children hit, pinch, bite, slap, and grab when their emotions cause them to act before they can think about doing something else.

Children learn to manage aggression when supportive adults help them learn other skills and connect consequences with aggression. Using aggression to stop aggression only teaches children that they must submit to adults who are bigger and more powerful. It does not help children gain control over aggressive behavior or replace it with more appropriate skills. Replacing aggressive behavior with more sophisticated skills is a process—just like learning to express feelings appropriately is a lifelong task. Children take the first steps in the first three years.

The following are some examples of ways supportive teachers can meet aggression with consequences from the earliest stage.

- When a toddler grabs a toy away from a friend, explain that the friend had the toy first and return the toy to the friend. Offer another idea about how to get the toy back. Tell the toddler to put out his hand, asking the friend with a gesture to put the toy in his hand. If the toddler falls apart when you do this, remove him from the situation until he is calm enough to return to play.
- Give toddlers the words to use when they are having trouble communicating with each other. When a child screams for help because he lost a toy to a friend, focus your help on the child who is unable to use language, whether gestural or expressive, to get his needs met. Go over near the child, showing him that you are his ally and will help him work it out. First check out what is going on by asking, "What's happening?" Offer a suggestion about what he might try to get his needs met. If the child is unable to use gestures or language, then you provide the words for him. You might say something like "Did you want him to take your toy?" If the child says "no," then help him say no to the child who took the toy. "Then tell him with words, I don't want you to take my toy. Give it back to me!"

Early experiences with the consequences of aggression help children learn over time that aggressive behavior doesn't accomplish much. After this lesson is learned, children can begin the process of becoming assertive enough to prevent being victimized and becoming authoritative enough to be seen as a leader. Both of these important lessons will never be learned unless both teachers and parents help children learn to manage normal aggression and convert it into constructive assertion and problem solving.

Dealing with Oppositional Behavior in Toddlers

During the second year of life, toddlers begin to develop a view of themselves as separate and independent from their parents and teachers. Because they have gained control over their bodies, toddlers are now capable of moving away from the adults in their world, exploring and discovering things that are out of reach, and taking care of some of their own needs, such as eating, drinking, and undressing by themselves.

As they try these new skills and abilities, and practice being separate and independent, toddlers alternate between being pleased about these new-found abilities and being frightened and scared by them. Teachers see this ambivalence as their toddlers handle one situation without problems and the next by falling apart and needing to reconnect with Mom or Dad or teacher before recovering. They also see it when children are tired, hungry, excited, or ill. In these situations, toddlers vacillate between wanting to be independent and separate and wanting to be dependent, cared for, connected, and supported.

Although toddlers are developing a sense of themselves as separate, they are just developing the ability to control their impulses, to wait, or to accurately predict the consequences of their independent behavior. Because of this, children get upset when teachers help them control their impulses, ask them to wait, or apply consequences. The result is a kind of meltdown that is the precursor to temper tantrums. Opposition can be very intense and emotional. It can also be upsetting to children and to their teachers.

Psychologists tell us that this is a universal and crucial stage for toddler development. It happens to all toddlers. If this is the case, what can teachers do to assist toddlers in gaining the psychological and emotional skills they need to move on? Here are some ideas.

Stanley Greenspan and Nancy Greenspan, authors of ***First Feelings: Milestones in the Emotional Development of Your Baby and Child*** (1989), say that toddlers need three things from teachers to get through this stage. The first is emotional support. Toddlers need emotional support for appropriate behavior and emotional support when they lose control. Teachers can provide this by being understanding and empathetic. Empathy implies that you understand and accept the feelings that children have, even when these feelings are negative ones such as anger or rage.

The second thing toddlers need is many opportunities to be in control. When you think about it, toddlers have little control over their lives. Parents decide when to get up, when to eat, what to wear, when to take a nap, what food goes on the plate, etc. Teachers decide when to go outside, whether or not particular toys and materials are available, and when to have snack. Teachers need to work hard to plan things for toddlers to control. Milk or juice? Two cookies or two crackers? Shoes off or on? Giving toddlers meaningful control over these small decisions empowers them to practice controlling what is happening in a positive way. Often, having positive experiences with control will diminish the amount of oppositional or resistant behavior toddlers have.

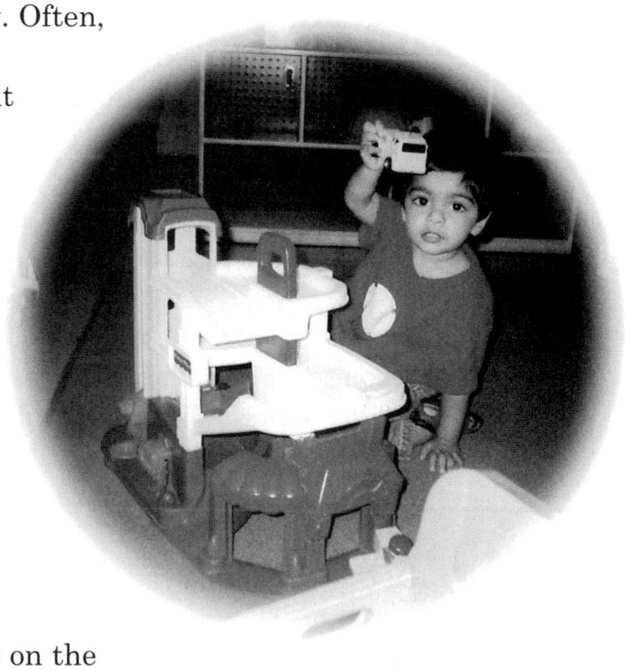

The third thing that toddlers need is limits. Without limits, children are not sure of where the safe space for experimentation starts and stops. Because toddlers are still unable to manage without the support and protection of adults, a lack of limits feels like being physically and emotionally abandoned. Limits on behavior during this stage are crucial to helping toddlers feel competent about separation and independence.

On the other hand, much of what toddlers do is on the edge. Teachers may feel that they are constantly limiting children's behavior. Good advice at this stage is to make a few nonnegotiable rules and use a lot of redirection, distraction, and ignoring of behavior that isn't related to the few important rules. Otherwise, you will feel like you are correcting toddlers all the time. Be realistic. Most oppositional behavior emerges when teachers expect toddlers to handle situations that are beyond their ability. Having realistic expectations for toddlers is crucial.

Keep your own feelings under control. If you are angry, anxious, or stressed, toddlers will know their behavior is working. Focus on the behavior rather than how you feel about it. This gives toddlers information to use in deciding whether to be resistant or not. Comments such as, "Your feet make noise when you tap them on the floor" instead of "You are driving me crazy with that tapping noise" help toddlers see the impact of their behavior on others.

Tell toddlers what you want them to do rather than saying "No!" or "Don't!" Remember that toddlers are trying to feel competent and independent. Nos and don'ts tell them that they have failed.

Negative statement	Positive statement
Stop running!	Walk! March! Crawl!
Don't throw sand!	Leave the sand in the sandbox.
Don't touch.	Put your hands in your pockets.
Don't whine.	Use a regular voice.
Don't touch the markers.	Put that in my hand.

Change the environment. Where children live and play is a minefield for an independence-seeking toddler. Tables and chairs look very much like climbing structures. Doors are there to be opened. Things that cause an action or reaction are fascinating. Rather than deal with constant limit-setting, change the environment. Put safety latches on doors that need them. Create a place to climb that is safe. Any effort teachers put into this area will make the life in a toddler classroom calmer and less combative.

Finally, be patient. This is a developmental stage. It is part of the process of becoming a competent, independent three-year-old. Viewed this way, a toddler's stretch for independence and autonomy will give way to increasing skills and abilities and a view of the world that says, "I can do it!"

Handling Temper Tantrums

During toddlerhood, children struggle to develop a sense of themselves as separate. This process, called differentiation or individuation, actually starts at birth and lasts well into young adulthood. It is the process of becoming a separate and successful individual. Toddler teachers must view this process as a positive one—even when it seems to present so many difficulties.

The first step in differentiation is related to control—who is in charge of me, my body, and my emotions? Early in children's lives, adults are in complete charge. Now, it is time for toddlers to begin to take charge of some of their own behavior. Development drives children to experiment with when they can take charge. This process of transferring some responsibility for control from adults to children usually results in children losing exactly what adults are striving to help them gain—control!

When toddlers feel angry, frustrated, or helpless, they may kick, scream, and flop on the ground. Tantrums are a normal, natural, and inevitable part of growing up. That does not make them fun. Make a plan now for how you will handle it when toddlers begin to tantrum in your classroom.

The first step of the plan is preventive in nature. Help children have some control over their lives. Find ways they can practice and demonstrate emerging competence and emerging control. Start small. Maybe your toddlers can help you pick up the toys that are on the floor. Or choose between walking outside or crawling like a bug or marching like a band. Giving toddlers choices gives them experience with making decisions and having them turn out successfully. This experience is crucial in helping toddlers make good choices about whether or not to throw a temper tantrum.

Be sure to reward appropriate progress in taking charge. When a child shows competence in climbing on the climber, eating with a spoon or fork, or pulling on his own socks, reward these early attempts at independence and self-control with lots of hugs, kisses, and encouragement.

Pick a place for toddlers to be out of control in the classroom. The tantrum place needs to be the place teachers will take children for all tantrums. Make sure the tantrum place is safe. Then, plan to take children to the special tantrum place when they are out of control. Make sure to say calmly to the tantrumming child that he is free to stay out of control as long as he likes—remember, part of this stage is learning that you can take charge of your own behavior. Choosing whether you want to scream for one minute or 10 is certainly taking charge of your own behavior!

It is important to follow through with your response to tantrums. If children get attention from tantrums, they will last much longer than if they have no audience. Removing the audience—your self and the other children—quickly and calmly when tantrums occur is the best thing you can do to lessen the frequency of tantrumming. Go to another section of the room, far from the tantrumming child. Stay in touch visually, but focus on what is happening with the other children. Tell children who might be interested or fascinated by the tantrum what is going on and that the tantrumming child can rejoin the group when he is finished.

When a tantrum is over—it's over. Accept the child back into classroom life as if nothing has happened. Avoid the temptation to lecture or threaten after a tantrum is over. A casual statement such as, "I'm glad you're back under control" is all that is needed. As frustrating as tantrums can be for teachers, a calm, confident approach will go a long way toward helping children grow through the tantrumming stage.

Although temper tantrums are a developmentally normal step in becoming a competent, capable, child, intense and prolonged tantrums may indicate that a toddler is having emotional difficulty. When tantrums continue to intensify when the suggested strategies are used, teachers need to discuss their concerns with parents and seek support in helping the toddler move on emotionally and developmentally.

Conferencing with Parents of Toddlers

Parent conferences are an accepted part of any school. Conferences form the foundation of the communication system between parents and the programs in which children spend their day. But, the length of school day and the busy schedules of working parents often leave teachers wondering how to make this crucial part of the program a viable one.

Communicating with Parents of Toddlers Is Different

For parents of toddlers, parent conferences are actually part of a broader communication and conferencing system. The system is based on five underlying assumptions. The first assumption is that communication and, therefore, conferencing, need to take place more often. The twice-a-year format of preschool conferences is simply inadequate for both parents and children.

The second assumption is that family systems have many adjustments to make as they transition to parenthood. Parenting in the United States is a lonely endeavor. Close relatives, neighborhoods as community, and same age and stage friends have gone the way of the dinosaurs for most families. Further, the workplace is only just beginning to understand the challenges working parents are facing, and many families are separated from the support systems that once made parenting a shared experience. As a result, schools are the places new families connect with resources to help them become good parents. This new reality puts even more pressure on schools as they attempt to meet these new demands.

The third assumption is that parents of very young children are different from parents of older children. There is little argument that this is true, particularly for first-time parents. The question is what to do about it without totally exhausting teachers.

The fourth assumption is that a wider variety of formats are required for communicating and conferencing with parents of toddlers. One type of communication and conferencing is not enough.

A fifth assumption is that a communication and conferencing system has to provide a wider range of resources in a wider variety of formats. Parents of toddlers want and need more. They need more information from a wider variety of sources. They want more time to discuss their ideas and concerns with caring teachers. They need more support in understanding development and much more opportunity to understand the difference between their "ideal" views of what parents can or should do and what is realistic or practical to do.

Conferences Are Parent Education

Conferences are a component of parent education. There are five goals of parent education:

1. To help parents develop self-confidence in their own parenting style.
2. To increase their understanding of child development.

3. To enhance parenting skills so that parents are able to support their child's increasing developmental competence.
4. To empower parents to make good parenting decisions and choices.
5. To connect parents to resources.

To address each of these goals, it is necessary to re-conceptualize conferencing into a broader system.

Re-conceptualizing Conferencing

Re-conceptualizing conferencing into a more multidimensional approach lessens the teacher's feeling of being overwhelmed by toddler parents. Think of parent communication and conferencing as an ongoing, two-way communication system among parents, the school, and the teacher. The communication system includes four types of communication and conferencing:

1. Formal face-to-face conferences with written documentation.
2. Informal conferences in a written format.
3. Formal oral conferences that occur at checkpoints in the school schedule.
4. Informal oral conferences that occur as a part of the regular interface between the parent and the teacher.

Let's look at each of these types of communicating and conferencing.

Formal Conferences with Written Documentation

This is the traditional conference. Parents and the teacher sit down together to review some sort of written evaluation of the child's developmental repertoire. Anecdotal notes by the teacher, normative developmental assessment with checklists, samples of children's work, and summaries of the child's developmental stage are common components of this type of conference. Formal conferences with written documentation are an important part of the parent education process because they validate the importance of parental understanding of the child's age and stage.

- What are your observations about your child's experience at school?
- What are his or her most interesting characteristics?
- What concerns do you have about your child?
- What questions do you have about how your child spends his or her day?
- What plans should we make for your child in the next few weeks or months?
- Has anything changed in your family that we should be aware of?
- What has been your child's response to other children in the program?
- Is there anything we should change about your child's day at school?

What is often missing from the formal conference is an opportunity for the parents to let teachers know about their feelings, issues, or concerns. Formal conferences are often directed by the teacher, who shares information she or he has collected with the parents.

Help make parents a part of the formal conference process by asking them to identify things they would like to include or discuss. A series of open-ended questions to think about before the conference might be helpful to parents to stimulate their thinking about what they might want to discuss.

Informal Conferences with Written Documentation

Toddlers change so dramatically during the first three years. They go from helpless, dependent, puzzling newborns to walking, talking, and interacting toddlers. This is a dramatic and rapid process with many developmental changes and dilemmas. Parents, particularly first-time parents, need opportunities to understand and support this rapid developmental growth.

Because this development takes place so quickly, it must be shared as it happens. Parents of toddlers need help seeing the little changes that indicate developmental growth, not just the easily observable milestones such as putting words together to form a sentence or jumping. Informal written communication can fill this role. This communication is also called the anecdotal record (see page 536 in the Appendix). Observations of what happened, when it happened, where it happened, and with whom it happened are written down to consider later for implications or conclusions.

Seizing the opportunity to share this type of developmental data on a regular basis creates a wonderful dialogue between parents and teachers. Try using an inexpensive notebook for each toddler. Start by writing one anecdotal note a week about each child. Then send the notebook home and ask the parents to write one anecdotal note about what happens at home. This back and forth of observations—not opinions or judgments—hones skills for both parties. Teachers learn really to observe toddlers' behavior as a source of notes, and parents become good observers of their child's developmental growth.

Something else happens. Parents get a glimpse of what teachers do all day besides interact, support, stimulate, facilitate, change, toilet, feed, and comfort toddlers. Informal written communication reinforces that observing is a crucial part of the teacher's role as well as communicates that parents are important sources of information about their child's development. It also gives teachers the perfect opportunity to share other resources with parents. Written materials, videotapes, reference books, helping professionals, and support from other parents with similar experiences can all be offered to enhance the parent education process.

Formal Oral Conferences

What we share with parents is as important as what we don't share. Every teacher of toddlers knows that early exposure to books is an important curriculum activity that fosters a love of reading in later life. Books are read to toddlers in schools every day. But how often do we share with parents that we read to their child every day?

Building in checkpoints for regular exchanges between parents and their child's teachers is an important part of the conferencing system. ***Touchpoints*** (Brazelton, 1992) identifies points of development that offer pediatricians an opportunity to discuss upcoming developmental changes and progress. Perhaps we need a *Touchpoints*-like approach to formal oral conferencing!

Consider formal oral conferences at the end of the first full week of school, one month later, and at least quarterly thereafter. In addition, formal oral conferences might be helpful any time something is going to change—such as a teacher's schedule or a change in staffing.

Although this seems like a lot of conferences, they can take place fairly simply by telephone. The scheduling problems of face-to-face conferences are almost completely avoided.

Frequent connections such as these confirm that everyone is on the same page and that nothing is happening that needs attention. Structure the conferences so similar topics are covered each time. Setting up the conference this way will encourage efficient use of the time allotted and can prevent overlooking emerging problems. Keep the notes from the conversation each time to analyze for trends, continued concerns, or perhaps, even compliments to share with your director or other teachers.

Informal Oral Conferences

Informal oral conferences that occur as a part of the regular interface between parents and the child's teacher are the last type of conference. These take place daily during arrival or departure time. Don't overlook them as important and don't overlook them as conferences. Parents get their view of their child's experiences from these verbal exchanges. The amount and accuracy of these conversations can either build confidence or concern. Confidence builds if teachers show their connection with the toddler. Concern builds if opening and closing teachers aren't reliable reporters of the child's experience or can't share information with parents when asked.

Operational supports help. Written communication systems such as Communication Sheets (see page 537 in the Appendix), telephone calls from the child's primary teacher who arrives after the parent drops off the child or before the child leaves, and varying schedules, so parents see their child's teacher occasionally either upon arrival or departure all help. And, this is an ongoing staff development issue. Helping early and late teachers see the importance of arrival and departure interactions as crucial parent conferences is a topic worth discussing often.

Parents of toddlers do require teachers to invest in building a relationship with them. The outcome of the investment is parents whose parenting skills grow as their child matures and develops. Taking the time to set up and implement a multidimensional conferencing system makes conferences become parent education.

Child Abuse Prevention

The safety and well-being of the children in care and early education programs are of foremost concern, and, therefore, child abuse reporting laws must be taken very seriously. Teachers are required by federal law and the Code of Ethical Conduct and Statement of Commitment (1999) to report any suspected child abuse, regardless of who is suspect or where the abuse may have occurred. Judgment of actual abuse is not made by the teacher or the school principal or director. It is the responsibility of the appropriate agency, usually the department of human services, to investigate the allegation and make a judgment. The role of teachers is to report any conditions that indicate the possibility of suspected abuse or neglect.

Documentation of Suspected Abuse

The best way to assure thorough and accurate documentation of suspected child abuse is to have a system for anecdotally recording data on each child in the classroom on a regular basis. Communication Sheets (see page 537 in the Appendix) serve well for this purpose. Record any and all information related to the child as it comes to a teacher's attention.

Jason arrived at the center at 7:55 a.m. When he took off his hat, a silver dollar-size bump and bruise were noticed above his right eye. His mother reported that he had walked into the corner of the dining room table over the weekend.

For example, if a child arrives in your classroom with a scratch or bump on his cheek, a quick note of the date, time, and description of the scratch is recorded under the teacher comments section. Facts, not opinions, are recorded. Note the example on the left.

This account is accurate and factual and is also nonthreatening. It indicates when and where the injury was noticed and establishes the explanation given for the injury. It does not indicate that Jason is abused or neglected. It is just a record of the incident.

If Jason had repeated injuries or seemed to behave in a considerably different way after the injury, a report to the appropriate agency may be necessary. Or, if the teacher noticed a pattern in the injuries that Jason received, reporting might be considered. The better the records, the more likely the child's best interest will be served.

The same is true for even minor injuries that occur at the center. Record the information for parents to review when they pick up the child. Under no circumstances should accident information be hidden. Parents deserve to know even about minor injuries.

Teacher Competencies to Support Toddlers Expressing Feelings with Parents, Teachers, and Friends

Sometimes	Usually	Always	
☐	☐	☐	Checks toddlers periodically for wetness, asks the child first if he needs changing; reminds toddlers to check their bodies to see if they need to toilet, helps toddlers with toilet play as well as toilet training.
☐	☐	☐	Assures that children have frequent opportunities for success. Delights in each child's success, expresses kindness and support when children are struggling with developmental challenges, and supports children in learning from their mistakes.
☐	☐	☐	Invites children to play with each other; participates in play as a partner and a facilitator.
☐	☐	☐	Allows children to direct and manage their own play.
☐	☐	☐	Recognizes the toddlers' need for balance between independence and dependence.
☐	☐	☐	Uses vocabulary, materials, activities, and experiences that are suitable for the age, stage, temperament, and learning styles of children in her or his group.
☐	☐	☐	Exhibits flexibility in carrying out activity and experience plans.
☐	☐	☐	Shows imagination and spontaneity in building on children's interest for developing curriculum rather than depending exclusively on pre-prepared curriculum.
☐	☐	☐	Plans, implements, and evaluates parent-teacher conferences, intake interviews, and gradual enrollment.
☐	☐	☐	Models the recognition and expression of feelings by naming her or his own feelings.

Teacher Competencies to Support Toddlers Expressing Feelings with Parents, Teachers, and Friends (continued)

Sometimes	Usually	Always	
☐	☐	☐	Uses modeling and patterning as strategies for helping toddlers interact successfully.
☐	☐	☐	Understands that social roles and expectations for children in their family setting may be different from what is expected at school. Helps children make the transition between these two different sets of expectations and helps children behave appropriately in each.
☐	☐	☐	Serves as a social model by building a relationship with each child and family and by maintaining positive relationships with other teachers. Provides children with a break from social interaction or overstimulation as needed.
☐	☐	☐	Watches and observes children at play and throughout the school day. Uses observation to inform curriculum planning and provide insight into interactions with children.

Resources for Teachers

Brazelton, T.B. (1992). ***Touchpoints: The essential reference.*** Reading, MA: Addison Wesley.

Goleman, D. (1995). ***Emotional Intelligence.*** New York: Bantam Doubleday Dell.

Goleman, D. (1998). ***Working with emotional intelligence.*** New York: Bantam Doubleday Dell.

Greenspan, S. & N.T. Greenspan. (1989). ***First feelings: Milestones in the emotional development of your baby and child.*** New York: Penguin.

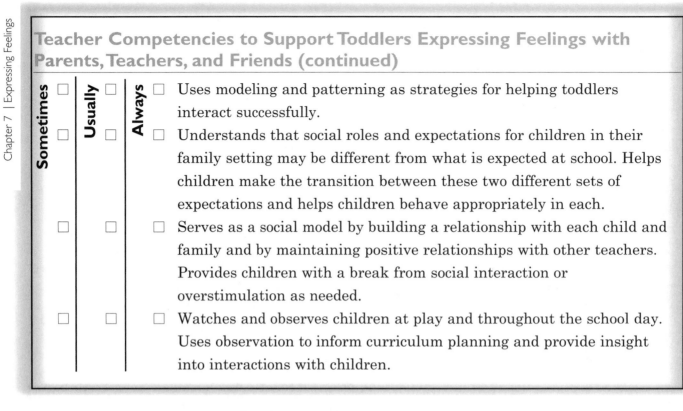

INNOVATIONS IN PARENT PARTNERSHIPS

School- or Teacher-initiated Activities

Supporting Possibilities

Help parents support their children's learning through gathering materials that will be needed in Storybook Classics and Water. Lists are provided at the end of each section, but posting the lists now will give parents ample time to save and find items you will need in the classroom.

Developmental Banners

Communicate with parents in a very special way. As children acquire milestones on the assessment instrument, communicate the child's progress to their parents by creating a developmental banner. For example, on a heavy sheet of paper help children create their handprints and footprints. Allow the prints to dry. Then add emotional developmental accomplishments in pen or thin marker. Don't forget the child's name and date. Parents will love this special type of communication. Or, take a picture of the child exhibiting the new skill and post the picture along with an anecdotal note recounting when you saw the skill used. Add these banners (or photographs of them) to the child's emerging portfolio.

Note: Developmental banners are individual in nature. A wall full of the same banner for each child is not appropriate. Make each banner specific to the child's emerging skills. Pick different domains of development to highlight for different children or focus on one or two children at a time, identifying new skills as they emerge.

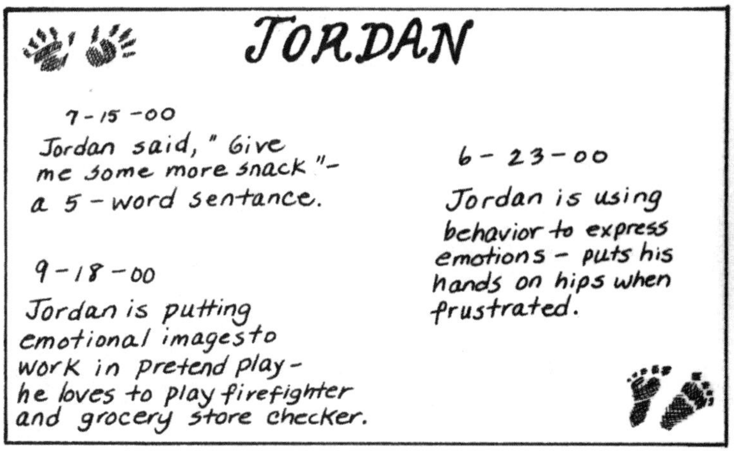

JORDAN
7-15-00
Jordan said, "Give me some more snack"- a 5-word sentance.
9-18-00
Jordan is putting emotional imagesto work in pretend play- he loves to play firefighter and grocery store checker.
6-23-00
Jordan is using behavior to express emotions - puts his hands on hips when frustrated.

Parent Participation Activities

Parent Day

Invite parents to visit at any time during Parent Day. Provide decorated nametags and have children's art "in process" as parents visit.

Terrific Toddler Celebration

Plan a time to celebrate terrific toddlerhood. During outdoor playtime, provide juice and crackers or cookies. Invite parents to join the celebration.

Parent Postcards

Share Parent Postcards with parents as they indicate an interest, at appropriate times during the enrollment cycle, or as developmental issues arise. (See page 548 in the Appendix for a sample dissemination schedule.) Copy Postcards. Cut if necessary. Address to parent(s) and place on Communication Sheet or hand out personally.

Managing Normal Aggression in Very Young Children

Every parent dreads the day when the teacher reports that his or her child is responsible for hurting another child. But that day will come. Aggression is a normal part of young children's experiences. Aggression results from powerful emotions that are not yet under the child's direct control. Children hit, pinch, bite, slap, and grab when their emotions cause them to act before they can think about doing something different.

Children learn to manage aggression when supportive adults help them learn other skills and connect consequences with aggression. Using aggression to stop aggression only teaches children that they must submit to adults who are bigger and more powerful. It does not help children gain control over aggressive behavior or replace it with more appropriate skills. Replacing aggressive behavior with more sophisticated skills is a process. Learning to express feelings appropriately is a lifelong task. The first steps are taken in the first three years.

The following are some examples of ways supportive parents can meet aggression with consequences from the earliest stage.

- When your toddler bites on your finger to get your attention, say that biting hurts, and walk away from him or her. Say that your finger is not for biting and don't let your child put your finger in his or her mouth again. What toddlers learn is the consequence of biting—close contact between parent and child goes away for a minute.

TO

Managing Normal Aggression in Very Young Children (continued)

- When your toddler grabs his or her sibling by the hair and pulls, separate the two and hold the child whose hair was pulled until he or she calms down and gets under control. Help the hurt sibling and tell the other sibling to stop pulling hair. Tell both children, "Pulling hair didn't solve the problem." Then offer an alternative such as, "Call me when you need help getting a toy back," or "Use words to tell her to stop."

- When your toddler grabs a toy away from his or her friend, explain that the friend had the toy first and return the toy to the friend. Offer another idea about how to get the toy back. Tell your toddler to put out his or her hand, asking the friend with a gesture to put the toy in his or her hand. If your child falls apart when you do this, remove your child from the situation until he or she is calm enough to return to play.

Early experiences with the consequences of aggression help children learn over time that aggressive behavior doesn't accomplish much. After this lesson is learned, children can begin the process of becoming assertive enough to prevent being victimized and becoming authoritative enough to be seen as a leader. Both of these important lessons will never be learned unless parents and teachers help children learn to manage normal aggression and convert it into constructive assertion and leadership.

TO

Dealing with Oppositional Behavior

During the second year of life, toddlers begin to develop a view of themselves as separate and independent from their parents. Because toddlers have gained control over their bodies, they are now capable of moving away from their parents, exploring and discovering things that are out of their immediate reach, and taking care of some of their own needs, such as eating and drinking by themselves.

As they try these new skills and abilities and practice being separate and independent from their parents, toddlers alternate between being pleased about these newfound abilities and being frightened and scared by them. Parents see this ambivalence as their toddler handles one situation without problems and the next by falling apart and needing to reconnect with Mom or Dad before recovering. They also see it when their toddler is tired, hungry, excited, or ill. In these situations, the toddler vacillates between wanting to be independent and separate and wanting to be dependent, cared for, connected, and supported.

Although your toddler is developing a sense of him- or herself as separate from you, he or she has not yet developed the ability to control impulses, to wait, or to predict the consequences of their newfound independent behavior. Because of this, your child gets upset when you help him or her control his or her impulses, ask the child to wait, or apply consequences. The result is a kind of meltdown that is the precursor to temper tantrums. Opposition can be very intense and emotional. It can also be upsetting to you and your child. Psychologists tell us that this is a universal and crucial stage for toddler development. It happens to all toddlers. If this is the case, what can you do to assist your toddler in gaining the psychological and emotional skills he or she needs to continue to develop? Here are some ideas.

Stanley Greenspan and Nancy Greenspan, authors of ***First Feelings: Milestones in the Emotional Development of Your Baby and Child***, say that your toddler needs three things to get through this stage. The first thing is lots of love. As your sweet infant becomes independent and separate as a toddler, your feelings as a parent may begin to change. Where did your compliant child go? Love, support for appropriate behavior, and emotional support for losing control are crucial for your toddler in this stage. You can provide this by being understanding and empathetic. Empathy implies that you understand and accept the feelings that your child has, even when these feelings are negative ones such as anger or rage.

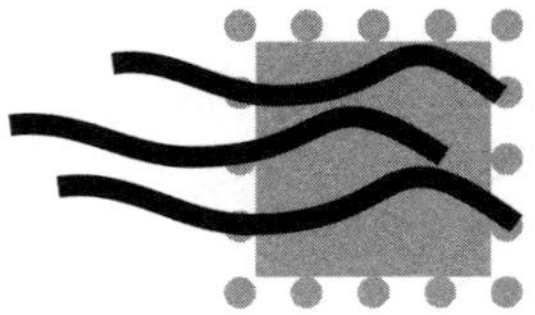

TO ______________

____

____

Dealing with Oppositional Behavior (continued)

The second thing your toddler needs is opportunities to be in control. When you think about it, your child has little direct control over his or her life. Parents decide when to get up, when to eat, what to wear, when to take a nap, what food goes on the plate, and so on. Work hard to find things for your toddler to control. Does he or she want a big bowl for cereal or a little bowl, white or red socks, milk or juice? Giving toddlers meaningful control over these small decisions empowers them to practice controlling what is happening in a positive way. Often, having positive experiences with control will diminish the amount of oppositional or resistant behavior your toddler has overall.

The third thing that your toddler needs is limits. Without limits, children are not sure of where the safe space for experimentation starts and stops. Because your toddler is still unable to manage without your support and protection, a lack of limits feels like being physically and emotionally abandoned. Limits on behavior during this stage are crucial to helping your toddler feel competent about separation and independence.

TO

Toddlers on the Edge

Much of what toddlers do is on the edge. Parents may feel that they are constantly limiting children's behavior. Good advice at this stage is to make a few nonnegotiable rules and use a lot of redirection, distraction, and ignoring of behavior that isn't related to the few important rules. Otherwise you will feel like you are correcting your toddler all the time.

Be realistic. Most oppositional behavior emerges when you expect your toddler to handle situations that are beyond her or his ability. Having realistic expectations for your toddler is crucial.

Keep your own feelings under control. If you are angry, anxious, or stressed, your toddler will know his or her behavior is working. Focus on the behavior rather than how you feel about it. Comments such as, "Your feet make noise when you tap them on the back of the car seat" instead of "You are driving me crazy with that kicking" help your toddler see the impact of his or her behavior on you.

Tell your toddler what you want him or her to do rather than saying "No!" or "Don't." Remember that your child is trying to feel competent and independent. "Nos" and "Don'ts" tell your toddler that he or she has failed.

Negative statement	Positive statement
Stop running!	Walk! March! Crawl!
Don't throw sand!	Leave the sand in the sand box.
Don't touch.	Put your hands in your pockets.
Don't whine.	Use a regular voice.
Don't touch the remote control.	Put that in my hand.

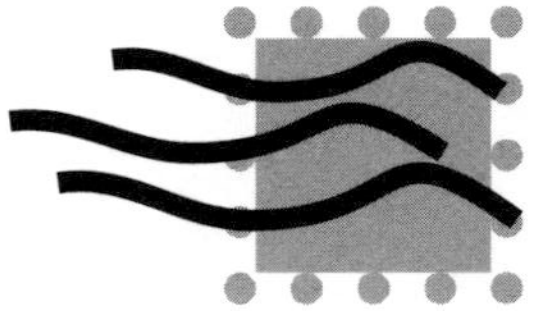

TO

Toddlers on the Edge (continued)

Change the environment. Where children live and play is a minefield for an independence-seeking toddler. Tables and chairs look very much like climbing structures. Doors are there to be opened. Things that cause an action or reaction are fascinating. Rather than deal with constant limit-setting, change the environment. Put safety latches on doors that need them. Put the remote control out of your toddler's reach. Create a place to climb that is safe. Any effort you put into this approach will make the life of your toddler and his or her family calmer and less combative.

Finally, be patient. This is a developmental stage. It is part of becoming a competent, independent three-year-old. Viewed this way, your toddler's stretch for independence and autonomy will give way to increasing skills and abilities and a view of the world that says "I can do it!"

TO

Handling Temper Tantrums

You've seen tantrums in action. A screaming child. An embarrassed and frustrated parent. Unsuccessful attempts to make the whole thing go away! During toddlerhood, children struggle to develop a sense of themselves as separate from their parents. This process, called differentiation, actually starts at birth and lasts well into young adulthood. It is the process of becoming a separate and successful individual.

The first step in differentiation is related to control—who is in charge of me, my body, and my emotions? Early in your child's life, you are in charge. Now, you want your toddler to begin to take charge of some of his or her own behavior. This process of transferring some responsibility for control usually results in children losing exactly what you are striving to help them gain—control!

When your toddler feels angry, frustrated, or helpless, he or she may kick, scream, and flop on the ground. Tantrums are a normal, natural, and inevitable part of growing up. That does not make them fun. Make a plan now for how you will handle it when your child begins to tantrum.

The first step of the plan is preventive in nature. Help your child have some control over his or her life. Start small. Maybe your toddler can help you pick out what he or she wants to wear from several choices. Giving your toddlers choices gives him or her experience with making decisions and having them turn out successfully. This experience is crucial in helping your toddler make good choices about whether or not to throw a temper tantrum.

Make sure to reward appropriate progress in taking charge. When your child shows competence in getting in or out of the car, eating with a spoon or fork, or pulling on his or her own socks, reward these early attempts at independence and self-control with lots of hugs, kisses, and compliments.

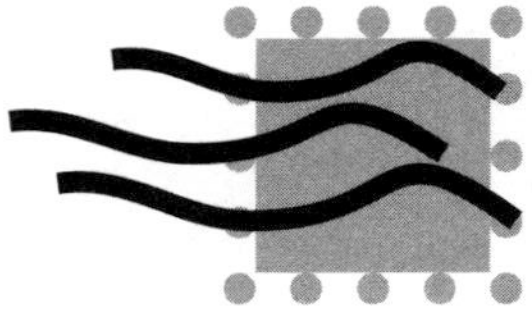

TO

Handling Temper Tantrums (continued)

Pick a place for your child to be out of control in your house. Make sure the tantrum place is safe. Then, plan to take your child to the special tantrum place when he or she is out of control. Make sure to tell your tantrumming child calmly that he or she is free to stay out of control as long as he or she likes—remember, part of this stage is learning that you can take charge of your own behavior. Choosing whether you want to scream for one minute or 10 is certainly taking charge of your own behavior!

It is important to follow through with your response to tantrums. If children get attention from tantrums, they will last much longer than if they have no audience. Removing yourself as an audience quickly and calmly when tantrums occur is the best thing you can do to lessen the frequency of tantrumming. If you are in a public place, consider stopping what you are doing and taking your child home to the tantrum place. Taking this behavior on quickly will prevent your child from learning that you can't control him or her or are intimidated by controlling him or her in public.

When a tantrum is over—it's over. Accept the child back into family life as if nothing has happened. Temper tantrums are a developmentally normal step in developing into a competent, capable, child. As frustrating as they can be for parents, a calm, confident approach will go a long way to preventing this stage from lasting very long.

Although temper tantrums are a developmentally normal step in becoming a competent, capable child, intense and prolonged tantrums may indicate that your toddler is having emotional difficulty. When tantrums continue to intensify across toddlerhood, or when the suggested strategies are used consistently and don't seem to work, discuss your concerns with your child's teacher or seek support in helping the toddler move on emotionally and developmentally from your pediatrician or another helping professional.

TO

Resources for Parents

Adams, C. & E. Fruge. (1996). ***Why children misbehave.*** Oakland, CA: New Harbinger.

Brazelton, T. B. (1992). ***Touchpoints: The essential reference.*** Reading, MA: Addison Wesley.

Greenspan, S. (1999). ***The six experiences that create intelligence and emotional growth in babies and young children.*** Reading, MA: Perseus Books.

Likona, T. (1994). ***Raising good children.*** New York: Bantam Doubleday Dell.

INNOVATIONS IN ENVIRONMENTS

Characteristics of Good Toddler Environments

Environments for young children contribute to how children grow and learn. This is especially true for toddler environments because of how toddlers learn and their special developmental needs. Equipment such as tables, chairs, storage bins and cabinets, carpet, and developmentally appropriate toys are necessary, but these are just the beginning of a well-prepared toddler classroom. Toddlers learn through their senses—from touching, tasting, smelling, and hearing. Most of their interactions are with things in the environment, both large things and small things.

Teachers need to take several issues into consideration when planning environments for toddlers. The first one is safety. Toddlers have a micro-focus—seeing and responding to things that adults never notice. Small items may be placed inside ears and noses. All items (including books) are chewed, and anything not strong enough to withstand the strength of toddler hands is torn apart.

Choke testers are not just for infant rooms. Small items that can pass through a choke tube have no place in the toddler environment. Additionally, teachers must think not only of the size of the whole item, but also of the size of parts of items if they are broken (wheels that come off vehicles are especially problematic).

A second consideration for the toddler environment has to do with the toddler's tendency to tantrum. During toddlerhood, children may have "meltdowns" where they need space to recover in sight of the supportive teacher. The "tantrumming place" in a toddler classroom is a safe place to get back under control. An open, visible area will work well. It can be a carpeted area, a soft cozy area with pillows, or a space separated by furniture from the rest of the classroom. Check carefully for sharp corners and other safety concerns.

Another consideration is accommodating the toddler's view of "mine." The toddler environment must support the toddler's need to have his belongings (and the collection of toys and materials that become his through possession) respected. "Mine" is a favorite word (and concept) for toddlers. They believe that everything they see in the environment is actually theirs.

Security items need special protection from other toddlers until children learn to put these special items in a safe place when they are not needed. Cubbies work if the child is able to turn the security item over to the teacher when it isn't needed. But most toddlers can't. So, establish a special location in your classroom for security items and help toddlers learn to take their favorite objects to this place to keep them safe.

Duplicate toys are a must in toddler classrooms. Because toddlers are parallel players, they need duplicate toys to enter into parallel play. When they get a good idea about playing from another child, toddlers want to replicate the idea. If he can't find the toys and materials to do so, getting the ones the other child has will become the focus of the interaction instead of picking up a duplicate toy and playing along.

A last characteristic of good toddler classrooms relates to toddler aggression. Toddlers have a tendency to use aggression, particularly biting, hitting, and grabbing, to get their needs met. They are still learning the language needed to negotiate these interactions successfully by themselves. They get frustrated trying to control their behaviors and manage their emotions. Overcrowding in the classroom can be a contributing factor. Give toddlers "elbow room," so they are not competing for the same space. Arrange the room to spread toddlers out in the available space, with one or two toddlers in each area. This kind of space utilization significantly lowers the amount of aggression that emerges from sharing a close space.

Environments teach. Carefully thought-out and arranged classrooms can function well and support emerging skills in toddlers. Take the time to make sure the classroom environment works.

Room Arrangement Guides Toddlers' Behavior

The way environments are arranged communicates many messages to children. Classroom arrangement gives children numerous clues about what to do and how to behave. When planned and arranged effectively, classrooms foster self-control and adaptive behavior.

Arrangements for toddlers need to allow for room to play alone, alongside, and with other children, leaving little open, nonfunctional space. The arrangement should clearly communicate the physical limits of play spaces, regulate children's behavior in each space, and control the use of materials within the space—all without direct intervention from an adult. For example, if classroom shelves are arranged in such a way that children can identify what toys go in which containers, toddlers will be more likely to put the toys in the containers and the containers back on the shelf. Conversely, if the middle of the classroom has plenty of room to run around, toddlers will use the space to run around, even if you don't want them to do so.

To evaluate whether your classroom arrangement communicates effectively to children, note the location of behavior problems in your classroom. If problems occur in certain areas of the room, reassess the arrangement of the physical space in the classroom.

Activities and Experiences vs. Centers

Most early childhood educators think of interest or learning centers as an essential part of any classroom setting. Yet, environments for toddlers are different because they are "groupie" in nature and tend to go where the action is. For this reason, teachers must bring activities and experiences to children and assist children in going to where the activities are. A wide range of activities and experiences must be available to toddlers. In each of the following Possibilities Plans, *Storybook Characters* and *Water*, activities and experiences are presented in the following areas:

- Dramatic Possibilities
- Sensory/Art Possibilities
- Curiosity Possibilities
- Construction Possibilities
- Literacy Possibilities
- Music Possibilities
- Movement Possibilities
- Outdoor Possibilities
- Project Possibilities
- Parent Participation Possibilities

Storybook Characters

WEB

Note: Using the techniques of webbing, teachers can follow the leads that children give them, as well as have an unlimited source of options. Always use the webs as a jumping-off point. The possibilities are endless!

PLANNING PAGES

Plan Possibilities

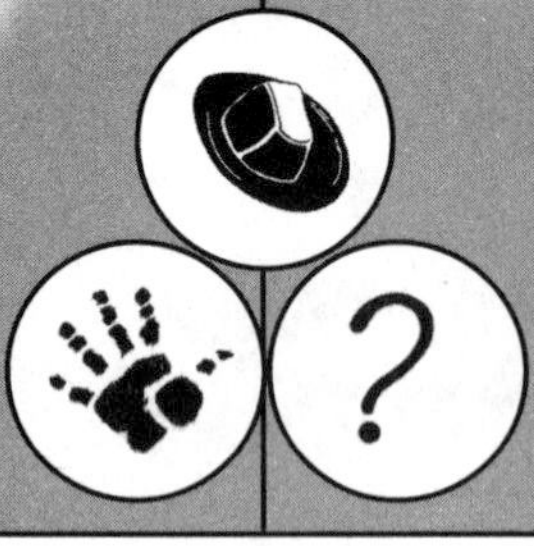

Dramatic

Stone Soup Cooking 490
Three Bears' Cottage 490
Big Red Barn 490

Sensory/Art

Barn Raising 491
Paper Plate Fingerpainting 491
Dirt and Water 492
Swimming Ducks 492

Curiosity

Oatmeal Porridge 492
Who's in the Barn? 493

Construction

Fill 'em Up 493
Duck Pond 494
Animals and Families 494

Literacy

Brown Bear, Brown Bear, What Do You See? 495
Individual Brown Bear Painting Book 495
The Very Hungry Caterpillar 495
Where the Wild Things Are 496
The Mitten 496
This Little Piggy 497

Music

There's a Little Flower . . . 497
Old MacDonald Had a Farm 498
Eensy Weensy Spider 498

Movement

Duck Puppets 499
Move to the Music 499
Bear Walking 499

Outdoor

Flowerpots 500
Paper Plate Kites 500
Storybook Characters Outdoors 501

Projects

Rainbow Big Fish 501

Parent Participation

Animal Sounds Tape 502
Stone Soup 502
Parent Postcard Process Is the Goal . . . 503

Storybook Characters

DRAMATIC POSSIBILITIES

Stone Soup Cooking

All ages

Materials

Stone Soup by Marcia Brown
Large pot
Large plastic spoon
Real or plastic vegetables
Crumpled brown paper (for stone)

Teacher Talk

Narrate as children place items in the pot and "cook." "Those are large carrots you are putting in the pot, Sue."

Read the story. Provide props and observe as children play.

Three Bears' Cottage

All ages

Materials

Three bowls, spoons, placemats
Three chairs
Three doll beds/cots
Goldilocks and the Three Bears story (any version)
Teddy bears

Provide props for this popular story. Observe how children use the props.

Big Red Barn

All ages

Materials

Large cardboard box
Child gardening toys
Red paint
Paintbrushes
Craft knife (teacher only)
Straw hats, overalls, plaid shirts, and work boots

Turn the area into a farm by adding a large cardboard box painted red (toddlers will enjoy painting in the sensory area or even outside), straw hats, denim overalls, plaid shirts, farm animals, gardening tools, and work boots as props. Observe children as they show interest in the barn and props. Watch for emerging play themes that can be supported with additional props (perhaps tractors and farm equipment).

SENSORY/ART POSSIBILITIES

Barn Raising

All ages

Materials
Red paint
Paintbrushes
Cardboard box
Newspaper to put under the box
Craft knife (teacher only)

Put a large cardboard box on newspaper in the sensory area. Add red paint and brushes. Paint the box red. When it is dry, cut windows and doors and add it to the Dramatic Possibilities area.

Paper Plate Fingerpainting

All ages

Materials
Paper plates
Fingerpaint

Teacher Talk
"You are painting in big circles on the paper plate."

Put one or two teaspoons of paint on each paper plate. Show children how to use their fingers to paint the plate.

Dirt and Water

All ages

Materials
Soil
Water in plastic spray/squirt bottles
Shovel
Pails
Smocks

Teacher Talk
"You mixed the water with the soil. How does that feel?"

Place the dirt in tubs in a sensory table. Add the squirt bottles and the props. Observe to see what happens.

Swimming Ducks

All ages

Materials
Water
Rubber ducks
Make Way for Ducklings by Robert McCloskey

Teacher Talk
"I hear a duck going quack!"

Place rubber ducks in the water table. Observe to see if children connect the ducks to the sounds that they make. Read *Make Way for Ducklings.*

CURIOSITY POSSIBILITIES

Oatmeal Porridge

All ages

Materials
Plastic pans
Dry oatmeal
Water
Plastic bowls
Plastic spoons

Teacher Talk
Describe the textures as children play. "That oatmeal is wet. This one is dry. That one squishes!"

Place dry oatmeal in one plastic pan, and oatmeal mixed with warm water in another plastic pan. Place plastic bowls and spoons in the plastic pans, so children can explore the different textures of oatmeal porridge.

Who's in the Barn?

All ages

Materials
Coffee can with lid
Red spray paint (teacher only)
Craft knife (teacher only)
Farm animal pictures

Teacher Talk
Connect the pictures of the animals to the sounds the animals make. "The pig goes 'oink.' The duck goes 'quack.' The cow goes 'moo.'"

Spray the coffee can with red spray paint. Use a craft knife to cut a four-inch-diameter circle in the can lid. Place the farm animal pictures inside the can. Snap the lid onto the can. Invite children to reach inside the can and pull out a picture. Explore the picture and see what the child says about it.

CONSTRUCTION POSSIBILITIES

Fill 'em Up

All ages

Materials
Wood or plastic blocks
Buckets

Teacher Talk
"Your bucket (pail) is full of blocks. Out they go! Peggy can put the blocks back in the bucket, too."

Provide small plastic buckets for toddlers to put the blocks in and take them out, or take buckets of blocks outside, so children can fill and dump them there.

Duck Pond

All ages

Materials
Rubber ducks
Blue butcher paper

Teacher Talk
"You have four ducks swimming in the pond, Tomeka. One, two, three, four."

Add rubber ducks and ponds created with blue butcher paper. Observe to see if the children connect the ducks to the ponds where they live.

Animals and Families

All ages

Materials
Plastic animal families (big animals and little animals)
Plastic tubs

Teacher Talk
"There is the big animal. Where is the baby?"

Add these props to the area and observe to see what the children do with them.

LITERACY POSSIBILITIES

Note: For this Possibilities Plan, select Storybook Classics that your children love to read over and over again. Create opportunities to read these favorites or select a few new books to become classics. Expand children's understanding of the classics by extending the story into the important domain of practice and pretend play. Some examples of how to do so are included, and teachers can create many more. See the list of books on page 505 for ideas about potential classics for your classroom.

Brown Bear, Brown Bear, What Do You See?

All ages

Materials

Brown Bear Brown Bear, What Do You See? by Bill Martin, Jr.
Brown bear puppet

Use a bear puppet as you read the story. Pause before you turn the page to see if children guess what the bear sees. Then, add hand puppets of the animals in the book to the Dramatic Possibilities area, so children can recreate this story again and again. Then, rewrite the book using pictures of the children in your group as the characters of the book. Finally, read the other books that are similar such as *Polar Bear, Polar Bear, What do You See?* by bill Martin, Jr.

Individual Brown Bear Painting Book

All ages

Materials

Paints in the colors used in *Brown Bear, Brown Bear, What Do You See?* by Bill Martin, Jr.
Paintbrushes
Paper
Hole punch
Yarn or metal rings

Use the sequence of colors in the Brown Bear book to create a book. Let children paint one page at a time, covering the page with paint. Let dry. Write the color words on the bottom of each page and put the colored pages together into a book with yarn or rings. Children can "read" the book, adding what they see to the color.

The Very Hungry Caterpillar

All ages

Materials

Poster board
Scissors (teacher only)
Markers
Tube sock
Colored markers
The Very Hungry Caterpillar by Eric Carle

Teacher Talk
"What is your favorite food to eat, Enrique? Talk about the different foods the caterpillar ate, the chrysalis, and the colors of the butterfly."

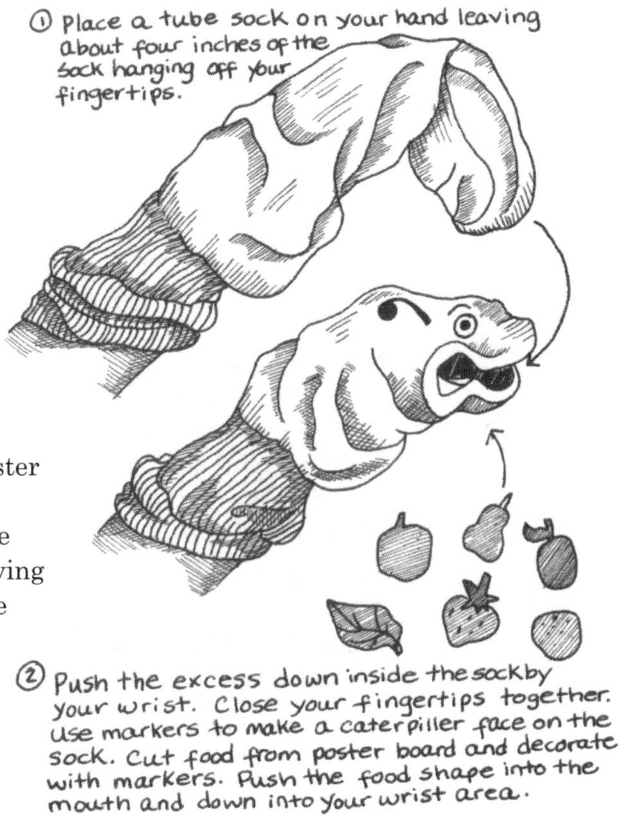
① Place a tube sock on your hand leaving about four inches of the sock hanging off your fingertips.
② Push the excess down inside the sock by your wrist. Close your fingertips together. Use markers to make a caterpiller face on the sock. Cut food from poster board and decorate with markers. Push the food shape into the mouth and down into your wrist area.

Cut the appropriate number of different foods the caterpillar ate from poster board. Decorate with markers. Place the tube sock on your hand, leaving about four inches of the sock hanging off your fingertips. Push the excess down inside the sock by your wrist. Close your fingertips together. Use markers to make a caterpillar face on the sock. Read the book to children. Let the caterpillar eat each food. (Push the food shape into the mouth and down into your wrist area.)

Where the Wild Things Are

All ages

Materials
Where the Wild Things Are by Maurice Sendak
Puppets that go along with the book
Basket

Toddlers enjoy reading books like this that have puppets to accompany the story. Place the book and the puppets in a basket, so they can be kept together. Use book baskets for individual as well as small group reading.

The Mitten

All ages

Materials
Animal pictures
Mitten
The Mitten by Jan Brett

Teacher Talk
Talk about the animals, mittens, and gloves. "Reginald, the glove has fingers. One, two, three, four, five fingers."

As you read the book, tuck the appropriate animal picture into the mitten. Give children an opportunity to tell the story in their own way using the props.

This Little Piggy

All ages

Materials
None

Teacher Talk
"Your little piggies are wiggling all the way home."

Touch each toe as you say the rhyme.

This Little Piggy
This little piggy went to market.
This little piggy stayed home.
This little piggy had roast beef.
This little piggy had none.
This little piggy cried, "Wee-wee, I
can't find my way home!"

MUSIC POSSIBILITIES

There's a Little Flower

All ages

Materials
None

Sing the following song with children. Sing to the tune "Have You Ever Seen a Lassie?"

There's a Little Flower
There's a little flower,
A flower, a flower.
There's a little flower,
On my garden path.

A flower so neat
It's a rose so sweet.
There's a little flower,
On my garden path.

Old MacDonald Had a Farm

All ages

Materials
None

Teacher Talk
"What else is on Old MacDonald's Farm?"

Sing the song and make a list of the animal sounds children make. See how long the list gets over time.

Old MacDonald Had a Farm
Old MacDonald had a farm, E-I-E-I-O.
And on his farm he had some cows, E-I-E-I-O.
With a moo-moo here, and a moo-moo there,
Here a moo, there a moo, everywhere a moo-moo.
Old MacDonald had a farm, E-I-E-I-O.

Continue with other animals:

Duck...quack-quack...
Pig...oink-oink...
Horse...neigh-neigh...

Eensy Weensy Spider

All ages

Materials
None

Sing the song and observe how children act out the words.

Eensy Weensy Spider
The eensy weensy spider
Walked up the waterspout. (Walk fingers up the arm.)
Down came the rain,
And washed the spider out. (Wiggle fingers downward.)
Out came the sun,
And dried up all the rain. (Big circle with arms overhead.)
And the eensy weensy spider,
Walked up the spout again. (Walk fingers up the arm.)

MOVEMENT POSSIBILITIES

___ Duck Puppets

All ages

Materials
Duck puppets

Repeat the "Five Little Ducks" rhyme using a duck hand puppet. Act out the rhyme and observe the variety of "waddles" children use.

Five Little Ducks
Five little ducks
That I once knew (Hold up five fingers.)
Fat ones, skinny ones,
Tall ones, too.
But the one little duck with the
Feather on his back (Wave hand behind back.)
He led the others with
A Quack! Quack! Quack! (Stoop down and waddle.)

___ Move to the Music

All ages

Materials
Scarves
Crepe paper streamers
Classical music

Teacher Talk
"You are dancing slowly like the music, Adrian."

Play classical music for children to move to the rhythm of the music. Show children how to move the scarves and streamers as they dance.

___ Bear Walking

All ages

Materials
None

Teacher Talk
"You are walking like a bear, Su Lin."

With toddlers, explore how bears walk.

OUTDOOR POSSIBILITIES

Flowerpots
All ages

Materials
Plastic flowerpots
Child's gardening tools
Soil

Teacher Talk
Talk with children about planting as they play. "Trish is filling up the pot and dumping it out again."

Fill the sand table with soil. Place a variety of sizes of plastic flowerpots in the dirt. Provide plastic gardening tools for children to fill and dump dirt in the pots.

Paper Plate Kites
All ages

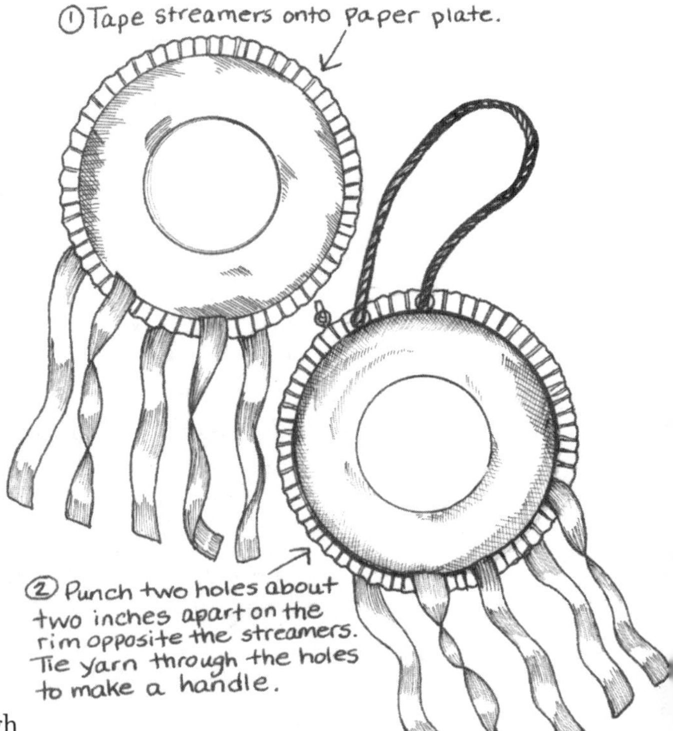
① Tape streamers onto paper plate.
② Punch two holes about two inches apart on the rim opposite the streamers. Tie yarn through the holes to make a handle.

Materials
Paper plates
Crepe paper streamers
Tape
Hole punch
Yarn

Teacher Talk
"Run fast, Terrelle. Make the streamers fly!"

Tape crepe paper streamers onto paper plate. Punch two holes about two inches apart on the rim opposite the streamers. Tie yarn through the holes to make a handle. Observe what children do as they play with the streamers.

Storybook Characters Outdoors

All ages

Materials
Hay bales
Small buckets
Plastic animals
Dress-up clothes

Outside is a wonderful place for playing out the roles talked about in this Possibilities Plan. Bring play props outside and help children get started.

PROJECT POSSIBILITIES

Rainbow Big Fish

All ages

Materials
Butcher paper
Tempera paint
Paintbrushes
Glue
Newspaper
Scissors
Colored paper scraps
Yarn

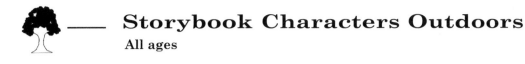

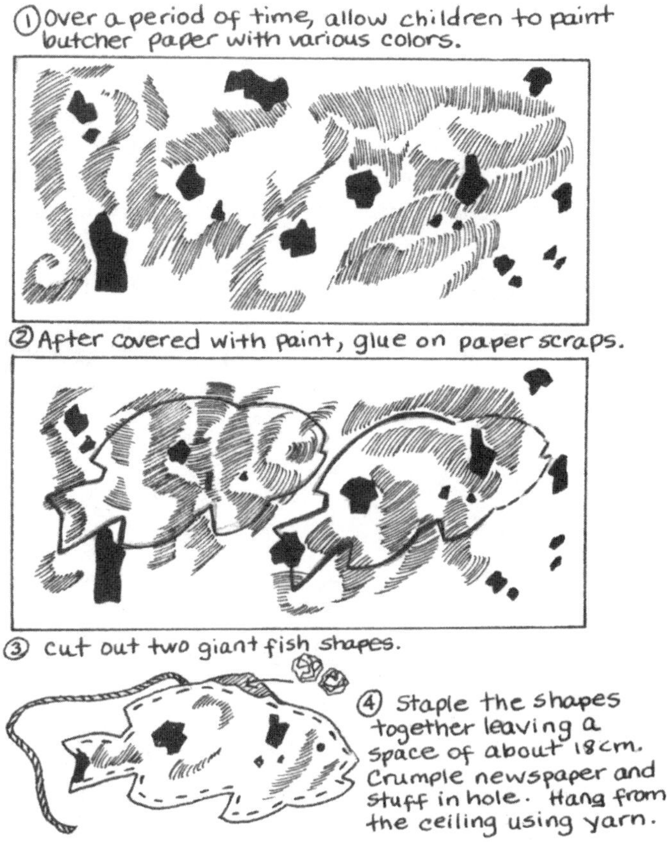

① Over a period of time, allow children to paint butcher paper with various colors.
② After covered with paint, glue on paper scraps.
③ cut out two giant fish shapes.
④ Staple the shapes together leaving a space of about 18cm. Crumple newspaper and stuff in hole. Hang from the ceiling using yarn.

Completely cover a table with large pieces of butcher paper. Over a period of time paint the paper with various colors of paint. After the entire surface is covered with paint, provide paper scraps and glue to add texture. Continue adding the paper scraps over a period of time. Cut two giant fish shapes. Staple the shapes together leaving a space of about 18 inches. Show toddlers how to crumple the newspapers and stuff them into the hole. Staple the edges together and hang from the ceiling using yarn. Take photographs throughout the project and create a display on the parent board to share with parents.

PARENT PARTICIPATION POSSIBILITIES

Animal Sounds Tape

Ask parents to help make a tape of farm animal sounds for children to listen to. Have a blank tape and a tape recorder set up, so parents can make their favorite animal sounds on the tape when they arrive in the afternoon. Children will delight in hearing parents' voices making animal sounds on tape.

Stone Soup

Invite parents to send vegetables to share in making stone soup. Read the story, then search for a suitable stone. Wash and clean the stone thoroughly. Put the vegetables in the sensory table with scrub brushes for children to clean. Help children tear or break the vegetables in to pieces, helping if necessary. Put the prepared vegetables in the pot with the stone. Cook the soup safely away from children. Invite parents to share the stone soup with children. Read the story for parents and children as they eat the soup.

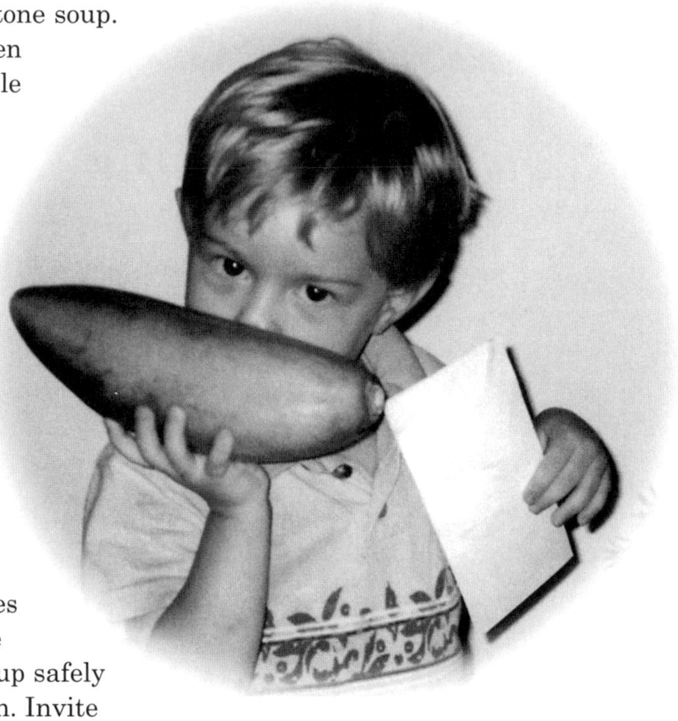

Postcard

The Parent Postcard in this section is designed to share with parents during the Possibilities Plan. The topic is a natural extension of the activities and experiences that you are planning and implementing for the toddlers in the classroom. Use the Postcard to connect parents to their children's learning.

Process Is the Goal

Because young children are living in the moment, the process—the experience of an activity, whether it is art, sensory, or music—is the goal. Sometimes adults have a hard time with this concept because we tend to look at the product or the accomplishment to determine whether we are pleased or displeased with our work. Young children have no interest in the final product, especially an art product. Art activities for toddlers are sensory in nature. They allow toddlers to explore the world around them.

Your child's teacher will be very careful to observe and then record observations of children as they interact during the day. Teachers may even take photographs to share with you to show what the process was like, even if the product isn't available.

Play is the work of children. As children play and interact with their environment and with significant adults in their lives, they are learning. As adults, we are challenged to stay in the moment just as toddlers do and enjoy the process.

TO

Concepts Learned in Storybook Characters

Concepts Learned

- Some things are small, medium, or large.
- I can count to three.
- Farmers take care of farm animals.
- Some farm animals live in a barn.
- I can make farm animal sounds.
- Ducks like water.
- Flowers grow in dirt.
- Seeds need sun, rain, and warm breezes to grow.
- Oatmeal feels different when wet or dry.
- I can move my body in many ways.
- Spiders make webs.
- Mittens are different from gloves.
- I can put on mittens.
- I like to hear stories.
- I can listen for sounds.
- Animals move in different ways.

Resources

Prop Boxes

Three Bears Box
- Goldilocks story (any version)
- Stuffed bears
- Goldilocks hat
- Three bowls/spoons

Red Barn
- *Big Red Barn* by Margaret Wise Brown
- Farm animals
- Plaid shirts
- Work boots
- Denim overalls
- Farm tools
- Straw hats
- Work gloves

The Very Hungry Caterpillar
- Caterpillar puppet
- Tube sock caterpillar puppet
- Food pieces
- *Very Hungry Caterpillar, The* by Eric Carle

Where the Wild Things Are
- Puppets of the wild things
- *Where the Wild Things Are* by Maurice Sendak

Stone Soup
- Large pot
- Plastic spoon
- Stone Soup story (any version)
- Variety of plastic vegetables

Picture File/Vocabulary

Barn
Bears
Ducks
Farm animals
Flowers
Nursery rhyme characters
Spiders
Stone
Vegetables

Books

Big Red Barn by Margaret Wise Brown (page 504)
Brown Bear, Brown Bear, What Do You See? by Bill Martin, Jr. (page 495)
Chicken Soup with Rice by Maurice Sendak
Corduroy by Don Freeman
Goldilocks and the Three Bears by James Marshall (page 490)
Make Way for Ducklings by Robert McCloskey (page 492)
Mitten, The by Jan Brett (page 496)
Planting a Rainbow by Lois Elhert
Polar Bear, Polar Bear, What Do You See? by Bill Martin, Jr. (page 495)
Rainbow Fish by Marcus Pfister
Stone Soup by Marcia Brown (page 490)
Very Busy Spider, The by Eric Carle
Very Hungry Caterpillar, The by Eric Carle (page 495)
Where the Wild Things Are by Maurice Sendak(page 496)
Who Took the Farmer's Hat? by Joan L. Nodset

Rhymes/Fingerplays

"Five Little Ducks" (page 499)
"This Little Piggy" (page 497)

Music/Songs

"Eensy Weensy Spider" (page 498)
"Old MacDonald Had a Farm" (page 498)
"There's a Little Flower" (page 497)

Toys and Materials

The following purchased items are important for this Possibilities Plan.

Brown Bear puppet
Brown paper
Butcher paper (including blue)
Child gardening tools
Classical music
Craft knife (teacher only)
Crepe paper streamers
Fingerpaints
Glue
Hole punch
Markers
Paintbrushes
Paper
Paper plates
Plastic animals
Plastic or real vegetables
Plastic pans
Puppets for *Where the Wild Things Are*
Red paint
Red spray paint (teacher only)
Rubber ducks
Rubber or wood farm animals and families
Scarves
Scissors
Smocks
Tape
Tempera paint (variety, including red)
Three child's chairs
Three cots
Three plastic bowls, spoons, and place mats
Three toy stuffed bears
Wood/plastic blocks
Yarn/metal rings

The following gathered items will help support this Possibilities Plan.

Animal pictures
Coffee can with lid
Colored paper scraps
Dry oatmeal
Farm animal pictures
Feed packets
Flower magazines and catalogs
Hay bales
Large cardboard boxes
Large metal pot
Large plastic spoon
Large prepared vegetables
Mittens
Newspapers
Plastic flowerpots
Plastic spray bottle
Plastic tubs
Scrub brushes
Small buckets
Soil
Stone
Straw hats, overalls, plaid shirts, and work boots
Tube socks

Water

WEB

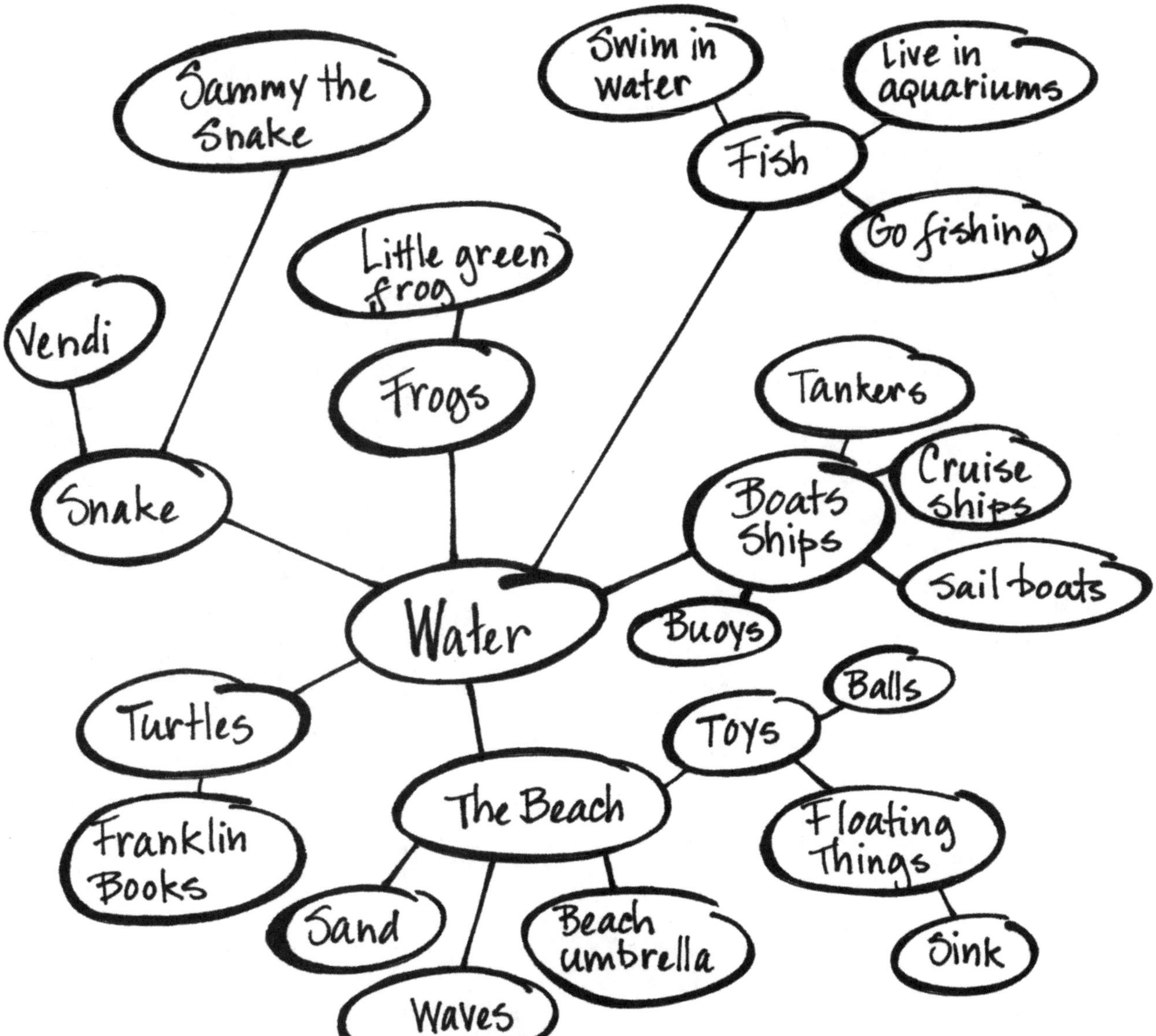

Note: Using the techniques of webbing, teachers can follow the leads that children give them, as well as have an unlimited source of options. Always use the webs as a jumping-off point. The possibilities are endless!

PLANNING PAGES

Plan Possibilities

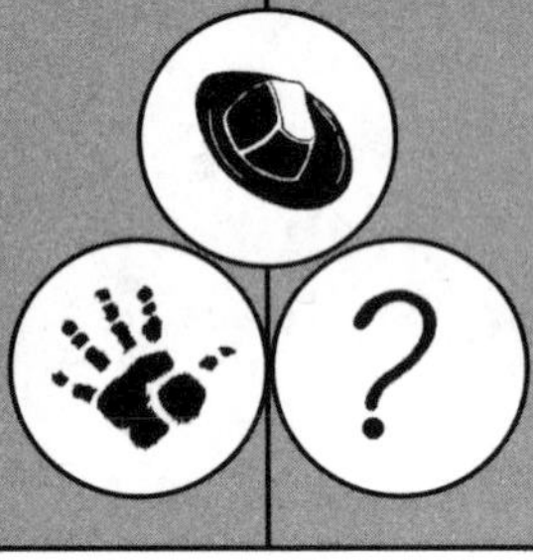

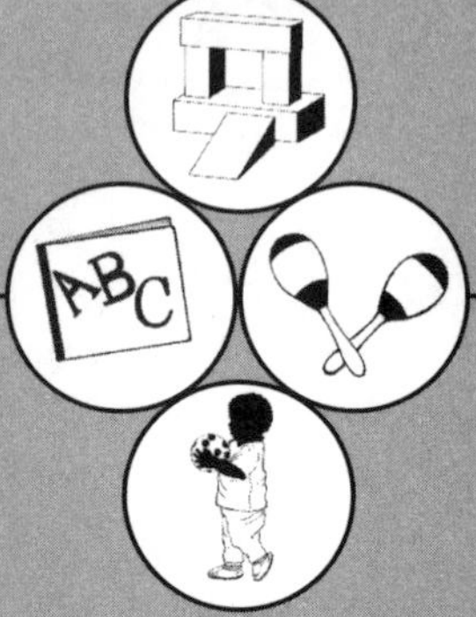

Dramatic

Box Boats 510
Rain Gear 510
Bathing Dolls 510
Froggie Comes to Play . . . 511

Sensory/Art

Warm Water. 511
Sponge Play 511
Coffee Filter Flowers 512
Bottle Boats 512
Rain Pictures 513

Curiosity

Soda Bottle Submarine . . 513
Water Bottles 513
Boat Float. 514
Will It Hold Water? 514

Construction

Blue Blocks 515
Boating Time 515
Fish Farm 515

Literacy

Frog Story 516
Water Pictures Book 517
Who Sank the Boat? 517
Rain Sounds 518
Floating Fish. 518
Jack and Jill 519

Music

Row, Row, Row
Your Boat. 519
Five Little Ducks 520
Over in the Meadow 521
Swim, Swim, Quack,
Quack. 521

Movement

The Little Ducks. 522
Frog Jumping 522

Outdoor

Jumped in the Boat 523
Car Wash 523
Roll on the Water 524
Slippery Goop 524
Jump the Water 524

Projects

Bubble Blowing. 525

Parent Participation

Water Animals 526
Parent Readers. 526
Parent Postcards
When Your Child's
Teacher Leaves 527
When Your Child's
Day Is Lengthened . . 528

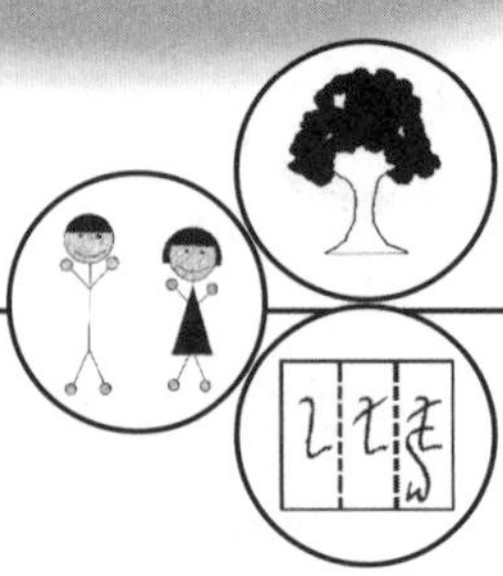

Water

Books

Alfie's Feet by Shirley Hughes
Boy, A Dog, and a Frog, A by Mercer Meyer
Bringing the Rain to Kapiti Plain by Verna Aardema 518
Fish Is Fish by Leo Leoni
Gone Fishing by Earlene Long
Jump! Frog! Jump! by Robert Karian 529
Make Way for Ducklings by Robert McCloskey 529
Mr. Bear's Boat by Thomas Graham
Mr. Gumpy's Outing by John Burningham
Peter Speir's Rain by Peter Speir 529
Swimmy by Leo Leoni 518
Who Sank the Boat? by Pamela Allen 517

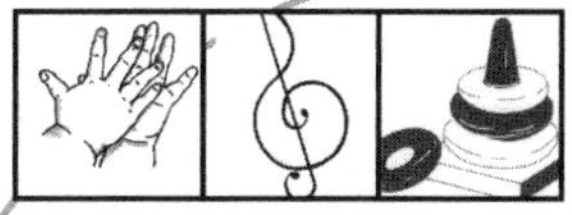

Rhymes/Fingerplays

"Frogs at the Pond" 516
"Jack and Jill" 519
"The Little Ducks" 522

Music/Songs

"Five Little Ducks" 520
"Jumped in the Boat" 523
"Over in the Meadow" 521
"Row, Row, Row, Your Boat" 519
"Swim, Swim, Quack, Quack" 521

Toys and Materials 532

DRAMATIC POSSIBILITIES

Box Boats

All ages

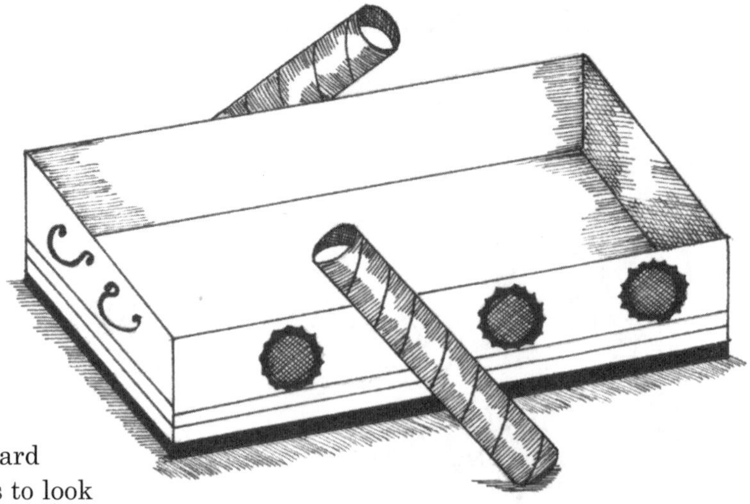

Materials
Large cardboard boxes
Paper towel tubes

Teacher Talk
"I see Alexis in the boat. Where are you going?"

Decorate a cardboard box with low sides to look like a boat and provide paper towel or wrapping paper tubes for oars. Observe children as they enjoy moving in and around the box.

Rain Gear

All ages

Materials
Raincoats
Rain hats
Rubber boots
Toy umbrellas with safety knobs on the ends of the umbrella points

Teacher Talk
"Joseph is dressed to go out in the rain."

Provide a variety of raincoats, ponchos, rain hats, and rubber boots for children to dress up for a rainy day. Supervise umbrellas carefully with children as they play.

Bathing Dolls

18-24 months

Materials
Plastic dishpans
Rubber dolls
Baby washcloths
Towels
Water

Teacher Talk
"Torrie, the doll's face needs to be washed."

Provide plastic pans with less than an inch of water in them. Add washcloths and towels. Observe children to see how they play.

Froggie Comes to Play

30-36 months

Materials
Frog puppet

Teacher Talk
Talk with children about characteristics of frogs as they play. "I see the frog hopping. Ribbit, ribbit."

Provide purchased or teacher-made frog puppets.

SENSORY/ART POSSIBILITIES

Warm Water

18-24 months

Materials
Warm water
Baby powder container

Teacher Talk
"How does the water feel, Suzanne?"

Fill the water table with warm water. Cut the bottom off a plastic baby powder container. Provide this and other items as children water play.

Sponge Play

18-24 months

Materials
Water table
Assorted shapes of sponges
Plastic pails

Teacher Talk
"Look, there's a duck-shaped sponge, Benjamin."

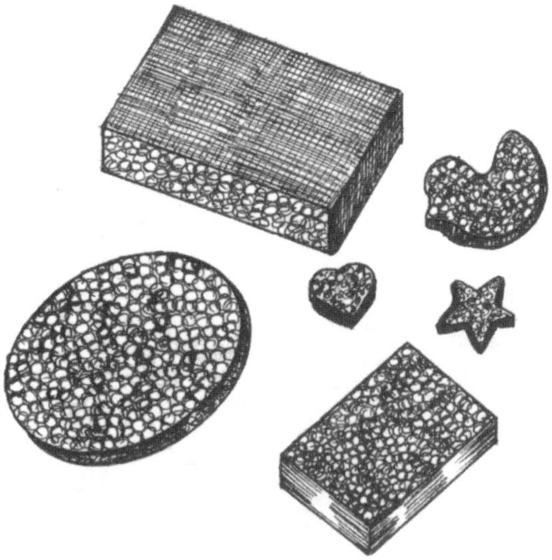

Place a variety of shapes, sizes, and colors of dense sponges in the water table. Do not use sponges that can be bitten into pieces as they pose a choke hazard. Supervise children as they explore floating, squeezing, and sorting the sponges into plastic pails.

Coffee Filter Flowers

24-30 months

Materials
Coffee filters
Water-based markers
Spray bottles of water

Teacher Talk
Talk about the materials, colors, designs, and the color changes as the colors blend together. "Which marker do you want, Shannon?"

Show children how to color coffee filters with water-based markers. Help children use a spray bottle of water to wet the coffee filter after making marks.

Bottle Boats

24-30 months

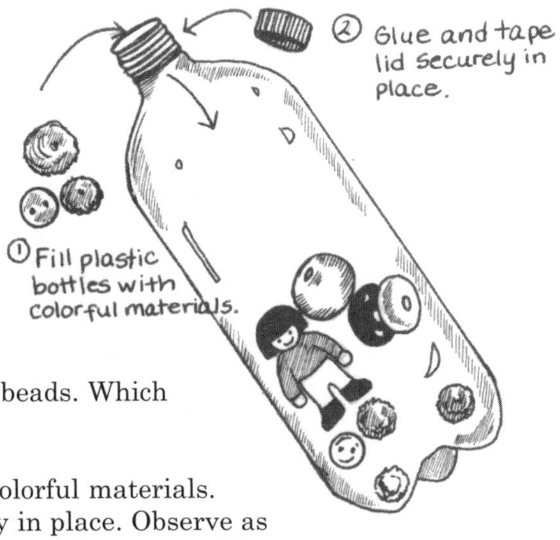

Materials
Plastic bottles
Colored beads, pompom balls, small toys
Tape
Glue
Water table

Teacher Talk
"I like this bottle with the red beads. Which bottle do you like, Eli?"

Fill clear plastic bottles with colorful materials. Glue and tape the lids securely in place. Observe as children explore the bottle boats in the water table.

Rain Pictures

30-36 months

Materials
Plastic squirt bottles
Powdered tempera paint
Paper
Water

Teacher Talk
Talk about colors and designs as children play. "Well, Niesha, let's see what happens when you squeeze the water onto the paper."

Dilute several colors of tempera paint with water. Show children how to use plastic squeeze bottles to squeeze the paint onto paper. As the paint falls, the drops will spatter on the paper to create interesting designs.

CURIOSITY POSSIBILITIES

Soda Bottle Submarine

18-24 months

Materials
Photos of children
Clear plastic bottles
Glue
Tape

Teacher Talk
"Look, Andy, there's a picture of Chaquin."

Drop pictures inside plastic bottles. Glue and tape the bottle lids securely in place. Place the photo submarines in the water table. Children will enjoy the pictures as they play with the submarines.

Water Bottles

18-24 months

Materials
Clear plastic bottles
Water
Foil confetti, glitter, sequins, shiny beads
Tape
Glue

Teacher Talk
"Louis, you can see the pretty colors move when you shake the bottle. That's it!"

Fill clear plastic bottle within two inches of the neck of the bottle. Place confetti, glitter, beads, spangles, or sequins inside the bottle. Glue and tape the lid securely in place. Children shake and/or roll the bottles to see the shiny colors move inside the bottles.

? Boat Float

24-30 months

Materials
Plastic boats
Plastic bottles
Aluminum foil boats
Fast food containers
Deli containers
Water table

Teacher Talk
"Which one of these boats do you like, Aubrey?"

Place boats made from a variety of materials in the water table. Observe as children experiment with the boats.

? Will It Hold Water?

30-36 months

Materials
Plastic cups, plastic bottles, margarine tubs
Colanders, sieves, berry baskets
Water table

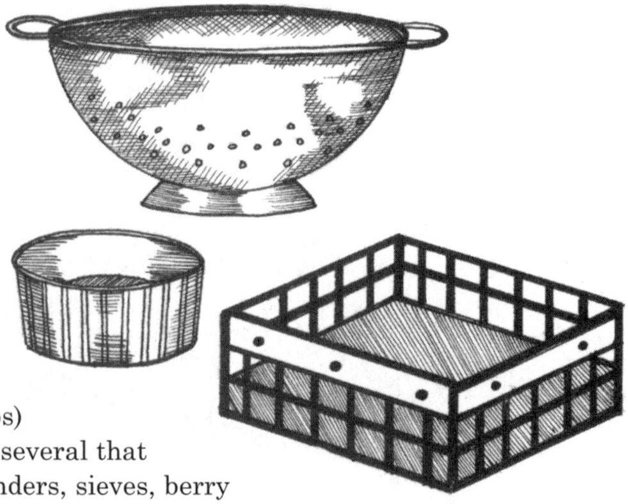

Teacher Talk
"The water runs through the colander, Rhianna." Ask children to examine each container and predict whether it will hold water.

Collect several containers (plastic cups, bottles, or margarine tubs) that will hold water and several that will not hold water (colanders, sieves, berry baskets). Place the containers in the water table and invite children to explore them.

CONSTRUCTION POSSIBILITIES

Blue Blocks

All ages

Materials
Blue construction paper or butcher paper
Tape

Cover some of the blocks with blue paper, so children can create bodies of water as they build.

Boating Time

All ages

Materials
Toy boats
Sailor hats, optional

Add toy boats to the blocks for children to use as they play. Sailor hats can also add to the boating fun!

Fish Farm

All ages

Materials
Toy fish
Construction paper
Markers
Plastic wading pool

Provide toy fish or make them using construction paper and markers. Place them with the blocks, so children can use them with the blocks as they play. A small rigid wading pool makes a great area in which children can build.

Frog Story

All ages

Materials

Flannel board
Five green felt frogs
Felt fish
Felt snake, alligator, lizard, and crane
Used dryer sheets
Markers
Scissors

Teacher Talk

Talk with children about the different characters, where the frogs could have gone, and life at the pond. "Where did the frogs go, Rebecca?"

Read the rhyme and place the felt characters on the board. Felt characters may be substituted with characters made from used dryer sheets. Trace the characters onto the sheets. Color them with markers and cut them out. As long as the dryer sheets are used, they will adhere to the felt boards.

Frogs at the Pond

Five little frogs
Were down at the pond,
Down at the pond at play.
Along came a hungry fish,
And chased one frog away.

Four little frogs
Were down at the pond,
Down at the pond at play.
Along came a wiggly snake,
And chased one frog away.

Three little frogs
Were down at the pond,
Down at the pond at play.
Along came a giant alligator,
And chased one frog away.

Two little frogs
Were down at the pond,
Down at the pond at play.

Along came a purple lizard,
And chased one frog away.

One little frog
Was down at the pond,
Down at the pond at play.
Along came a flying crane,
And chased the frog away.

Then no little frogs
Were down at the pond,
Down at the pond at play.
Where do you think the little frogs went
When they all hopped away?

Water Pictures Book

All ages

① Glue water pictures onto cardboard pages.
② Cut pages to fit into resealable bags. Place pages back to back inside the bags. Punch holes in the edge of the bags and join together with metal rings or yarn.

Materials
Water pictures from magazines
Cardboard pages
Resealable bags
Metal rings or yarn
Glue
Scissors
Hole punch

Teacher Talk
Enjoy talking about the pictures with children. "The fish are swimming in the ocean in this picture. There are three orange ones—one, two, three."

Glue water pictures (boats, floats, fish, fishing supplies) onto cardboard pages. Cut pages to fit into resealable bags. Place pages back to back inside the bags. Punch holes in the edge of the bags and join together with metal rings or short lengths of yarn.

Who Sank the Boat?

All ages

Materials
Who Sank the Boat by Pamela Allen
Clear plastic tub
Plastic boat
Plastic animals
Water

Teacher Talk
Talk about what happened to the boat. "Place the cow in the boat, Gunther."

Gather materials and props. As you read the story, children may wish to place the animals inside the boat.

Rain Sounds

All ages

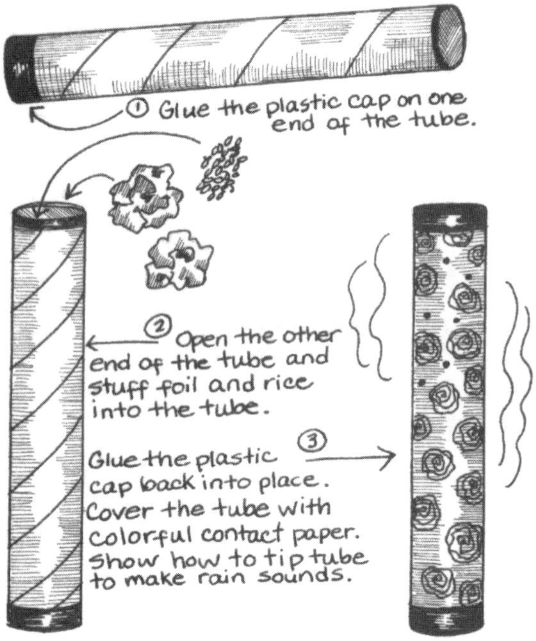

① Glue the plastic cap on one end of the tube.
② Open the other end of the tube and stuff foil and rice into the tube.
③ Glue the plastic cap back into place. Cover the tube with colorful contact paper. Show how to tip tube to make rain sounds.

Materials
Bringing the Rain to Kapiti Plain by Verna Aardema
Cardboard mailing tube with plastic caps on the ends
Aluminum foil
Dry rice
Colored contact paper

Teacher Talk
"The rainstick is making that sound, Mikala. Want it to start again?"

Glue the plastic cap on one end of the tube. Open one end of the mailing tube and stuff crumpled aluminum foil into the tube. Pour a cup of dry rice into the tube. Glue the plastic cap into place. Cover the tube with colorful contact paper. Read the storybook and then show children how to tip the tube over gently to make rain sounds.

Floating Fish

All ages

Materials
Resealable plastic bags
Blue hair gel (nontoxic)
Plastic fish
Glue
Tape
Swimmy by Leo Lionni

Teacher Talk
"You made the fish move, Justin."

Fill a resealable plastic bag with nontoxic blue hair gel. Place plastic fish into the gel. Glue and tape the opening securely closed. Read the storybook as children explore moving the fish inside the bag. Supervise this activity closely. Help toddlers keep the bags out of their mouths.

Jack and Jill

All ages

Materials
Felt characters for the rhyme
Flannel board

Teacher Talk
Talk about water from wells, the top and bottom of the hill, and falling down. "The water was in the bucket, Alise."

Recite the rhyme as you place the felt characters on the board. Children may want to place the characters once they are familiar with the rhyme.

Jack and Jill
Jack and Jill went up the hill
To fetch a pail of water.
Jack fell down and broke his crown,
And Jill came tumbling after.

MUSIC POSSIBILITIES

Row, Row, Row Your Boat

All ages

Materials
None

Sing the song with children. Show them how to act out the words of the song.

Row, Row, Row, Your Boat
Row, row, row, your boat (Make rowing motions.)
Gently down the stream. (Wiggle fingers.)
Merrily, merrily, merrily, merrily, (Circle pointer in the air.)
Life is but a dream. (Place folded hands under face.)

Five Little Ducks

All ages

Materials
None

Teacher Talk
"That's the way to make 'five' with your hand, Christina."

Sing the song and act out the words with children.

Five Little Ducks

Five little ducks went out to swim, (Hold up five fingers.)
Over the pond and far away. (Make swimming motions.)
Mama Duck called, Quack! Quack! Quack! (Open/close hands.)
And four little ducks came swimming back. (Hold up four fingers.)

Four little ducks went out to swim, (Hold up four fingers.)
Over the pond and far away. (Make swimming motions.)
Mama Duck called, Quack! Quack! Quack! (Open/close hands.)
And three little ducks came swimming back. (Hold up three fingers.)

Three little ducks went out to swim, (Hold up three fingers.)
Over the pond and far away. (Make swimming motions.)
Mama Duck called, Quack! Quack! Quack! (Open/close hands.)
And two little ducks came swimming back. (Hold up two fingers.)

Two little ducks went out to swim, (Hold up two fingers.)
Over the pond and far away. (Make swimming motions.)
Mama Duck called, Quack! Quack! Quack! (Open/close hands.)
And one little duck came swimming back. (Hold up one finger.)

One little duck went out to swim, (Hold up one finger.)

Over the pond and far away. (Make swimming motions.)
Mama Duck called, Quack! Quack! Quack! (Open/close hands.)
And no little ducks came swimming back. (Hold hands palms up.)

Father Duck said, Quack! Quack! Quack! (Big voice.)
And five little ducks came swimming back. (Hold up five fingers.)

Over in the Meadow

All ages

Materials
None

Teacher Talk
"That's the way to swim like a fish, Marla."

Sing "Over in the Meadow" with the children. Children can "swim" as they sing.

Swim, Swim, Quack, Quack

All ages

Materials
None

Teacher Talk
"Let's swim, Wesley. That's the way!"

Show children how to move and "quack" as you sing the song. Sing to the tune "My Bonnie Lies Over the Ocean."

Swim, Swim, Quack, Quack
Ducks like to swim in the water.
They stretch their webbed feet out in back.
Ducks like to swim in circles.
They swim and they swim and they quack.
Swim, swim, quack, quack!
They swim and they swim and they quack.
Swim, swim, quack, quack!
They swim and they swim and they quack.

MOVEMENT POSSIBILITIES

The Little Ducks

All ages

Materials
None

Teacher Talk
"Are you ready to waddle, Amadou?"

Show children how to act out the movements as you recite the following rhyme.

The Little Ducks

All the little ducklings (Children squat and waddle like ducks.)
Line up in a row.
Quack, quack, quack,
And away they go.

They follow their mother (Children follow the leader.)
Waddling to and fro.
Quack, quack, quack,
And away they go.

They jump in the water, (Make a diving motion.)
And bob up and down. (Bob up and down.)
Quack, quack, quack,
They swim all around. (Make a swimming motion.)

Frog Jumping

All ages

Materials
None

Teacher Talk
"You can jump like a frog, Ethan."

Make big and little frog jumps. Practice jumping during transitions or during playground time.

Jumped in the Boat

All ages

Materials

Large cardboard boxes

Teacher Talk

"That's the way to get in the boat, Cal."

Sing the song as children climb into and out of the cardboard box boats. The tune is "Paw, Paw Patch."

Jumped in the Boat

They jumped in the boat,
And the boat tipped over.
They jumped in the boat,
And the boat tipped over.
They jumped in the boat,
And the boat tipped over.
All the little boys and girls.

Car Wash

All ages

Materials

Large cardboard box
Crepe paper streamers
Tape
Craft knife
Scoot toys
Sprinkler hose
Buckets
Sponges

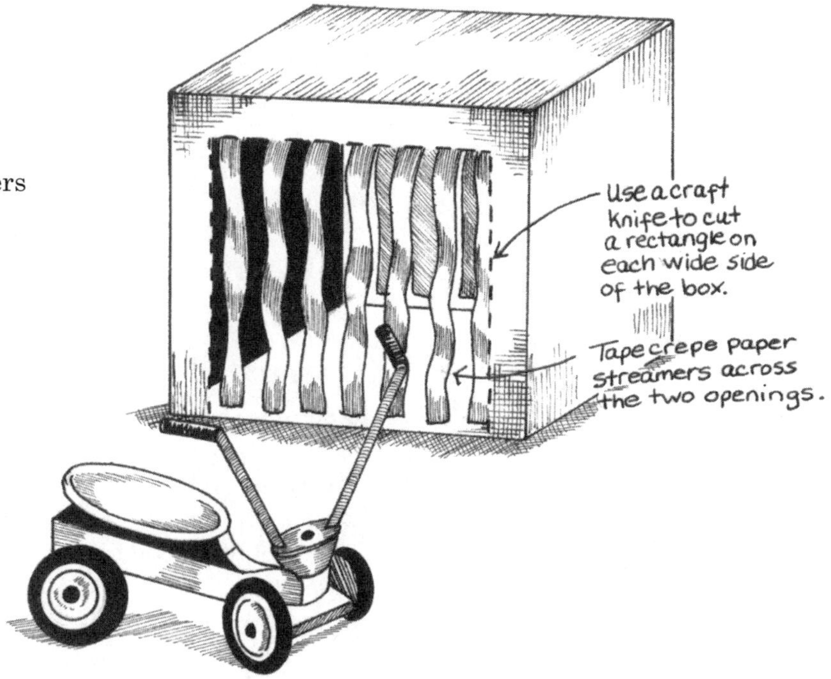
Use a craft knife to cut a rectangle on each wide side of the box.
Tape crepe paper streamers across the two openings.

Teacher Talk

"Here comes Jennifer through the car wash!"

Use a craft knife to cut a large rectangle from each wide side of the box. Tape crepe paper streamers across the two openings. Children ride the scoot toys through the car wash. Or, set up a real car wash with a sprinkler hose and really wash the cars. Provide sponges, scrub brushes, and buckets for the work.

Roll on the Water

18-24 months

Materials
Paint rollers
Paintbrushes
Roller tray
Water

Teacher Talk
"Kwan is painting the fence with water."

Fill a paint tray with water. Provide paint rollers and brushes, so children can "paint" the sidewalk, fence, the side of the building, or other playground structures with the paint roller.

Slippery Goop

24-30 months

Materials
Cornstarch
Water
Bowl
Water table
Food coloring

Teacher Talk
"How does the goop feel, Rodrico?"

Mix equal portions of water and cornstarch together in a bowl. Pour the mixture into the water table. Experiment with using food coloring to make goop in different colors. Children may want to use plastic cups as they explore the goop.

Jump the Water

30-36 months

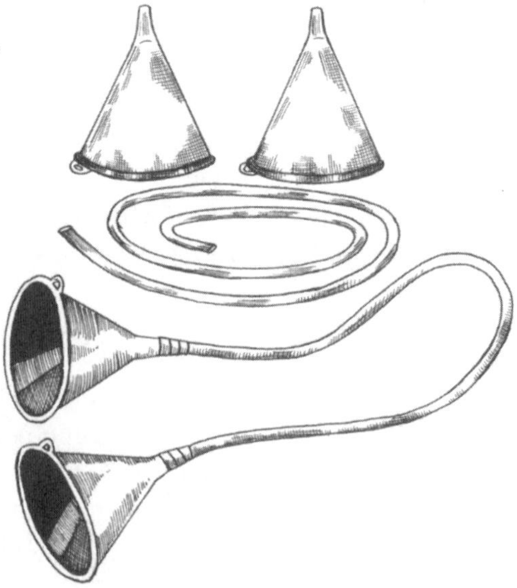

Materials
Two plastic funnels
Three feet of plastic tubing
Water
Food coloring

Teacher Talk
"Where does the water go, Kirsten?"

Fit funnels on each end of the plastic tubing. Secure the funnels with plastic tape. Children pour water into one or both funnels to see how water moves. A few drops of food coloring will make the water easier to see in the tubing.

PROJECT POSSIBILITIES

Bubble Blowing

All ages

Materials

Bubble recipe

Bubble makers, such as a plastic six-pack holder, plastic berry baskets, plastic paper plate holders, embroidery hoops, large plastic lids with centers removed, large plastic hoops

Plastic dishpans or large shallow pans

Teacher Talk

"Wow! See the bubbles Marcus is making, Julie."

Bubble Recipe

2 cups dishwashing soap, such as Joy

6 cups water

¾ cup light corn syrup

Revisit making bubbles again and again over a period of time. Mix ingredients and shake. Allow mixture to sit for a few hours. Pour bubble mixture into plastic dishpans or large shallow pans. Use one of the bubble makers. The mixture bubbles easily and makes strong bubbles that last long enough for children to see the colors. Be careful of slippery areas around the bubbles. Toddlers will have to practice making the bubbles, so provide bubble solution repeatedly for this practice. Bubble blowing is hard for toddlers. However, making bubbles this way isn't and can create some interesting experiences.

PARENT PARTICIPATION POSSIBILITIES

Water Animals

Ask parents to bring water animals such as a frog or fish for children to see. Check with parents for a source for tadpoles. Children would enjoy watching tadpoles turn into frogs.

Parent Readers

Invite parents to read stories with children. Parents may share a favorite book or use a book from your shelf to read to children. Let parents read to their own child or to two or three children together.

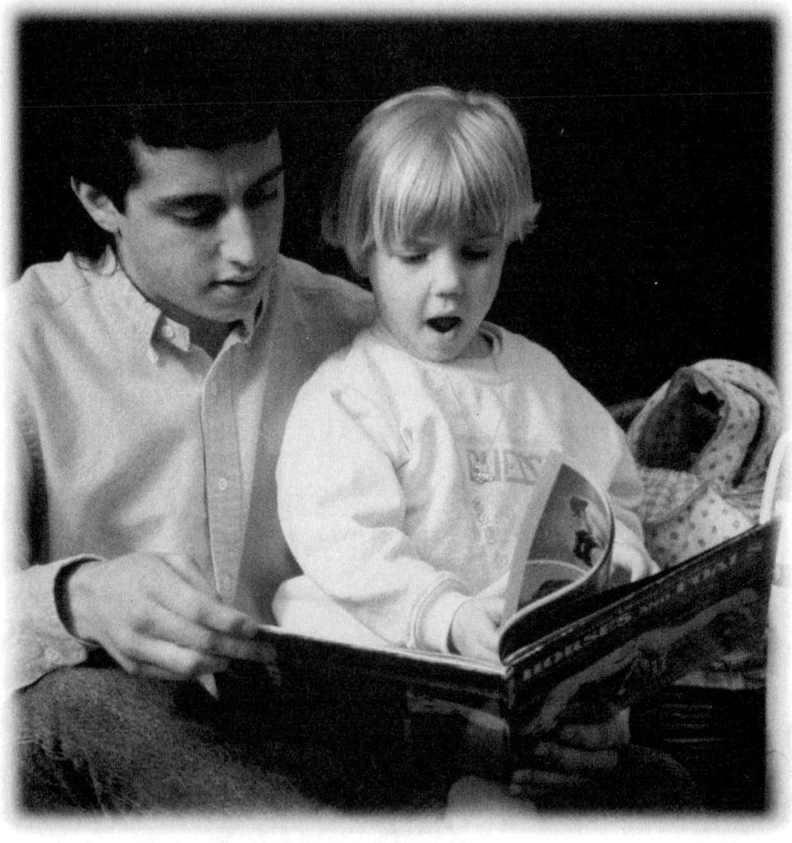

Parent Postcards

The Parent Postcards in this section are designed to share with parents during the Possibilities Plan. The topics are natural extensions of the activities and experiences that you are planning and implementing for the toddlers in the classroom. Use the Postcards to connect parents to their children's learning.

When Your Child's Teacher Leaves

It may be your worst fear. Your toddler has really started to adjust to school while you are at work. Then, wham! Something changes. Your child's favorite teacher leaves. You have a big project at work that requires a lot of extra time (and lengthens your child's day at school). The principal or director tells you a classroom change is coming up. Change is a challenge to everyone—children, teachers, and parents. Having a teacher leave is like riding up an escalator that abruptly jerks to a stop. Everything seems so unsure. What can parents do to help their toddler cope with change?

First of all, remember that everything isn't changing. As important as the teacher-child relationship is, it is one part of the big picture. Other areas will stay constant. Your child's schedule will probably remain the same. So, too, will the daily routine, the other children in the group, and the other adults in the classroom. Most importantly, you will stay constant. Continuity of group, schedule, activities, and friends can form a strong foundation for children to begin to adjust to a departing teacher. Work to keep as many other parts of your child's life as consistent as possible to help him or her adjust to a change in teachers.

Second, view adjusting to change as a transition. It may take as much as two to six weeks for everything to settle down again after a favorite teacher departs. Children are learning to accommodate changes. Adults may not like change, but they have many more adjustment skills than children do. In this case, time is a good friend.

Third, keep your schedule predictable. When your child loses a special teacher, he or she may wonder if you are going to leave, too. Keeping to your regular arrival and departure schedule reassures your child that you will be there for him or her. Say goodbye when you leave in the morning. Never sneak out while your child is playing. He or she may cry when you leave, but you will be able to remind your child that you will be back, reinforcing that you will always be there for him or her.

Fourth, welcome the new teacher. Your child will be cautious at first and will be looking to you for cues as to whether the new teacher is acceptable. Greet the teacher warmly, talk with her or him, and tell the teacher about your child. Give your toddler a chance to warm up before you encourage him or her to interact with the new teacher. Don't push too hard for interaction between your child and the new teacher. Adjustment to change takes time.

TO

When Your Child's Day Is Lengthened

Toddlers get better at handling change when parents and teachers make change a positive experience. Your child will have many changes in his or her life. Early experience with smooth, facilitated transitions will prepare him or her for adjusting to the inevitable change that permeates our lives.

Very young children have little perspective on time, but they have a powerful sense of sequence. Just watch your children in a toddler classroom during departure time. Although the children can't tell you with words who will come in the door next, the right child will be waiting close to the door for his or her parents to arrive. Even young children know the sequence of who arrives in what order.

Try to let your child's teacher know if your routine is going to change. Sometimes teachers can offset your child's discomfort about changes by preparing him or her for the change. Your child's teacher can alert your child that you will be a little out of sequence today and keep him or her from going into the waiting mode too soon.

TO ______________

____

____

Concepts Learned

Concepts Learned in Water

Water is warm and cool.
Water pours, sprinkles, and drips.
Rain is water.
Raincoats keep you dry when it rains.
Ducks swim in water.
Ducks waddle.
Frogs live in water.
Frogs jump.
Frogs catch insects with their tongues.
Fish live in water.
Fish swim with their fins.
We take a bath in water.
Plants need water to grow.
We drink water.
Water keeps us cool.
Boats float in water.
Some things float; some things sink.

Resources

Prop Boxes

Rain Gear
- *Bringing the Rain to Kapiti Plain* by Verna Aardema
- *Peter Spier's Rain* by Peter Spier
- Ponchos
- Rain hats
- Rain sticks
- Raincoats
- Rubber boots
- Toy umbrellas

Ducks
- Duck masks
- Duck puppets
- *Make Way for Ducklings* by Robert Mccloskey
- Rubber ducks

Frogs
- Frog mask
- Frog puppet
- *Jump! Frog! Jump!* by Robert Kalan
- Rubber frogs

Water Play

- Boats
- Buckets
- Plastic bottles of shiny materials
- Plastic colanders/sieves/ baskets
- Plastic cups/bowls
- Plastic funnels
- Plastic margarine containers
- Plastic tubing
- Scrub brushes
- Sponges
- Watering cans

Picture File/Vocabulary

- Aquarium
- Ducks
- Fish
- Frogs
- Ice
- Ocean
- Ponds
- Rain
- Snow
- Swimming pools
- Water buckets
- Water hose
- Water tanks
- Watering cans

Books

Alfie's Feet by Shirley Hughes
Boy, A Dog, and a Frog, A by Mercer Meyer
Bringing the Rain to Kapiti Plain by Verna Aardema (page 518)
Fish Is Fish by Leo Leoni
Gone Fishing by Earlene Long
Jump! Frog! Jump! by Robert Karian (page 529)
Make Way for Ducklings by Robert McCloskey (page 529)
Mr. Bear's Boat by Thomas Graham
Mr. Gumpy's Outing by John Burningham
Peter Speir's Rain by Peter Speir (page 529)
Swimmy by Leo Leoni (page 518)
Who Sank the Boat? by Pamela Allen (page 517)

Rhymes/Fingerplays

"Frogs at the Pond" (page 516)
"Jack and Jill" (page 519)
"The Little Ducks" (page 522)

Music/Songs

"Five Little Ducks" (page 520)
"Jumped in the Boat" (page 523)
"Over in the Meadow" (page 521)
"Row, Row, Row, Your Boat" (page 519)
"Swim, Swim, Quack, Quack" (page 521)

Toys and Materials

The following purchased items are important for this Possibilities Plan.

- Baby washcloths
- Blue hair gel (nontoxic, of course)
- Blue paper
- Cardboard pages
- Clear plastic tub
- Colored beads
- Colored contact paper
- Construction Paper
- Craft knife (teacher only)
- Felt animals (frogs, snake, alligator, lizard, and crane)
- Flannel board
- Foil confetti
- Frog puppet
- Glitter
- Glue
- Hole punch
- Jack and Jill story felt figures
- Large plastic lids
- Markers
- Metal rings/yarn
- Paintbrushes
- Paper
- Paper cups
- Party blower
- Plastic animals
- Plastic boats
- Plastic dishpans
- Plastic fish
- Plastic pails
- Plastic wading pool
- Plastic watering cans
- Pompoms
- Poster board
- Powdered tempera
- Resealable bags
- Rubber dolls
- Scissors
- Sequins
- Shiny beads
- Small toys
- Sponge shapes
- Tape
- Towels
- Toy boats
- Toy umbrellas
- Water table
- Water-based markers
- Wide craft sticks

Toys and Materials (continued)

The following gathered items will help support this Possibilities Plan.

Aluminum foil
Baby powder container
Berry baskets
Bubble recipe
Cardboard mailing tube
Clear plastic bottles
Coffee filters
Colanders and sieves
Cornstarch
Dry rice
Embroidery hoops
Fast food and deli containers
Large cardboard boxes
Large plastic lids
Large shallow pans
Magazine water pictures
Margarine tubs
Paper plate holders
Paper towel tubes
Photos of children
Plants in plastic pots
Plastic berry baskets
Plastic six-pack holder
Plastic spray/squirt bottles
Raincoats, hats, boots, and
umbrellas
Sailor hats
Used dryer sheets

Appendix Contents

Anecdotal Record

Child Date Time

What I observed

Teacher

Anecdotal Record

Child Date Time

What I observed

Teacher

Communication Sheet

CHILD'S NAME ____________________ **FOR THE WEEK OF** ____________________

DAY	BREAKFAST	TOTAL HOURS SLEPT	BEHAVIOR CHANGES NOTICED	PARENT COMMENTS/INSTRUCTIONS	FOODS EATEN		DIAPER CHANGES	NAPTIME		TEACHER COMMENTS
					SOLIDS	LIQUIDS		START	WOKE	
M	YES		YES				WET			
	NO		NO				BM			
T	YES		YES				WET			
	NO		NO				BM			
W	YES		YES				WET			
	NO		NO				BM			
Th	YES		YES				WET			
	NO		NO				BM			
F	YES		YES				WET			
	NO		NO				BM			

Books Read List

Book Title	Date
1.	
2.	
3.	
4.	
5.	
6.	
7.	
8.	
9.	
10.	
11.	
12.	
13.	
14.	
15.	
16.	
17.	
18.	
19.	
20.	
21.	
22.	
23.	
24.	
25.	
26.	
27.	
28.	
29.	
30.	

Accident/Incident Report

Name of injured party

Date of accident

Location of accident (address)

Site of accident (place in school)

What happened? Describe what took place.

Why did it happen? Give all of the facts—why? where? what? when? who? etc.

Accident/Incident Report (cont'd.)

What should be done to prevent this accident from recurring?

If the accident involved a child, how was the parent notified and by whom?

What was the parent's reaction?

What has been done so far to correct the situation?

With whom was this accident discussed, other than the child's parents?

Reported by

Date

Parent Visit Log

School Name ______________________________

Date	Name of Parent
1.	
2.	
3.	
4.	
5.	
6.	
7.	
8.	
9.	
10.	
11.	
12.	
13.	
14.	
15.	
16.	
17.	
18.	
19.	
20.	
21.	
22.	
23.	
24.	
25.	
26.	
27.	
28.	
29.	
30.	

Observation/Assessment Instruments

Transitioning to School

	18-24 months	24-30 months	30-36 months
S1	a. Experienced in separating from Mom and Dad; resists initial separation in new or unusual settings, but adjusts after a few moments.	b. Experienced with separating.	c. May get into difficulty seeking and exploring interesting stimuli.
S2	a. Actively seeks new and interesting stimuli; interested in everything in the environment.	b. May get into difficulty exploring interesting stimuli.	c. Seeks novel and interesting stimuli; when presented with familiar and novel stimuli, prefers novel ones.
S3	a. Resists transitions to unfamiliar or new settings or to settings that are not familiar and preferred.	b. Transitions to familiar people in familiar settings easily.	c. Transitions to most settings without distress; when distress occurs, can be comforted or distracted.
S4	a. Separation anxiety begins to resolve.	b. Stranger anxiety emerges.	c. Stranger anxiety begins to resolve.
S5	a. Prefers predictable routines and schedule; manages changes in schedule fairly well at the time but may experience problems later.	b. Ritualistic about routines and schedule—likes to do the same thing in the same way every time; exhibits ritualistic behavior around routines; likes routines the same way every time; needs warnings of anticipated transitions and still may resist them; melts down or tantrums when schedule is changed without reminders and preparation.	c. Adapts to changes in schedule when prepared in advance; abrupt or unplanned schedule changes still present problems; adapts more readily in familiar settings except when tired, hungry, or ill.
S6	a. Tries new food when presented; has strong food preferences.	b. Resists new foods on some days and not on others; reduces intake; may become picky eater or refuse to try new foods when offered. c. Has small selection of food preferences; still resists new food when presented; eats well on some days and not on others.	d. Food intake and preferences even out; will try new food after many presentations; needs encouragement to try new foods.
S7	a. Develops a sense of property rights; hoards toys and favorite objects.	b. Considers objects being played with as personal property.	c. Recognizes mine and not mine.

	18-24 months	24-30 months	30-36 months
R1	a. Calms self with verbal support from adults and transitional objects.	b. Calms self with verbal support from adults; may look for transitional objects to help with the calm-down process after verbal support is provided. Frequency of emotional outburst begins to diminish.	c. Calms self with only verbal support. Use of transitional objects begins to decline except at bedtime and when recovering from intense emotional outbursts.
R2	a Goes to mirror to look at self; makes faces, and shows emotions like laughing, crying, and so on.	b. Calls own name when looking at photographs or in the mirror.	c. Calls names of friends in photographs.
R3	a. Develops preferences for types of play and types of toys.	b. Develops play themes that are repeated again and again (such as mommy or firefighter).	c. Begins exploration of a wider range of play themes. Themes often come from new experiences.
R4	a. Perfects gross motor skills such as running, climbing, and riding push toys. Fine motor skills with manipulatives (simple puzzles, Duplos, and so on) are emerging.	b. Likes physical challenges such as running fast, jumping high, and going up and down stairs. Plays with preferred manipulatives for increasing periods of time.	c. Competently exhibits a wide range of physical skills. Begins to be interested in practicing skills such as throwing a ball, riding a tricycle, or completing a puzzle.
R5	a. Play may be onlooker, solitary, or parallel in nature.	b. Play is predominantly parallel in nature.	c. Exhibits associative play with familiar play partners.
R6	a. Exhibits symbolic play.	b. Practices and explores a wide variety of symbolic play themes and roles.	
R7	a. Objects to strangers presence; clings, cries, and seeks support when strangers are around.	b. Objection to strangers begins to diminish; may still be wary of strangers or new situations.	c. Is able to venture into strange or new situations if prepared in advance by adults.
R8	a. Uses single words to indicate needs and wants such as "muk" for "I want milk," or "bye bye" for "Let's go bye bye."	b. Uses phrases and 2- to 3-word sentences to indicate needs and wants.	c. Uses 4- to 6-word sentences to indicate needs and wants.
R9	a. Connects emotions with behaviors; uses language to express these connections.	b. Uses emotional ideas in play. c. Elaborates on emotional ideas and understanding to play with objects.	d. Begins emotional thinking; begins to understand emotional cause-and-effect relationships.
R10	a. Takes turns with toys and materials with adult support and facilitation.	b. Takes turns with toys and materials with friend, sometimes without adult support.	
R11	a. Experiments with behavior that accomplishes a goal; may bite, pinch, poke, scratch, push, and so on while trying to make things happen.	b. Begins to anticipate what might happen when actions are taken; chooses to make things happen if outcomes are desirable (for example, trade toys with a friend who will stay and play), and resists taking action if outcomes are undesirable (for example, teacher will put markers away if child chews on the tips).	

Exploring Roles

	18-24 months	24-30 months	30-36 months
ER1	a. Explores roles related to self and family.	b. Explores roles related to self, friends, family, and neighborhood.	c. Explores roles related to self, friends, family, neighborhood, and the community at large.
ER2	a. Is unable to choose or modify behavior in response to physical or social cues of situations; persists in behavior that doesn't work in situations.	b. Begins to choose or modify behavior in response to physical and social cues of situations; when one behavior isn't working, may stop and try something else.	c. Chooses and modifies behavior in response to the physical and social cues of a situation; tries to choose the behaviors that will get what he or she wants; can change behaviors if they are not working.
ER3	a. Does not understand the impact of own behavior on others.	b. Begins to understand the impact of own behavior on others; shows interest and awareness of the emotional behaviors of friends and others.	c. Understands the impact of own behavior on others; anticipates how friends or others will react.
ER4	a. Uses props to play roles; becomes the occupant of the role (is superman when wearing a cape or mommy when holding a baby). Prefers familiar roles.	b. Uses props to adopt roles; abandons roles when the props are removed; changes between familiar and favorite roles in dramatic play.	c. Can play roles with or without props. Transitions between roles frequently and easily (for example, can be the mommy, then the daddy, then the monster during same play period).

	18-24 months	24-30 months	30-36 months
CM1	a. Expressive vocabulary increases; uses about 200 words on a regular basis. Expressive language continues to be telegraphic, where single words may carry expanded meaning that is only understood by familiar caregivers.	b. Vocabulary size begins to grow rapidly; sentence length begins to increase with 3 or 4 words in some sentences.	c. Sentence length continues to grow. Four- to six-word sentences predominate expressive language. Vocabulary continues to expand; expressive vocabulary is adequate to make most needs and wants understood by others.
CM2	a. Uses a greater variety of sounds and sound combinations, simplifying the word if it is too complex (such as pane for plane, tephone for telephone); enjoys experimenting with inflection that sounds like adult speech although it is not yet understandable.	b. Rapid development of new sound combinations and new words that are understandable to adults. Begins to use language functionally—to ask for things and get needs met.	c. Is able to use language to get most needs and wants met by familiar caregivers.
CM3	a. Seeks vocal interactions with familiar people; can communicate needs and wants to familiar caregivers; begins to be wary of talking to strangers.	b. Resists interactions with strangers; hides, withdraws, or objects to encouragement to talk to strangers.	
CM4	a. 20-25% of language is intelligible to strangers. Parents and caregivers can understand more.	b. 60-65% of language is intelligible to strangers. Parents and caregivers understand most of the child's expressive language.	
CM5	a. "Reads" book from front to back; turns books right side up to look at them. b. Makes sounds that connect to pictures in books.	c. Listens to a complete story from beginning to end; asks to read familiar books over and over again.	d. Likes to look at books independently; "reads" books to self.
CM6	a. Actively experiments with the environment; follows visual displacement of objects.	b. Begins transition to symbolic thought. Uses formed mental images to solve problems. Thought processes relate to concrete experiences and objects.	c. Begins transition to pre-operational stage characterized by the beginning of symbolic thought and the use of mental images and words.

Problem Solving Assessment 18-36 months

	18-24 months	24-30 months	30-36 months
PS1	a. Interest in toileting is limited to watching; may show interest in flushing toilet, sitting on the toilet, or washing hands. Interest may wax and wane quickly.	b. Toilet play stage of toileting; interested in playing out toileting activities such as taking off diaper, sitting on the toilet, using toilet paper, flushing the toilet, and washing hands.	c. Toilet practice begins; likes to repeat toileting activities again and again, with or without success.
PS2	a. Activity level increases; requests and seeks out motor activities. Does not control activity level without adult support; resists adult support in modulating activity level.	b. Activity level continues to increase; continues to seek out motor activities. Begins to modulate activity levels with verbal and physical adult support.	c. Alternates between high levels of activity and periods of calm, quieter activity. Can modulate activity level with verbal reminders from adults.
PS3	a. On-task behavior begins to increase.	b. Able to sustain favorite activities for increasingly longer periods of time; extends on-task play time at favorite activities to 10 minutes. Still loses interest in other activities quickly.	c. Stays on task at favorite manipulative activities for sustained periods of time; extends on-task play time at favorite activities to 20 minutes. Still loses interest in other activities quickly.
PS4	a. Carries toys around from place to place. b. Undresses; takes off shoes, socks, and clothes. c. Turns door knob to open door.	d. Holds cup with one hand to drink. e. Shows preference for one hand.	f. Unzips zipper. g. Pulls pants up. h. Zips zipper.
PS5	a. Propels riding toys with feet. b. Runs; collapses to stop forward movement.	c. Goes up stairs without alternating feet, holding on to handrail. d. Runs; begins to control starting and stopping. e. Balances on one foot.	f. Goes up stairs alternating feet, holding on to handrail. g. Jumps up and down on two feet. h. Pedals tricycle.

Expressing Feelings with Parents, Teachers, and Friends

	18-24 months	24-30 months	30-36 months
E1	a. Begins to create mental images of emotional behaviors. b. Uses behavior to express emotions (i.e., stomps foot when angry, laughs when happy, etc.).	c. Distinguishes between emotions and the behaviors that go with that emotion.	d. Understands how one feeling relates to another (i.e., being disappointed about getting a toy and getting angry as a result of the disappointment).
E2	a. Emotional intensity is not regulated—minor and major events get similar reactions; falls apart easily.	b. Begins to regulate emotional intensity in some situations; falls apart less frequently.	c. Regulates emotional intensity most of the time; seldom falls apart. d. Figures out how to respond with appropriate emotions to most situations.
E3	a. Watches and remembers emotional behaviors exhibited by others; uses observations in future interactions.	b. Puts emotional mental images to work in pretend play; can make-believe or pretend to be angry, happy, sad, etc.	
E4	a. Knows rules that have been reinforced consistently but still needs reminders and physical adult support to comply.	b. Follows rules that have been reinforced consistently with verbal reminders and physical adult support.	c. Follows rules that have been reinforced consistently with just verbal reminders.
E5	a. Unable to label own feelings.	b. Can label some feelings; uses the same feeling to represent many feelings (i.e., mad for angry, frustrated, irritated, unhappy, etc.).	c. Labels most of his or her own feelings; can differentiate between similar emotions and label them appropriately.
E6	a. Unable to understand how others feel.	b. Begins to understand how others feel when observing others but not when he or she is a part of the interaction.	c. Understands how others feel when the behavior exhibited is consistent with the emotion being felt (i.e., angry child is yelling, stomping foot, saying, "No!").
E7	a. Has difficulty delaying gratification.	b. Can delay gratification for a short time when supported by adults.	c. Can delay gratification for a few minutes in most situations.
E8	a. Does not separate fantasy from reality.	b. Can switch from reality to fantasy.	c. Understands "real" and "not real."
E9	a. Ambivalent about being autonomous; wants to sometimes and doesn't want to at other times.	b. Independent behaviors are increasing; dependent behaviors are decreasing.	c. Independent behaviors are usually present.
E10	a. Has little control over impulses.	b. Controls impulses in some situations or with support from adults.	c. Most impulses are under control.
E11	a. Loses emotional control often and intensely.	b. Loss of emotional control is less frequent, less intense, and less prolonged.	c. Infrequently loses emotional control.

Dissemination Schedule for Postcards

There are two ways to disseminate postcards. The first strategy is to begin the dissemination along with the child's enrollment in school. If children enroll as toddlers, this strategy works well. It allows the teacher to select Postcards that are appropriate to the child's situation, the family's interests and parent education needs, and the school's desire to share information. When used in this fashion, postcards can be viewed as roughly chronological in order.

A second strategy for disseminating Postcards is to do so by topic as needs or interests arise. This approach allows teachers to pick and choose topics and Postcards that fit individual families' experiences and needs.

If you choose to disseminate Postcards as needs arise, notice that the Postcards are typically disseminated *before* the need to know and understand emerges chronologically. This makes the Postcards anticipatory preparation for the next stage and, therefore, parent education at its best. Don't hesitate to give parents a Postcard more than once—repetition assures that parents will have more than one opportunity to get, understand, and use the information provided. Some issues arise repeatedly and strategies to use need be refreshed.

Finally, supplement the Postcards printed in this curriculum with articles, ideas, and resources from other sources. There are many wonderful materials for parents available. When you discover one, add it to the curriculum to strengthen and supplement the topics that are included here.

Transitioning from Home to School: Months 18-20

Attachment Stage 4—Stranger Anxiety: What Parents Can Do
Creating an Arrival and Departure Ritual
Arrival and Departure Routines ARE Transitions
Always Say Goodbye
Thumb and Finger Sucking
Pacifiers
Transitional or Security Items
Just How Long Will Adjustment Take?

Use the following Postcards from the Possibilities Plan when you are doing related activities with children.

Me! And My Body Possibilities

Every Child Is Unique

You Are Your Child's Best Teacher

My Family Possibilities

We are Now Partners

Creating Partnerships—Two Way Communication

Making Friends: Months 20-24

Action/Reaction Biting: Help! My Child Got Bitten, Again!

Oh No! Not Again!: Handling Purposeful Biting

What Can Teachers Do to Prevent Purposeful Biting?

Additional Steps to Prevent Purposeful Biting

Teaching Social Skills to Reduce Biting

What Can Parents Do to Prevent Purposeful Biting?

Social Expectations for Toddlers

Expectations with Friends

Use the following Postcards from the Possibilities Plan when you are doing related activities with children.

My Neighborhood Possibilities

What Do Children Learn While They Play?

Transmitting Values to Your Child

Fruits and Vegetables Possibilities

Drive Time Activities

Preparing for Time Away from Your Child

Exploring Roles: Months 24-26

How Parents Support Exploring Roles

Facilitating Positive Self-concept in Your Child

Use the following Postcards from the Possibilities Plan when you are doing related activities with children.

Space Possibilities

Gender-Role Stereotyping

Sky Possibilities

Exploring Roles at Home

Preparing for Time Away from Your Child

Communicating with Parents, Teachers, and Friends: Months 26-28

What Is Developmentally Appropriate Care and Early Education for Toddlers?—The Role of the Teacher

What Is Developmentally Appropriate Care and Early Education for Toddlers?—The Role of Curriculum (Activities and Experiences)

Using Found and Discarded Items for Toys

Good Books for Toddlers
The Amazing Toddler Brain
How Toddlers Learn

Use the following Postcards from the Possibilities Plan when you are doing related activities with children.

Little Animals Possibilities
Teaching Your Child to Read
Tips for Reading to Your Toddler
Teaching Your Child to Write

Big Animals Possibilities
Supporting Brain Development at Home
Appropriate Expectations for Learning Academic Skills

Problem-Solving: Months 28-30

Picky Eaters: Helping Your Toddler Eat Healthy
Toileting: I'm Ready, But My Child Isn't
Natural and Logical Consequences
Setting Appropriate Limits

Use the following Postcards from the Possibilities Plan when you are doing related activities with children.

Construction Possibilities
Encouraging Independence and Autonomy
Continuing to Support Independence and Autonomy

Wheels Possibilities
Appropriate Expectations for Self-control
What If?

Expressing Feelings with Parents, Teachers, and Friends: Months 30-36

Managing Normal Aggression in Very Young Children
Dealing with Oppositional Behavior
Toddlers on the Edge

Use the following Postcards from the Possibilities Plan when you are doing related activities with children.

Storybook Characters Possibilities
Process Is the Goal

Water Possibilities
When Your Child's Teacher Leaves
When Your Child's Day Is Lengthened

Possibilities Planning

Like the old saying goes, "If we fail to plan, we plan to fail." Even though ***Innovations: The Comprehensive Toddler Curriculum*** is emergent in nature, planning is crucial. In fact, we see planning as being even more important when curriculum is emergent. To adequately prepare, teachers need to be aware of options and how, when, and where these options might present themselves. Viewed this way, curriculum is as much about what teachers do before interacting with children as it is about what teachers do during and after interactions.

The purpose of a Possibilities Plan is to focus attention on all of the dimensions of planning and to support the process of planning curriculum. In addition, the plan supports teachers' efforts to make both parents and other teachers aware of the focus, events, activities, experiences, and interactions that are being considered and provided for babies. The Possibilities Plan includes all the different aspects of curriculum presented in ***Innovations: The Comprehensive Toddler Curriculum***.

Unlike traditional lesson plans that provide only activities, the Possibilities Plan provides the big picture of possibilities that might emerge. It may cover a week, two weeks, or even a month. Possibilities Plans are designed to be living documents. Teachers may make additions, changes, or corrections to reflect children's experiences, reactions, preferences, emergent ideas, and changing development. You may find it helpful to use one color pen for your original Possibilities Plan, then other color pens to make changes in the plan that result from children's reactions or that influence what happens next, as well as to show how the children responded or reacted to what actually happens in the classroom.

The following list provides an overview of the different sections of the Possibilities Plan. Use the Possibilities Plan as it is (feel free to make additional copies), or modify it to reflect individual differences or preferences in format or space.

Parent Possibilities: Because parents are children's first and most important teachers, the Possibilities Plan begins with the parent involvement section. Include suggestions for both teacher-initiated activities as well as parent participation possibilities. Be sensitive to the range of parents' abilities to participate in activities by planning many different options.

Environmental Possibilities: Innovations: The Comprehensive Toddler Curriculum views environmental planning, preparation, and modification as a major responsibility for all teachers. Our colleagues in Reggio Emilia view the environment as the "extra" teacher in any classroom. A well-planned environment can communicate volumes to children, even very young children. Planned and prepared thoroughly and thoughtfully, the environment can support children's play and work, teachers' activities and work, and parents' comfort. When inadequately planned and prepared, environments can interfere or even conflict with children's ideas, development, and activity as well as with teachers' goals and parents' comfort. Included in this section is equipment and materials to make, add, take away, and change. When regularly considered, changes and modifications like these will keep the environment fresh and interesting for children, their parents, and their teachers.

Observation/Assessment Possibilities: A major focus of this curriculum is observation and assessment. Use indicators from the various developmental continua to cue teachers' observation as well as to create anecdotal documentation of children's emerging skills, abilities, reactions, responses, and emergent activities. A copy of the complete assessment form follows. Complete an assessment on each child for his or her portfolio and use it to discuss your observations and children's emerging skills with parents at formal conferences. Use the Possibilities Plan and the Communication Sheet to record brief notes concerning individual children's development and experiences or reactions to the plan.

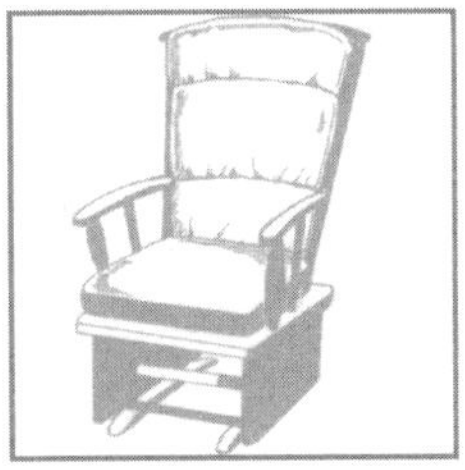

Interactive Experiences: Each chapter in the curriculum includes a list of important interactive experiences for young children. Often, these experiences emerge from warm, caring interactions and are rarely the result of planning or formal activities. Because the quality of children's experiences is so important and cumulative, it is important to remind teachers and parents that these interactions ARE curriculum. Use the lists in each developmental task as well as ones that emerge uniquely from your interactive teaching style and list them for parents (and teachers) to see. This validates these important experiences and reminds everyone that warm, positive interaction is the foundation of early childhood EDUCATION.

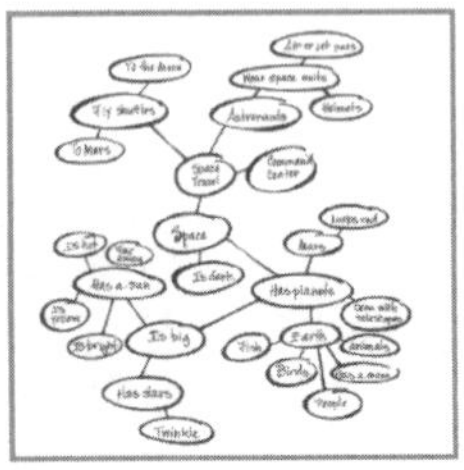

Web: A sample web is provided for each Possibilities Plan. Use it or create your own web including ideas and activities that your children might enjoy as well as to open up emergent possibilities. Then, you might use different ink colors to show how the web grows or changes as children show preferences for activities, experiences, materials, and so on. Further, these beginning webs can be used later as a platform for future planning as children grow and learn.

Possibilities: Choose from the many different possibilities provided. Initially, use the age guides at the beginning of each activity, then modify activities based on your observations of children's responses. Because so much of a toddler's day is involved with routines (diapering, eating, napping, and so on), you may need only a few activities listed. Remember the value of repetition for early brain development. Never hesitate to repeat popular activities more than once a day or for many subsequent days. At the same time, remember the value of novelty—add variety to the children's day to gently excite and challenge emerging skills and prevent boredom. Finally, include plenty of time for children to explore the stimulating environment you have planned and prepared.

Books: Include children's books that are favorites and that will support the other activities that the children will be experiencing. Read to children individually or in small groups each and every day.

Picture File/Vocabulary: Write the new vocabulary words you will be using in this section and indicate the pictures you will add to the classroom from your picture file. Including these additions to the plan will not only cue parents that you are supporting vocabulary development (and receptive language) but also that you are adding a wide variety of interest and images to the environment. It also gives parents an opportunity to support your teaching by adding photos and pictures from home and to replicate these early literacy ideas at home.

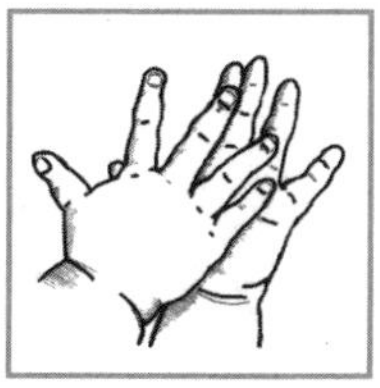

Rhymes/Fingerplays and Music/Songs: Include rhymes and music that you will be using during the course of the plan. Writing the titles of these important literacy activities and placing copies of the rhymes, fingerplays, and/or songs on the parent bulletin board or on the Communication Sheet supports developing literacy and reinforces parents as the primary educators of their children.

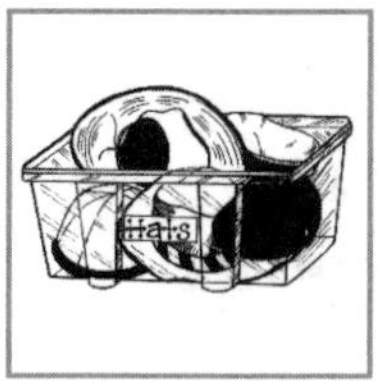

Prop Boxes: Items included in individual prop boxes can be listed in this section. Prop boxes are valuable resources for teachers because they help you collect, organize, and store materials and resources. Start by developing one prop box and you will be hooked! Storing items in clear plastic containers aides in quick identification of resources as curriculum emerges in your classroom. Listing prop boxes on your Possibilities Plan will also remind parents to support the collection of these valuable teaching resources.

When you are finished considering all of these possibilities, you will have a rich and interesting plan for you and your toddlers. Then, it will be time to relax and enjoy the educational experiences that you have prepared for children in your group—knowing that everything you do IS curriculum.

Possibilities

Parent Possibilities

Teacher-Initiated

Parent Participation

Innovations in Environments

Observation/Assessment Possibilities

Interactive Experiences

Plan

Web

Dramatic Possibilities

Art/Sensory Possibilities

Curiosity Possibilities

Music Possibilities

Movement Possibilities

Literacy Possibilities

Outdoor Possibilities

Project Possibilities

Books	Picture File Pictures/Vocabulary

Rhymes & Fingerplays	Music/Songs	Prop Boxes

Possibilities

Parent Possibilities

Teacher-Initiated	Anecdotal Note Calendar Video-diary on Helena, Brent
Parent Participation	Muffins for Mom Tuesday June 5 Star Gazing

Innovations in Environments

add side by side materials
- two consoles in Space Station
- duplicate helmets and air packs

provide play cues for Space Station
- add photos for picture file
- add puppets

put away farm animals/barn

Observation/Assessment Possibilities

Abby= E1n, E1a, E3b, Ex6b, E10b
Kaylee= E1q, E2q, E11b
Marco= E8a, E9b, E11c
Le= E4c, E5b, E6c, E11b
Brent= E1n, E1o, E3b, E10b

Interactive Experiences

- celebrate cultural differences-ask Marco's mother to read favorite story
- support feeling of belonging and add family photo to child's family photo book
- Make a "I did it" documentation
- Pair up Abby and Le for an activity to encourage cooperation

Plan

Web

Construction Possibilities Space Bldg; Astronauts Builder

Dramatic Possibilities Space Shuttle Command Center

Art/Sensory Possibilities Stars, Star Dust Collage, String Moons

Curiosity Possibilities Moon Bottles, Moon Puzzles, Moon Snacks

Music Possibilities Star Wars, Space Odyssey, Twinkle, Twinkle

Movement Possibilities Five Little Rockets

Literacy Possibilities Flip book What Next Baby Bear

Outdoor Possibilities Moon Walk, Box Rocket

Project Possibilities Build a Space Ship

Books

Papa Please Get the Moon for Me
Dogs in Space
Flip Books (teacher made)
Good Night Moon

Picture File Pictures/Vocabulary

Moon	Astronaut
Mars	Pluto
Planets	Rockets
Stars	Sun

Rhymes & Fingerplays

Five Little Rockets

Music/Songs

Twinkle, Twinkle

Prop Boxes

Space
Astronaut
Good Night Moon

Concepts Learned in Me and My Body

Concepts Learned

I can recognize myself in a mirror.
I can play interactive games.
I can play near another child.
I can point to named body parts (eyes, ears, nose, mouth, chin, elbow, arm, knee, ankle, wrist, and so on).
I can name body parts.
Eyes are for seeing.
Noses are for smelling.
Mouths are for eating.
Ears are for hearing.
I can play chase.
I can climb two- or three-step stairs.
I can roll a ball.
I can turn the pages of a book.
I can ride a small riding toy without pedals.
I can jump in place.
I can hop on one foot.
I can walk with balance.
I can walk on tiptoes.
I can match pictures.
I can name pictured items.
I can use glue sticks and art materials to create a project.
I can follow one-step and two-step directions.
I can take things off.
I can put things on.

Concepts Learned in My Family

Concepts Learned

I can identify my family members (mother, father, sister, brother) in photos.
I can identify extended family members (grandparents, aunts, uncles) in photos.
I can identify pets (dog, cat, bird).
I can do housework.
I can take care of babies.
I can take care of pets.
I can make pet sounds.
I can move like pets.
I can mix two colors to make a new color.
I can use different items to make sounds.
I can names textures (soft, hard, smooth, rough).
I can put thing in and take things out of boxes.
I can fill and dump.
I can use words to describe different sizes (big, little).
I can use liquid glue and glue sticks.
I can scribble with crayons.
I can turn pages in a book.
I can read picture books.
I can act out words to songs.
I can use hands and fingers to act out fingerplays.

Concepts Learned in My Neighborhood

Concepts Learned

I can play community workers.
I can play house.
I can experiment with a variety of textures.
I can explore filling and pouring.
I can play post office.
I can explore different sounds.
I can match colors.
I can put together simple puzzles.
I can explore the properties of magnets.
I can act out stories using a puppet.
I can enjoy looking at books.
I can turn pages in a book.
I can recognize basic colors.
I can recognize familiar symbols.
I can scribble on unlined paper.
I can name familiar places in the neighborhood.
I can play simple games with an adult.
I can develop large motor skills with legs and arms.
I can use fine motor skills with crayons, puzzles, and paintbrushes.
I can sing simple songs.
I can follow one- and two-step directions.
I can push riding toys with my feet.

Concepts Learned in Fruits and Vegetables

Concepts Learned

I can name familiar vegetables.
I can name familiar fruits.
I can pretend to cook.
I can set the table.
Fruits have different tastes.
I can identify a star shape.
I can match smells with appropriate fruits.
I can blow bubbles.
I can put puzzles together.
Plants need water.
I can sort.
I can match.
I can name pictures in books.
I can turn pages of a book.
I can listen to a story.
I can participate in a group story activity.
Carrots grow in the ground.
Strawberries have texture, scent, and taste good!
I can name vegetables.
I can predict what happens next in a story.
I can count to five.
I can follow directions in a song.
I can move my big muscles.
I can identify colors.
I can match colors.
I can walk on a designated path.
I can jump with two feet.
I can do cross-lateral body movements.
I can play dress up.
I can place collage materials.
I can glue.
Plants have green leaves.
I can care for living plants.
Plants grow from seeds.
Plants need sun and water.
Vegetables and fruits come from plants.

Concepts Learned in Space

Concepts Learned

Space is far away.
Space ships can go to space.
I can play space center activities.
Astronauts wear helmets and boots.
The moon is round.
The moon is in the sky.
I can see the moon at night.
Stars are in the night sky.
Stars twinkle.
Stars have points.
Rockets go to the moon.
Rockets go very fast.
Sand on Mars is red.
I can move my whole body to music.
I can sing simple songs.
I can recite simple rhymes.
I can use fine motor skills with my fingers.
I can be involved in imaginary play with sound effects.
I can throw.
I can jump.
I can put together simple puzzles.
I can stack more than two blocks.
I can glue.
I can use spatial awareness skills.
I can use creative materials for construction.
I can explore a variety of textures and materials.
I can use words for textures.

Concepts Learned in Sky

Concepts Learned

The sun is in the daytime sky.
The sun is yellow.
The sun is hot.
The sun warms the earth.
The sun helps living things grow.
The sun gives light.
The sun shines at the beach.
Clouds are white.
Clouds stay in the sky.
Clouds are soft.
Rain falls from the sky.
Rain is water.
Rain waters the flowers.
Raincoats keep people dry in the rain.
Rain makes sounds.
Rainbows have many colors.
Rainbows are in the sky at special times.
Rain and sunshine make rainbows.
Some textures are soft, rough, wet, or sandy.
I understand up and down, high and low.
Words can be written on paper.
I can make large motor movements to different music rhythms
I can strengthen my large muscles by riding toys.

Concepts Learned in Big Animals

Concepts Learned

Some animals are big.
Bears are big animals
Bears live in caves.
Bears eat berries.
Bears sleep in winter.
Bears growl.
Elephants are gray.
Elephants have trunks.
Elephants are big animals.
Elephants eat peanuts.
Cows are big animals.
Cows live on the farm.
Cows say "moo."
Horses are big animals.
Horses live in barns.
Horses say "neigh."
Things are heavy or light.
My body goes up and down.
Sandpaper feels rough.
Big animals move in different ways.
Big and little are opposites.
Lacing uses my finger muscles.
Puzzle pieces fit together to make a picture.
Fingers can turn pages in a book.
Acting out songs exercises large muscles.
Walking, running, and jumping are ways animals move.
Moving like animals is a part of pretending to be an animal.
Painting is a way to express feelings.
Moving my body makes me feel happy.
Big brushes paint big.

Concept Learned in Little Animals

Concepts Learned

Bunnies are soft animals.
Bunnies have long ears.
Bunnies eat carrots.
Bunnies hop.
Monkeys live in trees.
Monkeys are funny.
Monkeys eat fruit.
Monkeys swing from trees.
Monkeys have hands like mine.
Mice are very small animals.
Mice have long tails.
Mice scurry very fast.
Mice hide in holes.
Turtles live inside a hard shell.
Turtles crawl slowly.
Turtles are brown and green.
Some animals feel soft and fluffy.
Some animals have hard shells.
I can hop like a bunny.
I can swing my arms like a monkey.
I can crawl like a turtle.
All animals eat food.
All animals play.
Cotton balls are soft like a bunny.
I can make silly faces.
My body can move like animal bodies.
I can play follow-the-leader games.

Concepts Learned in Construction

Concepts Learned

Construction workers wear hard hats.
Construction workers wear tool belts.
Plumbers use pipes.
Hammers are for pounding nails.
Wrenches turn bolts.
Saws cut wood.
Measuring tapes measure the length of things.
Bulldozers make loud noises.
Bulldozers push piles of dirt.
Cement trucks carry wet cement to construction sites.
Cement trucks make grinding noises.
Dump trucks can carry heavy loads.
Dump trucks dump dirt and sand.
I can pound with a hammer.
Wet sand sticks together.
Dirt and water make mud.
I can use big boxes to make big buildings.
I can tell stories about construction machines.
I can name construction machines and familiar tools.
I can identify sounds tools make.
I can sing songs about trucks.
I can move my body in big ways.

Concepts Learned in Wheels

Concepts Learned

Cars have wheels.
Trucks have wheels.
Buses have wheels.
Police cars have wheels.
Fire trucks have wheels.
Some vehicles, such as cars and trucks, have four wheels.
Motorcycles and bicycles have two wheels.
Tricycles have three wheels.
Wheelbarrows have one wheel.
Trucks and buses have big wheels.
Skates and skateboards have little wheels.
Wheels roll.
Wheels are round.
Wheels help us move easier.
Push and pull toys have wheels.
Wheels are made of plastic, rubber, and metal.
Riding toys have wheels.
Wheels move around and around in a circle.

Concepts Learned in Storybook Characters

Concepts Learned

Some things are small, medium, or large.
I can count to three.
Farmers take care of farm animals.
Some farm animals live in a barn.
I can make farm animal sounds.
Ducks like water.
Flowers grow in dirt.
Seeds need sun, rain, and warm breezes to grow.
Oatmeal feels different when wet or dry.
I can move my body in many ways.
Spiders make webs.
Mittens are different from gloves.
I can put on mittens.
I like to hear stories.
I can listen for sounds.
Animals move in different ways.

Concepts Learned in Water

Concepts Learned

Water is warm and cool.
Water pours, sprinkles, and drips.
Rain is water.
Raincoats keep you dry when it rains.
Ducks swim in water.
Ducks waddle.
Frogs live in water.
Frogs jump.
Frogs catch insects with their tongues.
Fish live in water.
Fish swim with their fins.
We take a bath in water.
Plants need water to grow.
We drink water.
Water keeps us cool.
Boats float in water.
Some things float; some things sink.

Songs, Poems, Rhymes, and Fingerplays

Are You Sleeping?

Are you sleeping,
Are you sleeping,
Brother John, Brother John?
Morning bells are ringing,
Morning bells are ringing,
Ding, ding, dong!
Ding, ding, dong!

As I Was Walking

As I was walking down the street, (Children move in circle.)
Down the street, down the street,
A dump truck I chanced to meet.
Hi ho, hi ho, hi ho. (Stop moving and clap hands.)

Vroom! Vroom! Vroom!
And away it went. (Children move in circle.)
Away it went; away it went.
Vroom! Vroom! Vroom!
And away it went.
Hi ho, hi ho, hi ho. (Stop moving and clap hands.)

As I was walking down the street, (Children move in circle.)
Down the street, down the street.
A cement truck I chanced to meet.
Hi ho, hi ho, hi ho. (Stop moving and clap hands.)

Grrrh! Grrrh! Grrrh!
And away it went. (Move in circle.)
Away it went, away it went.
Grrrrh! Grrrh! Grrrh!
And away it went.
Hi ho, hi ho, hi ho. (Stop moving and clap hands.)

Bear Is Sleeping (Tune: "Are You Sleeping?")

Bear is sleeping.
Bear is sleeping.
In a cave, in a cave.
Snoring through the winter, snoring through the winter.
Snug and warm, snug and warm.

Big Steps, Little Steps

Big steps, big steps, big steps.
Little steps, little steps, little steps.
Big steps, little steps.
BIG STEPS!

Big Old Bear

Big old bear is nice and fat.
Ready for a winter's nap.
Big old bear is fast asleep.
Safe inside her cave so deep.
Big old bear is inside her den.
When it's spring, she'll growl again!

Clapping Hands (Tune: "Skip to My Lou")

Clap, clap, clap your hands.
Clap, clap, clap your hands.
Clap, clap, clap your hands.
Clap your hands like me.

Copy Me!

I put my hand on my head. (Hand on head.)
Copy me, copy me! (Child's hands on head.)
I put my hand on my knee. (Hand on knee.)
Copy me, copy me! (Child's hands on knee.)
Twiddle dee dee, twiddle dee, dee! (Hold hands and turn in a circle.)

Dancing Fingers (Tune: "London Bridges")

Dancing fingers dance so slow, dance so slow, dance so slow. (Move fingers slowly.)
Dancing fingers dance so fast, dance so fast, dance so fast. (Move fingers rapidly.)
Dancing fingers dance so high, dance so high, dance so high. (Move fingers above the head.)
Dancing fingers go to sleep, go to sleep, go to sleep. (Place palms of hands together.)
Night, night, fingers. (Place hands by the face.)

Did You Ever See? (Tune: "Did You Ever See a Lassie?")

Did you ever see an elephant, an elephant, an elephant?
Did you ever see an elephant,
Jump up and down?

Did you ever see a bear, a bear, a bear?
Did you ever see a bear,
Wiggle his nose?

(Continue with other animals.)

Did You Ever See a Cloud? (Tune: "Did You Ever See a Lassie?")

Did you ever see a cloud, a cloud, a cloud?
Did you ever see a cloud that looked like a sheep?
A fat one, a skinny one, a silly one, a funny one?
Did you ever see a cloud that looked like a sheep?

Did you ever see a cloud, a cloud, a cloud?
Did you ever see a cloud that looked like a car?
A big one, a little one, a fast one, a slow one.
Did you ever see a cloud that looked like a car?

Down by the Station

Down by the station
Early in the morning,
See the little puffer bellies
All in a row.

See the engine driver,
Pull the little throttle,
Puff, puff, toot, toot!
Off we go.

Drive the Truck (Tune: "Row, Row, Row Your Boat")

Drive, drive, drive the truck, (Pretend to steer the truck.)
Carefully down the road. (Nod head from side to side.)
Bumpity, bumpity, bumpity bump. (Move up and down from the knees.)
Listen to my horn! (Honk!)

Eensy Weensy Spider

The eensy weensy spider
Walked up the waterspout. (Walk fingers up the arm.)
Down came the rain,
And washed the spider out. (Wiggle fingers downward.)
Out came the sun,
And dried up all the rain. (Big circle with arms overhead.)
And the eensy weensy spider,
Walked up the spout again. (Walk fingers up the arm.)

Elephant Dancing (Tune: "The Mulberry Bush")

This is the way the elephants dance,
The elephants dance, the elephants dance.
This is the way the elephants dance,
On a bright and sunny morning.

Finger Family

Finger family up, (Wiggle fingers up.)
Finger family down, (Wiggle fingers down.)
Finger family dancing,
All around the town. (Wiggle fingers all around.)
Dance them on your shoulders. (Wiggle fingers on shoulders.)
Dance fingers on your head. (Wiggle fingers on top of head.)
Dance fingers on your knees, (Wiggle fingers on knees.)
And tuck them into bed. (Fold hands and put beside face.)

Five Little Ducks

Five little ducks went out to swim, (Hold up five fingers.)
Over the pond and far away. (Make swimming motions.)
Mama Duck called,
Quack! Quack! Quack! (Open/close hands.)
And four little ducks came swimming back. (Hold up four fingers.)

Four little ducks went out to swim, (Hold up four fingers.)
Over the pond and far away. (Make swimming motions.)
Mama Duck called,
Quack! Quack! Quack! (Open/close hands.)

And three little ducks came swimming back. (Hold up three fingers.)

Three little ducks went out to swim, (Hold up three fingers.)
Over the pond and far away. (Make swimming motions.)
Mama Duck called,
Quack! Quack! Quack! (Open/close hands.)
And two little ducks came swimming back. (Hold up two fingers.)

Two little ducks went out to swim, (Hold up two fingers.)
Over the pond and far away. (Make swimming motions.)
Mama Duck called,
Quack! Quack! Quack! (Open/close hands.)
And one little duck came swimming back. (Hold up one finger.)

One little duck went out to swim, (Hold up one finger.)
Over the pond and far away. (Make swimming motions.)
Mama Duck called,
Quack! Quack! Quack! (Open/close hands.)
And no little ducks came swimming back. (Hold hands palms up.)

Father Duck said,
Quack! Quack! Quack! (Big voice.)
And five little ducks came swimming back. (Hold up five fingers.)

Five Little Ducks

Five little ducks
That I once knew (Hold up five fingers.)
Fat ones, skinny ones
Tall ones, too.
But the one little duck with the
Feather on his back (Wave hand behind back.)
He led the others with
A Quack! Quack! Quack! (Stoop down and waddle.)

Five Little Monkeys

Five little monkeys jumping on the bed. (Hold up five fingers.)
One fell off and bumped his head. (Rub head.)
Mother called the doctor. (Hold hand like talking on phone.)
And the doctor said,
"No more monkeys jumping on the bed!" (Shake finger.)

(Repeat motions using the appropriate number of fingers.)

Four little monkeys jumping on the bed.
One fell off and bumped his head.
Mother called the doctor.
And the doctor said,
"No more monkeys jumping on the bed!"

Three little monkeys jumping on the bed.
One fell off and bumped his head.
Mother called the doctor.
And the doctor said,
"No more monkeys jumping on the bed!"

Two little monkeys jumping on the bed.
One fell off and bumped his head.
Mother called the doctor.
And the doctor said,
"No more monkeys jumping on the bed!"

One little monkey jumping on the bed.
One fell off and bumped his head.
Mother called the doctor.
And the doctor said,
"No more monkeys jumping on the bed!"

Five Little Rockets

Five little rockets flying in the sky,
Come in for a landing from way up high.

The first little rocket shining in the sun,
Is the first to land on runway number 1.

The second little rocket carrying its crew,
Lands very slowly on runway number 2.

The third little rocket, such a sight to see,
Lands quietly on runway number 3.

The fourth little rocket can't wait anymore.
And lands very quickly on runway number 4.

The fifth little rocket is the last to arrive,
And finally lands on runway number 5.

Five Little Trucks

Five little trucks driving down the road,
The first one said, "I'm carrying a heavy load."
The second one said, "I'm the color red."
The third one said, "I'm moving ahead."
The fourth one said, "I'm driving very slow."
The fifth one said, "Let's go and go and go!"

Food Song (Tune: "I've Been Working on the Railroad")

Red is the color for an apple to eat.
Red is the color for cherries, too.
Red is the color for strawberries.
I like red, don't you.

Yellow is the color for a great big pear.
Yellow is the color for lemonade, too.
Yellow is the color of a pineapple.
I like yellow, don't you?

Orange is the color of oranges.
Orange is the color for carrots, too.
Orange is the color of a jack-o-lantern.
I like orange, don't you?

Frogs at the Pond

Five little frogs
Were down at the pond,
Down at the pond at play.
Along came a hungry fish
And chased one frog away.

Four little frogs
Were down at the pond,
Down at the pond at play.
Along came a wiggly snake,
And chased one frog away.

Three little frogs
Were down at the pond,
Down at the pond at play.
Along came a giant alligator
And chased one frog away.

Two little frogs
Were down at the pond,
Down at the pond at play.
Along came a purple lizard,
And chased one frog away.

One little frog
Was down at the pond,
Down at the pond at play.
Along came a flying crane,
And chased the frog away.

Then no little frogs
Were down at the pond,
Down at the pond at play.
Where do you think the little frogs went
When they all hopped away?

The Frog Sits on a Log (tune: "The Farmer in the Dell")

The frog sits on a log.
His tongue is ever so long.
It reaches high to catch a fly.
The frog sits on a log.

Go In and Out the Neighborhood

Go in and out the neighborhood.
Go in and out the neighborhood.
Go in and out the neighborhood.
As you have done before.

Grandma (Tune: "I'm a Little Teapot")

I have a special Grandma, I like to see.
I love her and she loves me.
When I go to see her, we have fun,
From early morning 'til the day is done.

Grow Little Seed

I'm a little seed in the deep dark soil. (Children kneel on their knees, covering their eyes.)
The warm breezes blow. (Fan the kneeling children.)
The gentle rains fall. (Lightly spray water over the children.)
The hot sun calls the seeds to rise. (Children slowly get to their feet.)
The blue sky waits for the surprise. (Children stretch their arms high over their heads.)
Happy plants grow from seeds. (Children smile.)

The Hammer Song

Johnny hammers with one hammer, (Hammer with the right fist.)
One hammer, one hammer.

Johnny hammers with one hammer,
Then he hammers with two.

Johnny hammers with two hammers,
(Hammer with right and left fists.)
Two hammers, two hammers.
Johnny hammers with two hammers,
Then he hammers with three.
Then he goes to sleep. (Place folded hands under face.)

Heigh Ho the Derry O (Tune: "The Farmer in the Dell")

I'm riding on the bus, (Bounce up and down.)
I'm riding on the bus,
Heigh ho the derry o
I'm riding on the bus.

I hear the horns honking, (Make a beeping motion with hands.)
I hear the horns honking,
Heigh ho the derry o
I hear the horns honking.

I see the people walking, (Walk in place.)
I see the people walking,
Heigh ho the derry o,
I see the people walking.

I see the people jogging, (Jog in place.)
I see the people jogging,
Heigh ho the derry o,
I see the people jogging.

Here Is a House

Here is a house (Form a roof with hands over head.)
With an open door. (Open arms wide.)
Here are the windows, (Draw a square in the air.)
One, two, three, four. (Count with fingers.)

Here is the roof (Form a roof with hands over head.)
To keep warm and dry. (Hug yourself.)
Here is the chimney, (Raise arms higher as you say both lines.)
Way up high.
Here are the people, (Hold up both hands.)
So many, you see. (Wiggle fingers.)
And here is the place, (Form roof with hands over head.)
They like to be. (Nod "yes" and smile.)

Here's a Bunny

Here's a bunny with ears so funny. (Point to bunny's ears.)
And here's his hole in the ground. (Point to the table.)
A sound he hears,
And perks up his ears,
And pops right into the ground. (Make bunny go under the tabletop.)

Here They Are! (Tune: "Where Is Thumbkin?")

Where are your hands? Where are your hands?
Here they are! Here they are!
Clap them together. Clap them together.
Clap, clap, clap. Clap, clap, clap.
Where are your feet? Where are your feet?
Here they are! Here they are!
Stamp them on the floor. Stamp them on the floor.
Stamp, stamp, stamp. Stamp, stamp, stamp.

Hey, Diddle, Diddle

Hey, diddle, diddle the cat and the fiddle
The cow jumped over the moon.
The little dog laughed to see such sport,
And the dish ran away with the spoon.

Hickory, Dickory Dock

Hickory, dickory dock.
The mouse ran up the clock.
The clock struck one,
And down he'd run.
Hickory, dickory dock.

Hop a Little

Hop a little, jump a little,
One, two, three.
Run a little, clap a little,
Tap one knee.
Bend a little, stretch a little,
Wiggle your head.
Hop a little, jump a little

Houses, Houses, Everywhere! (Tune: "Twinkle, Twinkle Little Star")

Houses can be made of sticks.
Houses can be made of bricks.
Houses can be short or tall.
Houses can be big or small.
Houses here and houses there;
Houses, houses, everywhere!

I Am Eating (Tune: "Are You Sleeping?")

I am eating,
I am eating,
Something red, something red.
It is so delicious,
It is so delicious!
Yum, yum, yum,
Yum, yum, yum,

I Had a Little Turtle

I had a little turtle.
I kept him in a box. (Make a box shape with hands.)
He swam in the puddles, (Make swimming motions.)
And he climbed on the rocks. (Make climbing motions.)
He snapped at a mosquito. (Open and close hands quickly.)
He snapped at a flea. (Open and close hands quickly.)
He snapped at a minnow, (Open and close hands quickly.)
And he snapped at me! (Point to self.)
He caught the mosquito. (Clap hands.)
He caught the flea. (Clap hands.)
He caught the minnow. (Clap hands.)
But he didn't catch me! (Shake head and point to self.)

I'm Bringing Home a Baby Bumblebee

In bringing home a baby bumblebee, (Cup hands together.)
Won't my mommy be so proud of me? (Thumbs to chest.)
I'm bringing home a baby bumblebee— (Cup hands together.)
Ouch! He stung me! (Clap hands loudly.)

It's Raining, It's Pouring

It's raining. It's pouring,
The old man is snoring.
He snored so hard, he fell out of bed,
And bumped his head,
He couldn't get up in the morning.

I Wonder Where the Clouds All Go

When I look into the sky, (Hand on brow, looking up.)
I can see the clouds go by. (Flutter fingers.)
They don't ever make a sound (Put a finger to lips.)
Letting wind push them around. (Push with hands.)
Some go fast and some go slow. (Move hands fast, then slow.)
I wonder where the clouds all go. (Hand on brow, looking up.)

Jack and Jill

Jack and Jill went up the hill
To fetch a pail of water.
Jack fell down and broke his crown,
And Jill came tumbling after.

Jumped in the Boat (Tune: "Paw Paw Patch")

They jumped in the boat,
And the boat tipped over.
They jumped in the boat,
And the boat tipped over.
They jumped in the boat,
And the boat tipped over.
All the little boys and girls.

Jumping Feet

Jumping feet, jumping feet, jump, jump!
Up to the sky, away up high.
Jumping feet, jumping feet, jump, jump!

The Little Ducks

All the little ducklings (Squat and waddle like ducks.)
Line up in a row.
Quack, quack, quack,
And away they go.

They follow their mother (Children follow the leader.)
Waddling to and fro.
Quack, quack, quack,
And away they go.

They jump in the water, (Make a diving motion.)
And bob up and down. (Bob up and down.)

Quack, quack, quack,
They swim all around. (Make a swimming motion.)

London Bridge

London Bridge is falling down, (Make a bridge with clasped hands.)
Falling down, falling down. (Children walk under the bridge.)
London Bridge is falling down.
My fair lady (gentleman)! (Catch, hug, and release the last child.)

Mister Moon (Tune: "Where Is Thumbkin?")

O Mister Moon, Moon,
Bright and shiny Moon,
Won't you please,
Won't you please,
Shine down on me?
Shine down on me?
Won't you please?

O Mister Moon, Moon,
Bright and shiny Moon,
Won't you please,
Won't you please,
Set me fancy free?
Set me fancy free?
Won't you please?

The Moon Is Out Tonight

The moon is out tonight. (Make a big circle with arms.)
The stars are shining bright. (Wiggle fingers overhead.)
My mom says it's time for bed, (Rest head on hands.)
And she's right. Goodnight!

The Muffin Man

Oh, do you know the muffin man,
The muffin man, the muffin man?
Oh, do you know the muffin man,
Who lives in Drury Lane?

Oh, yes we know the muffin man,
The muffin man, the muffin man.
Oh, yes we know the muffin man,
Who lives on Drury Lane.

My Kitty

See my kitty,
My kitty has stripes.
My kitty wears pajamas,
Morning, noon, and night.

My Little Red Wagon (Tune: "Paw-Paw Patch")

Bumping along in my little red wagon.
Bumping along in my little red wagon.
Bumping along in my little red wagon,
All around the town.

The wheel fell off and the wagon tipped over.
The wheel fell off and the wagon tipped over.
The wheel fell off and the wagon tipped over,
Made me bump my head.

Oh, Do You Know Your Vegetables? (Tune: "The Muffin Man")

Oh, do you know your vegetables?
Vegetables, vegetables?
Oh, do you know your vegetables?
Veggies are so good for you!

Carrots, peas, and squash, and beans,
Broccoli, and salad greens,
Cabbage, corn, and tomatoes, too.
Veggies are so good for you!

Old MacDonald Had a Farm

Old MacDonald had a farm, E-I-E-I-O.
And on his farm he had some cows, E-I-E-I-O.
With a moo-moo here, and a moo-moo there,
Here a moo, there a moo, everywhere a moo-moo.
Old MacDonald had a farm, E-I-E-I-O.

Continue with other animals:
Duck...quack-quack
Pig...oink-oink
Horse...neigh-neigh, etc.

Old Mother Turtle (Tune: "Over in the Meadow")

Over in the meadow in the sand, in the sun,
Lived an old mother turtle and her little turtle one.
"Snap!' said the mother; "I snap!" said the one,
So they snapped and they snapped in the sand, in the sun.

One Elephant

One elephant went out to play,
Out on a spider's web one day.
He had such enormous fun,
He called for another elephant to come.

Over in the Meadow

Over in the meadow, in the water so blue,
Lived an old mother fish and her little fishes two.
"Swim!" said the mother. "We swim!" said the two.
So they swam and they swam in the water so blue.

Pat-a-Cake

Pat-a-cake, pat-a-cake, baker's man. (Clap hands.)
Bake me a cake as fast as you can.
Roll it, pat it and mark it with a "B." (Roll arms and pat hands.)
Put it in the oven for baby and me! (Hug self.)

Picking Some Big Ears (Tune: "Skip to My Lou")

Standing in the corn field out in the sun,
Picking some big ears one by one.
Cooking up the yellow corn, boy what fun!
Munching on sweet corn, yum, yum, yum!

Picking Up Potatoes (Tune: "The Paw Paw Patch")

Picking up potatoes and putting them in a basket,
Picking up potatoes and putting them in a basket,
Picking up potatoes and putting them in a basket,
Way down yonder in the potato patch!

Pop Goes the Bunny (Tune: "Pop Goes the Weasel")

'Round and 'round the cobbler's bench,
The monkey chased the bunny.
The monkey thought it was all in fun,'til
Pop! goes the bunny.

Rainbow Colors (Tune: "Twinkle, Twinkle Little Star")

When the rain falls from the sky,
Be sure to look way up high.
If the sun is shining there,
You will find a rainbow fair.
Red, orange, yellow, green, and blue,
And surely there's some purple. too.

Rain, Rain Go Away

Rain, rain go away,
Come again another day.
Rain, rain go away,
Little (child's name) wants to play.

Row, Row, Row, Your Boat

Row, row, row, your boat (Make rowing motions.)
Gently down the stream. (Wiggle fingers.)
Merrily, merrily, merrily, merrily, (Circle pointer in the air.)
Life is but a dream. (Place folded hands under face.)

Ring Around the Rosy

Ring around the rosy,
Pocket full of posies.
Ashes, ashes,
All fall down.

See the Wheels Go Round (Tune: "My Bonnie Lies Over the Ocean")

I love to play with my cars
And push them over the ground.
Sometimes I drive them on the sidewalks
And see the wheels go round,
Round, round, round, round.
I see the wheels go round, round, round,
Round, round, round, round.
I see the wheels go round.

Shake Your Shaker (Tune: "The Farmer in the Dell")

Shake your shaker high.
Shake your shaker low.
Shake it here and shake it there.
Now shake it by your toe!

Shaker Up (Tune: "Mary Had a Little Lamb')

Shaker, shaker, up, up, up (Shake bag above your head.)
Down, down, down. (Shake bag by knees.)
Up, up, up (Shake bag above your head.)
Shaker, shaker all around. (Turn in a circle.)
All around the town. (Shake bags in a big circle.)

Silly Face

These are my eye peepers, eye peepers, eye peepers.
These are my eye peepers. (Point to eyes.)
Now they're eye sleepers. (Close eyes.)
This is my nose beeper, nose beeper, nose beeper.
This is my nose beeper. (Point to nose.)
I can go beep! beep! beep! (Touch the nose.)
This is my mouth eater, mouth eater, mouth eater.
This is my mouth eater. (Point to the mouth.)
Munch! Munch! Munch! (Make chewing motions.)

The Store

This is the store. (Put finger tips together for a roof.)
This is the door. (Hold hands apart.)
The windows are shiny, (Pretend to polish windows.)
And so is the floor. (Pretend to polish the floor.)
Here we buy our food, (Pretend to eat.)
This is our favorite store. (Give a "thumbs up.")

The Sun

The sun gets up from its bed,
And marches across the sky all day.
At noon it stands right overhead,
And at night it goes away.

Swim, Swim, Quack, Quack (Tune: "My Bonnie Lies Over the Ocean')

Ducks like to swim in the water.
They stretch their webbed feet out in back.
Ducks like to swim in circles.
They swim and they swim, and they quack.
Swim, swim, quack, quack!
They swim and they swim, and they quack.
Swim, swim, quack, quack!
They swim and they swim, and they quack.

The Dump Truck Song (Tune: "The Wheels on the Bus")

The front end loader fills up the truck, (Scooping motion with both hands.)
Fills up the truck, fills up the truck.
The front-end loader fills up the truck,
At the construction site.

The dump truck dumps out the dirt, (Make a dumping motion with both hands.)
Dumps out the dirt, dumps out the dirt.
The dump truck dumps out the dirt,
At the construction site.

The driver of the dump truck waves hello, (Wave hello.)
Waves hello, waves hello.
The driver of the dump truck waves hello
At the construction site.

There's a Little Flower (Tune: "Have You Ever Seen a Lassie?")

There's a little flower,
A flower, a flower.
There's a little flower,
On my garden path.

A flower so neat,
It's a rose so sweet.
There's a little flower,
On my garden path.

There's an Animal (Tune: "Put Your Finger in the Air")

There's an animal on my head, on my head.
There's an animal on my head, on my head.
There's an animal on my head,
Oh, I wish I were in bed.
There's an animal on my head.

There's an animal on my nose, on my nose.
There's an animal on my nose, on my nose.
There's an animal on my nose,
Oh, I wish it smelled like a rose.
There's an animal on my nose, on my nose.

There's an animal on my knee, on my knee.
There's an animal on my knee, on my knee.
There's an animal on my knee,
Oh, I hope it's not a bee.
There's an animal on my knee.

This Cow (Touch children's fingers as you say the rhyme.)

This cow eats grass.
This cow eats hay.
This cow drinks water.
This cow runs away.
This cow just moos all day.

This Little Piggy

This little piggy went to market.
This little piggy stayed home.
This little piggy had roast beef.
This little piggy had none.
This little piggy cried, "Wee-wee, I can't find my way home!"

This Is My Turtle

This is my turtle, (Make a fist with thumb extended.)
He lives in a shell. (Hide thumb inside fist.)
He likes his home very well.
He pokes his head out
When he wants to eat. (Extend thumb.)
He pulls it back in
When he wants to sleep. (Hide thumb inside fist.)

This Is Our Neighborhood

This is our neighborhood where (child's name) lives.
This is our neighborhood where (child's name) lives.
Where is (child's name)? (Look all around.)
Where is (child's name)? (Look all around.)
Here he (she) is! (Hug named child.)
Here he (she) is! (Hug named child.)

This Is the Family

This is the father short and stout. (Thumb)
This is the mother with children about. (Index finger)
This is the brother, tall you see. (Middle finger)
This is the sister with a toy on her knee. (Ring finger)
This is the baby sure to grow. (Pinky finger)
And here is the family all in a row. (All five fingers)

This Is the Way (Tune: "The Mulberry Bush")

This is the way we hammer the nails, (Hammer one fist on top of the other fist.)
Hammer the nails, hammer the nails.
This is the way we hammer the nails,
On a bright and sunny morning.

This is the way we saw the wood, (Make sawing motion.)
Saw the wood, saw the wood.
This is the way we saw the wood,
On a bright and sunny morning.

This is the way we tighten the bolt, (Pretend to use a wrench.)
Tighten the bolt, tighten the bolt.
This is the way we tighten the bolt,
On a bright and sunny morning.

This is the way we shovel the dirt, (Pretend to shovel dirt.)
Shovel the dirt, shovel the dirt,
This is the way we shovel the dirt,
On a bright and sunny morning.

Thumb-in-the-Box

Thumb-in-the-Box, sit so still, (Make a fist by placing the thumb inside the fingers.)
Will you come out?
Yes, I will! (Pop thumb out of fist.)

Twinkle, Twinkle Little Star

Twinkle, Twinkle Little Star,
How I wonder what you are.
Up above the world so high,
Like a diamond in the sky.
Twinkle, Twinkle Little Star,
How I wonder what you are.

We Planted a Little Seed (Tune: "I'm a Little Teapot")

We planted a little seed in the dark, dark ground.
Out comes the warm sun, big and round.
Down comes the gentle rain, soft and slow.
Up comes the little seed, grow, seed, grow!

Wheels (Tune: "The Wheels on the Bus")

The wheels on the bus go round, and round,
Round and round, round and round.
The wheels on the bus go round and round,
All over town.

Winking Eyes

Here are my eyes,
One and two. (Point to eyes one at a time.)
I give a wink.
So can you! (Wink your eyes.)

References and Resources

Adams, C. & E. Fruge. (1996). *Why children misbehave.* Oakland, CA: New Harbinger.

Albrecht, K.M. & M. Ward. (1989). Growing pains. *Pre-K Today*, 36, 54-55.

American Public Health Association/American Academy of Pediatrics. (1992). *Caring for our children: National health and safety performance standards: Guidelines for out-of-home child care programs.* Washington, D.C: American Public Health Association/American Academy of Pediatrics.

Bailey, B. (1997). *I love you rituals.* Oviedo, FL: Loving Guidance.

Bailey, B. (1998). *10 principles of positive discipline.* Oviedo, FL: Loving Guidance.

Belsky, J. (1988). The "effects" of infant day care reconsidered. *Early Childhood Research Quarterly*, 3, 235-272.

Berk, L.E. (1994). Vygotsky's Theory: The importance of make-believe play. *Young Children,* 50(1), 30-39.

Bernhardt, J.L. (2000). A primary caregiving system for infants and toddlers: Best for everyone involved. *Young Children,* 55(2), 74-82,

Blecher-Sass, H. (1997). Good-byes can build trust. *Young Children*, 52(7), 12-15.

Bodrova, E. & D.J. Leong. (1995). *Tools of the mind: The Vygotskyian approach to early childhood education.* New York: Prentice Hall.

Brazelton, T. B. (1992). *Touchpoints: The essential reference.* Reading, MA: Addison-Wesley.

Bredekamp., S. (1987). *Developmentally appropriate practice in early childhood programs serving children from birth to age 8* (exp. ed.). Washington, DC: National Association for the Education of Young Children (NAEYC).

Bredekamp, S. & C. Copple. (1997). *Developmentally appropriate practice in early childhood programs,* Revised edition. Washington, DC: National Association for the Education of Young Children (NAEYC).

California Department of Education. (1990). *Flexible, fearful, or fiesty: The different temperaments of infants and toddlers* {videotape}. Sacramento, CA.

Carnegie Corporation of New York. (1994). *Starting Points: Meeting the needs of our youngest children.* New York: Carnegie Corporation of New York.

Carter, M. (2000). Literacy development: Back to the real basics. *Child Care Information Exchange,* 14-17.

Catlin, C. (1996). *More toddlers together: The complete planning guide for a toddler curriculum, volume II.* Beltsville, MD: Gryphon House.

Catlin, C. (1994). *Toddlers together: The complete planning guide for a toddler curriculum.* Beltsville, MD: Gryphon House.

Cherry, C. (1976). *Creative play for the developing child: Early lifehood education through play.* Belmont, CA: Fearon.

Chess, S. & A. Thomas. (1987). *Know your child.* New York: Basic Books.

Clark, S. (1996). Tips for feeding picky eaters. *Texas Child Care*, Winter, 2-7.

Cooper, P. (1993). *When stories come to school: Telling, writing, and performing stories in the early childhood classroom.* New York: Teachers and Writers.

Crary, E. (1993). *Without spanking or spoiling.* Seattle, WA: Parenting Press.

Curry, N.E. & C.N. Johnson. (1990). *Beyond self-esteem: Developing a genuine sense of human value.* Washington, DC: National Association for the Education of Young Children (NAEYC).

Dreikurs, R. (1964). *Children: The challenge.* New York: Hawthorne/Dutton.

Edwards, C., L. Gandini & G. Forman. (1994). *The one hundred languages of children: The Reggio Emilia approach to early childhood education.* Norwood, NJ: Ablex.

Edwards, C., L. Gandini & G. Forman. (1998). *The one hundred languages of children: The Reggio Emilia approach to early childhood education—advanced reflections.* Norwood, NJ: Ablex.

Erickson, E.H. (1950). *Childhood and society.* New York: Norton.

Erickson, E.H. (1963). *Childhood and society.* New York: Norton.

Fein, G.G., A. Gariboldi, & R. Boni. (1993). The adjustment of infants and toddlers to group care: The first six months. *Early Childhood Research Quarterly*, 8, 1-14.

Gardner, H. (1983). *Frames of the mind: The theory of multiple intelligences.* New York: Basic Books.

Gerber, M. (1979). *Resources for infant educarers: A manual for parents and professionals.* Los Angeles: Resources for Infant Educarers.

Gerber, M. & A. Johnson. (1998). *Your self-confident baby.* New York: Wiley.

Glenn, H. & J. Nelson. (1998). *Raising self-reliant children in a self-indulgent world.* Rocklin, CA: Prima Publishing.

Goleman, D. (1995). *Emotional intelligence.* New York: Bantam Doubleday Dell.

Goleman, D. (1998). *Working with emotional intelligence.* New York: Bantam Doubleday Dell.

Gordon, I. (1970). *Baby learning through baby play.* New York: St. Martin's.

Greenman, J. (1988). *Caring spaces, learning places: Children's environments that work.* Redmond, WA: Exchange Press.

Greenman, J. & A. Stonehouse. (1996). *Prime times: A handbook for excellence in infant and toddler care.* St. Paul, MN: Redleaf Press.

Greenspan, S. (1999). *The six experiences that create intelligence and emotional growth in babies and young children.* Reading, MA: Perseus Books.

Greenspan, S. & N.T. Greenspan. (1989). *The essential partnership.* New York: Penguin.

Greenspan, S. & N.T. Greenspan. (1989). *First feelings: Milestones in the emotional development of your baby and child.* New York: Penguin.

Hast, F. & A. Hollyfield. (1999). *Infant and toddler experiences.* St. Paul, MN: Redleaf.

Herr, J. & T. Swim. (1999). *Creative resources for infants and toddlers.* Albany, NY: Delmar.

Hitz, R. & A. Driscoll. (1988). Praise or encouragement?: New insights and implications for early childhood teachers. *Young Children*, 43(5), 6-13.

Honig, A.S. (1982). *Playtime learning games for young children.* Syracuse, NY: Syracuse University Press.

Honig, A. (1989). *Love and learn: Discipline for young children.* Washington, DC: National Association for the Education of Young Children (NAEYC).

Honig, A. (1995). Singing with infants and toddlers. *Young Children*, 50(5), 72-78.

Honig, A. & H.E. Brody. (1996). *Talking with your baby: Family as the first school.* Syracuse, NY: Syracuse University Press.

Howes, C. & C.E. Hamilton. (1992). Children's relationships with caregivers: Mothers and child care teachers. *Child Development.* 64, 859-866.

Ilg, L.B. & F.L. Ames. (1976). *Your two year old.* New York: Delacorte Press.

Katz, L. & P. McClellan. (1997). *Fostering social competence: The teacher's role.* Washington, DC; National Association for the Education of Young Children (NAEYC).

Kendrick, A.S., R. Kaufman, & K.P. Messinger. (1988). *Healthy young children: A manual for programs.* Washington, DC: National Association for the Education of Young Children (NAEYC).

Kovach, B.A. & D.A. Da Ros. (1998). Respectful, individual, and responsive caregiving for infants: The key to successful care in group settings. *Young Children*, 53(3), 61-64.

Lally, J.R. (1995). The impact of child care policies and practices on infant/toddler identity formation. *Young Children*, 51(1), 58-67.

Leach, P. (1997). *Your baby and child: From birth to five*. New York: Knopf.

Leavitt, R.L. (1994). *Power and emotion in infant-toddler day care*. Albany, NY: State University of New York Press.

Likona, T. (1994). *Raising good children*. New York: Bantam Doubleday Dell.

Marion, M. (1998). *Guidance of young children*. New York: Prentice Hall.

McMullen, M.B. (1999). Achieving best practices in infant and toddler care and education. *Young Children*, 54(4), 69-75.

Miller, K. (2000). *Ages and stages*. West Palm Beach, FL: TelShare.

Miller, K. (1984). *More things to do with toddlers and twos*. West Palm Beach, FL: Telshare.

Miller, K. (1984). *Things to do with toddlers and twos*. West Palm Beach, FL: Telshare.

Miller, K. (1999). *Simple steps: Developmental activities for infants, toddlers, and two-year-olds*. Beltsville, MD: Gryphon House.

Mitchell, G. (1998). *A very practical guide to discipline with young children*. West Palm Beach, FL: Telshare.

National Academy of Early Childhood Programs. (1991). *Accreditation criteria and procedures*. Washington, DC: National Academy of Early Childhood Programs.

National Association for the Education of Young Children. (1996). NAEYC position statement: Responding to linguistic and cultural diversity—Recommendations for effective early childhood education. *Young Children*, 51(2), 4-12.

Neugebauer, B. (1992). *Alike and different: Exploring our humanity with children*. Washington, DC: National Association for the Education of Young Children (NAEYC).

Neuman, S., C. Copple & S. Bredekamp. (2000). *Learning to Read and Write: Developmentally Appropriate Practices for Young Children*. Washington, DC: National Association for the Education of Young Children (NAEYC).

Okagaki, L. & K.E. Diamond. (2000). Responding to cultural and linguistic differences in the beliefs and practices of families with young children. *Young Children*, 55(1), 74-80.

Parten, M.B. (1932). Social participation among preschool children. *Journal of Abnormal Psychology*, 27, 243-269.

Pelegrini, A.S. & C.D. Glickman. (1990). Measuring kindergartners' social competence, *Young Children,* 45(4), 40-44.

Piaget, J. (1977). *The origins of intelligence in children*. New York: International Universities Press.

Piaget, J. (1962). *Play, dreams, and imitation in childhood*. (C. Gattegno & F.M. Hodgson, Trans.) New York: Norton.

Powell, D.R. (1998). Reweaving parents into the fabric of early childhood programs. *Young Children*, 53(5), 60-67.

Raikes, H. (1993). Relationship duration in infant care: Time with high-ability teacher and infant-teacher attachment. *Early Childhood Research Quarterly,* 8, 309-325.

Raikes, H. (1996). A secure base for babies: Applying attachment concepts to the infant care setting. *Young Children*. 51(5), 50-67.

Ratlev, M. (1994). Universal precautions in early intervention and child care. *Infants and children*, 6(3), 54-64.

Reisenberg, J. (1995). Reflections on quality infant care. *Young Children*, 50(6), 23-25.

Rockwell, R., D. Hoge & B. Searcy. (1999). *Linking language and literacy: Simple language and literacy throughout the curriculum*. Beltsville, MD: Gryphon House.

Rogers, C.S. & J.K. Sawyer. (1988). *Play in the lives of children*. Washington, D.C.: National Association for the Education of Young Children (NAEYC).

Schiller, P. (1999). *Start smart: Building brain power in the early years*. Beltsville, MD: Gryphon House.

Schweinhart, L. & D.P. Weikert. (1996). *Lasting differences: The High/Scope preschool curriculum comparison through age 23*. Monographs of the High/Scope Educational Research Foundation, #12, Ypsilanti, MI: High/Scope Press.

Shelov, S. (1998) *Caring for your baby and child*. New York: Bantam, Doubleday, Dell.

Shore, R. (1997). *Rethinking the brain: New insights into early development*. New York: Families and Work.

Silberg, J. (2000). *125 brain games for toddlers and twos*. Beltsville, MD: Gryphon House.

Silberg, J. (1993). *Games to play with toddlers.* Beltsville, MD: Gryphon House.

Silberg, J. (1993). *Games to play with two year olds*. Beltsville, MD: Gryphon House.

Silberg, J. (1996). *More games to play with toddlers*. Beltsville, MD: Gryphon House.

Stonehouse, A. (1988). *How does it feel?: Child care from a parent's perspective*. Redmond, WA: Exchange Press.

Tabors, P.O. (1998). What early childhood educators need to know: Developing programs for linguistically and culturally diverse children and families. *Young Children*, 53(6), 20-26.

Teaching Tolerance Project. (1997). *Starting small: Teaching tolerance in preschool and the early grades*. Montgomery, AL: Southern Poverty Law Center.

Wardle, F. (1995). How young children build images of themselves. *Child Care Information Exchange*, 104, 44-47.

Wong, D.L., M. Hockenberry-Eaton, M.L. Winkelstein, D. Wilson, & E. Ahmann. (1999). *Nursing care of infants and children*. New York: Mosby.

Index

10 Principles of Positive Discipline by Becky Bailey, 67
125 Brain Games for Toddlers and Twos by J. Silberg, 319, 308

18–24 months

cognitive development, 289
communicating, 283
construction possibilities, 79, 102–103, 172, 198–199, 268–269, 330–331, 330–331, 353–354, 414–415, 436, 493–494, 515
curiosity possibilities, 77, 100–102, 169–170, 197, 243–245, 267–268, 329–330, 412–413, 434–435, 492–493, 513–514
dramatic possibilities, 74, 96, 166, 194–195, 238–240, 264, 326–327, 350–351, 410, 432–433, 490–491, 510–511
exploring roles, 217
expressing feelings, 455
food guide, 381
language behaviors, 286
literacy possibilities, 79–80, 103–104, 173, 199–201, 246–247, 269–270, 331–333, 415–417, 437–438, 494–497, 516–519
making friends, 123
motor skills, 371
movement possibilities, 83, 107, 177–178, 202–204, 250–251, 273, 335–337, 357, 419–420, 441–443, 499–500, 522
music possibilities, 81–82, 105–106, 175–177, 201, 249–250, 271–272, 333–334, 355, 417–419, 439–441, 497–498, 519–521
outdoor possibilities, 84–85, 108–109, 204, 252–253, 274–275, 358–359, 420–422, 443–444, 500–501, 523–524
problem-solving, 369
project possibilities, 86–87, 110, 181–182, 205–206, 254, 275, 337, 359–360, 422, 445, 501, 525
sensory/art possibilities, 75–76, 98–99, 168, 195–197, 240–242, 265–266, 327–328, 351–352, 75–76
transitioning to school, 39

24–30 months

communicating, 283
construction possibilities, 79, 102–103, 172, 268–269, 330–331, 330–331, 353–354, 414–415, 436, 493–494, 515
curiosity possibilities, 78, 100–102, 170–171, 197–198, 243–245, 267–268, 329–330, 412–413, 434–435, 492–493, 514
dramatic possibilities, 74, 96, 166–167, 194, 238–240, 264, 326–327, 350–351, 410, 432–433, 490–491, 510
exploring roles, 217
expressing feelings, 455
food guide, 381

language behaviors, 287
literacy possibilities, 80–81, 103–105, 174, 199–200, 246–247, 269–270, 331–333, 415–417, 437–438, 494–497, 516–519
making friends, 123
motor skills, 371
movement possibilities, 83–84, 107, 178–179, 202–204, 250–251, 273, 335–337, 357–358, 419–420, 441–443, 499–500, 522
music possibilities, 82–83, 105–106, 175–177, 201, 249–250, 271–272, 333–334, 355–356, 417–419, 439–441, 497–498, 519–521
outdoor possibilities, 85, 108–109, 180–181, 205, 252–253, 274–275, 358–359, 420–422, 443–444, 500–501, 523–524
problem-solving, 369
project possibilities, 86–87, 110, 181–182, 205–206, 254, 275, 337, 359–360, 422, 445, 501, 525
sensory/art possibilities, 75–77, 98–99, 168–169, 195–197, 240–242, 265–266, 327–328, 351
transitioning to school, 39

30–36 months

communicating, 283
construction possibilities, 79, 102–103, 172, 199, 268–269, 330–331, 353–354, 414–415, 436–437, 493–494, 515
curiosity possibilities, 78, 100–102, 171–172, 198, 243–245, 267–268, 329–330, 412–414, 434–436, 492–493, 514
dramatic possibilities, 75, 97, 167, 194–195, 238–240, 264, 326–327, 350–351, 410–411, 432–433, 490–491, 510–511
exploring roles, 217
expressing feelings, 455
food guide, 381
language behaviors, 287
literacy possibilities, 81, 103–105, 174–175, 199–200, 246–247, 269–270, 331–333, 415–417, 437–439, 494–497, 516–519
making friends, 123
motor skills, 371
movement possibilities, 84, 107–108, 179–180, 202–204, 250–251, 273, 335–337, 357, 419–420, 441–443, 499–500, 522
music possibilities, 82–83, 105–106, 175–177, 201–202, 249–250, 271–272, 333–334, 356–357, 417–419, 439–441, 497–498, 519–521
outdoor possibilities, 85–86, 108–109, 181, 205, 252–253, 274–275, 358–359, 420–422, 443–444, 500–501, 523–524
problem-solving, 369
project possibilities, 86–87, 110, 181–182, 254–255, 275, 337, 359–360, 422, 445, 501, 525
sensory/art possibilities, 75–77, 98–100, 195–197, 240–242, 265–266, 327–328, 169, 351
transitioning to school, 39

2–7 years

cognitive development, 289

A

Accidents
parent postcard, 447–448
"Achieving Best Practices in Infant and Toddler Care," by M. B. McMullen, 141
Adams, C., 390, 484
"The Adjustment of Infants and Toddlers to Group Care," by G. G. Fein, A. Gariboldi, & R. Boni, 140
Ads, 166, 189, 437, 452
Aftershave, 142
Ages and Stages by K. Miller, 57, 67, 402
Aggression, 462–463
parent postcard, 477
Albrecht, Ward, 134
Alfie's Feet by Shirley Hughes, 509, 531
Alike and Different by B. Neugebauer, 57, 227
Allergies, 194, 337
Alligators
felt, 516, 532
Aluminum foil, 238, 241, 243, 260, 267, 279, 518, 533
boats, 514
American Academy of Pediatrics, 383, 385
Ames, F. L., 136
Anecdotal note, 21, 470
calendar, 228
Animals. See also Big animals possibilities plan; Little animals possibilities plan
block figures, 414, 422, 427, 506
felt, 532
homes, 326–327, 332, 336, 350–351
pictures, 343, 493, 496, 506
plastic, 259, 328, 330–331, 345, 351, 353, 359, 366, 494, 501, 504, 506, 517, 532
shapes, 327, 334, 336, 345
stuffed, 25, 108–109, 116, 119, 259, 260, 232, 326, 336, 337, 345, 350–351, 366, 490, 504, 506
water, 526
Apples, 194, 211
plastic, 350
shapes, 202
Aprons, 416, 427
construction, 410, 425
Architectural blocks, 421, 427
Are You My Mother? by P. D. Eastman, 349, 364

Art possibilities
18–24 months, 75–76, 98–99, 168, 195–197, 240–242, 265–266, 327–328, 351–352, 75–76
24–30 months, 75–77, 98–99, 168–169, 195–197, 240–242, 265–266, 327–328, 351
30–36 months, 75–77, 98–100, 195–197, 240–242, 265–266, 327–328, 169, 351
big animals, 327–328
construction, 411-412
fruits and vegetables, 195–197
introduction to, 25–26
little animals, 351–352
me and my body, 75–77
my family, 98–100
my neighborhood, 168–169
sky, 265–266
space, 240–242
storybook characters, 491-492
water, 511-513
wheels, 433-434
Assessment
communicating, 282–283
comparisons, 19
developmentally appropriate practice, 19–21
exploring roles, 217
expressing feelings, 454–455
facilitating attachment, 51
giving feedback, 22
introduction to, 14, 18–22
making friends, 122–123
problem-solving, 368–369
toddlers, 42–43
transitioning to school, 38–39
using strategies, 21
Autonomy
parent postcard, 423–424

B

Baby formula, 381
Baby Learning Through Play by I. Gordon, 57, 141
Baby powder containers, 511, 533
Bags
beach, 264
diaper, 96
fast food, 167, 174
grocery, 97, 120, 166, 181–182, 186, 189, 194, 211, 332, 437, 452
money, 186
paper, 178, 189, 330, 337
plastic, 386
resealable, 81, 104, 119, 171, 174, 182, 188, 200, 245, 260, 360, 517–518, 532
shoe, 90
shopping, 90
tote, 109, 120, 207
Balance beams, 403
Balance scales, 330
Balls
sock, 252
soft, 86, 92
yarn, 252
Bananas, 194
flavoring, 198
plastic, 350
Banners, 391
developmental, 475
Baskets, 74, 92, 175, 198, 204, 211, 350, 358, 366, 406
berry, 197, 205, 514, 525, 530, 533
laundry, 86, 92
shopping, 186, 194
Bathtub mats, 77, 241, 260
Beach chairs, 264, 279
Beach towels, 264, 277, 279
Beach umbrellas, 264, 279
Beads, 170, 189, 512–513, 532
Beanbags, 252, 442, 451
Beans, 82, 92, 103, 120, 381
Bear's Bicycle by Emilie McCloud, 431, 450
Bear's Busy Family by Stella Blackstone, 95, 117
Bears, 329, 334, 336
puppets, 332, 495, 506
puzzles, 333, 345
shapes, 336
stuffed, 259, 260, 326, 343, 345, 490, 504, 506
Bedrova, E., 308
Beds, 96, 119
Bells, 82, 92, 170, 186, 189
Belsky, J., 50
Berk, L. E., 126
Bernhardt, J. L., 128
Berries, 329
plastic, 205
Berry baskets, 197, 205, 514, 525, 530, 533
Beyond Self-Esteem by N. E. Curry & C. N. Johnson, 227
Bicycle Race by Donald Crew, 431, 450
Bicycles
helmets, 432, 452
wheels, 449
Big animals possibilities plan
concepts learned, 342
construction possibilities, 330–331
curiosity possibilities, 329–330
dramatic possibilities, 326–326
literacy possibilities, 331–333
movement possibilities, 335
music possibilities, 333–334
outdoor possibilities, 336–337
parent participation, 337–338
parent postcards, 338–341

project possibilities, 337
resources, 325, 343–346
sensory/art possibilities, 326–327
web, 323
Big Red Barn by Margaret Wise Brown, 489, 504–505
The Biggest Nose by Kathy Caple, 325, 344
The Biggest Truck by David Lyon, 409, 426
Biting, 136–139, 462–463
anticipation, 137
dealing with parents, 138–139
guidelines, 138
parent postcards, 144–155
prevention, 136
shadowing, 137
social skills, 137–138
substitution, 137
three types, 136
Blankets, 96, 117, 119, 326, 364, 366, 404
Bleach, 303, 386, 405
Block figures, 414, 427
Blocks, 26, 27, 68, 70, 92, 178, 189, 255, 414, 420, 427, 436, 451, 515
architectural, 421, 427
box, 198–199
cardboard, 422
foam, 68, 159
homemade, 87
milk cartons, 422
picture, 79
plastic, 421, 427, 493, 506
shoebox, 422
Styrofoam, 422
tree, 374
castle, 374
unit, 374, 422
wooden, 102, 119, 493, 506
Blueberries for Sal by Robert McCloskey, 325, 344
Boats, 512, 515, 530, 532
aluminum foil, 514
plastic, 514
plastic, 517, 532
Bones, rubber, 108, 120
Books, 27–28, 68, 72, 304, 320, 404, 526 (See also Resources)
farm, 343
for parents, 67, 157, 319
homemade, 58, 79, 81, 104–105, 173, 200, 247–248, 269–260, 415–417, 437–438, 495–496, 517
zoo, 343
Boots
rubber, 167, 186, 189, 239, 259, 260, 264, 278, 279, 510, 529, 533
space, 239
work, 410, 421, 425, 490, 504, 506
Bottles
2-liter, 99, 103, 170, 289, 240, 260
baby 96, 117, 119
plastic, 82, 92, 120, 169, 171, 182, 189, 243–244, 260, 313, 330, 351, 366, 512–514, 530, 533
spray, 202, 274, 303, 492, 506, 512, 533
squirt, 513, 533
suntan lotion, 264, 277, 279
Bowls, 98, 119, 166, 181, 188, 244, 265, 267, 337, 352, 366, 490, 492, 504, 506, 524, 530
fish, 351, 366
Boxes, 67, 79, 87, 93, 101, 102, 120, 255, 351, 366
cereal, 171, 182, 189
copy paper, 97, 120, 253, 260
cracker, 103, 120
dog food, 108, 120
food, 97, 116, 166, 171, 182, 189, 198–199, 351, 366
large, 108–110, 120, 167, 181–182, 189, 238, 239, 252, 260, 313, 336, 490, 491, 506, 510, 523, 533
lunch, 96, 117, 410, 421, 425, 427
money, 432, 449, 451, 452
muffin mix, 166, 189
oatmeal, 255, 260
pizza, 186, 198, 452
shoe, 101, 120, 167, 172, 182, 189, 198, 255, 260, 437, 438, 452
small, 353
turtle food, 351, 366
A Boy, a Dog, and a Frog by Mercer Mayer, 509, 531
Brain development
parent postcards, 361–362
Brain-based care, 295–297
Brazelton, T. B., 129–130, 402, 471, 474, 484
Bread and Jam for Frances by Russell Hoban, 95, 117
Bredekamp, S., 19–20, 47, 290–291, 308
Briefcases, 96, 117
Bringing the Rain to Kapiti Plain by Verna Aardema, 263, 278, 509, 518, 529, 531
Brody, H. E., 308
Brown Bear, Brown Bear, What Do You See? by Bill Martin, Jr., 325, 344, 489, 495, 505
Brushes, 259, 260
scrub, 502, 506, 530
Bubble makers, 525
Bubble mix, 197, 533
recipe, 535
Bubble wrap, 76, 77, 92
Buckets, 252, 260, 277, 343, 492, 493, 501, 523, 530
Bulldozers, 415, 421, 427
Bus driver clothes, 432
Busy boxes, 26
Butcher paper, 75–76, 92, 206, 254, 260, 279, 327, 337, 345, 350, 366, 419, 427, 436, 445, 451, 494, 501, 506, 515
Butter, 381
tubs, 206
Buttermilk, 265

C

California State Dept. of Education, 44
Cameras, 111, 167, 188, 255, 337, 345
  disposable, 142, 182
Caps for Sale by Esphyr Slobodkina, 349, 364
Caps, 364, 366
Cardboard, 77, 79, 81, 92, 99, 120, 168, 189, 197, 260, 279, 308, 329, 345, 411, 412, 415, 427, 452, 517, 532
  bear shapes, 336
  blocks, 422
  box lids, 195
  circles, 186, 241, 436
  corrugated, 173
  fruit shapes, 202, 205, 211
  moon shapes, 254
  squares, 275
  stars, 240, 249, 254
  steering wheels, 432, 449
  sun shapes, 273
  tubes, 99, 101, 120, 249, 255, 260, 267, 279, 350, 366, 510, 518, 533
Caring for Your Baby and Child by S. Shelov, 402
Carnegie Task Force, 50
Carpeting, 70
  roads, 353, 366
  rolls, 350, 366
  scraps, 77
The Carrot Seed by Ruth Krauss, 199, 206, 211, 212
Carrots, 199, 206, 211, 358, 366
  plastic, 364, 366
  shapes, 202
Cars, 52, 353, 366, 422, 433, 434, 439, 444, 451
  magazines, 452
  police, 185
  tires, 443, 449, 452
Carter, Margie, 308
Carts, 158
  shopping, 97, 166, 188, 432, 451
  storage, 432, 451
Cash registers, 166, 186, 188, 194, 211
Cassette tapes, 28, 111, 119, 238, 309, 336, 345, 414, 427, 502
  classical music, 499, 506
  instrumental music, 273
  Star Wars music, 250
Castle blocks, 374
Cat in the Hat by Dr. Seuss, 73, 91, 95, 116–117
Catalogs, 80, 92, 320, 506
Caterpillars
  puppets, 495–496, 504
Cats, 351
  stuffed, 109
CD players, 250, 273, 336, 499
CDs, 28, 336
  classical music, 499, 506
  instrumental music, 273
  Star Wars music, 250
Cellophane, 268, 279
Cement trucks, 421, 427
Cereal, 352, 366, 381
  boxes, 171, 182, 189, 198
Chairs, 320,70, 432, 451, 490, 506
  beach, 264, 279
Chalk, 265, 320, 331, 345, 439, 451
  colored, 328, 345
Chalkboard, 439, 451
Changing papers, 385
Changing table, 385–386
Chart paper, 270, 279, 332, 345
Charts, 320
Cheese, 381, 434
Chef's hat, 211
Cherish Me by Joyce Thomas, 73, 91
Chess, S., 43, 57
Chicken Soup with Rice by Maurice Sendak, 489, 505
Child development
  attachment, 42–43
  brain, 284–285, 315–317
  communicating, 284–294
  creativity, 4612–462
  emotional, 456–457, 459–461
  exploring roles, 218–221
  expressing feelings, 456–457
  intellectual, 287–289
  introduction to, 14, 22
  language, 285–287
  literacy, 290–292
  making friends, 124–127
  Parten, 125
  physical, 370–371
  Piaget, 124–125
  play, 124–127
  principles, 40–41
  problem-solving, 370–373
  self-concept, 218–219
  stimulating growth, 297–299
  temperament, 43–45
  toddler characteristics, 42
  toilet training, 371–373
  transitioning to school, 40–45
  Vygotsky, 126
Childhood and Society by E. H. Erickson, 140, 227
Children: The Challenge by R. Dreikurs, 390
"Children's Relationships with Caregivers," by C. Howes & C. E. Hamilton, 141
Choke tubes, 386
Clark, S., 381, 390
Clay, 320
Climbers, 69, 159, 402–404
Clipboards, 166, 188
Clocks, 259, 260

pictures, 354, 366
Cloud Book by Tomie dePaola, 263, 278
Coats
rain, 167, 186, 189, 264, 278, 279, 510, 529, 533
suit, 91, 96, 117
Coffee cans, 493, 506
Coffee filters, 512, 533
Colanders, 514, 530, 533
Collage materials, 110, 120, 168, 189
Color Farm by Lois Ehlert, 325, 344
Color Fun by Deni Brown, 193, 211, 212
Combs, 259, 260
Communicating, 18, 281–366
child development, 284–294
environments, 319–321
interactive experiences, 294–295
introduction, 281–282
observation/assessment, 282–283
parent partnerships, 308–309
parent postcards, 308–318
possibilities plans, 323–366
resources, 308, 319
teacher competencies, 307
teaching innovations, 295–308
with parents, 468
Communication sheets, 21–22, 58, 305, 309, 386–387, 389, 391, 471
Computer paper, 385
Concepts learned
big animals, 342
construction, 425
fruits and vegetables, 210
introduction to, 30–31
little animals, 363
me and my body, 90
my family, 116
my neighborhood, 185
sky, 277
space, 258
storybook characters, 504
water, 529
wheels, 449
Conferences, 467–472
as education, 468–469
formal, 469–470
formal/oral, 471
informal, 470
informal/oral, 471–472
reconceptualizing, 469
Confetti, 244, 260
foil, 514, 532
Construction possibilities
18–24 months, 79, 102–103, 172, 198–199, 268–269, 330–331, 330–331, 353–354, 414–415, 436, 493–494, 515
24–30 months, 79, 102–103, 172, 268–269, 330–331, 330–331, 353–354, 414–415, 436, 493–494, 515
30–36 months, 79, 102–103, 172, 199, 268–269, 330–331, 353–354, 414–415, 436–437, 493–494, 515
big animals, 330–331
construction, 414–415
fruits and vegetables, 198–199
introduction to, 27
little animals, 353–354
me and my body, 79
my family, 102–103
my neighborhood, 172
sky, 268–269
space, 172
storybook characters, 493–494
water, 515
wheels, 436–437
Construction aprons, 410, 425
Construction magazines, 425
Construction paper, 170, 181, 186, 189, 200, 242, 254, 260, 266, 279, 355, 366, 437, 451, 515, 515, 532
Construction possibilities plan, 172, 407–428
construction possibilities, 414–415
curiosity possibilities, 412–414
dramatic possibilities, 410–411
literacy possibilities, 415–417
movement possibilities, 419–420
music possibilities, 417–419
outdoor possibilities, 420–422
parent participation, 422–423
parent postcards, 423–424
project possibilities, 422
resources, 409, 426–428
sensory/art possibilities, 411–412
web, 407
Construction site mats, 426
Construction vehicles, 70, 414, 416, 419, 421–422, 426–427, 451
Contact paper, 79, 92, 102, 103, 119, 168, 172, 182, 188, 267, 279, 308, 333, 345, 427
colored, 518, 532
Containers, 267, 303, 337
baby powder, 511, 533
deli, 514, 533
fast food, 167, 189, 238, 514, 533
margarine, 206, 514, 530
plastic, 274, 279
Cookies, 111, 381, 475
boxes, 198
cutters, 168, 189
sheets, 168, 189
Cooling racks, 100
Cooper, P., 304, 308
Copier machine, 79, 101, 110, 120, 167
Copple, C. 19–20, 47, 308, 290–291

Copy Cat! by Deborah Chancellor, 73, 91
Copy paper boxes, 120, 253, 260
Corduroy by Don Freeman, 489, 505
Corn syrup, 525
Corn
  on the cob, 194, 195, 203
  plastic, 203
Cornmeal, 101, 119
Cornstarch, 265, 279, 524, 533
Cots, 490, 506
Cotton
  balls, 198
  batting, 77
Coveralls, 239, 259, 260
Cows, 335
  flannel, 247, 260
  plastic, 259, 260
Crackers, 381, 434, 475
  boxes, 103, 120, 198
Craft knives, 97, 101, 119, 181, 197, 238–240, 245, 249, 252–253, 260, 329, 336, 345, 351–352, 366, 490–491, 493, 506, 523, 532
Craft sticks, 269, 532
Cranes, felt, 516, 532
Crary, E., 390
Crayons, 26, 92, 98, 166, 174, 188, 253, 305, 320, 331, 345, 425, 427, 434, 438, 451
Creative Resources for Infants and Toddlers by J. Herr & T. Swim, 34, 319
Creativity, 461–462
Crepe paper, 250, 260, 499, 500, 506, 523
Cups
  measuring, 169, 189, 267
  paper, 329, 352, 366, 421, 427, 532
  plastic, 98, 119, 196, 211, 238, 260, 274, 279, 353, 514, 530
Curiosity possibilities
  18–24 months, 77, 100–102, 169–170, 197, 243–245, 267–268, 329–330, 412–413, 434–435, 492–493, 513–514
  24–30 months, 78, 100–102, 170–171, 197–198, 243–245, 267–268, 329–330, 412–413, 434–435, 492–493, 514
  30–36 months, 78, 100–102, 171–172, 198, 243–245, 267–268, 329–330, 412–414, 434–436, 492–493, 514
  big animals, 329–330
  construction, 412–414
  fruits and vegetables, 197–198
  introduction to, 26–27
  little animals, 352-353
  me and my body, 77–78
  my family, 100–102
  my neighborhood, 169–172
  sky, 267–268
  space, 243–245
  storybook characters, 492–493
  water, 513–514
  wheels, 434–436
Curious George by H. A. and Margaret Rey, 349, 364
Curriculum planning process, 32–36
  observation, 34–36
Curry, N. E., 19, 219, 227
Curtains, 74, 92, 413, 435, 452
  shower, 78, 274, 279
Cushions, 69, 402–403
Cutting board, 196, 206

D

Da Ros, D. A., 51, 129, 130
Deep in the Forest by Brinton Turkel, 325, 344
Deli containers, 515, 533
Delivery props, 443, 452
Description, 297
Developmental assessment instruments, 22
Developmental challenges, 306–307
Developmental tasks, 18 (See also Child Development)
Developmentally Appropriate Practice in Early Childhood Programs by S. Bredekamp & Copple, C., 57
Diamond, K. E., 308
Diaper bags, 96, 117, 119
Diapering, 70, 385–386, 404
  disposable gloves, 385
Dirt, 181, 189, 403, 411, 420, 492
  red, 241
Discipline
  biting, 136–139, 462–462
  exploring roles, 225–226
  expressing feelings, 462–467
  limit-setting, 465
  making friends, 133–139
  managing aggression, 462–463, 477
  natural consequences, 378–379
  oppositional behavior, 463–466, 478–479
  problem-solving, 133–135, 378–380
  setting limits, 379–380
  temper tantrums, 466–467, 480–483
  transitioning to school, 54–55
Dish mops, 99, 120
Dishes, 195, 211
  shallow, 206
Dishpans, 181, 188, 189, 510, 525, 532
Dishwashing soap, 525
Distraction, 54
Documentation
  formal conferences, 469–470
  informal conferences, 470
Dogs in Space by Nancy Coffelt, 237, 248, 259

Dogs, 351
dishes, 108, 120
food boxes, 108, 120
stuffed, 108–109, 119
Dollhouses, 259, 260
Dolls, 25, 68, 96, 97, 100, 117, 119, 510, 532
clothes, 117
Don't Forget the Bacon by Pat Hutchins, 165, 187
Doughnuts for dad breakfast, 228
Dramatic possibilities, 169–172
18–24 months, 74, 96, 166, 194–195, 238–240, 264, 326–327, 350–351, 410, 432–433, 490–491, 510–511
24–30 months, 74, 96, 166–167, 194, 238–240, 264, 326–327, 350–351, 410, 432–433, 490–491, 510
30–36 months, 75, 97, 167, 194–195, 238–240, 264, 326–327, 350–351, 410–411, 432–433, 490–491, 510–511
big animals, 326–327
construction, 410–411
emotional development, 459
fruits and vegetables, 194–195
introduction to, 25
little animals, 350–351
me and my body, 74–75
my family, 96–97
my neighborhood, 166–167
sky, 264
space, 238–240
storybook characters, 490–491
water, 510–511
wheels, 432–433
Dreikurs, R., 390
Dress-up clothes, 25, 73, 91, 96, 117, 120, 167, 343, 432, 490, 501, 504, 506
Dress-Up Time! by Tom Arna, 73, 91
Driscoll, A., 227
Driver's uniform, 451
cap, 451
Drive-time activities, 208
Dryer sheets, 516, 533
Ducks
masks, 529
prop box, 509, 529
puppets, 499, 529
rubber, 492, 494, 506, 529
Duct tape, 76, 92, 100, 119, 238, 240, 260
Dump trucks, 415, 421, 427
Duplos, 374

E

Easels, 98, 119, 205, 320
Edwards, C., 27, 131, 140, 233
The Effects of Infant Day Care Reconsidered by J. Belsky, 57
Eggs, 381
cartons, 77
plastic, 343
Elastic, 197, 327, 345
Electrician's tape, 169, 189
Elephants, 326–327–328, 331, 333, 335–337
puppets, 345
toys, 345
Embroidery hoops, 525, 533
Emotional development, 456–457
facilitating, 459–461
E*motional Intelligence* by D. Goleman, 308, 474
Emotional intelligence, 301–302
Encouragement, 225–226
Envelopes, 167, 174, 189
Environments
accessible toys, 158–159
centers vs. experiences, 69–70, 161, 234, 321, 405, 486
characteristics, 484485
climbers, 69, 159
communicating, 319–321
cues and props, 231–233
exploring roles, 231–234
expressing feelings, 484–485
introduction to, 24
literacy-rich, 320–321
making friends, 157–161
meltdown places, 67–68
mirrors, 233–234
multiple intelligences, 319–320
multiple levels, 159
outdoor, 402–404
parallel play, 231
problem-solving, 402–405
room arrangement, 486
sanitation, 404–405
toy safety, 233
transitioning to school, 67–70
Erickson, E. H., 129, 219, 227
The Essential Partnership by S. Greenspan & N.T. Greenspan, 57, 227
Expansion plus, 298
Exploring roles, 18, 215–279
child development, 218–221
environments, 231–234
interactive experiences, 221
introduction, 215–216
observation/assessment, 217
parent partnerships, 227–230
parent postcards, 229–230, 257, 276
possibilities plans, 235–279
resources, 227, 259–260, 277–279
teacher competencies, 226

teaching innovations, 222–227
Expressing feelings, 18, 453–533
child development, 456–457
environments, 484–485
interactive experiences, 457–458
introduction, 453–454
observation/assessment, 454–455
parent partnerships, 474–475
parent postcards, 475–483
possibilities plans, 487–533
resources, 474
teacher competencies, 473–474
teaching innovations, 459–474
Expressive language, 287

F

Fabric, 425
felt, 110, 120, 168, 173, 189, 270, 279, 345, 438
paint pens, 239, 260
scraps, 173, 240, 260
textured, 77
trim, 110
Fall by Chris L. Demarest, 193, 211, 212
Family diversity, 47–48
Family interviews, 58
Family-centered practices, 224–225
Farm Morning by David McPhail, 325, 344
Fast food
bags, 167, 174
containers, 167, 189, 238, 514, 533
Fearful children, 44
Feeding dishes, 117, 351
Feisty children, 44
Felt board, 176
Felt, 173, 270, 279, 345, 438, 451, 516
animals, 532
Jack & Jill characters, 519, 532
scraps, 110, 120, 168, 189
Fences, 205, 353, 524
chain-link, 108
plastic, 330, 345
Film, 337, 345
Finger paints, 26, 99, 119, 168, 188, 241, 260, 320, 491, 506
Finger sucking. See Thumb sucking
Fingerplays, 28, 422–433
"Finger Family," 95, 107–108
"Five Little Rockets," 237, 250–251, 259
"Five Little Trucks," 431, 443, 450
"Monkeys Jumping on the Bed," 349, 356–357, 365
"The Store," 165, 178, 187
"This Cow," 325, 335, 344
"This Is My Turtle," 349, 357, 365
"This Is the Family," 95, 107, 118
"Thumb in the Box," 73, 83, 91
Fire Fighters by Norma Simon, 165, 186–187
Fire Truck (Box Car Series), 165, 186–187
Firefighter helmets, 186
Fireman Small to the Rescue by Wong Herbert Lee, 165, 186–187
First Feelings by S. Greenspan & N.T. Greenspan, 141, 464, 474
Fish Is Fish by Leo Leonni, 509, 531
Fish, 381, 501, 526
bowls, 351, 366
plastic, 518, 532
toy, 515
Flannel board, 173, 188, 247, 260, 270, 279, 345, 516, 519, 532
Flashlights, 185, 186, 364, 366
Flexible children, 44
Flexible, Fearful, or Feisty by the California Dept. of Education, 57
Floor time, 460–461
Flour, 101, 119, 168, 267, 279
pans, 320
Flowerpots, 500, 506, 533
Flowers
coffee filter, 512
magazines, 506
Foam blocks, 68, 159
Foil confetti, 514, 532
Food
allergies, 194, 337
boxes, 97, 103, 116, 120, 166, 182, 189, 198–199, 351, 366
cardboard shapes, 211
coloring, 169, 189, 243, 260, 265, 274, 279, 359, 366, 524
flavorings, 76, 92, 197–198
guide, 381
plastic, 211
Forman, G., 27, 131, 140, 233
Fostering Social Competence by E. Katz & P. McClellan, 141, 227
Franklin in the Dark by Paulette Bourgeois, 349, 364
Freezer, 244
Friends. See Making friends
Froggy Gets Dressed by Jonathan London, 73, 91
Frogs, 526
felt, 516, 532
masks, 529
prop box, 509, 529
puppets, 511, 529, 532
rubber, 529
Front-end loaders, 415, 427
Fruge, E., 390, 484
Fruit crates, 199
Fruits and vegetables possibilities plan
concepts learned, 210

construction possibilities, 198–199
curiosity possibilities, 197–198
dramatic possibilities, 194–195
literacy possibilities, 199–201
movement possibilities, 202–204
music possibilities, 201–202
outdoor possibilities, 204–205
parent participation, 207
parent postcards, 208–209
project possibilities, 205–206
resources, 193, 211–212
sensory/art possibilities, 195–197
web, 191
Fruits, 194, 196, 345, 381
flavorings, 198
pictures, 200, 206
plastic, 199, 205, 350, 366
shapes, 202, 205
snacks, 207
Funnels, 98, 119, 524, 530
Furniture, 70, 404, 490

G

Games to Play with Toddlers by J. Silberg, 34, 319
Games to Play with Two Year Olds by J. Silberg, 34, 319
Gandini, L., 27, 131, 140
Garden hose, 167, 186, 189, 274, 279, 523
Gardening containers, 199, 211, 533
Gardening tools, 343, 490, 500, 504, 506
Gender role stereotyping, 257
Gerber, M., 53, 57, 129, 130, 140–141, 158, 297
Gerbils, 351, 360
Gift wrap, 87, 142
tubes, 267, 279
The Gigantic Turnip by Aleksei Tolstoy, 193, 212
Glitter, 243, 244, 260, 313, 513, 532
Gloves, 80, 91, 93
disposable, 385
work, 421, 504
Glue, 77, 79, 81, 82, 92, 99, 101–105, 110, 119, 166, 169–174, 176, 181, 188, 200, 242–244, 247, 249, 260, 269, 275, 313, 330, 337, 345, 366, 412, 415, 416, 427, 437–438, 451, 501, 506, 512–513, 517–518, 532
sticks, 76, 92, 206, 248, 254
Goldilocks and the Three Bears by James Marshall, 489, 490, 505
Goleman, D., 301–302, 308, 474
Gone Fishing by Earlene Long, 95, 117, 509, 531
Goodnight Moon by Margaret Wise Brown, 237, 248, 259
Gordon, I., 53, 130
Gradual enrollment, 48–49, 58
Grandfather Twilight by Barbara Helen Berger, 237, 259
Greenman, J., 128, 130
Greenspan, N. T., 219, 227. 456, 460, 464, 474
Greenspan, S., 158, 219, 227, 456, 460, 464, 474, 484
Grocery bags, 97, 120, 166, 181–182, 186, 189, 194, 211, 332, 437, 452
Group participation, 52–53
Guidance of Young Children by M. Marion, 390
Guidance. See Discipline
Guinea pigs, 360
Gym mats, 29

H

Hair gel, 244, 260, 518, 532
Hamilton, C. E., 130
Hammers, 108, 119
Hamsters, 360
Handkerchiefs, 142
Handwashing, 385–386
Happy Birthday Moon by Frank Asch, 237, 259
Hard hats, 117, 421, 425–426
Harrington, Brooke, 34–36
Harry the Dirty Dog by Gene Zion, 95, 116–117
Hats, 25, 74, 91, 92, 96
caps, 364, 366
chef, 211
driver, 449, 451
firefighter, 167, 188
Goldilocks, 504
hard, 117, 421, 425–426
police, 167, 188, 185
rain, 264, 278, 279, 510, 529, 533
sailor, 515, 533
space helmet, 238
straw, 490, 504, 506
sun, 264, 277, 279
Hay bales, 501, 506
Headbands, 364
Health policies, 383–389
accidents, 389
conversations, 386–387
diapering, 385–386
illness, 383–384
sanitation, 404–405
sending children home, 387–389
toddler safety, 384
Healthy Young Children by A. S. Kendrick, R. Kaufman, & K. P. Messinger, 390
Helicopters, 268
Helmets
bicycle, 432, 452
firefighter, 186
motorcycle, 432, 452
space, 238
Herr, J., 319
Hitz, R., 227
Hoge, D., 308

Hole punches, 79, 81, 92, 103, 104, 119, 173, 174, 182, 188, 200, 247, 248, 260, 269, 415, 416, 427, 437, 451, 495, 500, 506, 517, 532
Honig, A. S., 128, 302, 308, 402
Hoops, 442, 451, 525, 533
embroidery, 525, 533
A House Is a House for Me by Mary Anne Hoberman, 165, 187
House plans, 425
How Can I Get There? by Pamela Cote, 165, 187
How Do I Feel? by Pamela Cote, 73, 91
How Does It Feel? by A. Stonehouse, 57
"How Young Children Build Images of Themselves" by F. Wardle, 227
Howes, C., 130
HVAC building plans, 410

I

I Eat Fruit! by Hannah Tofts, 193, 212
I Eat Vegetables! by Hannah Tofts, 193, 211, 212
I Love You Rituals by Becky Bailey, 67
Ice cream, 279
cartons, 238, 256, 452
scoops, 279
If You Give a Moose a Muffin by Laura Joffe Numeroff, 165, 187
Ignoring, 55
Ilg, L. B., 136
Illness, 383–384
sending children home, 387–398
Imagery stage, 289
"Impact of Child Care Policies," by J. R. Lally, 141
In a People House by Theo Le Seig, 165, 187
In My House by Susan Hood, 95, 117, 117
Independence
parent postcard, 423–424
Infant and Toddler Experiences by F. Hast & A. Hollyfield, 34
Inkpads, 78, 92
Interactive experiences
communicating, 294–295
exploring roles, 221
expressing feelings, 457–458
guidelines, 46
introduction to, 14, 22–23
making friends, 127–128
problem-solving skills, 373
transitioning to school, 45–46
Intuitive stage, 289
It Looked Like Spilt Milk by Charles G. Shaw, 263, 278
It's Mine by Leo Lionni, 73, 91

J

Jack-in-the-box toys, 26, 355
Jack-o-lantern shapes, 202
Jars, 26, 82, 169, 189
Jelly, 337, 345
Jessie Bear, What Will You Wear? by Nancy W. Carlstrom, 73, 91
Johnson, A., 19, 129, 130
Johnson, C. N., 219, 227
Joy dishwashing soap, 525
Jump! Frog! Jump! by Roberg Karian, 509, 529, 531
Just Like Home by Elizabeth Miller, 165, 187

K

Katie and the Big Snow by Virginia Lee Burton, 409, 426
Katz, E., 127
Katz, L., 227
Kaufman, R., 381, 390
Kendrick, A. S., 381, 390
Key rings, 25
Keyboards, 260, 289
Keys, 117
Kites, 500
Kittens, 259, 260
Knives, 196, 206
craft, 97, 101, 119, 181, 197, 238–240, 245, 249, 252–253, 260, 329, 336, 345, 351–352, 366, 490–491, 493, 506, 523, 532
Know Your Child by S. Chess & A. Thomas, 57
Kovach, B. A., 51, 129, 130

L

Labels, 299, 303, 320
Lally, J. R., 128, 129, 141
Laminate, 58, 142, 182, 308, 333
Lasting Differences by L. Schweinhart & D. P. Weikert, 57
Laundry baskets, 86, 92
Lawn mowers, 444, 451
Lazy Susans, 433, 434, 452
Leaves, 353
Leavitt, R. L., 129, 141
Lemonade, 111, 196–197
Lemons, 196
flavoring, 198
juice containers, 211
Leo the Late Bloomer by Robert Kraus, 95, 117
Leong, D. J., 308
Letter to Amy by Ezra Jack Keats, 165, 187

Letters, 167, 189
Lids
 bottles, 512
 cardboard box, 195
 coffee can, 493, 506
 plastic, 103, 120, 168, 189, 253, 260, 518, 525, 532, 533
 screw-on, 189, 198
 shoebox, 101, 331, 438
Lighting, 69
Likona, T., 484
Limit-setting, 379–380, 465
 parent postcard, 400–401
Linking Language and Literacy by R. Rockwell, D. Hoge, & B. Searcy, 308
Liquid starch, 279
Listen to the Rain by J. Endicott, J. Archambault, & B. Martin, Jr., 263, 278
Literacy, 290–292
 environments, 320–321
 parent postcards, 338–341
Literacy possibilities
 18–24 months, 79–80, 103–104, 173, 199–201, 246–247, 269–270, 331–333, 415–417, 437–438, 494–497, 516–519
 24–30 months, 80–81, 103–105, 174, 199–200, 246–247, 269–270, 331–333, 415–417, 437–438, 494–497, 516–519
 30–36 months, 81, 103–105, 174–175, 199–200, 246–247, 269–270, 331–333, 415–417, 437–439, 494–497, 516–519
 big animals, 331–333
 construction, 415–417
 fruits and vegetables, 199–201
 introduction to, 27–28
 little animals, 354-355
 me and my body, 79–81
 my family, 103–105
 my neighborhood, 173–175
 sky, 269–270
 space, 246–247
 storybook characters, 494–497
 supporting, 303–306
 transitioning to school, 79–81, 103–105
 water, 516–519
 wheels, 437–439
"Literacy Development," by Margie Carter, 308
Little animals possibilities plan
 concepts learned, 363
 construction possibilities, 353–354
 curiosity possibilities, 352–353
 dramatic possibilities, 350–351
 literacy possibilities, 354–355
 movement possibilities, 357–358
 music possibilities, 355–357
 outdoor possibilities, 358–359
 parent participation, 360
 parent postcards, 361–362
 project possibilities, 359–360
 resources, 349, 364–365
 sensory/art possibilities, 351–352
 web, 347
The Little Engine That Could by Watty Piper, 431, 450
The Little Mouse, the Red Ripe Strawberry, and the Very Hungry Bear by Don & Audrey Wood, 193, 200, 211, 212
Lizards, 351
 felt, 516, 532
Logical consequences, 378–379
Love and Learn by A. Honig, 402
Lunch boxes, 96, 117, 410, 421, 425, 427

M

Macaroni, 381
 boxes, 198
Magazines, 76, 79–81, 93, 102, 120, 172, 189, 275, 304, 320, 331, 359, 366, 517, 533
 auto, 437, 451
 construction, 425
 farm, 343
 flower, 506
 zoo, 343
Magic slates, 320
Magical School Bus: Lost in Outer Space by Joanna Cole, 237, 259
Magnets, 142, 171, 188, 435, 451
Magnifying glasses, 78, 92
Mailing tubes, 518, 533
Make Way for Ducklings by Robert McCloskey, 489, 492, 505, 509, 529, 531
Making friends, 18, 121–214
 child development, 124–127
 environments, 157–171
 interactive experiences, 127–128
 introduction, 121–122
 observations, 122–123
 parent partnerships, 142–143
 parent postcards, 144–157, 183–184, 208–209
 possibilities plans, 163–214
 resources, 140–141, 157, 185–189, 211–213
 teacher competencies, 140
 teaching innovations, 128–141
Manipulatives, 26, 68, 70, 374
Margarine, 381
 tubs, 206, 514, 530
Marion, M., 390
Markers, 92, 101, 119, 167, 168, 171–174, 181, 188, 200, 206, 207, 247, 249, 252, 260, 270, 279, 305, 320, 332, 333, 345, 353, 355, 366, 415, 427, 437, 438, 443, 451, 495, 506, 515, 516, 532

permanent, 80, 86, 92, 169, 239, 245
water-based, 512, 532
Marshmallows, 245, 260
Martin's Hats by Joan W. Blos, 73, 91
Masking tape, 99, 241
Masks, 529
Matching games, 170–171, 200, 360
McClellan, P., 127, 227
McMullen, M. B., 129, 130, 141
Me and my body possibilities plan
concepts learned, 90
construction possibilities, 79
curiosity possibilities, 77–78
dramatic possibilities, 74–75
literacy possibilities, 79–81
movement possibilities, 83–84
music possibilities, 81–83
outdoor possibilities, 84–86
parent participation, 87
parent postcards, 88–89
project possibilities, 86–87
resources, 73, 90–92
sensory/art possibilities, 75–77
web, 71
Measuring cups, 169, 189, 267
"Measuring Kindergartners' Social Competence," by A. S. Pelegrini & C. D. Glickman, 141
Measuring spoons, 92, 178, 189
Measuring tapes, 410, 425, 427
Medical kits, 167
Messinger, K. P., 381, 390
Metal objects, 171, 189
Metal rings, 79, 92, 103–104, 119, 173, 174, 182, 188, 248, 260, 269, 415, 437, 451, 495, 506, 517, 532
Mice, 351, 360
puppets, 354, 366
toy, 259, 260
Mid-day reunions, 142
Mike Mulligan by Virginia Lee Burton, 409, 416, 426
Milk, 381
cartons, 422
jugs, 238, 260
The Milk Makers by Gail Gibbons, 325, 344
Miller, K., 319, 402
Mine by Miriam Cohen, 73, 91
Mineral oil, 169, 189
Mirrors, 26–27, 70, 74, 78, 91, 92, 167, 188, 233–234, 435, 451
Mitchell, G., 390
The Mitten by Jan Brett, 489, 496, 505
Mittens, 259, 260, 496, 506
Modeling, 133–134
Money
bags, 186
boxes, 432, 449, 451, 452
play, 166, 186, 188, 194, 211
Monkeys, 350, 356–357
plastic, 364
stuffed, 350, 366
Moo Baa La La La by Sandra Boynton, 165, 186–187
Moongame by Frank Asch, 237, 259
More Games to Play with Toddlers by J. Silberg, 34, 319
More Things to Do with Toddlers and Twos by K. Miller, 34, 319
More Toddlers Together by C. Catlin, 34
Motor skills, 370–371
supporting, 374–375
Motorcycles, 445
helmets, 432, 452
Movement possibilities
18–24 months, 83, 107, 177–178, 202–204, 250–251, 273, 335–337, 357, 419–420, 441–443, 499–500, 522
24–30 months, 83–84, 107, 178–179, 202–204, 250–251, 273, 335–337, 357–358, 419–420, 441–443, 499–500, 522
30–36 months, 84, 107–108, 179–180, 202–204, 250–251, 273, 335–337, 357, 419–420, 441–443, 499–500, 522
big animals, 335–337
construction, 419–420
fruits and vegetables, 202–204
introduction to, 29
little animals, 357–358
me and my body, 83–84
my family, 107–108
my neighborhood, 177–180
sky, 273
space, 250–251
storybook characters, 499–500
water, 522
wheels, 441–443
Mr. Bear's Boat by Thomas Graham, 509, 531
Mr. Griggs Work by Cynthia Rylant, 165, 187
Mr. Gumpy's Outing by John Burningham, 509, 531
Mud Puddle by Robert Munsch, 409, 426
Muffins, 175, 228
breakfast for moms, 228
mix boxes, 189
tins, 166, 170, 188, 189
Multiculturalism
dolls, 25
family diversity, 47–48
supporting, 299–300
Multiple intelligences, 301–302
environments, 319–320
Murmel, Murmel, Murmel by Robert Munsch, 409, 426
Music possibilities
18–24 months, 81–82, 105–106, 175–177, 201, 249–250, 271–272, 333–334, 355, 417–419, 439–441, 497–498, 519–521
24–30 months, 82–83, 105–106, 175–177, 201, 249–250, 271–272, 333–334, 355–356,

417–419, 439–441, 497–498, 519–521
30–36 months, 82–83, 105–106, 175–177, 201–202, 249–250, 271–272, 333–334, 356–357, 417–419, 439–441, 497–498, 519–521
big animals, 333–334
construction, 417–419
fruits and vegetables, 201–202
introduction to, 28–29
little animals, 355–357
me and my body, 81–83
my family, 105–106
my neighborhood, 175–177
sky, 271–272
space, 249–250
storybook characters, 497–498
water, 519–521
wheels, 439–441
Music, 99, 279
classical, 499
instrumental, 273
Star Wars, 250
My family possibilities plan
concepts learned, 116
construction possibilities, 102–103
curiosity possibilities, 100–102
dramatic possibilities, 96–97
literacy possibilities, 103–105
movement possibilities, 107–108
music possibilities, 105–106
outdoor possibilities, 108–109
parent participation, 111
parent postcards, 111–115
project possibilities, 110
resources, 95, 116–120
sensory/art possibilities, 98–100
web, 93
My neighborhood possibilities plan
concepts learned, 185
construction possibilities, 172
curiosity possibilities, 169–172
dramatic possibilities, 166–167
literacy possibilities, 173–175
movement possibilities, 177–180
music possibilities, 175–177
outdoor possibilities, 180–181
parent participation, 182
parent postcards, 183–184
project possibilities, 181–182
resources, 165, 186–189
sensory/art possibilities, 168–169
web, 163
My Sister and Me Outside by Lucy Dickens, 95, 117

N

The Napping House by Audrey Woods, 95, 117
National Academy of Early Childhood Programs, 20
National Assn. for the Education of Young Children, 18, 227, 308
Natural consequences, 378–379
parent postcard, 399
Necklaces
picture, 182, 308
Neighborhood Trucker by Louise Borden, 409, 426
Neugebauer, B., 227
Neuman, S., 290–291, 308
Newspaper, 79, 102, 120, 172, 181, 189, 198, 304, 385, 491, 501, 506
No Elephants Allowed by Deborah Robinson, 343
Noisemakers, 82, 92, 103, 109, 170, 178, 189
Nonverbal cues, 46, 459
Not the Piano, Mrs. Medley! by Evan Levine, 431, 450
Notebooks, 105, 119, 320, 320
Notes, 391
Nutrition, 381–383
24-hour food guide, 381
picky eaters, 382–383

O

Oatmeal, 492, 506
boxes, 255, 260
Observation/assessment
communicating, 283
comparisons, 19
developmentally appropriate practice, 19–21
exploring roles, 217
expressing feelings, 454–455
facilitating attachment, 51
giving feedback, 22
in curriculum planning, 34–36
introduction, 14, 18–22
making friends, 122–123
problem-solving, 368–369
transitioning to school, 38–39
using strategies, 21
Oils, 381
mineral, 169, 189
salad, 267, 279
Okagaki, L., 308
Old Henry by John W. Blos, 165, 187
Old MacDonald Had a Farm by Holly Berry, 165, 186, 187
The One Hundred Languages of Children by C. Edwards, L. Gandini, & G. Forman, 140
Oppositional behavior, 463–466
parent postcards, 478–479

Oranges, 194
flavoring, 198
plastic, 350
shapes, 202
Origins of Intelligence in Children by J. Piaget, 308
Outdoor possibilities
18–24 months, 84–85, 108–109, 204, 252–253, 274–275, 358–359, 420–422, 443–444, 500–501, 523–524
24–30 months, 85, 108–109, 180–181, 205, 252–253, 274–275, 358–359, 420–422, 443–444, 500–501, 523–524
30–36 months, 85–86, 108–109, 181, 205, 252–253, 274–275, 358–359, 420–422, 443–444, 500–501, 523–524
big animals, 336-337
construction, 420–421
environments, 402–404
fruits and vegetables, 204–205
introduction to, 29
little animals, 358–359
me and my body, 84–86
my family, 108–109
my neighborhood, 180–181
sky, 174–275
space, 252–253
storybook characters, 500–501
supporting physical development, 375
water, 523–525
wheels, 443–444
Oven racks, 100
Overalls, 490, 504, 506

P

Pacifiers
parent postcard, 63
Paddles, 268, 279
Pails, 492, 511, 532
Paintbrushes, 75, 76, 78, 86, 92, 97, 98, 109, 119, 181, 188, 205, 238–240, 242, 245, 252–254, 265, 269, 279, 320, 327, 490–491, 495, 501, 506, 524, 532
Paints, 76, 87, 97–99, 101, 109, 119, 180, 181, 188, 195, 205, 230, 238, 240, 241, 245, 252–254, 260, 265, 269, 279, 336, 350, 352, 366, 412, 427, 433, 434, 445, 451, 490–491, 495, 506
acrylic, 75, 92
fabric, 239, 260
finger 491, 26, 99, 119, 168, 188, 241, 260, 320, 506
rollers, 524
spray, 75, 92, 239, 243, 260, 493, 506
tempera, 92, 241, 244, 254, 266, 274, 279, 327, 345, 359, 366, 501, 506, 513, 532
washable, 78, 86, 327, 345
Pans, 100, 195, 211
flour, 320
plastic, 265, 279, 411–412, 427, 451, 492, 506
shallow, 525, 533
Pantyhose, 252, 260
Papa, Please Get the Moon for Me by Eric Carle, 237, 259
Paper, 26, 58, 76, 78, 86–87, 92, 98, 100, 110, 119, 166, 168, 172, 174, 188, 195, 205, 241, 242, 244, 255, 260, 265, 279, 305, 320, 352, 366, 412, 416, 426, 427, 433, 434, 438, 451, 475, 495, 506, 513, 532
bags, 330, 337
cups, 329, 352, 366, 421, 427, 532
strips, 85, 120, 168, 189, 501, 506
Paper plates, 248–249, 260, 268–269, 279, 366, 416, 427, 434, 437, 451, 491, 500, 506
colored, 435, 451
holders, 433, 452, 525, 533
Paper towels, 75, 92, 385–386
tubes, 99, 101, 120, 249, 255, 260, 510, 533
Parallel play, 231
Parallel talk, 298
Parent brag board, 391
Parent day, 475
Parent participation possibilities
big animals, 337–338
construction, 422–423
fruits and vegetables, 207
introduction to, 14, 24, 30
little animals, 360
me and my body, 87
my family, 111
my neighborhood, 182
sky, 275
space, 255–256
storybook characters, 502–503
water, 526–528
wheels, 445
Parent partnerships
communicating, 308–309
exploring roles, 227–230
expressing feelings, 474–475
introduction to, 23–24
making friends, 142–143
problem-solving, 391
transitioning to school, 58–67
Parent postcards, 197
communicating, 309–318, 338–341, 361–362
exploring roles, 229–230, 257, 276
expressing feelings, 475–483, 503, 527–528
introduction to, 23–24, 30
making friends, 143–157, 183–184, 208–209
problem-solving, 391–401, 423–424, 446–448
transitioning to school, 58–66, 88–89, 111–115
Parent teas, 142, 309

Parents
    books for, 67, 157, 402, 484
    conferences, 467–472
    giving feedback, 22
    validating, 132–133
Party blowers, 532
Patterning, 133–134, 304
Patty's Pumpkin Patch by Teri Sloat, 193, 212
Peanut butter, 337, 381
Peanuts, 337, 345
Pears, 194
    shapes, 202
Pencils, 185, 186, 174, 320, 415, 427, 438, 451
Pens, 87, 110, 205, 206, 255, 445
    fabric paint, 239
People, block figures, 414, 422, 427, 506
Pet brushes, 116
Pet Show by Ezra Jack Keats, 349, 365
Peter Rabbit by Beatrix Potter, 349, 365, 364
Peter Speir's Rain by Peter Speir, 509, 529, 531
Pets, 116, 359–360
Phone books, 320
Photo albums, 104, 359–350
Photographs, 47–48, 58, 79, 92, 102–105, 110, 120, 142, 167, 182, 189, 359, 366, 475, 513, 533
Piaget, J., 124–125, 302–303, 308
    theory of cognitive development, 288–289
Pickin' Peas by Margaret Read MacDonald & Pat Cummins, 193, 212
Picky eaters, 382–383
    parent postcard, 391
Picnic by Emily Arnold McCully, 193, 211, 212
Picture blocks, 72
Picture files
    big animals, 343
    construction, 426
    fruits and vegetables, 211
    introduction to, 31–32
    little animals, 364
    me and my body, 91
    my family, 117
    my neighborhood, 186
    sky, 278
    space, 259
    storybook characters, 505
    water, 530
    wheels, 450
Pictures, 76, 79, 81, 101, 102, 120, 174, 176, 189, 200, 201, 206, 247–248, 259–260, 269–271, 275, 279, 299, 308, 337, 343, 354, 359–360, 366, 391, 413, 415–416, 435, 437, 439, 452, 493, 496, 506, 517, 533
Pie tins, 182, 352, 366
Pigs by Robert Munsch, 431, 450
Pillowcases, 142
Pillows, 142, 264, 279, 326, 343
Pineapples, 196
    flavoring, 198
    shapes, 202
Pinecones, 353
Pipes, plastic, 410
Pitchers, 169, 189, 196, 211
Pizza boards, 99, 120, 245, 260
Pizza boxes, 186, 198, 452
Pizza Man by Marjorie Pillar, 165, 187
Placemats, 490, 506
Planes, 268
Planting a Rainbow by Lois Ehlert, 263, 270, 278, 489, 505
Plants, 533
Plastic
    animals, 259, 260, 328, 330–331, 345, 351, 353, 359, 364, 366, 494, 501, 504, 506, 517, 532
    blocks, 421, 427, 493, 506
    boats, 514, 517, 532
    bottles, 82, 92, 99, 103, 120, 169–171, 182, 189, 243–244, 260, 289, 240, 260, 313, 330, 351, 366, 512–514, 530, 533
    bubble wrap, 76, 77, 92
    color paddles, 268, 279
    containers, 267, 274, 279
    cups, 98, 119, 211, 238, 260, 274, 279, 353, 514, 530
    eggs, 343
    feeding dish, 108, 351
    fish, 518, 532
    flowerpots, 506, 533
    food, 211
    fruits, 199, 205, 350, 366
    hammers, 108, 119
    hoops, 442, 451
    jars, 26, 82, 169
    joint pieces, 410
    keys, 117
    lids, 103, 120, 168, 189, 253, 260, 525, 532, 533
    pans, 265, 279, 411–412, 427, 451, 492, 506
    pipes, 410
    resealable bags, 81, 104, 119, 171, 174, 182, 188, 200, 245, 260, 360, 386, 517–518, 532
    rings, 92, 178, 189
    six-pack holders, 525, 533
    spatulas, 100
    spoons, 98, 100, 119, 166, 181, 188, 195, 211, 266, 279, 490, 492, 505, 506
    tools, 410, 413, 416, 425, 427
    trays, 254
    tubing, 524, 530
    vegetables, 195, 199, 211, 364, 366, 505, 506
    wheels, 449
Plastic-coated shelving, 100
Plates
    colored, 435, 451
    holders, 433, 452, 525, 533

paper, 248–249, 260, 268–269, 279, 366, 416, 427, 434, 437, 451, 500, 506
Platforms, 68
Play in the Lives of Children by C. S. Rogers & J. K. Sawyer, 141
Play with Me by Marie Hall Ets, 349, 365
Play, 124–127
cues and props, 231–233
parallel, 231
parent postcard, 183
Parten, 125
Piaget, 124–125
six types, 126
Vygotsky, 126
Play, Dreams, and Imitation in Childhood by J. Piaget, 141
Playdough, 188, 320
homemade, 168, 267
Plungers, 412, 427
Polar Bear, Polar Bear, What Do You See? by Bill Martin, Jr., 489, 495, 505
Pompoms, 512, 532
Ponchos, 278, 529
Portfolios, 475
Possibilities plans
big animals, 323–346
construction, 407–428
fruits and vegetables, 191–214
introduction to, 24–32
little animals, 347–366
me and my body, 71–92
my family, 93–120
my neighborhood, 163–190
resources, 31–32
sky, 261–279
space, 235–260
storybook characters, 487–506
water, 507–533
wheels, 429–452
Poster board, 79, 81, 92, 101, 104, 119, 173, 174, 180, 188, 200, 204, 205, 247, 252–253, 260, 326, 333, 336, 345, 353, 366, 415, 443, 451, 495, 532
Potato chip canisters, 102, 120
Potatoes, 194, 198, 204
Pots, 195, 211, 490, 505, 506
Potting soil, 199, 206, 211, 411, 420, 492, 500, 506
Pounding benches, 411, 427
Powell, D. R., 129, 141
Power and Emotion in Infant-Toddler Day Care by R. L. Leavitt, 141
"Praise or Encouragement?" by R. Hitz & A. Driscoll, 227
Pre-conceptual stage, 289
Pre-enrollment visit, 58
Pre-operational stage, 289
Pretzels, 245, 260, 352, 366
A Primary Caregiving System for Infants and Toddlers by J. L. Bernhardt, 140
Primary teaching, 128–130
Prime Times by J. Greenman & A. Stonehouse, 141
Print-making, 195–196, 241–242, 352, 412, 433–434, 445
Prisms, 268, 279
Problem-solving, 367–452
child development, 370–373
environments, 402–405
interactive experiences, 373
observation/assessment, 368–369
parent partnerships, 391
parent postcards, 392–401
possibilities plans, 407–452
resources, 390, 402
teacher competencies, 390
teaching innovations, 374–389
Project possibilities
18–24 months, 86–87, 110, 181–182, 205–206, 254, 275, 337, 359–360, 422, 445, 501, 525
24–30 months, 86–87, 110, 181–182, 205–206, 254, 275, 337, 359–360, 422, 445, 501, 525
30–36 months, 86–87, 110, 181–182, 254–255, 275, 337, 359–360, 422, 445, 501, 525
big animals, 337
construction, 422
fruits and vegetables, 205–206
introduction to, 29
little animals, 359–360
me and my body, 86–87
my family, 110
my neighborhood, 181–182
sky, 275
space, 254–255
storybook characters, 501
water, 525
wheels, 445
Prop boxes
astronaut, 237, 259
babies, 95, 117
beach, 277
bear cave, 325–326, 343
big machines, 409, 425
bunny, 349, 364
bus driver, 431, 449
carrot seed, 193, 211
construction worker, 409, 416–417, 425
cooking, 193, 211
dress-up, 73, 90
ducks, 509, 529
elephant, 325, 343
farm, 325–326, 343
firefighter, 186
frogs, 509, 529
goodnight moon, 237, 259
grocery store, 186

mommies and daddies, 95, 117
monkey, 349, 364
pets, 95, 116
pizza delivery, 186
police, 185
rain, 278, 509, 529
red barn, 489, 504
red, rip strawberry, 193, 211
shoes, 73, 90
stone soup, 489, 505
three bears, 489, 504
turtle, 349, 364
vegetable market, 193, 211
very hungry caterpillar, 193, 211, 489, 504
water play, 509, 530
wheels, 431, 449
where the wild things are, 489, 504
zoo, 325–326, 343
Pull toys, 451
Puppets, 80, 104, 119, 211, 259, 269, 332, 337, 345, 354, 364, 366, 495, 496, 499, 504, 506, 511, 529, 532
Purses, 25, 91, 117, 186
Push toys, 336, 345, 403, 444, 451
Puzzles, 26, 68, 413, 427
homemade, 171, 197, 245, 333
pegged, 374

R

Rabbits, 351, 354–355, 358, 360
puppets, 354, 364
stuffed, 259, 260, 351, 366
Racks
metal, 100
shoe, 90
wooden, 100
Raikes, 128
Rain hats, 264, 278, 279, 510, 529, 533
Rain sticks, 529
homemade, 518
Rainbow Fish by Marcus Pfister, 489, 505
A Rainbow of My Own by Don Freeman, 263, 278
Raincoats, 167, 186, 189, 264, 278, 279, 510, 529, 533
Raising Good Children by T. Likona, 157, 484
Raising Self-Reliant Children in a Self-Indulgent World by H. Glenn & J. Nelson, 157
Raisins, 245, 260, 352, 366
Rakes, 444
Ratlev, M., 340
Receptive language, 287
Reciprocity, 53
language, 285–286
Redirection, 54–55
"Reflections on Quality Infant Care," by J. Reisenberg, 141
Reggio Emilia school, 27, 461
Reisenberg, J., 128, 141
"Relationship Duration in Infant Care," by H. Raikes, 141
Resources for Infant Educarers by M. Gerber, 57, 140–141
Resources
big animals, 343–345
construction, 426–428
for parents, 67, 319, 402, 484
fruits and vegetables, 211–212
introduction to, 23, 31–32
little animals, 364–365
me and my body, 90–92
my family, 116-118
my neighborhood, 185–189
sky, 277–279
space, 258-260
storybook characters, 504–506
water, 529–533
wheels, 449–452
"Respectful, Individual, and Responsive Caregiving for Infants," by B. A. Kovach & D. A. Da Ros, 57, 141
"Responding to Cultural and Linguistic Differences," by L. Okagaki & K. E. Diamond, 308
Rethinking the Brain by R. Shore, 141, 308
"Reweaving Parents into the Fabric of Early Childhood Programs," by D. R. Powell, 141
Rhinos, 327–328
Rhymes, 28, 570-579
"As I Was Walking," 409, 419–420, 426
"Big Old Bear," 325, 332, 344
"Big Steps, Little Steps," 165, 178, 187
"Copy Me," 165, 180, 187
"Five Little Ducks," 489, 499, 505
"Frogs at the Pond," 509, 516–517, 531
"Grow Little Seed," 193, 203, 212
"Here Is a House," 165, 179, 187
"Here's a Bunny," 349, 354–355, 365
"Hey, Diddle, Diddle," 237, 247, 259
"Hickory, Dickory Dock," 349, 354, 365
"Hop a Little," 73, 84, 91
"I Had a Little Turtle," 349, 357–358, 365
"I Wonder Where the Clouds All Go," 263, 272, 278
"Jack and Jill," 509, 519, 531
"Jumping Feet," 73, 83, 91
"The Little Ducks," 509, 522, 531
"The Moon Is Out," 237, 251, 259
"One Elephant," 325, 331, 344
"Riding in the Car," 431, 450
"Silly Face," 73, 84, 91
"The Sun," 263, 269, 278
"There Was a Little Turtle," 208
"This Is Our Neighborhood," 165, 177, 187
"This Little Piggy," 489, 497, 505
"The Truck Driver," 409, 426
"Winking Eyes," 91

Ribbons, 110, 120, 168, 189
Rice, 82, 92, 103, 120, 267, 279, 330, 381, 518, 533
Riding toys, 84, 92, 109, 119, 159, 180, 336, 345, 403
Rings
key, 25
metal, 79, 92, 103–104, 119, 173, 174, 182, 188, 248, 260, 269, 415, 437, 451, 495, 506, 517, 532
plastic, 92, 178, 189
silver, 427
Rituals, 58–62
Road carpets, 353, 366
Road mats, 436, 451
Rocket ships, 259
Rocks, 243, 253, 502, 506
Rockwell, R., 308
Rolling pins, 168, 189
Rosie's Walk by Pat Hutchins, 165, 187
Routines, 300
Rubber
boots, 167, 186, 189, 259, 260, 264, 278, 279, 108, 120, 239, 510, 529, 533
ducks, 492, 494, 506, 529
frogs, 529
spatulas, 108
Rulers, 410, 425, 427
The Runaway Bunny by Margaret Wise Brown, 95, 118

S

Safety, 233, 384
accidents, 389
choke tubes, 386
Sailor hats, 515, 533
Salad oil, 267, 279
Salad spinners, 434, 451
Salt, 168, 242, 260
shakers, 198, 242, 260, 412
Sand, 25, 101, 119, 171, 189, 241, 254, 327–328, 330, 359, 366, 403, 412, 420, 421, 435, 452
box, 328, 345, 421
pails, 277
table, 241, 98, 119, 366, 411–412, 444, 427, 451
trays, 320
Sandpaper, 77, 173, 265, 279, 328
Sanitation, 404–405
Scarves, 250, 260, 499, 506
Schiller, P., 308, 319
School Bus by Donald Crews, 431, 450
School buses, 445
Schweinhart, L., 51, 57
Scissors, 76, 80, 92, 101, 103, 105, 119, 166, 170–174, 188, 200, 204, 238, 241, 252, 254, 260, 268, 270, 279, 328, 333, 336, 345, 350, 355, 366, 427, 435, 438, 451, 495, 501, 506, 516, 517, 532
Scoops, 98, 119, 279
Scooting toys, 523
Scrub brushes, 502, 506, 530
Searcy, R., 308
Security items
parent postcard, 64
Self-concept. See Exploring roles
Self-control
parent postcard, 446
Self-talk, 298
Sensory/art possibilities
18–24 months, 75–76, 168, 195–197, 240–242, 265–266, 327–328, 351–352, 411–412, 433–434, 491–492, 511–512
24–30 months, 75–76, 98–99, 168–169, 195–197, 240–242, 265–266, 327–328, 351, 411–412, 433–434, 491–492, 512
30–34 months, 75–77, 98–100, 327–328, 169, 195–197, 240–242, 265–266 , 351, 411–412, 433–434, 491–492, 513
big animals, 327–328
construction, 411–412
fruits and vegetables, 195–197
introduction to, 25–26
little animals, 351–352
me and my body, 75–77
my family, 98–100
my neighborhood, 168–169
sky, 265–266
space, 240–242
storybook characters, 491–492
water, 511–513
wheels, 433–434
Sensory table, 25, 337, 502
outside, 359
Separation
postcards, 209
rituals, 58–62, 65–66
security items, 63–64
Sequins, 513, 532
Shape sorters, 374
Shaving cream, 266, 279, 327, 345, 359, 366
Sheet protectors, 359, 366
Sheets, 326, 343
Shelov, S., 402
Shelving, 158, 232, 304, 486
plastic-coated, 100
Shirts, 343, 490, 504, 506
Shoeboxes, 101, 120, 167, 172, 182, 189, 198, 255, 260, 422, 437, 438, 452
lids, 331, 438
Shoes, 73, 75, 90, 91, 92
bags, 90
high heels, 117
laces, 329, 345, 435, 451
rack, 90
Shopping bags, 90

The Shopping Basket by John Burningham, 165, 187
Shopping baskets, 186, 194
Shopping carts, 97, 166, 188, 432, 451
Shore, R., 129, 233, 284, 308
Shovels, 277, 492
Shower curtains, 78, 92, 274, 279
Sieves, 514, 530, 533
Signs, 211, 304, 320, 391
Silberg, J., 308, 319
Silver rings, 427
Simple Steps by K. Miller, 34, 319
"Singing with Infants and Toddlers," by A. S. Honig, 141
Sirens, 186
Six Experiences That Create Intelligence and Emotional Growth in Babies and Young Children by S. Greenspan, 484
Sky All Around by Anna G. Hines, 237, 259
Sky possibilities plan, 261–279
  concepts learned, 277
  construction possibilities, 268–269
  curiosity possibilities, 267–268
  dramatic possibilities, 264
  literacy possibilities, 269–270
  movement possibilities, 273
  music possibilities, 271–272
  outdoor possibilities, 274–275
  parent participation, 275
  parent postcards, 276
  project possibilities, 275
  resources, 263, 278–279
  sensory/art possibilities, 265–266
  web, 261
Sleep shirts, 109, 120
Sleeping by Jan Ormerod, 117–118
Smelling jars, 198
Smocks, 411, 416, 427, 492, 506
Snacks, 175, 194, 196–197, 200, 207, 245, 329, 337, 352, 358, 434–435, 502
Snakes, felt, 516, 532
Soap, 385–386
  dishwashing, 525
"Social Participation among Preschool Children," by M. B. Parten, 141
Socks, 74, 78, 92, 259, 260, 327, 343, 353, 366, 405, 504, 506
  balls, 252
Songs, 422–423
  "Are You Sleeping?" 95, 106, 118
  "Bear Is Sleeping," 325, 334, 344
  "Clapping Hands," 73, 82, 92
  "Dancing Fingers," 92
  "Did You Ever See a Cloud?" 263, 271–272, 278
  "Did You Ever See?" 325, 333, 344
  "Down by the Station," 431, 440–441, 450
  "Drive the Truck," 409, 420, 426
  "The Dump Truck Song," 409, 418–419, 426
  "Eensy Weensy Spider," 489, 498, 505
  "Elephant Dancing," 325, 335, 344
  "Five Little Ducks," 509, 520–521, 531
  "Food Song," 193, 202, 212
  "Go In and Out the Neighborhood," 165, 177, 187
  "Grandma," 95, 106, 118
  "The Hammer Song," 409, 417, 426
  "Heigh Ho the Derry O," 431, 441–442, 450
  "Here They Are!" 73, 82, 92
  "Houses, Houses, Everywhere," 165, 176, 187
  "I Am Eating," 193, 212
  "I'm Bringing Home a Baby Bumblebee," 95, 106, 118
  "It's Raining, It's Pouring," 263, 271, 278
  "Jumped in the Boat," 509, 523, 531
  "London Bridge," 165, 176, 187
  "Merrily We Roll Along," 431, 450
  "Mister Moon," 237, 249, 260
  "The Muffin Man," 165, 175, 187
  "Musical Fingers," 92
  "My Little Red Wagon," 431, 441, 450
  "Oh, Do You Know Your Vegetables?" 193, 201, 212
  "Old MacDonald Had a Farm," 489, 498, 505
  "Old Mother Turtle," 349, 355–356, 365
  "Over in the Meadow," 509, 521, 531
  "Pat-a-Cake," 165, 170, 1877
  "Picking Some Big Ears," 193, 203, 212
  "Picking Up Potatoes," 193, 204, 212
  "Pop Goes the Bunny," 349, 355, 365
  "Rain, Rain, Go Away," 263, 271, 278
  "Rainbow Colors," 263, 272, 278
  "Ring Around the Rosy," 431, 440, 450
  "Rock-a-Bye, Baby," 96
  "Row, Row, Row Your Boat," 509, 519, 531
  "See the Wheels Go Round," 431, 439, 450
  "Shake Your Shaker," 73, 83, 92
  "Shaker Up," 165, 179, 187
  "Swim, Swim, Quack, Quack," 509, 521, 531
  "There's a Little Flower," 489, 497, 505
  "There's an Animal," 325, 334, 344
  "This Is the Way," 409, 417–418, 426
  "Twinkle, Twinkle, Little Star," 237, 249–250, 260
  "We Planted a Little Seed," 193, 203, 212
  "Wheels," 431, 440, 450
Space possibilities plan, 235–260
  concepts learned, 258
  construction possibilities, 246
  curiosity possibilities, 243–245
  dramatic possibilities, 238–240
  helmets, 259
  literacy possibilities, 247–248
  movement possibilities, 250–251
  music possibilities, 249–250
  outdoor possibilities, 252–253
  parent participation, 255–256
  parent postcards, 256–257

project possibilities, 254–255
resources, 237, 259–260
sensory/art possibilities, 240–242
web, 235
Spatulas, 100, 108, 120, 168, 189
Spelling, 292–294
Sponges, 75, 92, 99, 120, 254, 345, 352, 366, 451, 511, 523, 530, 532
Spools, 253, 260
Spoons, 490, 504, 506
large, 108, 120, 490, 505, 506
measuring, 92, 178, 189
plastic, 92, 98, 100, 119, 166, 181, 188, 195, 211, 266, 279, 492
rubber, 100
wooden, 120
Spray bottles, 202, 274, 303, 492, 506, 512, 533
Spray paints, 75, 92, 239, 243, 260, 493, 506
Sprinkler, 523
Squirrel Nutkin by Beatrix Potter, 349, 365
Squirt bottles, 492, 513, 533
Stamps, 167, 175, 189
Stapler, 501
Star Builders, 374
Stars, 240, 242, 249, 254
confetti, 244, 260
Start Smart by P. Schiller, 308, 319
Starting Points by the Carnegie Foundation of New York, 57
Starting Small by the Teaching Tolerance Project, 57
Stone Soup by Marcia Brown, 489, 490, 502, 505
Stonehouse, A., 126, 128, 130
Storage carts, 432, 451
Storybook characters possibilities plan, 487–506
concepts learned, 504
construction possibilities, 493–494
curiosity possibilities, 492–493
dramatic possibilities, 490–491
literacy possibilities, 494–497
movement possibilities, 499–500
music possibilities, 497–498
outdoor possibilities, 500–501
parent participation, 502–503
parent postcard, 503
project possibilities, 501
resources, 489, 504–506
sensory/art possibilities, 491–492
web, 487
Stranger anxiety, 42–43
helping with, 50
parent postcard, 59
Straw hats, 490, 504, 506
Strawberries, 200, 211
flavoring, 197
shapes, 202
Streamers, 250, 260, 272, 279, 499, 500, 506, 523
The Street Cleaner by Annie Kubler, 165, 187
String, 58, 180, 189
Strollers, 96, 119, 432, 451
Stuffed animals, 108–109, 116, 119, 259, 260, 326, 336–337, 343, 345, 350–351, 366, 490, 504, 506
Styrofoam blocks, 422
Sugar, 196, 265, 381
Suit coats, 91, 96, 117
Sun hats, 264, 277, 279
Sun Up, Sun Down by Gail Gibbons, 263, 278
Sunglasses, 277, 279
Suntan lotion bottles, 264, 277, 279
The Supermarket by Gail Gibbons, 193, 211, 212
Swim, T., 319
Swimmy by Leo Leonni, 509, 518, 531

T

Tables, 70, 98, 119, 320
laminated, 168
Tabors, 299
Tadpoles, 526
Taking turns, 134–135
The Tale of the Turnip by Brian Alderson, 193, 212
Talking with Your Baby by A. Honig & H. E. Brody, 157, 308
Tape players, 238, 250, 273, 309, 336, 414, 427, 499, 502
Tape, 79, 82, 86, 92, 98, 101–103, 110, 119, 166, 168–172, 178, 180–181, 188, 198, 243–244, 253–255, 260, 267–269, 279, 330, 332, 345, 350, 352, 355–366, 422, 427, 434, 443, 451, 500, 506, 512, 513, 515, 518, 523, 532
duct, 76, 92, 100, 119, 238, 240, 260
electrician's, 169, 189
masking, 241, 99
packing, 239
shiny, 239, 260
Teacher competencies
communicating, 307
exploring roles, 226
expressing feelings, 473–474
introduction to, 23
making friends, 140
problem-solving, 390
transitioning to school, 56
Teaching innovations
brain-based care, 295–297
communicating, 295–308
continuity, 131
creating opportunities, 222
developmental challenges, 306–306
discipline, 225–226
emotional development, 459
exploring roles, 222–227
expressing feelings, 459–474

facilitating attachment, 49–51
family diversity, 47–48
family-centered practices, 224–225
floor time, 460–461
gradual enrollment, 48–49
group participation, 52–53
guidance/discipline, 54–55, 133–139, 378–380, 462–467
health policies, 383–389
interactive relationships, 223
introduction to, 14, 23
literacy, 303–306
making friends, 128–141
maximizing interactions, 53
multiple intelligences, 301–302
nutrition, 381–383
observing, 223–224
parent conferences, 467–472
physical development, 374–375
Piaget, 302–303
positive self-concept, 224
primary teaching, 128–130
problem-solving skills, 374–389
social development, 131–132
stimulating growth, 297–299
supporting creativity, 461–462
supporting diversity, 299–300
toilet training, 375–378
transitioning to school, 47–57
validating parents, 132–133
Telephone, 260, 259, 309
Temper tantrums, 466–467
parent postcards, 480–483
Tempera paints, 254, 266, 279, 345, 92, 501, 506
powdered, 241, 244, 266, 274, 279, 327, 359, 366, 513, 532
Temperament, 43–45
Ten, Nine, Eight by Molly Bang, 95, 118
Tertiary circular reaction stage, 289
Textured materials, 77, 92, 173, 353, 366
Things to Do with Toddlers and Twos by K. Miller, 34, 319
This Is the House that Jack Built by Pam Adams, 95, 117–118
This Is the Way We Go to School by Edith Baer, 431, 450
Thomas, A., 43, 57
Three-ring binders, 359, 366
Thumb sucking
parent postcard, 66
"Tips for Feeding Picky Eaters," by S. Clark, 390
Tires, 443, 452
Tissue paper, 110
Toddlers Together by C. Catlin, 34
Toilet tissue tubes, 99, 101, 120, 255, 260, 249
Toilet training, 371–373
parent postcards, 392–398
stages, 372
supporting, 375–378
Tools by Byron Barton, 95, 118
Tools of the Mind by E. Bodrova & D. J. Leong, 308
Tools, 410, 413, 416, 425, 427
belts, 421, 422, 425
boxes, 410, 425, 427
caddy, 427
gardening, 500, 504, 506
yard, 444, 451
Tote bags, 109, 120, 207
Touch and Feel: Clothes by Deni Brown, 73, 91
Touch and Feel: Home by Deni Brown, 95, 117–118
Touchpoints by T. B. Brazelton, 67, 140, 157, 402, 471, 474, 484
Towels, 510, 532
beach, 264, 277, 279
hand, 142
paper, 385–386, 75, 92
Toys
small, 512, 532
swaps, 142, 227
Trading, 134
Transitioning to school, 18, 37–120
child development, 40–45
environments, 67–70
interactive experiences, 45–46
introduction, 37–38
observation/assessment, 38–39
parent partnerships, 58–67
parent postcards, 59–66, 88–89, 112–115
possibilities plans, 71–120
resources, 57, 67, 90–92, 116–120
teacher competencies, 56
teaching innovations, 47–57
Trashy Town by Andrea Zimmerman, 165, 187
Trays, 445
plastic, 254
roller, 524
Tricycles, 403
The Trouble with Elephants by Chris Riddle, 343
Truck by Donald Crew, 409, 426, 431, 450
Truck Song by Diane Siebert, 409, 426
Trucks by Anne Rockwell, 409, 426
Trucks by Gail Gibbons, 409, 426
Trucks, 52, 331, 345, 353, 366, 422, 435, 436, 444, 445
construction, 414–416, 419, 421, 422, 426, 427, 451
fire, 186
tires, 443, 452
T-shirts, 142
Tubes
cardboard, 99, 101, 120, 249, 255, 260, 267, 279, 350, 366, 510, 533
gift wrap, 267, 269
mailing, 518, 533
paper towel, 99, 101, 120, 249, 255, 260, 510, 533
toilet tissue, 99, 101, 120, 255, 260, 249

Tubing, 524, 530
Tubs, 100, 120, 167, 189, 494, 506
clear, 517, 532
margarine, 206, 514
Turtle food boxes, 351, 366
Turtles, 351–352, 355–358
plastic, 351–352, 366
puppets, 364, 366
Typewriters, 238, 260

U

Ugly Vegetables by Grace Lin, 193, 212
Umbrellas, 350, 366, 510, 529, 532, 533
beach, 264, 279
Uniforms, 96, 117, 167, 185, 188, 449, 451
Unit blocks, 374, 422
"Universal Precautions in Early Interventions and Child Care," by M. Ratlev, 390

V

Vacuum cleaners, 432, 451
Values
parent postcard, 184
Vegetable crates, 199
Vegetables, 194, 211, 381, 490, 502, 506
plastic, 195, 199, 211, 490, 505, 506
shapes, 204
Velcro fasteners, 74, 92, 176, 188
The Very Busy Spider by Eric Carle, 489, 505
The Very Hungry Caterpillar by Eric Carle, 193, 211, 212, 489, 495–496, 504–505
A Very Practical Guide to Discipline with Young Children by G. Mitchell, 390
Video diaries, 228
Visit logs, 142
Vocabulary files
big animals, 343
construction, 426
introduction to, 31–32
little animals, 364
me and my body, 91
my family, 117
my neighborhood, 186
sky, 278
space, 259
storybook characters, 505
water, 530
wheels, 450
Vocabulary-building, 298–299
Vygotsky's Theory by L. E. Berk, 140

W

Wading pools, 515, 532
Wagons, 420, 427, 442
Walking away, 135
Wallets, 166, 186, 188, 449
Wallpaper samples, 77, 173
Wardle, F., 219, 227
Washable paints, 327, 345
Washcloths, 78, 100, 120, 351, 366, 510, 532
Water possibilities plan, 487–506
concepts learned, 529
construction possibilities, 515
curiosity possibilities, 513–514
dramatic possibilities, 510–511
literacy possibilities, 516–519
movement possibilities, 522
music possibilities, 519–521
outdoor possibilities, 523–525
parent participation, 526–528
parent postcard, 527–528
project possibilities, 525
resources, 509, 529–533
sensory/art possibilities, 511–513
web, 507
Water, 25, 168–169, 181, 189, 196, 202, 206, 243, 265, 267, 274, 279, 303, 313, 351, 359, 381, 385–386, 405, 411, 421, 492, 502, 510, 511–513, 517, 524, 525
cooler, 421, 427
prop box, 509, 530
table, 169, 188, 243–244, 260, 266, 274, 279, 351, 359, 366, 511–514, 524, 532
Watering cans, 530, 532
The Way to Start a Day by Byrd Baylor, 263, 278
Webs
big animals, 323
construction, 407
fruits and vegetables, 191
little animals, 347
me and my body, 71
my family, 93
my neighborhood, 163
sky, 261
space, 235
storybook characters, 487
wheels, 429
water, 507
Weikert, D. P., 51, 57
What Color Is It? by Elisabeth Ivanosky, 193, 211, 212
What Color Is It? by Pamela Cote, 73, 91
What Next, Baby Bear? by Jill Murphy, 237, 259
Wheelbarrows, 420, 422, 427, 444, 451
Wheels Go Round by Margaret Miller, 439, 449–450
The Wheels on the Bus by Maryanne Kovalski, 95, 117–118, 431, 449–450
Wheels possibilities plan, 419–452
construction possibilities, 436–437
curiosity possibilities, 434–436
dramatic possibilities, 432–433
literacy possibilities, 437–439

movement possibilities, 441–443
music possibilities, 439–441
outdoor possibilities, 443–444
parent participation, 445
parent postcards, 446–448
project possibilities, 445
resources, 431, 449–452
sensory/art possibilities, 433–434
web, 419
When I Get Bigger by Mercer Mayer, 73, 91
When I Was Little by Toyomi Igus, 73, 91
When Stories Come to School by P. Cooper, 308
Where Can I Go? by Pamela Cote, 165, 187
Where Do Bears Sleep? by Barbara Shook Hazen, 325, 343, 344
Where the Wild Things Are by Maurice Sendak, 489, 496, 504–505
Whistle for Willie by Ezra Jack Keats, 95, 118
Who Sank the Boat? by Pamela Allen, 509, 517, 531
Who Took the Farmer's Hat? by Joan L. Nodset, 73, 91, 489, 505
Whose Hat? by Margaret Miller, 73, 91
Whose Shoe? by Margaret Miller, 73, 90–91
Why Children Misbehave by C. Adams & E. Fruge, 390, 484
Why the Sun and Moon Live in the Sky by Elphinston Dayrell, 237, 259, 263, 278
Windows, 68
Without Spanking or Spoiling by E. Crary, 390
Wood blocks, 493, 506
animals, 414, 422, 427, 506
Work boots, 410, 421, 425, 490, 504, 506
Working with Emotional Intelligence by D. Goleman, 474
Wrenches, 410
Writing pads, 425
Writing skills, 291–292
parent postcards, 341

Y

Yard tools, 444, 451
Yarn, 58, 79, 81, 92, 99, 104, 108, 119, 174, 182, 188, 200, 247–248, 260, 308, 345, 416, 427, 495, 500, 501, 506, 517, 532
balls, 252, 260
Yogurt, 381
Young Children by H. Blecher-Sass, 57
Your Baby and Child by P. Leach, 67
Your Self-Confident Baby by M. Gerber & A. Johnson, 57, 141
Your Two Year Old by L. B. Ilg & F. L. Ames, 67, 141
Yum! Yum! by Kate Gleason, 193, 212